The
Poetical Works
of
James Russell
Lowell

THE CAMBRIDGE EDITIONS

The Poetical Works of James Russell Lowell

Cambridge Edition

Revised and with a New Introduction
by Marjorie R. Kaufman

Houghton Mifflin Company Boston

1978

Library of Congress Cataloging in Publication Data

Lowell, James Russell, 1819–1891.
   The poetical works of James Russell Lowell.

   Includes index.
   I. Kaufman, Marjorie Ruth, 1922–
PS2305.A1   1978   811′.3   77-17274
ISBN 0-395-25726-3

Printed in the United States of America

V 10 9 8 7 6 5 4 3 2 1

EDITOR'S NOTE

THREE previously uncollected poems have been added to this edition within the text of the Introduction; they have been chosen, from among over two hundred uncollected or unpublished poems, primarily because they easily demonstrate a satiric vigor in Lowell's poetry after the Civil War, a vigor usually assumed to be lacking in the work of his later years.*

Horace Scudder, who edited the original Cambridge volume, was a careful, not wholly uncritical editor and biographer of Lowell. The chief weakness of the generally sound edition he prepared lies in the distribution of the apparatus Lowell added to each series of *The Biglow Papers* as he readied them for publication. In a brief paragraph at the end of Scudder's prefatory note to the First Series (p. 167), he indicates all is in order, and Lowell's work begins with "Notices of an Independent Press." But the "Glossary" and "Index" Lowell prepared for the First Series and later expanded to include the Second Series is separated from the Papers themselves and appears as Appendices II and III at the back of the volume. The dislocations in the Second Series are more violent and complex: on p. 216, after printing the title and Lowell's epigraphs, Scudder inserts his own prefatory note, which is immediately followed by one of Lowell's once most popular poems, "The Courtin'." Only in the penultimate paragraph of his note (col. 1, p. 217) does Scudder partially describe his rearrangement of materials. Lowell's own preface to the Second Series, an important study of Yankee dialects, has been removed to Appendix I in this edition, though Scudder did excerpt a paragraph from it to introduce "The Courtin'." In short, because the arrangement in the text is misleading, the reader should be wholly aware that not only the press notices but the glossary to *The Biglow Papers* are an integral part of its satiric framing, tongue-in-cheek pedantic paraphernalia whose deadpan comedy is treated in Scudder's edition as if it were literally serious scholarship. The "Glossary" and "Index," while accurate, are full of play, some of it quite sharp-edged. Under "Sogerin'," for instance, one finds "*soldiering;* a barbarous amusement common among men in the savage state"; under "Zack, Ole," not Zachary Taylor but "a second Washington, an antislavery slaveholder, a humane buyer and seller of men and women, a Christian hero generally." The same extension of the central satire can be found among the subjects itemized in the "Index."

Appendix IV may also be misleading. Without clear distinctions, Scudder conflates his notes to certain poems of this edition with notes, made at Lowell's

---

* These poems first came to my attention in the careful edition of Thelma Smith, *The Uncollected Poems of James Russell Lowell* (Philadelphia: University of Pennsylvania Press, 1950).

request, to accompany complete editions of *The Biglow Papers*. The latter run from col. 2, p. 471, to the top of col. 1, p. 479; the "I" on p. 471 refers to Lowell, then, not Scudder.

For this edition, Appendix V, as originally compiled by Scudder, has been expanded to include the substantially longer list of poems he identified for his two-volume biography of JRL as well as titles of previously uncollected and unpublished poems, currently available in two modern texts.

Because I have viewed the function of the Introduction as critical rather than biographical — it replaces Scudder's Biographical Sketch — I have added an annotated chronology of Lowell's life. I hope the reader will glance at it before reading the introductory essay, which was written with it in mind.

MARJORIE R. KAUFMAN

EDITOR'S NOTE TO FIRST EDITION

THE present Cambridge Edition of Mr. Lowell's poems contains, substantially in the order established by the author, the poems included by him not long before his death in the definitive Riverside Edition of his writings, and in addition the small group contained in the *Last Poems*, collected by his literary executor, Mr. Charles Eliot Norton. In the brief Prefatory Note to the four volumes of his Poems in the Riverside Edition, Mr. Lowell said : —

"There are a great many pieces in these volumes, especially in the first of them, which I would gladly suppress or put into the Coventry of smaller print in an appendix. But 'ilka mon maun dree his weird,' and the avenging *litera scripta manet* is that of the over-hasty author. Owing to the unjust distinction made by the law between literary and other property, most of what I published prematurely has lost the protection of copyright, and is reprinted by others against my will. I cannot shake off the burthen of my early indiscretions if I would. The best way, perhaps, is to accept with silent contrition the consequences of one's own mistakes, and I have, after much hesitation, consented to the reprinting of the old editions without excision.

"I must confess, however, that I have attained this pitch of self-sacrifice only by compulsion, and should have greatly preferred to increase the value of this collection by lessening its bulk. The judicious reader will, I fear, distinguish only too easily what I should wish, in parliamentary phrase, 'to be taken as read.' As we grow older, we grow the more willing to say, as Petrarca in Landor's *Pentameron* says to Boccaccio, 'We neither of us are such poets as we thought ourselves when we were younger.' "

The Editor of this volume has not felt at liberty either to add poems left by the author in the deepening obscurity of old mazagines, or to follow the probable judgment of Mr. Lowell in reducing any of his collected verse to the lower terms of an appendix.

The method followed in the other volumes of the Cambridge series has been observed in this. The head-notes are occupied mainly with the history of the several poems ; criticism has been given only when the author himself was the critic. The Publishers and Editor desire to make acknowledgment to Mr. Norton, the editor, and Messrs. Harper & Brothers, the publishers, for their courtesy in allowing a liberal use to be made of *Letters of James Russell Lowell*, and special thanks are due Mr. Norton for the valuable aid which he has given the editor in the preparation of the volume.

HORACE E. SCUDDER

CONTENTS

CONTENTS

CONTENTS

CHRONOLOGY OF LOWELL'S LIFE

1819 22 FEBRUARY. James Russell Lowell born, third son and fifth child of Rev. Charles Lowell, minister of the West Church, Boston, and Harriet Spence Lowell ("It pleased her to fancy herself descended from the hero of one of the most famous ballads 'Sir Patrick Spens'" [Scudder]), at "Elmwood," Cambridge, Mass.

1834–38 Attends Harvard College. Is "rusticated" to Concord in senior year but writes the Class Poem, which college authorities forbid him to read while not in residence. Poem published by subscription of classmates (reprinted in Thelma Smith's *The Uncollected Poems of JRL* [Phila., 1950], pp. 217–248).

1840 AUGUST. Unenthusiastically takes LL.B. at Dane College Law School (Harvard). Delegate to Anti-Slavery Convention, Boston. Engaged to Maria White, feminist, abolitionist, transcendentalist, poet — member of Elizabeth Peabody's circle and auditor at Margaret Fuller's lecture series.

1841 JANUARY. *A Year's Life*, his first volume of poetry, dedicated to Maria White, "Gentle Una."

1842 Poems in *Arcturus, Democratic Review, The Dial, Graham's Magazine*, etc.; poetry and prose in anti-slavery publications, e.g. *The Liberty Bell, National Anti-Slavery Standard;* prose series on "Old English Dramatists" (Ford, Chapman, Massinger, Webster), in *Boston Miscellany.*

1843 JANUARY–MARCH. With Robert Carter, edits new periodical, *The Pioneer:* the first issue includes Poe's "The Tell-Tale Heart" and poems of Jones Very, Elizabeth Barrett; the second, Hawthorne's "The Hall of Fantasy," Poe's "Leonora."
DECEMBER. *Poems*, dedicated to William Page, painter and friend. Reviewed widely and extravagantly in the U.S. and England, sells 1500 copies.

1844 *Conversations on Some of the Old Poets*, literary essays, including revised "Old Dramatists," and commentary on Chaucer, natural religion, Life, Art, abolition, etc., dedicated to his father. First edition, 1000 copies, sold out in three months.
26 DECEMBER. Marries Maria White and moves temporarily to Philadelphia, active in all contemporary reform movements from radical Garrisonian point of view, including women's rights, working conditions of factory hands, Graham's diets, and temperance acts.

1845 JUNE. Returns to Elmwood, via New York: meets Poe for first time to mutual disillusion. Income mostly from anti-slavery journals, primarily the *National Anti-Slavery Standard.*
31 DECEMBER. Blanche, first daughter, born.

1846 Continues abolitionist publication, now under contract to the *Standard.*
FEBRUARY–MAY. Writes unsigned series of historical essays on anti-slavery movement for London *Daily News*, Charles Dickens, editor.
17 JUNE. First *Biglow Paper*, Boston *Courier.*

1847   19 MARCH. Blanche dies.
       9 SEPTEMBER. Mabel, second daughter, born.
       DECEMBER. *Poems*, Second Series, including fine lyric on Blanche's death,
       "She Came and Went": "As, at one bound, our swift spring heaps/ The
       orchards full of bloom and scent,/ So clove her May my wintry steps; — /
       I only know she came and went" (p. 89).

1848–50 Over forty-five articles on various aspects of reform and abolition to
       the *National Anti-Slavery Standard*.

1848   *A Fable for Critics*, satirical poem in rhymed couplets, delights wide audi-
       ence, including Longfellow and Ruskin, and infuriates Poe. 3000 copies
       rapidly sold. *The Biglow Papers*, First Series, extended satire, prose,
       and poetry against the Mexican War, in Yankee dialect.
       17 DECEMBER. *The Vision of Sir Launfal*, long, immensely popular quasi-
       medieval poem: "What is so rare as a day in June?"

1849   16 JULY. Rose, third daughter, born.

1850   Contractual arrangement with the *Standard* ends.
       2 FEBRUARY. Rose dies. Lowell refuses formal funeral and walks alone
       to Mount Auburn cemetery for burial.
       APRIL. Harriet Spence Lowell, JRL's mother, dies.
       22 DECEMBER. Walter, fourth child and only son, born.

1851   12 JULY. The Lowells leave for extended stay in Europe, renting the
       Brownings' rooms in Casa Guidi in Florence and Julia Ward Howe's in
       Rome.

1852   9 JUNE. Walter dies of measles in Rome. Tour through Germany, Swit-
       zerland, France (Paris), and England.
       2 OCTOBER. Sail for home with Thackeray and Arthur Hugh Clough as
       fellow passengers.

1853   Writes one chapter of a novel. Begins a series of satiric travel poems for
       Putnam's Monthly, "Our Own, His Wanderings and Personal Adventures"
       (see "Aladdin" [p. 300] and "Fragments of an Unfinished Poem" [p. 158]
       for only collected publication), but stops, on editor's suggestion, when series
       proves unsuccessful. Works on project first conceived in 1849, long poem
       to be called "The Nooning." Takes summer hiking trip to Maine, the
       source for "A Moosehead Journal" (in *Fireside Travels*, 1864).
       27 OCTOBER. Maria White Lowell dies of tuberculosis. "The waters have
       gone over me."

1854   Desolated. Publishes three prose sketches, including "A Moosehead Jour-
       nal" and "Cambridge Thirty Years Ago." Edits Donne, Marvell, Dryden;
       does biographical introductions of Wordsworth and Keats in *British Poets*
       series.

1855   Prepares privately printed volume of *The Poems of Maria Lowell*.
       9 JANUARY. Gives first of twelve Lowell Institute lectures on English
       poets so successfully that the series is immediately oversubscribed.
       FEBRUARY. Following Ticknor and Longfellow, accepts appointment as
       Smith Professor of Modern Languages and Literature at Harvard.
       MARCH–APRIL. On lecture tour through Mid-West.
       4 JUNE. Leaves for Europe (Dresden) to study German and Spanish in
       preparation for Harvard appointment.

1856   AUGUST. Returns to Cambridge but rents out Elmwood.
       SEPTEMBER. Begins teaching at Harvard.

1857 JUNE. First editor of *The Atlantic Monthly: A Magazine of Literature, Art, and Politics*.
16 SEPTEMBER. Marries Frances Dunlap, Mabel's governess since Maria's death.

1858–60 Teaches; edits; writes over forty reviews and political commentary for *The Atlantic*.

1859 Thomas Hughes (*Tom Brown's School Days*) edits English edition of *The Biglow Papers*, establishing Lowell's international reputation.

1861 Lowells move back to Elmwood.
JANUARY. Charles Lowell, JRL's father, dies.
MAY. Lowell resigns as editor of *The Atlantic*.
OCTOBER. William Lowell Putnam, nephew, dies in Civil War battle at Ball's Bluff.

1862 JANUARY–JUNE. First six of *Biglow Papers*, Second Series, appear in *The Atlantic*. James Jackson Lowell, nephew, killed in Seven Days' Battle with Col. Robert Gould Shaw (see "Memoriae Positum," [p. 337]).

1864 Co-editor with Charles Eliot Norton of *The North American Review:* for first issue (January), writes extended essay, "The President's Policy," drawing special praise from Lincoln and wide pamphlet distribution.
OCTOBER. Charles Russell Lowell, nephew and husband of Shaw's sister, killed at Cedar Creek. *Fireside Travels*, collection of informal essays.

1865 21 JULY. "Commemoration Ode" delivered at Harvard memorial service for students who died in the war.

1866 *Biglow Papers*, Second Series (eleven papers), dedicated to Judge Rockwood Hoar, Grant's attorney general.

1867 JANUARY. "Fitz Adam's Story," seven-hundred-line poem from uncompleted "Nooning" (see 1853) in *The Atlantic*.

1868 *Under the Willows and Other Poems*, first volume of poetry in twenty years: most written before 1863; a few before 1848. "God, how bad they seem now!"

1870 *The Cathedral* (originally titled "A Day at Chartres"), dedicated to James T. Fields. Ruskin "couldn't put it down." *Among My Books*, First Series, literary essays.

1871 Continues as co-editor of the *North American Review*, now with Henry Adams. *My Study Windows*, essays.

1872 Resigns Harvard professorship after sixteen years.
9 JULY. Sails, with Mrs. Lowell, for two-year stay in Europe, with the newly married Henry Adamses and Francis Parkman as fellow passengers.

1872–73 Seven months in Paris, where Henry James is frequent companion.

1873 JUNE. Honorary degree, Doctor of Civil Law, from Oxford University. Travels down Rhine with Leslie Stephen.
OCTOBER. Lowells move to Italy. Writes memorial ode on Louis Agassiz (publ., *Atlantic*, 1874).

1874 Accepts reappointment to Harvard.
JUNE. Receives Doctor of Civil Law degree from Cambridge University.
4 JULY. Lowells return to U.S. and Cambridge, Mass. Lowell offered and refuses ambassadorial post to Russia.

1875 Completes essays on Spenser, Milton, Dante; revisions of Wordsworth and Keats for *Among My Books*, Second Series (publ. 1876), dedicated to Emerson.

1876 Attends Republican National Convention as representative of Eighth

Congressional District, Mass., against James Blaine's nomination for president and in favor of Rutherford B. Hayes. Offered and refuses Republican nomination to Congress but is successfully nominated as presidential elector.

1877 FEBRUARY. Delivers course of twenty lectures on medieval literature of France, Spain, and Italy at Johns Hopkins.

MAY. Accepts appointment by Hayes as American minister to Spain.

14 JULY. Lowells sail for three-year stay in Madrid.

Three Memorial Poems, Lowell's odes for 1876 Centennial, all originally published in *The Atlantic*.

1879 JUNE. Frances Lowell suffers severe attack of typhus, or brain tumor, never fully recovering and enduring long periods of disability and apparent madness.

1880 JANUARY. Appointed American minister to the Court of St. James's.

MAY. Moves to London to remain until 1885, a successful and popular ambassador and frequent speaker, especially for literary occasions: principal speaker at Westminster Abbey Memorial Dedication for Coleridge; also Fielding and Pepys.

1882 Named godfather of Virginia Stephen (Woolf).

1883 Elected Lord Rector of St. Andrews University, Scotland, by overwhelming number of undergraduates but declared ineligible as an "alien": "An alien? Go to! If fresh genial wit/ In good sound Saxon speech be not genuine grit,/ If the wisdom and mirth he has put into verse for us/ Don't make him a 'native,' why so much the worse for us" (*Punch* 85 [Dec. 1, 1883], 255).

1884 APRIL. Receives D.Litt. from Edinburgh University at its Tercentenary celebration.

6 OCTOBER. "Democracy," inaugural address as president of Birmingham and Midland Institute, Birmingham, England.

Elected president of Wordsworth Society.

1885 Lowell refuses offer to stand for first professorship in English Language and Literature at Oxford. "Had he consented to stand," comments the London *Times*, "not even a Board determined to sink Literature in Philology could have passed over his claims."

19 FEBRUARY. Frances Dunlap Lowell dies in England.

MARCH. Lowell recalled as ambassador by new Cleveland administration.

JUNE. Returns to U.S. and daughter's home in Southborough, Mass.

SEPTEMBER. Offers one-semester course in Dante at Harvard.

1886 *Democracy and Other Addresses*, volume of English speeches.

APRIL. Summers in England, as he will for each of the next four years.

1887 MARCH. Series of Lowell Institute lectures on "Old Dramatists."

1888 Accepts D. Litt. from University of Bologna on its 800th anniversary.

Heartsease and Rue, volume of poetry collected from past thirty years, including "Agassiz" ode. *Political Essays*.

1889 FEBRUARY. Special issue of the *Boston Critic*, celebrating Lowell's seventieth birthday; among contributors are Gladstone and Tennyson.

NOVEMBER. Returns at last to Elmwood and begins to prepare ten-volume edition of his work.

1890 *Writings of James Russell Lowell*. Riverside Edition. 10 volumes. Includes prose — literary and political — and poetry.

1891 12 AUGUST. JRL dies of cancer at Elmwood.

1893   28 NOVEMBER. Dedication of window and bust in Chapter House, Westminster Abbey:

> The window . . . consists of three lights. In the centre is the figure of Sir Launfal . . . below is an angel with the Holy Grail, and in the lowest compartment the incident of Sir Launfal and the leper is represented. The right light has the figure of St. Botolph, the patron saint of the church of Boston, Lincolnshire, from which the Massachusetts city, Lowell's birthplace, derived its name; below is the landing of the Pilgrim Fathers. The light on the left contains the figure of St. Ambrose, one of the reputed authors of *Te Deum Laudamus;* below is a group representing the emancipation of the slaves. In trefoils above the side-lights are shields bearing the arms of the United States and the United Kingdom. (The London *Times,* 29 November 1893)

Leslie Stephen was the principal speaker; guests included T. H. Huxley, Gosse, Darwin, George Meredith, Mrs. Humphry Ward, and the widow of Matthew Arnold.

1895   *Last Poems of James Russell Lowell.*

INTRODUCTION

For James Fisk, Jr., An Epitaph

World, Flesh, and Devil gave him all they could,
Wealth, harlots, wine and disbelief in good;
Fame, too, he bought, our modern kind of fame,
The morning-column reeking with his name;
Lifelong he never did his lusts deny
One pleasure sin could give, or money buy.
The halter bilked, a pandar's coward shot
Sent him to where he — nay, I had forgot;
That's *passé*, so they tell us who should know,
Put out with milk and water years ago;
No retribution, then? Yes, something worse
Than angry justice e'er distilled in verse;
He had (could shame or vengeance this exceed?)
Living, Gould's friendship, dead, the tears of Tweed!

(1872)

PERHAPS if more poems like this sonnet had been permitted to enter the canon of James Russell Lowell as first he and then, posthumously, his first editors defined it, something of the man and his work might still remain in the American consciousness. With such evidence to hand in the 1930's, Vernon Louis Parrington's strike at the Boston Brahmins — Longfellow, Whittier, Holmes, Lowell — might have been tempered; the resulting eclipse, less than total. Without such stanzas, Parrington easily found the whole group of once-beloved poets overly precious and erudite, too removed from the "real" life of the streets, to deserve any further serious consideration:

> The essence of the genteel tradition was a refined ethicism, that professed to discover the highest virtue in shutting one's eyes to disagreeable fact, and the highest law of convention. Gone were the franker days. . . . Every smutch of the natural man [was] bleached out in the pure sunshine of manners. . . . Literature was conceived of as belonging to the library and drawing-room, and it must observe drawing-room amenities. Only a vulgarian would lug a spade there. Any venture into realism was likely to prove libidinous, and surely to be common.

More recent social historians have qualified Parrington's generalities; and Howard Nemerov has found a slender core of Longfellow's poetry worth preserving in a modern edition, as both Donald Hall and Robert Penn Warren have of

Whittier's. But no one has yet tried to recover any of Lowell's verse; and virtually no line of his poetry is remembered by Americans born after the Second World War. Irving Howe, in a 1970 three-volume anthology called *The Literature of America*, can find only one complete Lowell poem worth preserving, the first *Biglow Paper*, and a 170-line fragment from *A Fable for Critics*. "Lowell," he notes in his introduction, "is the one [of all the Brahmins] whose work seems most to have faded."

This reissuing of the authorized collected poems, the only volume of Lowell's poetry in print, will not make him rise from his grave. Between these covers lies no hidden Melville or neglected Tuckerman to unveil; in fact, it will be all too easy for the reader to find much that had been better never set in type:

> Light of triumph in her eyes,
> Eleanor her apron ties;
> As she pushes back her sleeves,
> High resolve her bosom heaves.
> Hasten, cook! impel the fire
> To the pace of her desire;
> As you hope to save your soul,
> Bring a virgin casserole,
> Brightest bring of silver spoons, —
> Eleanor makes macaroons!
> ("Eleanor Makes Macaroons," p. 408)

Lowell's lawyer suggested the suppression of the Fisk "Epitaph" for fear of a Gould libel suit, but the poet had no friend or critic generous enough to warn him of the larger libel against himself that lay in the public preservation of "Eleanor" and her ilk. Such poems are not infrequent, especially in *Heartsease and Rue*, Lowell's own last collection; and their presence alone makes Howe's melancholy judgment sound like respectful restraint. And yet, side by side with "Eleanor" sit such accurately observed and finely felt little lyrics as the one on the phoebe (p. 399) as well as one of Lowell's major achievements, the Agassiz memorial ode (p. 374).

In short, the reader who picks up this book holds the corpus of Lowell's poetry, not only a mixed bag of forms and genres (ballads, lyrics, long narratives, sonnets, parodies, odes), of moods and tones (satiric, elegiac, playfully humorous, melancholic, rapt), but also poems of widely ranging quality. The adventure of making his own small selection of a pertinent Lowell, from work spread across the last fifty years of the nineteenth century, lies all before him. And, because Lowell's work, good and bad, has been so thoroughly ignored, the pleasure of fresh discovery is abundant and real.

What follows are certain observations which may help encourage and sustain that undertaking. For instance, during the years of protest against the Vietnam war, literary and social historians, wishing wisely to attach their positions against government policy to a convincing American tradition, returned to the essays of Thoreau and resurrected the antiwar poems of Melville. Not many, I

suspect, thought of digging beneath the moss grown over Lowell to uncover his
more outspoken — and in his own time, at least, more powerful — stance:

> Ez fer war, I call it murder,—
> There you hev it plain and flat . . .

Although the accuracy, originality, and ingenuity of Lowell's use of vernacular
speech in *The Biglow Papers* was adequately recognized by Walter Blair in
Native American Humor in 1937, his work has been excluded, as far as I know,
from the major rhetorical studies, begun in the 1950's by such men as Henry Nash
Smith, that dignified the art of *Huckleberry Finn*. Had Lowell's contribution to
the method been subjected to a similar examination, we might already know that
a quarter of a century before Twain's achievement, the poet was displaying the
same invention on surprisingly similar materials with much the same effect:
the artistic freedom gained by the use of vernacular rather than literary speech
to attack official but morally decayed institutions and attitudes, a freedom created
when the artist chooses a hero and an idiom not from his own world but from
the bottom of the social and cultural heap. None of the characters who people
Jaalam Centre, the home town of Lowell's rustic poet, Hosea Biglow, glow with
the innocent warmth and health of Mark Twain's boy and his companion, Jim.
But through a wide range of authentic Yankee voices — from the theological
pedant Rev. Homer Wilbur, who transmits Biglow's poems to the press, and
Increase D'Ophace, Esq., the local politician, to Birdofredum Sawin, a wastrel
and Mexican War volunteer who ultimately marries a Confederate widow and
attempts to become a slaveholder himself — Lowell achieves, with great satirical
subtlety, a penetrating political analysis of the morally shoddy that extends be-
yond the immediate issues of old presidential campaigns and pro-slavery debates
with which the *Papers* ostensibly deal. A few lines from Sawin's first letter
home, after he has been seduced into enlisting to fight Mexicans by the usual re-
cruitment propaganda — "I felt, ez sister Patience sez, a little mite histericky" —
will illustrate Lowell's procedure. Sawin, dismayed by the discrepancy between
what he is doing and the official language describing it, quotes Colonel Caleb
Cushing, the actual U.S. military hero of that shameful engagement, as saying:

> Thet our nation's bigger 'n theirn an' so its rights air bigger,
> An' thet it's all to make 'em free thet we air pullin' trigger,
> The Anglo-Saxondom's idee 's abreakin' 'em to pieces,
> An' thet idee 's thet every man doos jest wut he damn pleases;

and comments, with a blunt deflation of the high-sounding rhetoric behind which
American imperialism seems to make its way:

> Ef I don't make his meanin' clear, perhaps in some respex I can,
> I know thet "every man" don't mean a nigger or a Mexican . . .

Incidentally, modern awareness of Lowell's Biglow characters would allow
Birdofredum Sawin (whom George Cruikshank, Dickens's illustrator, drew for

the English edition of the *Papers*) his rightful place beside Poe's Brevet
Brigadier-General John A. B. C. Smith, in "The Man That Was Used Up," as a
prototype for Lemuel Pitkin in Nathanael West's *A Cool Million*. Together, the
three shape a minor type among the figures in American black humor: the hero
who is literally dismembered ("used up") in the service of his country. Sawin,
after the Mexican War, is left with but one eye, one hand, and one leg to
stand on.

And, although Hosea Biglow, older and more tutored than Huck, can never
draw a sunrise as startlingly new as the one Huck sees from the raft, he can
speak of nature in New England, consciously rejecting literary convention and
sounding at least a prefatory note of wonder:

> . . . May-day seldom looks
> Up in the country ez it doos in books;
> . . . .
> I, country-born an' bred, know where to find
> Some blooms thet make the season suit the mind,
> An' seem to metch the doubtin' bluebird's notes, —
> Half-vent'rin' liverworts in furry coats,
> Bloodroots, whose rolled-up leaves ef you oncurl,
> Each on 'em 's cradle to a baby-pearl, —
> But these are jes' Spring's pickets; sure ez sin,
> The rebble frosts 'll try to drive 'em in;
> . . . .
> Though I own up I like our back'ard springs
> Thet kind o' haggle with their greens an' things,
> An' when you 'most give up, 'uthout more words
> Toss the fields full o' blossoms, leaves, an' birds;
> Thet's Northun natur', slow an' apt to doubt,
> But when it *doos* git stirred, ther' 's no gin-out!

(p. 261)

Lowell's sensitivity to the New England countryside and its peculiar seasons, his
accurate ear for the rhythms of its regional speech, was not limited, however, to
vernacular expression. When he speaks in the voice of an educated New England
traveler, the twentieth-century reader can hear a diction and a tone he has al-
ready learned to admire in the poetry of Robert Frost:

> "Well, there I lingered all October through,
> In that sweet atmosphere of hazy blue,
> So leisurely, so soothing, so forgiving,
> That sometimes makes New England fit for living.
> I watched the landscape, erst so granite glum,
> Bloom like the south side of a ripening plum,
> And each rock-maple on the hillside make
> His ten days' sunset doubled in the lake;
> The very stone walls draggling up the hills
> Seemed touched, and wavered in their roundhead wills.
> Ah! there 's a deal of sugar in the sun!

> Tap me in Indian summer, I should run
> A juice to make rock-candy of, — but then
> We get such weather scarce one year in ten."
> ("Fitz Adam's Story," p. 416)

The search for an unfaded Lowell need not be restricted, however, to his early experiments in areas where later writers find their main achievements. Among his contemporaries, Lowell was exceptionally well read in classical and modern European and English literature (see the Chronology for transatlantic recognition of this fact) ; he was especially drawn to Chaucer, Spenser, the minor Elizabethans, the medieval lays of all the Romance languages, Dante. Unfortunately, literary allusions, even deliberate paraphrase and partial quotation, so permeate his serious verse that it is often hard to hear Lowell's own voice. What he viewed as added richness now, sadly, works almost to exclude the later, less literate reader, unskilled as we are in catching and appreciating echoes. Yet more remains open to our enjoyment than may at first appear. It takes little knowledge of the poetry of Wordsworth, for instance, to recognize the device of the young Lowell protesting, in a sonnet sequence, the older poet's defense of capital punishment by using Wordsworth's own form and diction (and the values it professes) as the very basis of the charge against his views:

> And always 't is the saddest sight to see
> An old man faithless in Humanity.
> ("The Same Continued," XVI, p. 23)

Nor, when one knows these lines, does it seem extravagant to find them a more effective condemnation than Browning's better known

> Just for a handful of silver he left us,
> Just for a riband to stick in his coat —
> ("The Lost Leader")

In the long run, the only run from which Lowell's poetry can now be viewed, the best remains generally available without elaborate annotation. Little need be said about *The Biglow Papers* and *A Fable for Critics* in this context; any student of American literature is likely to have caught sight of a snippet or two from either long work. Appearing as early as 1848, *A Fable* not only demonstrates Lowell's wide and thoughtful reading of contemporary American writers, particularly of the North and East (Poe complained of the neglect of Southern writers, though he himself was included) ; it also shows the sharpness and objectivity of his critical acumen, rare for its day, and often expressed with enough pithiness and wit to warrant quotation still, on writers such as Cooper and Emerson, Longfellow and Hawthorne, and even Lowell himself.

For instance, on Emerson:

> A Greek head on right Yankee shoulders, whose range
> Has Olympus for one pole, for t' other the Exchange . . .
> (p. 127)

Or, after praising Cooper's timeless creation in Natty Bumppo:

> His Indians, with proper respect be it said,
> Are just Natty Bumppo, daubed over with red,
> . . . .
> And the women he draws from one model don't vary,
> All sappy as maples and flat as a prairie.
>
> (p. 135)

Or Whittier, whose

> . . . failures arise (though he seem not to know it)
> From the very same cause that has made him a poet, —
> A fervor of mind which knows no separation
> 'Twixt simple excitement and pure inspiration . . .
>
> (p. 132)

Or, most frequently quoted:

> There comes Poe, with his raven, like Barnaby Rudge,
> Three fifths of him genius and two fifths sheer fudge,
> . . . .
> Who has written some things quite the best of their kind,
> But the heart somehow seems all squeezed out by the mind . . .
>
> (p. 140)

Or, on himself:

> There is Lowell, who's striving Parnassus to climb
> With a whole bale of *isms* tied together with rhyme,
> . . . .
> The top of the hill he will ne'er come nigh reaching
> Till he learns the distinction 'twixt singing and preaching . . .
>
> (pp. 144–45)

Cursed by a great facility and a broad interest, Lowell wrote much and hastily, seldom rewrote, tinkered rather than revised. Thus, as is true of his other long poems, *A Fable* suffers from inadequate pruning: rhyme-serving lines; mere palaver; framing devices, modeled on traditional antecedents, that grow too elaborate for their original function but remain, clotting the whole, merely because they were put in at the start. The temptation to skip dozens of couplets is almost irresistible; yet patience with the entire poem can be rewarding. In its apparently most arid stretches, there are oases of wit — at the least, of atrocious punning. Phoebus Apollo's lament for the loss of Daphne, changed to a laurel tree, is for better or worse typical:

> "Ah! It went to my heart, and the memory still grieves,
> To see those loved graces all taking their leaves;
> Those charms beyond speech, so enchanting but now,

As they left me forever, each making its bough!
If her tongue *had* a tang sometimes more than was right,
Her new bark is worse than ten times her old bite."

(p. 118)

But knowledge of the whole work has substantive importance as well, an importance infrequently noted simply because the poem is seldom read in its entirety (Edmund Wilson is a significant exception here) — that is, an awareness of it as a major document of American literary criticism rather than a random collection of happy epigraphs. It is the first extended statement of its kind and quality in American letters, undertaken as something other than pure puffery of native writers over British. Because it appears just before the major works of the mid-century — *The Scarlet Letter*, 1849; *Moby Dick*, 1850; *Walden*, 1854; *Leaves of Grass*, 1855 — Lowell's essay, with its echoes of Byron's "English Bards and Scotch Reviewers" and Leigh Hunt's *The Feast of the Poets*, serves to sum up and delimit the first half-century of American literature, and points, accurately, to the directions it will soon take in its first great ripening.

Seventy years ago, when it still mattered, critics customarily spoke of 1848 as Lowell's *annus mirabilis;* that year saw not only the publication of his second volume of poetry, the First Series of *The Biglow Papers*, and *A Fable*, but also Lowell's contribution to the matter of Arthur, *The Vision of Sir Launfal*. His Grail story of Launfal and the leper is pleasant enough, though not particularly distinguished either as poetry or narrative. It was nevertheless immediately and immensely popular and continued to be so over at least the next fifty years. In fact the editors of the *New York Times* crossword puzzle assume its most famous lines are usable in 1977 as clues "up" or "down." The magic that lies in "And what is so rare as a day in June?/ Then, if ever, come perfect days . . ." and has struck so congenial a chord in the American imagination that it vibrates across the revolutions of taste and custom that separate us from the young Lowell and his first audience, I find hard to understand or feel. For the reader curious about the history of American sensibility, the poem remains a major document.

What little of Lowell's poetry has survived without subsequent revaluation predates the Civil War. It was the later work, written when Lowell's chief occupations were centered elsewhere — as editor, essayist, teacher, diplomat — that apparently justifies the charges exemplified in Parrington's comment. Yet on reconsideration now, almost fifty years after Parrington, perhaps something may be salvaged from the wreckage — some poetry, no longer seen as absolutely of the first quality but important enough to conserve. Aside from the tumescence already mentioned in all of Lowell's long poems, the most serious barrier for the modern reader willing to uncover the genuine poetry embedded in the occasional odes Lowell composed in the 1870's and '80's, is the form itself. For Lowell, fully aware of the majestic tradition of the ode, the choice of genre was inevitable, given the circumstances impelling their composition: the memorial ceremony for Harvard students killed in the Civil War; three celebrations of the national Centennial in 1875–76; the death of Agassiz; the impulse to contribute his own expression to the poetic documents that record the Victorian intellectual's crisis of faith. The classical precedents, the long tradition, the formal diction, the attendant imagery of personified abstraction that, in Lowell's eyes, worked to elevate the subjects of the New World to the importance accorded the ancients, now serve only to make the odes appear more "old-fashioned" and remote from present concerns than I think they actually are.

The truth of this generalization may be quickly tested if one takes a passage from the Centennial ode "For the Fourth of July 1876" and reads it in relation to a poem Lowell published at about the same time but viewed as ephemeral newspaper verse and hence properly treated more colloquially. First, then, from the ode:

> Murmur of many voices in the air
> Denounces us degenerate,
> Unfaithful guardians of a noble fate,
> And prompts indifference or despair:
> Is this the country that we dreamed in youth,
> Where wisdom and not numbers should have weight,
> . . . .
> Where shams should cease to dominate
> In household, church, and state?
> Is this Atlantis? This the unpoisoned soil,
> . . . .
> Where parasitic greed no more should coil
> Round Freedom's stem to bend awry and blight
> . . . .
> Is this debating club where boys dispute,
> And wrangle o'er their stolen fruit,
> The Senate . . . ?   (p. 372)

Aside from the last few lines, which remain fresh, is the emotion of the rest of the passage lost to us? Can we perceive passionate indignation when its high dudgeon is expressed in stately rhythms and statuesque diction — do we see, with at least a shadow of the outrage intended, the "robber barons" of the railroads and finance, the vote-buyers, the rabble-rousing corrupters of Grant's second administration, or our own equivalents to these, — when we are asked to picture "parasitic greed," blighting and perverting that once-strong plant, "Freedom"? Or are we left with lifeless unsignifying words? The following poem makes sufficiently evident that, *pace* Parrington, Lowell could perfectly well lug a spade into the muck-heap when he thought spades the proper vehicle:

The World's Fair, 1876

> Columbia, puzzled what she should display
> Of true home-make on her Centennial Day,
> Asked Brother Jonathan: he scratched his head,
> Whittled a while reflectively, and said,
> "You're [sic] own invention and own making, too?

Why, any child could tell ye what to do:
Show 'em your Civil Service, and explain
How all men's loss is everybody's gain;
Show your new patent to increase your rents
By paying quarters for collecting cents;
Show your short cut to cure financial ills
By making paper-collars current bills;
Show your new bleaching-process, cheap and brief,
To wit: a jury chosen by the thief;
Show your State Legislatures; show your Rings;
And challenge Europe to produce such things
As high officials sitting half in sight
To share the plunder and to fix things right;
If that don't fetch her, why, you only need
To show your latest style in martyrs — Tweed:
She'll find it hard to hide her spiteful tears
At such advance in one poor hundred years."

Perhaps, after all, it really is too late and we cannot be moved by the abstracted "unfaithful guardians of a noble fate"; we need the specificity of those "high officials sitting half in sight/ To share the plunder . . ." For popular periodicals, Lowell spoke out concretely until a few months before he died. In May 1890, for instance, he sent these verses to *The Nation:*

The Infant Prodigy

A veteran entered at my gate
    With locks as cherry-blossoms white;
His clothes proclaimed a prosperous fate,
    His boots were arrogantly bright.

The hat was glossy on his head,
    Gold-rimmed his eye-glass, gold his chain,
In genial curves his waistcoat spread,
    And golden-headed was his cane.

Without a preface thus he spoke,
    "I've called to get my annual due";
Whereat I too the silence broke
    With, "Who, respected sir, are you?

"What is your claim against me, pray?
    A many-childed man am I,
Hard-pinched my monthly bills to pay,
    And prices rule perversely high."

"Not know me? Everybody knows
    And gladly gives his mite," quoth he,
"Why, I'm a babe in swaddling clo'es,
    I am an Infant Industry."

"Forgive me, Reverend Shape," I cried,
    "You set my faith a heavy task;
This infancy which seems your pride,
    Is it your *second*, may I ask?

"Or have you, where so many failed,
 The key to life's Elixir found?
You look like one who never ailed,
 In wind and limb sedately sound."

"You doubt my word? (Excuse these tears,
 They flow for you and not for me;)
Young man, for more than seventy years
 I've been an Infant Industry.
"Your father rued my helpless lot,
 Lifelong he handed me his fee
Nor ever asked himself for what;
 He *loved* an Infant Industry."

Quoth I, "He paid my ransom then
 From further tribute, small or great;
Besides, if I can judge of men,
 Since that, you've grown to man's estate."

He murmured, as I bowed him out,
 "The world is getting worse and worse;
This fellow almost makes me doubt
 Whether I've not been changed at nurse.

"But no, this hat, this cane, these boots,
 This suit in London made by P.,
Convince me to the very roots
 I am an Infant Industry."

Until he vanished from my sight
 These words came floating back to me:
"Yes, 'spite of Time, in Reason's spite,
 I *am* an Infant Industry!"

Before returning to the odes and while we are, so to speak, still among the spades, it should be noted that the Fisk "Epitaph," "The World's Fair," and "The Infant Prodigy" are here added to this volume for the first time. Neither Lowell nor Horace Scudder, the original editor, thought it proper to include them, though Scudder liked "The World's Fair" well enough to smuggle it into his two-volume authorized biography of the poet. They did, however, include other similar verses, often elevated by Latin titles, which may now, ironically, prevent a reader from even glancing at them: "Credidmus Jovem Regnare" (p. 423), for instance —

> [God] gone, I felt a moment's spasm,
> But calmed myself with Protoplasm,
> A finer name, and, what is more,
> As enigmatic as before;
> Greek, too . . .

Or, the Juvenalian satire, "Tempora Mutantur" (p. 425), which treats centrally the moral corruption implicit in the political euphemism, the act of eschewing the blunt spade:

> And there 's a subtle influence that springs
> From words to modify our sense of things.
> A plain distinction grows obscure of late:
>
> . . . .
>
> But now that "Statesmanship" is just a way
> To dodge the primal curse and make it pay,
>
> . . . .
>
> With generous curve we draw the moral line:
> Our swindlers are permitted to resign;
> Their guilt is wrapped in deferential names,
> And twenty sympathize for one that blames.
>
> . . . .
>
> Steal but enough, the world is unsevere, —
> Tweed is a statesman, Fisk a financier . . .

The cutting edge of such couplets remains sharp.

To an age like ours where advertising slogans indicate that "TRAD is trendy!" it may even be possible to attend to the far better poetry of the later odes. Mocked though they were by adherents of the avant garde literary movements of the turn of the century (pure aestheticism or ash can naturalism), the odes nonetheless made a deep impression on two writers of that next generation who fit into no popular fashion of their time but whose stature now is unquestioned: Henry James and Henry Adams.

James (whom Martin Duberman, Lowell's finest modern biographer, finds still his best literary critic) wrote two major essays on the man and his work in the years immediately following Lowell's death: a memorial essay in *The Atlantic Monthly* (1892) and an introduction to some Lowell selections for an 1897 anthology of "the world's best literature." In both he points to the "Harvard Commemoration Ode" (p. 340) as the best thing Lowell did in verse. For James, "the air of the study [so] mingles [there] with the hot breath of passion," that the verses "translate with equal exaltation and veracity the highest national mood." James is also shrewd enough, however, to add a necessary caveat: "— even if it be of the very nature of the English ode to show us always, at its best, something of the chill of the poetic Exercise." I find it hard to recapture what James calls "the great historic throb" in Lowell's lines; they seem now too book-bound. When they do break free, however, they can still move. Consider, for instance, Lowell's formulation of the traditional question, Can these dead be long remembered? —

> But, when we vanish hence,
> Shall they lie forceless in the dark below,
> Save to make green their little length of sods,
> Or deepen pansies for a year or two,
> Who now to us are shining-sweet as gods?
> Was dying all they had the skill to do?
>
> (p. 346)

Or this glimpse of Lincoln, about whose high stature Lowell was sure long be-
fore most of his contemporaries:

> Nothing of Europe here,
> . . . .
> The kindly-earnest, brave, foreseeing man,
> Sagacious, patient, dreading praise, not blame,
> New birth of our new soil, the first American.
>   (p. 344)

Yet there is nothing for us in such lines of the magnificence we find in "When
Lilacs Last in the Dooryard Bloom'd"; Lowell's ode has importance as an his-
torical document, but its pulse has faded.

That is less true of his other major elegiac ode, the ode on the death of his
friend and Harvard colleague, the great Swiss-born naturalist, Louis Agassiz.
James thought "Agassiz" (p. 374) "a summary of all of [Lowell's] vigors and
felicities, his most genial achievement, and . . . the truest expression of his
poetic nature." Consciously reaching back to *Lycidas* in structure and diction,
and to the classical elegies behind the English tradition from which Milton's great
ode flows, Lowell does more than echo and allude here. Perhaps because the
poem was uncommissioned and so came as a spontaneous expression of a felt
need, perhaps because Lowell wrote it in Rome, a little removed from the ex-
pectations of Cambridge — whatever the cause, the Agassiz ode shows more
innovation than the others. It is of course daring only for Lowell, who viewed
all sudden change in literature, all attempts at a large originality, as a clear
bid for instant mortality. But into the stately slow march of the Elegy, with
its customary procession of present and absent mourners, he introduced, for
instance, with a play of wit and melancholy humor (itself a rarity in elegiac
verse) a meeting of the Saturday Club and vignettes of its members. In the
Agassiz ode, then, Lowell not only adopts a tradition but significantly adapts it.
And although the poem again illustrates Lowell's inability or reluctance to em-
ploy what James calls "an economy of means," much of it remains highly
readable — from its opening allusion to the telegraph ("The electric nerve, whose
instantaneous thrill/ Makes next-door gossips of the antipodes") to passage after
passage of what seem to me happy verbal inventions:

> He had a habitude of mountain air;
> He brought wide outlook where he went,
>   And could on sunny uplands dwell
> Of prospects sweeter than the pastures fair
>   High-hung of viny Neufchâtel;
>   Nor, surely, did he miss
>   Some pale, imaginary bliss
> Of earlier sights whose inner landscape still was Swiss.
> . . . .
>
>   . . . it may be he had trod
> Outside the plain old path of *God thus spake*,
>   But God to him was very God,
>   And not a visionary wraith,

Skulking in murky corners of the mind,
    And he was sure to be
Somehow, somewhere, imperishable as He,
Not with His essence mystically combined,
As some high spirits long, but whole and free,
A perfected and conscious Agassiz.

(pp. 380–81)

Both James and Henry Adams remember afternoons or evenings in Lowell's study at Elmwood where, as Smith Professor of Modern Languages, he read Dante with those Harvard undergraduates who chose to come by. For James, who knew Lowell best when he served as American ambassador to Great Britain, the older New Englander came to represent the quintessential American man of letters. For Adams, who returned to Harvard as Lowell's colleague and acted with him for a time as co-editor of *The North American Review*, Lowell was more than a loved and respected friend. Certain of his attitudes, and the images in which they were cast, worked deeply to influence Adams's own. Thus, James speaks comfortably of "the mellow, witty wisdom" of Lowell's ode "The Cathedral" (p. 349); while, according to Ernest Samuels (in his definitive biography of Adams), the poem's effect on Adams was profound enough to warrant our later attention to it for that reason if no other. "In [Adams's] life-long search for the meaning of these Gothic symbols," Samuels observes, "a poetic chart already existed."

Professor James Russell Lowell, his associate on the *North American*, had recently hymned the glory of Chartres Cathedral in . . . a poem which must now have taken on a richer meaning to Lowell's former proselyte [i.e., Henry Adams]. Its mood strongly presages that of Adams's own *Mont St. Michel and Chartres*. . . . "The Cathedral," filled with religious nostalgia and the anguish of the unwilling skeptic, could not help but speak directly to Henry's heart.

(*The Young Henry Adams* [Cambridge, Mass., 1967], pp. 209–10)

Although, like the "Agassiz," this ode, originally entitled "A Day at Chartres," needs pruning, the lines that so influenced Adams and brought unstinting praise (along with editorial suggestions) from Leslie Stephen and John Ruskin can, I suspect, be heard again — perhaps because we, too, at the close of another century, are again experiencing "a crisis of faith." In any case, much of the poem seems far less "faded" than it did even a decade ago.

Looking up suddenly, I found mine eyes
Confronted with the minster's vast repose.
Silent and gray as forest-leaguered cliff
Left inland by the ocean's slow retreat, . . .
Remembering shocks of surf that clomb and fell,
Spume-sliding down the baffled decuman,
It [Chartres] rose before me, patiently remote
From the great tides of life it breasted once,
Hearing the noise of men as in a dream.

. . . .

I seem to have heard it said by learnëd folk
Who drench you with œsthetics till you feel
As if all beauty were a ghastly bore,

. . . .
That Gothic is not Grecian, therefore worse ;

. . . .
The Grecian gluts me with its perfectness,
Unanswerable as Euclid, self-contained,
The one thing finished in this hasty world,
Forever finished . . .

. . . .
But ah ! this other, this that never ends,
Still climbing, luring fancy still to climb,

. . . .
Graceful, grotesque, with ever new surprise
Of hazardous caprices sure to please,
Heavy as nightmare, airy-light as fern,
Imagination's very self in stone !

. . . .
I looked, and owned myself a happy Goth.
                                        (pp. 352–53)

Lowell's "happy Goth" reached his apotheosis over seventy years ago with the publication of *Mont Saint-Michel and Chartres*. But the influence of Lowell's sensibility and spirit — even of the emblematic figures he raised — does not end there. It can be found again in the attitudes and in the poetry of one of the major writers of our own time. Although Richard Ellman finds Robert Lowell an "unexpected" offshoot from the family tree that includes his great-great uncle, James Russell, there are in fact surprising affinities. Both men, for instance, point, markedly and gratuitously, to a trace of Jewish blood : the elder Lowell was sure the Russells were Jewish and said so, frequently ; the younger begins his autobiographical sketch, *Life Studies*, not with Cabots speaking to Lowells, but with his great-great-grandfather, Mordecai Myers. More fundamentally, both poets, living through periods of social and political upheaval in the United States — bad wars (with Mexico and in Vietnam), violent struggles for the extention of civil rights to blacks, large-scale political corruption — are not only on the same side in each instance but view protest as a proper function of their poetry. Through the work of each writer runs a deep patriotism, conservatively based on a vigorous commitment to ethical idealism, that results in satire, often bitter in tone — the kind that makes unsympathetic bureaucrats label their poems "radical" and, ironically, "un-American." They even share a figure who symbolizes for each of them the bravest and the best : Colonel Robert Gould Shaw, the young Bostonian who led the first company of free Negro troops into the Civil War and was killed with them in battle in South Carolina in July 1863. "I would rather," James Russell wrote Shaw's mother, "have my name known and blest, as his will be, through all the hovels of an outcast race, than blaring from all the trumpets of repute." (For the rest of this letter, see Scudder's headnote to JRL's elegy for Shaw, "Memoriæ Positum" [p. 337].) When Robert Lowell, the more gifted poet of the two, turned his hand to attack the destruction of individual human worth in the past by the technological savagery of the present — a theme in every way congenial to the elder Lowell — he cast it as an elegiac ode, "For the Union Dead": its central figure, Robert Shaw and the Saint-Gaudens bas-relief Boston raised in his honor; its original title, "Colonel Shaw and the Massachusetts 54th." Given all the obvious differences in time, talent, and temperament that separate the poets, the portrait of Shaw in James Lowell's elegiac ode is remarkably akin to the Shaw of "For the Union Dead." From "Memoriæ Positum" (1864):

> Brave, good, and true,
> I see him stand before me now,
> And read again on that young brow,
> Where every hope was new,
> *How sweet were life!* Yet, by the mouth firm-set,
> And look made up for Duty's utmost debt,
> I could divine he knew
> That death within the sulphurous hostile lines,
> In the mere wreck of nobly-pitched designs,
> Plucks heart's-ease, and not rue.

From "For the Union Dead" (1959):

> He has an angry wrenlike vigilance,
> a greyhound's gentle tautness;
>
> He is out of bounds now. He rejoices in man's lovely,
> peculiar pleasure to choose life and die —
> when he leads his black soldiers to death,
> he cannot bend his back.

A measure of the personal importance to James Russell Lowell of Shaw and of the ode he wrote in his memory may be taken from the fact that he plucked a phrase from the poem for the title of the last collection of poetry he published, twenty-five years later: *Heartsease and Rue.*

As this introduction is being written, the Northern Illinois University Press has announced the publication of a modern critical edition of *The Biglow Papers*, First Series, the first edition to appear since 1890. I do not think it a wind-testing straw, catching early vibrations of a Lowell renascence. But it, and this refreshed edition of Lowell's collected poems, may help break the seal that generations of unexamined assumptions have placed on Lowell's work. Reacting to the overpraise of his own contemporaries and eager, rightly, to point to the strengths of writers like Whitman whom those same contemporaries neglected, later critics have consistently pointed to Lowell's *failures*. Now, with Whitman's reputation safe, with the recovery of the fragile and eccentric but genuine poetry of artists like Henry Tuckerman and Jones Very, we may at last be able to afford a place to the *successes* of Lowell. Examined without the political prejudices of the past and freed from the necessity to confront the expectations of antithetic critical "schools," much of that poetry can still please the reader — if by nothing more, then by that happy "shock of recognition" experienced by Ulysses Grant's most recent biographer, William McFeely, when he discovered that Lowell's last poem, "On a Bust of General Grant" (p. 439), expressed his thesis, that his view of Grant was also Lowell's: ". . . the eternal law/ That who can saddle Opportunity/ Is God's elect." James Russell Lowell was not granted such election. Yet the alternative need not be the damnation of oblivion. In addition to its importance to literary history, much of the poetry remains its own excuse for being.

MARJORIE R. KAUFMAN

February 1977
South Hadley, Mass.

EARLIER POEMS

THE first book of poetry issued by Lowell, if we except the pamphlet containing his *Class Poem*, was *A Year's Life*, published in 1841 by C. C. Little and J. Brown, Boston. It contained thirty-two poems and songs and thirty-five sonnets, besides a *l'envoi* headed "Goe, Little Booke," and a dedication addressed, though not formally, to Miss Maria White, to whom he had become engaged in the fall of 1840.

> The gentle Una I have loved,
> The snowy maiden, pure and mild,
> Since ever by her side I roved
> Through ventures strange, a wondering child,
> In fantasy a Red Cross Knight
> Burning for her dear sake to fight.
>
> If there be one who can, like her,
> Make sunshine in life's shady places,
> One in whose holy bosom stir
> As many gentle household graces, —
> And such I think there needs must be, —
> Will she accept this book from me?

The poems which filled the volume had appeared in *The Knickerbocker*, *The Southern Literary Messenger*, and some of the Boston newspapers. How little value the author set upon the contents of this first volume is evident when one discovers that on making his first general collection of poems in 1849, he retained but seven of those printed in *A Year's Life*. He continued to contribute to the magazines of his time, especially to *The Democratic Review*, *Graham's Magazine*, *The Boston Miscellany*, and *The Pioneer*, the last named being a very short-lived magazine which he conducted in company with Mr. Robert Carter, and in 1843 he issued a second volume of *Poems*, in which he gathered the product of the intervening time, whether printed or in manuscript. The division *Earlier Poems*, first used in the collection dated 1877, contains but seven of the poems, two of them being sonnets included in *A Year's Life*. Of the thirty-five poems and thirty-seven sonnets printed in the 1843 volume of *Poems*, seven poems and thirteen sonnets were silently dropped from later collections, and the poems included in the two volumes were distributed mainly between the two divisions *Earlier Poems* and *Miscellaneous Poems*.

THRENODIA

As first printed in *The Knickerbocker* magazine for May, 1839, this poem bore the title *Threnodia on an Infant*, and was signed H. P., the initials for Hugh Perceval, a pseudonym which Lowell used occasionally at the outset of his career. In a letter to G. B. Loring, upon the appearance of the poem, Lowell says that his brother Robert animadverted on the irregular metre of the *Threnodia;* "but as I think," he adds, "very unphilosophically and without much perception of the *true* rules of poetry. In my opinion no verse ought to be longer than the writer can sensibly make it. It has been this senseless stretching of verses to make them octo- or deka-syllabic or what not, that has brought such an abundance of useless epithets on the shoulders of poor English verse."

GONE, gone from us! and shall we see
Those sibyl-leaves of destiny,
Those calm eyes, nevermore?

Those deep, dark eyes so warm and bright,
Wherein the fortunes of the man
Lay slumbering in prophetic light,
In characters a child might scan?
So bright, and gone forth utterly!
Oh stern word — Nevermore!

The stars of those two gentle eyes
Will shine no more on earth;
Quenched are the hopes that had their
    birth,
As we watched them slowly rise,
Stars of a mother's fate;
And she would read them o'er and o'er,
Pondering, as she sate,
Over their dear astrology,
Which she had conned and conned before,
Deeming she needs must read aright
What was writ so passing bright.
And yet, alas! she knew not why,
Her voice would falter in its song,

And tears would slide from out her eye,
Silent, as they were doing wrong.
Oh stern word — Nevermore !

   The tongue that scarce had learned to
     claim
An entrance to a mother's heart
By that dear talisman, a mother's name,
Sleeps all forgetful of its art !
I loved to see the infant soul
(How mighty in the weakness
Of its untutored meekness !)
Peep timidly from out its nest,
His lips, the while,
Fluttering with half-fledged words,
Or hushing to a smile
That more than words expressed,
When his glad mother on him stole
And snatched him to her breast !
Oh, thoughts were brooding in those eyes,
That would have soared like strong-winged
     birds
Far, far into the skies,
Gladding the earth with song,
And gushing harmonies,
Had he but tarried with us long !
Oh stern word — Nevermore !

   How peacefully they rest,
Crossfolded there
Upon his little breast,
Those small, white hands that ne'er were
     still before,
But ever sported with his mother's hair,
Or the plain cross that on her breast she
     wore !
Her heart no more will beat
To feel the touch of that soft palm,
That ever seemed a new surprise
Sending glad thoughts up to her eyes
To bless him with their holy calm, —
Sweet thoughts ! they made her eyes as
     sweet.
How quiet are the hands
That wove those pleasant bands !
But that they do not rise and sink
With his calm breathing, I should think
That he were dropped asleep.
Alas ! too deep, too deep
Is this his slumber !
Time scarce can number
The years ere he shall wake again.
Oh, may we see his eyelids open then !
Oh stern word — Nevermore !

   As the airy gossamere,
Floating in the sunlight clear,
Where'er it toucheth clingeth tightly,
Round glossy leaf or stump unsightly,
So from his spirit wandered out
Tendrils spreading all about,
Knitting all things to its thrall
With a perfect love of all:
Oh stern word — Nevermore !

   He did but float a little way
Adown the stream of time,
With dreamy eyes watching the ripples
     play,
Or hearkening their fairy chime;
His slender sail
Ne'er felt the gale;
He did but float a little way,
And, putting to the shore
While yet 't was early day,
Went calmly on his way,
To dwell with us no more !
No jarring did he feel,
No grating on his shallop's keel;
A strip of silver sand
Mingled the waters with the land
Where he was seen no more:
Oh stern word — Nevermore !

   Full short his journey was; no dust
Of earth unto his sandals clave;
The weary weight that old men must,
He bore not to the grave.
He seemed a cherub who had lost his way
And wandered hither, so his stay
With us was short, and 't was most meet
That he should be no delver in earth's clod,
Nor need to pause and cleanse his feet
To stand before his God:
Oh blest word — Evermore !

THE SIRENS

   This poem in *A Year's Life* is dated Nan-
tasket, July, 1840.

THE sea is lonely, the sea is dreary,
The sea is restless and uneasy;
Thou seekest quiet, thou art weary,
Wandering thou knowest not whither; —
Our little isle is green and breezy,
Come and rest thee !   Oh come hither,
Come to this peaceful home of ours,
    Where evermore

The low west-wind creeps panting up the
    shore
To be at rest among the flowers;
Full of rest, the green moss lifts,
   As the dark waves of the sea
Draw in and out of rocky rifts,
   Calling solemnly to thee
With voices deep and hollow, —
     " To the shore
    Follow! Oh, follow!
    To be at rest forevermore!
     Forevermore!"

Look how the gray old Ocean
From the depth of his heart rejoices,
Heaving with a gentle motion,
When he hears our restful voices;
List how he sings in an undertone,
Chiming with our melody;
And all sweet sounds of earth and air
Melt into one low voice alone,
That murmurs over the weary sea,
And seems to sing from everywhere, —
" Here mayst thou harbor peacefully,
Here mayst thou rest from the aching oar;
   Turn thy curvëd prow ashore,
And in our green isle rest forevermore!
    Forevermore!"
And Echo half wakes in the wooded hill,
   And, to her heart so calm and deep,
   Murmurs over in her sleep,
Doubtfully pausing and murmuring still,
    " Evermore!"
     Thus, on Life's weary sea,
     Heareth the marinere
     Voices sweet, from far and near,
     Ever singing low and clear,
     Ever singing longingly.

Is it not better here to be,
Than to be toiling late and soon?
In the dreary night to see
Nothing but the blood-red moon
Go up and down into the sea;
Or, in the loneliness of day,
   To see the still seals only
Solemnly lift their faces gray,
   Making it yet more lonely?
Is it not better than to hear
Only the sliding of the wave
Beneath the plank, and feel so near
A cold and lonely grave,
A restless grave, where thou shalt lie
Even in death unquietly?
Look down beneath thy wave-worn bark,

Lean over the side and see
The leaden eye of the sidelong shark
   Upturnëd patiently,
   Ever waiting there for thee:
Look down and see those shapeless forms,
   Which ever keep their dreamless sleep
   Far down within the gloomy deep,
And only stir themselves in storms,
Rising like islands from beneath,
And snorting through the angry spray,
As the frail vessel perisheth
In the whirls of their unwieldy play;
   Look down! Look down!
Upon the seaweed, slimy and dark,
That waves its arms so lank and brown,
   Beckoning for thee!
Look down beneath thy wave-worn bark
   Into the cold depth of the sea!
   Look down! Look down!
    Thus, on Life's lonely sea,
    Heareth the marinere
    Voices sad, from far and near,
    Ever singing full of fear,
    Ever singing dreadfully.

Here all is pleasant as a dream;
The wind scarce shaketh down the dew,
The green grass floweth like a stream
    Into the ocean's blue;
     Listen! Oh, listen!
Here is a gush of many streams,
   A song of many birds,
And every wish and longing seems
Lulled to a numbered flow of words, —
     Listen! Oh, listen!
Here ever hum the golden bees
Underneath full-blossomed trees,
At once with glowing fruit and flowers
    crowned; —
So smooth the sand, the yellow sand,
That thy keel will not grate as it touches
    the land;
All around with a slumberous sound,
The singing waves slide up the strand,
And there, where the smooth, wet pebbles be,
The waters gurgle longingly,
As if they fain would seek the shore,
To be at rest from the ceaseless roar,
To be at rest forevermore, —
     Forevermore.
    Thus, on Life's gloomy sea,
    Heareth the marinere
    Voices sweet, from far and near,
    Ever singing in his ear,
   " Here is rest and peace for thee!"

IRENÉ

The indirect as well as direct references to Maria White are frequent in these early poems. Lowell, in a letter to G. B. Loring shortly after this poem appeared, wrote: " Maria fills my ideal and I satisfy hers, and I mean to live as one beloved by such a woman should live. She is every way noble. People have called *Irené* a beautiful piece of poetry. And so it is. It owes all its beauty to her."

HERS is a spirit deep, and crystal-clear;
Calmly beneath her earnest face it lies,
Free without boldness, meek without a
    fear,
Quicker to look than speak its sympathies;
Far down into her large and patient eyes
I gaze, deep-drinking of the infinite,
As, in the mid-watch of a clear, still night,
I look into the fathomless blue skies.

So circled lives she with Love's holy
    light,
That from the shade of self she walketh
    free;
The garden of her soul still keepeth she
An Eden where the snake did never enter;
She hath a natural, wise sincerity,
A simple truthfulness, and these have lent
    her
A dignity as moveless as the centre;
So that no influence of our earth can stir
Her steadfast courage, nor can take away
The holy peacefulness, which night and
    day,
Unto her queenly soul doth minister.

Most gentle is she; her large charity
(An all unwitting, childlike gift in her)
Not freer is to give than meek to bear;
And, though herself not unacquaint with
    care,
Hath in her heart wide room for all that
    be, —
Her heart that hath no secrets of its own,
But open is as eglantine full blown.
Cloudless forever is her brow serene,
Speaking calm hope and trust within her,
    whence
Welleth a noiseless spring of patience,
That keepeth all her life so fresh, so green
And full of holiness, that every look,
The greatness of her woman's soul reveal-
    ing,

Unto me bringeth blessing, and a feeling
As when I read in God's own holy book.

A graciousness in giving that doth make
The small'st gift greatest, and a sense
    most meek
Of worthiness, that doth not fear to take
From others, but which always fears to
    speak
Its thanks in utterance, for the giver's
    sake; —
The deep religion of a thankful heart,
Which rests instinctively in Heaven's clear
    law
With a full peace, that never can depart
From its own steadfastness; — a holy awe
For holy things, — not those which men
    call holy,
But such as are revealèd to the eyes
Of a true woman's soul bent down and
    lowly
Before the face of daily mysteries; —
A love that blossoms soon, but ripens
    slowly
To the full goldenness of fruitful prime,
Enduring with a firmness that defies
All shallow tricks of circumstance and
    time,
By a sure insight knowing where to cling,
And where it clingeth never withering; —
These are Irené's dowry, which no fate
Can shake from their serene, deep-builded
    state.

In-seeing sympathy is hers, which chas-
    teneth
No less than loveth, scorning to be bound
With fear of blame, and yet which ever
    hasteneth
To pour the balm of kind looks on the
    wound,
If they be wounds which such sweet teach-
    ing makes,
Giving itself a pang for others' sakes;
No want of faith, that chills with sidelong
    eye,
Hath she ; no jealousy, no Levite pride
That passeth by upon the other side;
For in her soul there never dwelt a lie.
Right from the hand of God her spirit
    came
Unstained, and she hath ne'er forgotten
    whence
It came, nor wandered far from thence,
But laboreth to keep her still the same,

Near to her place of birth, that she may
  not
Soil her white raiment with an earthly
  spot.

Yet sets she not her soul so steadily
Above, that she forgets her ties to earth,
But her whole thought would almost seem
  to be
How to make glad one lowly human
  hearth;
For with a gentle courage she doth strive
In thought and word and feeling so to live
As to make earth next heaven; and her
  heart
Herein doth show its most exceeding worth,
That, bearing in our frailty her just part,
She hath not shrunk from evils of this life,
But hath gone calmly forth into the strife,
And all its sins and sorrows hath withstood
With lofty strength of patient womanhood:
For this I love her great soul more than
  all,
That, being bound, like us, with earthly
  thrall,
She walks so bright and heaven-like there-
  in, —
Too wise, too meek, too womanly, to sin.

Like a lone star through riven storm-
  clouds seen
By sailors, tempest-tost upon the sea,
Telling of rest and peaceful heavens nigh,
Unto my soul her star-like soul hath been,
Her sight as full of hope and calm to
  me; —
For she unto herself hath builded high
A home serene, wherein to lay her head,
Earth's noblest thing, a Woman perfected.

SERENADE

FROM the close-shut windows gleams no
  spark,
The night is chilly, the night is dark,
The poplars shiver, the pine-trees moan,
My hair by the autumn breeze is blown,
Under thy window I sing alone,
Alone, alone, ah woe ! alone !

The darkness is pressing coldly around,
The windows shake with a lonely sound,
The stars are hid and the night is drear,
The heart of silence throbs in thine ear,

In thy chamber thou sittest alone,
Alone, alone, ah woe ! alone !

The world is happy, the world is wide,
Kind hearts are beating on every side;
Ah, why should we lie so coldly curled
Alone in the shell of this great world ?
Why should we any more be alone ?
Alone, alone, ah woe ! alone !

Oh, 't is a bitter and dreary word,
The saddest by man's ear ever heard !
We each are young, we each have a heart,
Why stand we ever coldly apart ?
Must we forever, then, be alone ?
Alone, alone, ah woe ! alone !

WITH A PRESSED FLOWER

THIS little blossom from afar
Hath come from other lands to thine;
For, once, its white and drooping star
Could see its shadow in the Rhine.

Perchance some fair-haired German maid
Hath plucked one from the selfsame stalk,
And numbered over, half afraid,
Its petals in her evening walk.

"He loves me, loves me not," she cries;
"He loves me more than earth or heaven!"
And then glad tears have filled her eyes
To find the number was uneven.

And thou must count its petals well,
Because it is a gift from me;
And the last one of all shall tell
Something I 've often told to thee.

But here at home, where we were born,
Thou wilt find blossoms just as true,
Down-bending every summer morn,
With freshness of New England dew.

For Nature, ever kind to love,
Hath granted them the same sweet tongue,
Whether with German skies above,
Or here our granite rocks among.

THE BEGGAR

A BEGGAR through the world am I,
From place to place I wander by.

Fill up my pilgrim's scrip for me,
For Christ's sweet sake and charity !

A little of thy steadfastness,
Rounded with leafy gracefulness,
Old oak, give me,
That the world's blasts may round me blow,
And I yield gently to and fro,
While my stout-hearted trunk below
And firm-set roots unshaken be.

Some of thy stern, unyielding might,
Enduring still through day and night
Rude tempest-shock and withering blight,
That I may keep at bay
The changeful April sky of chance
And the strong tide of circumstance, —
Give me, old granite gray.

Some of thy pensiveness serene,
Some of thy never-dying green,
Put in this scrip of mine,
That griefs may fall like snow-flakes light,
And deck me in a robe of white,
Ready to be an angel bright,
O sweetly mournful pine.

A little of thy merriment,
Of thy sparkling, light content,
Give me, my cheerful brook,
That I may still be full of glee
And gladsomeness, where'er I be,
Though fickle fate hath prisoned me
In some neglected nook.

Ye have been very kind and good
To me, since I 've been in the wood;
Ye have gone nigh to fill my heart;
But good-by, kind friends, every one,
I 've far to go ere set of sun;
Of all good things I would have part,
The day was high ere I could start,
And so my journey 's scarce begun.

Heaven help me ! how could I forget
To beg of thee, dear violet !
Some of thy modesty,
That blossoms here as well, unseen,
As if before the world thou 'dst been,
Oh, give, to strengthen me.

MY LOVE

Not as all other women are
Is she that to my soul is dear;

Her glorious fancies come from far,
Beneath the silver evening-star,
And yet her heart is ever near.

Great feelings hath she of her own,
Which lesser souls may never know;
God giveth them to her alone,
And sweet they are as any tone
Wherewith the wind may choose to blow.

Yet in herself she dwelleth not,
Although no home were half so fair;
No simplest duty is forgot,
Life hath no dim and lowly spot
That doth not in her sunshine share.

She doeth little kindnesses,
Which most leave undone, or despise:
For naught that sets one heart at ease,
And giveth happiness or peace,
Is low-esteemèd in her eyes.

She hath no scorn of common things,
And, though she seem of other birth,
Round us her heart intwines and clings,
And patiently she folds her wings
To tread the humble paths of earth.

Blessing she is : God made her so,
And deeds of week-day holiness
Fall from her noiseless as the snow,
Nor hath she ever chanced to know
That aught were easier than to bless.

She is most fair, and thereunto
Her life doth rightly harmonize;
Feeling or thought that was not true
Ne'er made less beautiful the blue
Unclouded heaven of her eyes.

She is a woman: one in whom
The spring-time of her childish years
Hath never lost its fresh perfume,
Though knowing well that life hath room
For many blights and many tears.

I love her with a love as still
As a broad river's peaceful might,
Which, by high tower and lowly mill,
Seems following its own wayward will,
And yet doth ever flow aright.

And, on its full, deep breast serene,
Like quiet isles my duties lie;
It flows around them and between,

And makes them fresh and fair and green,
Sweet homes wherein to live and die.

SUMMER STORM

UNTREMULOUS in the river clear,
Toward the sky's image, hangs the imaged
    bridge;
So still the air that I can hear
The slender clarion of the unseen midge;
    Out of the stillness, with a gathering
        creep,
Like rising wind in leaves, which now de-
    creases,
Now lulls, now swells, and all the while
    increases,
    The huddling trample of a drove of
        sheep
Tilts the loose planks, and then as gradu-
    ally ceases
    In dust on the other side ; life's emblem
        deep,
A confused noise between two silences,
Finding at last in dust precarious peace.
On the wide marsh the purple-blossomed
    grasses
    Soak up the sunshine; sleeps the brim-
        ming tide,
Save when the wedge-shaped wake in si-
    lence passes
    Of some slow water-rat, whose sinuous
        glide
Wavers the sedge's emerald shade from
    side to side;
But up the west, like a rock-shivered surge,
    Climbs a great cloud edged with sun-
        whitened spray;
Huge whirls of foam boil toppling o'er its
    verge,
    And falling still it seems, and yet it
        climbs alway.

    Suddenly all the sky is hid
    As with the shutting of a lid,
    One by one great drops are falling
        Doubtful and slow,
    Down the pane they are crookedly crawl-
        ing,
        And the wind breathes low;
    Slowly the circles widen on the river,
        Widen and mingle, one and all;
    Here and there the slenderer flowers
        shiver,
        Struck by an icy rain-drop's fall.

Now on the hills I hear the thunder mutter,
    The wind is gathering in the west;
The upturned leaves first whiten and flutter,
    Then droop to a fitful rest;
Up from the stream with sluggish flap
    Struggles the gull and floats away;
Nearer and nearer rolls the thunder-clap, —
    We shall not see the sun go down to-day:
Now leaps the wind on the sleepy marsh,
    And tramples the grass with terrified feet,
The startled river turns leaden and harsh,
    You can hear the quick heart of the
        tempest beat.

    Look ! look ! that livid flash !
And instantly follows the rattling thunder,
    As if some cloud-crag, split asunder,
    Fell, splintering with a ruinous crash,
On the Earth, which crouches in silence
    under;
    And now a solid gray wall of rain
Shuts off the landscape, mile by mile;
    For a breath's space I see the blue wood
        again,
And ere the next heart-beat, the wind-
    hurled pile,
    That seemed but now a league aloof,
    Bursts crackling o'er the sun-parched
        roof;
Against the windows the storm comes dash-
    ing,
Through tattered foliage the hail tears
    crashing,
        The blue lightning flashes,
        The rapid hail clashes,
        The white waves are tumbling,
        And, in one baffled roar,
        Like the toothless sea mumbling
        A rock-bristled shore,
        The thunder is rumbling
        And crashing and crumbling, —
    Will silence return nevermore ?

        Hush !   Still as death,
        The tempest holds his breath
        As from a sudden will;
    The rain stops short, but from the eaves
    You see it drop, and hear it from the
        leaves,
        All is so bodingly still;
        Again, now, now, again
    Plashes the rain in heavy gouts,
        The crinkled lightning
        Seems ever brightening,
        And loud and long

Again the thunder shouts
    His battle-song, —
    One quivering flash,
    One wildering crash,
Followed by silence dead and dull,
    As if the cloud, let go,
    Leapt bodily below
To whelm the earth in one mad over-
      throw,
    And then a total lull.

    Gone, gone, so soon !
No more my half-dazed fancy there,
Can shape a giant in the air,
No more I see his streaming hair,
The writhing portent of his form; —
    The pale and quiet moon
Makes her calm forehead bare,
And the last fragments of the storm,
Like shattered rigging from a fight at sea,
Silent and few, are drifting over me.

LOVE

TRUE Love is but a humble, low-born
    thing,
And hath its food served up in earthen
    ware;
It is a thing to walk with, hand in hand,
Through the everydayness of this work-
    day world,
Baring its tender feet to every flint,
Yet letting not one heart-beat go astray
From Beauty's law of plainness and con-
    tent;
A simple, fireside thing, whose quiet smile
Can warm earth's poorest hovel to a home;
Which, when our autumn cometh, as it
    must,
And life in the chill wind shivers bare and
    leafless,
Shall still be blest with Indian-summer
    youth
In bleak November, and, with thankful
    heart,
Smile on its ample stores of garnered fruit,
As full of sunshine to our aged eyes
As when it nursed the blossoms of our
    spring.
Such is true Love, which steals into the
    heart
With feet as silent as the lightsome dawn
That kisses smooth the rough brows of the
    dark.

And hath its will through blissful gentle-
    ness,
Not like a rocket, which, with passionate
    glare,
Whirs suddenly up, then bursts, and leaves
    the night
Painfully quivering on the dazed eyes;
A love that gives and takes, that seeth
    faults,
Not with flaw-seeking eyes like needle
    points,
But loving-kindly ever looks them down
With the o'ercoming faith that still for-
    gives;
A love that shall be new and fresh each
    hour,
As is the sunset's golden mystery,
Or the sweet coming of the evening-star,
Alike, and yet most unlike, every day,
And seeming ever best and fairest *now;*
A love that doth not kneel for what it
    seeks,
But faces Truth and Beauty as their peer,
Showing its worthiness of noble thoughts
By a clear sense of inward nobleness;
A love that in its object findeth not
All grace and beauty, and enough to sate
Its thirst of blessing, but, in all of good
Found there, sees but the Heaven-implanted
    types
Of good and beauty in the soul of man,
And traces, in the simplest heart that beats,
A family-likeness to its chosen one,
That claims of it the rights of brotherhood.
For love is blind but with the fleshly eye,
That so its inner sight may be more clear;
And outward shows of beauty only so
Are needful at the first, as is a hand
To guide and to uphold an infant's steps:
Fine natures need them not: their earnest
    look
Pierces the body's mask of thin disguise,
And beauty ever is to them revealed,
Behind the unshapeliest, meanest lump of
    clay,
With arms outstretched and eager face
    ablaze,
Yearning to be but understood and loved.

TO PERDITA, SINGING

THY voice is like a fountain,
    Leaping up in clear moonshine;
Silver, silver, ever mounting,

Ever sinking,
Without thinking,
To that brimful heart of thine.
Every sad and happy feeling,
Thou hast had in bygone years,
Through thy lips comes stealing, stealing,
Clear and low;
All thy smiles and all thy tears
In thy voice awaken,
And sweetness, wove of joy and woe,
From their teaching it hath taken:
Feeling and music move together,
Like a swan and shadow ever
Floating on a sky-blue river
In a day of cloudless weather.

It hath caught a touch of sadness,
Yet it is not sad;
It hath tones of clearest gladness,
Yet it is not glad;
A dim, sweet twilight voice it is
Where to-day's accustomed blue
Is over-grayed with memories,
With starry feelings quivered through.

Thy voice is like a fountain
Leaping up in sunshine bright,
And I never weary counting
Its clear droppings, lone and single,
Or when in one full gush they mingle,
Shooting in melodious light.

Thine is music such as yields
Feelings of old brooks and fields,
And, around this pent-up room,
Sheds a woodland, free perfume;
Oh, thus forever sing to me!
Oh, thus forever!
The green, bright grass of childhood bring
to me,
Flowing like an emerald river,
And the bright blue skies above!
Oh, sing them back, as fresh as ever,
Into the bosom of my love, —
The sunshine and the merriment,
The unsought, evergreen content,
Of that never cold time,
The joy, that, like a clear breeze, went
Through and through the old time!

Peace sits within thine eyes,
With white hands crossed in joyful rest,
While, through thy lips and face, arise
The melodies from out thy breast;
She sits and sings,

With folded wings
And white arms crost,
" Weep not for bygone things,
They are not lost:
The beauty which the summer time
O'er thine opening spirit shed,
The forest oracles sublime
That filled thy soul with joyous dread,
The scent of every smallest flower
That made thy heart sweet for an hour,
Yea, every holy influence,
Flowing to thee, thou knewest not whence,
In thine eyes to-day is seen,
Fresh as it hath ever been;
Promptings of Nature, beckonings sweet,
Whatever led thy childish feet,
Still will linger unawares
The guiders of thy silver hairs;
Every look and every word
Which thou givest forth to-day,
Tell of the singing of the bird
Whose music stilled thy boyish play."

Thy voice is like a fountain,
Twinkling up in sharp starlight,
When the moon behind the mountain
Dims the low East with faintest white,
Ever darkling,
Ever sparkling,
We know not if 't is dark or bright;
But, when the great moon hath rolled round,
And, sudden-slow, its solemn power
Grows from behind its black, clear-edgëd
bound,
No spot of dark the fountain keepeth,
But, swift as opening eyelids, leapeth
Into a waving silver flower.

THE MOON

My soul was like the sea,
Before the moon was made,
Moaning in vague immensity,
Of its own strength afraid,
Unrestful and unstaid.
Through every rift it foamed in vain,
About its earthly prison,
Seeking some unknown thing in pain,
And sinking restless back again,
For yet no moon had risen:
Its only voice a vast dumb moan,
Of utterless anguish speaking,
It lay unhopefully alone,
And lived but in an aimless seeking.

So was my soul; but when 't was full
    Of unrest to o'erloading,
A voice of something beautiful
    Whispered a dim foreboding,
And yet so soft, so sweet, so low,
It had not more of joy than woe;

And, as the sea doth oft lie still,
    Making its waters meet,
As if by an unconscious will,
    For the moon's silver feet,
So lay my soul within mine eyes
When thou, its guardian moon, didst rise.

And now, howe'er its waves above
    May toss and seem uneaseful,
One strong, eternal law of Love,
    With guidance sure and peaceful,
As calm and natural as breath,
Moves its great deeps through life and death.

REMEMBERED MUSIC

A FRAGMENT

THICK-RUSHING, like an ocean vast
    Of bisons the far prairie shaking,
The notes crowd heavily and fast
As surfs, one plunging while the last
    Draws seaward from its foamy breaking.

Or in low murmurs they began,
    Rising and rising momently,
As o'er a harp Æolian
A fitful breeze, until they ran
    Up to a sudden ecstasy.

And then, like minute-drops of rain
    Ringing in water silverly,
They lingering dropped and dropped again,
Till it was almost like a pain
    To listen when the next would be.

SONG

TO M. L.

A LILY thou wast when I saw thee first,
    A lily-bud not opened quite,
    That hourly grew more pure and white,
By morning, and noontide, and evening
    nursed:
    In all of nature thou hadst thy share;

        Thou wast waited on
        By the wind and sun;
    The rain and the dew for thee took care;
    It seemed thou never couldst be more
        fair.

A lily thou wast when I saw thee first,
    A lily-bud; but oh, how strange,
    How full of wonder was the change,
When, ripe with all sweetness, thy full
    bloom burst!
    How did the tears to my glad eyes start,
        When the woman-flower
        Reached its blossoming hour,
And I saw the warm deeps of thy golden
    heart!

Glad death may pluck thee, but never before
    The gold dust of thy bloom divine
    Hath dropped from thy heart into mine,
To quicken its faint germs of heavenly lore;
For no breeze comes nigh thee but carries
    away
        Some impulses bright
        Of fragrance and light,
Which fall upon souls that are lone and
    astray,
To plant fruitful hopes of the flower of
    day.

ALLEGRA

I WOULD more natures were like thine,
    That never casts a glance before,
Thou Hebe, who thy heart's bright wine
    So lavishly to all dost pour,
That we who drink forget to pine,
    And can but dream of bliss in store.

Thou canst not see a shade in life;
    With sunward instinct thou dost rise,
And, leaving clouds below at strife,
    Gazest undazzled at the skies,
With all their blazing splendors rife,
    A songful lark with eagle's eyes.

Thou wast some foundling whom the
    Hours
    Nursed, laughing, with the milk of
    Mirth;
Some influence more gay than ours
    Hath ruled thy nature from its birth,
As if thy natal stars were flowers
    That shook their seeds round thee on
    earth.

And thou, to lull thine infant rest,
  Wast cradled like an Indian child;
All pleasant winds from south and west
  With lullabies thine ears beguiled,
Rocking thee in thine oriole's nest,
  Till Nature looked at thee and smiled.

Thine every fancy seems to borrow
  A sunlight from thy childish years,
Making a golden cloud of sorrow,
  A hope-lit rainbow out of tears, —
Thy heart is certain of to-morrow,
  Though 'yond to-day it never peers.

I would more natures were like thine,
  So innocently wild and free,
Whose sad thoughts, even, leap and shine,
  Like sunny wavelets in the sea,
Making us mindless of the brine,
  In gazing on the brilliancy.

THE FOUNTAIN

Into the sunshine,
  Full of the light,
Leaping and flashing
  From morn till night;

Into the moonlight,
  Whiter than snow,
Waving so flower-like
  When the winds blow;

Into the starlight
  Rushing in spray,
Happy at midnight,
  Happy by day;

Ever in motion,
  Blithesome and cheery,
Still climbing heavenward,
  Never aweary;

Glad of all weathers,
  Still seeming best,
Upward or downward,
  Motion thy rest;

Full of a nature
  Nothing can tame,
Changed every moment,
  Ever the same;

Ceaseless aspiring,
  Ceaseless content,

Darkness or sunshine
  Thy element;

Glorious fountain,
  Let my heart be
Fresh, changeful, constant,
  Upward, like thee !

ODE

I

In the old days of awe and keen-eyed
    wonder,
  The Poet's song with blood-warm truth
      was rife;
He saw the mysteries which circle under
  The outward shell and skin of daily life.
Nothing to him were fleeting time and
    fashion,
  His soul was led by the eternal law;
There was in him no hope of fame, no pas-
    sion,
  But with calm, godlike eyes he only saw.
He did not sigh o'er heroes dead and
    buried,
  Chief - mourner at the Golden Age's
      hearse,
Nor deem that souls whom Charon grim
    had ferried
  Alone were fitting themes of epic verse:
He could believe the promise of to-morrow,
  And feel the wondrous meaning of to-
      day;
He had a deeper faith in holy sorrow
  Than the world's seeming loss could take
      away.
To know the heart of all things was his
    duty,
  All things did sing to him to make him
      wise,
And, with a sorrowful and conquering
    beauty,
  The soul of all looked grandly from his
      eyes.
He gazed on all within him and without
    him,
  He watched the flowing of Time's steady
      tide,
And shapes of glory floated all about him
  And whispered to him, and he prophe-
      sied.
Than all men he more fearless was and
    freer,

And all his brethren cried with one ac-
    cord, —
"Behold the holy man ! Behold the Seer !
Him who hath spoken with the unseen
    Lord ! "
He to his heart with large embrace had
    taken
    The universal sorrow of mankind,
And, from that root, a shelter never shaken,
    The tree of wisdom grew with sturdy
    rind.
He could interpret well the wondrous voices
    Which to the calm and silent spirit come;
He knew that the One Soul no more rejoices
    In the star's anthem than the insect's
    hum.
He in his heart was ever meek and humble,
    And yet with kingly pomp his numbers
    ran,
As he foresaw how all things false should
    crumble
    Before the free, uplifted soul of man:
And, when he was made full to overflowing
    With all the loveliness of heaven and
    earth,
Out rushed his song, like molten iron glow-
    ing,
    To show God sitting by the humblest
    hearth.
With calmest courage he was ever ready
    To teach that action was the truth of
    thought,
And, with strong arm and purpose firm and
    steady,
    An anchor for the drifting world he
    wrought.
So did he make the meanest man partaker
Of all his brother-gods unto him gave;
All souls did reverence him and name him
    Maker,
    And when he died heaped temples on his
    grave.
And still his deathless words of light are
    swimming
    Serene throughout the great deep infinite
Of human soul, unwaning and undimming,
    To cheer and guide the mariner at night.

II

But now the Poet is an empty rhymer
    Who lies with idle elbow on the grass,
And fits his singing, like a cunning timer,
    To all men's prides and fancies as they
    pass.

Not his the song, which, in its metre holy,
    Chimes with the music of the eternal
    stars,
Humbling the tyrant, lifting up the lowly,
    And sending sun through the soul's prison-
    bars.
Maker no more, — oh no ! unmaker rather,
    For he unmakes who doth not all put
    forth
The power given freely by our loving Father
    To show the body's dross, the spirit's
    worth.
Awake ! great spirit of the ages olden !
    Shiver the mists that hide thy starry lyre,
And let man's soul be yet again beholden
    To thee for wings to soar to her desire.
Oh, prophesy no more to-morrow's splendor,
    Be no more shamefaced to speak out for
    Truth,
Lay on her altar all the gushings tender,
    The hope, the fire, the loving faith of
    youth !
Oh, prophesy no more the Maker's coming,
    Say not his onward footsteps thou canst
    hear
In the dim void, like to the awful humming
    Of the great wings of some new-lighted
    sphere !
Oh, prophesy no more, but be the Poet !
    This longing was but granted unto thee
That, when all beauty thou couldst feel and
    know it,
    That beauty in its highest thou shouldst
    be.
O thou who moanest tost with sealike long-
    ings,
    Who dimly hearest voices call on thee,
Whose soul is overfilled with mighty throng-
    ings
    Of love, and fear, and glorious agony,
Thou of the toil-strung hands and iron sinews
    And soul by Mother Earth with freedom
    fed,
In whom the hero-spirit yet continues,
    The old free nature is not chained or
    dead,
Arouse ! let thy soul break in music-thun-
    der,
    Let loose the ocean that is in thee pent,
Pour forth thy hope, thy fear, thy love, thy
    wonder,
    And tell the age what all its signs have
    meant.
Where'er thy wildered crowd of brethren
    jostles,

Where'er there lingers but a shadow of
wrong,
There still is need of martyrs and apos-
tles,
There still are texts for never-dying song:
From age to age man's still aspiring spirit
Finds wider scope and sees with clearer
eyes,
And thou in larger measure dost inherit
What made thy great forerunners free
and wise.
Sit thou enthronëd where the Poet's moun-
tain
Above the thunder lifts its silent peak,
And roll thy songs down like a gathering
fountain,
They all may drink and find the rest they
seek.
Sing ! there shall silence grow in earth and
heaven,
A silence of deep awe and wondering;
For, listening gladly, bend the angels, even,
To hear a mortal like an angel sing.

III

Among the toil-worn poor my soul is seek-
ing
For who shall bring the Maker's name to
light,
To be the voice of that almighty speaking
Which every age demands to do it right.
Proprieties our silken bards environ;
He who would be the tongue of this wide
land
Must string his harp with chords of sturdy
iron
And strike it with a toil-imbrownëd hand;
One who hath dwelt with Nature well at-
tended,
Who hath learnt wisdom from her mystic
books,
Whose soul with all her countless lives hath
blended,
So that all beauty awes us in his looks;
Who not with body's waste his soul hath
pampered,
Who as the clear northwestern wind is
free,
Who walks with Form's observances un-
hampered,
And follows the One Will obediently;
Whose eyes, like windows on a breezy sum-
mit,
Control a lovely prospect every way;

Who doth not sound God's sea with earthly
plummet,
And find a bottom still of worthless clay ;
Who heeds not how the lower gusts are
working,
Knowing that one sure wind blows on
above,
And sees, beneath the foulest faces lurking,
One God-built shrine of reverence and
love;
Who sees all stars that wheel their shining
marches
Around the centre fixed of Destiny,
Where the encircling soul serene o'erarches
The moving globe of being like a sky;
Who feels that God and Heaven's great
deeps are nearer
Him to whose heart his fellow-man is
nigh,
Who doth not hold his soul's own freedom
dearer
Than that of all his brethren, low or
high;
Who to the Right can feel himself the truer
For being gently patient with the wrong,
Who sees a brother in the evil-doer,
And finds in Love the heart's-blood of his
song; —
This, this is he for whom the world is wait-
ing
To sing the beatings of its mighty heart,
Too long hath it been patient with the grat-
ing
Of scrannel-pipes, and heard it misnamed
Art.
To him the smiling soul of man shall listen,
Laying awhile its crown of thorns aside,
And once again in every eye shall glisten
The glory of a nature satisfied.
His verse shall have a great commanding
motion,
Heaving and swelling with a melody
Learnt of the sky, the river, and the ocean,
And all the pure, majestic things that be.
Awake, then, thou ! we pine for thy great
presence
To make us feel the soul once more sub-
lime,
We are of far too infinite an essence
To rest contented with the lies of Time.
Speak out ! and lo ! a hush of deepest won-
der
Shall sink o'er all this many-voicëd scene,
As when a sudden burst of rattling thunder
Shatters the blueness of a sky serene.

THE FATHERLAND

WHERE is the true man's fatherland?
　Is it where he by chance is born?
　Doth not the yearning spirit scorn
In such scant borders to be spanned?
　Oh yes! his fatherland must be
　As the blue heaven wide and free!

Is it alone where freedom is,
　Where God is God and man is man?
　Doth he not claim a broader span
For the soul's love of home than this?
　Oh yes! his fatherland must be
　As the blue heaven wide and free!

Where'er a human heart doth wear
　Joy's myrtle-wreath or sorrow's gyves,
　Where'er a human spirit strives
After a life more true and fair,
　There is the true man's birthplace grand,
　His is a world-wide fatherland!

Where'er a single slave doth pine,
　Where'er one man may help another, —
　Thank God for such a birthright, bro-
　　ther, —
That spot of earth is thine and mine!
　There is the true man's birthplace grand,
　His is a world-wide fatherland!

THE FORLORN

THE night is dark, the stinging sleet,
　Swept by the bitter gusts of air,
Drives whistling down the lonely street,
　And glazes on the pavement bare.

The street-lamps flare and struggle dim
　Through the gray sleet-clouds as they
　　pass,
Or, governed by a boisterous whim,
　Drop down and rustle on the glass.

One poor, heart-broken, outcast girl
　Faces the east-wind's searching flaws,
And, as about her heart they whirl,
　Her tattered cloak more tightly draws.

The flat brick walls look cold and bleak,
　Her bare feet to the sidewalk freeze;
Yet dares she not a shelter seek,
　Though faint with hunger and disease.

The sharp storm cuts her forehead bare,
　And, piercing through her garments thin,
Beats on her shrunken breast, and there
　Makes colder the cold heart within.

She lingers where a ruddy glow
　Streams outward through an open shut-
　　ter,
Adding more bitterness to woe,
　More loneliness to desertion utter.

One half the cold she had not felt
　Until she saw this gush of light
Spread warmly forth, and seem to melt
　Its slow way through the deadening night.

She hears a woman's voice within,
　Singing sweet words her childhood knew,
And years of misery and sin
　Furl off, and leave her heaven blue.

Her freezing heart, like one who sinks
　Outwearied in the drifting snow,
Drowses to deadly sleep and thinks
　No longer of its hopeless woe:

Old fields, and clear blue summer days,
　Old meadows, green with grass, and trees
That shimmer through the trembling haze
　And whiten in the western breeze,

Old faces, all the friendly past
　Rises within her heart again,
And sunshine from her childhood cast
　Makes summer of the icy rain.

Enhaloed by a mild, warm glow,
　From man's humanity apart,
She hears old footsteps wandering slow
　Through the lone chambers of the heart.

Outside the porch before the door,
　Her cheek upon the cold, hard stone,
She lies, no longer foul and poor,
　No longer dreary and alone.

Next morning something heavily
　Against the opening door did weigh,
And there, from sin and sorrow free,
　A woman on the threshold lay.

A smile upon the wan lips told
　That she had found a calm release,
And that, from out the want and cold,
　The song had borne her soul in peace.

For, whom the heart of man shuts out,
  Sometimes the heart of God takes in,
And fences them all round about
  With silence mid the world's loud din;

And one of his great charities
  Is Music, and it doth not scorn
To close the lids upon the eyes
  Of the polluted and forlorn;

Far was she from her childhood's home,
  Farther in guilt had wandered thence,
Yet thither it had bid her come
  To die in maiden innocence.

MIDNIGHT

The moon shines white and silent
  On the mist, which, like a tide
Of some enchanted ocean,
  O'er the wide marsh doth glide,
Spreading its ghost-like billows
  Silently far and wide.

A vague and starry magic
  Makes all things mysteries,
And lures the earth's dumb spirit
  Up to the longing skies;
I seem to hear dim whispers,
  And tremulous replies.

The fireflies o'er the meadow
  In pulses come and go;
The elm-trees' heavy shadow
  Weighs on the grass below;
And faintly from the distance
  The dreaming cock doth crow.

All things look strange and mystic,
  The very bushes swell
And take wild shapes and motions,
  As if beneath a spell;
They seem not the same lilacs
  From childhood known so well.

The snow of deepest silence
  O'er everything doth fall,
So beautiful and quiet,
  And yet so like a pall;
As if all life were ended,
  And rest were come to all.

O wild and wondrous midnight,
  There is a might in thee

To make the charmèd body
  Almost like spirit be,
And give it some faint glimpses
  Of immortality!

A PRAYER

God! do not let my loved one die,
  But rather wait until the time
That I am grown in purity
  Enough to enter thy pure clime,
Then take me, I will gladly go,
So that my love remain below!

Oh, let her stay! She is by birth
  What I through death must learn to be;
We need her more on our poor earth
  Than thou canst need in heaven with thee:
She hath her wings already, I
Must burst this earth-shell ere I fly.

Then, God, take me! We shall be near,
  More near than ever, each to each:
Her angel ears will find more clear
  My heavenly than my earthly speech;
And still, as I draw nigh to thee,
Her soul and mine shall closer be.

THE HERITAGE

The rich man's son inherits lands,
  And piles of brick and stone, and gold,
And he inherits soft white hands,
  And tender flesh that fears the cold,
  Nor dares to wear a garment old;
A heritage, it seems to me,
One scarce would wish to hold in fee.

The rich man's son inherits cares;
  The bank may break, the factory burn,
A breath may burst his bubble shares,
  And soft white hands could hardly earn
  A living that would serve his turn;
A heritage, it seems to me,
One scarce would wish to hold in fee.

The rich man's son inherits wants,
  His stomach craves for dainty fare;
With sated heart, he hears the pants
  Of toiling hinds with brown arms bare,
  And wearies in his easy-chair;
A heritage, it seems to me,
One scarce would wish to hold in fee.

What doth the poor man's son inherit ?
　Stout muscles and a sinewy heart,
A hardy frame, a hardier spirit;
　King of two hands, he does his part
In every useful toil and art;
A heritage, it seems to me,
A king might wish to hold in fee.

What doth the poor man's son inherit ?
　Wishes o'erjoyed with humble things,
A rank adjudged by toil-won merit,
　Content that from employment springs,
A heart that in his labor sings;
A heritage, it seems to me,
A king might wish to hold in fee.

What doth the poor man's son inherit ?
　A patience learned of being poor,
Courage, if sorrow come, to bear it,
　A fellow-feeling that is sure
To make the outcast bless his door;
A heritage, it seems to me,
A king might wish to hold in fee.

O rich man's son ! there is a toil
　That with all others level stands;
Large charity doth never soil,
　But only whiten, soft white hands;
This is the best crop from thy lands,
A heritage, it seems to me,
Worth being rich to hold in fee.

O poor man's son ! scorn not thy state;
　There is worse weariness than thine,
In merely being rich and great;
　Toil only gives the soul to shine,
And makes rest fragrant and benign;
A heritage, it seems to me,
Worth being poor to hold in fee.

Both, heirs to some six feet of sod,
　Are equal in the earth at last;
Both, children of the same dear God,
　Prove title to your heirship vast
By record of a well-filled past;
A heritage, it seems to me,
Well worth a life to hold in fee.

THE ROSE: A BALLAD

I

IN his tower sat the poet
　Gazing on the roaring sea,

" Take this rose," he sighed, " and throw it
　Where there 's none that loveth me.
On the rock the billow bursteth
　And sinks back into the seas,
But in vain my spirit thirsteth
　So to burst and be at ease.
Take, O sea ! the tender blossom
　That hath lain against my breast;
On thy black and angry bosom
　It will find a surer rest.
Life is vain, and love is hollow,
　Ugly death stands there behind,
Hate and scorn and hunger follow
　Him that toileth for his kind."
Forth into the night he hurled it,
　And with bitter smile did mark
How the surly tempest whirled it
　Swift into the hungry dark.
Foam and spray drive back to leeward,
　And the gale, with dreary moan,
Drifts the helpless blossom seaward,
　Through the breakers all alone.

II

Stands a maiden, on the morrow,
　Musing by the wave-beat strand,
Half in hope and half in sorrow,
　Tracing words upon the sand:
" Shall I ever then behold him
　Who hath been my life so long,
Ever to this sick heart fold him,
　Be the spirit of his song ?
Touch not, sea, the blessed letters
　I have traced upon thy shore,
Spare his name whose spirit fetters
　Mine with love forevermore ! "
Swells the tide and overflows it,
　But, with omen pure and meet,
Brings a little rose, and throws it
　Humbly at the maiden's feet.
Full of bliss she takes the token,
　And, upon her snowy breast,
Soothes the ruffled petals broken
　With the ocean's fierce unrest.
" Love is thine, O heart ! and surely
　Peace shall also be thine own,
For the heart that trusteth purely
　Never long can pine alone."

III

In his tower sits the poet,
　Blisses new and strange to him
Fill his heart and overflow it
　With a wonder sweet and dim.

Up the beach the ocean slideth
  With a whisper of delight,
And the moon in silence glideth
  Through the peaceful blue of night.
Rippling o'er the poet's shoulder
Flows a maiden's golden hair,
Maiden lips, with love grown bolder,
  Kiss his moon-lit forehead bare.
" Life is joy, and love is power,
  Death all fetters doth unbind,
Strength and wisdom only flower
  When we toil for all our kind.
Hope is truth, — the future giveth
  More than present takes away,
And the soul forever liveth
  Nearer God from day to day."
Not a word the maiden uttered,
  Fullest hearts are slow to speak,
But a withered rose-leaf fluttered
  Down upon the poet's cheek.

SONG

Violet ! sweet violet !
Thine eyes are full of tears;
    Are they wet
    Even yet
With the thought of other years ?
Or with gladness are they full,
For the night so beautiful,
And longing for those far-off spheres ?

  Loved one of my youth thou wast,
  Of my merry youth,
    And I see,
    Tearfully,
All the fair and sunny past,
All its openness and truth,
  Ever fresh and green in thee
As the moss is in the sea.

  Thy little heart, that hath with love
  Grown colored like the sky above,
  On which thou lookest ever, —
    Can it know
    All the woe
Of hope for what returneth never,
All the sorrow and the longing
To these hearts of ours belonging ?

  Out on it ! no foolish pining
    For the sky
    Dims thine eye,
Or for the stars so calmly shining;

Like thee let this soul of mine
Take hue from that wherefor I long,
Self-stayed and high, serene and strong,
Not satisfied with hoping — but divine.

  Violet ! dear violet !
  Thy blue eyes are only wet
With joy and love of Him who sent thee,
And for the fulfilling sense
Of that glad obedience
Which made thee all that Nature meant
    thee !

ROSALINE

Thou look'dst on me all yesternight,
Thine eyes were blue, thy hair was bright
As when we murmured our troth-plight
Beneath the thick stars, Rosaline !
Thy hair was braided on thy head,
As on the day we two were wed,
Mine eyes scarce knew if thou wert dead,
But my shrunk heart knew, Rosaline !

The death-watch ticked behind the wall,
The blackness rustled like a pall,
The moaning wind did rise and fall
Among the bleak pines, Rosaline !
My heart beat thickly in mine ears:
The lids may shut out fleshly fears,
But still the spirit sees and hears,
Its eyes are lidless, Rosaline !

A wildness rushing suddenly,
A knowing some ill shape is nigh,
A wish for death, a fear to die,
Is not this vengeance, Rosaline ?
A loneliness that is not lone,
A love quite withered up and gone,
A strong soul ousted from its throne,
What wouldst thou further, Rosaline ?

'T is drear such moonless nights as these,
Strange sounds are out upon the breeze,
And the leaves shiver in the trees,
And then thou comest, Rosaline !
I seem to hear the mourners go,
With long black garments trailing slow,
And plumes anodding to and fro,
As once I heard them, Rosaline !

Thy shroud is all of snowy white,
And, in the middle of the night,
Thou standest moveless and upright,
Gazing upon me, Rosaline !

There is no sorrow in thine eyes,
But evermore that meek surprise, —
O God ! thy gentle spirit tries
To deem me guiltless, Rosaline !

Above thy grave the robin sings,
And swarms of bright and happy things
Flit all about with sunlit wings,
But I am cheerless, Rosaline !
The violets in the hillock toss,
The gravestone is o'ergrown with moss;
For nature feels not any loss,
But I am cheerless, Rosaline !

I did not know when thou wast dead;
A blackbird whistling overhead
Thrilled through my brain; I would have
        fled,
But dared not leave thee, Rosaline !
The sun rolled down, and very soon,
Like a great fire, the awful moon
Rose, stained with blood, and then a swoon
Crept chilly o'er me, Rosaline !

The stars came out; and, one by one,
Each angel from his silver throne
Looked down and saw what I had done:
I dared not hide me, Rosaline !
I crouched; I feared thy corpse would cry
Against me to God's silent sky,
I thought I saw the blue lips try
To utter something, Rosaline !

I waited with a maddened grin
To hear that voice all icy thin
Slide forth and tell my deadly sin
To hell and heaven, Rosaline !
But no voice came, and then it seemed,
That, if the very corpse had screamed,
The sound like sunshine glad had streamed
Through that dark stillness, Rosaline !

And then, amid the silent night,
I screamed with horrible delight,
And in my brain an awful light
Did seem to crackle, Rosaline !
It is my curse ! sweet memories fall
From me like snow, and only all
Of that one night, like cold worms, crawl
My doomed heart over, Rosaline !

Why wilt thou haunt me with thine eyes,
Wherein such blessed memories,
Such pitying forgiveness lies,
Than hate more bitter, Rosaline !

Woe 's me ! I know that love so high
As thine, true soul, could never die,
And with mean clay in churchyard lie, —
Would it might be so, Rosaline !

A REQUIEM

AY, pale and silent maiden,
    Cold as thou liest there,
Thine was the sunniest nature
    That ever drew the air;
The wildest and most wayward,
    And yet so gently kind,
Thou seemedst but to body
    A breath of summer wind.

Into the eternal shadow
    That girds our life around,
Into the infinite silence
    Wherewith Death's shore is bound,
Thou hast gone forth, belovëd !
    And I were mean to weep,
That thou hast left Life's shallows,
    And dost possess the Deep.

Thou liest low and silent,
    Thy heart is cold and still,
Thine eyes are shut forever,
    And Death hath had his will;
He loved and would have taken,
    I loved and would have kept,
We strove, — and he was stronger,
    And I have never wept.

Let him possess thy body,
    Thy soul is still with me,
More sunny and more gladsome
    Than it was wont to be:
Thy body was a fetter
    That bound me to the flesh,
Thank God that it is broken,
    And now I live afresh !

Now I can see thee clearly;
    The dusky cloud of clay,
That hid thy starry spirit,
    Is rent and blown away:
To earth I give thy body,
    Thy spirit to the sky,
I saw its bright wings growing,
    And knew that thou must fly.

Now I can love thee truly,
    For nothing comes between

The senses and the spirit,
  The seen and the unseen;
Lifts the eternal shadow,
  The silence bursts apart,
And the soul's boundless future
  Is present in my heart.

A PARABLE

Worn and footsore was the Prophet,
  When he gained the holy hill;
"God has left the earth," he murmured,
  "Here his presence lingers still.

"God of all the olden prophets,
  Wilt thou speak with men no more ?
Have I not as truly served thee
  As thy chosen ones of yore ?

"Hear me, guider of my fathers,
  Lo ! a humble heart is mine;
By thy mercy I beseech thee
  Grant thy servant but a sign !"

Bowing then his head, he listened
  For an answer to his prayer;
No loud burst of thunder followed,
  Not a murmur stirred the air:

But the tuft of moss before him
  Opened while he waited yet,
And, from out the rock's hard bosom,
  Sprang a tender violet.

"God ! I thank thee," said the Prophet;
  "Hard of heart and blind was I,
Looking to the holy mountain
  For the gift of prophecy.

"Still thou speakest with thy children
  Freely as in eld sublime;
Humbleness, and love, and patience,
  Still give empire over time.

"Had I trusted in my nature,
  And had faith in lowly things,
Thou thyself wouldst then have sought me,
  And set free my spirit's wings.

"But I looked for signs and wonders,
  That o'er men should give me sway;
Thirsting to be more than mortal,
  I was even less than clay.

"Ere I entered on my journey,
  As I girt my loins to start,
Ran to me my little daughter,
  The belovëd of my heart;

"In her hand she held a flower,
  Like to this as like may be,
Which, beside my very threshold,
  She had plucked and brought to me."

SONG

O moonlight deep and tender,
  A year and more agone,
Your mist of golden splendor
  Round my betrothal shone !

O elm-leaves dark and dewy,
  The very same ye seem,
The low wind trembles through ye,
  Ye murmur in my dream !

O river, dim with distance,
  Flow thus forever by,
A part of my existence
  Within your heart doth lie !

O stars, ye saw our meeting,
  Two beings and one soul,
Two hearts so madly beating
  To mingle and be whole !

O happy night, deliver
  Her kisses back to me,
Or keep them all, and give her
  A blissful dream of me !

SONNETS

I

TO A. C. L.

A. C. L. was Mrs. Anna Cabot Lowell (Mrs.
Charles Lowell), the wife of the eldest brother
of the poet, and mother of those gallant bro-
thers, Charles and James, who fell in the war
for the union, and to whom Lowell refers in
the tenth of the second series of *Biglow Papers*.

Through suffering and sorrow thou hast
    passed
To show us what a woman true may be:
They have not taken sympathy from thee,
Nor made thee any other than thou wast,

Save as some tree, which, in a sudden
    blast,
Sheddeth those blossoms, that are weakly
    grown,
Upon the air, but keepeth every one
Whose strength gives warrant of good fruit
    at last:
So thou hast shed some blooms of gayety,
But never one of steadfast cheerfulness;
Nor hath thy knowledge of adversity
Robbed thee of any faith in happiness,
But rather cleared thine inner eyes to see
How many simple ways there are to bless.

II

WHAT were I, Love, if I were stripped of
    thee,
If thine eyes shut me out whereby I live,
Thou, who unto my calmer soul dost give
Knowledge, and Truth, and holy Mystery,
Wherein Truth mainly lies for those who
    see
Beyond the earthly and the fugitive,
Who in the grandeur of the soul believe,
And only in the Infinite are free?
Without thee I were naked, bleak, and
    bare
As yon dead cedar on the sea-cliff's brow;
And Nature's teachings, which come to me
    now,
Common and beautiful as light and air,
Would be as fruitless as a stream which still
Slips through the wheel of some old ruined
    mill.

III

I WOULD not have this perfect love of ours
Grow from a single root, a single stem,
Bearing no goodly fruit, but only flowers
That idly hide life's iron diadem:
It should grow alway like that Eastern
    tree
Whose limbs take root and spread forth
    constantly;
That love for one, from which there doth
    not spring
Wide love for all, is but a worthless thing.
Not in another world, as poets prate,
Dwell we apart above the tide of things,
High floating o'er earth's clouds on faery
    wings;
But our pure love doth ever elevate
Into a holy bond of brotherhood
All earthly things, making them pure and
    good.

IV

" FOR this true nobleness I seek in vain,
In woman and in man I find it not;
I almost weary of my earthly lot,
My life-springs are dried up with burning
    pain."
Thou find'st it not? I pray thee look
    again,
Look *inward* through the depths of thine
    own soul.
How is it with thee?   Art thou sound and
    whole?
Doth narrow search show thee no earthly
    stain?
BE NOBLE! and the nobleness that lies
In other men, sleeping, but never dead,
Will rise in majesty to meet thine own;
Then wilt thou see it gleam in many eyes,
Then will pure light around thy path be
    shed,
And thou wilt nevermore be sad and lone.

V

TO THE SPIRIT OF KEATS

GREAT soul, thou sittest with me in my
    room,
Uplifting me with thy vast, quiet eyes,
On whose full orbs, with kindly lustre, lies
The twilight warmth of ruddy ember-
    gloom:
Thy clear, strong tones will oft bring sud-
    den bloom
Of hope secure, to him who lonely cries,
Wrestling with the young poet's agonies,
Neglect and scorn, which seem a certain
    doom:
Yes! the few words which, like great
    thunder-drops,
Thy large heart down to earth shook doubt-
    fully,
Thrilled by the inward lightning of its
    might,
Serene and pure, like gushing joy of light,
Shall track the eternal chords of Destiny,
After the moon-led pulse of ocean stops.

VI

GREAT Truths are portions of the soul of
    man;
Great souls are portions of Eternity;
Each drop of blood that e'er through true
    heart ran
With lofty message, ran for thee and me;

For God's law, since the starry song began,
Hath been, and still forevermore must be,
That every deed which shall outlast Time's
  span
Must spur the soul to be erect and free;
Slave is no word of deathless lineage
  sprung;
Too many noble souls have thought and
  died,
Too many mighty poets lived and sung,
And our good Saxon, from lips purified
With martyr-fire, throughout the world
  hath rung
Too long to have God's holy cause denied.

VII

I ASK not for those thoughts, that sudden
  leap
From being's sea, like the isle-seeming
  Kraken,
With whose great rise the ocean all is
  shaken
And a heart-tremble quivers through the
  deep;
Give me that growth which some perchance
  deem sleep,
Wherewith the steadfast coral-stems uprise,
Which, by the toil of gathering energies,
Their upward way into clear sunshine
  keep,
Until, by Heaven's sweetest influences,
Slowly and slowly spreads a speck of green
Into a pleasant island in the seas,
Where, mid tall palms, the cane-roofed
  home is seen,
And wearied men shall sit at sunset's hour,
Hearing the leaves and loving God's dear
  power.

VIII

TO M. W., ON HER BIRTHDAY

MAIDEN, when such a soul as thine is born,
The morning - stars their ancient music
  make,
And, joyful, once again their song awake,
Long silent now with melancholy scorn;
And thou, not mindless of so blest a morn,
By no least deed its harmony shalt break,
But shalt to that high chime thy footsteps
  take,
Through life's most darksome passes un-
  forlorn;
Therefore from thy pure faith thou shalt
  not fall,

Therefore shalt thou be ever fair and free,
And in thine every motion musical
As summer air, majestic as the sea,
A mystery to those who creep and crawl
Through Time, and part it from Eternity.

IX

MY Love, I have no fear that thou shouldst
  die;
Albeit I ask no fairer life than this,
Whose numbering-clock is still thy gentle
  kiss,
While Time and Peace with hands en-
  lockèd fly;
Yet care I not where in Eternity
We live and love, well knowing that there is
No backward step for those who feel the
  bliss
Of Faith as their most lofty yearnings
  high:
Love hath so purified my being's core,
Meseems I scarcely should be startled,
  even,
To find, some morn, that thou hadst gone
  before;
Since, with thy love, this knowledge too
  was given,
Which each calm day doth strengthen
  more and more,
That they who love are but one step from
  Heaven.

X

I CANNOT think that thou shouldst pass
  away,
Whose life to mine is an eternal law,
A piece of nature that can have no flaw,
A new and certain sunrise every day;
But, if thou art to be another ray
About the Sun of Life, and art to live
Free from what part of thee was fugitive,
The debt of Love I will more fully pay,
Not downcast with the thought of thee so
  high,
But rather raised to be a nobler man,
And more divine in my humanity,
As knowing that the waiting eyes which
  scan
My life are lighted by a purer being,
And ask high, calm-browed deeds, with it
  agreeing.

XI

THERE never yet was flower fair in vain,
Let classic poets rhyme it as they will;
The seasons toil that it may blow again,

And summer's heart doth feel its every ill;
Nor is a true soul ever born for naught;
Wherever any such hath lived and died,
There hath been something for true free-
    dom wrought,
Some bulwark levelled on the evil side:
Toil on, then, Greatness ! thou art in the
    right,
However narrow souls may call thee
    wrong;
Be as thou wouldst be in thine own clear
    sight,
And so thou shalt be in the world's erelong;
For worldlings cannot, struggle as they
    may,
From man's great soul one great thought
    hide away.

XII

SUB PONDERE CRESCIT

THE hope of Truth grows stronger, day by
    day;
I hear the soul of Man around me waking,
Like a great sea, its frozen fetters break-
    ing,
And flinging up to heaven its sunlit spray,
Tossing huge continents in scornful play,
And crushing them, with din of grinding
    thunder,
That makes old emptinesses stare in won-
    der;
The memory of a glory passed away
Lingers in every heart, as, in the shell,
Resounds the bygone freedom of the sea,
And every hour new signs of promise tell,
That the great soul shall once again be free,
For high, and yet more high, the murmurs
    swell
Of inward strife for truth and liberty.

XIII

BELOVED, in the noisy city here,
The thought of thee can make all turmoil
    cease;
Around my spirit, folds thy spirit clear
Its still, soft arms, and circles it with
    peace;
There is no room for any doubt or fear
In souls so overfilled with love's increase,
There is no memory of the bygone year
But growth in heart's and spirit's perfect
    ease:
How hath our love, half nebulous at first,

Rounded itself into a full-orbed sun !
How have our lives and wills (as haply erst
They were, ere this forgetfulness begun)
Through all their earthly distances out-
    burst,
And melted, like two rays of light in one !

XIV

ON READING WORDSWORTH'S SONNETS IN DEFENCE OF CAPITAL PUNISHMENT

These sonnets, XIV–XIX, when printed in
The Democratic Review for May, 1842, bore
merely the title *Sonnets.*

As the broad ocean endlessly upheaveth,
With the majestic beating of his heart,
The mighty tides, whereof its rightful part
Each sea-wide bay and little weed receiv-
    eth,
So, through his soul who earnestly believeth,
Life from the universal Heart doth flow,
Whereby some conquest of the eternal
    Woe,
By instinct of God's nature, he achieveth:
A fuller pulse of this all-powerful beauty
Into the poet's gulf-like heart doth tide,
And he more keenly feels the glorious duty
Of serving Truth, despised and crucified, —
Happy, unknowing sect or creed, to rest,
And feel God flow forever through his
    breast.

XV

THE SAME CONTINUED

ONCE hardly in a cycle blossometh
A flower-like soul ripe with the seeds of
    song,
A spirit foreordained to cope with wrong,
Whose divine thoughts are natural as
    breath,
Who the old Darkness thickly scattereth
With starry words, that shoot prevailing
    light
Into the deeps, and wither, with the blight
Of serene Truth, the coward heart of
    Death:
Woe, if such spirit thwart its errand high,
And mock with lies the longing soul of
    man !
Yet one age longer must true Culture lie,
Soothing her bitter fetters as she can,
Until new messages of love outstart
At the next beating of the infinite Heart.

XVI

THE SAME CONTINUED

THE love of all things springs from love of
    one;
Wider the soul's horizon hourly grows,
And over it with fuller glory flows
The sky-like spirit of God; a hope begun
In doubt and darkness 'neath a fairer sun
Cometh to fruitage, if it be of Truth;
And to the law of meekness, faith, and
    ruth,
By inward sympathy, shall all be won:
This thou shouldst know, who, from the
    painted feature
Of shifting Fashion, couldst thy brethren
    turn
Unto the love of ever-youthful Nature,
And of a beauty fadeless and eterne;
And always 't is the saddest sight to see
An old man faithless in Humanity.

XVII

THE SAME CONTINUED

A POET cannot strive for despotism;
His harp falls shattered ; for it still must be
The instinct of great spirits to be free,
And the sworn foes of cunning barbarism:
He who has deepest searched the wide
    abysm
Of that life-giving Soul which men call
    fate,
Knows that to put more faith in lies and
    hate
Than truth and love is the true atheism:
Upward the soul forever turns her eyes:
The next hour always shames the hour be-
    fore;
One beauty, at its highest, prophesies
That by whose side it shall seem mean and
    poor;
No Godlike thing knows aught of less and
    less,
But widens to the boundless Perfectness.

XVIII

THE SAME CONTINUED

THEREFORE think not the Past is wise
    alone,
For Yesterday knows nothing of the Best,
And thou shalt love it only as the nest
Whence glory-wingèd things to Heaven
    have flown:

To the great Soul only are all things
    known;
Present and future are to her as past,
While she in glorious madness doth fore-
    cast
That perfect bud, which seems a flower
    full-blown
To each new Prophet, and yet always opes
Fuller and fuller with each day and hour,
Heartening the soul with odor of fresh
    hopes,
And longings high, and gushings of wide
    power,
Yet never is or shall be fully blown
Save in the forethought of the Eternal
    One.

XIX

THE SAME CONCLUDED

FAR 'yond this narrow parapet of Time,
With eyes uplift, the poet's soul should
    look
Into the Endless Promise, nor should brook
One prying doubt to shake his faith sub-
    lime;
To him the earth is ever in her prime
And dewiness of morning; he can see
Good lying hid, from all eternity,
Within the teeming womb of sin and
    crime;
His soul should not be cramped by any bar,
His nobleness should be so Godlike high,
That his least deed is perfect as a star,
His common look majestic as the sky,
And all o'erflooded with a light from far,
Undimmed by clouds of weak mortality.

XX

TO M. O. S.

Mary Orne Story, sister to William Wetmore
Story, afterward married to George Ticknor
Curtis.

MARY, since first I knew thee, to this hour,
My love hath deepened, with my wiser
    sense
Of what in Woman is to reverence;
Thy clear heart, fresh as e'er was forest-
    flower,
Still opens more to me its beauteous
    dower; —
But let praise hush, — Love asks no
    evidence
To prove itself well-placed; we know not
    whence

It gleans the straws that thatch its humble
    bower:
We can but say we found it in the heart,
Spring of all sweetest thoughts, arch foe of
    blame,
Sower of flowers in the dusty mart,
Pure vestal of the poet's holy flame, —
This is enough, and we have done our part
If we but keep it spotless as it came.

XXI

OUR love is not a fading, earthly flower:
Its wingèd seed dropped down from Para-
    dise,
And, nursed by day and night, by sun and
    shower,
Doth momently to fresher beauty rise:
To us the leafless autumn is not bare,
Nor winter's rattling boughs lack lusty
    green.
Our summer hearts make summer's ful-
    ness, where
No leaf, or bud, or blossom may be seen:
For nature's life in love's deep life doth lie,
Love, — whose forgetfulness is beauty's
    death,
Whose mystic key these cells of Thou and I
Into the infinite freedom openeth,
And makes the body's dark and narrow
    grate
The wide-flung leaves of Heaven's own
    palace-gate.

XXII

IN ABSENCE

THESE rugged, wintry days I scarce could
    bear,
Did I not know that, in the early spring,
When wild March winds upon their er-
    rands sing,
Thou wouldst return, bursting on this still
    air,
Like those same winds, when, startled from
    their lair,
They hunt up violets, and free swift brooks
From icy cares, even as thy clear looks
Bid my heart bloom, and sing, and break
    all care:
When drops with welcome rain the April
    day,
My flowers shall find their April in thine
    eyes,
Save there the rain in dreamy clouds doth
    stay,

As loath to fall out of those happy skies;
Yet sure, my love, thou art most like to
    May,
That comes with steady sun when April
    dies.

XXIII

WENDELL PHILLIPS

HE stood upon the world's broad thresh-
    old; wide
The din of battle and of slaughter rose;
He saw God stand upon the weaker side,
That sank in seeming loss before its foes:
Many there were who made great haste
    and sold
Unto the cunning enemy their swords,
He scorned their gifts of fame, and power,
    and gold,
And, underneath their soft and flowery
    words,
Heard the cold serpent hiss; therefore he
    went
And humbly joined him to the weaker
    part,
Fanatic named, and fool, yet well content
So he could be the nearer to God's heart,
And feel its solemn pulses sending blood
Through all the widespread veins of end-
    less good.

XXIV

THE STREET

THEY pass me by like shadows, crowds on
    crowds,
Dim ghosts of men, that hover to and fro,
Hugging their bodies round them like thin
    shrouds
Wherein their souls were buried long ago:
They trampled on their youth, and faith,
    and love,
They cast their hope of human-kind away,
With Heaven's clear messages they madly
    strove,
And conquered, — and their spirits turned
    to clay:
Lo! how they wander round the world,
    their grave,
Whose ever-gaping maw by such is fed,
Gibbering at living men, and idly rave,
" We only truly live, but ye are dead."
Alas! poor fools, the anointed eye may
    trace
A dead soul's epitaph in every face!

XXV

I GRIEVE not that ripe Knowledge takes
    away
The charm that Nature to my childhood
    wore,
For, with that insight, cometh, day by day,
A greater bliss than wonder was before;
The real doth not clip the poet's wings, —
To win the secret of a weed's plain heart
Reveals some clue to spiritual things,
And stumbling guess becomes firm-footed
    art:
Flowers are not flowers unto the poet's
    eyes,
Their beauty thrills him by an inward
    sense;
He knows that outward seemings are but
    lies,
Or, at the most, but earthly shadows,
    whence
The soul that looks within for truth may
    guess
The presence of some wondrous heavenli-
    ness.

XXVI

TO J. R. GIDDINGS

GIDDINGS, far rougher names than thine
    have grown
Smoother than honey on the lips of men;
And thou shalt aye be honorably known,
As one who bravely used his tongue and pen,
As best befits a freeman, — even for those
To whom our Law's unblushing front de-
    nies
A right to plead against the lifelong woes
Which are the Negro's glimpse of Free-
    dom's skies:
Fear nothing, and hope all things, as the
    Right
Alone may do securely; every hour
The thrones of Ignorance and ancient
    Night
Lose somewhat of their long-usurpëd
    power,
And Freedom's lightest word can make
    them shiver
With a base dread that clings to them for-
    ever.

XXVII

I THOUGHT our love at full, but I did err;
Joy's wreath drooped o'er mine eyes; I
    could not see

That sorrow in our happy world must be
Love's deepest spokesman and interpreter:
But, as a mother feels her child first stir
Under her heart, so felt I instantly
Deep in my soul another bond to thee
Thrill with that life we saw depart from
    her;
O mother of our angel child ! twice dear !
Death knits as well as parts, and still, I
    wis,
Her tender radiance shall infold us here,
Even as the light, borne up by inward bliss,
Threads the void glooms of space without
    a fear,
To print on farthest stars her pitying kiss.

L'ENVOI

WHETHER my heart hath wiser grown or
    not,
In these three years, since I to thee in-
    scribed,
Mine own betrothed, the firstlings of my
    muse, —
Poor windfalls of unripe experience,
Young buds plucked hastily by childish
    hands
Not patient to await more full-blown flow-
    ers, —
At least it hath seen more of life and men,
And pondered more, and grown a shade
    more sad;
Yet with no loss of hope or settled trust
In the benignness of that Providence
Which shapes from out our elements awry
The grace and order that we wonder at,
The mystic harmony of right and wrong,
Both working out His wisdom and our
    good:
A trust, Beloved, chiefly learned of thee,
Who hast that gift of patient tenderness,
The instinctive wisdom of a woman's heart.

They tell us that our land was made for
    song,
With its huge rivers and sky-piercing
    peaks,
Its sealike lakes and mighty cataracts,
Its forests vast and hoar, and prairies wide,
And mounds that tell of wondrous tribes
    extinct.
But Poesy springs not from rocks and
    woods;
Her womb and cradle are the human heart,

And she can find a nobler theme for song
In the most loathsome man that blasts the
sight
Than in the broad expanse of sea and shore
Between the frozen deserts of the poles.
All nations have their message from on
high,
Each the messiah of some central thought,
For the fulfilment and delight of Man:
One has to teach that labor is divine;
Another Freedom; and another Mind;
And all, that God is open-eyed and just,
The happy centre and calm heart of all.

Are, then, our woods, our mountains, and
our streams,
Needful to teach our poets how to sing ?
O maiden rare, far other thoughts were ours,
When we have sat by ocean's foaming
marge,
And watched the waves leap roaring on the
rocks,
Than young Leander and his Hero had,
Gazing from Sestos to the other shore.
The moon looks down and ocean worships
her,
Stars rise and set, and seasons come and go
Even as they did in Homer's elder time,
But we behold them not with Grecian eyes:
Then they were types of beauty and of
strength,
But now of freedom, unconfined and pure,
Subject alone to Order's higher law.
What cares the Russian serf or Southern
slave
Though we should speak as man spake
never yet
Of gleaming Hudson's broad magnificence,
Or green Niagara's never-ending roar ?
Our country hath a gospel of her own
To preach and practise before all the
world, —
The freedom and divinity of man,
The glorious claims of human brother-
hood, —
Which to pay nobly, as a freeman should,
Gains the sole wealth that will not fly
away, —
And the soul's fealty to none but God.
These are realities, which make the shows
Of outward Nature, be they ne'er so grand,
Seem small, and worthless, and contempti-
ble.
These are the mountain-summits for our
bards,

Which stretch far upward into heaven it-
self,
And give such widespread and exulting
view
Of hope, and faith, and onward destiny,
That shrunk Parnassus to a molehill
dwindles.
Our new Atlantis, like a morning-star,
Silvers the mirk face of slow-yielding
Night,
The herald of a fuller truth than yet
Hath gleamed upon the upraised face of
Man
Since the earth glittered in her stainless
prime, —
Of a more glorious sunrise than of old
Drew wondrous melodies from Memnon
huge,
Yea, draws them still, though now he sit
waist-deep
In the ingulfing flood of whirling sand,
And look across the wastes of endless gray,
Sole wreck, where once his hundred-gated
Thebes
Pained with her mighty hum the calm,
blue heaven:
Shall the dull stone pay grateful orisons,
And we till noonday bar the splendor out,
Lest it reproach and chide our sluggard
hearts,
Warm-nestled in the down of Prejudice,
And be content, though clad with angel-
wings,
Close-clipped, to hop about from perch to
perch,
In paltry cages of dead men's dead
thoughts ?
Oh, rather, like the skylark, soar and sing,
And let our gushing songs befit the dawn
And sunrise, and the yet unshaken dew
Brimming the chalice of each full-blown
hope,
Whose blithe front turns to greet the
growing day !
Never had poets such high call before,
Never can poets hope for higher one,
And, if they be but faithful to their trust,
Earth will remember them with love and joy,
And oh, far better, God will not forget.
For he who settles Freedom's principles
Writes the death-warrant of all tyranny;
Who speaks the truth stabs Falsehood to
the heart,
And his mere word makes despots tremble
more

Than ever Brutus with his dagger could.
Wait for no hints from waterfalls or
    woods,
Nor dream that tales of red men, brute
    and fierce,
Repay the finding of this Western World,
Or needed half the globe to give them
    birth:
Spirit supreme of Freedom! not for this
Did great Columbus tame his eagle soul
To jostle with the daws that perch in
    courts;
Not for this, friendless, on an unknown sea,
Coping with mad waves and more mutin-
    ous spirits,
Battled he with the dreadful ache at heart
Which tempts, with devilish subtleties of
    doubt,
The hermit of that loneliest solitude,
The silent desert of a great New Thought;
Though loud Niagara were to-day struck
    dumb,
Yet would this cataract of boiling life
Rush plunging on and on to endless deeps,
And utter thunder till the world shall
    cease, —
A thunder worthy of the poet's song,
And which alone can fill it with true life.
The high evangel to our country granted

Could make apostles, yea, with tongues of
    fire,
Of hearts half-darkened back again to
    clay!
'T is the soul only that is national,
And he who pays true loyalty to that
Alone can claim the wreath of patriotism.

Beloved! if I wander far and oft
From that which I believe, and feel, and
    know,
Thou wilt forgive, not with a sorrowing
    heart,
But with a strengthened hope of better
    things;
Knowing that I, though often blind and
    false
To those I love, and oh, more false than
    all
Unto myself, have been most true to thee,
And that whoso in one thing hath been
    true
Can be as true in all. Therefore thy hope
May yet not prove unfruitful, and thy love
Meet, day by day, with less unworthy
    thanks,
Whether, as now, we journey hand in hand,
Or, parted in the body, yet are one
In spirit and the love of holy things.

MISCELLANEOUS POEMS

WHEN Lowell published his second volume, *Poems*, in 1843, he opened it with *A Legend of Brittany*, and dedicated it in the following letter to the painter, William Page: —

MY DEAR FRIEND, —
    The love between us, which can now look back upon happy years of still enlarging confidence, and forward, with a sure trust in its own prophecy of yet deeper and tenderer sympathies, as long as life shall remain to us, stands in no need, I am well aware, of so poor a voucher as an Epistle Dedicatory. True, it is one of Love's chiefest charms, that it must still take special pains to be superfluous in seeking out ways to declare itself, — but for these it demands no publicity, and wishes no acknowledgment. But the admiration which one soul feels for another loses half its worth, if it let slip any opportunity of making itself heard and felt by that strange Abbot of Unreason which we call the World. For the humblest man's true admiration is no uncer-

tain oracle of the verdict of Posterity, — the unerring tribunal where Genius is at last allowed the right of trial by its peers, and to which none but sincere and real Greatness can appeal with an unwavering heart. There the false witnesses of to-day will be unable to appear, being fled to some hospitable Texas in the realms of Limbo, beyond the sphere of its jurisdiction and the summons of its apparitors.
    I have never seen the works of the Great Masters of your Art, but I have studied their lives, and sure I am that no nobler, gentler, or purer spirit than yours was ever anointed by the Eternal Beauty to bear that part of her divine message which it belongs to the Great Painter to reveal. The sympathy of sister pursuits, of an agreeing artistic faith, and, yet more, of a common hope for the final destiny of man, has not been wanting to us, and now you will forgive the pride I feel in having this advantage over you, namely, of telling that admiration in public which I have never stinted to utter in private. You will believe, that, as

your winning that fadeless laurel, which you
deserve, and which will one day surely be
yours, can never heighten my judgment of you,
so nothing that is not in your own control will
ever lower it, and that I shall think as simply
of you when the World's opinion has overtaken
my own, as now.

As the swiftly diverging channels of Life
bear wider and wider apart from us the friends
who hoisted sail with us as fellow-mariners,
when we cast off for the voyage, and as some,

even, who are yet side by side with us, no
longer send back to us an answering cheer, we
are drawn the more closely to those that re-
main, and I would fain hope that this joining
of our names will always be one of our not
least happy memories.

And so, with all best wishes,
            I remain always your friend,
                            J. R. LOWELL.
CAMBRIDGE, December 15, 1843.

A LEGEND OF BRITTANY

Lowell was in high spirits when he was at
work on *A Legend of Brittany*. "I am now
at work," he writes to G. B. Loring, under
date of June 15, 1843, "on a still longer poem
[than Prometheus] in the *ottava rima*, to be the
first in my forthcoming volume. I feel more
and more assured every day that I shall yet do
something that will keep my name (and per-
haps my body) alive. My wings were never so
light and strong as now."

A Legend of Brittany and most of the other
poems in the volume which it opened belong
in the category referred to by him in his *Prefa-
tory Note*, of pieces which he "would gladly
suppress or put into the Coventry of smaller
print in an appendix." Their value is chiefly
in the record they contain of his poetic devel-
opment and his temperament.

PART FIRST

I

FAIR as a summer dream was Margaret,
    Such dream as in a poet's soul might
        start,
Musing of old loves while the moon doth
        set:
    Her hair was not more sunny than her
        heart,
Though like a natural golden coronet
    It circled her dear head with careless
        art,
Mocking the sunshine, that would fain
        have lent
To its frank grace a richer ornament.

II

His loved one's eyes could poet ever speak,
    So kind, so dewy, and so deep were
        hers, —
But, while he strives, the choicest phrase,
        too weak,
    Their glad reflection in his spirit blurs;

As one may see a dream dissolve and
        break
Out of his grasp when he to tell it stirs,
Like that sad Dryad doomed no more to
        bless
The mortal who revealed her loveliness.

III

She dwelt forever in a region bright,
    Peopled with living fancies of her own,
Where naught could come but visions of
        delight,
    Far, far aloof from earth's eternal moan:
A summer cloud thrilled through with rosy
        light,
    Floating beneath the blue sky all alone,
Her spirit wandered by itself, and won
A golden edge from some unsetting sun.

IV

The heart grows richer that its lot is poor,
    God blesses want with larger sympa-
        thies,
Love enters gladliest at the humble door,
    And makes the cot a palace with his
        eyes;
So Margaret's heart a softer beauty wore,
    And grew in gentleness and patience
        wise,
For she was but a simple herdsman's child,
A lily chance-sown in the rugged wild.

V

There was no beauty of the wood or field
    But she its fragrant bosom-secret knew,
Nor any but to her would freely yield
    Some grace that in her soul took root
        and grew:
Nature to her shone as but now revealed,
    All rosy-fresh with innocent morning
        dew,
And looked into her heart with dim, sweet
        eyes
That left it full of sylvan memories.

VI

Oh, what a face was hers to brighten light,
  And give back sunshine with an added
    glow,
To wile each moment with a fresh delight,
  And part of memory's best contentment
    grow !
Oh, how her voice, as with an inmate's
    right,
  Into the strangest heart would welcome
    go,
And make it sweet, and ready to become
Of white and gracious thoughts the chosen
    home !

VII

None looked upon her but he straightway
    thought
  Of all the greenest depths of country
    cheer,
And into each one's heart was freshly
    brought
  What was to him the sweetest time of
    year,
So was her every look and motion fraught
  With out-of-door delights and forest
    lere;
Not the first violet on a woodland lea
Seemed a more visible gift of Spring than
  she.

VIII

Is love learned only out of poets' books ?
  Is there not somewhat in the dropping
    flood,
And in the nunneries of silent nooks,
  And in the murmured longing of the
    wood,
That could make Margaret dream of love-
    lorn looks,
  And stir a thrilling mystery in her blood
More trembly secret than Aurora's tear
Shed in the bosom of an eglatere ?

IX

Full many a sweet forewarning hath the
    mind,
  Full many a whispering of vague desire,
Ere comes the nature destined to unbind
  Its virgin zone, and all its deeps in-
    spire, —
Low stirrings in the leaves, before the wind
  Wake all the green strings of the forest
    lyre,

Faint heatings in the calyx, ere the rose
Its warm voluptuous breast doth all un-
  close.

X

Long in its dim recesses pines the spirit,
  Wildered and dark, despairingly alone;
Though many a shape of beauty wander
    near it,
  And many a wild and half-remembered
    tone
Tremble from the divine abyss to cheer it,
  Yet still it knows that there is only one
Before whom it can kneel and tribute bring,
At once a happy vassal and a king.

XI

To feel a want, yet scarce know what it is,
  To seek one nature that is always new,
Whose glance is warmer than another's
    kiss,
  Whom we can bare our inmost beauty to,
Nor feel deserted afterwards, — for this
  But with our destined co-mate we can
    do, —
Such longing instinct fills the mighty scope
Of the young soul with one mysterious
  hope.

XII

So Margaret's heart grew brimming with
    the lore
  Of love's enticing secrets; and although
She had found none to cast it down before,
  Yet oft to Fancy's chapel she would go
To pay her vows — and count the rosary
    o'ër
  Of her love's promised graces: — haply
    so
Miranda's hope had pictured Ferdinand
Long ere the gaunt wave tossed him on the
    strand.

XIII

A new-made star that swims the lonely
    gloom,
  Unwedded yet and longing for the sun,
Whose beams, the bride-gifts of the lavish
    groom,
  Blithely to crown the virgin planet run,
Her being was, watching to see the bloom
  Of love's fresh sunrise roofing one by
    one
Its clouds with gold, a triumph-arch to be
For him who came to hold her heart in fee.

XIV

Not far from Margaret's cottage dwelt a
    knight
Of the proud Templars, a sworn celibate,
Whose heart in secret fed upon the light
And dew of her ripe beauty, through the
    grate
Of his close vow catching what gleams he
    might
Of the free heaven, and cursing all too late
The cruel faith whose black walls hemmed
    him in
And turned life's crowning bliss to deadly
    sin.

XV

For he had met her in the wood by chance,
    And, having drunk her beauty's wilder-
        ing spell,
His heart shook like the pennon of a lance
That quivers in a breeze's sudden swell,
And thenceforth, in a close-infolded trance,
    From mistily golden deep to deep he fell ;
Till earth did waver and fade far away
Beneath the hope in whose warm arms he
    lay.

XVI

A dark, proud man he was, whose half-
    blown youth
Had shed its blossoms even in opening,
Leaving a few that with more winning ruth
Trembling around grave manhood's stem
    might cling,
More sad than cheery, making, in good
    sooth,
    Like the fringed gentian, a late autumn
        spring:
A twilight nature, braided light and gloom,
A youth half-smiling by an open tomb.

XVII

Fair as an angel, who yet inly wore
    A wrinkled heart foreboding his near
        fall;
Who saw him alway wished to know him
    more,
As if he were some fate's defiant thrall
And nursed a dreaded secret at his core;
    Little he loved, but power the most of all,
And that he seemed to scorn, as one who
    knew
By what foul paths men choose to crawl
    thereto.

XVIII

He had been noble, but some great deceit
    Had turned his better instinct to a vice:
He strove to think the world was all a
    cheat,
That power and fame were cheap at any
    price,
That the sure way of being shortly great
    Was even to play life's game with loaded
        dice,
Since he had tried the honest play and
    found
That vice and virtue differed but in sound.

XIX

Yet Margaret's sight redeemed him for a
    space
    From his own thraldom; man could
        never be
A hypocrite when first such maiden grace
    Smiled in upon his heart; the agony
Of wearing all day long a lying face
    Fell lightly from him, and, a moment
        free,
Erect with wakened faith his spirit stood
And scorned the weakness of his demon-
    mood.

XX

Like a sweet wind-harp to him was her
    thought,
    Which would not let the common air
        come near,
Till from its dim enchantment it had caught
    A musical tenderness that brimmed his
        ear
With sweetness more ethereal than aught
    Save silver-dropping snatches that whil-
        ere
Rained down from some sad angel's faith-
    ful harp
To cool her fallen lover's anguish sharp.

XXI

Deep in the forest was a little dell
    High overarchëd with the leafy sweep
Of a broad oak, through whose gnarled
    roots there fell
    A slender rill that sung itself to sleep,
Where its continuous toil had scooped a well
    To please the fairy folk; breathlessly deep
The stillness was, save when the dreaming
    brook
From its small urn a drizzly murmur shook.

XXII

The wooded hills sloped upward all around
  With gradual rise, and made an even rim,
So that it seemed a mighty casque un-
    bound
  From some huge Titan's brow to lighten
    him,
Ages ago, and left upon the ground,
  Where the slow soil had mossed it to the
    brim,
Till after countless centuries it grew
Into this dell, the haunt of noontide dew.

XXIII

Dim vistas, sprinkled o'er with sun-flecked
    green,
  Wound through the thickset trunks on
    every side,
And, toward the west, in fancy might be
    seen
  A Gothic window in its blazing pride,
When the low sun, two arching elms be-
    tween,
  Lit up the leaves beyond, which, autumn-
    dyed
With lavish hues, would into splendor start,
Shaming the labored panes of richest art.

XXIV

Here, leaning once against the old oak's
    trunk,
  Mordred, for such was the young Tem-
    plar's name,
Saw Margaret come; unseen, the falcon
    shrunk
  From the meek dove; sharp thrills of
    tingling flame
Made him forget that he was vowed a
    monk,
  And all the outworks of his pride o'er-
    came:
Flooded he seemed with bright delicious
    pain,
As if a star had burst within his brain.

XXV

Such power hath beauty and frank inno-
    cence:
  A flower bloomed forth, that sunshine
    glad to bless,
Even from his love's long leafless stem;
    the sense
  Of exile from Hope's happy realm grew
    less,

And thoughts of childish peace, he knew
    not whence,
  Thronged round his heart with many an
    old caress,
Melting the frost there into pearly dew
That mirrored back his nature's morning-
    blue.

XXVI

She turned and saw him, but she felt no
    dread,
  Her purity, like adamantine mail,
Did so encircle her; and yet her head
  She drooped, and made her golden hair
    her veil,
Through which a glow of rosiest lustre
    spread,
  Then faded, and anon she stood all pale,
As snow o'er which a blush of northern-light
Suddenly reddens, and as soon grows
    white.

XXVII

She thought of Tristrem and of Lancilot,
  Of all her dreams, and of kind fairies'
    might,
And how that dell was deemed a haunted
    spot,
  Until there grew a mist before her sight,
And where the present was she half forgot,
  Borne backward through the realms of
    old delight, —
Then, starting up awake, she would have
    gone,
Yet almost wished it might not be alone.

XXVIII

How they went home together through the
    wood,
  And how all life seemed focussed into one
Thought-dazzling spot that set ablaze the
    blood,
  What need to tell ? Fit language there
    is none
For the heart's deepest things. Who ever
    wooed
  As in his boyish hope he would have done ?
For, when the soul is fullest, the hushed
    tongue
Voicelessly trembles like a lute unstrung.

XXIX

But all things carry the heart's messages
  And know it not, nor doth the heart well
    know,

But Nature hath her will; even as the
    bees,
Blithe go-betweens, fly singing to and fro
With the fruit-quickening pollen; — hard
    if these
    Found not some all unthought-of way to
        show
Their secret each to each; and so they did,
And one heart's flower-dust into the other
    slid.

XXX

Young hearts are free; the selfish world it
    is
    That turns them miserly and cold as
        stone,
And makes them clutch their fingers on
    the bliss
    Which but in giving truly is their
        own; —
She had no dreams of barter, asked not
    his,
    But gave hers freely as she would have
        thrown
A rose to him, or as that rose gives forth
Its generous fragrance, thoughtless of its
    worth.

XXXI

Her summer nature felt a need to bless,
    And a like longing to be blest again;
So, from her sky-like spirit, gentleness
    Dropt ever like a sunlit fall of rain,
And his beneath drank in the bright caress
    As thirstily as would a parchèd plain,
That long hath watched the showers of
    sloping gray
For ever, ever, falling far away.

XXXII

How should she dream of ill ? the heart
    filled quite
    With sunshine, like the shepherd's-clock
        at noon,
Closes its leaves around its warm delight;
    Whate'er in life is harsh or out of tune
Is all shut out, no boding shade of blight
    Can pierce the opiate ether of its swoon:
Love is but blind as thoughtful justice is,
But naught can be so wanton-blind as bliss.

XXXIII

All beauty and all life he was to her;
    She questioned not his love, she only
        knew

That she loved him, and not a pulse could
    stir
    In her whole frame but quivered through
        and through
With this glad thought, and was a minister
    To do him fealty and service true,
Like golden ripples hasting to the land
To wreck their freight of sunshine on the
    strand.

XXXIV

O dewy dawn of love ! O hopes that are
    Hung high, like the cliff-swallow's peril-
        ous nest,
Most like to fall when fullest, and that
    jar
    With every heavier billow ! O unrest
Than balmiest deeps of quiet sweeter far !
    How did ye triumph now in Margaret's
        breast,
Making it readier to shrink and start
Than quivering gold of the pond - lily's
    heart !

XXXV

Here let us pause: oh, would the soul
    might ever
    Achieve its immortality in youth,
When nothing yet hath damped its high
    endeavor
    After the starry energy of truth !
Here let us pause, and for a moment sever
    This gleam of sunshine from the sad
        unruth
That sometime comes to all, for it is good
To lengthen to the last a sunny mood.

PART SECOND

I

As one who, from the sunshine and the
    green,
    Enters the solid darkness of a cave,
Nor knows what precipice or pit unseen
    May yawn before him with its sudden
        grave,
And, with hushed breath, doth often for-
    ward lean,
    Dreaming he hears the plashing of a
        wave
Dimly below, or feels a damper air
From out some dreary chasm, he knows
    not where;

II

So, from the sunshine and the green of
    love,
We enter on our story's darker part;
And, though the horror of it well may
    move
An impulse of repugnance in the heart,
Yet let us think, that, as there's naught
    above
The all-embracing atmosphere of Art,
So also there is naught that falls below
Her generous reach, though grimed with
    guilt and woe.

III

Her fittest triumph is to show that good
    Lurks in the heart of evil evermore,
That love, though scorned, and outcast,
    and withstood,
    Can without end forgive, and yet have
        store;
God's love and man's are of the selfsame
    blood,
    And He can see that always at the door
Of foulest hearts the angel-nature yet
Knocks to return and cancel all its debt.

IV

It ever is weak falsehood's destiny
    That her thick mask turns crystal to let
        through
The unsuspicious eyes of honesty;
    But Margaret's heart was too sincere
        and true
Aught but plain truth and faithfulness to
    see,
    And Mordred's for a time a little grew
To be like hers, won by the mild reproof
Of those kind eyes that kept all doubt
    aloof.

V

Full oft they met, as dawn and twilight
    meet
    In northern climes; she full of growing
        day
As he of darkness, which before her feet
    Shrank gradual, and faded quite away,
Soon to return; for power had made love
    sweet
    To him, and, when his will had gained
        full sway,
The taste began to pall; for never power
Can sate the hungry soul beyond an hour.

VI

He fell as doth the tempter ever fall,
    Even in the gaining of his loathsome
        end;
God doth not work as man works, but
    makes all
    The crooked paths of ill to goodness
        tend;
Let him judge Margaret! If to be the
    thrall
    Of love, and faith too generous to defend
Its very life from him she loved, be sin,
What hope of grace may the seducer win?

VII

Grim-hearted world, that look'st with Le-
    vite eyes
    On those poor fallen by too much faith in
        man,
She that upon thy freezing threshold lies,
    Starved to more sinning by thy savage
        ban,
Seeking that refuge because foulest vice
    More godlike than thy virtue is, whose
        span
Shuts out the wretched only, is more free
To enter heaven than thou shalt ever be!

VIII

Thou wilt not let her wash thy dainty feet
    With such salt things as tears, or with
        rude hair
Dry them, soft Pharisee, that sit'st at meat
    With him who made her such, and
        speak'st him fair,
Leaving God's wandering lamb the while to
    bleat
    Unheeded, shivering in the pitiless air:
Thou hast made prisoned virtue show more
    wan
And haggard than a vice to look upon.

IX

Now many months flew by, and weary
    grew
    To Margaret the sight of happy things;
Blight fell on all her flowers, instead of
    dew;
    Shut round her heart were now the joy-
        ous wings
Wherewith it wont to soar; yet not un-
    true,
    Though tempted much, her woman's
        nature clings

To its first pure belief, and with sad eyes
Looks backward o'er the gate of Paradise.

X

And so, though altered Mordred came less
   oft,
   And winter frowned where spring had
     laughed before
In his strange eyes, yet half her sadness
   doffed,
   And in her silent patience loved him
     more:
Sorrow had made her soft heart yet more
   soft,
   And a new life within her own she bore
Which made her tenderer, as she felt it
   move
Beneath her breast, a refuge for her love.

XI

This babe, she thought, would surely bring
   him back,
   And be a bond forever them between;
Before its eyes the sullen tempest-rack
   Would fade, and leave the face of heaven
     serene;
And love's return doth more than fill the
   lack,
   Which in his absence withered the heart's
     green:
And yet a dim foreboding still would flit
Between her and her hope to darken it.

XII

She could not figure forth a happy fate,
   Even for this life from heaven so newly
     come;
The earth must needs be doubly desolate
   To him scarce parted from a fairer
     home:
Such boding heavier on her bosom sate
   One night, as, standing in the twilight
     gloam,
She strained her eyes beyond that dizzy
   verge
At whose foot faintly breaks the future's
   surge.

XIII

Poor little spirit ! naught but shame and woe
   Nurse the sick heart whose lifeblood
     nurses thine:
Yet not those only ; love hath triumphed so,
   As for thy sake makes sorrow more
     divine:

And yet, though thou be pure, the world is
   foe
   To purity, if born in such a shrine;
And, having trampled it for struggling
   thence,
Smiles to itself, and calls it Providence.

XIV

As thus she mused, a shadow seemed to
   rise
   From out her thought, and turn to dreari-
     ness
All blissful hopes and sunny memories,
   And the quick blood would curdle up
     and press
About her heart, which seemed to shut its
   eyes
   And hush itself, as who with shuddering
     guess
Harks through the gloom and dreads e'en
   now to feel
Through his hot breast the icy slide of
   steel.

XV

But, at that heart-beat, while in dread she
   was,
   In the low wind the honeysuckles gleam,
A dewy thrill flits through the heavy
   grass,
   And, looking forth, she saw, as in a
     dream,
Within the wood the moonlight's shadowy
   mass:
   Night's starry heart yearning to hers
     doth seem,
And the deep sky, full-hearted with the
   moon,
Folds round her all the happiness of June.

XVI

What fear could face a heaven and earth
   like this ?
   What silveriest cloud could hang 'neath
     such a sky ?
A tide of wondrous and unwonted bliss
   Rolls back through all her pulses sud-
     denly,
As if some seraph, who had learned to
   kiss
   From the fair daughters of the world
     gone by,
Had wedded so his fallen light with hers,
Such sweet, strange joy through soul and
   body stirs.

XVII

Now seek we Mordred: he who did not fear
  The crime, yet fears the latent conse-
    quence:
If it should reach a brother Templar's ear,
  It haply might be made a good pretence
To cheat him of the hope he held most
    dear;
  For he had spared no thought's or deed's
    expense,
That by and by might help his wish to clip
Its darling bride, — the high grandmaster-
  ship.

XVIII

The apathy, ere a crime resolved is done,
  Is scarce less dreadful than remorse for
    crime;
By no allurement can the soul be won
  From brooding o'er the weary creep of
    time:
Mordred stole forth into the happy sun,
  Striving to hum a scrap of Breton
    rhyme,
But the sky struck him speechless, and he
    tried
In vain to summon up his callous pride.

XIX

In the courtyard a fountain leaped alway,
  A Triton blowing jewels through his
    shell
Into the sunshine; Mordred turned away,
  Weary because the stone face did not tell
Of weariness, nor could he bear to-day,
  Heartsick, to hear the patient sink and
    swell
Of winds among the leaves, or golden bees
Drowsily humming in the orange-trees.

XX

All happy sights and sounds now came to
  him
  Like a reproach: he wandered far and
    wide,
Following the lead of his unquiet whim,
  But still there went a something at his
    side
That made the cool breeze hot, the sun-
    shine dim;
  It would not flee, it could not be defied,
He could not see it, but he felt it there,
By the damp chill that crept among his
  hair.

XXI

Day wore at last; the evening-star arose,
  And throbbing in the sky grew red and
    set;
Then with a guilty, wavering step he goes
  To the hid nook where they so oft had
    met
In happier season, for his heart well knows
  That he is sure to find poor Margaret
Watching and waiting there with love-lorn
  breast
Around her young dream's rudely scattered
  nest.

XXII

Why follow here that grim old chronicle
  Which counts the dagger-strokes and
    drops of blood ?
Enough that Margaret by his mad steel
    fell,
  Unmoved by murder from her trusting
    mood,
Smiling on him as Heaven smiles on Hell,
  With a sad love, remembering when he
    stood
Not fallen yet, the unsealer of her heart,
Of all her holy dreams the holiest part.

XXIII

His crime complete, scarce knowing what
  he did,
  (So goes the tale,) beneath the altar
    there
In the high church the stiffening corpse he
  hid,
  And then, to 'scape that suffocating air,
Like a scared ghoul out of the porch he
    slid;
  But his strained eyes saw blood-spots
    everywhere,
And ghastly faces thrust themselves be-
    tween
His soul and hopes of peace with blasting
  mien.

XXIV

His heart went out within him like a spark
  Dropt in the sea; wherever he made
    bold
To turn his eyes, he saw, all stiff and stark,
  Pale Margaret lying dead; the lavish
    gold
Of her loose hair seemed in the cloudy dark
  To spread a glory, and a thousand-fold

More strangely pale and beautiful she
    grew:
Her silence stabbed his conscience through
    and through.

XXV

Or visions of past days, — a mother's eyes
    That smiled down on the fair boy at her
    knee,
Whose happy upturned face to hers re-
    plies, —
    He saw sometimes: or Margaret mourn-
    fully
Gazed on him full of doubt, as one who
    tries
To crush belief that does love injury;
Then she would wring her hands, but soon
    again
Love's patience glimmered out through
    cloudy pain.

XXVI

Meanwhile he dared not go and steal away
    The silent, dead-cold witness of his sin;
He had not feared the life, but that dull
    clay,
    Those open eyes that showed the death
    within,
Would surely stare him mad; yet all the
    day
    A dreadful impulse, whence his will could
    win
No refuge, made him linger in the aisle,
Freezing with his wan look each greeting
    smile.

XXVII

Now, on the second day there was to be
A festival in church: from far and near
Came flocking in the sunburnt peasantry,
    And knights and dames with stately an-
    tique cheer,
Blazing with pomp, as if all faërie
    Had emptied her quaint halls, or, as it
    were,
The illuminated marge of some old book,
While we were gazing, life and motion took.

XXVIII

When all were entered, and the roving eyes
    Of all were stayed, some upon faces
    bright,
Some on the priests, some on the traceries
    That decked the slumber of a marble
    knight,

And all the rustlings over that arise
    From recognizing tokens of delight,
When friendly glances meet, — then silent
    ease
Spread o'er the multitude by slow degrees.

XXIX

Then swelled the organ: up through choir
    and nave
    The music trembled with an inward thrill
Of bliss at its own grandeur: wave on wave
    Its flood of mellow thunder rose, until
The hushed air shivered with the throb it
    gave,
    Then, poising for a moment, it stood still,
And sank and rose again, to burst in spray
That wandered into silence far away.

XXX

Like to a mighty heart the music seemed,
    That yearns with melodies it cannot
    speak,
Until, in grand despair of what it dreamed,
    In the agony of effort it doth break,
Yet triumphs breaking; on it rushed and
    streamed
    And wantoned in its might, as when a
    lake,
Long pent among the mountains, bursts its
    walls
And in one crowding gush leaps forth and
    falls.

XXXI

Deeper and deeper shudders shook the air,
    As the huge bass kept gathering heavily,
Like thunder when it rouses in its lair,
    And with its hoarse growl shakes the low-
    hung sky,
It grew up like a darkness everywhere,
    Filling the vast cathedral; — suddenly,
From the dense mass a boy's clear treble
    broke
Like lightning, and the full-toned choir
    awoke.

XXXII

Through gorgeous windows shone the sun
    aslant,
    Brimming the church with gold and pur-
    ple mist,
Meet atmosphere to bosom that rich chant,
    Where fifty voices in one strand did twist
Their varicolored tones, and left no want
    To the delighted soul, which sank abyssed

In the warm music cloud, while, far be-
    low,
The organ heaved its surges to and fro.

XXXIII

As if a lark should suddenly drop dead
    While the blue air yet trembled with its
        song,
So snapped at once that music's golden
        thread,
    Struck by a nameless fear that leapt along
From heart to heart, and like a shadow
        spread
    With instantaneous shiver through the
        throng,
So that some glanced behind, as half aware
A hideous shape of dread were standing
    there.

XXXIV

As when a crowd of pale men gather round,
    Watching an eddy in the leaden deep,
From which they deem the body of one
        drowned
    Will be cast forth, from face to face doth
        creep
An eager dread that holds all tongues fast
        bound
    Until the horror, with a ghastly leap,
Starts up, its dead blue arms stretched aim-
        lessly,
Heaved with the swinging of the careless
    sea, —

XXXV

So in the faces of all these there grew,
    As by one impulse, a dark, freezing awe,
Which with a fearful fascination drew
    All eyes toward the altar; damp and
        raw
The air grew suddenly, and no man knew
    Whether perchance his silent neighbor
        saw
The dreadful thing which all were sure
        would rise
To scare the strained lids wider from their
    eyes.

XXXVI

The incense trembled as it upward sent
    Its slow, uncertain thread of wandering
        blue,
As 't were the only living element
    In all the church, so deep the stillness
        grew;

It seemed one might have heard it, as it
    went,
    Give out an audible rustle, curling
        through
The midnight silence of that awestruck air,
More hushed than death, though so much
    life was there.

XXXVII

Nothing they saw, but a low voice was
        heard
    Threading the ominous silence of that
        fear,
Gentle and terrorless as if a bird,
    Wakened by some volcano's glare, should
        cheer
The murk air with his song; yet every
        word
    In the cathedral's farthest arch seemed
        near,
As if it spoke to every one apart,
Like the clear voice of conscience in each
    heart.

XXXVIII

" O Rest, to weary hearts thou art most
        dear !
    O Silence, after life's bewildering din,
Thou art most welcome, whether in the sear
    Days of our age thou comest, or we win
Thy poppy-wreath in youth ! then where-
        fore here
    Linger I yet, once free to enter in
At that wished gate which gentle Death
        doth ope,
Into the boundless realm of strength and
    hope ?

XXXIX

" Think not in death my love could ever
        cease;
    If thou wast false, more need there is
        for me
Still to be true; that slumber were not
        peace,
    If 't were unvisited with dreams of thee:
And thou hadst never heard such words as
        these,
    Save that in heaven I must forever be
Most comfortless and wretched, seeing this
Our unbaptizëd babe shut out from bliss.

XL

" This little spirit with imploring eyes
    Wanders alone the dreary wild of space;

The shadow of his pain forever lies
  Upon my soul in this new dwelling-
    place;
His loneliness makes me in Paradise
  More lonely, and, unless I see his face,
Even here for grief could I lie down and
    die,
Save for my curse of immortality.

XLI

"World after world he sees around him
    swim
  Crowded with happy souls, that take no
    heed
Of the sad eyes that from the night's faint
    rim
  Gaze sick with longing on them as they
    speed
With golden gates, that only shut on him;
  And shapes sometimes from hell's
    abysses freed
Flap darkly by him, with enormous sweep
Of wings that roughen wide the pitchy
    deep.

XLII

"I am a mother, — spirits do not shake
  This much of earth from them, — and I
    must pine
Till I can feel his little hands, and take
  His weary head upon this heart of mine;
And, might it be, full gladly for his sake
  Would I this solitude of bliss resign
And be shut out of heaven to dwell with
    him
Forever in that silence drear and dim.

XLIII

"I strove to hush my soul, and would not
    speak
  At first, for thy dear sake; a woman's love
Is mighty, but a mother's heart is weak,
  And by its weakness overcomes; I strove
To smother bitter thoughts with patience
    meek,
  But still in the abyss my soul would rove,
Seeking my child, and drove me here to
    claim
The rite that gives him peace in Christ's
    dear name.

XLIV

"I sit and weep while blessed spirits sing;
  I can but long and pine the while they
    praise,

And, leaning o'er the wall of heaven, I
    fling
  My voice to where I deem my infant
    strays,
Like a robbed bird that cries in vain to
    bring
  Her nestlings back beneath her wings'
    embrace;
But still he answers not, and I but know
That heaven and earth are both alike in
    woe."

XLV

Then the pale priests, with ceremony due,
  Baptized the child within its dreadful
    tomb
Beneath that mother's heart, whose instinct
    true
  Star-like had battled down the triple
    gloom
Of sorrow, love, and death: young maidens,
    too,
  Strewed the pale corpse with many a
    milkwhite bloom,
And parted the bright hair, and on the
    breast
Crossed the unconscious hands in sign of
    rest.

XLVI

Some said, that, when the priest had
    sprinkled o'er
  The consecrated drops, they seemed to
    hear
A sigh, as of some heart from travail sore
  Released, and then two voices singing
    clear,
Misereatur Deus, more and more
  Fading far upward, and their ghastly
    fear
Fell from them with that sound, as bodies
    fall
From souls upspringing to celestial hall.

PROMETHEUS

In a letter to G. B. Loring, dated June 15, 1843, Lowell writes: "I have been very happy for the last day or two in writing a long poem in blank verse on Prometheus, the Greek archetype of St. Simeon Stylites, the first reformer and locofoco of the Greek Mythology. It will be quite worth your while to read it when it is printed. I hope to see it in the July number of the *Democratic Review*, but fear it was too late, having only been sent on this morning. It is the longest and best poem I have ever written, and overrunning with true radicalism and antislavery. I think that it will open the eyes of some folk and make them think that I am a poet, whatever they may say."

After the appearance of the poem, he regrets the absence of any public notice, and acknowledges thus an appreciative letter from his friend Charles F. Briggs : "Although such great names as Goethe, Byron, and Shelley have all handled the subject in modern times, you will find that I have looked at it from a somewhat new point of view. I have made it *radical*, and I believe that no poet in this age can write much that is good unless he give himself up to this tendency. For radicalism has now for the first time taken a distinctive and acknowledged shape of its own. So much of its spirit as poets in former ages have attained (and from their purer organization they could not fail of some) was by instinct rather than by reason. It has never till now been seen to be one of the two great wings that upbear the universe."

ONE after one the stars have risen and set,
Sparkling upon the hoarfrost on my chain:
The Bear, that prowled all night about the fold
Of the North-star, hath shrunk into his den,
Scared by the blithesome footsteps of the Dawn,
Whose blushing smile floods all the Orient;
And now bright Lucifer grows less and less,
Into the heaven's blue quiet deep - withdrawn.
Sunless and starless all, the desert sky
Arches above me, empty as this heart
For ages hath been empty of all joy,
Except to brood upon its silent hope,
As o'er its hope of day the sky doth now.
All night have I heard voices: deeper yet
The deep low breathing of the silence grew,
While all about, muffled in awe, there stood
Shadows, or forms, or both, clear-felt at heart,
But, when I turned to front them, far along
Only a shudder through the midnight ran,
And the dense stillness walled me closer round.
But still I heard them wander up and down
That solitude, and flappings of dusk wings
Did mingle with them, whether of those hags
Let slip upon me once from Hades deep,

Or of yet direr torments, if such be,
I could but guess; and then toward me came
A shape as of a woman: very pale
It was, and calm; its cold eyes did not move,
And mine moved not, but only stared on them.
Their fixëd awe went through my brain like ice;
A skeleton hand seemed clutching at my heart,
And a sharp chill, as if a dank night fog
Suddenly closed me in, was all I felt:
And then, methought, I heard a freezing sigh,
A long, deep, shivering sigh, as from blue lips
Stiffening in death, close to mine ear. I thought
Some doom was close upon me, and I looked
And saw the red moon through the heavy mist,
Just setting, and it seemed as it were falling,
Or reeling to its fall, so dim and dead
And palsy-struck it looked. Then all sounds merged
Into the rising surges of the pines,
Which, leagues below me, clothing the gaunt loins
Of ancient Caucasus with hairy strength,
Sent up a murmur in the morning wind,
Sad as the wail that from the populous earth
All day and night to high Olympus soars,
Fit incense to thy wicked throne, O Jove!

Thy hated name is tossed once more in scorn
From off my lips, for I will tell thy doom.
And are these tears? Nay, do not triumph, Jove !
They are wrung from me but by the agonies
Of prophecy, like those sparse drops which fall
From clouds in travail of the lightning, when
The great wave of the storm high-curled and black
Rolls steadily onward to its thunderous break.
Why art thou made a god of, thou poor type

Of anger, and revenge, and cunning force?
True Power was never born of brutish
    Strength,
Nor sweet Truth suckled at the shaggy
    dugs
Of that old she-wolf. Are thy thunder-
    bolts,
That quell the darkness for a space, so
    strong
As the prevailing patience of meek Light,
Who, with the invincible tenderness of
    peace,
Wins it to be a portion of herself?
Why art thou made a god of, thou, who
    hast
The never-sleeping terror at thy heart,
That birthright of all tyrants, worse to bear
Than this thy ravening bird on which I
    smile?
Thou swear'st to free me, if I will unfold
What kind of doom it is whose omen flits
Across thy heart, as o'er a troop of doves
The fearful shadow of the kite. What
    need
To know that truth whose knowledge can-
    not save?
Evil its errand hath, as well as Good;
When thine is finished, thou art known no
    more:
There is a higher purity than thou,
And higher purity is greater strength;
Thy nature is thy doom, at which thy heart
Trembles behind the thick wall of thy
    might.
Let man but hope, and thou art straight-
    way chilled
With thought of that drear silence and deep
    night
Which, like a dream, shall swallow thee
    and thine:
Let man but will, and thou art god no
    more,
More capable of ruin than the gold
And ivory that image thee on earth.
He who hurled down the monstrous Titan-
    brood
Blinded with lightnings, with rough thun-
    ders stunned,
Is weaker than a simple human thought.
My slender voice can shake thee, as the
    breeze,
That seems but apt to stir a maiden's hair,
Sways huge Oceanus from pole to pole;
For I am still Prometheus, and foreknow
In my wise heart the end and doom of all.

Yes, I am still Prometheus, wiser grown
By years of solitude, — that holds apart
The past and future, giving the soul room
To search into itself, — and long commune
With this eternal silence; — more a god,
In my long-suffering and strength to meet
With equal front the direst shafts of fate,
Than thou in thy faint-hearted despotism,
Girt with thy baby-toys of force and wrath.
Yes, I am that Prometheus who brought
    down
The light to man, which thou, in selfish
    fear,
Hadst to thyself usurped, — his by sole
    right,
For Man hath right to all save Tyranny, —
And which shall free him yet from thy frail
    throne.
Tyrants are but the spawn of Ignorance,
Begotten by the slaves they trample on,
Who, could they win a glimmer of the
    light,
And see that Tyranny is always weakness,
Or Fear with its own bosom ill at ease,
Would laugh away in scorn the sand-wove
    chain
Which their own blindness feigned for ada-
    mant.
Wrong ever builds on quicksands, but the
    Right
To the firm centre lays its moveless base.
The tyrant trembles, if the air but stir
The innocent ringlets of a child's free hair,
And crouches, when the thought of some
    great spirit,
With world-wide murmur, like a rising
    gale,
Over men's hearts, as over standing corn,
Rushes, and bends them to its own strong
    will.
So shall some thought of mine yet circle
    earth,
And puff away thy crumbling altars, Jove!

And, wouldst thou know of my supreme
    revenge,
Poor tyrant, even now dethroned in heart,
Realmless in soul, as tyrants ever are,
Listen! and tell me if this bitter peak,
This never-glutted vulture, and these
    chains
Shrink not before it; for it shall befit
A sorrow-taught, unconquered Titan-heart.
Men, when their death is on them, seem to
    stand

On a precipitous crag that overhangs
The abyss of doom, and in that depth to see,
As in a glass, the features dim and vast
Of things to come, the shadows, as it
    seems,
Of what have been. Death ever fronts the
    wise;
Not fearfully, but with clear promises
Of larger life, on whose broad vans up-
    borne,
Their outlook widens, and they see beyond
The horizon of the Present and the Past,
Even to the very source and end of things.
Such am I now: immortal woe hath made
My heart a seer, and my soul a judge
Between the substance and the shadow of
    Truth.
The sure supremeness of the Beautiful,
By all the martyrdoms made doubly sure
Of such as I am, this is my revenge,
Which of my wrongs builds a triumphal
    arch,
Through which I see a sceptre and a
    throne.
The pipings of glad shepherds on the hills,
Tending the flocks no more to bleed for
    thee;
The songs of maidens pressing with white
    feet
The vintage on thine altars poured no more;
The murmurous bliss of lovers underneath
Dim grapevine bowers whose rosy bunches
    press
Not half so closely their warm cheeks, un-
    paled
By thoughts of thy brute lust; the hive-
    like hum
Of peaceful commonwealths, where sun-
    burnt Toil
Reaps for itself the rich earth made its own
By its own labor, lightened with glad
    hymns
To an omnipotence which thy mad bolts
Would cope with as a spark with the vast
    sea, —
Even the spirit of free love and peace,
Duty's sure recompense through life and
    death, —
These are such harvests as all master-
    spirits
Reap, haply not on earth, but reap no less
Because the sheaves are bound by hands
    not theirs;
These are the bloodless daggers where-
    withal

They stab fallen tyrants, this their high re-
    venge:
For their best part of life on earth is when,
Long after death, prisoned and pent no
    more,
Their thoughts, their wild dreams even,
    have become
Part of the necessary air men breathe:
When, like the moon, herself behind a
    cloud,
They shed down light before us on life's
    sea,
That cheers us to steer onward still in
    hope.
Earth with her twining memories ivies o'er
Their holy sepulchres; the chainless sea,
In tempest or wide calm, repeats their
    thoughts;
The lightning and the thunder, all free
    things,
Have legends of them for the ears of men.
All other glories are as falling stars,
But universal Nature watches theirs:
Such strength is won by love of human-
    kind.

Not that I feel that hunger after fame,
Which souls of a half-greatness are beset
    with;
But that the memory of noble deeds
Cries shame upon the idle and the vile,
And keeps the heart of Man forever up
To the heroic level of old time.
To be forgot at first is little pain
To a heart conscious of such high intent
As must be deathless on the lips of men;
But, having been a name, to sink and be
A something which the world can do with-
    out,
Which, having been or not, would never
    change
The lightest pulse of fate, — this is indeed
A cup of bitterness the worst to taste,
And this thy heart shall empty to the
    dregs.
Endless despair shall be thy Caucasus,
And memory thy vulture; thou wilt find
Oblivion far lonelier than this peak.
Behold thy destiny ! Thou think'st it much
That I should brave thee, miserable god !
But I have braved a mightier than thou,
Even the sharp tempting of this soaring
    heart,
Which might have made me, scarcely less
    than thou,

A god among my brethren weak and blind,
Scarce less than thou, a pitiable thing
To be down-trodden into darkness soon.
But now I am above thee, for thou art
The bungling workmanship of fear, the
    block
That awes the swart Barbarian; but I
Am what myself have made, — a nature
    wise
With finding in itself the types of all,
With watching from the dim verge of the
    time
What things to be are visible in the gleams
Thrown forward on them from the lumi-
    nous past,
Wise with the history of its own frail
    heart,
With reverence and with sorrow, and with
    love,
Broad as the world, for freedom and for
    man.

Thou and all strength shall crumble, ex-
    cept Love,
By whom, and for whose glory, ye shall
    cease:
And, when thou 'rt but a weary moaning
    heard
From out the pitiless gloom of Chaos, I
Shall be a power and a memory,
A name to fright all tyrants with, a light
Unsetting as the pole-star, a great voice
Heard in the breathless pauses of the
    fight
By truth and freedom ever waged with
    wrong,
Clear as a silver trumpet, to awake
Far echoes that from age to age live on
In kindred spirits, giving them a sense
Of boundless power from boundless suffer-
    ing wrung:
And many a glazing eye shall smile to see
The memory of my triumph (for to meet
Wrong with endurance, and to overcome
The present with a heart that looks beyond,
Are triumph), like a prophet eagle, perch
Upon the sacred banner of the Right.
Evil springs up, and flowers, and bears no
    seed,
And feeds the green earth with its swift
    decay,
Leaving it richer for the growth of truth;
But Good, once put in action or in thought,
Like a strong oak, doth from its boughs
    shed down

The ripe germs of a forest. Thou, weak
    god,
Shalt fade and be forgotten ! but this soul,
Fresh-living still in the serene abyss,
In every heaving shall partake, that grows
From heart to heart among the sons of
    men, —
As the ominous hum before the earthquake
    runs
Far through the Ægean from roused isle
    to isle, —
Foreboding wreck to palaces and shrines,
And mighty rents in many a cavernous
    error
That darkens the free light to man: — This
    heart,
Unscarred by thy grim vulture, as the truth
Grows but more lovely 'neath the beaks
    and claws
Of Harpies blind that fain would soil it,
    shall
In all the throbbing exultations share
That wait on freedom's triumphs, and in
    all
The glorious agonies of martyr-spirits,
Sharp lightning-throes to split the jagged
    clouds
That veil the future, showing them the
    end,
Pain's thorny crown for constancy and
    truth,
Girding the temples like a wreath of stars.
This is a thought, that, like the fabled
    laurel,
Makes my faith thunder-proof; and thy
    dread bolts
Fall on me like the silent flakes of snow
On the hoar brows of aged Caucasus:
But, oh, thought far more blissful, they
    can rend
This cloud of flesh, and make my soul a
    star !

Unleash thy crouching thunders now, O
    Jove !
Free this high heart, which, a poor captive
    long,
Doth knock to be let forth, this heart
    which still,
In its invincible manhood, overtops
Thy puny godship, as this mountain doth
The pines that moss its roots. Oh, even
    now,
While from my peak of suffering I look
    down,

Beholding with a far-spread gush of hope
The sunrise of that Beauty, in whose face,
Shone all around with love, no man shall
    look
But straightway like a god he be uplift
Unto the throne long empty for his sake,
And clearly oft foreshadowed in brave
    dreams
By his free inward nature, which nor thou,
Nor any anarch after thee, can bind
From working its great doom, — now, now
    set free
This essence, not to die, but to become
Part of that awful Presence which doth
    haunt
The palaces of tyrants, to scare off,
With its grim eyes and fearful whisperings
And hideous sense of utter loneliness,
All hope of safety, all desire of peace,
All but the loathed forefeeling of blank
    death, —
Part of that spirit which doth ever brood
In patient calm on the unpilfered nest
Of man's deep heart, till mighty thoughts
    grow fledged
To sail with darkening shadow o'er the
    world,
Filling with dread such souls as dare not
    trust
In the unfailing energy of Good,
Until they swoop, and their pale quarry
    make
Of some o'erbloated wrong, — that spirit
    which
Scatters great hopes in the seed-field of
    man,
Like acorns among grain, to grow and be
A roof for freedom in all coming time !

But no, this cannot be; for ages yet,
In solitude unbroken, shall I hear
The angry Caspian to the Euxine shout,
And Euxine answer with a muffled roar,
On either side storming the giant walls
Of Caucasus with leagues of climbing foam
(Less, from my height, than flakes of
    downy snow),
That draw back baffled but to hurl again,
Snatched up in wrath and horrible turmoil,
Mountain on mountain, as the Titans erst,
My brethren, scaling the high seat of Jove,
Heaved Pelion upon Ossa's shoulders
    broad
In vain emprise.   The moon will come and
    go

With her monotonous vicissitude;
Once beautiful, when I was free to walk
Among my fellows, and to interchange
The influence benign of loving eyes,
But now by aged use grown wearisome; —
False thought ! most false ! for how could
    I endure
These crawling centuries of lonely woe
Unshamed by weak complaining, but for
    thee,
Loneliest, save me, of all created things,
Mild-eyed Astarte, my best comforter,
With thy pale smile of sad benignity ?

    Year after year will pass away and seem
To me, in mine eternal agony,
But as the shadows of dumb summer
    clouds,
Which I have watched so often darkening
    o'er
The vast Sarmatian plain, league-wide at
    first,
But, with still swiftness, lessening on and
    on
Till cloud and shadow meet and mingle
    where
The gray horizon fades into the sky,
Far, far to northward.   Yes, for ages yet
Must I lie here upon my altar huge,
A sacrifice for man.   Sorrow will be,
As it hath been, his portion; endless doom,
While the immortal with the mortal linked
Dreams of its wings and pines for what it
    dreams,
With upward yearn unceasing.   Better
    so:
For wisdom is stern sorrow's patient child,
And empire over self, and all the deep
Strong charities that make men seem like
    gods;
And love, that makes them be gods, from
    her breasts
Sucks in the milk that makes mankind one
    blood.
Good never comes unmixed, or so it seems,
Having two faces, as some images
Are carved, of foolish gods ; one face is
    ill;
But one heart lies beneath, and that is
    good,
As are all hearts, when we explore their
    depths.
Therefore, great heart, bear up ! thou art
    but type
Of what all lofty spirits endure, that fain

Would win men back to strength and
    peace through love:
Each hath his lonely peak, and on each
    heart
Envy, or scorn, or hatred, tears lifelong
With vulture beak; yet the high soul is
    left;
And faith, which is but hope grown wise,
    and love
And patience which at last shall overcome.

THE SHEPHERD OF KING AD-
METUS

THERE came a youth upon the earth,
    Some thousand years ago,
Whose slender hands were nothing worth,
Whether to plough, or reap, or sow.

Upon an empty tortoise-shell
    He stretched some chords, and drew
Music that made men's bosoms swell
Fearless, or brimmed their eyes with dew.

Then King Admetus, one who had
    Pure taste by right divine,
Decreed his singing not too bad
To hear between the cups of wine:

And so, well pleased with being soothed
    Into a sweet half-sleep,
Three times his kingly beard he smoothed,
And made him viceroy o'er his sheep.

His words were simple words enough,
    And yet he used them so,
That what in other mouths was rough
In his seemed musical and low.

Men called him but a shiftless youth,
    In whom no good they saw;
And yet, unwittingly, in truth,
They made his careless words their law.

They knew not how he learned at all,
    For idly, hour by hour,
He sat and watched the dead leaves fall,
Or mused upon a common flower.

It seemed the loveliness of things
    Did teach him all their use,
For, in mere weeds, and stones, and
    springs,
He found a healing power profuse.

Men granted that his speech was wise,
    But, when a glance they caught
Of his slim grace and woman's eyes,
They laughed, and called him good-for-
    naught.

Yet after he was dead and gone,
    And e'en his memory dim,
Earth seemed more sweet to live upon,
More full of love, because of him.

And day by day more holy grew
    Each spot where he had trod,
Till after-poets only knew
Their first-born brother as a god.

THE TOKEN

IT is a mere wild rosebud,
    Quite sallow now, and dry,
Yet there 's something wondrous in it,
    Some gleams of days gone by,
Dear sights and sounds that are to me
The very moons of memory,
And stir my heart's blood far below
Its short-lived waves of joy and woe.

Lips must fade and roses wither,
    All sweet times be o'er;
They   only   smile,   and,   murmuring
    "Thither !"
    Stay with us no more:
And yet ofttimes a look or smile,
Forgotten in a kiss's while,
Years after from the dark will start,
And flash across the trembling heart.

Thou hast given me many roses,
    But never one, like this,
O'erfloods both sense and spirit
    With such a deep, wild bliss;
We must have instincts that glean up
Sparse drops of this life in the cup,
Whose taste shall give us all that we
Can prove of immortality.

Earth's stablest things are shadows,
    And, in the life to come,
Haply some chance-saved trifle
    May tell of this old home:
As now sometimes we seem to find,
In a dark crevice of the mind,
Some relic, which, long pondered o'er,
Hints faintly at a life before.

AN INCIDENT IN A RAILROAD CAR

HE spoke of Burns: men rude and rough
Pressed round to hear the praise of one
Whose heart was made of manly, simple
  stuff,
  As homespun as their own.

And, when he read, they forward leaned,
Drinking, with thirsty hearts and ears,
His brook-like songs whom glory never
  weaned
  From humble smiles and tears.

Slowly there grew a tender awe,
Sun-like, o'er faces brown and hard,
As if in him who read they felt and saw
  Some presence of the bard.

It was a sight for sin and wrong
And slavish tyranny to see,
A sight to make our faith more pure and
  strong
  In high humanity.

I thought, these men will carry hence
Promptings their former life above,
And something of a finer reverence
  For beauty, truth, and love.

God scatters love on every side
Freely among his children all,
And always hearts are lying open wide,
  Wherein some grains may fall.

There is no wind but soweth seeds
Of a more true and open life,
Which burst, unlooked for, into high-souled
  deeds,
  With wayside beauty rife.

We find within these souls of ours
Some wild germs of a higher birth,
Which in the poet's tropic heart bear flowers
  Whose fragrance fills the earth.

Within the hearts of all men lie
These promises of wider bliss,
Which blossom into hopes that cannot die,
  In sunny hours like this.

All that hath been majestical
In life or death, since time began,
Is native in the simple heart of all,
  The angel heart of man.

And thus, among the untaught poor,
Great deeds and feelings find a home,
That cast in shadow all the golden lore
  Of classic Greece and Rome.

O mighty brother-soul of man,
Where'er thou art, in low or high,
Thy skyey arches with exulting span
  O'er-roof infinity!

All thoughts that mould the age begin
Deep down within the primitive soul,
And from the many slowly upward win
  To one who grasps the whole:

In his wide brain the feeling deep
That struggled on the many's tongue
Swells to a tide of thought, whose surges
  leap
  O'er the weak thrones of wrong.

All thought begins in feeling, — wide
In the great mass its base is hid,
And, narrowing up to thought, stands
  glorified,
  A moveless pyramid.

Nor is he far astray, who deems
That every hope, which rises and grows
  broad
In the world's heart, by ordered impulse
  streams
  From the great heart of God.

God wills, man hopes: in common souls
Hope is but vague and undefined,
Till from the poet's tongue the message
  rolls
  A blessing to his kind.

Never did Poesy appear
So full of heaven to me, as when
I saw how it would pierce through pride
  and fear
  To the lives of coarsest men.

It may be glorious to write
Thoughts that shall glad the two or
  three
High souls, like those far stars that come in
  sight
  Once in a century; —

But better far it is to speak
One simple word, which now and then
Shall waken their free nature in the weak
And friendless sons of men;

To write some earnest verse or line,
Which, seeking not the praise of art,
Shall make a clearer faith and manhood
shine
In the untutored heart.

He who doth this, in verse or prose,
May be forgotten in his day,
But surely shall be crowned at last with
those
Who live and speak for aye.

RHŒCUS

GOD sends his teachers unto every age,
To every clime, and every race of men,
With revelations fitted to their growth
And shape of mind, nor gives the realm of
Truth
Into the selfish rule of one sole race:
Therefore each form of worship that hath
swayed
The life of man, and given it to grasp
The master-key of knowledge, reverence,
Infolds some germs of goodness and of
right;
Else never had the eager soul, which
loathes
The slothful down of pampered ignorance,
Found in it even a moment's fitful rest.

There is an instinct in the human heart
Which makes that all the fables it hath
coined,
To justify the reign of its belief
And strengthen it by beauty's right divine,
Veil in their inner cells a mystic gift,
Which, like the hazel twig, in faithful
hands,
Points surely to the hidden springs of
truth.
For, as in nature naught is made in vain,
But all things have within their hull of
use
A wisdom and a meaning which may speak
Of spiritual secrets to the ear
Of spirit; so, in whatso'er the heart
Hath fashioned for a solace to itself,
To make its inspirations suit its creed,

And from the niggard hands of falsehood
wring
Its needful food of truth, there ever is
A sympathy with Nature, which reveals,
Not less than her own works, pure gleams
of light
And earnest parables of inward lore.
Hear now this fairy legend of old Greece,
As full of gracious youth, and beauty still
As the immortal freshness of that grace
Carved for all ages on some Attic frieze.

A youth named Rhœcus, wandering in
the wood,
Saw an old oak just trembling to its fall,
And, feeling pity of so fair a tree,
He propped its gray trunk with admiring
care,
And with a thoughtless footstep loitered
on.
But, as he turned, he heard a voice behind
That murmured "Rhœcus!" 'T was as if
the leaves,
Stirred by a passing breath, had murmured
it,
And, while he paused bewildered, yet again
It murmured "Rhœcus!" softer than a
breeze.
He started and beheld with dizzy eyes
What seemed the substance of a happy
dream
Stand there before him, spreading a warm
glow
Within the green glooms of the shadowy
oak.
It seemed a woman's shape, yet far too fair
To be a woman, and with eyes too meek
For any that were wont to mate with gods.
All naked like a goddess stood she there,
And like a goddess all too beautiful
To feel the guilt-born earthliness of shame.
"Rhœcus, I am the Dryad of this tree,"
Thus she began, dropping her low-toned
words
Serene, and full, and clear, as drops of dew,
"And with it I am doomed to live and die;
The rain and sunshine are my caterers,
Nor have I other bliss than simple life;
Now ask me what thou wilt, that I can
give,
And with a thankful joy it shall be thine."

Then Rhœcus, with a flutter at the heart,
Yet by the prompting of such beauty bold,
Answered: "What is there that can satisfy

The endless craving of the soul but love ?
Give me thy love, or but the hope of that
Which must be evermore my nature's
    goal."
After a little pause she said again,
But with a glimpse of sadness in her tone,
"I give it, Rhœcus, though a perilous gift;
An hour before the sunset meet me here."
And straightway there was nothing he
    could see
But the green glooms beneath the shadowy
    oak,
And not a sound came to his straining ears
But the low trickling rustle of the leaves,
And far away upon an emerald slope
The falter of an idle shepherd's pipe.

Now, in those days of simpleness and
    faith,
Men did not think that happy things were
    dreams
Because they overstepped the narrow bourn
Of likelihood, but reverently deemed
Nothing too wondrous or too beautiful
To be the guerdon of a daring heart.
So Rhœcus made no doubt that he was
    blest,
And all along unto the city's gate
Earth seemed to spring beneath him as he
    walked,
The clear, broad sky looked bluer than its
    wont,
And he could scarce believe he had not
    wings,
Such sunshine seemed to glitter through
    his veins
Instead of blood, so light he felt and
    strange.

Young Rhœcus had a faithful heart
    enough,
But one that in the present dwelt too
    much,
And, taking with blithe welcome whatso-
    e'er
Chance gave of joy, was wholly bound in
    that,
Like the contented peasant of a vale,
Deemed it the world, and never looked
    beyond.
So, haply meeting in the afternoon
Some comrades who were playing at the
    dice,
He joined them, and forgot all else be-
    side.

The dice were rattling at the merriest,
And Rhœcus, who had met but sorry luck,
Just laughed in triumph at a happy throw,
When through the room there hummed a
    yellow bee
That buzzed about his ear with down-
    dropped legs
As if to light. And Rhœcus laughed and
    said,
Feeling how red and flushed he was with
    loss,
"By Venus ! does he take me for a rose ? "
And brushed him off with rough, impa-
    tient hand.
But still the bee came back, and thrice
    again
Rhœcus did beat him off with growing
    wrath.
Then through the window flew the wounded
    bee,
And Rhœcus, tracking him with angry
    eyes,
Saw a sharp mountain-peak of Thessaly
Against the red disk of the setting sun,—
And instantly the blood sank from his
    heart,
As if its very walls had caved away.
Without a word he turned, and, rushing
    forth,
Ran madly through the city and the gate,
And o'er the plain, which now the wood's
    long shade,
By the low sun thrown forward broad and
    dim,
Darkened wellnigh unto the city's wall.

Quite spent and out of breath he reached
    the tree,
And, listening fearfully, he heard once
    more
The low voice murmur "Rhœcus ! " close
    at hand:
Whereat he looked around him, but could
    see
Naught but the deepening glooms beneath
    the oak.
Then sighed the voice, "O Rhœcus ! never-
    more
Shalt thou behold me or by day or night,
Me, who would fain have blessed thee with
    a love
More ripe and bounteous than ever yet
Filled up with nectar any mortal heart:
But thou didst scorn my humble messen-
    ger,

And sent'st him back to me with bruisèd
  wings.
We spirits only show to gentle eyes,
We ever ask an undivided love,
And he who scorns the least of Nature's
  works
Is thenceforth exiled and shut out from all.
Farewell! for thou canst never see me
  more."

Then Rhœcus beat his breast, and
  groaned aloud,
And cried, " Be pitiful! forgive me yet
This once, and I shall never need it
  more!"
"Alas!" the voice returned, "'t is thou
  art blind,
Not I unmerciful; I can forgive,
But have no skill to heal thy spirit's eyes;
Only the soul hath power o'er itself."
With that again there murmured "Never-
  more!"
And Rhœcus after heard no other sound,
Except the rattling of the oak's crisp
  leaves,
Like the long surf upon a distant shore,
Raking the sea-worn pebbles up and down.
The night had gathered round him: o'er
  the plain
The city sparkled with its thousand lights,
And sounds of revel fell upon his ear
Harshly and like a curse; above, the sky,
With all its bright sublimity of stars,
Deepened, and on his forehead smote the
  breeze:
Beauty was all around him and delight,
But from that eve he was alone on earth.

THE FALCON

I KNOW a falcon swift and peerless
  As e'er was cradled in the pine;
No bird had ever eye so fearless,
  Or wing so strong as this of mine.

The winds not better love to pilot
  A cloud with molten gold o'errun,
Than him, a little burning islet,
  A star above the coming sun.

For with a lark's heart he doth tower,
  By a glorious upward instinct drawn;
No bee nestles deeper in the flower
  Than he in the bursting rose of dawn.

No harmless dove, no bird that singeth,
  Shudders to see him overhead;
The rush of his fierce swooping bringeth
  To innocent hearts no thrill of dread.

Let fraud and wrong and baseness shiver,
  For still between them and the sky
The falcon Truth hangs poised forever
  And marks them with his vengeful eye.

TRIAL

I

WHETHER the idle prisoner through his
  grate
Watches the waving of the grass-tuft small,
Which, having colonized its rift i' th' wall,
Accepts God's dole of good or evil fate,
And from the sky's just helmet draws its
  lot
Daily of shower or sunshine, cold or hot;—
Whether the closer captive of a creed,
Cooped up from birth to grind out endless
  chaff,
Sees through his treadmill-bars the noonday
  laugh,
And feels in vain his crumpled pinions
  breed;—
Whether the Georgian slave look up and
  mark,
With bellying sails puffed full, the tall
  cloud-bark
Sink northward slowly,—thou alone seem'st
  good,
Fair only thou, O Freedom, whose desire
Can light in muddiest souls quick seeds of
  fire,
And strain life's chords to the old heroic
  mood.

II

Yet are there other gifts more fair than
  thine,
Nor can I count him happiest who has never
Been forced with his own hand his chains to
  sever,
And for himself find out the way divine;
He never knew the aspirer's glorious pains,
He never earned the struggle's priceless
  gains.
Oh, block by block, with sore and sharp
  endeavor,
Lifelong we build these human natures up
Into a temple fit for Freedom's shrine,

And Trial ever consecrates the cup
Wherefrom we pour her sacrificial wine.

A GLANCE BEHIND THE CUR-TAIN

This poem, printed in *The Democratic Review* for September, 1843, is most probably the one to which Lowell refers in a letter to C. F. Briggs, already quoted in the head-note to *Prometheus*: "I have sent another poem to O'Sullivan, still more radical than *Prometheus*, and in some respects better, though, from its subject, incapable of so high a strain as that." Elsewhere in this letter he appears to give it the title *Cromwell*.

It is interesting to turn back five years to the summer of Lowell's graduation and listen to what he says to G. B. Loring: "A plan has been running in my head for some time, of writing a sort of dramatic poem on the subject of Cromwell. Those old Roundheads have never had justice done them. They have only been held up as canting, psalm-singing, hypocritical rascals; as a sort of foil for the open-hearted Cavalier. But it were a strange thing, indeed, if there were not somewhat in such men as Milton, Sidney, Hampden, Selden, and Pym. It always struck me that there was more true poetry in those old fiery-eyed, buff-belted warriors, with their deep, holy enthusiasm for liberty and democracy, political and religious; with their glorious trust in the arm of the Lord in battle — than in the dashing, ranting Cavaliers, who wished to restore their king that they might give vent to their passions, and go to sleep again in the laps of their mistresses, deaf to the cries of the poor and the oppressed."

WE see but half the causes of our deeds,
Seeking them wholly in the outer life,
And heedless of the encircling spirit-world,
Which, though unseen, is felt, and sows in us
All germs of pure and world-wide purposes.
From one stage of our being to the next
We pass unconscious o'er a slender bridge,
The momentary work of unseen hands,
Which crumbles down behind us; looking back,
We see the other shore, the gulf between,
And, marvelling how we won to where we stand,
Content ourselves to call the builder Chance.
We trace the wisdom to the apple's fall,
Not to the birth-throes of a mighty Truth
Which, for long ages in blank Chaos dumb,

Yet yearned to be incarnate, and had found
At last a spirit meet to be the womb
From which it might be born to bless mankind, —
Not to the soul of Newton, ripe with all
The hoarded thoughtfulness of earnest years,
And waiting but one ray of sunlight more
To blossom fully.

But whence came that ray?
We call our sorrows Destiny, but ought
Rather to name our high successes so.
Only the instincts of great souls are Fate,
And have predestined sway: all other things,
Except by leave of us, could never be.
For Destiny is but the breath of God
Still moving in us, the last fragment left
Of our unfallen nature, waking oft
Within our thought, to beckon us beyond
The narrow circle of the seen and known,
And always tending to a noble end,
As all things must that overrule the soul,
And for a space unseat the helmsman, Will.
The fate of England and of freedom once
Seemed wavering in the heart of one plain man:
One step of his, and the great dial-hand,
That marks the destined progress of the world
In the eternal round from wisdom on
To higher wisdom, had been made to pause
A hundred years. That step he did not take, —
He knew not why, nor we, but only God, —
And lived to make his simple oaken chair
More terrible and soberly august,
More full of majesty than any throne,
Before or after, of a British king.

Upon the pier stood two stern-visaged men,
Looking to where a little craft lay moored,
Swayed by the lazy current of the Thames,
Which weltered by in muddy listlessness.
Grave men they were, and battlings of fierce thought
Had trampled out all softness from their brows,
And ploughed rough furrows there before their time,
For other crop than such as homebred Peace
Sows broadcast in the willing soil of Youth.

Care, not of self, but for the common-weal,
Had robbed their eyes of youth, and left
    instead
A look of patient power and iron will,
And something fiercer, too, that gave
    broad hint
Of the plain weapons girded at their sides.
The younger had an aspect of command, —
Not such as trickles down, a slender
    stream,
In the shrunk channel of a great descent,
But such as lies entowered in heart and
    head,
And an arm prompt to do the 'hests of
    both.
His was a brow where gold were out of
    place,
And yet it seemed right worthy of a crown
(Though he despised such), were it only
    made
Of iron, or some serviceable stuff
That would have matched his brownly
    rugged face.
The elder, although such he hardly seemed
(Care makes so little of some five short
    years),
Had a clear, honest face, whose rough-
    hewn strength
Was mildened by the scholar's wiser heart
To sober courage, such as best befits
The unsullied temper of a well - taught
    mind,
Yet so remained that one could plainly
    guess
The hushed volcano smouldering under-
    neath.
He spoke: the other, hearing, kept his
    gaze
Still fixed, as on some problem in the sky.

"O CROMWELL, we are fallen on evil
    times !
There was a day when England had wide
    room
For honest men as well as foolish kings:
But now the uneasy stomach of the time
Turns squeamish at them both. Therefore
    let us
Seek out that savage clime, where men as
    yet
Are free: there sleeps the vessel on the tide,
Her languid canvas drooping for the wind;
Give us but that, and what need we to fear
This Order of the Council ? The free
    waves

Will not say No to please a wayward king,
Nor will the winds turn traitors at his
    beck:
All things are fitly cared for, and the Lord
Will watch as kindly o'er the exodus
Of us his servants now, as in old time.
We have no cloud or fire, and haply we
May not pass dry-shod through the ocean-
    stream;
But, saved or lost, all things are in His
    hand."
So spake he, and meantime the other stood
With wide gray eyes still reading the blank
    air,
As if upon the sky's blue wall he saw
Some mystic sentence, written by a hand,
Such as of old made pale the Assyrian
    king,
Girt with his satraps in the blazing feast.

"HAMPDEN ! a moment since, my pur-
    pose was
To fly with thee, — for I will call it flight,
Nor flatter it with any smoother name, —
But something in me bids me not to go;
And I am one, thou knowest, who, un-
    moved
By what the weak deem omens, yet give
    heed
And reverence due to whatsoe'er my soul
Whispers of warning to the inner ear.
Moreover, as I know that God brings
    round
His purposes in ways undreamed by us,
And makes the wicked but his instruments
To hasten their own swift and sudden fall,
I see the beauty of his providence
In the King's order: blind, he will not let
His doom part from him, but must bid it
    stay
As 't were a cricket, whose enlivening
    chirp
He loved to hear beneath his very hearth.
Why should we fly ? Nay, why not rather
    stay
And rear again our Zion's crumbled walls,
Not, as of old the walls of Thebes were
    built,
By minstrel twanging, but, if need should
    be,
With the more potent music of our swords ?
Think'st thou that score of men beyond the
    sea
Claim more God's care than all of England
    here ?

No: when He moves His arm, it is to aid
Whole peoples, heedless if a few be
  crushed,
As some are ever, when the destiny
Of man takes one stride onward nearer
  home.
Believe me, 't is the mass of men He
  loves;
And, where there is most sorrow and most
  want,
Where the high heart of man is trodden
  down
The most, 't is not because He hides His
  face
From them in wrath, as purblind teachers
  prate:
Not so: there most is He, for there is He
Most needed. Men who seek for Fate
  abroad
Are not so near His heart as they who dare
Frankly to face her where she faces them,
On their own threshold, where their souls
  are strong
To grapple with and throw her; as I once,
Being yet a boy, did cast this puny king,
Who now has grown so dotard as to deem
That he can wrestle with an angry realm,
And throw the brawned Antæus of men's
  rights.
No, Hampden! they have half-way con-
  quered Fate
Who go half-way to meet her, — as will I.
Freedom hath yet a work for me to do;
So speaks that inward voice which never yet
Spake falsely, when it urged the spirit on
To noble emprise for country and mankind.
And, for success, I ask no more than
  this, —
To bear unflinching witness to the truth.
All true whole men succeed; for what is
  worth
Success's name, unless it be the thought,
The inward surety, to have carried out
A noble purpose to a noble end,
Although it be the gallows or the block?
'T is only Falsehood that doth ever need
These outward shows of gain to bolster her.
Be it we prove the weaker with our swords;
Truth only needs to be for once spoke out,
And there 's such music in her, such
  strange rhythm,
As makes men's memories her joyous
  slaves,
And clings around the soul, as the sky
  clings

Round the mute earth, forever beautiful,
And, if o'erclouded, only to burst forth
More all-embracingly divine and clear:
Get but the truth once uttered, and 't is
  like
A star new-born, that drops into its place,
And which, once circling in its placid
  round,
Not all the tumult of the earth can shake.

  "What should we do in that small colony
Of pinched fanatics, who would rather
  choose
Freedom to clip an inch more from their
  hair,
Than the great chance of setting England
  free?
Not there, amid the stormy wilderness,
Should we learn wisdom; or if learned,
  what room
To put it into act, — else worse than
  naught?
We learn our souls more, tossing for an
  hour
Upon this huge and ever-vexëd sea
Of human thought, where kingdoms go to
  wreck
Like fragile bubbles yonder in the stream,
Than in a cycle of New England sloth,
Broke only by a petty Indian war,
Or quarrel for a letter more or less
In some hard word, which, spelt in either
  way,
Not their most learnëd clerks can under-
  stand.
New times demand new measures and new
  men;
The world advances, and in time outgrows
The laws that in our fathers' day were
  best;
And, doubtless, after us, some purer
  scheme
Will be shaped out by wiser men than we,
Made wiser by the steady growth of truth.
We cannot hale Utopia on by force;
But better, almost, be at work in sin,
Than in a brute inaction browse and sleep.
No man is born into the world whose work
Is not born with him; there is always work,
And tools to work withal, for those who
  will;
And blessëd are the horny hands of toil!
The busy world shoves angrily aside
The man who stands with arms akimbo set,
Until occasion tells him what to do;

And he who waits to have his task marked
   out
Shall die and leave his errand unfulfilled.
Our time is one that calls for earnest deeds:
Reason and Government, like two broad
   seas,
Yearn for each other with outstretchèd
   arms
Across this narrow isthmus of the throne,
And roll their white surf higher every day.
One age moves onward, and the next builds
   up
Cities and gorgeous palaces, where stood
The rude log-huts of those who tamed the
   wild,
Rearing from out the forests they had
   felled
The goodly framework of a fairer state;
The builder's trowel and the settler's axe
Are seldom wielded by the selfsame hand;
Ours is the harder task, yet not the less
Shall we receive the blessing for our toil
From the choice spirits of the aftertime.
My soul is not a palace of the past,
Where outworn creeds, like Rome's gray
   senate, quake,
Hearing afar the Vandal's trumpet hoarse,
That shakes old systems with a thunder-fit.
The time is ripe, and rotten-ripe, for
   change;
Then let it come: I have no dread of what
Is called for by the instinct of mankind;
Nor think I that God's world will fall
   apart
Because we tear a parchment more or less.
Truth is eternal, but her effluence,
With endless change, is fitted to the hour;
Her mirror is turned forward to reflect
The promise of the future, not the past.
He who would win the name of truly great
Must understand his own age and the next,
And make the present ready to fulfil
Its prophecy, and with the future merge
Gently and peacefully, as wave with wave.
The future works out great men's pur-
   poses;
The present is enough for common souls,
Who, never looking forward, are indeed
Mere clay, wherein the footprints of their
   age
Are petrified forever: better those
Who lead the blind old giant by the hand
From out the pathless desert where he
   gropes,
And set him onward in his darksome way.

I do not fear to follow out the truth,
Albeit along the precipice's edge.
Let us speak plain: there is more force in
   names
Than most men dream of; and a lie may
   keep
Its throne a whole age longer, if it skulk
Behind the shield of some fair-seeming
   name.
Let us call tyrants *tyrants*, and maintain
That only freedom comes by grace of God,
And all that comes not by His grace must
   fall;
For men in earnest have no time to waste
In patching fig-leaves for the naked truth.

" I will have one more grapple with the
   man
Charles Stuart: whom the boy o'ercame,
The man stands not in awe of. I, per-
   chance,
Am one raised up by the Almighty arm
To witness some great truth to all the
   world.
Souls destined to o'erleap the vulgar lot,
And mould the world unto the scheme of
   God,
Have a fore-consciousness of their high
   doom,
As men are known to shiver at the heart
When the cold shadow of some coming ill
Creeps slowly o'er their spirits unawares.
Hath Good less power of prophecy than
   Ill ?
How else could men whom God hath called
   to sway
Earth's rudder, and to steer the bark of
   Truth,
Beating against the tempest tow'rd her
   port,
Bear all the mean and buzzing grievances,
The petty martyrdoms, wherewith Sin
   strives
To weary out the tethered hope of Faith ?
The sneers, the unrecognizing look of
   friends,
Who worship the dead corpse of old king
   Custom,
Where it doth lie in state within the
   Church,
Striving to cover up the mighty ocean
With a man's palm, and making even the
   truth
Lie for them, holding up the glass reversed,
To make the hope of man seem farther off ?

My God ! when I read o'er the bitter lives
Of men whose eager hearts were quite too
    great
To beat beneath the cramped mode of the
    day,
And see them mocked at by the world they
    love,
Haggling with prejudice for pennyworths
Of that reform which their hard toil will
    make
The common birthright of the age to
    come, —
When I see this, spite of my faith in God,
I marvel how their hearts bear up so long;
Nor could they but for this same prophecy,
This inward feeling of the glorious end.

"Deem me not fond; but in my warmer
    youth,
Ere my heart's bloom was soiled and brushed
    away,
I had great dreams of mighty things to
    come;
Of conquest, whether by the sword or pen
I knew not; but some conquest I would
    have,
Or else swift death: now wiser grown in
    years,
I find youth's dreams are but the flutterings
Of those strong wings whereon the soul
    shall soar
In after time to win a starry throne;
And so I cherish them, for they were lots,
Which I, a boy, cast in the helm of Fate.
Now will I draw them, since a man's right
    hand,
A right hand guided by an earnest soul,
With a true instinct, takes the golden
    prize
From out a thousand blanks.   What men
    call luck
Is the prerogative of valiant souls,
The fealty life pays its rightful kings.
The helm is shaking now, and I will stay
To pluck my lot forth; it were sin to flee!"

So they two turned together; one to die,
Fighting for freedom on the bloody field;
The other, far more happy, to become
A name earth wears forever next her heart;
One of the few that have a right to rank
With the true Makers: for his spirit
    wrought
Order from Chaos; proved that right di-
    vine

Dwelt only in the excellence of truth;
And far within old Darkness' hostile lines
Advanced and pitched the shining tents of
    Light.
Nor shall the grateful Muse forget to tell,
That — not the least among his many
    claims
To deathless honor — he was MILTON's
    friend,
A man not second among those who lived
To show us that the poet's lyre demands
An arm of tougher sinew than the sword.

A CHIPPEWA LEGEND

ἀλγεινὰ μέν μοι καὶ λέγειν ἐστὶν τάδε,
ἄλγος δὲ σιγᾶν.
        ÆSCHYLUS, *Prom. Vinct.* 197, 198.

For the leading incidents in this tale I am
indebted to the very valuable *Algic Researches*
of Henry R. Schoolcraft, Esq.   J. R. L.

THE old Chief, feeling now wellnigh his
    end,
Called his two eldest children to his side,
And gave them, in few words, his parting
    charge!
"My son and daughter, me ye see no more;
The happy hunting - grounds await me,
    green
With change of spring and summer through
    the year:
But, for remembrance, after I am gone,
Be kind to little Sheemah for my sake:
Weakling he is and young, and knows not
    yet
To set the trap, or draw the seasoned bow;
Therefore of both your loves he hath more
    need,
And he, who needeth love, to love hath
    right;
It is not like our furs and stores of corn,
Whereto we claim sole title by our toil,
But the Great Spirit plants it in our hearts,
And waters it, and gives it sun, to be
The common stock and heritage of all:
Therefore be kind to Sheemah, that your-
    selves
May not be left deserted in your need."

Alone, beside a lake, their wigwam stood,
Far from the other dwellings of their tribe;
And, after many moons, the loneliness
Wearied the elder brother, and he said,

"Why should I dwell here far from men,
    shut out
From the free, natural joys that fit my age?
Lo, I am tall and strong, well skilled to
    hunt,
Patient of toil and hunger, and not yet
Have seen the danger which I dared not
    look
Full in the face; what hinders me to be
A mighty Brave and Chief among my
    kin?"
So, taking up his arrows and his bow,
As if to hunt, he journeyed swiftly on,
Until he gained the wigwams of his tribe,
Where, choosing out a bride, he soon for-
    got,
In all the fret and bustle of new life,
The little Sheemah and his father's charge.

Now when the sister found her brother
    gone,
And that, for many days, he came not back,
She wept for Sheemah more than for her-
    self;
For Love bides longest in a woman's heart,
And flutters many times before he flies,
And then doth perch so nearly, that a word
May lure him back to his accustomed nest;
And Duty lingers even when Love is gone,
Oft looking out in hope of his return;
And, after Duty hath been driven forth,
Then Selfishness creeps in the last of all,
Warming her lean hands at the lonely
    hearth,
And crouching o'er the embers, to shut out
Whatever paltry warmth and light are left,
With avaricious greed, from all beside.
So, for long months, the sister hunted wide,
And cared for little Sheemah tenderly;
But, daily more and more, the loneliness
Grew wearisome, and to herself she sighed,
"Am I not fair? at least the glassy pool,
That hath no cause to flatter, tells me so;
But, oh, how flat and meaningless the tale,
Unless it tremble on a lover's tongue!
Beauty hath no true glass, except it be
In the sweet privacy of loving eyes."
Thus deemed she idly, and forgot the lore
Which she had learned of nature and the
    woods,
That beauty's chief reward is to itself,
And that Love's mirror holds no image
    long
Save of the inward fairness, blurred and
    lost

Unless kept clear and white by Duty's care.
So she went forth and sought the haunts of
    men,
And, being wedded, in her household cares,
Soon, like the elder brother, quite forgot
The little Sheemah and her father's charge.

But Sheemah, left alone within the lodge,
Waited and waited, with a shrinking heart,
Thinking each rustle was his sister's step,
Till hope grew less and less, and then went
    out,
And every sound was changed from hope
    to fear.
Few sounds there were: — the dropping of
    a nut,
The squirrel's chirrup, and the jay's harsh
    scream,
Autumn's sad remnants of blithe Summer's
    cheer,
Heard at long intervals, seemed but to
    make
The dreadful void of silence silenter.
Soon what small store his sister left was
    gone,
And, through the Autumn, he made shift
    to live
On roots and berries, gathered in much
    fear
Of wolves, whose ghastly howl he heard
    ofttimes,
Hollow and hungry, at the dead of night.
But Winter came at last, and, when the
    snow,
Thick-heaped for gleaming leagues o'er
    hill and plain,
Spread its unbroken silence over all,
Made bold by hunger, he was fain to glean
(More sick at heart than Ruth, and all
    alone)
After the harvest of the merciless wolf,
Grim Boaz, who, sharp-ribbed and gaunt,
    yet feared
A thing more wild and starving than him-
    self;
Till, by degrees, the wolf and he grew
    friends,
And shared together all the winter
    through.

Late in the Spring, when all the ice was
    gone,
The elder brother, fishing in the lake,
Upon whose edge his father's wigwam
    stood,

Heard a low moaning noise upon the shore:
Half like a child it seemed, half like a
wolf,
And straightway there was something in
his heart
That said, "It is thy brother Sheemah's
voice."
So, paddling swiftly to the bank, he saw,
Within a little thicket close at hand,
A child that seemed fast changing to a
wolf,
From the neck downward, gray with
shaggy hair,
That still crept on and upward as he
looked.
The face was turned away, but well he
knew
That it was Sheemah's, even his brother's
face.
Then with his trembling hands he hid his
eyes,
And bowed his head, so that he might not
see
The first look of his brother's eyes, and
cried,
"O Sheemah! O my brother, speak to
me!
Dost thou not know me, that I am thy
brother?
Come to me, little Sheemah, thou shalt
dwell
With me henceforth, and know no care or
want!"
Sheemah was silent for a space, as if
'T were hard to summon up a human
voice,
And, when he spake, the voice was as a
wolf's:
"I know thee not, nor art thou what thou
say'st;
I have none other brethren than the
wolves,
And, till thy heart be changed from what
it is,
Thou art not worthy to be called their
kin."
Then groaned the other, with a choking
tongue,
"Alas! my heart is changed right bitterly;
'T is shrunk and parched within me even
now!"
And, looking upward fearfully, he saw
Only a wolf that shrank away and ran,
Ugly and fierce, to hide among the woods.

STANZAS ON FREEDOM

MEN! whose boast it is that ye
Come of fathers brave and free,
If there breathe on earth a slave,
Are ye truly free and brave?
If ye do not feel the chain,
When it works a brother's pain,
Are ye not base slaves indeed,
Slaves unworthy to be freed?

Women! who shall one day bear
Sons to breathe New England air,
If ye hear, without a blush,
Deeds to make the roused blood rush
Like red lava through your veins,
For your sisters now in chains, —
Answer! are ye fit to be
Mothers of the brave and free?

Is true Freedom but to break
Fetters for our own dear sake,
And, with leathern hearts, forget
That we owe mankind a debt?
No! true freedom is to share
All the chains our brothers wear,
And, with heart and hand, to be
Earnest to make others free!

They are slaves who fear to speak
For the fallen and the weak;
They are slaves who will not choose
Hatred, scoffing, and abuse,
Rather than in silence shrink
From the truth they needs must think;
They are slaves who dare not be
In the right with two or three.

COLUMBUS

I have partly written a poem on *Columbus* to
match with *Prometheus* and *Cromwell*. I like
it better than either in point *of artistic merit.*
J. R. L. to C. F. Briggs, September 18, 1844.

THE cordage creaks and rattles in the
wind,
With whims of sudden hush; the reeling
sea
Now thumps like solid rock beneath the
stern,
Now leaps with clumsy wrath, strikes
short, and, falling

Crumbled to whispery foam, slips rustling
   down
The broad backs of the waves, which jostle
   and crowd
To fling themselves upon that unknown
   shore,
Their used familiar since the dawn of
   time,
Whither this foredoomed life is guided on
To sway on triumph's hushed, aspiring
   poise
One glittering moment, then to break ful-
   filled.

How lonely is the sea's perpetual swing,
The melancholy wash of endless waves,
The sigh of some grim monster undescried,
Fear-painted on the canvas of the dark,
Shifting on his uneasy pillow of brine !
Yet night brings more companions than the
   day
To this drear waste; new constellations
   burn,
And fairer stars, with whose calm height
   my soul
Finds nearer sympathy than with my herd
Of earthen souls, whose vision's scanty ring
Makes me its prisoner to beat my wings
Against the cold bars of their unbelief,
Knowing in vain my own free heaven be-
   yond.
O God ! this world, so crammed with eager
   life,
That comes and goes and wanders back to
   silence
Like the idle wind, which yet man's shap-
   ing mind
Can make his drudge to swell the longing
   sails
Of highest endeavor, — this mad, unthrift
   world,
Which, every hour, throws life enough
   away
To make her deserts kind and hospitable,
Lets her great destinies be waved aside
By smooth, lip-reverent, formal infidels,
Who weigh the God they not believe with
   gold,
And find no spot in Judas, save that he,
Driving a duller bargain than he ought,
Saddled his guild with too cheap precedent.
O Faith ! if thou art strong, thine opposite
Is mighty also, and the dull fool's sneer
Hath ofttimes shot chill palsy through the
   arm

Just lifted to achieve its crowning deed,
And made the firm-based heart, that would
   have quailed
The rack or fagot, shudder like a leaf
Wrinkled with frost, and loose upon its
   stem.
The wicked and the weak, by some dark
   law,
Have a strange power to shut and rivet
   down
Their own horizon round us, to unwing
Our heaven-aspiring visions, and to blur
With surly clouds the Future's gleaming
   peaks,
Far seen across the brine of thankless
   years.
If the chosen soul could never be alone
In deep mid-silence, open-doored to God,
No greatness ever had been dreamed or
   done;
Among dull hearts a prophet never grew;
The nurse of full-grown souls is solitude.

The old world is effete; there man with
   man
Jostles, and, in the brawl for means to live,
Life is trod underfoot, — Life, the one
   block
Of marble that's vouchsafed wherefrom to
   carve
Our great thoughts, white and godlike, to
   shine down
The future, Life, the irredeemable block,
Which one o'er-hasty chisel-dint oft mars,
Scanting our room to cut the features out
Of our full hope, so forcing us to crown
With a mean head the perfect limbs, or
   leave
The god's face glowing o'er a satyr's trunk,
Failure's brief epitaph.

               Yes, Europe's world
Reels on to judgment; there the common
   need,
Losing God's sacred use, to be a bond
'Twixt Me and Thee, sets each one scowl-
   ingly
O'er his own selfish hoard at bay; no state,
Knit strongly with eternal fibres up
Of all men's separate and united weals,
Self-poised and sole as stars, yet one as
   light,
Holds up a shape of large Humanity
To which by natural instinct every man
Pays loyalty exulting, by which all

Mould their own lives, and feel their pulses
 filled
With the red, fiery blood of the general
 life,
Making them mighty in peace, as now in
 war
They are, even in the flush of victory,
 weak,
Conquering that manhood which should
 them subdue.
And what gift bring I to this untried
 world ?
Shall the same tragedy be played anew,
And the same lurid curtain drop at last
On one dread desolation, one fierce crash
Of that recoil which on its makers God
Lets Ignorance and Sin and Hunger make,
Early or late ? Or shall that common-
 wealth
Whose potent unity and concentric force
Can draw these scattered joints and parts
 of men
Into a whole ideal man once more,
Which sucks not from its limbs the life
 away,
But sends it flood-tide and creates itself
Over again in every citizen,
Be there built up ? For me, I have no
 choice;
I might turn back to other destinies,
For one sincere key opes all Fortune's doors;
But whoso answers not God's earliest call
Forfeits or dulls that faculty supreme
Of lying open to his genius
Which makes the wise heart certain of its
 ends.

Here am I; for what end God knows, not I;
Westward still points the inexorable soul:
Here am I, with no friend but the sad sea,
The beating heart of this great enterprise,
Which, without me, would stiffen in swift
 death;
This have I mused on, since mine eye could
 first
Among the stars distinguish and with joy
Rest on that God-fed Pharos of the north,
On some blue promontory of heaven lighted
That juts far out into the upper sea;
To this one hope my heart hath clung for
 years,
As would a foundling to the talisman
Hung round his neck by hands he knew not
 whose;
A poor, vile thing and dross to all beside,

Yet he therein can feel a virtue left
By the sad pressure of a mother's hand,
And unto him it still is tremulous
With palpitating haste and wet with tears,
The key to him of hope and humanness,
The coarse shell of life's pearl, Expectancy.
This hope hath been to me for love and
 fame,
Hath made me wholly lonely on the earth,
Building me up as in a thick-ribbed tower,
Wherewith enwalled my watching spirit
 burned,
Conquering its little island from the Dark,
Sole as a scholar's lamp, and heard men's
 steps,
In the far hurry of the outward world,
Pass dimly forth and back, sounds heard in
 dream.
As Ganymede by the eagle was snatched
 up
From the gross sod to be Jove's cup-bearer,
So was I lifted by my great design:
And who hath trod Olympus, from his eye
Fades not that broader outlook of the gods;
His life's low valleys overbrow earth's
 clouds,
And that Olympian spectre of the past
Looms towering up in sovereign memory,
Beckoning his soul from meaner heights of
 doom.
Had but the shadow of the Thunderer's
 bird,
Flashing athwart my spirit, made of me
A swift-betraying vision's Ganymede,
Yet to have greatly dreamed precludes low
 ends;
Great days have ever such a morning-red,
On such a base great futures are built up,
And aspiration, though not put in act,
Comes back to ask its plighted troth again,
Still watches round its grave the unlaid
 ghost
Of a dead virtue, and makes other hopes,
Save that implacable one, seem thin and
 bleak
As shadows of bare trees upon the snow,
Bound freezing there by the unpitying
 moon.

While other youths perplexed their mando-
 lins,
Praying that Thetis would her fingers
 twine
In the loose glories of her lover's hair,
And wile another kiss to keep back day,

I, stretched beneath the many-centuried
shade
Of some writhed oak, the wood's Laocoön,
Did of my hope a dryad mistress make,
Whom I would woo to meet me privily,
Or underneath the stars, or when the
moon
Flecked all the forest floor with scattered
pearls.
O days whose memory tames to fawning
down
The surly fell of Ocean's bristled neck !

I know not when this hope enthralled me
first,
But from my boyhood up I loved to hear
The tall pine-forests of the Apennine
Murmur their hoary legends of the sea,
Which hearing, I in vision clear beheld
The sudden dark of tropic night shut down
O'er the huge whisper of great watery
wastes,
The while a pair of herons trailingly
Flapped inland, where some league-wide
river hurled
The yellow spoil of unconjectured realms
Far through a gulf's green silence, never
scarred
By any but the North-wind's hurrying
keels.
And not the pines alone; all sights and
sounds
To my world-seeking heart paid fealty,
And catered for it as the Cretan bees
Brought honey to the baby Jupiter,
Who in his soft hand crushed a violet,
Godlike foremusing the rough thunder's
gripe;
Then did I entertain the poet's song,
My great Idea's guest, and, passing o'er
That iron bridge the Tuscan built to hell,
I heard Ulysses tell of mountain-chains
Whose adamantine links, his manacles,
The western main shook growling, and
still gnawed.
I brooded on the wise Athenian's tale
Of happy Atlantis, and heard Björne's
keel
Crunch the gray pebbles of the Vinland
shore:
I listened, musing, to the prophecy
Of Nero's tutor-victim; lo, the birds
Sing darkling, conscious of the climbing
dawn.
And I believed the poets; it is they

Who utter wisdom from the central deep,
And, listening to the inner flow of things,
Speak to the age out of eternity.

Ah me ! old hermits sought for solitude
In caves and desert places of the earth,
Where their own heart-beat was the only
stir
Of living thing that comforted the year;
But the bald pillar-top of Simeon,
In midnight's blankest waste, were popu-
lous,
Matched with the isolation drear and deep
Of him who pines among the swarm of
men,
At once a new thought's king and pris-
oner,
Feeling the truer life within his life,
The fountain of his spirit's prophecy,
Sinking away and wasting, drop by drop,
In the ungrateful sands of sceptic ears.
He in the palace-aisles of untrod woods
Doth walk a king; for him the pent-up
cell
Widens beyond the circles of the stars,
And all the sceptred spirits of the past
Come thronging in to greet him as their
peer;
But in the market-place's glare and throng
He sits apart, an exile, and his brow
Aches with the mocking memory of its
crown.
Yet to the spirit select there is no choice;
He cannot say, This will I do, or that,
For the cheap means putting Heaven's
ends in pawn,
And bartering his bleak rocks, the freehold
stern
Of destiny's first-born, for smoother fields
That yield no crop of self-denying will;
A hand is stretched to him from out the
dark,
Which grasping without question, he is led
Where there is work that he must do for
God.
The trial still is the strength's complement,
And the uncertain, dizzy path that scales
The sheer heights of supremest purposes
Is steeper to the angel than the child.
Chances have laws as fixed as planets have,
And disappointment's dry and bitter root,
Envy's harsh berries, and the choking
pool
Of the world's scorn, are the right mother-
milk

To the tough hearts that pioneer their
kind,
And break a pathway to those unknown
realms
That in the earth's broad shadow lie en-
thralled;
Endurance is the crowning quality,
And patience all the passion of great
hearts;
These are their stay, and when the leaden
world
Sets its hard face against their fateful
thought,
And brute strength, like the Gaulish con-
queror,
Clangs his huge glaive down in the other
scale,
The inspired soul but flings his patience
in,
And slowly that outweighs the ponderous
globe, —
One faith against a whole earth's unbe-
lief,
One soul against the flesh of all mankind.

Thus ever seems it when my soul can hear
The voice that errs not; then my triumph
gleams,
O'er the blank ocean beckoning, and all
night
My heart flies on before me as I sail;
Far on I see my lifelong enterprise,
That rose like Ganges mid the freezing
snows
Of a world's solitude, sweep broadening
down,
And, gathering to itself a thousand streams,
Grow sacred ere it mingle with the sea;
I see the ungated wall of chaos old,
With blocks Cyclopean hewn of solid night,
Fade like a wreath of unreturning mist
Before the irreversible feet of light; —
And lo, with what clear omen in the east
On day's gray threshold stands the eager
dawn,
Like young Leander rosy from the sea
Glowing at Hero's lattice !

One day more
These muttering shoalbrains leave the
helm to me:
God, let me not in their dull ooze be
stranded;
Let not this one frail bark, to hollow which

I have dug out the pith and sinewy heart
Of my aspiring life's fair trunk, be so
Cast up to warp and blacken in the sun,
Just as the opposing wind 'gins whistle off
His cheek-swollen pack, and from the lean-
ing mast
Fortune's full sail strains forward !

One poor day ! —
Remember whose and not how short it is !
It is God's day, it is Columbus's.
A lavish day ! One day, with life and
heart,
Is more than time enough to find a world.

AN INCIDENT OF THE FIRE
AT HAMBURG

THE tower of old Saint Nicholas soared up-
ward to the skies,
Like some huge piece of Nature's make, the
growth of centuries;
You could not deem its crowding spires a
work of human art,
They seemed to struggle lightward from a
sturdy living heart.

Not Nature's self more freely speaks in
crystal or in oak,
Than, through the pious builder's hand, in
that gray pile she spoke;
And as from acorn springs the oak, so,
freely and alone,
Sprang from his heart this hymn to God,
sung in obedient stone.

It seemed a wondrous freak of chance, so
perfect, yet so rough,
A whim of Nature crystallized slowly in
granite tough;
The thick spires yearned towards the sky
in quaint harmonious lines,
And in broad sunlight basked and slept,
like a grove of blasted pines.

Never did rock or stream or tree lay claim
with better right
To all the adorning sympathies of shadow
and of light;
And, in that forest petrified, as forester
there dwells
Stout Herman, the old sacristan, sole lord
of all its bells.

Surge leaping after surge, the fire roared
   onward red as blood,
Till half of Hamburg lay engulfed beneath
   the eddying flood;
For miles away the fiery spray poured
   down its deadly rain,
And back and forth the billows sucked,
   and paused, and burst again.

From square to square with tiger leaps
   panted the lustful fire,
The air to leeward shuddered with the
   gasps of its desire;
And church and palace, which even now
   stood whelmed but to the knee,
Lift their black roofs like breakers lone
   amid the whirling sea.

Up in his tower old Herman sat and
   watched with quiet look;
His soul had trusted God too long to be at
   last forsook;
He could not fear, for surely God a path-
   way would unfold
Through this red sea for faithful hearts, as
   once He did of old.

But scarcely can he cross himself, or on his
   good saint call,
Before the sacrilegious flood o'erleaped the
   church-yard wall;
And, ere a *pater* half was said, mid smoke
   and crackling glare,
His island tower scarce juts its head above
   the wide despair.

Upon the peril's desperate peak his heart
   stood up sublime;
His first thought was for God above, his
   next was for his chime;
"Sing now and make your voices heard in
   hymns of praise," cried he,
"As did the Israelites of old, safe walking
   through the sea !

"Through this red sea our God hath made
   the pathway safe to shore;
Our promised land stands full in sight;
   shout now as ne'er before ! "
And as the tower came crashing down, the
   bells, in clear accord,
Pealed forth the grand old German hymn,
    — "All good souls, praise the
   Lord ! "

THE SOWER

I saw a Sower walking slow
   Across the earth, from east to west;
His hair was white as mountain snow,
   His head drooped forward on his breast.

With shrivelled hands he flung his seed,
   Nor ever turned to look behind;
Of sight or sound he took no heed;
   It seemed he was both deaf and blind.

His dim face showed no soul beneath,
   Yet in my heart I felt a stir,
As if I looked upon the sheath,
   That once had held Excalibur.

I heard, as still the seed he cast,
   How, crooning to himself, he sung,
" I sow again the holy Past,
   The happy days when I was young.

" Then all was wheat without a tare,
   Then all was righteous, fair, and true;
And I am he whose thoughtful care
   Shall plant the Old World in the New.

" The fruitful germs I scatter free,
   With busy hand, while all men sleep;
In Europe now, from sea to sea,
   The nations bless me as they reap."

Then I looked back along his path,
   And heard the clash of steel on steel,
Where man faced man, in deadly wrath,
   While clanged the tocsin's hurrying peal.

The sky with burning towns flared red,
   Nearer the noise of fighting rolled,
And brothers' blood, by brothers shed,
   Crept curdling over pavements cold.

Then marked I how each germ of truth
   Which through the dotard's fingers ran
Was mated with a dragon's tooth
   Whence there sprang up an arméd man.

I shouted, but he could not hear;
   Made signs, but these he could not see;
And still, without a doubt or fear,
   Broadcast he scattered anarchy.

Long to my straining ears the blast
   Brought faintly back the words he sung:

"I sow again the holy Past,
 The happy days when I was young."

HUNGER AND COLD

SISTERS two, all praise to you,
With your faces pinched and blue;
To the poor man you 've been true
  From of old:
You can speak the keenest word,
You are sure of being heard,
From the point you 're never stirred,
  Hunger and Cold!

Let sleek statesmen temporize;
Palsied are their shifts and lies
When they meet your bloodshot eyes,
  Grim and bold;
Policy you set at naught,
In their traps you 'll not be caught,
You 're too honest to be bought,
  Hunger and Cold!

Bolt and bar the palace door;
While the mass of men are poor,
Naked truth grows more and more
  Uncontrolled;
You had never yet, I guess,
Any praise for bashfulness,
You can visit sans court-dress,
  Hunger and Cold!

While the music fell and rose,
And the dance reeled to its close,
Where her round of costly woes
  Fashion strolled,
I beheld with shuddering fear
Wolves' eyes through the windows peer;
Little dream they you are near,
  Hunger and Cold!

When the toiler's heart you clutch,
Conscience is not valued much,
He recks not a bloody smutch
  On his gold:
Everything to you defers,
You are potent reasoners,
At your whisper Treason stirs,
  Hunger and Cold!

Rude comparisons you draw.
Words refuse to sate your maw,
Your gaunt limbs the cobweb law
  Cannot hold:

You 're not clogged with foolish pride,
But can seize a right denied:
Somehow God is on your side,
  Hunger and Cold!

You respect no hoary wrong
More for having triumphed long;
Its past victims, haggard throng
  From the mould
You unbury: swords and spears
Weaker are than poor men's tears,
Weaker than your silent years,
  Hunger and Cold!

Let them guard both hall and bower;
Through the window you will glower,
Patient till your reckoning hour
  Shall be tolled;
Cheeks are pale, but hands are red,
Guiltless blood may chance be shed,
But ye must and will be fed,
  Hunger and Cold!

God has plans man must not spoil,
Some were made to starve and toil,
Some to share the wine and oil,
  We are told:
Devil's theories are these,
Stifling hope and love and peace,
Framed your hideous lusts to please,
  Hunger and Cold!

Scatter ashes on thy head,
Tears of burning sorrow shed,
Earth! and be by Pity led
  To Love's fold;
Ere they block the very door
With lean corpses of the poor,
And will hush for naught but gore,
  Hunger and Cold!

THE LANDLORD

WHAT boot your houses and your lands?
  In spite of close-drawn deed and fence,
Like water, 'twixt your cheated hands,
They slip into the graveyard's sands,
  And mock your ownership's pretence.

How shall you speak to urge your right,
  Choked with that soil for which you lust?
The bit of clay, for whose delight
You grasp, is mortgaged, too; Death might
  Foreclose this very day in dust.

Fence as you please, this plain poor man,
 Whose only fields are in his wit,
Who shapes the world, as best he can,
According to God's higher plan,
 Owns you, and fences as is fit.

Though yours the rents, his incomes wax
 By right of eminent domain;
From factory tall to woodman's axe,
All things on earth must pay their tax,
 To feed his hungry heart and brain.

He takes you from your easy-chair,
 And what he plans that you must do;
You sleep in down, eat dainty fare, —
He mounts his crazy garret-stair
 And starves, the landlord over you.

Feeding the clods your idlesse drains,
 You make more green six feet of soil;
His fruitful word, like suns and rains,
Partakes the seasons' bounteous pains,
 And toils to lighten human toil.

Your lands, with force or cunning got,
 Shrink to the measure of the grave;
But Death himself abridges not
The tenures of almighty thought,
 The titles of the wise and brave.

TO A PINE-TREE

Lowell's friend C. F. Briggs called the poet's
attention to Coleridge's lines in *The Ancient
Mariner*,

> " And ice, mast high, came floating by
> As green as emerald,"

as perhaps the literary justification of " crags
of green ice " in the penultimate stanza of this
poem, — but maintained nevertheless that the
epithet *green* was not true to nature. In his
reply Lowell wrote : " I did not have Cole-
ridge's lines in my mind when I wrote my
verses. Coleridge had a fine, true eye, and I
would gladly accept him (if I wanted any aid)
in confirmation. I did trust my own eye.
When I was a boy, my favorite sport was sail-
ing upon Fresh Pond in summer, and in winter
helping the hardy reapers to get in their har-
vest of ice, and never was a field of wheat in
July of a more lovely green. You have doubt-
less seen ice-*bugs* (as most people entomologi-
cally pronounce it), and they may not be green,
though I think they are described as of all
colors. But my ice was fresh-water ice, and I
am right about it."

FAR up on Katahdin thou towerest,
 Purple-blue with the distance and vast;
Like a cloud o'er the lowlands thou lower-
  est,
 That hangs poised on a lull in the blast,
  To its fall leaning awful.

In the storm, like a prophet o'ermaddened,
 Thou singest and tossest thy branches;
Thy heart with the terror is gladdened,
 Thou forebodest the dread avalanches,
  When whole mountains swoop vale-
   ward.

In the calm thou o'erstretchest the valleys
 With thine arms, as if blessings implor-
  ing,
Like an old king led forth from his palace,
 When his people to battle are pouring
  From the city beneath him.

To the lumberer asleep 'neath thy gloom-
  ing
 Thou dost sing of wild billows in motion,
Till he longs to be swung mid their boom-
  ing
 In the tents of the Arabs of ocean,
  Whose finned isles are their cattle.

For the gale snatches thee for his lyre,
 With mad hand crashing melody frantic,
While he pours forth his mighty desire
 To leap down on the eager Atlantic,
  Whose arms stretch to his playmate.

The wild storm makes his lair in thy
  branches,
 Swooping thence on the continent under;
Like a lion, crouched close on his haunches,
 There awaiteth his leap the fierce thun-
  der,
  Growling low with impatience.

Spite of winter, thou keep'st thy green
  glory,
 Lusty father of Titans past number !
The snow-flakes alone make thee hoary,
 Nestling close to thy branches in slum-
  ber,
  And thee mantling with silence.

Thou alone know'st the splendor of winter,
 Mid thy snow-silvered, hushed precipices,
Hearing crags of green ice groan and splin-
  ter,

And then plunge down the muffled
    abysses
  In the quiet of midnight.

Thou alone know'st the glory of summer,
  Gazing down on thy broad seas of forest,
On thy subjects that send a proud mur-
    mur
  Up to thee, to their sachem, who tower-
    est
  From thy bleak throne to heaven.

SI DESCENDERO IN INFERNUM, ADES

O WANDERING dim on the extremest edge
  Of God's bright providence, whose spirits
    sigh
Drearily in you, like the winter sedge
  That shivers o'er the dead pool stiff and
    dry,
  A thin, sad voice, when the bold wind
    roars by
  From the clear North of Duty, —
Still by cracked arch and broken shaft I
    trace
That here was once a shrine and holy place
  Of the supernal Beauty,
  A child's play-altar reared of stones and
    moss,
  With wilted flowers for offering laid
    across,
Mute recognition of the all-ruling Grace.

How far are ye from the innocent, from
    those
  Whose hearts are as a little lane serene,
Smooth-heaped from wall to wall with un-
    broke snows,
  Or in the summer blithe with lamb-
    cropped green,
  Save the one track, where naught more
    rude is seen
  Than the plump wain at even
Bringing home four months' sunshine
    bound in sheaves !
How far are ye from those ! yet who be-
    lieves
  That ye can shut out heaven ?
  Your souls partake its influence, not in
    vain
  Nor all unconscious, as that silent lane
Its drift of noiseless apple-blooms receives.

Looking within myself, I note how thin
  A plank of station, chance, or prosperous
    fate,
Doth fence me from the clutching waves of
    sin;
  In my own heart I find the worst man's
    mate,
  And see not dimly the smooth-hingëd
    gate
  That opes to those abysses
Where ye grope darkly, — ye who never
    knew
On your young hearts love's consecrating
    dew,
  Or felt a mother's kisses,
  Or home's restraining tendrils round you
    curled;
Ah, side by side with heart's-ease in this
    world
The fatal nightshade grows and bitter rue !

One band ye cannot break, — the force that
    clips
  And grasps your circles to the central
    light;
Yours is the prodigal comet's long ellipse,
  Self - exiled to the farthest verge of
    night;
  Yet strives with you no less that inward
    might
  No sin hath e'er imbruted;
The god in you the creed-dimmed eye
    eludes;
The Law brooks not to have its solitudes
  By bigot feet polluted;
  Yet they who watch your God-compelled
    return
May see your happy perihelion burn
Where the calm sun his unfledged planets
    broods.

TO THE PAST

WONDROUS and awful are thy silent halls,
  O kingdom of the past !
There lie the bygone ages in their palls,
  Guarded by shadows vast;
  There all is hushed and breathless,
Save when some image of old error falls
Earth worshipped once as deathless.

There sits drear Egypt, mid beleaguering
    sands,
  Half woman and half beast.

The burnt-out torch within her mouldering
  hands
   That once lit all the East;
A dotard bleared and hoary,
There Asser crouches o'er the blackened
  brands
   Of Asia's long-quenched glory.

Still as a city buried 'neath the sea
   Thy courts and temples stand;
Idle as forms on wind-waved tapestry
   Of saints and heroes grand,
Thy phantasms grope and shiver,
Or watch the loose shores crumbling si-
  lently
   Into Time's gnawing river.

Titanic shapes with faces blank and dun,
   Of their old godhead lorn,
Gaze on the embers of the sunken sun,
   Which they misdeem for morn;
   And yet the eternal sorrow
In their unmonarched eyes says day is done
   Without the hope of morrow.

O realm of silence and of swart eclipse,
   The shapes that haunt thy gloom
Make signs to us and move their withered
  lips
   Across the gulf of doom;
   Yet all their sound and motion
Bring no more freight to us than wraiths
  of ships
   On the mirage's ocean.

And if sometimes a moaning wandereth
   From out thy desolate halls,
If some grim shadow of thy living death
   Across our sunshine falls
   And scares the world to error,
The eternal life sends forth melodious
  breath
   To chase the misty terror.

Thy mighty clamors, wars, and world-
  noised deeds
   Are silent now in dust,
Gone like a tremble of the huddling reeds
   Beneath some sudden gust;
   Thy forms and creeds have vanished,
Tossed out to wither like unsightly weeds
   From the world's garden banished.

Whatever of true life there was in thee
   Leaps in our age's veins;

Wield still thy bent and wrinkled em-
  pery,
   And shake thine idle chains;—
   To thee thy dross is clinging,
For us thy martyrs die, thy prophets
  see,
   Thy poets still are singing.

Here, mid the bleak waves of our strife
  and care,
   Float the green Fortunate Isles
Where all thy hero-spirits dwell, and share
   Our martyrdoms and toils;
   The present moves attended
With all of brave and excellent and fair
   That made the old time splendid.

TO THE FUTURE

O LAND of Promise! from what Pisgah's
  height
   Can I behold thy stretch of peaceful
  bowers,
Thy golden harvests flowing out of sight,
   Thy nestled homes and sun-illumined
  towers?
   Gazing upon the sunset's high-heaped
  gold,
Its crags of opal and of chrysolite,
   Its deeps on deeps of glory, that un-
  fold
   Still brightening abysses,
   And blazing precipices,
Whence but a scanty leap it seems to
  heaven,
   Sometimes a glimpse is given
Of thy more gorgeous realm, thy more un-
  stinted blisses.

O Land of Quiet! to thy shore the surf
   Of the perturbèd Present rolls and sleeps;
Our storms breathe soft as June upon thy
  turf
   And lure out blossoms; to thy bosom
  leaps,
As to a mother's, the o'erwearied heart,
Hearing far off and dim the toiling mart,
   The hurrying feet, the curses without
  number,
   And, circled with the glow Elysian
   Of thine exulting vision,
Out of its very cares wooes charms for
  peace and slumber.

To thee the earth lifts up her fettered
  hands
  And cries for vengeance; with a pitying
    smile
Thou blessest her, and she forgets her
  bands,
  And her old woe-worn face a little while
Grows young and noble; unto thee the
  Oppressor
    Looks, and is dumb with awe;
    The eternal law,
Which makes the crime its own blindfold
  redresser,
Shadows his heart with perilous foreboding,
  And he can see the grim-eyed Doom
  From out the trembling gloom
Its silent-footed steeds towards his palace
  goading.

What promises hast thou for Poets' eyes,
  A-weary of the turmoil and the wrong!
To all their hopes what overjoyed replies!
  What undreamed ecstasies for blissful
    song!
Thy happy plains no war-trump's brawling
  clangor
  Disturbs, and fools the poor to hate the
    poor;
The humble glares not on the high with
  anger;
  Love leaves no grudge at less, no greed
    for more;
In vain strives Self the godlike sense to
  smother;
    From the soul's deeps
    It throbs and leaps;
The noble 'neath foul rags beholds his long-
  lost brother.

To thee the Martyr looketh, and his fires
  Unlock their fangs and leave his spirit
    free;
To thee the Poet mid his toil aspires,
  And grief and hunger climb about his
    knee,
Welcome as children; thou upholdest
  The lone Inventor by his demon haunted;
The Prophet cries to thee when hearts are
  coldest,
  And gazing o'er the midnight's bleak
    abyss,
  Sees the drowsed soul awaken at thy
    kiss,
And stretch its happy arms and leap up
  disenchanted.

Thou bringest vengeance, but so loving-
  kindly
  The guilty thinks it pity; taught by thee,
Fierce tyrants drop the scourges where-
  with blindly
  Their own souls they were scarring; con-
    querors see
With horror in their hands the accursed
  spear
  That tore the meek One's side on Cal-
    vary,
And from their trophies shrink with
  ghastly fear;
    Thou, too, art the Forgiver,
The beauty of man's soul to man reveal-
  ing;
    The arrows from thy quiver
Pierce Error's guilty heart, but only pierce
  for healing.

Oh, whither, whither, glory-wingèd dreams,
  From out Life's sweat and turmoil would
    ye bear me?
Shut, gates of Fancy, on your golden
  gleams, —
  This agony of hopeless contrast spare me!
Fade, cheating glow, and leave me to my
  night!
  He is a coward, who would borrow
  A charm against the present sorrow
From the vague Future's promise of de-
  light:
  As life's alarums nearer roll,
  The ancestral buckler calls,
  Self-clanging from the walls
In the high temple of the soul;
Where are most sorrows, there the poet's
  sphere is,
  To feed the soul with patience,
  To heal its desolations
With words of unshorn truth, with love
  that never wearies.

HEBE

I SAW the twinkle of white feet,
I saw the flash of robes descending;
Before her ran an influence fleet,
That bowed my heart like barley bending.

As, in bare fields, the searching bees
Pilot to blooms beyond our finding,
  It led me on, by sweet degrees
Joy's simple honey-cells unbinding.

Those Graces were that seemed grim
    Fates;
With nearer love the sky leaned o'er me;
The long-sought Secret's golden gates
On musical hinges swung before me.

I saw the brimmed bowl in her grasp
Thrilling with godhood; like a lover
    I sprang the proffered life to clasp; —
The beaker fell; the luck was over.

The Earth has drunk the vintage up;
    What boots it patch the goblet's splin-
      ters?
Can Summer fill the icy cup,
Whose treacherous crystal is but Winter's?

O spendthrift haste! await the Gods;
The nectar crowns the lips of Patience;
    Haste scatters on unthankful sods
The immortal gift in vain libations.

Coy Hebe flies from those that woo,
And shuns the hands would seize upon her;
    Follow thy life, and she will sue
To pour for thee the cup of honor.

THE SEARCH

I WENT to seek for Christ,
    And Nature seemed so fair
That first the woods and fields my youth
    enticed,
    And I was sure to find him there:
    The temple I forsook,
    And to the solitude
Allegiance paid; but winter came and
    shook
The crown and purple from my wood;
His snows, like desert sands, with scornful
    drift,
    Besieged the columned aisle and palace-
      gate;
My Thebes, cut deep with many a solemn
    rift,
    But epitaphed her own sepulchred state:
Then I remembered whom I went to seek,
And blessed blunt Winter for his counsel
    bleak.

Back to the world I turned,
    For Christ, I said, is King;
So the cramped alley and the hut I
    spurned,

As far beneath his sojourning:
    Mid power and wealth I sought,
    But found no trace of him,
And all the costly offerings I had brought
    With sudden rust and mould grew dim:
I found his tomb, indeed, where, by their
    laws,
    All must on stated days themselves im-
      prison,
Mocking with bread a dead creed's grin-
    ning jaws,
    Witless how long the life had thence
      arisen;
Due sacrifice to this they set apart,
Prizing it more than Christ's own living
    heart.

So from my feet the dust
    Of the proud World I shook;
Then came dear Love and shared with me
    his crust,
    And half my sorrow's burden took.
    After the World's soft bed,
    Its rich and dainty fare,
Like down seemed Love's coarse pillow to
    my head,
    His cheap food seemed as manna rare;
Fresh-trodden prints of bare and bleeding
    feet,
    Turned to the heedless city whence I
      came,
Hard by I saw, and springs of worship
    sweet
    Gushed from my cleft heart smitten by
      the same;
Love looked me in the face and spake no
    words,
    But straight I knew those footprints were
      the Lord's.

I followed where they led,
    And in a hovel rude,
With naught to fence the weather from
    his head,
    The King I sought for meekly stood;
    A naked, hungry child
    Clung round his gracious knee,
And a poor hunted slave looked up and
    smiled
    To bless the smile that set him free;
New miracles I saw his presence do, —
    No more I knew the hovel bare and poor,
The gathered chips into a wood-pile grew
    The broken morsel swelled to goodly
      store;

I knelt and wept: my Christ no more I seek,
His throne is with the outcast and the
weak.

THE PRESENT CRISIS

Dated December, 1844.

WHEN a deed is done for Freedom, through
the broad earth's aching breast
Runs a thrill of joy prophetic, trembling
on from east to west,
And the slave, where'er he cowers, feels
the soul within him climb
To the awful verge of manhood, as the
energy sublime
Of a century bursts full-blossomed on the
thorny stem of Time.

Through the walls of hut and palace shoots
the instantaneous throe,
When the travail of the Ages wrings
earth's systems to and fro;
At the birth of each new Era, with a recog-
nizing start,
Nation wildly looks at nation, standing
with mute lips apart,
And glad Truth's yet mightier man-child
leaps beneath the Future's heart.

So the Evil's triumph sendeth, with a
terror and a chill,
Under continent to continent, the sense of
coming ill,
And the slave, where'er he cowers, feels
his sympathies with God
In hot tear-drops ebbing earthward, to be
drunk up by the sod,
Till a corpse crawls round unburied, delv-
ing in the nobler clod.

For mankind are one in spirit, and an in-
stinct bears along,
Round the earth's electric circle, the swift
flash of right or wrong;
Whether conscious or unconscious, yet
Humanity's vast frame
Through its ocean-sundered fibres feels the
gush of joy or shame; —
In the gain or loss of one race all the rest
have equal claim.

Once to every man and nation comes the
moment to decide,

In the strife of Truth with Falsehood, for
the good or evil side;
Some great cause, God's new Messiah,
offering each the bloom or blight,
Parts the goats upon the left hand, and the
sheep upon the right,
And the choice goes by forever 'twixt that
darkness and that light.

Hast thou chosen, O my people, on whose
party thou shalt stand,
Ere the Doom from its worn sandals shakes
the dust against our land ?
Though the cause of Evil prosper, yet 't is
Truth alone is strong,
And, albeit she wander outcast now, I see
around her throng
Troops of beautiful, tall angels, to enshield
her from all wrong.

Backward look across the ages and the
beacon-moments see,
That, like peaks of some sunk continent,
jut through Oblivion's sea;
Not an ear in court or market for the low
foreboding cry
Of those Crises, God's stern winnowers,
from whose feet earth's chaff must fly;
Never shows the choice momentous till the
judgment hath passed by.

Careless seems the great Avenger; history's
pages but record
One death-grapple in the darkness 'twixt
old systems and the Word;
Truth forever on the scaffold, Wrong for-
ever on the throne, —
Yet that scaffold sways the future, and, be-
hind the dim unknown,
Standeth God within the shadow, keeping
watch above his own.

We see dimly in the Present what is small
and what is great,
Slow of faith how weak an arm may turn
the iron helm of fate,
But the soul is still oracular; amid the
market's din,
List the ominous stern whisper from the
Delphic cave within, —
" They enslave their children's children who
make compromise with sin."

Slavery, the earth-born Cyclops, fellest of
the giant brood,

Sons of brutish Force and Darkness, who
    have drenched the earth with blood,
Famished in his self-made desert, blinded
    by our purer day,
Gropes in yet unblasted regions for his
    miserable prey; —
Shall we guide his gory fingers where our
    helpless children play ?

Then to side with Truth is noble when we
    share her wretched crust,
Ere her cause bring fame and profit, and
    't is prosperous to be just;
Then it is the brave man chooses, while the
    coward stands aside,
Doubting in his abject spirit, till his Lord
    is crucified,
And the multitude make virtue of the faith
    they had denied.

Count me o'er earth's chosen heroes, —
    they were souls that stood alone,
While the men they agonized for hurled
    the contumelious stone,
Stood serene, and down the future saw the
    golden beam incline
To the side of perfect justice, mastered by
    their faith divine,
By one man's plain truth to manhood and
    to God's supreme design.

By the light of burning heretics Christ's
    bleeding feet I track,
Toiling up new Calvaries ever with the
    cross that turns not back,
And these mounts of anguish number how
    each generation learned
One new word of that grand *Credo* which
    in prophet-hearts hath burned
Since the first man stood God-conquered
    with his face to heaven upturned.

For Humanity sweeps onward: where to-
    day the martyr stands,
On the morrow crouches Judas with the
    silver in his hands;
Far in front the cross stands ready and the
    crackling fagots burn,
While the hooting mob of yesterday in
    silent awe return
To glean up the scattered ashes into His-
    tory's golden urn.

'T is as easy to be heroes as to sit the idle
    slaves

Of a legendary virtue carved upon our
    father's graves,
Worshippers of light ancestral make the
    present light a crime; —
Was the Mayflower launched by cowards,
    steered by men behind their time ?
Turn those tracks toward Past or Future,
    that make Plymouth Rock sublime ?

They were men of present valor, stalwart
    old iconoclasts,
Unconvinced by axe or gibbet that all vir-
    tue was the Past's;
But we make their truth our falsehood,
    thinking that hath made us free,
Hoarding it in mouldy parchments, while
    our tender spirits flee
The rude grasp of that great Impulse which
    drove them across the sea.

They have rights who dare maintain them;
    we are traitors to our sires,
Smothering in their holy ashes Freedom's
    new-lit altar-fires;
Shall we make their creed our jailer ?
    Shall we, in our haste to slay,
From the tombs of the old prophets steal
    the funeral lamps away
To light up the martyr-fagots round the
    prophets of to-day ?

New occasions teach new duties; Time
    makes ancient good uncouth;
They must upward still, and onward, who
    would keep abreast of Truth;
Lo, before us gleam her camp-fires ! we
    ourselves must Pilgrims be,
Launch our Mayflower, and steer boldly
    through the desperate winter sea,
Nor attempt the Future's portal with the
    Past's blood-rusted key.

AN INDIAN–SUMMER REVERIE

    The reader familiar with Lowell's life will
readily recognize the local references which
occur in this poem. To others it may be worth
while to point out that the village smithy is
the same as that commemorated by Long-
fellow, that Allston lived in the section of
Cambridge known as Cambridgeport, that some
of the old willows at the causey's end still
stand, and that the group is the one which
gave the name to *Under the Willows*.

WHAT visionary tints the year puts on,
When falling leaves falter through mo-
tionless air
Or numbly cling and shiver to be gone !
How shimmer the low flats and pastures
bare,
As with her nectar Hebe Autumn fills
The bowl between me and those distant
hills,
And smiles and shakes abroad her misty,
tremulous hair !

No more the landscape holds its
wealth apart,
Making me poorer in my poverty,
But mingles with my senses and my
heart;
My own projected spirit seems to me
In her own reverie the world to steep;
'T is she that waves to sympathetic
sleep,
Moving, as she is moved, each field and hill
and tree.

How fuse and mix, with what unfelt
degrees,
Clasped by the faint horizon's languid
arms,
Each into each, the hazy distances !
The softened season all the landscape
charms;
Those hills, my native village that
embay,
In waves of dreamier purple roll away,
And floating in mirage seem all the glim-
mering farms.

Far distant sounds the hidden chicka-
dee
Close at my side; far distant sound the
leaves;
The fields seem fields of dream, where
Memory
Wanders like gleaning Ruth; and as the
sheaves
Of wheat and barley wavered in the
eye
Of Boaz as the maiden's glow went by,
So tremble and seem remote all things the
sense receives.

The cock's shrill trump that tells of
scattered corn,
Passed breezily on by all his flapping
mates,

Faint and more faint, from barn to
barn is borne,
Southward, perhaps to far Magellan's
Straits;
Dimly I catch the throb of distant
flails;
Silently overhead the hen-hawk sails,
With watchful, measuring eye, and for his
quarry waits.

The sobered robin, hunger-silent now,
Seeks cedar-berries blue, his autumn
cheer;
The chipmunk, on the shingly shag-
bark's bough,
Now saws, now lists with downward eye
and ear,
Then drops his nut, and, cheeping,
with a bound
Whisks to his winding fastness under-
ground;
The clouds like swans drift down the
streaming atmosphere.

O'er yon bare knoll the pointed cedar
shadows
Drowse on the crisp, gray moss; the
ploughman's call
Creeps faint as smoke from black,
fresh-furrowed meadows;
The single crow a single caw lets fall;
And all around me every bush and
tree
Says Autumn's here, and Winter soon
will be,
Who snows his soft, white sleep and silence
over all.

The birch, most shy and ladylike of
trees,
Her poverty, as best she may, retrieves,
And hints at her foregone gentilities
With some saved relics of her wealth of
leaves;
The swamp-oak, with his royal purple
on,
Glares red as blood across the sinking
sun,
As one who proudlier to a falling fortune
cleaves.

He looks a sachem, in red blanket
wrapt,
Who, mid some council of the sad-garbed
whites,

Erect and stern, in his own memories
  lapt,
With distant eye broods over other
  sights,
Sees the hushed wood the city's flare
  replace,
The wounded turf heal o'er the rail-
  way's trace,
And roams the savage Past of his un-
  dwindled rights.

The red-oak, softer-grained, yields all
  for lost,
And, with his crumpled foliage stiff and
  dry,
After the first betrayal of the frost,
Rebuffs the kiss of the relenting sky;
  The chestnuts, lavish of their long-hid
    gold,
  To the faint Summer, beggared now
    and old,
Pour back the sunshine hoarded 'neath her
  favoring eye.

The ash her purple drops forgivingly
And sadly, breaking not the general
  hush;
  The maple-swamps glow like a sunset
    sea,
  Each leaf a ripple with its separate
    flush;
All round the wood's edge creeps the
  skirting blaze
Of bushes low, as when, on cloudy
  days,
Ere the rain fall, the cautious farmer burns
  his brush.

O'er yon low wall, which guards one
  unkempt zone,
Where vines and weeds and scrub-oaks
  intertwine
Safe from the plough, whose rough,
  discordant stone
Is massed to one soft gray by lichens
  fine,
  The tangled blackberry, crossed and
    recrossed, weaves
  A prickly network of ensanguined
    leaves;
Hard by, with coral beads, the prim black-
  alders shine.

Pillaring with flame this crumbling
  boundary,

Whose loose blocks topple 'neath the
  ploughboy's foot,
Who, with each sense shut fast except
  the eye,
Creeps close and scares the jay he hoped
  to shoot,
  The woodbine up the elm's straight
    stem aspires,
  Coiling it, harmless, with autumnal
    fires;
In the ivy's paler blaze the martyr oak
  stands mute.

Below, the Charles, a stripe of nether
  sky,
Now hid by rounded apple-trees between,
Whose gaps the misplaced sail sweeps
  bellying by,
Now flickering golden through a wood-
  land screen,
  Then spreading out, at his next turn
    beyond,
  A silver circle like an inland pond —
Slips seaward silently through marshes
  purple and green.

Dear marshes! vain to him the gift of
  sight
Who cannot in their various incomes share,
From every season drawn, of shade
  and light,
Who sees in them but levels brown and
  bare;
  Each change of storm or sunshine
    scatters free
  On them its largess of variety,
For Nature with cheap means still works
  her wonders rare.

In Spring they lie one broad expanse
  of green,
O'er which the light winds run with
  glimmering feet:
Here, yellower stripes track out the
  creek unseen,
There, darker growths o'er hidden
  ditches meet;
  And purpler stains show where the
    blossoms crowd,
  As if the silent shadow of a cloud
Hung there becalmed, with the next breath
  to fleet.

All round, upon the river's slippery
  edge,

Witching to deeper calm the drowsy tide,
Whispers and leans the breeze-entan-
gling sedge;
Through emerald glooms the lingering
waters slide,
Or, sometimes wavering, throw back
the sun,
And the stiff banks in eddies melt and
run
Of dimpling light, and with the current
seem to glide.

In Summer 't is a blithesome sight to
see,
As, step by step, with measured swing,
they pass,
The wide-ranked mowers wading to
the knee,
Their sharp scythes panting through the
wiry grass;
Then, stretched beneath a rick's shade
in a ring,
Their nooning take, while one begins
to sing
A stave that droops and dies 'neath the
close sky of brass.

Meanwhile that devil-may-care, the
bobolink,
Remembering duty, in mid-quaver stops
Just ere he sweeps o'er rapture's
tremulous brink,
And 'twixt the winrows most demurely
drops,
A decorous bird of business, who pro-
vides
For his brown mate and fledglings six
besides,
And looks from right to left, a farmer mid
his crops.

Another change subdues them in the
Fall,
But saddens not; they still show merrier
tints,
Though sober russet seems to cover
all;
When the first sunshine through their
dew-drops glints,
Look how the yellow clearness,
streamed across,
Redeems with rarer hues the season's
loss,
As Dawn's feet there had touched and left
their rosy prints.

Or come when sunset gives its fresh-
ened zest,
Lean o'er the bridge and let the ruddy
thrill,
While the shorn sun swells down the
hazy west,
Glow opposite ; — the marshes drink
their fill
And swoon with purple veins, then
slowly fade
Through pink to brown, as eastward
moves the shade,
Lengthening with stealthy creep, of Si-
mond's darkening hill.

Later, and yet ere Winter wholly
shuts,
Ere through the first dry snow the run-
ner grates,
And the loath cart-wheel screams in
slippery ruts,
While firmer ice the eager boy awaits,
Trying each buckle and strap beside
the fire,
And until bedtime plays with his de-
sire,
Twenty times putting on and off his new-
bought skates; —

Then, every morn, the river's banks
shine bright
With smooth plate - armor, treacherous
and frail,
By the frost's clinking hammers forged
at night,
'Gainst which the lances of the sun pre-
vail,
Giving a pretty emblem of the day
When guiltier arms in light shall melt
away,
And states shall move free-limbed, loosed
from war's cramping mail.

And now those waterfalls the ebbing
river
Twice every day creates on either side
Tinkle, as through their fresh-sparred
grots they shiver
In grass-arched channels to the sun de-
nied;
High flaps in sparkling blue the far-
heard crow,
The silvered flats gleam frostily below,
Suddenly drops the gull and breaks the
glassy tide.

But crowned in turn by vying seasons
three,
Their winter halo hath a fuller ring;
This glory seems to rest immovably, —
The others were too fleet and vanish-
ing;
When the hid tide is at its highest
flow,
O'er marsh and stream one breathless
trance of snow
With brooding fulness awes and hushes
everything.

The sunshine seems blown off by the
bleak wind,
As pale as formal candles lit by day;
Gropes to the sea the river dumb and
blind;
The brown ricks, snow-thatched by the
storm in play,
Show pearly breakers combing o'er
their lee,
White crests as of some just enchanted
sea,
Checked in their maddest leap and hanging
poised midway.

But when the eastern blow, with rain
aslant,
From mid-sea's prairies green and rolling
plains
Drives in his wallowing herds of bil-
lows gaunt,
And the roused Charles remembers in
his veins
Old Ocean's blood and snaps his
gyves of frost,
That tyrannous silence on the shores is
tost
In dreary wreck, and crumbling desolation
reigns.

Edgewise or flat, in Druid-like device,
With leaden pools between or gullies
bare,
The blocks lie strewn, a bleak Stone-
henge of ice;
No life, no sound, to break the grim
despair,
Save sullen plunge, as through the
sedges stiff
Down crackles riverward some thaw-
sapped cliff,
Or when the close-wedged fields of ice
crunch here and there.

But let me turn from fancy-pictured
scenes
To that whose pastoral calm before me
lies:
Here nothing harsh or rugged inter-
venes;
The early evening with her misty dyes
Smooths off the ravelled edges of the
nigh,
Relieves the distant with her cooler sky,
And tones the landscape down, and soothes
the wearied eyes.

There gleams my native village, dear
to me,
Though higher change's waves each day
are seen,
Whelming fields famed in boyhood's
history,
Sanding with houses the diminished
green;
There, in red brick, which softening
time defies,
Stand square and stiff the Muses'
factories; —
How with my life knit up is every well-
known scene !

Flow on, dear river ! not alone you flow
To outward sight, and through your
marshes wind;
Fed from the mystic springs of long-
ago,
Your twin flows silent through my world
of mind:
Grow dim, dear marshes, in the even-
ing's gray !
Before my inner sight ye stretch away,
And will forever, though these fleshly eyes
grow blind.

Beyond the hillock's house-bespotted
swell,
Where Gothic chapels house the horse
and chaise,
Where quiet cits in Grecian temples
dwell,
Where Coptic tombs resound with prayer
and praise,
Where dust and mud the equal year
divide,
There gentle Allston lived, and
wrought, and died,
Transfiguring street and shop with his
illumined gaze.

Virgilium vidi tantum, — I have seen
But as a boy, who looks alike on all,
  That misty hair, that fine Undine-like
    mien,
Tremulous as down to feeling's faintest
    call; —
  Ah, dear old homestead! count it to
    thy fame
  That thither many times the Painter
    came; —
One elm yet bears his name, a feathery tree
    and tall.

Swiftly the present fades in memory's
    glow, —
Our only sure possession is the past;
  The village blacksmith died a month
    ago,
And dim to me the forge's roaring blast;
  Soon fire - new mediævals we shall
    see
  Oust the black smithy from its chest-
    nut-tree,
And that hewn down, perhaps, the beehive
    green and vast.

How many times, prouder than king
    on throne,
Loosed from the village school-dame's
    A's and B's,
  Panting have I the creaky bellows
    blown,
And watched the pent volcano's red in-
    crease,
  Then paused to see the ponderous
    sledge, brought down
  By that hard arm voluminous and
    brown,
From the white iron swarm its golden van-
    ishing bees.

Dear native town! whose choking elms
    each year
With eddying dust before their time turn
    gray,
  Pining for rain, — to me thy dust is
    dear;
It glorifies the eve of summer day,
  And when the westering sun half
    sunken burns,
  The mote-thick air to deepest orange
    turns,
The westward horseman rides through
    clouds of gold away,

So palpable, I 've seen those unshorn
    few,
The six old willows at the causey's end
  (Such trees Paul Potter never dreamed
    nor drew),
Through this dry mist their checkering
    shadows send,
  Striped, here and there, with many a
    long-drawn thread,
  Where streamed through leafy chinks
    the trembling red,
Past which, in one bright trail, the hang-
    bird's flashes blend.

Yes, dearer far thy dust than all that
    e'er,
Beneath the awarded crown of victory,
  Gilded the blown Olympic charioteer;
Though lightly prized the ribboned
    parchments three,
  Yet *collegisse juvat,* I am glad
  That here what colleging was mine I
    had, —
It linked another tie, dear native town,
    with thee!

Nearer art thou than simply native
    earth,
My dust with thine concedes a deeper
    tie;
  A closer claim thy soil may well put
    forth,
Something of kindred more than sympa-
    thy;
  For in thy bounds I reverently laid
    away
  That blinding anguish of forsaken
    clay,
That title I seemed to have in earth and
    sea and sky,

That portion of my life more choice to
    me
(Though brief, yet in itself so round and
    whole)
Than all the imperfect residue can
    be; —
The Artist saw his statue of the soul
  Was perfect; so, with one regretful
    stroke,
  The earthen model into fragments
    broke,
And without her the impoverished seasons
    roll.

THE GROWTH OF THE LEGEND

A FRAGMENT

A LEGEND that grew in the forest's hush
Slowly as tear-drops gather and gush,
When a word some poet chanced to say
Ages ago, in his careless way,
Brings our youth back to us out of its
    shroud
Clearly as under yon thunder-cloud
I see that white sea-gull. It grew and
    grew,
From the pine-trees gathering a sombre
    hue,
Till it seems a mere murmur out of the
    vast
Norwegian forests of the past;
And it grew itself like a true Northern
    pine,
First a little slender line,
Like a mermaid's green eyelash, and then
    anon
A stem that a tower might rest upon,
Standing spear-straight in the waist-deep
    moss,
Its bony roots clutching around and across,
As if they would tear up earth's heart in
    their grasp
Ere the storm should uproot them or make
    them unclasp;
Its cloudy boughs singing, as suiteth the
    pine,
To snow-bearded sea-kings old songs of the
    brine,
Till they straightened and let their staves
    fall to the floor,
Hearing waves moan again on the perilous
    shore
Of Vinland, perhaps, while their prow
    groped its way
'Twixt the frothed gnashing tusks of some
    ship-crunching bay.

So, pine-like, the legend grew, strong-
    limbed and tall,
As the Gypsy child grows that eats crusts
    in the hall;
It sucked the whole strength of the earth
    and the sky,
Spring, Summer, Fall, Winter, all brought
    it supply;
'T was a natural growth, and stood fear-
    lessly there,

True part of the landscape as sea, land, and
    air;
For it grew in good times, ere the fashion
    it was
To force these wild births of the woods
    under glass,
And so, if 't is told as it should be told,
Though 't were sung under Venice's moon-
    light of gold,
You would hear the old voice of its mother,
    the pine,
Murmur sealike and northern through
    every line,
And the verses should grow, self-sustained
    and free,
Round the vibrating stem of the melody,
Like the lithe moonlit limbs of the parent
    tree.

Yes, the pine is the mother of legends;
    what food
For their grim roots is left when the thou-
    sand-yeared wood,
The dim-aisled cathedral, whose tall arches
    spring
Light, sinewy, graceful, firm-set as the
    wing
From Michael's white shoulder, is hewn and
    defaced
By iconoclast axes in desperate waste,
And its wrecks seek the ocean it prophesied
    long,
Cassandra-like, crooning its mystical song ?
Then the legends go with them, — even yet
    on the sea
A wild virtue is left in the touch of the tree,
And the sailor's night-watches are thrilled
    to the core
With the lineal offspring of Odin and Thor.

Yes, wherever the pine-wood has never let
    in,
Since the day of creation, the light and the
    din
Of manifold life, but has safely conveyed
From the midnight primeval its armful of
    shade,
And has kept the weird Past with its child-
    faith alive
Mid the hum and the stir of To-day's busy
    hive,
There the legend takes root in the age-
    gathered gloom,
And its murmurous boughs for their sagas
    find room.

Where Aroostook, far-heard, seems to sob
  as he goes
Groping down to the sea 'neath his moun-
  tainous snows;
Where the lake's frore Sahara of never-
  tracked white,
When the crack shoots across it, complains
  to the night
With a long, lonely moan, that leagues
  northward is lost,
As the ice shrinks away from the tread of
  the frost;
Where the lumberers sit by the log-fires
  that throw
Their own threatening shadows far round
  o'er the snow,
When the wolf howls aloof, and the waver-
  ing glare
Flashes out from the blackness the eyes of
  the bear,
When the wood's huge recesses, half-
  lighted, supply
A canvas where Fancy her mad brush may
  try,
Blotting in giant Horrors that venture not
  down
Through the right-angled streets of the
  brisk, whitewashed town,
But skulk in the depths of the measureless
  wood
Mid the Dark's creeping whispers that
  curdle the blood,
When the eye, glanced in dread o'er the
  shoulder, may dream,
Ere it shrinks to the camp-fire's companion-
  ing gleam,
That it saw the fierce ghost of the Red
  Man crouch back
To the shroud of the tree-trunk's invincible
  black;
There the old shapes crowd thick round
  the pine-shadowed camp,
Which shun the keen gleam of the scholarly
  lamp,
And the seed of the legend finds true Nor-
  land ground,
While the border-tale's told and the can-
  teen flits round.

A CONTRAST

THY love thou sentest oft to me,
  And still as oft I thrust it back;
Thy messengers I could not see

In those who everything did lack,
  The poor, the outcast and the black.

Pride held his hand before mine eyes,
  The world with flattery stuffed mine ears;
I looked to see a monarch's guise,
  Nor dreamed thy love would knock for
    years,
  Poor, naked, fettered, full of tears.

Yet, when I sent my love to thee,
  Thou with a smile didst take it in,
And entertain'dst it royally,
  Though grimed with earth, with hunger
    thin,
  And leprous with the taint of sin.

Now every day thy love I meet,
  As o'er the earth it wanders wide,
With weary step and bleeding feet,
  Still knocking at the heart of pride
  And offering grace, though still denied.

EXTREME UNCTION

Go ! leave me, Priest; my soul would be
  Alone with the consoler, Death;
Far sadder eyes than thine will see
  This crumbling clay yield up its breath;
These shrivelled hands have deeper stains
  Than holy oil can cleanse away,
Hands that have plucked the world's coarse
    gains
  As erst they plucked the flowers of May.

Call, if thou canst, to these gray eyes
  Some faith from youth's traditions
    wrung;
This fruitless husk which dustward dries
  Hath been a heart once, hath been young;
On this bowed head the awful Past
  Once laid its consecrating hands;
The Future in its purpose vast
  Paused, waiting my supreme commands.

But look ! whose shadows block the door ?
  Who are those two that stand aloof ?
See ! on my hands this freshening gore
  Writes o'er again its crimson proof !
My looked-for death-bed guests are met;
  There my dead Youth doth wring its
    hands,
And there, with eyes that goad me yet,
  The ghost of my Ideal stands !

God bends from out the deep and says,
  "I gave thee the great gift of life;
Wast thou not called in many ways ?
  Are not my earth and heaven at strife ?
I gave thee of my seed to sow,
  Bringest thou me my hundred-fold ? "
Can I look up with face aglow,
  And answer, " Father, here is gold " ?

I have been innocent; God knows
  When first this wasted life began,
Not grape with grape more kindly grows,
  Than I with every brother-man :
Now here I gasp ; what lose my kind,
  When this fast ebbing breath shall
    part ?
What bands of love and service bind
  This being to a brother heart ?

Christ still was wandering o'er the earth
  Without a place to lay his head;
He found free welcome at my hearth,
  He shared my cup and broke my bread:
Now, when I hear those steps sublime,
  That bring the other world to this,
My snake-turned nature, sunk in slime,
  Starts sideway with defiant hiss.

Upon the hour when I was born,
  God said, " Another man shall be,"
And the great Maker did not scorn
  Out of himself to fashion me;
He sunned me with his ripening looks,
  And Heaven's rich instincts in me grew,
As effortless as woodland nooks
  Send violets up and paint them blue.

Yes, I who now, with angry tears,
  Am exiled back to brutish clod,
Have borne unquenched for fourscore years
  A spark of the eternal God;
And to what end ?   How yield I back
  The trust for such high uses given ?
Heaven's light hath but revealed a track
  Whereby to crawl away from heaven.

Men think it is an awful sight
  To see a soul just set adrift
On that drear voyage from whose night
  The ominous shadows never lift;
But 't is more awful to behold
  A helpless infant newly born,
Whose little hands unconscious hold
  The keys of darkness and of morn.

Mine held them once; I flung away
  Those keys that might have open set
The golden sluices of the day,
  But clutch the keys of darkness yet;
I hear the reapers singing go
  Into God's harvest; I, that might
With them have chosen, here below
  Grope shuddering at the gates of night.

O glorious Youth, that once wast mine !
  O high Ideal ! all in vain
Ye enter at this ruined shrine
  Whence worship ne'er shall rise again;
The bat and owl inhabit here,
  The snake nests in the altar-stone,
The sacred vessels moulder near,
  The image of the God is gone.

THE OAK

WHAT gnarlëd stretch, what depth of
    shade, is his !
  There needs no crown to mark the for-
    est's king;
How in his leaves outshines full summer's
    bliss !
  Sun, storm, rain, dew, to him their trib-
    ute bring,
Which he with such benignant royalty
  Accepts, as overpayeth what is lent;
All nature seems his vassal proud to be,
  And cunning only for his ornament.

How towers he, too, amid the billowed
    snows,
  An unquelled exile from the summer's
    throne,
Whose plain, uncinctured front more kingly
    shows,
  Now that the obscuring courtier leaves
    are flown.
His boughs make music of the winter air,
  Jewelled with sleet, like some cathedral
    front
Where clinging snow-flakes with quaint art
    repair
  The dints and furrows of time's envious
    brunt.

How doth his patient strength the rude
    March wind
  Persuade to seem glad breaths of sum-
    mer breeze,
And win the soil that fain would be unkind,

To swell his revenues with proud in-
crease !
He is the gem; and all the landscape wide
(So doth his grandeur isolate the sense)
Seems but the setting, worthless all beside,
An empty socket, were he fallen thence.

So, from oft converse with life's wintry
gales,
Should man learn how to clasp with
tougher roots
The inspiring earth; how otherwise avails
The leaf - creating sap that sunward
shoots ?
So every year that falls with noiseless
flake
Should fill old scars up on the storm-
ward side,
And make hoar age revered for age's sake,
Not for traditions of youth's leafy pride.

So, from the pinched soil of a churlish fate,
True hearts compel the sap of sturdier
growth,
So between earth and heaven stand simply
great,
That these shall seem but their attend-
ants both;
For nature's forces with obedient zeal
Wait on the rooted faith and oaken will;
As quickly the pretender's cheat they feel,
And turn mad Pucks to flout and mock
him still.

Lord ! all thy works are lessons; each con-
tains
Some emblem of man's all-containing
soul;
Shall he make fruitless all thy glorious
pains,
Delving within thy grace an eyeless
mole ?
Make me the least of thy Dodona-grove,
Cause me some message of thy truth to
bring,
Speak but a word through me, nor let thy
love
Among my boughs disdain to perch and
sing.

AMBROSE

NEVER, surely, was holier man
Than Ambrose, since the world began;
With diet spare and raiment thin
He shielded himself from the father of sin;
With bed of iron and scourgings oft,
His heart to God's hand as wax made soft.

Through earnest prayer and watchings
long
He sought to know 'tween right and wrong,
Much wrestling with the blessed Word
To make it yield the sense of the Lord,
That he might build a storm-proof creed
To fold the flock in at their need.

At last he builded a perfect faith,
Fenced round about with *The Lord thus
saith;*
To himself he fitted the doorway's size,
Meted the light to the need of his eyes,
And knew, by a sure and inward sign,
That the work of his fingers was divine.

Then Ambrose said, " All those shall die
The eternal death who believe not as I; "
And some were boiled, some burned in fire,
Some sawn in twain, that his heart's desire,
For the good of men's souls might be satis-
fied
By the drawing of all to the righteous side.

One day, as Ambrose was seeking the truth
In his lonely walk, he saw a youth
Resting himself in the shade of a tree;
It had never been granted him to see
So shining a face, and the good man
thought
'T were pity he should not believe as he
ought.

So he set himself by the young man's side,
And the state of his soul with questions
tried;
But the heart of the stranger was hardened
indeed,
Nor received the stamp of the one true
creed;
And the spirit of Ambrose waxed sore to
find
Such features the porch of so narrow a
mind.

" As each beholds in cloud and fire
The shape that answers his own desire,
So each," said the youth, " in the Law shall
find
The figure and fashion of his mind;

And to each in his mercy hath God allowed
His several pillar of fire and cloud."

The soul of Ambrose burned with zeal
And holy wrath for the young man's weal:
"Believest thou then, most wretched
    youth,"
Cried he, "a dividual essence in Truth?
I fear me thy heart is too cramped with sin
To take the Lord in his glory in."

Now there bubbled beside them where they
    stood
A fountain of waters sweet and good;
The youth to the streamlet's brink drew
    near
Saying, "Ambrose, thou maker of creeds,
    look here!"
Six vases of crystal then he took,
And set them along the edge of the brook.

"As into these vessels the water I pour,
There shall one hold less, another more,
And the water unchanged, in every case,
Shall put on the figure of the vase;
O thou, who wouldst unity make through
    strife,
Canst thou fit this sign to the Water of
    Life?"

When Ambrose looked up, he stood alone,
The youth and the stream and the vases
    were gone;
But he knew, by a sense of humbled grace,
He had talked with an angel face to face,
And felt his heart change inwardly,
As he fell on his knees beneath the tree.

ABOVE AND BELOW

I

O DWELLERS in the valley-land,
    Who in deep twilight grope and cower,
Till the slow mountain's dial-hand
    Shorten to noon's triumphal hour,
While ye sit idle, do ye think
    The Lord's great work sits idle too?
That light dare not o'erleap the brink
    Of morn, because 't is dark with you?

Though yet your valleys skulk in night,
    In God's ripe fields the day is cried,
And reapers, with their sickles bright,
    Troop, singing, down the mountain-side:

Come up, and feel what health there is
    In the frank Dawn's delighted eyes,
As, bending with a pitying kiss,
    The night-shed tears of Earth she dries!

The Lord wants reapers: oh, mount up,
    Before night comes, and says, "Too
        late!"
Stay not for taking scrip or cup,
    The Master hungers while ye wait;
'T is from these heights alone your eyes
    The advancing spears of day can see,
That o'er the eastern hill-tops rise,
    To break your long captivity.

II

Lone watcher on the mountain-height,
    It is right precious to behold
The first long surf of climbing light
    Flood all the thirsty east with gold;
But we, who in the shadow sit,
    Know also when the day is nigh,
Seeing thy shining forehead lit
    With his inspiring prophecy.

Thou hast thine office; we have ours;
    God lacks not early service here,
But what are thine eleventh hours
    He counts with us for morning cheer;
Our day, for Him, is long enough,
    And when He giveth work to do,
The bruisèd reed is amply tough
    To pierce the shield of error through.

But not the less do thou aspire
    Light's earlier messages to preach;
Keep back no syllable of fire,
    Plunge deep the rowels of thy speech.
Yet God deems not thine aeried sight
    More worthy than our twilight dim;
For meek Obedience, too, is Light,
    And following that is finding Him.

THE CAPTIVE

IT was past the hour of trysting,
    But she lingered for him still;
Like a child, the eager streamlet
    Leaped and laughed adown the hill,
Happy to be free at twilight
    From its toiling at the mill.

Then the great moon on a sudden
    Ominous, and red as blood,

Startling as a new creation,
  O'er the eastern hilltop stood,
Casting deep and deeper shadows
  Through the mystery of the wood.

Dread closed vast and vague about her,
  And her thoughts turned fearfully
To her heart, if there some shelter
  From the silence there might be,
Like bare cedars leaning inland
  From the blighting of the sea.

Yet he came not, and the stillness
  Dampened round her like a tomb;
She could feel cold eyes of spirits
  Looking on her through the gloom,
She could hear the groping footsteps
  Of some blind, gigantic doom.

Suddenly the silence wavered
  Like a light mist in the wind,
For a voice broke gently through it,
  Felt like sunshine by the blind,
And the dread, like mist in sunshine,
  Furled serenely from her mind.

" Once my love, my love forever,
  Flesh or spirit, still the same,
If I failed at time of trysting,
  Deem thou not my faith to blame;
I, alas, was made a captive,
  As from Holy Land I came.

" On a green spot in the desert,
  Gleaming like an emerald star,
Where a palm-tree, in lone silence,
  Yearning for its mate afar,
Droops above a silver runnel,
  Slender as a scimitar,

" There thou 'lt find the humble postern
  To the castle of my foe;
If thy love burn clear and faithful,
  Strike the gateway, green and low,
Ask to enter, and the warder
  Surely will not say thee no."

Slept again the aspen silence,
  But her loneliness was o'er;
Round her soul a motherly patience
  Clasped its arms forevermore;
From her heart ebbed back the sorrow,
  Leaving smooth the golden shore.

Donned she now the pilgrim scallop,
  Took the Pilgrim staff in hand;

Like a cloud-shade flitting eastward,
  Wandered she o'er sea and land;
And her footsteps in the desert
  Fell like cool rain on the sand.

Soon, beneath the palm-tree's shadow,
  Knelt she at the postern low;
And thereat she knocked full gently,
  Fearing much the warder's no;
All her heart stood still and listened,
  As the door swung backward slow.

There she saw no surly warder
  With an eye like bolt and bar;
Through her soul a sense of music
  Throbbed, and, like a guardian Lar,
On the threshold stood an angel,
  Bright and silent as a star.

Fairest seemed he of God's seraphs,
  And her spirit, lily-wise,
Opened when he turned upon her
  The deep welcome of his eyes,
Sending upward to that sunlight
  All its dew for sacrifice.

Then she heard a voice come onward
  Singing with a rapture new,
As Eve heard the songs in Eden,
  Dropping earthward with the dew;
Well she knew the happy singer,
  Well the happy song she knew.

Forward leaped she o'er the threshold,
  Eager as a glancing surf;
Fell from her the spirit's languor,
  Fell from her the body's scurf;
'Neath the palm next day some Arabs
  Found a corpse upon the turf.

THE BIRCH-TREE

RIPPLING through thy branches goes the
    sunshine,
Among thy leaves that palpitate forever;
Ovid in thee a pining Nymph had pris-
    oned,
The soul once of some tremulous inland
    river,
Quivering to tell her woe, but, ah! dumb,
    dumb forever!

While all the forest, witched with slum-
    berous moonshine,

Holds up its leaves in happy, happy still-
ness,
Waiting the dew, with breath and pulse
suspended,
I hear afar thy whispering, gleamy islands,
And track thee wakeful still amid the
wide-hung silence.

On the brink of some wood-nestled lakelet,
Thy foliage, like the tresses of a Dryad,
Dripping round thy slim white stem, whose
shadow
Slopes quivering down the water's dusky
quiet,
Thou shrink'st as on her bath's edge would
some startled Naiad.

Thou art the go-between of rustic lovers;
Thy white bark has their secrets in its
keeping;
Reuben writes here the happy name of Pa-
tience,
And thy lithe boughs hang murmuring and
weeping
Above her, as she steals the mystery from
thy keeping.

Thou art to me like my belovëd maiden,
So frankly coy, so full of trembly confi-
dences;
Thy shadow scarce seems shade, thy pat-
tering leaflets
Sprinkle their gathered sunshine o'er my
senses,
And Nature gives me all her summer con-
fidences.

Whether my heart with hope or sorrow
tremble,
Thou sympathizest still; wild and unquiet,
I fling me down; thy ripple, like a river,
Flows valleyward, where calmness is, and
by it
My heart is floated down into the land of
quiet.

AN INTERVIEW WITH MILES
STANDISH

I SAT one evening in my room,
In that sweet hour of twilight
When blended thoughts, half light, half
gloom,
Throng through the spirit's skylight;
The flames by fits curled round the bars,

Or up the chimney crinkled,
While embers dropped like falling stars,
And in the ashes tinkled.

I sat and mused; the fire burned low,
And, o'er my senses stealing,
Crept something of the ruddy glow
That bloomed on wall and ceiling;
My pictures (they are very few,
The heads of ancient wise men)
Smoothed down their knotted fronts, and
grew
As rosy as excisemen.

My antique high-backed Spanish chair
Felt thrills through wood and leather,
That had been strangers since whilere,
Mid Andalusian heather,
The oak that built its sturdy frame
His happy arms stretched over
The ox whose fortunate hide became
The bottom's polished cover.

It came out in that famous bark,
That brought our sires intrepid,
Capacious as another ark
For furniture decrepit;
For, as that saved of bird and beast
A pair for propagation,
So has the seed of these increased
And furnished half the nation.

Kings sit, they say, in slippery seats;
But those slant precipices
Of ice the northern voyager meets
Less slippery are than this is;
To cling therein would pass the wit
Of royal man or woman,
And whatsoe'er can stay in it
Is more or less than human.

I offer to all bores this perch,
Dear well-intentioned people
With heads as void as week-day church,
Tongues longer than the steeple;
To folks with missions, whose gaunt eyes
See golden ages rising, —
Salt of the earth! in what queer Guys
Thou 'rt fond of crystallizing!

My wonder, then, was not unmixed
With merciful suggestion,
When, as my roving eyes grew fixed
Upon the chair in question,
I saw its trembling arms enclose

A figure grim and rusty,
Whose doublet plain and plainer hose
Were something worn and dusty.

Now even such men as Nature forms
Merely to fill the street with,
Once turned to ghosts by hungry worms,
Are serious things to meet with;
Your penitent spirits are no jokes,
And, though I 'm not averse to
A quiet shade, even they are folks
One cares not to speak first to.

Who knows, thought I, but he has come,
By Charon kindly ferried,
To tell me of a mighty sum
Behind my wainscot buried ?
There is a buccaneerish air
About that garb outlandish —
Just then the ghost drew up his chair
And said, " My name is Standish.

" I come from Plymouth, deadly bored
With toasts, and songs, and speeches,
As long and flat as my old sword,
As threadbare as my breeches:
They understand us Pilgrims ! they,
Smooth men with rosy faces,
Strength's knots and gnarls all pared away,
And varnish in their places !

" We had some toughness in our grain,
The eye to rightly see us is
Not just the one that lights the brain
Of drawing-room Tyrtæuses:
They talk about their Pilgrim blood,
Their birthright high and holy !
A mountain-stream that ends in mud
Methinks is melancholy.

" He had stiff knees, the Puritan,
That were not good at bending;
The homespun dignity of man
He thought was worth defending;
He did not, with his pinchbeck ore,
His country's shame forgotten,
Gild Freedom's coffin o'er and o'er,
When all within was rotten.

" These loud ancestral boasts of yours,
How can they else than vex us ?
Where were your dinner orators
When slavery grasped at Texas ?
Dumb on his knees was every one
That now is bold as Cæsar;

Mere pegs.to hang an office on
Such stalwart men as these are."

" Good sir," I said, " you seem much
stirred;
The sacred compromises " —
" Now God confound the dastard word !
My gall thereat arises:
Northward it hath this sense alone,
That you, your conscience blinding,
Shall bow your fool's nose to the stone,
When slavery feels like grinding.

" 'T is shame to see such painted sticks
In Vane's and Winthrop's places,
To see your spirit of Seventy-six
Drag humbly in the traces,
With slavery's lash upon her back,
And herds of office-holders
To shout applause, as, with a crack,
It peels her patient shoulders.

" *We* forefathers to such a rout ! —
No, by my faith in God's word ! "
Half rose the ghost, and half drew out
The ghost of his old broadsword,
Then thrust it slowly back again,
And said, with reverent gesture,
" No, Freedom, no! blood should not stain
The hem of thy white vesture.

" I feel the soul in me draw near
The mount of prophesying;
In this bleak wilderness I hear
A John the Baptist crying;
Far in the east I see upleap
The streaks of first forewarning,
And they who sowed the light shall reap
The golden sheaves of morning.

" Child of our travail and our woe,
Light in our day of sorrow,
Through my rapt spirit I foreknow
The glory of thy morrow;
I hear great steps, that through the shade
Draw nigher still and nigher,
And voices call like that which bade
The prophet come up higher."

I looked, no form mine eyes could find,
I heard the red cock crowing,
And through my window-chinks the wind
A dismal tune was blowing;
Thought I, My neighbor Buckingham
Hath somewhat in him gritty,

Some Pilgrim-stuff that hates all sham,
And he will print my ditty.

ON THE CAPTURE OF FUGITIVE SLAVES NEAR WASHINGTON

In a letter to Edward M. Davis written from Elmwood July 24, 1845, Lowell says : " I blew another ' dolorous and jarring blast ' in the *Courier* the other day, which you will probably see in the *Liberator* of this week or next. I was impelled to write by the account of the poor fugitives who were taken near Washington. I think it has done some good. At any rate, it has set two gentlemen together by the ears about Dissolution, and they are hammering away at each other in the *Courier*." The blast was the following stanzas.

LOOK on who will in apathy, and stifle they who can,
The sympathies, the hopes, the words, that make man truly man;
Let those whose hearts are dungeoned up with interest or with ease
Consent to hear with quiet pulse of loathsome deeds like these !

I first drew in New England's air, and from her hardy breast
Sucked in the tyrant-hating milk that will not let me rest;
And if my words seem treason to the dullard and the tame,
'T is but my Bay-State dialect, — our fathers spake the same !

Shame on the costly mockery of piling stone on stone
To those who won our liberty, the heroes dead and gone,
While we look coldly on and see law-shielded ruffians slay
The men who fain would win their own, the heroes of to-day !

Are we pledged to craven silence ? Oh, fling it to the wind,
The parchment wall that bars us from the least of human kind,
That makes us cringe and temporize, and dumbly stand at rest,
While Pity's burning flood of words is red-hot in the breast !

Though we break our fathers' promise, we have nobler duties first;
The traitor to Humanity is the traitor most accursed;
Man is more than Constitutions; better rot beneath the sod,
Than be true to Church and State while we are doubly false to God !

We owe allegiance to the State; but deeper, truer, more,
To the sympathies that God hath set within our spirit's core;
Our country claims our fealty; we grant it so, but then
Before Man made us citizens, great Nature made us men.

He 's true to God who 's true to man ; wherever wrong is done,
To the humblest and the weakest, 'neath the all-beholding sun,
That wrong is also done to us; and they are slaves most base,
Whose love of right is for themselves, and not for all their race.

God works for all. Ye cannot hem the hope of being free
With parallels of latitude, with mountain-range or sea.
Put golden padlocks on Truth's lips, be callous as ye will,
From soul to soul, o'er all the world, leaps one electric thrill.

Chain down your slaves with ignorance, ye cannot keep apart,
With all your craft of tyranny, the human heart from heart:
When first the Pilgrims landed on the Bay State's iron shore,
The word went forth that slavery should one day be no more.

Out from the land of bondage 't is decreed our slaves shall go,
And signs to us are offered, as erst to Pharaoh ;
If we are blind, their exodus, like Israel's of yore,
Through a Red Sea is doomed to be, whose surges are of gore.

'T is ours to save our brethren, with peace
and love to win
Their darkened hearts from error, ere they
harden it to sin;
But if before his duty man with listless
spirit stands,
Erelong the Great Avenger takes the work
from out his hands.

TO THE DANDELION

DEAR common flower, that grow'st be-
side the way,
Fringing the dusty road with harmless
gold,
First pledge of blithesome May,
Which children pluck, and, full of pride
uphold,
High-hearted buccaneers, o'erjoyed that
they
An Eldorado in the grass have found,
Which not the rich earth's ample
round
May match in wealth, thou art more dear
to me
Than all the prouder summer-blooms
may be.

Gold such as thine ne'er drew the Span-
ish prow
Through the primeval hush of Indian seas,
Nor wrinkled the lean brow
Of age, to rob the lover's heart of ease;
'T is the Spring's largess, which she scat-
ters now
To rich and poor alike, with lavish hand,
Though most hearts never understand
To take it at God's value, but pass by
The offered wealth with unrewarded eye.

Thou art my tropics and mine Italy;
To look at thee unlocks a warmer clime;
The eyes thou givest me
Are in the heart, and heed not space or
time:
Not in mid June the golden-cuirassed
bee
Feels a more summer-like warm ravish-
ment
In the white lily's breezy tent,
His fragrant Sybaris, than I, when first
From the dark green thy yellow circles
burst.

Then think I of deep shadows on the
grass,
Of meadows where in sun the cattle graze,
Where, as the breezes pass,
The gleaming rushes lean a thousand ways,
Of leaves that slumber in a cloudy mass,
Or whiten in the wind, of waters blue
That from the distance sparkle through
Some woodland gap, and of a sky above,
Where one white cloud like a stray lamb
doth move.

My childhood's earliest thoughts are
linked with thee;
The sight of thee calls back the robin's
song,
Who, from the dark old tree
Beside the door, sang clearly all day long,
And I, secure in childish piety,
Listened as if I heard an angel sing
With news from heaven, which he
could bring
Fresh every day to my untainted ears
When birds and flowers and I were
happy peers.

How like a prodigal doth nature seem,
When thou, for all thy gold, so common art!
Thou teachest me to deem
More sacredly of every human heart,
Since each reflects in joy its scanty gleam
Of heaven, and could some wondrous secret
show,
Did we but pay the love we owe,
And with a child's undoubting wisdom
look
On all these living pages of God's book.

THE GHOST–SEER

This poem was printed March 8, 1845, in the
Broadway Journal, edited by C. F. Briggs.
In a letter accompanying the poem Lowell
confesses his dissatisfaction with the execution
as compared with the conception, and adds:
" Written in the metre which I have chosen it
is perhaps too long, but the plot would have
sufficed for quite a long and elaborate poem,
into which a good deal of reflection and ex-
perience might have been compressed."

YE who, passing graves by night,
Glance not to the left or right,
Lest a spirit should arise,
Cold and white, to freeze your eyes,

Some weak phantom, which your doubt
Shapes upon the dark without
From the dark within, a guess
At the spirit's deathlessness,
Which ye entertain with fear
In your self-built dungeon here,
Where ye sell your God-given lives
Just for gold to buy you gyves, —
Ye without a shudder meet
In the city's noonday street,
Spirits sadder and more dread
Than from out the clay have fled,
Buried, beyond hope of light,
In the body's haunted night !
See ye not that woman pale ?
There are bloodhounds on her trail !
Bloodhounds two, all gaunt and lean,
(For the soul their scent is keen,)
Want and Sin, and Sin is last,
They have followed far and fast;
Want gave tongue, and, at her howl,
Sin awakened with a growl.
Ah, poor girl ! she had a right
To a blessing from the light;
Title-deeds to sky and earth
God gave to her at her birth;
But, before they were enjoyed,
Poverty had made them void,
And had drunk the sunshine up
From all nature's ample cup,
Leaving her a first-born's share
In the dregs of darkness there.
Often, on the sidewalk bleak,
Hungry, all alone, and weak,
She has seen, in night and storm,
Rooms o'erflow with firelight warm,
Which, outside the window-glass,
Doubled all the cold, alas !
Till each ray that on her fell
Stabbed her like an icicle,
And she almost loved the wail
Of the bloodhounds on her trail.
Till the floor becomes her bier,
She shall feel their pantings near,
Close upon her very heels,
Spite of all the din of wheels;
Shivering on her pallet poor,
She shall hear them at the door
Whine and scratch to be let in,
Sister bloodhounds, Want and Sin !

Hark ! that rustle of a dress,
Stiff with lavish costliness !
Here comes one whose cheek would flush
But to have her garment brush

'Gainst the girl whose fingers thin
Wove the weary broidery in,
Bending backward from her toil,
Lest her tears the silk might soil,
And, in midnights chill and murk,
Stitched her life into the work,
Shaping from her bitter thought
Heart's-ease and forget-me-not,
Satirizing her despair
With the emblems woven there.
Little doth the wearer heed
Of the heart-break in the brede;
A hyena by her side
Skulks, down-looking, — it is Pride.
He digs for her in the earth,
Where lie all her claims of birth,
With his foul paws rooting o'er
Some long-buried ancestor,
Who perhaps a statue won
By the ill deeds he had done,
By the innocent blood he shed,
By the desolation spread
Over happy villages,
Blotting out the smile of peace.
There walks Judas, he who sold
Yesterday his Lord for gold,
Sold God's presence in his heart
For a proud step in the mart;
He hath dealt in flesh and blood;
At the bank his name is good;
At the bank, and only there,
'T is a marketable ware.
In his eyes that stealthy gleam
Was not learned of sky or stream,
But it has the cold, hard glint
Of new dollars from the mint.
Open now your spirit's eyes,
Look through that poor clay disguise
Which has thickened, day by day,
Till it keeps all light at bay,
And his soul in pitchy gloom
Gropes about its narrow tomb,
From whose dank and slimy walls
Drop by drop the horror falls.
Look ! a serpent lank and cold
Hugs his spirit fold on fold;
From his heart, all day and night,
It doth suck God's blessed light.
Drink it will, and drink it must,
Till the cup holds naught but dust;
All day long he hears it hiss,
Writhing in its fiendish bliss;
All night long he sees its eyes
Flicker with foul ecstasies,
As the spirit ebbs away

Into the absorbing clay.
Who is he that skulks, afraid
Of the trust he has betrayed,
Shuddering if perchance a gleam
Of old nobleness should stream
Through the pent, unwholesome room,
Where his shrunk soul cowers in gloom,
Spirit sad beyond the rest
By more instinct for the best ?
'T is a poet who was sent
For a bad world's punishment,
By compelling it to see
Golden glimpses of To Be,
By compelling it to hear
Songs that prove the angels near;
Who was sent to be the tongue
Of the weak and spirit-wrung,
Whence the fiery-winged Despair
In men's shrinking eyes might flare.
'T is our hope doth fashion us
To base use or glorious:
He who might have been a lark
Of Truth's morning, from the dark
Raining down melodious hope
Of a freer, broader scope,
Aspirations, prophecies,
Of the spirit's full sunrise,
Chose to be a bird of night,
That, with eyes refusing light,
Hooted from some hollow tree
Of the world's idolatry.
'T is his punishment to hear
Sweep of eager pinions near,
And his own vain wings to feel
Drooping downward to his heel,
All their grace and import lost,
Burdening his weary ghost:
Ever walking by his side
He must see his angel guide,
Who at intervals doth turn
Looks on him so sadly stern,
With such ever-new surprise
Of hushed anguish in her eyes,
That it seems the light of day
From around him shrinks away,
Or drops blunted from the wall
Built around him by his fall.
Then the mountains, whose white peaks
Catch the morning's earliest streaks,
He must see, where prophets sit,
Turning east their faces lit,
Whence, with footsteps beautiful,
To the earth, yet dim and dull,
They the gladsome tidings bring
Of the sunlight's hastening:

Never can these hills of bliss
Be o'erclimbed by feet like his !

But enough ! Oh, do not dare
From the next the veil to tear,
Woven of station, trade, or dress,
More obscene than nakedness,
Wherewith plausible culture drapes
Fallen Nature's myriad shapes !
Let us rather love to mark
How the unextinguished spark
Still gleams through the thin disguise
Of our customs, pomps, and lies,
And, not seldom blown to flame,
Vindicates its ancient claim.

STUDIES FOR TWO HEADS

The second of these studies was from A.
Bronson Alcott. See *Letters* II. 349, where
Lowell has something to say of the ease with
which he wrote at the time of this poem, *i. e.*
before 1850. He was under an engagement
at this time to write constantly for the *Anti-
Slavery Standard*, and he threw off many
poems as part of the fulfilment of his engage-
ment. The spur to activity came when his
own mind was fertile, and some of his best
known and most spontaneous work appeared
at this time.

I

SOME sort of heart I know is hers, —
  I chanced to feel her pulse one night;
A brain she has that never errs,
  And yet is never nobly right;
It does not leap to great results,
  But, in some corner out of sight,
  Suspects a spot of latent blight,
And, o'er the impatient infinite,
She bargains, haggles, and consults.

Her eye, — it seems a chemic test
  And drops upon you like an acid;
It bites you with unconscious zest,
  So clear and bright, so coldly placid;
It holds you quietly aloof,
  It holds, — and yet it does not win you;
It merely puts you to the proof
  And sorts what qualities are in you;
It smiles, but never brings you nearer,
  It lights, — her nature draws not nigh;
'T is but that yours is growing clearer
  To her assays; — yes, try and try,
  You 'll get no deeper than her eye.

There, you are classified: she 's gone
  Far, far away into herself;
Each with its Latin label on,
Your poor components, one by one,
  Are laid upon their proper shelf
In her compact and ordered mind,
And what of you is left behind
Is no more to her than the wind;
In that clear brain, which, day and night,
  No movement of the heart e'er jostles,
Her friends are ranged on left and right, —
Here, silex, hornblende, sienite;
  There, animal remains and fossils.

And yet, O subtile analyst,
  That canst each property detect
Of mood or grain, that canst untwist
  Each tangled skein of intellect,
And with thy scalpel eyes lay bare
Each mental nerve more fine than air, —
O brain exact, that in thy scales
Canst weigh the sun and never err,
  For once thy patient science fails,
  One problem still defies thy art; —
Thou never canst compute for her
The distance and diameter
  Of any simple human heart.

II

Hear him but speak, and you will feel
  The shadows of the Portico
Over your tranquil spirit steal,
  To modulate all joy and woe
To one subdued, subduing glow;
Above our squabbling business-hours,
Like Phidian Jove's, his beauty lowers,
His nature satirizes ours;
  A form and front of Attic grace,
  He shames the higgling market-place,
And dwarfs our more mechanic powers.

What throbbing verse can fitly render
That face so pure, so trembling-tender?
  Sensation glimmers through its rest,
It speaks unmanacled by words,
  As full of motion as a nest
That palpitates with unfledged birds;
  'T is likest to Bethesda's stream,
Forewarned through all its thrilling springs,
  White with the angel's coming gleam,
And rippled with his fanning wings.

Hear him unfold his plots and plans,
And larger destinies seem man's ;
You conjure from his glowing face

The omen of a fairer race;
With one grand trope he boldly spans
  The gulf wherein so many fall,
  'Twixt possible and actual;
His first swift word, talaria-shod,
Exuberant with conscious God,
Out of the choir of planets blots
The present earth with all its spots.

Himself unshaken as the sky,
His words, like whirlwinds, spin on high
  Systems and creeds pellmell together;
'T is strange as to a deaf man's eye,
  While trees uprooted splinter by,
  The dumb turmoil of stormy weather;
Less of iconoclast than shaper,
His spirit, safe behind the reach
Of the tornado of his speech,
  Burns calmly as a glowworm's taper.

So great in speech, but, ah ! in act
  So overrun with vermin troubles,
The coarse, sharp-cornered, ugly fact
  Of life collapses all his bubbles:
Had he but lived in Plato's day,
He might, unless my fancy errs,
Have shared that golden voice's sway
  O'er barefooted philosophers.
Our nipping climate hardly suits
The ripening of ideal fruits:
His theories vanquish us all summer,
But winter makes him dumb and dumber;
To see him mid life's needful things
  Is something painfully bewildering;
He seems an angel with clipt wings
  Tied to a mortal wife and children,
And by a brother seraph taken
In the act of eating eggs and bacon.
Like a clear fountain, his desire
  Exults and leaps toward the light,
In every drop it says " Aspire ! "
  Striving for more ideal height;
And as the fountain, falling thence,
  Crawls baffled through the common gut-
    ter,
So, from his speech's eminence,
He shrinks into the present tense,
  Unkinged by foolish bread and butter.

Yet smile not, worldling, for in deeds
  Not all of life that 's brave and wise is;
He strews an ampler future's seeds,
  'T is your fault if no harvest rises;
Smooth back the sneer; for is it naught
  That all he is and has is Beauty's ?

By soul the soul's gains must be wrought,
The Actual claims our coarser thought,
The Ideal hath its higher duties.

ON A PORTRAIT OF DANTE
BY GIOTTO

CAN this be thou who, lean and pale,
  With such immitigable eye
Didst look upon those writhing souls in
    bale,
  And note each vengeance, and pass by
Unmoved, save when thy heart by chance
Cast backward one forbidden glance,
  And saw Francesca, with child's glee,
  Subdue and mount thy wild-horse knee
And with proud hands control its fiery
    prance ?

With half-drooped lids, and smooth, round
    brow,
  And eye remote, that inly sees
Fair Beatrice's spirit wandering now
  In some sea-lulled Hesperides,
Thou movest through the jarring street,
Secluded from the noise of feet
  By her gift-blossom in thy hand,
  Thy branch of palm from Holy Land; —
No trace is here of ruin's fiery sleet.

Yet there is something round thy lips
  That prophesies the coming doom,
The soft, gray herald-shadow ere the
    eclipse
Notches the perfect disk with gloom;
A something that would banish thee,
And thine untamed pursuer be,
  From men and their unworthy fates,
  Though Florence had not shut her gates,
And Grief had loosed her clutch and let
  thee free.

Ah ! he who follows fearlessly
  The beckonings of a poet-heart
Shall wander, and without the world's de-
    cree,
  A banished man in field and mart;
Harder than Florence' walls the bar
Which with deaf sternness holds him far
  From home and friends, till death's re-
    lease,
  And makes his only prayer for peace,
Like thine, scarred veteran of a lifelong
    war !

ON THE DEATH OF A
FRIEND'S CHILD

This poem was printed in the *Democratic
Review*, October, 1844, and the friend was
doubtless C. F. Briggs. See the letter of con-
solation addressed to him in August, *Letters* I.
78–81.

DEATH never came so nigh to me before,
Nor showed me his mild face: oft had I
    mused
Of calm and peace and safe forgetfulness,
Of folded hands, closed eyes, and heart at
    rest,
And slumber sound beneath a flowery turf,
Of faults forgotten, and an inner place
Kept sacred for us in the heart of friends;
But these were idle fancies, satisfied
With the mere husk of this great mystery,
And dwelling in the outward shows of
    things.
Heaven is not mounted to on wings of
    dreams,
Nor doth the unthankful happiness of
    youth
Aim thitherward, but floats from bloom to
    bloom,
With earth's warm patch of sunshine well
    content:
'T is sorrow builds the shining ladder up,
Whose golden rounds are our calamities,
Whereon our firm feet planting, nearer
    God
The spirit climbs, and hath its eyes un-
    sealed.

True is it that Death's face seems stern
    and cold,
When he is sent to summon those we love,
But all God's angels come to us disguised;
Sorrow and sickness, poverty and death,
One after other lift their frowning masks,
And we behold the seraph's face beneath,
All radiant with the glory and the calm
Of having looked upon the front of God.
With every anguish of our earthly part
The spirit's sight grows clearer; this was
    meant
When Jesus touched the blind man's lids
    with clay.
Life is the jailer, Death the angel sent
To draw the unwilling bolts and set us free.
He flings not ope the ivory gate of Rest, —
Only the fallen spirit knocks at that, —

But to benigner regions beckons us,
To destinies of more rewarded toil.
In the hushed chamber, sitting by the dead,
It grates on us to hear the flood of life
Whirl rustling onward, senseless of our
    loss.
The bee hums on; around the blossomed
    vine
Whirs the light humming-bird; the cricket
    chirps;
The locust's shrill alarum stings the ear;
Hard by, the cock shouts lustily; from
    farm to farm,
His cheery brothers, telling of the sun,
Answer, till far away the joyance dies:
We never knew before how God had filled
The summer air with happy living sounds;
All round us seems an overplus of life,
And yet the one dear heart lies cold and
    still.
It is most strange, when the great miracle
Hath for our sakes been done, when we
    have had
Our inwardest experience of God,
When with his presence still the room ex-
    pands,
And is awed after him, that naught is
    changed,
That Nature's face looks unacknowledging,
And the mad world still dances heedless on
After its butterflies, and gives no sign.
'T is hard at first to see it all aright:
In vain Faith blows her trump to summon
    back
Her scattered troop: yet, through the
    clouded glass
Of our own bitter tears, we learn to look
Undazzled on the kindness of God's face;
Earth is too dark, and Heaven alone shines
    through.

It is no little thing, when a fresh soul
And a fresh heart, with their unmeasured
    scope
For good, not gravitating earthward yet,
But circling in diviner periods,
Are sent into the world, — no little thing,
When this unbounded possibility
Into the outer silence is withdrawn.
Ah, in this world, where every guiding
    thread
Ends suddenly in the one sure centre,
    death,
The visionary hand of Might-have-been
Alone can fill Desire's cup to the brim !

How changed, dear friend, are thy part and
    thy child's !
He bends above *thy* cradle now, or holds
His warning finger out to be thy guide;
Thou art the nursling now; he watches
    thee
Slow learning, one by one, the secret things
Which are to him used sights of every day;
He smiles to see thy wondering glances
    con
The grass and pebbles of the spirit-world,
To thee miraculous; and he will teach
Thy knees their due observances of prayer.
Children are God's apostles, day by day
Sent forth to preach of love, and hope, and
    peace;
Nor hath thy babe his mission left undone.
To me, at least, his going hence hath given
Serener thoughts and nearer to the skies,
And opened a new fountain in my heart
For thee, my friend, and all: and oh, if
    Death
More near approaches meditates, and clasps
Even now some dearer, more reluctant
    hand,
God, strengthen thou my faith, that I may
    see
That 't is thine angel, who, with loving
    haste,
Unto the service of the inner shrine,
Doth waken thy belovëd with a kiss.

EURYDICE

HEAVEN's cup held down to me I drain,
The sunshine mounts and spurs my brain;
Bathing in grass, with thirsty eye
I suck the last drop of the sky;
With each hot sense I draw to the lees
The quickening out-door influences,
And empty to each radiant comer
A supernaculum of summer:
Not, Bacchus, all thy grosser juice
Could bring enchantment so profuse,
Though for its press each grape-bunch had
The white feet of an Oread.

Through our coarse art gleam, now and
    then,
The features of angelic men:
'Neath the lewd Satyr's veiling paint
Glows forth the Sibyl, Muse, or Saint;
The dauber's botch no more obscures
The mighty master's portraitures.

And who can say what luckier beam
The hidden glory shall redeem,
For what chance clod the soul may wait
To stumble on its nobler fate,
Or why, to his unwarned abode,
Still by surprises comes the God ?
Some moment, nailed on sorrow's cross,
May mediate a whole youth's loss,
Some windfall joy, we know not whence,
Redeem a lifetime's rash expense,
And, suddenly wise, the soul may mark,
Stripped of their simulated dark,
Mountains of gold that pierce the sky,
Girdling its valleyed poverty.

I feel ye, childhood's hopes, return,
With olden heats my pulses burn, —
Mine be the self-forgetting sweep,
The torrent impulse swift and wild,
Wherewith Taghkanic's rockborn child
Dares gloriously the dangerous leap,
And, in his sky-descended mood,
Transmutes each drop of sluggish blood,
By touch of bravery's simple wand,
To amethyst and diamond,
Proving himself no bastard slip,
But the true granite-cradled one,
Nursed with the rock's primeval drip,
The cloud-embracing mountain's son !

Prayer breathed in vain ! no wish's sway
Rebuilds the vanished yesterday;
For plated wares of Sheffield stamp
We gave the old Aladdin's lamp;
'T is we are changed; ah, whither went
That undesigned abandonment,
That wise, unquestioning content,
Which could erect its microcosm
Out of a weed's neglected blossom,
Could call up Arthur and his peers
By a low moss's clump of spears,
Or, in its shingle trireme launched,
Where Charles in some green inlet
        branched,
Could venture for the golden fleece
And dragon-watched Hesperides,
Or, from its ripple-shattered fate,
Ulysses' chances re-create ?
When, heralding life's every phase,
There glowed a goddess-veiling haze,
A plenteous, forewarning grace,
Like that more tender dawn that flies
Before the full moon's ample rise ?
Methinks thy parting glory shines
Through yonder grove of singing pines;

At that elm-vista's end I trace
Dimly thy sad leave-taking face,
Eurydice ! Eurydice !
The tremulous leaves repeat to me
Eurydice ! Eurydice !
No gloomier Orcus swallows thee
Than the unclouded sunset's glow;
Thine is at least Elysian woe;
Thou hast Good's natural decay,
And fadest like a star away
Into an atmosphere whose shine
With fuller day o'ermasters thine,
Entering defeat as 't were a shrine;
For us, — we turn life's diary o'er
To find but one word, — Nevermore.

SHE CAME AND WENT

As a twig trembles, which a bird
    Lights on to sing, then leaves unbent,
So is my memory thrilled and stirred; —
    I only know she came and went.

As clasps some lake, by gusts unriven,
    The blue dome's measureless content,
So my soul held that moment's heaven; —
    I only know she came and went.

As, at one bound, our swift spring heaps
    The orchards full of bloom and scent,
So clove her May my wintry sleeps; —
    I only know she came and went.

An angel stood and met my gaze,
    Through the low doorway of my tent;
The tent is struck, the vision stays; —
    I only know she came and went.

Oh, when the room grows slowly dim,
    And life's last oil is nearly spent,
One gush of light these eyes will brim,
    Only to think she came and went.

THE CHANGELING

I HAD a little daughter,
    And she was given to me
To lead me gently backward
    To the Heavenly Father's knee,
That I, by the force of nature,
    Might in some dim wise divine
The depth of his infinite patience
    To this wayward soul of mine.

I know not how others saw her,
  But to me she was wholly fair,
And the light of the heaven she came from
  Still lingered and gleamed in her hair;
For it was as wavy and golden,
  And as many changes took,
As the shadows of sun-gilt ripples   .
  On the yellow bed of a brook.

To what can I liken her smiling
  Upon me, her kneeling lover,
How it leaped from her lips to her eye-
    lids,
  And dimpled her wholly over,
Till her outstretched hands smiled also,
  And I almost seemed to see
The very heart of her mother
  Sending sun through her veins to me !

She had been with us scarce a twelve-
    month,
  And it hardly seemed a day,
When a troop of wandering angels
  Stole my little daughter away;
Or perhaps those heavenly Zingari
  But loosed the hampering strings,
And when they had opened her cage-door,
  My little bird used her wings.

But they left in her stead a changeling,
  A little angel child,
That seems like her bud in full blossom,
  And smiles as she never smiled:
When I wake in the morning, I see it
  Where she always used to lie,
And I feel as weak as a violet
  Alone 'neath the awful sky.

As weak, yet as trustful also;
  For the whole year long I see
All the wonders of faithful Nature
  Still worked for the love of me;
Winds wander, and dews drip earthward,
  Rain falls, suns rise and set,
Earth whirls, and all but to prosper
  A poor little violet.

This child is not mine as the first was,
  I cannot sing it to rest,
I cannot lift it up fatherly
  And bliss it upon my breast:
Yet it lies in my little one's cradle
  And sits in my little one's chair,
And the light of the heaven she 's gone to
  Transfigures its golden hair.

THE PIONEER

WHAT man would live coffined with
    brick and stone,
  Imprisoned from the healing touch of
    air,
  And cramped with selfish landmarks
    everywhere,
When all before him stretches, furrowless
    and lone,
  The unmapped prairie none can fence or
    own ?

What man would read and read the self-
    same faces,
  And, like the marbles which the wind-
    mill grinds,
  Rub smooth forever with the same
    smooth minds,
This year retracing last year's, every
    year's, dull traces,
  When there are woods and un-penfolded
    spaces ?

What man o'er one old thought would
    pore and pore,
  Shut like a book between its covers
    thin
  For every fool to leave his dog's-ears
    in,
When solitude is his, and God forevermore,
  Just for the opening of a paltry door ?

What man would watch life's oozy
    element
  Creep Letheward forever, when he
    might
  Down some great river drift beyond
    men's sight,
To where the undethronëd forest's royal
    tent
  Broods with its hush o'er half a conti-
    nent ?

What man with men would push and al-
    tercate,
  Piecing out crooked means to crooked
    ends,
  When he can have the skies and woods
    for friends,
Snatch back the rudder of his undismantled
    fate,
  And in himself be ruler, church, and
    state ?

Cast leaves and feathers rot in last year's
    nest,
  The wingëd brood, flown thence, new
    dwellings plan;
  The serf of his own Past is not a man;
To change and change is life, to move and
    never rest; —
  Not what we are, but what we hope, is
    best.

The wild, free woods make no man halt
    or blind;
  Cities rob men of eyes and hands and
    feet,
  Patching one whole of many incom-
    plete;
The general preys upon the individual
    mind,
  And each alone is helpless as the wind.

Each man is some man's servant; every
    soul
  Is by some other's presence quite dis-
    crowned;
  Each owes the next through all the
    imperfect round,
Yet not with mutual help; each man is his
    own goal,
  And the whole earth must stop to pay
    him toll.

Here, life the undiminished man de-
    mands;
  New faculties stretch out to meet new
    wants;
  What Nature asks, that Nature also
    grants;
Here man is lord, not drudge, of eyes and
    feet and hands,
  And to his life is knit with hourly
    bands.

Come out, then, from the old thoughts
    and old ways,
  Before you harden to a crystal cold
  Which the new life can shatter, but
    not mould;
Freedom for you still waits, still, looking
    backward, stays,
  But widens still the irretrievable space.

LONGING

Of all the myriad moods of mind
  That through the soul come thronging,

Which one was e'er so dear, so kind,
  So beautiful as Longing?
The thing we long for, that we are
  For one transcendent moment,
Before the Present poor and bare
  Can make its sneering comment.

Still, through our paltry stir and strife,
  Glows down the wished Ideal,
And Longing moulds in clay what Life
  Carves in the marble Real;
To let the new life in, we know,
  Desire must ope the portal;
Perhaps the longing to be so
  Helps make the soul immortal.

Longing is God's fresh heavenward will
  With our poor earthward striving;
We quench it that we may be still
  Content with merely living;
But, would we learn that heart's full scope
  Which we are hourly wronging,
Our lives must climb from hope to hope
  And realize our longing.

Ah! let us hope that to our praise
  Good God not only reckons
The moments when we tread his ways,
  But when the spirit beckons, —
That some slight good is also wrought
  Beyond self-satisfaction,
When we are simply good in thought,
  Howe'er we fail in action.

ODE TO FRANCE

FEBRUARY, 1848

I

As, flake by flake, the beetling avalanches
  Build up their imminent crags of noise-
    less snow,
Till some chance thrill the loosened ruin
    launches
  In unwarned havoc on the roofs below,
So grew and gathered through the silent
    years
  The madness of a People, wrong by
    wrong.
There seemed no strength in the dumb
    toiler's tears,
  No strength in suffering; but the Past
    was strong:
The brute despair of trampled centuries

Leaped up with one hoarse yell and
　　snapped its bands,
Groped for its right with horny, callous
　　hands,
And stared around for God with bloodshot
　　eyes.
What wonder if those palms were all too
　　hard
For nice distinctions, — if that mænad
　　throng —
They whose thick atmosphere no bard
Had shivered with the lightning of his
　　song,
Brutes with the memories and desires of
　　men,
Whose chronicles were writ with iron
　　pen,
　　In the crooked shoulder and the fore-
　　　head low,
　　Set wrong to balance wrong,
　　And physicked woe with woe ?

II

They did as they were taught; not theirs
　　the blame,
If men who scattered firebrands reaped the
　　flame:
They trampled Peace beneath their sav-
　　age feet,
And by her golden tresses drew
Mercy along the pavement of the street.
O Freedom ! Freedom ! is thy morning-
　　dew
　　So gory red ? Alas, thy light had
　　　ne'er
　　Shone in upon the chaos of their lair !
They reared to thee such symbol as they
　　knew,
　　And worshipped it with flame and
　　　blood,
　　A Vengeance, axe in hand, that stood
Holding a tyrant's head up by the clotted
　　hair.

III

What wrongs the Oppressor suffered, these
　　we know;
　　These have found piteous voice in song
　　　and prose;
But for the Oppressed, their darkness and
　　their woe,
　　Their grinding centuries, — what Muse
　　　had those ?
Though hall and palace had nor eyes nor
　　ears,

Hardening a people's heart to senseless
　　stone,
Thou knewest them, O Earth, that drank
　　their tears,
　　O Heaven, that heard their inarticulate
　　　moan !
They noted down their fetters, link by
　　link;
Coarse was the hand that scrawled, and
　　red the ink;
　　Rude was their score, as suits unlettered
　　　men,
Notched with a headsman's axe upon a
　　block:
What marvel if, when came the avenging
　　shock,
　　'T was Atë, not Urania, held the pen ?

IV

With eye averted, and an anguished frown,
　　Loathingly glides the Muse through
　　　scenes of strife,
Where, like the heart of Vengeance up
　　and down,
　　Throbs in its framework the blood-
　　　muffled knife;
Slow are the steps of Freedom, but her feet
　　Turn never backward: hers no bloody
　　　glare ;
Her light is calm, and innocent, and sweet,
　　And where it enters there is no despair :
Not first on palace and cathedral spire
Quivers and gleams that unconsuming fire;
　　While these stand black against her
　　　morning skies,
The peasant sees it leap from peak to peak
　　Along his hills; the craftsman's burning
　　　eyes
Own with cool tears its influence mother-
　　meek;
It lights the poet's heart up like a star;
Ah ! while the tyrant deemed it still
　　afar,
And twined with golden threads his futile
　　snare,
　　That swift, convicting glow all round
　　　him ran;
'T was close beside him there,
Sunrise whose Memnon is the soul of man.

V

O Broker-King, is this thy wisdom's fruit ?
A dynasty plucked out as 't were a weed
Grown rankly in a night, that leaves no
　　seed !

Could eighteen years strike down no deeper
    root ?
But now thy vulture eye was turned on
    Spain;
A shout from Paris, and thy crown falls off,
    Thy race has ceased to reign,
And thou become a fugitive and scoff:
Slippery the feet that mount by stairs of
    gold,
And weakest of all fences one of steel;
    Go and keep school again like him of
      old,
The Syracusan tyrant; — thou mayst feel
Royal amid a birch-swayed commonweal !

VI

Not long can he be ruler who allows
    His time to run before him; thou wast
      naught
Soon as the strip of gold about thy brows
    Was no more emblem of the People's
      thought:
Vain were thy bayonets against the foe
    Thou hadst to cope with; thou didst
      wage
War not with Frenchmen merely; — no,
    Thy strife was with the Spirit of the Age,
The invisible Spirit whose first breath di-
    vine
    Scattered thy frail endeavor,
And, like poor last year's leaves, whirled
    thee and thine
      Into the Dark forever !

VII

Is here no triumph ?   Nay, what though
The yellow blood of Trade meanwhile
    should pour
Along its arteries a shrunken flow,
And the idle canvas droop around the
    shore ?
      These do not make a state,
      Nor keep it great;
    I think God made
The earth for man, not trade;
And where each humblest human creature
Can stand, no more suspicious or afraid,
Erect and kingly in his right of nature,
To heaven and earth knit with harmonious
    ties, —
Where I behold the exultation
Of manhood glowing in those eyes
    That had been dark for ages,
      Or only lit with bestial loves and
      rages,

There I behold a Nation:
    The France which lies
Between the Pyrenees and Rhine
    Is the least part of France;
I see her rather in the soul whose shine
Burns through the craftsman's grimy
    countenance,
    In the new energy divine
      Of Toil's enfranchised glance.

VIII

    And if it be a dream,
If the great Future be the little Past
'Neath a new mask, which drops and
    shows at last
The same weird, mocking face to balk
    and blast,
Yet, Muse, a gladder measure suits the
    theme,
    And the Tyrtæan harp
Loves notes more resolute and sharp,
Throbbing, as throbs the bosom, hot and
    fast:
      Such visions are of morning,
      Theirs is no vague forewarning,
The dreams which nations dream come true,
    And shape the world anew;
      If this be a sleep,
      Make it long, make it deep,
O Father, who sendest the harvests men reap!
      While Labor so sleepeth,
      His sorrow is gone,
    No longer he weepeth,
    But smileth and steepeth
      His thoughts in the dawn;
He heareth Hope yonder
    Rain, lark-like, her fancies,
His dreaming hands wander
    Mid heart's-ease and pansies;
" 'T is a dream ! 'T is a vision ! "
    Shrieks Mammon aghast;
" The day's broad derision
    Will chase it at last;
    Ye are mad, ye have taken
    A slumbering kraken
    For firm land of the Past ! "
Ah ! if he awaken,
    God shield us all then,
If this dream rudely shaken
    Shall cheat him again !

IX

Since first I heard our North-wind blow,
Since first I saw Atlantic throw
On our grim rocks his thunderous snow,

I loved thee, Freedom; as a boy
The rattle of thy shield at Marathon
　　Did with a Grecian joy
　　　Through all my pulses run;
But I have learned to love thee now
Without the helm upon thy gleaming brow,
　　A maiden mild and undefiled
Like her who bore the world's redeeming
　　child;
　　And surely never did thine altars glance
With purer fires than now in France;
　While, in their clear white flashes,
　　Wrong's shadow, backward cast,
　Waves cowering o'er the ashes
　　Of the dead, blaspheming Past,
O'er the shapes of fallen giants,
　His own unburied brood,
Whose dead hands clench defiance
　　At the overpowering Good:
And down the happy future runs a flood
　　Of prophesying light;
It shows an Earth no longer stained with
　blood,
Blossom and fruit where now we see the bud
　Of Brotherhood and Right.

ANTI-APIS

PRAISEST Law, friend ? We, too, love it
　much as they that love it best;
'T is the deep, august foundation, whereon
　Peace and Justice rest;
On the rock primeval, hidden in the Past
　its bases be,
Block by block the endeavoring Ages built
　it up to what we see.

But dig down: the Old unbury; thou shalt
　find on every stone
That each Age hath carved the symbol of
　what god to them was known,
Ugly shapes and brutish sometimes, but
　the fairest that they knew;
If their sight were dim and earthward, yet
　their hope and aim were true.

Surely as the unconscious needle feels the
　far-off loadstar draw,
So strives every gracious nature to at-one
　itself with law;
And the elder Saints and Sages laid their
　pious framework right
By a theocratic instinct covered from the
　people's sight.

As their gods were, so their laws were;
　Thor the strong could reave and
　steal,
So through many a peaceful inlet tore the
　Norseman's eager keel;
But a new law came when Christ came,
　and not blameless, as before,
Can we, paying him our lip-tithes, give our
　lives and faiths to Thor.

Law is holy: ay, but what law ? Is there
　nothing more divine
Than the patched-up broils of Congress,
　venal, full of meat and wine ?
Is there, say you, nothing higher ? Naught,
　God save us ! that transcends
Laws of cotton texture, wove by vulgar
　men for vulgar ends ?

Did Jehovah ask their counsel, or submit
　to them a plan,
Ere he filled with loves, hopes, longings,
　this aspiring heart of man ?
For their edict does the soul wait, ere it
　swing round to the pole
Of the true, the free, the God-willed, all
　that makes it be a soul ?

Law is holy; but not your law, ye who
　keep the tablets whole
While ye dash the Law to pieces, shatter it
　in life and soul;
Bearing up the Ark is lightsome, golden
　Apis hid within,
While we Levites share the offerings, richer
　by the people's sin.

Give to Cæsar what is Cæsar's ? yes, but
　tell me, if you can,
Is this superscription Cæsar's here upon
　our brother man ?
Is not here some other's image, dark and
　sullied though it be,
In this fellow-soul that worships, struggles
　Godward even as we ?

It was not to such a future that the May-
　flower's prow was turned,
Not to such a faith the martyrs clung, ex-
　ulting as they burned;
Not by such laws are men fashioned, ear-
　nest, simple, valiant, great
In the household virtues whereon rests the
　unconquerable state.

Ah ! there is a higher gospel, overhead the
  God-roof springs,
And each glad, obedient planet like a
  golden shuttle sings
Through the web which Time is weaving
  in his never-resting loom,
Weaving seasons many - colored, bringing
  prophecy to doom.

Think you Truth a farthing rushlight, to
  be pinched out when you will
With your deft official fingers, and your
  politicians' skill ?
Is your God a wooden fetish, to be hidden
  out of sight
That his block eyes may not see you do the
  thing that is not right ?

But the Destinies think not so; to their
  judgment-chamber lone
Comes no noise of popular clamor, there
  Fame's trumpet is not blown;
Your majorities they reck not; that you
  grant, but then you say
That you differ with them somewhat, —
  which is stronger, you or they ?

Patient are they as the insects that build
  islands in the deep;
They hurl not the bolted thunder, but their
  silent way they keep;
Where they have been that we know;
  where empires towered that were
  not just;
Lo ! the skulking wild fox scratches in a
  little heap of dust.

A PARABLE

SAID Christ our Lord, " I will go and see
How the men, my brethren, believe in me."
He passed not again through the gate of
  birth,
But made himself known to the children of
  earth.

Then said the chief priests, and rulers, and
  kings,
" Behold, now, the Giver of all good things;
Go to, let us welcome with pomp and state
Him who alone is mighty and great."

With carpets of gold the ground they
  spread
Wherever the Son of Man should tread,

And in palace-chambers lofty and rare
They lodged him, and served him with
  kingly fare.

Great organs surged through arches dim
Their jubilant floods in praise of him;
And in church, and palace, and judgment-
  hall,
He saw his own image high over all.

But still, wherever his steps they led,
The Lord in sorrow bent down his head,
And from under the heavy foundation
  stones,
The son of Mary heard bitter groans.

And in church, and palace, and judgment-
  hall,
He marked great fissures that rent the wall,
And opened wider and yet more wide
As the living foundation heaved and sighed.

" Have ye founded your thrones and altars,
  then,
On the bodies and souls of living men ?
And think ye that building shall endure,
Which shelters the noble and crushes the
  poor ?

" With gates of silver and bars of gold
Ye have fenced my sheep from their
  Father's fold;
I have heard the dropping of their tears
In heaven these eighteen hundred years."

" O Lord and Master, not ours the guilt,
We build but as our fathers built;
Behold thine images, how they stand,
Sovereign and sole, through all our land.

" Our task is hard, — with sword and flame
To hold thine earth forever the same,
And with sharp crooks of steel to keep
Still, as thou leftest them, thy sheep."

Then Christ sought out an artisan,
A low-browed, stunted, haggard man,
And a motherless girl, whose fingers thin
Pushed from her faintly want and sin.

These set he in the midst of them,
And as they drew back their garment-
  hem,
For fear of defilement, " Lo, here," said he,
" The images ye have made of me !"

ODE

WRITTEN FOR THE CELEBRATION OF THE INTRODUCTION OF THE COCHITUATE WATER INTO THE CITY OF BOSTON

The public system of water works in Boston dates from October 25, 1848, when with much ceremony the water of Lake Cochituate, formerly called Long Pond, was turned into the reservoir which then occupied the site of the present extension of the State House, and a stream was conducted into the Frog Pond on Boston Common, where the pressure gave head to a fine jet. Besides the Ode, a selection was sung from the oratorio of *Elijah*, and addresses were made by the mayor and the chairman of the water commissioners.

My name is Water: I have sped
  Through strange, dark ways, untried before,
By pure desire of friendship led,
  Cochituate's ambassador;
He sends four royal gifts by me:
Long life, health, peace, and purity.

I'm Ceres' cup-bearer; I pour,
  For flowers and fruits and all their kin,
Her crystal vintage, from of yore
  Stored in old Earth's selectest bin,
Flora's Falernian ripe, since God
The wine-press of the deluge trod.

In that far isle whence, iron-willed,
  The New World's sires their bark unmoored,
The fairies' acorn-cups I filled
  Upon the toadstool's silver board,
And, 'neath Herne's oak, for Shakespeare's sight,
Strewed moss and grass with diamonds bright.

No fairies in the Mayflower came,
  And, lightsome as I sparkle here,
For Mother Bay State, busy dame,
  I've toiled and drudged this many a year,
Throbbed in her engines' iron veins,
Twirled myriad spindles for her gains.

I, too, can weave: the warp I set
  Through which the sun his shuttle throws,
And, bright as Noah saw it, yet
  For you the arching rainbow glows,
A sight in Paradise denied
To unfallen Adam and his bride.

When Winter held me in his grip,
  You seized and sent me o'er the wave,
Ungrateful! in a prison-ship;
  But I forgive, not long a slave,
For, soon as summer south-winds blew,
Homeward I fled, disguised as dew.

For countless services I'm fit,
  Of use, of pleasure, and of gain,
But lightly from all bonds I flit,
  Nor lose my mirth, nor feel a stain;
From mill and wash-tub I escape,
And take in heaven my proper shape.

So, free myself, to-day, elate
  I come from far o'er hill and mead,
And here, Cochituate's envoy, wait
  To be your blithesome Ganymede,
And brim your cups with nectar true
That never will make slaves of you.

LINES

SUGGESTED BY THE GRAVES OF TWO ENGLISH SOLDIERS ON CONCORD BATTLE-GROUND

THE same good blood that now refills
The dotard Orient's shrunken veins,
The same whose vigor westward thrills,
Bursting Nevada's silver chains,
Poured here upon the April grass,
Freckled with red the herbage new;
On reeled the battle's trampling mass,
Back to the ash the bluebird flew.

Poured here in vain; — that sturdy blood
Was meant to make the earth more green,
But in a higher, gentler mood
Than broke this April noon serene;
Two graves are here: to mark the place,
At head and foot, an unhewn stone,
O'er which the herald lichens trace
The blazon of Oblivion.

These men were brave enough, and true
To the hired soldier's bull-dog creed;
What brought them here they never knew,
They fought as suits the English breed:

They came three thousand miles, and died,
To keep the Past upon its throne;
Unheard, beyond the ocean tide,
Their English mother made her moan.

The turf that covers them no thrill
Sends up to fire the heart and brain;
No stronger purpose nerves the will,
No hope renews its youth again:
From farm to farm the Concord glides,
And trails my fancy with its flow;
O'erhead the balanced hen-hawk slides,
Twinned in the river's heaven below.

But go, whose Bay State bosom stirs,
Proud of thy birth and neighbor's right,
Where sleep the heroic villagers
Borne red and stiff from Concord fight;
Thought Reuben, snatching down his gun,
Or Seth, as ebbed the life away,
What earthquake rifts would shoot and run
World-wide from that short April fray?

What then? With heart and hand they
    wrought,
According to their village light;
'T was for the Future that they fought,
Their rustic faith in what was right.
Upon earth's tragic stage they burst
Unsummoned, in the humble sock;
Theirs the fifth act; the curtain first
Rose long ago on Charles's block.

Their graves have voices; if they threw
Dice charged with fates beyond their ken,
Yet to their instincts they were true,
And had the genius to be men.
Fine privilege of Freedom's host,
Of humblest soldiers for the Right! —
Age after age ye hold your post,
Your graves send courage forth, and
    might.

TO ——

WE, too, have autumns, when our leaves
Drop loosely through the dampened air,
When all our good seems bound in sheaves,
And we stand reaped and bare.

Our seasons have no fixed returns,
Without our will they come and go;
At noon our sudden summer burns,
Ere sunset all is snow.

But each day brings less summer cheer,
Crimps more our ineffectual spring,
And something earlier every year
Our singing birds take wing.

As less the olden glow abides,
And less the chillier heart aspires,
With drift-wood beached in past spring-
    tides
We light our sullen fires.

By the pinched rushlight's starving beam
We cower and strain our wasted sight,
To stitch youth's shroud up, seam by seam,
In the long arctic night.

It was not so — we once were young —
When Spring, to womanly Summer turn-
    ing,
Her dew-drops on each grass-blade strung,
In the red sunrise burning.

We trusted then, aspired, believed
That earth could be remade to-morrow;
Ah, why be ever undeceived?
Why give up faith for sorrow?

O thou, whose days are yet all spring,
Faith, blighted one, is past retrieving;
Experience is a dumb, dead thing;
The victory 's in believing.

FREEDOM

In a letter to Mr. Norton, written June 29, 1859, Mr. Lowell refers to English comments on the Austro-Italian war, then in its early stages, and alludes to a quotation which Mr. Bright had made from his writings. "But," he says, "I fear he thinks me too much of a Quaker. In my *Poems* there are some verses on 'Freedom' written in '48 or '49. They ended thus as originally written. I left the verses out only because I did not think them good, — not because I did not like the sentiment. I have strength of mind enough not to change a word — though I see how much better I might make it." He then copies the lines which below are separated from the poem by a long dash, and adds: "I think it must have been written in 1848, for I remember that, as I first composed it, it had 'Fair Italy' instead of 'Humanity.'"

ARE we, then, wholly fallen? Can it be
That thou, North wind, that from thy
    mountains bringest

Their spirit to our plains, and thou, blue
    sea,
Who on our rocks thy wreaths of freedom
    flingest, —
As on an altar, — can it be that ye
Have wasted inspiration on dead ears,
Dulled with the too familiar clank of
    chains ?
The people's heart is like a harp for years
Hung where some petrifying torrent rains
Its slow - incrusting spray: the stiffened
    chords
Faint and more faint make answer to the
    tears
That drip upon them: idle are all words:
Only a golden plectrum wakes the tone
Deep buried 'neath that ever-thickening
    stone.

We are not free: doth Freedom, then, con-
    sist
In musing with our faces toward the Past,
While petty cares and crawling interests
    twist
Their spider-threads about us, which at last
Grow strong as iron chains, to cramp and
    bind
In formal narrowness heart, soul, and
    mind ?
Freedom is recreated year by year,
In hearts wide open on the Godward side,
In souls calm-cadenced as the whirling
    sphere,
In minds that sway the future like a tide.
No broadest creeds can hold her, and no
    codes;
She chooses men for her august abodes,
Building them fair and fronting to the
    dawn;
Yet, when we seek her, we but find a few
Light   footprints, leading morn - ward
    through the dew:
Before the day had risen, she was gone.

And we must follow: swiftly runs she on,
And, if our steps should slacken in despair,
Half turns her face, half smiles through
    golden hair,
Forever yielding, never wholly won:
That is not love which pauses in the race
Two close-linked names on fleeting sand
    to trace;
Freedom gained yesterday is no more ours;
Men gather but dry seeds of last year's
    flowers;

Still there 's a charm ungranted, still a
    grace,
Still rosy Hope, the free, the unattained,
Makes us Possession's languid hand let
    fall;
'T is but a fragment of ourselves is gained,
The Future brings us more, but never all.

And, as the finder of some unknown realm,
Mounting a summit whence he thinks to
    see
On either side of him the imprisoning sea,
Beholds, above the clouds that overwhelm
The valley-land, peak after snowy peak
Stretch out of sight, each like a silver
    helm
Beneath its plume of smoke, sublime and
    bleak,
And what he thought an island finds to be
A continent to him first oped, — so we
Can from our height of Freedom look along
A boundless future, ours if we be strong;
Or if we shrink, better remount our ships
And, fleeing God's express design, trace
    back
The hero-freighted Mayflower's prophet-
    track
To Europe entering her blood-red eclipse.

Therefore of Europe now I will not doubt,
For the broad foreheads surely win the
    day,
And brains, not crowns or soul-gelt armies,
    weigh
In Fortune's scales: such dust she brushes
    out.
Most gracious are the conquests of the
    Word,
Gradual and silent as a flower's increase,
And the best guide from old to new is
    Peace —
Yet, Freedom, thou canst sanctify the
    sword !

Bravely to do whate'er the time demands,
Whether with pen or sword, and not to
    flinch,
This is the task that fits heroic hands;
So are Truth's boundaries widened inch by
    inch.
I do not love the Peace which tyrants
    make;
The calm she breeds let the sword's light-
    ning break !

It is the tyrants who have beaten out
Ploughshares and pruning-hooks to spears
   and swords,
And shall I pause and moralize and doubt?
Whose veins run water let him mete his
   words!
Each fetter sundered is the whole world's
   gain!
And rather than humanity remain
A pearl beneath the feet of Austrian swine,
Welcome to me whatever breaks a chain.
That surely is of God, and all divine!

BIBLIOLATRES

Bowing thyself in dust before a Book,
And thinking the great God is thine alone,
O rash iconoclast, thou wilt not brook
What gods the heathen carves in wood and
   stone,
As if the Shepherd who from the outer
   cold
Leads all his shivering lambs to one sure
   fold
Were careful for the fashion of his crook.

There is no broken reed so poor and base,
No rush, the bending tilt of swamp-fly
   blue,
But He therewith the ravening wolf can
   chase,
And guide his flock to springs and pastures
   new;
Through ways unlooked for, and through
   many lands,
Far from the rich folds built with human
   hands,
The gracious footprints of his love I trace.

And what art thou, own brother of the clod,
That from his hand the crook wouldst
   snatch away
And shake instead thy dry and sapless rod,
To scare the sheep out of the wholesome
   day?
Yea, what art thou, blind, unconverted
   Jew,
That with thy idol-volume's covers two
Wouldst make a jail to coop the living
   God?

Thou hear'st not well the mountain organ-
   tones
By prophet ears from Hor and Sinai caught,

Thinking the cisterns of those Hebrew
   brains
Drew dry the springs of the All-knower's
   thought,
Nor shall thy lips be touched with living
   fire,
Who blow'st old altar-coals with sole
   desire
To weld anew the spirit's broken chains.

God is not dumb, that He should speak no
   more;
If thou hast wanderings in the wilder-
   ness
And find'st not Sinai, 't is thy soul is poor;
There towers the Mountain of the Voice no
   less,
Which whoso seeks shall find, but he who
   bends,
Intent on manna still and mortal ends,
Sees it not, neither hears its thundered
   lore.

Slowly the Bible of the race is writ,
And not on paper leaves nor leaves of stone;
Each age, each kindred, adds a verse to it,
Texts of despair or hope, of joy or moan.
While swings the sea, while mists the
   mountains shroud,
While thunder's surges burst on cliffs of
   cloud,
Still at the prophets' feet the nations sit.

BEAVER BROOK

. . . "Don't you like the poem [*Beaver
Brook*] I sent you last week? I was inclined
to think pretty well of it, but I have not seen
it in print yet. The little mill stands in a val-
ley between one of the spurs of Wellington
Hill and the main summit, just on the edge of
Waltham. It is surely one of the loveliest
spots in the world. It is one of my lions, and
if you will make me a visit this spring I will
take you up to hear it roar, and I will show you
'the oaks' — the largest, I fancy, left in the
country." *Letters* I. 149. The poem was sent
to Mr. Gay for the *Standard*. These oaks are
now known as the Waverley Oaks, and are to
be preserved.

Hushed with broad sunlight lies the hill,
   And, minuting the long day's loss,
The cedar's shadow, slow and still,
   Creeps o'er its dial of gray moss.

Warm noon brims full the valley's cup,
  The aspen's leaves are scarce astir;
Only the little mill sends up
  Its busy, never-ceasing burr.

Climbing the loose-piled wall that hems
  The road along the mill-pond's brink,
From 'neath the arching barberry-stems,
  My footstep scares the shy chewink.

Beneath a bony buttonwood
  The mill's red door lets forth the din;
The whitened miller, dust-imbued,
  Flits past the square of dark within.

No mountain torrent's strength is here;
  Sweet Beaver, child of forest still,
Heaps its small pitcher to the ear,
  And gently waits the miller's will.

Swift slips Undine along the race
  Unheard, and then, with flashing bound,
Floods the dull wheel with light and grace,
  And, laughing, hunts the loath drudge
     round.

The miller dreams not at what cost
  The quivering millstones hum and whirl,

Nor how for every turn are tost
  Armfuls of diamond and of pearl.

But Summer cleared my happier eyes
  With drops of some celestial juice,
To see how Beauty underlies
  Forevermore each form of use.

And more; methought I saw that flood,
  Which now so dull and darkling steals,
Thick, here and there, with human blood,
  To turn the world's laborious wheels.

No more than doth the miller there,
  Shut in our several cells, do we
Know with what waste of beauty rare
  Moves every day's machinery.

Surely the wiser time shall come
  When this fine overplus of might,
No longer sullen, slow, and dumb,
  Shall leap to music and to light.

In that new childhood of the Earth
  Life of itself shall dance and play,
Fresh blood in Time's shrunk veins make
    mirth,
  And labor meet delight half-way.

MEMORIAL VERSES

KOSSUTH

A RACE of nobles may die out,
  A royal line may leave no heir;
Wise Nature sets no guards about
  Her pewter plate and wooden ware.

But they fail not, the kinglier breed,
  Who starry diadems attain;
To dungeon, axe, and stake succeed
  Heirs of the old heroic strain.

The zeal of Nature never cools,
  Nor is she thwarted of her ends;
When gapped and dulled her cheaper tools,
  Then she a saint and prophet spends.

Land of the Magyars! though it be
  The tyrant may relink his chain,
Already thine the victory,
  As the just Future measures gain.

Thou hast succeeded, thou hast won
  The deathly travail's amplest worth;
A nation's duty thou hast done,
  Giving a hero to our earth.

And he, let come what will of woe,
  Hath saved the land he strove to save;
No Cossack hordes, no traitor's blow,
  Can quench the voice shall haunt his
    grave.

" I Kossuth am: O Future, thou
  That clear'st the just and blott'st the vile,
O'er this small dust in reverence bow,
  Remembering what I was erewhile.

" I was the chosen trump wherethrough
  Our God sent forth awakening breath;
Came chains? Came death? The strain
    He blew
  Sounds on, outliving chains and death."

TO LAMARTINE

1848

I DID not praise thee when the crowd,
'Witched with the moment's inspira-
tion,
Vexed thy still ether with hosannas loud,
And stamped their dusty adoration;
I but looked upward with the rest,
And, when they shouted Greatest, whis-
pered Best.

They raised thee not, but rose to thee,
Their fickle wreaths about thee fling-
ing;
So on some marble Phœbus the swol'n sea
Might leave his worthless seaweed
clinging,
But pious hands, with reverent care,
Make the pure limbs once more sublimely
bare.

Now thou 'rt thy plain, grand self again,
Thou art secure from panegyric,
Thou who gav'st politics an epic strain,
And actedst Freedom's noblest lyric;
This side the Blessed Isles, no tree
Grows green enough to make a wreath for
thee.

Nor can blame cling to thee; the snow
From swinish footprints takes no stain-
ing,
But, leaving the gross soils of earth below,
Its spirit mounts, the skies regaining,
And unresentful falls again,
To beautify the world with dews and rain.

The highest duty to mere man vouchsafed
Was laid on thee, — out of wild chaos,
When the roused popular ocean foamed
and chafed
And vulture War from his Imaus
Snuffed blood, to summon homely Peace,
And show that only order is release.

To carve thy fullest thought, what though
Time was not granted ? Aye in his-
tory,
Like that Dawn's face which baffled Angelo
Left shapeless, grander for its mystery,
Thy great Design shall stand, and day
Flood its blind front from Orients far
away.

Who says thy day is o'er ? Control,
My heart, that bitter first emotion;
While men shall reverence the steadfast
soul,
The heart in silent self-devotion
Breaking, the mild, heroic mien,
Thou 'lt need no prop of marble, Lamar-
tine.

If France reject thee, 't is not thine,
But her own, exile that she utters;
Ideal France, the deathless, the divine,
Will be where thy white pennon flut-
ters,
As once the nobler Athens went
With Aristides into banishment.

No fitting metewand hath To-day
For measuring spirits of thy stature;
Only the Future can reach up to lay
The laurel on that lofty nature,
Bard, who with some diviner art
Hast touched the bard's true lyre, a nation's
heart.

Swept by thy hand, the gladdened chords,
Crashed now in discords fierce by
others,
Gave forth one note beyond all skill of
words,
And chimed together, We are brothers.
O poem unsurpassed ! it ran
All round the world, unlocking man to
man.

France is too poor to pay alone
The service of that ample spirit;
Paltry seem low dictatorship and throne,
Weighed with thy self - renouncing
merit;
They had to thee been rust and loss;
Thy aim was higher, — thou hast climbed
a Cross !

TO JOHN GORHAM PALFREY

Dr. Palfrey, whose name is for students as-
sociated mainly with his *History of New Eng-
land,* was one of the most consistent and firm
anti-slavery men of his day. Chosen to Con-
gress as a Whig member, he refused to support
the Whig candidate for the Speakership of the
House, because he was assured that the candi-
date, Mr. Winthrop, would not use his position
to obstruct the extension of the slave power.

This incident called out the fourth of the first series of *Biglow Papers*.

THERE are who triumph in a losing
  cause,
Who can put on defeat, as 't were a wreath
Unwithering in the adverse popular breath,
  Safe from the blasting demagogue's ap-
    plause;
  'T is they who stand for Freedom and
    God's laws.

And so stands Palfrey now, as Marvell
  stood,
Loyal to Truth dethroned, nor could be
  wooed
  To trust the playful tiger's velvet paws:
And if the second Charles brought in decay
Of ancient virtue, if it well might wring
Souls that had broadened 'neath a nobler
  day,
  To see a losel, marketable king
Fearfully watering with his realm's best
  blood
  Cromwell's quenched bolts, that erst had
    cracked and flamed,
Scaring, through all their depths of courtier
  mud,
  Europe's crowned bloodsuckers, — how
    more ashamed
Ought we to be, who see Corruption's flood
Still rise o'er last year's mark, to mine
  away
  Our brazen idol's feet of treacherous
    clay!

O utter degradation! Freedom turned
  Slavery's vile bawd, to cozen and betray
  To the old lecher's clutch a maiden prey,
If so a loathsome pander's fee be earned!
  And we are silent, — we who daily tread
A soil sublime, at least, with heroes'
  graves! —
  Beckon no more, shades of the noble
    dead!
Be dumb, ye heaven-touched lips of winds
  and waves!
  Or hope to rouse some Coptic dullard,
    hid
Ages ago, wrapt stiffly, fold on fold,
With cerements close, to wither in the cold,
  Forever hushed, and sunless pyramid!

Beauty and Truth, and all that these
  contain,

Drop not like ripened fruit about our feet;
  We climb to them through years of
    sweat and pain;
  Without long struggle, none did e'er at-
    tain
The downward look from Quiet's blissful
  seat:
  Though present loss may be the hero's
    part,
  Yet none can rob him of the victor heart
Whereby the broad-realmed future is sub-
  dued,
  And Wrong, which now insults from tri-
    umph's car,
  Sending her vulture hope to raven far,
Is made unwilling tributary of Good.

O Mother State, how quenched thy Sinai
  fires!
  Is there none left of thy stanch May-
    flower breed?
No spark among the ashes of thy sires,
  Of Virtue's altar-flame the kindling
    seed?
Are these thy great men, these that cringe
  and creep,
  And writhe through slimy ways to place
    and power? —
How long, O Lord, before thy wrath shall
  reap
  Our frail-stemmed summer prosperings
    in their flower?
Oh for one hour of that undaunted stock
That went with Vane and Sidney to the
  block!

Oh for a whiff of Naseby, that would
  sweep,
  With its stern Puritan besom, all this
    chaff
From the Lord's threshing-floor! Yet
  more than half
The victory is attained, when one or two,
  Through the fool's laughter and the
    traitor's scorn,
  Beside thy sepulchre can bide the morn,
Crucified Truth, when thou shalt rise
  anew.

TO W. L. GARRISON

"Some time afterward, it was reported to me by the city officers that they had ferreted out the paper and its editor; that his office was an obscure hole, his only visible auxiliary a negro boy, and his supporters a few very insignificant persons of all colors." — *Letter of H. G. Otis.*

This significant sentence printed at its head gave the key-note to the following poem, but it is interesting to read the characterization of Garrison drawn by Mr. Lowell at this same time, in a letter to C. F. Briggs dated March 26, 1848. " I do not agree with the abolitionists in their disunion and non-voting theories. They treat ideas as ignorant persons do cherries. They think them unwholesome unless they are swallowed, stones and all. Garrison is so used to standing alone that, like Daniel Boone, he moves away as the world creeps up to him, and goes farther into the wilderness. He considers every step a step forward, though it be over the edge of a precipice. But, with all his faults (and they are the faults of his position) he is a great and extraordinary man. His work may be over, but it has been a great work. . . . I respect Garrison (respect does not include love). Remember that Garrison was so long in a position where he alone was right and all the world wrong, that such a position has created in him a habit of mind which may remain, though circumstances have wholly changed. Indeed a mind of that cast is essential to a Reformer. Luther was as infallible as any man that ever held St. Peter's keys." *Letters* I. 125, 126.

In a small chamber, friendless and unseen,
  Toiled o'er his types one poor, unlearned young man;
The place was dark, unfurnitured, and mean;
  Yet there the freedom of a race began.

Help came but slowly ; surely no man yet
  Put lever to the heavy world with less:
What need of help ? He knew how types were set,
  He'had a dauntless spirit, and a press.

Such earnest natures are the fiery pith,
  The compact nucleus, round which systems grow;
Mass after mass becomes inspired therewith,
  And whirls impregnate with the central glow.

O Truth ! O Freedom ! how are ye still born
  In the rude stable, in the manger nurst !

What humble hands unbar those gates of morn
  Through which the splendors of the New Day burst !

What ! shall one monk, scarce known beyond his cell,
  Front Rome's far-reaching bolts, and scorn her frown ?
Brave Luther answered YES; that thunder's swell
  Rocked Europe, and discharmed the triple crown.

Whatever can be known of earth we know,
  Sneered Europe's wise men, in their snail-shells curled;
No ! said one man in Genoa, and that No
  Out of the darkness summoned this New World.

Who is it will not dare himself to trust ?
  Who is it hath not strength to stand alone ?
Who is it thwarts and bilks the inward MUST ?
  He and his works, like sand, from earth are blown.

Men of a thousand shifts and wiles, look here !
  See one straightforward conscience put in pawn
To win a world; see the obedient sphere
  By bravery's simple gravitation drawn !

Shall we not heed the lesson taught of old,
  And by the Present's lips repeated still,
In our own single manhood to be bold,
  Fortressed in conscience and impregnable will ?

We stride the river daily at its spring,
  Nor, in our childish thoughtlessness, foresee
What myriad vassal streams shall tribute bring,
  How like an equal it shall greet the sea.

O small beginnings, ye are great and strong,
  Based on a faithful heart and weariless brain !
Ye build the future fair, ye conquer wrong,
  Ye earn the crown, and wear it not in vain.

ON THE DEATH OF CHARLES TURNER TORREY

The Martyr Torrey was the name applied to this clergyman, who gave up his professional life in order to devote himself to the anti-slavery cause in Maryland. He was con-demned to long imprisonment for aiding in the escape of slaves, but died in the penitentiary, May, 1846, of disease brought on by ill usage. His body was taken to Boston, and the funeral made a profound impression on the community.

WOE worth the hour when it is crime
  To plead the poor dumb bondman's cause,
When all that makes the heart sublime,
The glorious throbs that conquer time,
  Are traitors to our cruel laws !

He strove among God's suffering poor
  One gleam of brotherhood to send;
The dungeon oped its hungry door
To give the truth one martyr more,
  Then shut, — and here behold the end !

O Mother State ! when this was done,
  No pitying throe thy bosom gave;
Silent thou saw'st the death-shroud spun,
And now thou givest to thy son
  The stranger's charity, — a grave.

Must it be thus forever ? No !
  The hand of God sows not in vain,
Long sleeps the darkling seed below,
The seasons come, and change, and go,
  And all the fields are deep with grain.

Although our brother lie asleep,
  Man's heart still struggles, still aspires;
His grave shall quiver yet, while deep
Through the brave Bay State's pulses leap
  Her ancient energies and fires.

When hours like this the senses' gush
  Have stilled, and left the spirit room,
It hears amid the eternal hush
The swooping pinions' dreadful rush,
  That bring the vengeance and the
      doom; —

Not man's brute vengeance, such as rends
  What rivets man to man apart, —
God doth not so bring round his ends,
But waits the ripened time, and sends
  His mercy to the oppressor's heart.

ELEGY ON THE DEATH OF DR. CHANNING

I DO not come to weep above thy pall,
  And mourn the dying-out of noble
      powers;
The poet's clearer eye should see, in all
  Earth's seeming woe, seed of immortal
      flowers.

Truth needs no champions: in the infinite
      deep
  Of everlasting Soul her strength abides,
From Nature's heart her mighty pulses
      leap,
  Through Nature's veins her strength,
      undying, tides.

Peace is more strong than war, and gentle-
      ness,
  Where force were vain, makes conquest
      o'er the wave;
And love lives on and hath a power to
      bless,
  When they who loved are hidden in the
      grave.

The sculptured marble brags of death-
      strewn fields,
  And Glory's epitaph is writ in blood;
But Alexander now to Plato yields,
  Clarkson will stand where Wellington
      hath stood.

I watch the circle of the eternal years,
  And read forever in the storied page
One lengthened roll of blood, and wrong,
      and tears,
  One onward step of Truth from age to
      age.

The poor are crushed; the tyrants link
      their chain;
  The poet sings through narrow dun-
      geon-grates;
Man's hope lies quenched; and, lo ! with
      steadfast gain
  Freedom doth forge her mail of adverse
      fates.

Men slay the prophets; fagot, rack, and
      cross
  Make up the groaning record of the
      past;

But Evil's triumphs are her endless loss,
    And sovereign Beauty wins the soul at
        last.

No power can die that ever wrought for
    Truth;
    Thereby a law of Nature it became,
And lives unwithered in its blithesome
      youth,
    When he who called it forth is but a
      name.

Therefore I cannot think thee wholly gone;
    The better part of thee is with us still;
Thy soul its hampering clay aside hath
      thrown,
    And only freer wrestles with the Ill.

Thou livest in the life of all good things;
    What words thou spak'st for Freedom
      shall not die;
Thou sleepest not, for now thy Love hath
      wings
    To soar where hence thy Hope could
      hardly fly.

And often, from that other world, on this
    Some gleams from great souls gone be-
      fore may shine,
To shed on struggling hearts a clearer bliss,
    And clothe the Right with lustre more
      divine.

Thou art not idle: in thy higher sphere
    Thy spirit bends itself to loving tasks,
And strength to perfect what it dreamed
      of here
Is all the crown and glory that it asks.

For sure, in Heaven's wide chambers, there
    is room
    For love and pity, and for helpful deeds;
Else were our summons thither but a doom
To life more vain than this in clayey
      weeds.

From off the starry mountain-peak of song,
    Thy spirit shows me, in the coming time,
An earth unwithered by the foot of wrong,
    A race revering its own soul sublime.

What wars, what martyrdoms, what crimes,
    may come,
    Thou knowest not, nor I; but God will
      lead

The prodigal soul from want and sorrow
    home,
    And Eden ope her gates to Adam's seed.

Farewell! good man, good angel now!
    this hand
Soon, like thine own, shall lose its cun-
      ning too;
Soon shall this soul, like thine, bewildered
    stand,
    Then leap to thread the free, unfathomed
      blue:

When that day comes, oh, may this hand
    grow cold,
    Busy, like thine, for Freedom and the
      Right;
Oh, may this soul, like thine, be ever bold
    To face dark Slavery's encroaching
      blight!

This laurel-leaf I cast upon thy bier;
    Let worthier hands than these thy wreath
      intwine;
Upon thy hearse I shed no useless tear, —
    For us weep rather thou in calm divine!

TO THE MEMORY OF HOOD

ANOTHER star 'neath Time's horizon
    dropped,
To gleam o'er unknown lands and seas;
Another heart that beat for freedom
    stopped, —
    What mournful words are these!

O Love Divine, that claspest our tired
    earth,
    And lullest it upon thy heart,
Thou knowest how much a gentle soul is
    worth
    To teach men what thou art!

His was a spirit that to all thy poor
    Was kind as slumber after pain:
Why ope so soon thy heaven-deep Quiet's
    door
    And call him home again?

Freedom needs all her poets: it is they
    Who give her aspirations wings,
And to the wiser law of music sway
    Her wild imaginings.

Yet thou hast called him, nor art thou un-
kind,
O Love Divine, for 't is thy will
That gracious natures leave their love be-
hind
To work for Mercy still.

Let laurelled marbles weigh on other
tombs,
Let anthems peal for other dead,
Rustling the bannered depth of minster-
glooms
With their exulting spread.

His epitaph shall mock the short-lived
stone,
No lichen shall its lines efface,
He needs these few and simple lines
alone
To mark his resting-place: —

"Here lies a Poet. Stranger, if to thee
His claim to memory be obscure,
If thou wouldst learn how truly great was
he,
Go, ask it of the poor."

THE VISION OF SIR LAUNFAL

THIS poem was written apparently early in 1848, for in a letter to Mr. Briggs, dated February 1 of that year, Lowell, referring to it, says: " The new poem I spoke of is a sort of a story, and more likely to be popular than what I write generally. Maria thinks very highly of it. I shall probably publish it by itself next summer." The poem was published in the middle of December, 1848, and in an exuberant letter to Mr. Briggs shortly after it appeared, Lowell wrote : " Last night . . . I walked to Watertown over the snow with the new moon before me and a sky exactly like that in Page's evening landscape. Orion was rising behind me, and, as I stood on the hill just before you enter the village, the stillness of the fields around me was delicious, broken only by the tinkle of a little brook which runs too swiftly for Frost to catch it. My picture of the brook in *Sir Launfal* was drawn from it." The following note was prefixed to the poem by its author.

According to the mythology of the Romancers, the San Greal, or Holy Grail, was the cup

out of which Jesus partook of the Last Supper with his disciples. It was brought into England ·by Joseph of Arimathea, and remained there, an object of pilgrimage and adoration, for many years in the keeping of his lineal descendants. It was incumbent upon those who had charge of it to be chaste in thought, word, and deed; but one of the keepers having broken this condition, the Holy Grail disappeared. From that time it was a favorite enterprise of the knights of Arthur's court to go in search of it. Sir Galahad was at last successful in finding it, as may be read in the seventeenth book of the Romance of King Arthur. Tennyson has made Sir Galahad the subject of one of the most exquisite of his poems.

The plot (if I may give that name to anything so slight) of the following poem is my own, and, to serve its purposes, I have enlarged the circle of competition in search of the miraculous cup in such a manner as to include, not only other persons than the heroes of the Round Table, but also a period of time subsequent to the supposed date of King Arthur's reign.

PRELUDE TO PART FIRST

OVER his keys the musing organist,
Beginning doubtfully and far away,
First lets his fingers wander as they list,
And builds a bridge from Dreamland for
his lay:
Then, as the touch of his loved instrument
Gives hope and fervor, nearer draws his
theme,
First guessed by faint auroral flushes sent
Along the wavering vista of his dream.

Not only around our infancy
Doth heaven with all its splendors lie;
Daily, with souls that cringe and plot,
We Sinais climb and know it not.

Over our manhood bend the skies;
Against our fallen and traitor lives
The great winds utter prophecies;
With our faint hearts the mountain
strives;
Its arms outstretched, the druid wood
Waits with its benedicite;

And to our age's drowsy blood
  Still shouts the inspiring sea.

Earth gets its price for what Earth gives
    us;
  The beggar is taxed for a corner to die
    in,
The priest hath his fee who comes and
    shrives us,
  We bargain for the graves we lie in;
At the devil's booth are all things sold,
Each ounce of dross costs its ounce of
    gold;
For a cap and bells our lives we pay,
Bubbles we buy with a whole soul's task-
    ing:
'T is heaven alone that is given away,
'T is only God may be had for the ask-
    ing;
No price is set on the lavish summer;
June may be had by the poorest comer.

And what is so rare as a day in June ?
  Then, if ever, come perfect days;
Then Heaven tries earth if it be in tune,
  And over it softly her warm ear lays;
Whether we look, or whether we listen,
We hear life murmur, or see it glisten;
Every clod feels a stir of might,
  An instinct within it that reaches and
    towers,
And, groping blindly above it for light,
  Climbs to a soul in grass and flowers;
The flush of life may well be seen
  Thrilling back over hills and valleys;
The cowslip startles in meadows green,
  The buttercup catches the sun in its
    chalice,
And there 's never a leaf nor a blade too
    mean
  To be some happy creature's palace;
The little bird sits at his door in the sun,
  Atilt like a blossom among the leaves,
And lets his illumined being o'errun
  With the deluge of summer it receives;
His mate feels the eggs beneath her wings,
And the heart in her dumb breast flutters
    and sings;
He sings to the wide world, and she to her
    nest, —
  In the nice ear of Nature which song is the
    best ?

Now is the high-tide of the year,
  And whatever of life hath ebbed away

Comes flooding back with a ripply cheer,
  Into every bare inlet and creek and
    bay;
Now the heart is so full that a drop over-
    fills it,
We are happy now because God wills it;
No matter how barren the past may have
    been,
'T is enough for us now that the leaves are
    green;
We sit in the warm shade and feel right
    well
How the sap creeps up and the blossoms
    swell;
We may shut our eyes, but we cannot help
    knowing
That skies are clear and grass is grow-
    ing;
The breeze comes whispering in our ear,
That dandelions are blossoming near,
  That maize has sprouted, that streams
    are flowing,
That the river is bluer than the sky,
That the robin is plastering his house hard
    by ;
And if the breeze kept the good news
    back,
For other couriers we should not lack;
  We could guess it all by yon heifer's
    lowing, —
And hark ! how clear bold chanticleer,
Warmed with the new wine of the year,
  Tells all in his lusty crowing !

Joy comes, grief goes, we know not how;
Everything is happy now,
  Everything is upward striving;
'T is as easy now for the heart to be
    true
As for grass to be green or skies to be
    blue, —
'T is the natural way of living:
Who knows whither the clouds have fled ?
  In the unscarred heaven they leave no
    wake;
And the eyes forget the tears they have
    shed,
  The heart forgets its sorrow and ache;
The soul partakes the season's youth,
  And the sulphurous rifts of passion and
    woe
Lie deep 'neath a silence pure and smooth,
  Like burnt-out craters healed with snow.
What wonder if Sir Launfal now
Remembered the keeping of his vow ?

PART FIRST

I

" My golden spurs now bring to me,
  And bring to me my richest mail,
For to-morrow I go over land and sea
  In search of the Holy Grail;
Shall never a bed for me be spread,
Nor shall a pillow be under my head,
  Till I begin my vow to keep;
Here on the rushes will I sleep,
And perchance there may come a vision
  true
Ere day create the world anew."
  Slowly Sir Launfal's eyes grew dim,
  Slumber fell like a cloud on him,
And into his soul the vision flew.

II

The crows flapped over by twos and threes,
In the pool drowsed the cattle up to their
  knees,
  The little birds sang as if it were
  The one day of summer in all the year,
And the very leaves seemed to sing on the
  trees:
The castle alone in the landscape lay
Like an outpost of winter, dull and gray:
'T was the proudest hall in the North
  Countree,
And never its gates might opened be,
Save to lord or lady of high degree;
Summer besieged it on every side,
But the churlish stone her assaults defied;
She could not scale the chilly wall,
Though around it for leagues her pavilions
  tall
Stretched left and right,
Over the hills and out of sight;
  Green and broad was every tent,
  And out of each a murmur went
Till the breeze fell off at night.

III

The drawbridge dropped with a surly clang,
And through the dark arch a charger
  sprang,
Bearing Sir Launfal, the maiden knight,
In his gilded mail, that flamed so bright
It seemed the dark castle had gathered all
Those shafts the fierce sun had shot over
  its wall
  In his siege of three hundred summers
  long,

And, binding them all in one blazing sheaf,
  Had cast them forth: so, young and
  strong,
And lightsome as a locust-leaf,
Sir Launfal flashed forth in his maiden
  mail,
To seek in all climes for the Holy Grail.

IV

It was morning on hill and stream and tree,
  And morning in the young knight's
  heart;
Only the castle moodily
Rebuffed the gifts of the sunshine free,
  And gloomed by itself apart;
The season brimmed all other things up
Full as the rain fills the pitcher-plant's cup.

V

As Sir Launfal made morn through the
  darksome gate,
  He was 'ware of a leper, crouched by the
  same,
Who begged with his hand and moaned as
  he sate;
  And a loathing over Sir Launfal came;
The sunshine went out of his soul with a
  thrill,
  The flesh 'neath his armor 'gan shrink
  and crawl,
And midway its leap his heart stood still
  Like a frozen waterfall;
For this man, so foul and bent of stature,
Rasped harshly against his dainty nature,
And seemed the one blot on the summer
  morn, —
So he tossed him a piece of gold in scorn.

VI

The leper raised not the gold from the
  dust:
" Better to me the poor man's crust,
Better the blessing of the poor,
Though I turn me empty from his door;
That is no true alms which the hand can
  hold;
He gives only the worthless gold
  Who gives from a sense of duty;
But he who gives but a slender mite,
And gives to that which is out of sight,
  That thread of the all-sustaining Beauty
Which runs through all and doth all
  unite, —
The hand cannot clasp the whole of his
  alms,

The heart outstretches its eager palms,
For a god goes with it and makes it store
To the soul that was starving in darkness
    before."

PRELUDE TO PART SECOND

Down swept the chill wind from the moun-
    tain peak,
    From the snow five thousand summers
        old;
On open wold and hilltop bleak
    It had gathered all the cold,
And whirled it like sleet on the wanderer's
    cheek;
It carried a shiver everywhere
From the unleafed boughs and pastures
    bare;
The little brook heard it and built a roof
'Neath which he could house him, winter-
    proof;
All night by the white stars' frosty gleams
He groined his arches and matched his
    beams;
Slender and clear were his crystal spars
As the lashes of light that trim the stars:
He sculptured every summer delight
In his halls and chambers out of sight;
Sometimes his tinkling waters slipt
Down through a frost-leaved forest-crypt,
Long, sparkling aisles of steel-stemmed
    trees
Bending to counterfeit a breeze;
Sometimes the roof no fretwork knew
But silvery mosses that downward grew;
Sometimes it was carved in sharp relief
With quaint arabesques of ice-fern leaf;
Sometimes it was simply smooth and clear
For the gladness of heaven to shine
    through, and here
He had caught the nodding bulrush-tops
And hung them thickly with diamond
    drops,
That crystalled the beams of moon and sun,
And made a star of every one :
No mortal builder's most rare device
Could match this winter-palace of ice;
'T was as if every image that mirrored lay
In his depths serene through the summer
    day,
Each fleeting shadow of earth and sky,
    Lest the happy model should be lost,
Had been mimicked in fairy masonry
    By the elfin builders of the frost.

Within the hall are song and laughter,
    The cheeks of Christmas glow red and
        jolly,
And sprouting is every corbel and rafter
    With lightsome green of ivy and holly;
Through the deep gulf of the chimney
    wide
Wallows the Yule-log's roaring tide;
The broad flame-pennons droop and flap
    And belly and tug as a flag in the wind;
Like a locust shrills the imprisoned sap,
    Hunted to death in its galleries blind;
And swift little troops of silent sparks,
    Now pausing, now scattering away as in
        fear,
Go threading the soot-forest's tangled darks
    Like herds of startled deer.

But the wind without was eager and sharp,
Of Sir Launfal's gray hair it makes a harp,
    And rattles and wrings
    The icy strings,
Singing, in dreary monotone,
A Christmas carol of its own,
    Whose burden still, as he might guess,
    Was "Shelterless, shelterless, shelter-
        less !"
The voice of the seneschal flared like a
    torch
As he shouted the wanderer away from the
    porch,
And he sat in the gateway and saw all
    night
    The great hall-fire, so cheery and bold,
    Through the window-slits of the castle
        old,
Build out its piers of ruddy light
Against the drift of the cold.

PART SECOND

I

There was never a leaf on bush or tree,
The bare boughs rattled shudderingly;
The river was dumb and could not speak,
    For the weaver Winter its shroud had
        spun;
A single crow on the tree-top bleak
    From his shining feathers shed off the
        cold sun;
Again it was morning, but shrunk and cold,
As if her veins were sapless and old,
And she rose up decrepitly
For a last dim look at earth and sea.

II

Sir Launfal turned from his own hard gate,
For another heir in his earldom sate;
An old, bent man, worn out and frail,
He came back from seeking the Holy
    Grail;
Little he recked of his earldom's loss,
No more on his surcoat was blazoned the
    cross,
But deep in his soul the sign he wore,
The badge of the suffering and the poor.

III

Sir Launfal's raiment thin and spare
Was idle mail 'gainst the barbèd air,
For it was just at the Christmas time;
So he mused, as he sat, of a sunnier clime,
And sought for a shelter from cold and
    snow
In the light and warmth of long-ago;
He sees the snake-like caravan crawl
O'er the edge of the desert, black and
    small,
Then nearer and nearer, till, one by one,
He can count the camels in the sun,
As over the red-hot sands they pass
To where, in its slender necklace of grass,
The little spring laughed and leapt in the
    shade,
And with its own self like an infant played,
And waved its signal of palms.

IV

"For Christ's sweet sake, I beg an alms ; "
The happy camels may reach the spring,
But Sir Launfal sees only the grewsome
    thing,
The leper, lank as the rain-blanched bone,
That cowers beside him, a thing as lone
And white as the ice-isles of Northern
    seas
In the desolate horror of his disease.

V

And Sir Launfal said, " I behold in thee
An image of Him who died on the tree;
Thou also hast had thy crown of thorns,
Thou also hast had the world's buffets and
    scorns,
And to thy life were not denied
The wounds in the hands and feet and
    side:
Mild Mary's Son, acknowledge me;
Behold, through him, I give to thee ! "

VI

Then the soul of the leper stood up in his
    eyes
    And looked at Sir Launfal, and straight-
        way he
Remembered in what a haughtier guise
    He had flung an alms to leprosie,
When he girt his young life up in gilded
    mail
And set forth in search of the Holy Grail.
The heart within him was ashes and dust;
He parted in twain his single crust,
He broke the ice on the streamlet's brink,
And gave the leper to eat and drink,
'T was a mouldy crust of coarse brown
    bread,
    'T was water out of a wooden bowl, —
Yet with fine wheaten bread was the leper
    fed,
    And 't was red wine he drank with his
        thirsty soul.

VII

As Sir Launfal mused with a downcast
    face,
A light shone round about the place;
The leper no longer crouched at his side,
But stood before him glorified,
Shining and tall and fair and straight
As the pillar that stood by the Beautiful
    Gate, —
Himself the Gate whereby men can
Enter the temple of God in Man.

VIII

His words were shed softer than leaves
    from the pine,
And they fell on Sir Launfal as snows on
    the brine,
That mingle their softness and quiet in one
With the shaggy unrest they float down
    upon;
And the voice that was softer than silence
    said,
" Lo, it is I, be not afraid !
In many climes, without avail,
Thou hast spent thy life for the Holy Grail;
Behold, it is here, — this cup which thou
Didst fill at the streamlet for me but now;
This crust is my body broken for thee,
This water his blood that died on the tree;
The Holy Supper is kept, indeed,
In whatso we share with another's need;
Not what we give, but what we share,

For the gift without the giver is bare;
Who gives himself with his alms feeds three,
Himself, his hungering neighbor, and me."

IX

Sir Launfal awoke as from a swound:
"The Grail in my castle here is found!
Hang my idle armor up on the wall,
Let it be the spider's banquet-hall;
He must be fenced with stronger mail
Who would seek and find the Holy Grail."

X

The castle gate stands open now,
    And the wanderer is welcome to the hall
As the hangbird is to the elm-tree bough;

No longer scowl the turrets tall,
The Summer's long siege at last is o'er;
When the first poor outcast went in at the
    door,
She entered with him in disguise,
And mastered the fortress by surprise;
There is no spot she loves so well on
    ground,
She lingers and smiles there the whole year
    round;
The meanest serf on Sir Launfal's land
Has hall and bower at his command;
And there's no poor man in the North
    Countree
But is lord of the earldom as much as he.

LETTER FROM BOSTON

THIS letter was written to Mr. James Miller McKim, who had succeeded Whittier as editor of *The Pennsylvania Freeman*, where the verses were first published.

December, 1846.

DEAR M——

        By way of saving time,
I 'll do this letter up in rhyme,
Whose slim stream through four pages flows
Ere one is packed with tight-screwed prose,
Threading the tube of an epistle,
Smooth as a child's breath through a whistle.

The great attraction now of all
Is the "Bazaar" at Faneuil Hall,
Where swarm the anti-slavery folks
As thick, dear Miller, as your jokes.
There 's GARRISON, his features very
Benign for an incendiary,
Beaming forth sunshine through his glasses
On the surrounding lads and lasses,
(No bee could blither be, or brisker,) —
A Pickwick somehow turned John Ziska,
His bump of firmness swelling up
Like a rye cupcake from its cup.
And there, too, was his English tea-set,
Which in his ear a kind of flea set
His Uncle Samuel for its beauty
Demanding sixty dollars duty,
('T was natural Sam should serve his trunk
    ill,
For G., you know, has cut his uncle,)
Whereas, had he but once made tea in 't,
His uncle's ear had had the flea in 't,
There being not a cent of duty
On any pot that ever drew tea.

There was MARIA CHAPMAN, too,

With her swift eyes of clear steel-blue,
The coiled-up mainspring of the Fair,
Originating everywhere
The expansive force without a sound
That whirls a hundred wheels around,
Herself meanwhile as calm and still
As the bare crown of Prospect Hill;
A noble woman, brave and apt,
Cumæan sibyl not more rapt,
Who might, with those fair tresses shorn,
The Maid of Orleans' casque have worn,
Herself the Joan of our Ark,
For every shaft a shining mark.

And there, too, was ELIZA FOLLEN,
Who scatters fruit-creating pollen
Where'er a blossom she can find
Hardy enough for Truth's north wind,
Each several point of all her face
Tremblingly bright with the inward grace,
As if all motion gave it light
Like phosphorescent seas at night.

There jokes our EDMUND, plainly son
Of him who bearded Jefferson,
A non-resistant by conviction,
But with a bump in contradiction,
So that whene'er it gets a chance
His pen delights to play the lance,
And — you may doubt it, or believe it—
Full at the head of Joshua Leavitt
The very calumet he.'d launch,
And scourge him with the olive branch.
A master with the foils of wit,

'T is natural he should love a hit;
A gentleman, withal, and scholar,
Only base things excite his choler,
And then his satire 's keen and thin
As the lithe blade of Saladin.
Good letters are a gift apart,
And his are gems of Flemish art,
True offspring of the fireside Muse,
Not a rag-gathering of news
Like a new hopfield which is all poles,
But of one blood with Horace Walpole's.

There, with one hand behind his back,
Stands PHILLIPS buttoned in a sack,
Our Attic orator, our Chatham;
Old fogies, when he lightens at 'em,
Shrivel like leaves; to him 't is granted
Always to say the word that 's wanted,
So that he seems but speaking clearer
The tiptop thought of every hearer;
Each flash his brooding heart lets fall
Fires what 's combustible in all,
And sends the applauses bursting in
Like an exploded magazine.
His eloquence no frothy show,
The gutter's street-polluted flow,
No Mississippi's yellow flood
Whose shoalness can't be seen for mud; —
So simply clear, serenely deep,
So silent-strong its graceful sweep,
None measures its unrippling force
Who has not striven to stem its course;
How fare their barques who think to play
With smooth Niagara's mane of spray,
Let Austin's total shipwreck say.
He never spoke a word too much —
Except of Story, or some such,
Whom, though condemned by ethics strict,
The heart refuses to convict.

Beyond, a crater in each eye,
Sways brown, broad-shouldered PILLS-
          BURY,
Who tears up words like trees by the roots,
A Theseus in stout cow-hide boots,
The wager of eternal war
Against that loathsome Minotaur
To whom we sacrifice each year
The best blood of our Athens here,
(Dear M., pray brush up your Lempriere.)
A terrible denouncer he,
Old Sinai burns unquenchably
Upon his lips; he well might be a
Hot-blazing soul from fierce Judea,
Habakkuk, Ezra, or Hosea.

His words are red hot iron searers,
And nightmare-like he mounts his hearers,
Spurring them like avenging Fate, or
As Waterton his alligator.

Hard by, as calm as summer even,
Smiles the reviled and pelted STEPHEN,
The unappeasable Boanerges
To all the Churches and the Clergies,
The grim *savant* who, to complete
His own peculiar cabinet,
Contrived to label 'mong his kicks
One from the followers of Hicks;
Who studied mineralogy
Not with soft book upon the knee,
But learned the properties of stones
By contact sharp of flesh and bones,
And made the *experimentum crucis*
With his own body's vital juices;
A man with caoutchouc endurance,
A perfect gem for life insurance,
A kind of maddened John the Baptist,
To whom the harshest word comes aptest,
Who, struck by stone or brick ill-starred,
Hurls back an epithet as hard,
Which, deadlier than stone or brick,
Has a propensity to stick.
His oratory is like the scream
Of the iron-horse's frenzied steam
Which warns the world to leave wide space
For the black engine's swerveless race.
Ye men with neckcloths white, I warn
          you —
Habet a whole haymow *in cornu.*

A Judith, there, turned Quakeress,
Sits ABBY in her modest dress,
Serving a table quietly,
As if that mild and downcast eye
Flashed never, with its scorn intense,
More than Medea's eloquence.
So the same force which shakes its dread
Far-blazing blocks o'er Ætna's head,
Along the wires in silence fares
And messages of commerce bears.
No nobler gift of heart and brain,
No life more white from spot or stain,
Was e'er on Freedom's altar laid
Than hers, the simple Quaker maid.

These last three (leaving in the lurch
Some other themes) assault the Church,
Who therefore writes them in her lists
As Satan's limbs and atheists;
For each sect has one argument

Whereby the rest to hell are sent,
Which serve them like the Graiæ's tooth,
Passed round in turn from mouth to
    mouth; —
If any *ism* should arise,
Then look on it with constable's eyes,
Tie round its neck a heavy *athe-*,
And give it kittens' hydropathy.
This trick with other (useful very) tricks
Is laid to the Babylonian *meretrix*,
But 't was in vogue before her day
Wherever priesthoods had their way,
And Buddha's Popes with this struck dumb
The followers of Fi and Fum.

Well, if the world, with prudent fear
Pay God a seventh of the year,
And as a Farmer, who would pack
All his religion in one stack,
For this world works six days in seven
And idles on the seventh for Heaven,
Expecting, for his Sunday's sowing,
In the next world to go a-mowing
The crop of all his meeting-going; —
If the poor Church, by power enticed,
Finds none so infidel as Christ,

Quite backward reads his Gospel meek,
(As 't were in Hebrew writ, not Greek,)
Fencing the gallows and the sword
With conscripts drafted from his word,
And makes one gate of Heaven so wide
That the rich orthodox might ride
Through on their camels, while the poor
Squirm through the scant, unyielding door,
Which, of the Gospel's straitest size,
Is narrower than bead-needles' eyes,
What wonder World and Church should
    call
The true faith atheistical?

Yet, after all, 'twixt you and me,
Dear Miller, I could never see
That Sin's and Error's ugly smirch
Stained the walls only of the Church;
There are good priests, and men who take
Freedom's torn cloak for lucre's sake;
I can't believe the Church so strong,
As some men do, for Right or Wrong.
But, for this subject (long and vext)
I must refer you to my next,
As also for a list exact
Of goods with which the Hall was packed.

A FABLE FOR CRITICS

In a Prefatory Note which Mr. Lowell prefixed to a later issue of this poem, the history of its inception and publication is thus briefly told: "This *jeu d'esprit* was extemporized, I may fairly say, so rapidly was it written, purely for my own amusement and with no thought of publication. I sent daily instalments of it to a friend in New York, the late Charles F. Briggs. He urged me to let it be printed, and I at last consented to its anonymous publication. The secret was kept till after several persons had laid claim to its authorship." In the *Letters* it is possible to get a closer view of the author at work. In a letter to Mr. Briggs, written November 13, 1847, he says: "My satire remains just as it was. About six hundred lines I think are written. I left it because I wished to finish it in one mood of mind, and not to get that and my serious poems in the new volume entangled. It is a rambling, disjointed affair, and I may alter the form of it, but if I can get it read, I know it will take. I intend to give it some serial title and continue it at intervals." On the last day of the same year, he writes to his correspondent: "I have been hard at work copying my satire, that I might get it (what was finished of it, at least) to you by New-Year's Day as a present. As it is, I can only send the first part. It was all written with one impulse and was the work of not a great many hours, but it was written in good spirits (*con amore*, as Leupp said he used to smoke), and therefore seems to me to have a hearty and easy swing about it that is pleasant. But I was interrupted midway by being obliged to get ready the copy for my volume, and I have never been able to weld my present mood upon the old one without making an ugly swelling at the joint.

"I wish you to understand that I make you a New-Year's gift, not of the manuscript, but of the thing itself. I wish you to get it printed (if you think the sale will warrant it) for your own benefit. At the same time I am desirous of retaining my copyright, in order that, if circumstances render it desirable, I may still possess a control over it. Therefore, if you think it would repay publishing (*I* have no doubt of it, or I should not offer it to you) I wish you would enter the copyright in your own name, and then make a transfer to me in ' consideration of,' etc.

"I am making as particular directions as if I were drawing my will, but I have a sort of presentiment (which I never had in regard to anything else) that this little bit of pleasantry will *take*. Perhaps I have said too much of the Centurion. But it was only the comicality of his *character* that attracted me — for the man himself personally never entered my head. But the sketch is clever ? "

Again under date of March 26, 1848: " Since I sent you the first half, I have written something about Willis and about Longfellow — and I am waiting for pleasanter weather in order to finish it. I want to get my windows open and to write in the fresh air. I ought not to have sent you any part of it till I had finished it entirely. I feel a sense of responsibility which hinders my pen from running along as it ought in such a theme. I wish the last half to be as jolly and unconstrained as the first. If you had not praised what I sent you, I dare say you would have had the whole of it ere this. Praise is the only thing that can make me feel any doubt of myself." Six

weeks later he wrote, May 12 : " When I can sit at my open window and my friendly leaves hold their hands before my eyes to prevent their wandering to the landscape, I can sit down and write. I have begun upon the *Fable* again fairly, and am making some headway. I think with what I sent you (which I believe was about five hundred lines) it will make something over a thousand. I have done, since I sent the first half, Willis, Longfellow, Bryant, Miss Fuller, and Mrs. Child. In Longfellow's case I have attempted no characterization. The same (in a degree) may be said of S. M. F. With her I have been perfectly good-humored, but I have a fancy that what I say will stick uncomfortably. It will make you laugh. So will L. M. C. After S. M. F. I make a short digression on bores in general, which has some drollery. Willis I think good. Bryant is funny, and as fair as I could make it, immitigably just. Indeed I have endeavored to be so in all."

The volume was affectionately inscribed to Charles F. Briggs, and furnished with the following rhymed title page and preliminary note, a second note being prefixed to a second edition.

Reader ! walk up at once (it will soon be too late), and buy at a perfectly ruinous rate

A FABLE FOR CRITICS:

OR, BETTER,

(I LIKE, AS A THING THAT THE READER'S FIRST FANCY MAY STRIKE, AN OLD-FASHIONED TITLE-PAGE, SUCH AS PRESENTS A TABULAR VIEW OF THE VOLUME'S CONTENTS),

A GLANCE AT A FEW OF OUR LITERARY PROGENIES

(MRS. MALAPROP'S WORD)

FROM THE TUB OF DIOGENES ;

A VOCAL AND MUSICAL MEDLEY,

THAT IS,

A SERIES OF JOKES

By A Wonderful Quiz,

WHO ACCOMPANIES HIMSELF WITH A RUB-A-DUB-DUB, FULL OF SPIRIT AND GRACE, ON THE TOP OF THE TUB.

Set forth in October, the 21st day, In the year '48, G. P. Putnam, Broadway.

IT being the commonest mode of procedure, I premise a few candid remarks

TO THE READER : —

This trifle, begun to please only myself and my own private fancy, was laid on the shelf. But some friends, who had seen it, induced me, by dint of saying they liked it, to put it in print. That is, having come to that very conclusion, I asked their advice when 't would make no confusion. For though (in the gentlest of ways) they had hinted it was scarce worth the while, I should doubtless have printed it.

I began it, intending a Fable, a frail, slender thing, rhyme-ywinged, with a sting in its tail. But, by addings and alterings not previously planned, digressions chance-hatched, like birds' eggs in the sand, and dawdlings to suit every whimsey's demand (always freeing the bird which I held in my hand, for the two perched, perhaps out of reach, in the tree), — it grew by degrees to the size which you see. I was like the old woman that carried the calf, and my neighbors, like hers, no doubt, wonder and laugh; and when, my strained arms with their grown burthen full, I call it my Fable, they call it a bull.

Having scrawled at full gallop (as far as that goes) in a style that is neither good verse nor bad prose, and being a person whom nobody knows, some people will say I am rather more free with my readers than it is becoming to be, that I seem to expect them to wait on my leisure in following wherever I wander at pleasure, that, in short, I take more than a young author's lawful ease, and laugh in a queer way so like Mephistopheles, that the Public will doubt, as they grope through my rhythm, if in truth I am making fun *of* them or *with* them.

So the excellent Public is hereby assured that the sale of my book is already secured. For there is not a poet throughout the whole land but will purchase a copy or two out of hand, in the fond expectation of being amused in it, by seeing his betters cut up and abused in it. Now, I find, by a pretty exact calculation, there are something like ten thousand bards in the nation, of that special variety whom the Review and Magazine critics call *lofty* and *true*, and about thirty thousand (*this* tribe is increasing) of the kinds who are termed *full of promise* and *pleasing*. The Public will see by a glance at this schedule, that they cannot expect me to be over-sedulous about courting *them*, since it seems I have got enough fuel made sure of for boiling my pot.

As for such of our poets as find not their names mentioned once in my pages, with praises or blames, let them SEND IN THEIR CARDS, without further DELAY, to my friend G. P. PUTNAM, Esquire, in Broadway, where a LIST will be kept with the strictest regard to the day and the hour of receiving the card. Then, taking them up as I chance to have time (that is, if their names can be twisted in rhyme), I will honestly give each his PROPER POSITION, at the rate of ONE AUTHOR to each NEW EDITION. Thus a PREMIUM is offered sufficiently HIGH (as the magazines say when they tell their best lie) to induce bards to CLUB their resources and buy the balance of every edition, until they have all of them fairly been run through the mill.

One word to such readers (judicious and wise) as read books with something behind the mere eyes, of whom in the country, perhaps, there are two, including myself, gentle reader, and you. All the characters sketched in this slight *jeu d'esprit*, though, it may be, they seem, here and there, rather free, and drawn from a somewhat too cynical standpoint, are *meant* to be faithful, for that is the grand point, and none but an owl would feel sore at a rub from a jester who tells you, without any subterfuge, that he sits in Diogenes' tub.

A PRELIMINARY NOTE TO THE SECOND EDITION,

though it well may be reckoned, of all composition, the species at once most delightful and healthy, is a thing which an author, unless he be wealthy and willing to pay for that kind of delight, is not, in all instances, called on to write, though there are, it is said, who, their spirits to cheer, slip in a new title-page three times a year, and in this way snuff up an imaginary savor of that sweetest of dishes, the popular favor, — much as if a starved painter should fall to and treat the Ugolino inside to a picture of meat.

You remember (if not, pray turn backward and look) that, in writing the preface which ushered my book, I treated you, excellent Public, not merely with a cool disregard, but downright cavalierly. Now I would not take back the least thing I then said, though I thereby could butter both sides of my bread, for I never could see that an author owed aught to the people he solaced, diverted, or taught ; and, as for mere fame, I have long ago learned that the persons by whom it is finally earned are those with whom *your* verdict weighed not a pin, unsustained by the higher court sitting within.

But I wander from what I intended to say, — that you have, namely, shown such a liberal way of thinking, and so much æsthetic perception of anonymous worth in the handsome reception you gave to my book, spite of some private piques (having bought the first thousand in barely two weeks), that I think, past a doubt, if you measured the phiz of yours most devotedly, Wonderful Quiz, you would find that its vertical section was shorter, by an inch and two tenths, or 'twixt that and a quarter.

You have watched a child playing — in

those wondrous years when belief is not bound to the eyes and the ears, and the vision divine is so clear and unmarred, that each baker of pies in the dirt is a bard ? Give a knife and a shingle, he fits out a fleet, and, on that little mud-puddle over the street, his fancy, in purest good faith, will make sail round the globe with a puff of his breath for a gale, will visit, in barely ten minutes, all climes, and do the Columbus-feat hundreds of times. Or, suppose the young poet fresh stored with delights from that Bible of childhood, the Arabian Nights, he will turn to a crony and cry, " Jack, let 's play that I am a Genius ! " Jacky straightway makes Aladdin's lamp out of a stone, and, for hours, they enjoy each his own supernatural powers. This is all very pretty and pleasant, but then suppose our two urchins have grown into men, and both have turned authors, — one says to his brother, " Let 's play we 're the American somethings or other, — say Homer or Sophocles, Goethe or Scott (only let them be big enough, no matter what). Come, you shall be Byron or Pope, which you choose: I 'll be Coleridge, and both shall write mutual reviews." So they both (as mere strangers) before many days send each other a cord of anonymous bays. Each, piling his epithets, smiles in his sleeve to see what his friend can be made to believe; each, reading the other's unbiased review, thinks — Here 's pretty high praise, but no more than my due. Well, we laugh at them both, and yet make no great fuss when the same farce is acted to benefit us. Even I, who, if asked, scarce a month since, what Fudge meant, should have answered, the dear Public's critical judgment, begin to think sharp-witted Horace spoke sooth when he said that the Public *sometimes* hit the truth.

In reading these lines, you perhaps have a vision of a person in pretty good health and condition ; and yet, since I put forth my primary edition, I have been crushed, scorched, withered, used up and put down (by Smith with the cordial assistance of Brown), in all, if you put any faith in my rhymes, to the number of ninety-five several times, and, while I am writing, — I tremble to think of it, for I may at this moment be just on the brink of it, — Molybdostom,

angry at being omitted, has begun a critique, — am I not to be pitied ? [1]

Now I shall not crush *them* since, indeed, for that matter, no pressure I know of could render them flatter ; nor wither, nor scorch them, — no action of fire could make either them or their articles drier ; nor waste time in putting them down — I am thinking not their own self-inflation will keep them from sinking ; for there 's this contradiction about the whole bevy, — though without the least weight, they are awfully heavy. No, my dear honest bore, *surdo fabulam narras*, they are no more to me than a rat in the arras. I can walk with the Doctor, get facts from the Don, or draw out the Lambish quintessence of John, and feel nothing more than a half-comic sorrow, to think that they all will be lying to-morrow tossed carelessly up on the waste-paper shelves, and forgotten by all but their half-dozen selves. Once snug in my attic, my fire in a roar, I leave the whole pack of them outside the door. With Hakluyt or Purchas I wander away to the black northern seas or barbaric Cathay ; get *fou* with O'Shanter, and sober me then with that builder of brick-kilnish dramas, rare Ben ; snuff Herbert, as holy as a flower on a grave ; with Fletcher wax tender, o'er Chapman grow brave ; with Marlowe or Kyd take a fine poet-rave ; in Very, most Hebrew of Saxons, find peace ; with Lycidas welter on vext Irish seas ; with Webster grow wild, and climb earthward again, down by mystical Browne's Jacob's-ladder-like brain, to that spiritual Pepys (Cotton's version) Montaigne ; find a new depth in Wordsworth, undreamed of before, that marvel, a poet divine who can bore. Or, out of my study, the scholar thrown off, Nature holds up her shield 'gainst the sneer and the scoff ; the landscape, forever consoling and kind, pours her wine and her oil on the smarts of the mind. The waterfall, scattering its vanishing gems ; the tall grove of hemlocks, with moss on their stems, like plashes of sunlight ; the pond in the woods, where no foot but mine and the bittern's intrudes, where pitcher-plants purple and gentians

[1] The wise Scandinavians probably called their bards by the queer-looking title of Scald in a delicate way, as it were, just to hint to the world the hot water they always get into.

hard by recall to September the blue of
June's sky; these are all my kind neigh-
bors, and leave me no wish to say aught to
you all, my poor critics, but — pish! I 've
buried the hatchet : I 'm twisting an allu-
mette out of one of you now, and relight-
ing my calumet. In your private capaci-
ties, come when you please, I will give you
my hand and a fresh pipe apiece.

As I ran through the leaves of my poor
little book, to take a fond author's first
tremulous look, it was quite an excitement
to hunt the *errata*, sprawled in as birds'
tracks are in some kinds of strata (only
these made things crookeder). Fancy an
heir that a father had seen born well-
featured and fair, turning suddenly wry-
nosed, club-footed, squint-eyed, hair-lipped,
wapper-jawed, carrot-haired, from a pride
become an aversion, — my case was yet
worse. A club-foot (by way of a change)
in a verse, I might have forgiven, an *o*'s
being wry, a limp in an *e*, or a cock in an
i, — but to have the sweet babe of my
brain served in *pi!* I am not queasy-
stomached, but such a Thyestean banquet
as that was quite out of the question.

In the edition now issued no pains are
neglected, and my verses, as orators say,
stand corrected. Yet some blunders re-
main of the Public's own make, which I
wish to correct for my personal sake. For
instance, a character drawn in pure fun
and condensing the traits of a dozen in one,
has been, as I hear, by some persons ap-
plied to a good friend of mine, whom to
stab in the side, as we walked along chat-
ting and joking together, would not be *my*
way. I can hardly tell whether a question
will ever arise in which he and I should by
any strange fortune agree, but meanwhile
my esteem for him grows as I know him,
and, though not the best judge on earth of
a poem, he knows what it is he is saying
and why, and is honest and fearless, two
good points which I have not found so rife
I can easily smother my love for them,
whether on my side or t' other.

For my other *anonymi*, you may be sure
that I know what is meant by a caricature,
and what by a portrait. There *are* those
who think it is capital fun to be spattering
their ink on quiet, unquarrelsome folk, but
the minute the game changes sides and the
others begin it, they see something savage

and horrible in it. As for me I respect
neither women nor men for their gender,
nor own any sex in a pen. I choose just
to hint to some causeless unfriends that, as
far as I know, there are always two ends
(and one of them heaviest, too) to a staff,
and two parties also to every good laugh.

A FABLE FOR CRITICS

PHŒBUS, sitting one day in a laurel-
tree's shade,
Was reminded of Daphne, of whom it was
made,
For the god being one day too warm in his
wooing,
She took to the tree to escape his pursuing;
Be the cause what it might, from his offers
she shrunk,
And, Ginevra-like, shut herself up in a
trunk;
And, though 't was a step into which he
had driven her,
He somehow or other had never forgiven
her;
Her memory he nursed as a kind of a tonic,
Something bitter to chew when he 'd play
the Byronic,
And I can't count the obstinate nymphs
that he brought over
By a strange kind of smile he put on when
he thought of her.
"My case is like Dido's," he sometimes re-
marked;
"When I last saw my love, she was fairly
embarked
In a laurel, as *she* thought — but (ah, how
Fate mocks!)
She has found it by this time a very bad
box;
Let hunters from me take this saw when
they need it, —
You 're not always sure of your game when
you 've treed it.
Just conceive such a change taking place
in one's mistress!
What romance would be left? — who can
flatter or kiss trees?
And, for mercy's sake, how could one keep
up a dialogue
With a dull wooden thing that will live
and will die a log, —
Not to say that the thought would forever
intrude

That you 've less chance to win her the more she is wood ?
Ah ! it went to my heart, and the memory still grieves,
To see those loved graces all taking their leaves;
Those charms beyond speech, so enchanting but now,
As they left me forever, each making its bough !
If her tongue *had* a tang sometimes more than was right,
Her new bark is worse than ten times her old bite."

Now, Daphne — before she was happily treeified —
Over all other blossoms the lily had deified,
And when she expected the god on a visit
('T was before he had made his intentions explicit),
Some buds she arranged with a vast deal of care,
To look as if artlessly twined in her hair,
Where they seemed, as he said, when he paid his addresses,
Like the day breaking through the long night of her tresses;
So whenever he wished to be quite irresistible,
Like a man with eight trumps in his hand at a whist-table
(I feared me at first that the rhyme was untwistable,
Though I might have lugged in an allusion to Cristabel), —
He would take up a lily, and gloomily look in it,
As I shall at the ——, when they cut up my book in it.

Well, here, after all the bad rhyme I 've been spinning,
I 've got back at last to my story's beginning:
Sitting there, as I say, in the shade of his mistress,
As dull as a volume of old Chester mysteries,
Or as those puzzling specimens which, in old histories,
We read of his verses — the Oracles, namely, —
(I wonder the Greeks should have swallowed them tamely,

For one might bet safely whatever he has to risk,
They were laid at his door by some ancient Miss Asterisk,
And so dull that the men who retailed them out-doors
Got the ill name of augurs, because they were bores, —)
First, he mused what the animal substance or herb is
Would induce a mustache, for you know he 's *imberbis ;*
Then he shuddered to think how his youthful position
Was assailed by the age of his son the physician ;
At some poems he glanced, had been sent to him lately,
And the metre and sentiment puzzled him greatly;
"Mehercle ! I 'd make such proceeding felonious, —
Have they all of them slept in the cave of Trophonius ?
Look well to your seat, 't is like taking an airing
On a corduroy road, and that out of repairing;
It leads one, 't is true, through the primitive forest,
Grand natural features, but then one has no rest;
You just catch a glimpse of some ravishing distance,
When a jolt puts the whole of it out of existence, —
Why not use their ears, if they happen to have any ? "
— Here the laurel-leaves murmured the name of poor Daphne.

"Oh, weep with me, Daphne," he sighed, "for you know it 's
A terrible thing to be pestered with poets !
But, alas, she is dumb, and the proverb holds good,
She never will cry till she 's out of the wood !
What would n't I give if I never had known of her ?
'T were a kind of relief had I something to groan over:
If I had but some letters of hers, now, to toss over,

I might turn for the nonce a Byronic phi-
losopher,
And bewitch all the flats by bemoaning the
loss of her.
One needs something tangible, though, to
begin on, —
A loom, as it were, for the fancy to spin
on;
What boots all your grist ? it can never be
ground
Till a breeze makes the arms of the wind-
mill go round;
(Or, if 't is a water-mill, alter the meta-
phor,
And say it won't stir, save the wheel be
well wet afore,
Or lug in some stuff about water 'so
dreamily,' —
It is not a metaphor, though, 't is a sim-
ile) ;
A lily, perhaps, would set *my* mill a-going,
For just at this season, I think, they are
blowing.
Here, somebody, fetch one; not very far
hence
They 're in bloom by the score, 't is but
climbing a fence;
There 's a poet hard by, who does nothing
but fill his
Whole garden, from one end to t' other,
with lilies;
A very good plan, were it not for satiety,
One longs for a weed here and there, for
variety;
Though a weed is no more than a flower in
disguise,
Which is seen through at once, if love give
a man eyes."

Now there happened to be among Phœ-
bus's followers,
A gentleman, one of the omnivorous swal-
lowers,
Who bolt every book that comes out of
the press,
Without the least question of larger or
less,
Whose stomachs are strong at the expense
of their head, —
For reading new books is like eating new
bread,
One can bear it at first, but by gradual
steps he
Is brought to death's door of a mental
dyspepsy.

On a previous stage of existence, our
Hero
Had ridden outside, with the glass below
zero;
He had been, 't is a fact you may safely
rely on,
Of a very old stock a most eminent
scion, —
A stock all fresh quacks their fierce boluses
ply on,
Who stretch the new boots Earth 's unwill-
ing to try on,
Whom humbugs of all shapes and sorts
keep their eye on,
Whose hair 's in the mortar of every new
Zion,
Who, when whistles are dear, go directly
and buy one,
Who think slavery a crime that we must
not say fie on,
Who hunt, if they e'er hunt at all, with the
lion
(Though they hunt lions also, whenever
they spy one),
Who contrive to make every good fortune
a wry one,
And at last choose the hard bed of honor
to die on,
Whose pedigree, traced to earth's earliest
years,
Is longer than anything else but their
ears; —
In short, he was sent into life with the
wrong key,
He unlocked the door, and stept forth a
poor donkey.
Though kicked and abused by his bipedal
betters
Yet he filled no mean place in the kingdom
of letters;
Far happier than many a literary hack,
He bore only paper-mill rags on his
back
(For it makes a vast difference which side
the mill
One expends on the paper his labor and
skill);
So, when his soul waited a new transmi-
gration,
And Destiny balanced 'twixt this and that
station,
Not having much time to expend upon
bothers,
Remembering he 'd had some connection
with authors,

And considering his four legs had grown
    paralytic, —
She set him on two, and he came forth a
    critic.

Through his babyhood no kind of pleas-
    ure he took
In any amusement but tearing a book;
For him there was no intermediate stage
From babyhood up to straight-laced mid-
    dle age;
There were years when he did n't wear
    coat-tails behind,
But a boy he could never be rightly de-
    fined;
Like the Irish Good Folk, though in length
    scarce a span,
From the womb he came gravely, a little
    old man;
While other boys' trousers demanded the
    toil
Of the motherly fingers on all kinds of
    soil,
Red, yellow, brown, black, clayey, gravelly,
    loamy,
He sat in the corner and read Viri Romæ.
He never was known to unbend or to revel
    once
In base, marbles, hockey, or kick up the
    devil once;
He was just one of those who excite the
    benevolence
Of your old prigs who sound the soul's
    depths with a ledger,
And are on the lookout for some young
    men to "edger-
cate," as they call it, who won't be too
    costly,
And who 'll afterward take to the ministry
    mostly;
Who always wear spectacles, always look
    bilious,
Always keep on good terms with each
    mater-familias
Throughout the whole parish, and manage
    to rear
Ten boys like themselves, on four hundred
    a year:
Who, fulfilling in turn the same fearful
    conditions,
Either preach through their noses, or go
    upon missions.

In this way our Hero got safely to col-
    lege,

Where he bolted alike both his commons
    and knowledge;
A reading-machine, always wound up and
    going,
He mastered whatever was not worth the
    knowing,
Appeared in a gown, with black waistcoat
    of satin,
To spout such a Gothic oration in Latin
That Tully could never have made out a
    word in it
(Though himself was the model the author
    preferred in it),
And grasping the parchment which gave
    him in fee
All the mystic and-so-forths contained in
    A. B.,
He was launched (life is always compared
    to a sea)
With just enough learning, and skill for
    the using it,
To prove he 'd a brain, by forever confus-
    ing it.
So worthy St. Benedict, piously burning
With the holiest zeal against secular learn-
    ing,
Nesciensque scienter, as writers express it,
Indoctusque sapienter a Roma recessit.

'T would be endless to tell you the
    things that he knew,
Each a separate fact, undeniably true,
But with him or each other they 'd nothing
    to do;
No power of combining, arranging, dis-
    cerning,
Digested the masses he learned into learn-
    ing;
There was one thing in life he had practical
    knowledge for
(And this, you will think, he need scarce
    go to college for), —
Not a deed would he do, nor a word would
    he utter,
Till he 'd weighed its relations to plain
    bread and butter.
When he left Alma Mater, he practised his
    wits
In compiling the journals' historical bits, —
Of shops broken open, men falling in
    fits,
Great fortunes in England bequeathed to
    poor printers,
And cold spells, the coldest for many past
    winters, —

Then, rising by industry, knack, and address,
Got notices up for an unbiased press,
With a mind so well poised, it seemed equally made for
Applause or abuse, just which chanced to be paid for:
From this point his progress was rapid and sure,
To the post of a regular heavy reviewer.

And here I must say he wrote excellent articles
On Hebraical points, or the force of Greek particles;
They filled up the space nothing else was prepared for,
And nobody read that which nobody cared for;
If any old book reached a fiftieth edition,
He could fill forty pages with safe erudition:
He could gauge the old books by the old set of rules,
And his very old nothings pleased very old fools;
But give him a new book, fresh out of the heart,
And you put him at sea without compass or chart, —
His blunders aspired to the rank of an art;
For his lore was engraft, something foreign that grew in him,
Exhausting the sap of the native and true in him,
So that when a man came with a soul that was new in him,
Carving new forms of truth out of Nature's old granite,
New and old at their birth, like Le Verrier's planet,
Which, to get a true judgment, themselves must create
In the soul of their critic the measure and weight,
Being rather themselves a fresh standard of grace,
To compute their own judge, and assign him his place,
Our reviewer would crawl all about it and round it,
And, reporting each circumstance just as he found it,
Without the least malice, — his record would be

Profoundly æsthetic as that of a flea,
Which, supping on Wordsworth, should print, for our sakes,
Recollections of nights with the Bard of the Lakes,
Or, lodged by an Arab guide, ventured to render a
Comprehensive account of the ruins at Denderah.

As I said, he was never precisely unkind,
The defect in his brain was just absence of mind;
If he boasted, 't was simply that he was self-made,
A position which I, for one, never gainsaid,
My respect for my Maker supposing a skill
In his works which our Hero would answer but ill;
And I trust that the mould which he used may be cracked, or he,
Made bold by success, may enlarge his phylactery,
And set up a kind of a man-manufactory, —
An event which I shudder to think about, seeing
That Man is a moral, accountable being.

He meant well enough, but was still in the way,
As dunces still are, let them be where they may;
Indeed, they appear to come into existence
To impede other folks with their awkward assistance;
If you set up a dunce on the very North pole
All alone with himself, I believe, on my soul,
He 'd manage to get betwixt somebody's shins,
And pitch him down bodily, all in his sins,
To the grave polar bears sitting round on the ice,
All shortening their grace, to be in for a slice;
Or, if he found nobody else there to pother,
Why, one of his legs would just trip up the other,
For there 's nothing we read of in torture's inventions,
Like a well-meaning dunce, with the best of intentions.

A terrible fellow to meet in society,
Not the toast that he buttered was ever so
    dry at tea;
There he 'd sit at the table and stir in his
    sugar,
Crouching close for a spring, all the while,
    like a cougar;
Be sure of your facts, of your measures
    and weights,
Of your time, — he 's as fond as an Arab of
    dates;
You 'll be telling, perhaps, in your comical
    way,
Of something you 've seen in the course of
    the day;
And, just as you 're tapering out the con-
    clusion,
You venture an ill-fated classic allusion, —
The girls have all got their laughs ready,
    when, whack !
The cougar comes down on your thunder-
    struck back !
You had left out a comma, — your Greek's
    put in joint,
And pointed at cost of your story's whole
    point.
In the course of the evening, you find
    chance for certain
Soft speeches to Anne, in the shade of the
    curtain:
You tell her your heart can be likened to
    one flower,
" And that, O most charming of women, 's
    the sunflower,
Which turns " — here a clear nasal voice,
    to your terror,
From outside the curtain, says, " That's all
    an error."
As for him, he 's — no matter, he never
    grew tender,
Sitting after a ball, with his feet on the
    fender,
Shaping somebody's sweet features out of
    cigar smoke
(Though he 'd willingly grant you that
    such doings are smoke);
All women he damns with *mutabile semper*,
And if ever he felt something like love's
    distemper,
'T was tow'rds a young lady who spoke
    ancient Mexican,
And assisted her father in making a lexi-
    con;
Though I recollect hearing him get quite
    ferocious

About Mary Clausum, the mistress of Gro-
    tius,
Or something of that sort, — but, no more
    to bore ye
With character-painting, I 'll turn to my
    story.

Now, Apollo, who finds it convenient
    sometimes
To get his court clear of the makers of
    rhymes,
The *genus*, I think it is called, *irritabile*,
Every one of whom thinks himself treated
    most shabbily,
And nurses a — what is it ? — *immedicabile*,
Which keeps him at boiling-point, hot for a
    quarrel,
As bitter as wormwood, and sourer than
    sorrel,
If any poor devil but look at a laurel; —
Apollo, I say, being sick of their rioting
(Though he sometimes acknowledged their
    verse had a quieting
Effect after dinner, and seemed to sug-
    gest a
Retreat to the shrine of a tranquil siesta),
Kept our Hero at hand, who, by means of
    a bray,
Which he gave to the life, drove the rabble
    away;
And if that would n't do, he was sure to
    succeed,
If he took his review out and offered to
    read;
Or, failing in plans of this milder descrip-
    tion,
He would ask for their aid to get up a
    subscription,
Considering that authorship was n't a rich
    craft,
To print the " American drama of Witch-
    craft."
" Stay, I 'll read you a scene," — but he
    hardly began,
Ere Apollo shrieked " Help ! " and the
    authors all ran:
And once, when these purgatives acted
    with less spirit,
And the desperate case asked a remedy
    desperate,
He drew from his pocket a foolscap epistle
As calmly as if 't were a nine-barrelled
    pistol,
And threatened them all with the judg-
    ment to come,

Of " A wandering Star's first impressions
  of Rome."
" Stop ! stop ! " with their hands o'er their
  ears, screamed the Muses,
" He may go off and murder himself, if he
  chooses,
'T was a means self-defence only sanctioned
  his trying,
'T is mere massacre now that the enemy 's
  flying;
If he 's forced to 't again, and we happen
  to be there,
Give us each a large handkerchief soaked
  in strong ether."

I called this a " Fable for Critics ; "
  you think it 's
More like a display of my rhythmical
  trinkets;
My plot, like an icicle, 's slender and slip-
  pery,
Every moment more slender, and likely
  to slip awry,
And the reader unwilling *in loco desipere*
Is free to jump over as much of my frip-
  pery
As he fancies, and, if he 's a provident
  skipper, he
May have like Odysseus control of the
  gales,
And get safe to port, ere his patience quite
  fails;
Moreover, although 't is a slender return
For your toil and expense, yet my paper
  will burn,
And, if you have manfully struggled thus
  far with me,
You may e'en twist me up, and just light
  your cigar with me:
If too angry for that, you can tear me in
  pieces,
And my *membra disjecta* consign to the
  breezes,
A fate like great Ratzau's, whom one of
  those bores,
Who beflead with bad verses poor Louis
  Quatorze,
Describes (the first verse somehow ends
  with *victoire*),
As *dispersant partout et ses membres et sa
  gloire;*
Or, if I were over-desirous of earning
A repute among noodles for classical learn-
  ing,
I could pick you a score of allusions, i-wis,

As new as the jests of *Didaskalos tis;*
Better still, I could make out a good solid
  list
From authors recondite who do not exist, —
But that would be naughty: at least, I
  could twist
Something out of Absyrtus, or turn your
  inquiries
After Milton's prose metaphor, drawn from
  Osiris;
But, as Cicero says he won't say this or that
(A fetch, I must say, most transparent and
  flat),
After saying whate'er he could possibly
  think of, —
I simply will state that I pause on the
  brink of
A mire, ankle-deep, of deliberate confusion,
Made up of old jumbles of classic allusion:
So, when you were thinking yourselves to
  be pitied,
Just conceive how much harder your teeth
  you 'd have gritted,
An 't were not for the dulness I 've kindly
  omitted.

I 'd apologize here for my many digres-
  sions,
Were it not that I 'm certain to trip into
  fresh ones
('T is so hard to escape if you get in their
  mesh once);
Just reflect, if you please, how 't is said by
  Horatius,
That Mæonides nods now and then, and,
  my gracious !
It certainly does look a little bit ominous
When he gets under way with *ton d'
  apameibomenos.*
(Here a something occurs which I 'll just
  clap a rhyme to,
And say it myself, ere a Zoilus have time
  to, —
Any author a nap like Van Winkle's may
  take,
If he only contrive to keep readers awake,
But he 'll very soon find himself laid on
  the shelf,
If *they* fall a-nodding when he nods him-
  self.)

Once for all, to return, and to stay, will
  I, nill I —
When Phœbus expressed his desire for a
  lily,

Our Hero, whose homœopathic sagacity
With an ocean of zeal mixed his drop of
    capacity,
Set off for the garden as fast as the wind
(Or, to take a comparison more to my
    mind,
As a sound politician leaves conscience be-
    hind),
And leaped the low fence, as a party hack
    jumps
O'er his principles, when something else
    turns up trumps.

He was gone a long time, and Apollo,
    meanwhile,
Went over some sonnets of his with a file,
For, of all compositions, he thought that the
    sonnet
Best repaid all the toil you expended upon
    it;
It should reach with one impulse the end of
    its course,
And for one final blow collect all of its
    force;
Not a verse should be salient, but each one
    should tend
With a wave-like up-gathering to break at
    the end;
So, condensing the strength here, there
    smoothing a wry kink,
He was killing the time, when up walked
    Mr. D—— ;
At a few steps behind him, a small man in
    glasses
Went dodging about, muttering, "Murder-
    ers ! asses !"
From out of his pocket a paper he 'd take,
With a proud look of martyrdom tied to
    its stake,
And, reading a squib at himself, he 'd say,
    " Here I see
'Gainst American letters a bloody conspir-
    acy,
They are all by my personal enemies writ-
    ten;
I must post an anonymous letter to Britain,
And show that this gall is the merest sug-
    gestion
Of spite at my zeal on the Copyright ques-
    tion,
For, on this side the water, 't is prudent to
    pull
O'er the eyes of the public their national
    wool,
By accusing of slavish respect to John Bull

All American authors who have more or
    less
Of that anti-American humbug — success,
While in private we 're always embracing
    the knees
Of some twopenny editor over the seas,
And licking his critical shoes, for you
    know 't is
The whole aim of our lives to get one Eng-
    lish notice;
My American puffs I would willingly burn
    all
(They 're all from one source, monthly,
    weekly, diurnal)
To get but a kick from a transmarine jour-
    nal !"

So, culling the gibes of each critical
    scorner
As if they were plums, and himself were
    Jack Horner,
He came cautiously on, peeping round every
    corner,
And into each hole where a weasel might
    pass in,
Expecting the knife of some critic assassin,
Who stabs to the heart with a caricature,
Not so bad as those daubs of the Sun, to be
    sure,
Yet done with a dagger-o'-type, whose vile
    portraits
Disperse all one's good and condense all
    one's poor traits.

Apollo looked up, hearing footsteps ap-
    proaching,
And slipped out of sight the new rhymes
    he was broaching, —
"Good day, Mr. D——, I 'm happy to meet
With a scholar so ripe, and a critic so neat,
Who through Grub Street the soul of a
    gentleman carries ;
What news from that suburb of London and
    Paris
Which latterly makes such shrill claims to
    monopolize
The credit of being the New World's me-
    tropolis ?"

" Why, nothing of consequence, save this
    attack
On my friend there, behind, by some pitiful
    hack,
Who thinks every national author a poor
    one,

That is n't a copy of something that 's for-
eign,
And assaults the American Dick— "

"Nay, 't is clear
That your Damon there 's fond of a flea in
his ear,
And, if no one else furnished them gratis,
on tick
He would buy some himself, just to hear the
old click ;
Why, I honestly think, if some fool in Japan
Should turn up his nose at the ' Poems on
Man,'
(Which contain many verses as fine, by the
bye,
As any that lately came under my eye,)
Your friend there by some inward instinct
would know it,
Would get it translated, reprinted, and show
it ;
As a man might take off a high stock to
exhibit
The autograph round his own neck of the
gibbet ;
Nor would let it rest so, but fire column after
column,
Signed Cato, or Brutus, or something as
solemn,
By way of displaying his critical crosses,
And tweaking that poor transatlantic pro-
boscis,
His broadsides resulting (this last there 's no
doubt of)
In successively sinking the craft they 're
fired out of.
Now nobody knows when an author is hit,
If he have not a public hysterical fit ;
Let him only keep close in his snug garret's
dim ether,
And nobody 'd think of his foes — or of him
either ;
If an author have any least fibre of worth
in him,
Abuse would but tickle the organ of mirth
in him ;
All the critics on earth cannot crush with
their ban
One word that 's in tune with the nature of
man."

"Well, perhaps so ; meanwhile I have
brought you a book,
Into which if you 'll just have the goodness
to look,

You may feel so delighted (when once you
are through it)
As to deem it not unworth your while to re-
view it,
And I think I can promise your thoughts,
if you do,
A place in the next Democratic Review."

"The most thankless of gods you must
surely have thought me,
For this is the forty-fourth copy you 've
brought me ;
I have given them away, or at least I have
tried,
But I 've forty-two left, standing all side by
side
(The man who accepted that one copy
died), —
From one end of a shelf to the other they
reach,
' With the author's respects ' neatly written
in each.
The publisher, sure, will proclaim a Te
Deum,
When he hears of that order the British
Museum
Has sent for one set of what books were first
printed
In America, little or big, — for 't is hinted
That this is the first truly tangible hope he
Has ever had raised for the sale of a copy.
I 've thought very often 't would be a good
thing
In all public collections of books, if a wing
Were set off by itself, like the seas from the
dry lands,
Marked *Literature suited to desolate islands*,
And filled with such books as could never be
read
Save by readers of proofs, forced to do it
for bread, —
Such books as one 's wrecked on in small
country taverns,
Such as hermits might mortify over in
caverns,
Such as Satan, if printing had then been
invented,
As the climax of woe, would to Job have
presented,
Such as Crusoe might dip in, although there
are few so
Outrageously cornered by fate as poor Cru-
soe ;
And since the philanthropists just now are
banging

And gibbeting all who 're in favor of hang-
ing
(Though Cheever has proved that the Bible
and Altar
Were let down from Heaven at the end of a
halter,
And that vital religion would dull and grow
callous,
Unrefreshed, now and then, with a sniff of
the gallows), —
And folks are beginning to think it looks
odd,
To choke a poor scamp for the glory of
God;
And that He who esteems the Virginia reel
A bait to draw saints from their spiritual
weal,
And regards the quadrille as a far greater
knavery
Than crushing his African children with
slavery, —
Since all who take part in a waltz or cotil-
lon
Are mounted for hell on the Devil's own
pillion,
Who, as every true orthodox Christian well
knows,
Approaches the heart through the door of
the toes, —
That He, I was saying, whose judgments
are stored
For such as take steps in despite of his
word,
Should look with delight on the agonized
prancing
Of a wretch who has not the least ground
for his dancing,
While the State, standing by, sings a verse
from the Psalter
About offering to God on his favorite hal-
ter,
And, when the legs droop from their twitch-
ing divergence,
Sells the clothes to a Jew, and the corpse
to the surgeons; —
Now, instead of all this, I think I can di-
rect you all
To a criminal code both humane and effect-
ual; —
I propose to shut up every doer of wrong
With these desperate books, for such term,
short or long,
As, by statute in such cases made and pro-
vided,
Shall be by your wise legislators decided:

Thus: Let murderers be shut, to grow
wiser and cooler,
At hard labor for life on the works of
Miss ——;
Petty thieves, kept from flagranter crimes
by their fears,
Shall peruse Yankee Doodle a blank term
of years, —
That American Punch, like the English, no
doubt, —
Just the sugar and lemons and spirit left
out.

" But stay, here comes Tityrus Griswold,
and leads on
The flocks whom he first plucks alive, and
then feeds on, —
A loud-cackling swarm, in whose feathers
warm drest,
He goes for as perfect a — swan as the rest.

"There comes Emerson first, whose rich
words, every one,
Are like gold nails in temples to hang tro-
phies on,
Whose prose is grand verse, while his
verse, the Lord knows,
Is some of it pr— No, 't is not even
prose;
I 'm speaking of metres; some poems have
welled
From those rare depths of soul that have
ne'er been excelled;
They 're not epics, but that does n't matter
a pin,
In creating, the only hard thing 's to
begin;
A grass-blade 's no easier to make than an
oak;
If you 've once found the way, you 've
achieved the grand stroke;
In the worst of his poems are mines of rich
matter,
But thrown in a heap with a crash and a
clatter;
Now it is not one thing nor another alone
Makes a poem, but rather the general
tone,
The something pervading, uniting the
whole,
The before unconceived, unconceivable soul,
So that just in removing this trifle or that,
you
Take away, as it were, a chief limb of the
statue;

Roots, wood, bark, and leaves singly per-
    fect may be,
But, clapt hodge-podge together, they
    don't make a tree.

" But, to come back to Emerson (whom,
    by the way,
I believe we left waiting), — his is, we may
    say,
A Greek head on right Yankee shoulders,
    whose range
Has Olympus for one pole, for t' other the
    Exchange;
He seems, to my thinking (although I 'm
    afraid
The comparison must, long ere this, have
    been made),
A Plotinus-Montaigne, where the Egyp-
    tian's gold mist
And the Gascon's shrewd wit cheek-by-jowl
    coexist;
All admire, and yet scarcely six converts
    he 's got
To I don't (nor they either) exactly know
    what;
For though he builds glorious temples, 't is
    odd
He leaves never a doorway to get in a
    god.
'T is refreshing to old-fashioned people like
    me
To meet such a primitive Pagan as he,
In whose mind all creation is duly re-
    spected
As parts of himself — just a little pro-
    jected;
And who 's willing to worship the stars and
    the sun,
A convert to — nothing but Emerson.
So perfect a balance there is in his head,
That he talks of things sometimes as if
    they were dead;
Life, nature, love, God, and affairs of that
    sort,
He looks at as merely ideas; in short,
As if they were fossils stuck round in a
    cabinet,
Of such vast extent that our earth 's a mere
    dab in it;
Composed just as he is inclined to conjec-
    ture her,
Namely, one part pure earth, ninety-nine
    parts pure lecturer;
You are filled with delight at his clear
    demonstration,

Each figure, word, gesture, just fits the
    occasion,
With the quiet precision of science he 'll
    sort 'em,
But you can't help suspecting the whole a
    post mortem.

" There are persons, mole-blind to the
    soul's make and style,
Who insist on a likeness 'twixt him and
    Carlyle;
To compare him with Plato would be
    vastly fairer,
Carlyle 's the more burly, but E. is the
    rarer;
He sees fewer objects, but clearlier, true-
    lier,
If C. 's as original, E. 's more peculiar;
That he 's more of a man you might say of
    the one,
Of the other he 's more of an Emerson;
C. 's the Titan, as shaggy of mind as of
    limb, —
E. the clear-eyed Olympian, rapid and
    slim;
The one 's two thirds Norseman, the other
    half Greek,
Where the one 's most abounding, the
    other 's to seek;
C.'s generals require to be seen in the
    mass, —
E.'s specialties gain if enlarged by the glass;
C. gives nature and God his own fits of the
    blues,
And rims common-sense things with mysti-
    cal hues, —
E. sits in a mystery calm and intense,
And looks coolly around him with sharp
    common-sense ;
C. shows you how every-day matters unite
With the dim transdiurnal recesses of
    night, —
While E., in a plain, preternatural way,
Makes mysteries matters of mere every
    day;
C. draws all his characters quite *à la* Fu-
    seli, —
Not sketching their bundles of muscles and
    thews illy,
He paints with a brush so untamed and pro-
    fuse,
They seem nothing but bundles of muscles
    and thews ;
E. is rather like Flaxman, lines strait and
    severe,

And a colorless outline, but full, round, and
  clear ; —
To the men he thinks worthy he frankly
  accords
The design of a white marble statue in
  words.
C. labors to get at the centre, and then
Take a reckoning from there of his actions
  and men ;
E. calmly assumes the said centre as grant-
  ed,
And, given himself, has whatever is wanted.

" He has imitators in scores, who omit
No part of the man but his wisdom and
  wit, —
Who go carefully o'er the sky-blue of his
  brain,
And when he has skimmed it once, skim it
  again ;
If at all they resemble him, you may be sure
  it is
Because their shoals mirror his mists and
  obscurities,
As a mud-puddle seems deep as heaven for
  a minute,
While a cloud that floats o'er is reflected
  within it.

" There comes ——, for instance ; to see
  him 's rare sport,
Tread in Emerson's tracks with legs pain-
  fully short ;
How he jumps, how he strains, and gets red
  in the face,
To keep step with the mystagogue's natural
  pace !
He follows as close as a stick to a rocket,
His fingers exploring the prophet's each
  pocket.
Fie, for shame, brother bard ; with good fruit
  of your own,
Can't you let Neighbor Emerson's orchards
  alone ?
Besides, 't is no use, you 'll not find e'en a
  core, —
—— has picked up all the windfalls before.
They might strip every tree, and E. never
  would catch 'em,
His Hesperides have no rude dragon to
  watch 'em ;
When they send him a dishful, and ask him
  to try 'em,
He never suspects how the sly rogues came
  by 'em ;

He wonders why 't is there are none such
  his trees on,
And thinks 'em the best he has tasted this
  season.

" Yonder, calm as a cloud, Alcott stalks
  in a dream,
And fancies himself in thy groves, Aca-
  deme,
With the Parthenon nigh, and the olive-trees
  o'er him,
And never a fact to perplex him or bore
  him,
With a snug room at Plato's when night
  comes, to walk to,
And people from morning till midnight to
  talk to,
And from midnight till morning, nor snore
  in their listening ; —
So he muses, his face with the joy of it glis-
  tening,
For his highest conceit of a happiest state is
Where they 'd live upon acorns, and hear
  him talk gratis;
And indeed, I believe, no man ever talked
  better, —
Each sentence hangs perfectly poised to a
  letter ;
He seems piling words, but there 's royal
  dust hid
In the heart of each sky-piercing pyramid.
While he talks he is great, but goes out like
  a taper,
If you shut him up closely with pen, ink,
  and paper;
Yet his fingers itch for 'em from morning
  till night,
And he thinks he does wrong if he don't
  always write;
In this, as in all things, a lamb among men,
He goes to sure death when he goes to his
  pen.

" Close behind him is Brownson, his mouth
  very full
With attempting to gulp a Gregorian bull ;
Who contrives, spite of that, to pour out as
  he goes
A stream of transparent and forcible prose;
He shifts quite about, then proceeds to ex-
  pound
That 't is merely the earth, not himself, that
  turns round,
And wishes it clearly impressed on your
  mind

That the weathercock rules and not follows
the wind ;
Proving first, then as deftly confuting each
side,
With no doctrine pleased that 's not some-
where denied,
He lays the denier away on the shelf,
And then — down beside him lies gravely
himself.
He 's the Salt River boatman, who always
stands willing
To convey friend or foe without charging a
shilling,
And so fond of the trip that, when leisure 's
to spare,
He 'll row himself up, if he can't get a fare.
The worst of it is, that his logic 's so strong,
That of two sides he commonly chooses the
wrong ;
If there *is* only one, why, he 'll split it in two,
And first pummel this half, then that, black
and blue.
That white 's white needs no proof, but it
takes a deep fellow
To prove it jet-black, and that jet-black is
yellow.
He offers the true faith to drink in a
sieve, —
When it reaches your lips there 's naught
left to believe
But a few silly- (syllo-, I mean,) -gisms
that squat 'em
Like tadpoles, o'erjoyed with the mud at the
bottom.

" There is Willis, all *natty* and jaunty and
gay,
Who says his best things in so foppish a
way,
With conceits and pet phrases so thickly
o'erlaying 'em,
That one hardly knows whether to thank
him for saying 'em;
Over-ornament ruins both poem and prose,
Just conceive of a Muse with a ring in her
nose !
His prose had a natural grace of its own,
And enough of it, too, if he 'd let it alone;
But he twitches and jerks so, one fairly gets
tired,
And is forced to forgive where one might
have admired;
Yet whenever it slips away free and un-
laced,
It runs like a stream with a musical waste,

And gurgles along with the liquidest
sweep; —
'T is not deep as a river, but who 'd have it
deep ?
In a country where scarcely a village is
found
That has not its author sublime and pro-
found,
For some one to be slightly shallow 's a duty,
And Willis's shallowness makes half his
beauty.
His prose winds along with a blithe, gur-
gling error,
And reflects all of Heaven it can see in its
mirror:
'T is a narrowish strip, but it is not an arti-
fice;
'T is the true out-of-doors with its genuine
hearty phiz;
It is Nature herself, and there 's something
in that,
Since most brains reflect but the crown of a
hat.
Few volumes I know to read under a tree,
More truly delightful than his A l'Abri,
With the shadows of leaves flowing over
your book,
Like ripple-shades netting the bed of a
brook;
With June coming softly your shoulder to
look over,
Breezes waiting to turn every leaf of your
book over,
And Nature to criticise still as you read, —
The page that bears that is a rare one in-
deed.

" He 's so innate a cockney, that had he
been born
Where plain bare-skin 's the only full-dress
that is worn,
He 'd have given his own such an air that
you 'd say
'T had been made by a tailor to lounge in
Broadway.
His nature 's a glass of champagne with the
foam on 't,
As tender as Fletcher, as witty as Beau-
mont;
So his best things are done in the flush of
the moment;
If he wait, all is spoiled; he may stir it and
shake it,
But, the fixed air once gone, he can never
re-make it.

He might be a marvel of easy delightfulness,
If he would not sometimes leave the *r* out
of sprightfulness;
And he ought to let Scripture alone — 't is
self-slaughter,
For nobody likes inspiration-and-water.
He 'd have been just the fellow to sup at
the Mermaid,
Cracking jokes at rare Ben, with an eye to
the barmaid,
His wit running up as Canary ran down, —
The topmost bright bubble on the wave of
The Town.

" Here comes Parker, the Orson of par-
sons, a man
Whom the Church undertook to put under
her ban
(The Church of Socinus, I mean), — his
opinions
Being So- (ultra) -cinian, they shocked the
Socinians;
They believed — faith, I 'm puzzled — I
think I may call
Their belief a believing in nothing at all,
Or something of that sort; I know they all
went
For a general union of total dissent:
He went a step farther; without cough or
hem,
He frankly avowed he believed not in them;
And, before he could be jumbled up or pre-
vented,
From their orthodox kind of dissent he
dissented.
There was heresy here, you perceive, for
the right
Of privately judging means simply that
light
Has been granted to *me*, for deciding on
you;
And in happier times, before Atheism grew,
The deed contained clauses for cooking you
too:
Now at Xerxes and Knut we all laugh, yet
our foot
With the same wave is wet that mocked
Xerxes and Knut,
And we all entertain a secure private notion,
That our *Thus far!* will have a great weight
with the ocean.
'T was so with our liberal Christians: they
bore
With sincerest conviction their chairs to the
shore;

They brandished their worn theological
birches,
Bade natural progress keep out of the
Churches,
And expected the lines they had drawn to
prevail
With the fast - rising tide to keep out of
their pale;
They had formerly dammed the Pontifical
See,
And the same thing, they thought, would
do nicely for P. ;
But he turned up his nose at their mum-
ming and shamming,
And cared (shall I say ?) not a d—— for
their damming;
So they first read him out of their church,
and next minute
Turned round and declared he had never
been in it.
But the ban was too small or the man was
too big,
For he recks not their bells, books, and
candles a fig
(He scarce looks like a man who would *stay*
treated shabbily,
Sophroniscus' son's head o'er the features
of Rabelais); —
He bangs and bethwacks them,— their backs
he salutes
With the whole tree of knowledge torn up
by the roots;
His sermons with satire are plenteously
verjuiced,
And he talks in one breath of Confutzee,
Cass, Zerduscht,
Jack Robinson, Peter the Hermit, Strap,
Dathan,
Cush, Pitt (not the bottomless, *that* he 's
no faith in),
Pan, Pillicock, Shakespeare, Paul, Toots,
Monsieur Tonson,
Aldebaran, Alcander, Ben Khorat, Ben
Jonson,
Thoth, Richter, Joe Smith, Father Paul,
Judah Monis,
Musæus, Muretus, *hem*, — μ Scorpionis,
Maccabee, Maccaboy, Mac — Mac — ah !
Machiavelli,
Condorcet, Count d'Orsay, Conder, Say,
Ganganelli,
Orion, O'Connell, the Chevalier D'O,
(See the Memoirs of Sully,) τὸ πᾶν, the
great toe
Of the statue of Jupiter, now made to pass

For that of Jew Peter by good Romish
    brass,
(You may add for yourselves, for I find it
    a bore,
All the names you have ever, or not, heard
    before,
And when you 've done that — why, invent
    a few more).
His hearers can't tell you on Sunday be-
    forehand,
If in that day's discourse they 'll be Bibled
    or Koraned,
For he 's seized the idea (by his martyr-
    dom fired)
That all men (not orthodox) *may be* in-
    spired;
Yet though wisdom profane with his creed
    he may weave in,
He makes it quite clear what he *does n't*
    believe in,
While some, who decry him, think all
    Kingdom Come
Is a sort of a, kind of a, species of Hum,
Of which, as it were, so to speak, not a
    crumb
Would be left, if we did n't keep carefully
    mum,
And, to make a clean breast, that 't is per-
    fectly plain
That *all* kinds of wisdom are somewhat
    profane;
Now P.'s creed than this may be lighter or
    darker,
But in one thing, 't is clear, he has faith,
    namely — Parker;
And this is what makes him the crowd-
    drawing preacher,
There 's a background of god to each hard-
    working feature,
Every word that he speaks has been fierily
    furnaced
In the blast of a life that has struggled in
    earnest:
There he stands, looking more like a
    ploughman than priest,
If not dreadfully awkward, not graceful at
    least,
His gestures all downright and same, if
    you will,
As of brown-fisted Hobnail in hoeing a
    drill;
But his periods fall on you, stroke after
    stroke,
Like the blows of a lumberer felling an
    oak,

You forget the man wholly, you 're thank-
    ful to meet
With a preacher who smacks of the field
    and the street,
And to hear, you 're not over-particular
    whence,
Almost Taylor's profusion, quite Latimer's
    sense.

"There is Bryant, as quiet, as cool, and
    as dignified,
As a smooth, silent iceberg, that never is
    ignified,
Save when by reflection 't is kindled o'
    nights
With a semblance of flame by the chill
    Northern Lights.
He may rank (Griswold says so) first bard
    of your nation
(There 's no doubt that he stands in su-
    preme iceolation),
Your topmost Parnassus he may set his
    heel on,
But no warm applauses come, peal follow-
    ing peal on, —
He 's too smooth and too polished to hang
    any zeal on:
Unqualified merits, I 'll grant, if you
    choose, he has 'em,
But he lacks the one merit of kindling
    enthusiasm;
If he stir you at all, it is just, on my soul,
Like being stirred up with the very North
    Pole.

"He is very nice reading in summer,
    but *inter*
Nos, we don't want *extra* freezing in win-
    ter;
Take him up in the depth of July, my ad-
    vice is,
When you feel an Egyptian devotion to
    ices.
But, deduct all you can, there 's enough
    that 's right good in him,
He has a true soul for field, river, and
    wood in him;
And his heart, in the midst of brick walls,
    or where'er it is,
Glows, softens, and thrills with the tender-
    est charities —
To you mortals that delve in this trade-
    ridden planet ?
No, to old Berkshire's hills, with their
    limestone and granite.

If you 're one who *in loco* (add *foco* here) *desipis*,
You will get of his outermost heart (as I guess) a piece;
But you 'd get deeper down if you came as a precipice,
And would break the last seal of its inwardest fountain,
If you only could palm yourself off for a mountain.
Mr. Quivis, or somebody quite as discerning,
Some scholar who 's hourly expecting his learning,
Calls B. the American Wordsworth; but Wordsworth
May be rated at more than your whole tuneful herd 's worth.
No, don't be absurd, he 's an excellent Bryant;
But, my friends, you 'll endanger the life of your client,
By attempting to stretch him up into a giant:
If you choose to compare him, I think there are two per-
-sons fit for a parallel — Thomson and Cowper;[1]
I don't mean exactly, — there 's something of each,
There 's T.'s love of nature, C.'s penchant to preach;
Just mix up their minds so that C.'s spice of craziness
Shall balance and neutralize T.'s turn for laziness,
And it gives you a brain cool, quite frictionless, quiet,
Whose internal police nips the buds of all riot, —
A brain like a permanent strait-jacket put on
The heart that strives vainly to burst off a button, —
A brain which, without being slow or mechanic,
Does more than a larger less drilled, more volcanic;
He 's a Cowper condensed, with no craziness bitten,
And the advantage that Wordsworth before him had written.

[1] To demonstrate quickly and easily how per-
-versely absurd 't is to sound this name *Cowper*,
As people in general call him named *super*,
I remark that he rhymes it himself with horse-trooper.

"But, my dear little bardlings, don't prick up your ears
Nor suppose I would rank you and Bryant as peers;
If I call him an iceberg, I don't mean to say
There is nothing in that which is grand in its way;
He is almost the one of your poets that knows
How much grace, strength, and dignity lie in Repose;
If he sometimes fall short, he is too wise to mar
His thought's modest fulness by going too far;
'T would be well if your authors should all make a trial
Of what virtue there is in severe self-denial,
And measure their writings by Hesiod's staff,
Which teaches that all has less value than half.

"There is Whittier, whose swelling and vehement heart
Strains the strait-breasted drab of the Quaker apart,
And reveals the live Man, still supreme and erect,
Underneath the bemummying wrappers of sect;
There was ne'er a man born who had more of the swing
Of the true lyric bard and all that kind of thing;
And his failures arise (though he seem not to know it)
From the very same cause that has made him a poet, —
A fervor of mind which knows no separation
'Twixt simple excitement and pure inspiration,
As my Pythoness erst sometimes erred from not knowing
If 't were I or mere wind through her tripod was blowing;
Let his mind once get head in its favorite direction
And the torrent of verse bursts the dams of reflection,
While, borne with the rush of the metre along,

The poet may chance to go right or go
  wrong,
Content with the whirl and delirium of
  song;
Then his grammar's not always correct,
  nor his rhymes,
And he's prone to repeat his own lyrics
  sometimes,
Not his best, though, for those are struck
  off at white-heats
When the heart in his breast like a trip-
  hammer beats,
And can ne'er be repeated again any more
Than they could have been carefully plot-
  ted before:
Like old what's-his-name there at the bat-
  tle of Hastings
(Who, however, gave more than mere
  rhythmical bastings),
Our Quaker leads off metaphorical fights
For reform and whatever they call human
  rights,
Both singing and striking in front of the
  war,
And hitting his foes with the mallet of
  Thor;
Anne haec, one exclaims, on beholding his
  knocks,
Vestis filii tui, O leather-clad Fox?
Can that be thy son, in the battle's mid
  din,
Preaching brotherly love and then driving
  it in
To the brain of the tough old Goliath of
  sin,
With the smoothest of pebbles from Cas-
  taly's spring
Impressed on his hard moral sense with a
  sling?

"All honor and praise to the right-
  hearted bard
Who was true to The Voice when such
  service was hard,
Who himself was so free he dared sing for
  the slave
When to look but a protest in silence was
  brave;
All honor and praise to the women and men
Who spoke out for the dumb and the
  down-trodden then!
It needs not to name them, already for
  each
I see History preparing the statue and
  niche;

They were harsh, but shall *you* be so
  shocked at hard words
Who have beaten your pruning-hooks up
  into swords,
Whose rewards and hurrahs men are surer
  to gain
By the reaping of men and of women than
  grain?
Why should *you* stand aghast at their
  fierce wordy war, if
You scalp one another for Bank or for
  Tariff?
Your calling them cut-throats and knaves
  all day long
Does n't prove that the use of hard lan-
  guage is wrong;
While the World's heart beats quicker to
  think of such men
As signed Tyranny's doom with a bloody
  steel-pen,
While on Fourth-of-Julys beardless orators
  fright one
With hints at Harmodius and Aristogeiton,
You need not look shy at your sisters and
  brothers
Who stab with sharp words for the free-
  dom of others;—
No, a wreath, twine a wreath for the loyal
  and true
Who, for sake of the many, dared stand
  with the few,
Not of blood-spattered laurel for enemies
  braved,
But of broad, peaceful oak-leaves for citi-
  zens saved!

"Here comes Dana, abstractedly loiter-
  ing along,
Involved in a paulo-post-future of song,
Who'll be going to write what'll never be
  written
Till the Muse, ere he think of it, gives him
  the mitten,—
Who is so well aware of how things should
  be done,
That his own works displease him before
  they're begun,—
Who so well all that makes up good poetry
  knows,
That the best of his poems is written in
  prose;
All saddled and bridled stood Pegasus wait-
  ing,
He was booted and spurred, but he loitered
  debating;

In a very grave question his soul was immersed, —
Which foot in the stirrup he ought to put first;
And, while this point and that he judicially dwelt on,
He, somehow or other, had written Paul Felton,
Whose beauties or faults, whichsoever you see there,
You'll allow only genius could hit upon either.
That he once was the Idle Man none will deplore,
But I fear he will never be anything more;
The ocean of song heaves and glitters before him,
The depth and the vastness and longing sweep o'er him,
He knows every breaker and shoal on the chart,
He has the Coast Pilot and so on by heart,
Yet he spends his whole life, like the man in the fable,
In learning to swim on his library-table.

"There swaggers John Neal, who has wasted in Maine
The sinews and cords of his pugilist brain,
Who might have been poet, but that, in its stead, he
Preferred to believe that he was so already;
Too hasty to wait till Art's ripe fruit should drop,
He must pelt down an unripe and colicky crop;
Who took to the law, and had this sterling plea for it,
It required him to quarrel, and paid him a fee for it;
A man who's made less than he might have, because
He always has thought himself more than he was, —
Who, with very good natural gifts as a bard,
Broke the strings of his lyre out by striking too hard,
And cracked half the notes of a truly fine voice,
Because song drew less instant attention than noise.
Ah, men do not know how much strength is in poise,
That he goes the farthest who goes far enough,

And that all beyond that is just bother and stuff.
No vain man matures, he makes too much new wood;
His blooms are too thick for the fruit to be good;
'T is the modest man ripens, 't is he that achieves,
Just what's needed of sunshine and shade he receives;
Grapes, to mellow, require the cool dark of their leaves;
Neal wants balance; he throws his mind always too far,
Whisking out flocks of comets, but never a star;
He has so much muscle, and loves so to show it,
That he strips himself naked to prove he's a poet,
And, to show he could leap Art's wide ditch, if he tried,
Jumps clean o'er it, and into the hedge t' other side.
He has strength, but there's nothing about him in keeping;
One gets surelier onward by walking than leaping;
He has used his own sinews himself to distress,
And had done vastly more had he done vastly less;
In letters, too soon is as bad as too late ;
Could he only have waited he might have been great;
But he plumped into Helicon up to the waist,
And muddied the stream ere he took his first taste.

"There is Hawthorne, with genius so shrinking and rare
That you hardly at first see the strength that is there;
A frame so robust, with a nature so sweet,
So earnest, so graceful, so lithe and so fleet,
Is worth a descent from Olympus to meet;
'T is as if a rough oak that for ages had stood,
With his gnarled bony branches like ribs of the wood,
Should bloom, after cycles of struggle and scathe,
With a single anemone trembly and rathe;

His strength is so tender, his wildness so
meek,
That a suitable parallel sets one to seek, —
He's a John Bunyan Fouqué, a Puritan
Tieck;
When Nature was shaping him, clay was
not granted
For making so full-sized a man as she
wanted,
So, to fill out her model, a little she spared
From some finer-grained stuff for a woman
prepared,
And she could not have hit a more excellent
plan
For making him fully and perfectly man.
The success of her scheme gave her so much
delight,
That she tried it again, shortly after, in
Dwight;
Only, while she was kneading and shaping
the clay,
She sang to her work in her sweet childish
way,
And found, when she'd put the last touch
to his soul,
That the music had somehow got mixed
with the whole.

"Here's Cooper, who's written six vol-
umes to show
He's as good as a lord : well, let's grant
that he's so ;
If a person prefer that description of praise,
Why, a coronet's certainly cheaper than
bays;
But he need take no pains to convince us
he's not
(As his enemies say) the American Scott.
Choose any twelve men, and let C. read
aloud
That one of his novels of which he's most
proud,
And I'd lay any bet that, without ever
quitting
Their box, they'd be all, to a man, for ac-
quitting.
He has drawn you one character, though,
that is new,
One wildflower he's plucked that is wet
with the dew
Of this fresh Western world, and, the thing
not to mince,
He has done naught but copy it ill ever
since;
His Indians, with proper respect be it said,

Are just Natty Bumppo, daubed over with
red,
And his very Long Toms are the same
useful Nat,
Rigged up in duck pants and a sou'wester
hat
(Though once in a Coffin, a good chance
was found
To have slipped the old fellow away under-
ground).
All his other men-figures are clothes upon
sticks,
The *dernière chemise* of a man in a fix
(As a captain besieged, when his garrison's
small,
Sets up caps upon poles to be seen o'er the
wall);
And the women he draws from one model
don't vary,
All sappy as maples and flat as a prairie.
When a character's wanted, he goes to the
task
As a cooper would do in composing a cask;
He picks out the staves, of their qualities
heedful,
Just hoops them together as tight as is
needful,
And, if the best fortune should crown the
attempt, he
Has made at the most something wooden
and empty.

"Don't suppose I would underrate
Cooper's abilities;
If I thought you'd do that, I should feel
very ill at ease;
The men who have given to *one* character life
And objective existence are not very rife;
You may number them all, both prose-
writers and singers,
Without overrunning the bounds of your
fingers,
And Natty won't go to oblivion quicker
Than Adams the parson or Primrose the
vicar.

"There is one thing in Cooper I like,
too, and that is
That on manners he lectures his country-
men gratis;
Not precisely so either, because, for a
rarity,
He is paid for his tickets in unpopularity.
Now he may overcharge his American pic-
tures,

But you 'll grant there 's a good deal of
  truth in his strictures;
And I honor the man who is willing to sink
Half his present repute for the freedom to
  think,
And, when he has thought, be his cause
  strong or weak,
Will risk t' other half for the freedom to
  speak,
Caring naught for what vengeance the
  mob has in store,
Let that mob be the upper ten thousand or
  lower.

"There are truths you Americans need
  to be told,
And it never 'll refute them to swagger
  and scold;
John Bull, looking o'er the Atlantic, in
  choler
At your aptness for trade, says you worship
  the dollar;
But to scorn such eye-dollar-try 's what
  very few do,
And John goes to that church as often as
  you do.
No matter what John says, don't try to
  outcrow him,
'T is enough to go quietly on and outgrow
  him;
Like most fathers, Bull hates to see Num-
  ber One
Displacing himself in the mind of his son,
And detests the same faults in himself
  he 'd neglected
When he sees them again in his child's
  glass reflected;
To love one another you 're too like by
  half;
If he is a bull, you 're a pretty stout calf,
And tear your own pasture for naught but
  to show
What a nice pair of horns you 're begin-
  ning to grow.

"There are one or two things I should
  just like to hint,
For you don't often get the truth told you
  in print;
The most of you (this is what strikes all
  beholders)
Have a mental and physical stoop in the
  shoulders;
Though you ought to be free as the winds
  and the waves,

You 've the gait and the manners of run-
  away slaves;
Though you brag of your New World, you
  don't half believe in it;
And as much of the Old as is possible
  weave in it;
Your goddess of freedom, a tight, buxom
  girl,
With lips like a cherry and teeth like a
  pearl,
With eyes bold as Herë's, and hair floating
  free,
And full of the sun as the spray of the sea,
Who can sing at a husking or romp at a
  shearing,
Who can trip through the forests alone
  without fearing,
Who can drive home the cows with a song
  through the grass,
Keeps glancing aside into Europe's cracked
  glass,
Hides her red hands in gloves, pinches up
  her lithe waist,
And makes herself wretched with transma-
  rine taste;
She loses her fresh country charm when
  she takes
Any mirror except her own rivers and
  lakes.

"You steal Englishmen's books and
  think Englishmen's thought,
With their salt on her tail your wild eagle
  is caught;
Your literature suits its each whisper and
  motion
To what will be thought of it over the
  ocean;
The cast clothes of Europe your statesman-
  ship tries
And mumbles again the old blarneys and
  lies; —
Forget Europe wholly, your veins throb
  with blood,
To which the dull current in hers is but mud:
Let her sneer, let her say your experiment
  fails,
In her voice there 's a tremble e'en now
  while she rails,
And your shore will soon be in the nature
  of things
Covered thick with gilt drift-wood of cast-
  away kings,
Where alone, as it were in a Longfellow's
  Waif,

Her fugitive pieces will find themselves
  safe.
O my friends, thank your god, if you have
  one, that he
'Twixt the Old World and you set the gulf
  of a sea;
Be strong-backed, brown-handed, upright
  as your pines,
By the scale of a hemisphere shape your
  designs,
Be true to yourselves and this new nine-
  teenth age,
As a statue by Powers, or a picture by
  Page,
Plough, sail, forge, build, carve, paint,
  make all over new,
To your own New-World instincts contrive
  to be true,
Keep your ears open wide to the Future's
  first call,
Be whatever you will, but yourselves first
  of all,
Stand fronting the dawn on Toil's heaven-
  scaling peaks,
And become my new race of more practi-
  cal Greeks. —
Hem ! your likeness at present, I shudder
  to tell o't,
Is that you have your slaves, and the
  Greek had his helot."

Here a gentleman present, who had in
  his attic
More pepper than brains, shrieked, " The
  man 's a fanatic,
I 'm a capital tailor with warm tar and
  feathers,
And will make him a suit that 'll serve in
  all weathers;
But we 'll argue the point first, I 'm willing
  to reason 't,
Palaver before condemnation 's but decent;
So, through my humble person, Humanity
  begs
Of the friends of true freedom a loan of
  bad eggs."
But Apollo let one such a look of his show
  forth
As when ἤϊε νύκτι ἐοικώς, and so forth,
And the gentleman somehow slunk out of
  the way,
But, as he was going, gained courage to
  say, —
" At slavery in the abstract my whole soul
  rebels,

I am as strongly opposed to 't as any one
  else."
" Ay, no doubt, but whenever I 've hap-
  pened to meet
With a wrong or a crime, it is always con-
  crete,"
Answered Phœbus severely; then turning
  to us,
" The mistake of such fellows as just made
  the fuss
Is only in taking a great busy nation
For a part of their pitiful cotton-planta-
  tion. —
But there comes Miranda, Zeus ! where
  shall I flee to ?
She has such a penchant for bothering me
  too !
She always keeps asking if I don't observe a
Particular likeness 'twixt her and Minerva;
She tells me my efforts in verse are quite
  clever; —
She 's been travelling now, and will be
  worse than ever;
One would think, though, a sharp-sighted
  noter she 'd be
Of all that 's worth mentioning over the
  sea,
For a woman must surely see well, if she
  try,
The whole of whose being 's a capital I:
She will take an old notion, and make it
  her own,
By saying it o'er in her Sibylline tone,
Or persuade you 't is something tremen-
  dously deep,
By repeating it so as to put you to sleep;
And she well may defy any mortal to see
  through it,
When once she has mixed up her infinite
  me through it.
There is one thing she owns in her own
  single right,
It is native and genuine — namely, her
  spite;
Though, when acting as censor, she pri-
  vately blows
A censer of vanity 'neath her own nose."

Here Miranda came up, and said, " Phœ-
  bus ! you know
That the Infinite Soul has its infinite woe,
As I ought to know, having lived cheek by
  jowl,
Since the day I was born, with the Infinite
  Soul;

I myself introduced, I myself, I alone,
To my Land's better life authors solely my
    own,
Who the sad heart of earth on their shoul-
    ders have taken,
Whose works sound a depth by Life's
    quiet unshaken,
Such as Shakespeare, for instance, the
    Bible, and Bacon,
Not to mention my own works; Time's
    nadir is fleet,
And, as for myself, I 'm quite out of con-
    ceit " —

    " Quite out of conceit ! I 'm enchanted
        to hear it,"
Cried Apollo aside. " Who 'd have thought
    she was near it ?
To be sure, one is apt to exhaust those
    commodities
One uses too fast, yet in this case as odd it is
As if Neptune should say to his turbots
    and whitings,
' I 'm as much out of salt as Miranda's own
    writings '
(Which, as she in her own happy manner
    has said,
Sound a depth, for 't is one of the functions
    of lead).
She often has asked me if I could not find
A place somewhere near me that suited her
    mind;
I know but a single one vacant, which she,
With her rare talent that way, would fit to
    a T.
And it would not imply any pause or cessa-
    tion
In the work she esteems her peculiar voca-
    tion, —
She may enter on duty to-day, if she
    chooses,
And remain Tiring-woman for life to the
    Muses."

Miranda meanwhile has succeeded in
    driving
Up into a corner, in spite of their striving,
A small flock of terrified victims, and
    there,
With an I-turn-the-crank-of-the-Universe
    air
And a tone which, at least to *my* fancy, ap-
    pears
Not so much to be entering as boxing your
    ears,

Is unfolding a tale (of herself, I surmise,
For 't is dotted as thick as a peacock's with
    I's).
Apropos of Miranda, I 'll rest on my oars
And drift through a trifling digression on
    bores,
For, though not wearing ear-rings *in more
    majorum,*
Our ears are kept bored just as if we still
    wore 'em.
There was one feudal custom worth keep-
    ing, at least,
Roasted bores made a part of each well-
    ordered feast,
And of all quiet pleasures the very *ne plus*
Was in hunting wild bores as the tame
    ones hunt us.
Archæologians, I know, who have personal
    fears
Of this wise application of hounds and of
    spears,
Have tried to make out, with a zeal more
    than wonted,
'T was a kind of wild swine that our ances-
    tors hunted;
But I 'll never believe that the age which
    has strewn
Europe o'er with cathedrals, and otherwise
    shown
That it knew what was what, could by
    chance not have known
(Spending, too, its chief time with its buff
    on, no doubt)
Which beast 't would improve the world
    most to thin out.
I divide bores myself, in the manner of
    rifles,
Into two great divisions, regardless of tri-
    fles; —
There 's your smooth-bore and screw-bore,
    who do not much vary
In the weight of cold lead they respectively
    carry.
The smooth-bore is one in whose essence
    the mind
Not a corner nor cranny to cling by can
    find;
You feel as in nightmares sometimes, when
    you slip
Down a steep slated roof, where there 's
    nothing to grip;
You slide and you slide, the blank horror
    increases, —
You had rather by far be at once smashed
    to pieces;

You fancy a whirlpool below white and
  frothing,
And finally drop off and light upon — no-
  thing.
The screw-bore has twists in him, faint
  predilections
For going just wrong in the tritest direc-
  tions;
When he 's wrong he is flat, when he 's
  right he can't show it,
He 'll tell you what Snooks said about the
  new poet,[1]
Or how Fogrum was outraged by Tenny-
  son's Princess;
He has spent all his spare time and intel-
  lect since his
Birth in perusing, on each art and science,
Just the books in which no one puts any
  reliance,
And though *nemo*, we 're told, *horis omnibus
  sapit*,
The rule will not fit him, however you
  shape it,
For he has a perennial foison of sappiness;
He has just enough force to spoil half your
  day's happiness,
And to make him a sort of mosquito to be
  with,
But just not enough to dispute or agree
  with.

These sketches I made (not to be too
  explicit)
From two honest fellows who made me
  a visit,
And broke, like the tale of the Bear and
  the Fiddle,
My reflections on Halleck short off by the
  middle;
I sha'n't now go into the subject more
  deeply,
For I notice that some of my readers look
  sleep'ly;
I will barely remark that, 'mongst civilized
  nations,
There 's none that displays more exemplary
  patience
Under all sorts of boring, at all sorts of
  hours,
From all sorts of desperate persons, than
  ours.
Not to speak of our papers, our State legis-
  latures,

And other such trials for sensitive na-
  tures,
Just look for a moment at Congress, — ap-
  palled,
My fancy shrinks back from the phantom
  it called;
Why, there 's scarcely a member unworthy
  to frown
'Neath what Fourier nicknames the Boreal
  crown;
Only think what that infinite bore-pow'r
  could do
If applied with a utilitarian view;
Suppose, for example, we shipped it with
  care
To Sahara's great desert and let it bore
  there;
If they held one short session and did no-
  thing else,
They 'd fill the whole waste with Artesian
  wells.
But 't is time now with pen phonographic
  to follow
Through some more of his sketches our
  laughing Apollo: —

"There comes Harry Franco, and, as he
  draws near,
You find that 's a smile which you took for
  a sneer;
One half of him contradicts t' other; his
  wont
Is to say very sharp things and do very
  blunt;
His manner 's as hard as his feelings are
  tender,
And a *sortie* he 'll make when he means to
  surrender;
He 's in joke half the time when he seems
  to be sternest,
When he seems to be joking, be sure he 's
  in earnest;
He has common sense in a way that 's un-
  common,
Hates humbug and cant, loves his friends
  like a woman,
Builds his dislikes of cards and his friend-
  ships of oak,
Loves a prejudice better than aught but a
  joke,
Is half upright Quaker, half downright
  Come-outer,
Loves Freedom too well to go stark mad
  about her,
Quite artless himself, is a lover of Art,

---

[1] (If you call Snooks an owl, he will show by his looks
That he 's morally certain you 're jealous of Snooks.)

Shuts you out of his secrets and into his heart,
And though not a poet, yet all must admire
In his letters of Pinto his skill on the liar.

"There comes Poe, with his raven, like Barnaby Rudge,
Three fifths of him genius and two fifths sheer fudge,
Who talks like a book of iambs and pentameters,
In a way to make people of common sense damn metres,
Who has written some things quite the best of their kind,
But the heart somehow seems all squeezed out by the mind,
Who — But hey-day! What 's this? Messieurs Mathews and Poe,
You must n't fling mud-balls at Longfellow so,
Does it make a man worse that his character 's such
As to make his friends love him (as you think) too much?
Why, there is not a bard at this moment alive
More willing than he that his fellows should thrive;
While you are abusing him thus, even now
He would help either one of you out of a slough;
You may say that he 's smooth and all that till you 're hoarse,
But remember that elegance also is force;
After polishing granite as much as you will,
The heart keeps its tough old persistency still;
Deduct all you can, *that* still keeps you at bay;
Why, he 'll live till men weary of Collins and Gray.
I 'm not over-fond of Greek metres in English,
To me rhyme 's a gain, so it be not too jinglish,
And your modern hexameter verses are no more
Like Greek ones than sleek Mr. Pope is like Homer;
As the roar of the sea to the coo of a pigeon is,
So, compared to your moderns, sounds old Melesigenes;

I may be too partial, the reason, perhaps, o't is
That I 've heard the old blind man recite his own rhapsodies,
And my ear with that music impregnate may be,
Like the poor exiled shell with the soul of the sea,
Or as one can't bear Strauss when his nature is cloven
To its deeps within deeps by the stroke of Beethoven;
But, set that aside, and 't is truth that I speak,
Had Theocritus written in English, not Greek,
I believe that his exquisite sense would scarce change a line
In that rare, tender, virgin-like pastoral Evangeline.
That 's not ancient nor modern, its place is apart
Where time has no sway, in the realm of pure Art,
'T is a shrine of retreat from Earth's hubbub and strife
As quiet and chaste as the author's own life.

"There comes Philothea, her face all aglow,
She has just been dividing some poor creature's woe,
And can't tell which pleases her most, to relieve
His want, or his story to hear and believe;
No doubt against many deep griefs she prevails,
For her ear is the refuge of destitute tales;
She knows well that silence is sorrow's best food,
And that talking draws off from the heart its black blood,
So she 'll listen with patience and let you unfold
Your bundle of rags as 't were pure cloth of gold,
Which, indeed, it all turns to as soon as she 's touched it,
And (to borrow a phrase from the nursery) *muched* it;
She has such a musical taste, she will go
Any distance to hear one who draws a long bow;
She will swallow a wonder by mere might and main,

And thinks it Geometry's fault if she's fain
To consider things flat, inasmuch as they're
  plain;
Facts with her are accomplished, as French-
  men would say —
They will prove all she wishes them to
  either way, —
And, as fact lies on this side or that, we
  must try,
If we're seeking the truth, to find where it
  don't lie;
I was telling her once of a marvellous aloe
That for thousands of years had looked
  spindling and sallow,
And, though nursed by the fruitfullest
  powers of mud,
Had never vouchsafed e'en so much as a
  bud,
Till its owner remarked (as a sailor, you
  know,
Often will in a calm) that it never would
  blow,
For he wished to exhibit the plant, and de-
  signed
That its blowing should help him in raising
  the wind;
At last it was told him that if he should
  water
Its roots with the blood of his unmarried
  daughter
(Who was born, as her mother, a Calvinist,
  said,
With William Law's serious caul on her
  head),
It would blow as the obstinate breeze did
  when by a
Like decree of her father died Iphigenia;
At first he declared he himself would be
  blowed
Ere his conscience with such a foul crime
  he would load,
But the thought, coming oft, grew less dark
  than before,
And he mused, as each creditor knocked at
  his door,
If *this* were but done they would dun me no
  more;
I told Philothea his struggles and doubts,
And how he considered the ins and the outs
Of the visions he had, and the dreadful
  dyspepsy,
How he went to the seër that lives at Po'-
  keepsie,
How the seër advised him to sleep on it
  first,

And to read his big volume in case of the
  worst,
And further advised he should pay him five
  dollars
For writing 𝕳um, 𝕳um, on his wristbands
  and collars;
Three years and ten days these dark words
  he had studied
When the daughter was missed, and the
  aloe had budded;
I told how he watched it grow large and
  more large,
And wondered how much for the show he
  should charge, —
She had listened with utter indifference to
  this, till
I told how it bloomed, and, discharging its
  pistil
With an aim the Eumenides dictated, shot
The botanical filicide dead on the spot;
It had blown, but he reaped not his horrible
  gains,
For it blew with such force as to blow out
  his brains,
And the crime was blown also, because on
  the wad,
Which was paper, was writ 'Visitation of
  God,'
As well as a thrilling account of the deed
Which the coroner kindly allowed me to
  read.

"Well, my friend took this story up
  just, to be sure,
As one might a poor foundling that's laid
  at one's door;
She combed it and washed it and clothed it
  and fed it,
And as if 't were her own child most ten-
  derly bred it,
Laid the scene (of the legend, I mean) far
  away a-
-mong the green vales underneath Hima-
  laya,
And by artist-like touches, laid on here
  and there,
Made the whole thing so touching, I
  frankly declare
I have read it all thrice, and, perhaps I am
  weak,
But I found every time there were tears on
  my cheek.

"The pole, science tells us, the magnet
  controls,

But she is a magnet to emigrant Poles,
And folks with a mission that nobody
knows
Throng thickly about her as bees round a
rose;
She can fill up the *carets* in such, make
their scope
Converge to some focus of rational hope,
And, with sympathies fresh as the morn-
ing, their gall
Can transmute into honey, — but this is
not all;
Not only for those she has solace, oh
say,
Vice's desperate nursling adrift in Broad-
way,
Who clingest, with all that is left of thee
human,
To the last slender spar from the wreck of
the woman,
Hast thou not found one shore where those
tired drooping feet
Could reach firm mother-earth, one full
heart on whose beat
The soothed head in silence reposing could
hear
The chimes of far childhood throb back on
the ear ?
Ah, there 's many a beam from the foun-
tain of day
That, to reach us unclouded, must pass, on
its way,
Through the soul of a woman, and hers is
wide ope
To the influence of Heaven as the blue
eyes of Hope;
Yes, a great heart is hers, one that dares
to go in
To the prison, the slave-hut, the alleys of
sin,
And to bring into each, or to find there,
some line
Of the never completely out-trampled di-
vine;
If her heart at high floods swamps her
brain now and then,
'T is but richer for that when the tide ebbs
agen,
As, after old Nile has subsided, his plain
Overflows with a second broad deluge of
grain;
What a wealth would it bring to the nar-
row and sour
Could they be as a Child but for one little
hour !

"What ! Irving ? thrice welcome, warm
heart and fine brain,
You bring back the happiest spirit from
Spain,
And the gravest sweet humor, that ever
were there
Since Cervantes met death in his gentle
despair;
Nay, don't be embarrassed, nor look so be-
seeching,
I sha'n't run directly against my own
preaching,
And, having just laughed at their Raphaels
and Dantes,
Go to setting you up beside matchless Cer-
vantes;
But allow me to speak what I honestly
feel, —
To a true poet-heart add the fun of Dick
Steele,
Throw in all of Addison, *minus* the chill,
With the whole of that partnership's stock
and good-will,
Mix well, and while stirring, hum o'er, as
a spell,
The fine *old* English Gentleman, simmer it
well,
Sweeten just to your own private liking,
then strain,
That only the finest and clearest remain,
Let it stand out of doors till a soul it re-
ceives
From the warm lazy sun loitering down
through green leaves,
And you 'll find a choice nature, not wholly
deserving
A name either English or Yankee, — just
Irving.

"There goes, — but *stet nominis umbra*,
— his name
You 'll be glad enough, some day or other,
to claim,
And will all crowd about him and swear
that you knew him
If some English critic should chance to re-
view him.
The old *porcos ante ne projiciatis*
MARGARITAS, for him you have verified
gratis;
What matters his name ?   Why, it may be
Sylvester,
Judd, Junior, or Junius, Ulysses, or Nestor,
For aught *I* know or care; 't is enough
that I look

On the author of 'Margaret,' the first
  Yankee book
With the *soul* of Down East in 't, and things
  farther East,
As far as the threshold of morning, at
  least,
Where awaits the fair dawn of the simple
  and true,
Of the day that comes slowly to make all
  things new.
'T has a smack of pine woods, of bare field
  and bleak hill,
Such as only the breed of the Mayflower
  could till;
The Puritan 's shown in it, tough to the
  core,
Such as prayed, smiting Agag on red Mar-
  ston Moor:
With an unwilling humor, half choked by
  the drouth
In brown hollows about the inhospitable
  mouth;
With a soul full of poetry, though it has
  qualms
About finding a happiness out of the
  Psalms;
Full of tenderness, too, though it shrinks
  in the dark,
Hamadryad-like, under the coarse, shaggy
  bark;
That sees visions, knows wrestlings of God
  with the Will,
And has its own Sinais and thunderings
  still."

Here, "Forgive me, Apollo," I cried,
  " while I pour
My heart out to my birthplace: O loved
  more and more
Dear Baystate, from whose rocky bosom
  thy sons
Should suck milk, strong-will-giving, brave,
  such as runs
In the veins of old Greylock — who is it
  that dares
Call thee pedler, a soul wrapped in bank-
  books and shares ?
It is false ! She 's a Poet ! I see, as I
  write,
Along the far railroad the steam-snake
  glide white,
The cataract-throb of her mill-hearts I
  hear,
The swift strokes of trip-hammers weary
  my ear,

Sledges ring upon anvils, through logs the
  saw screams,
Blocks swing to their place, beetles drive
  home the beams: —
It is songs such as these that she croons to
  the din
Of her fast-flying shuttles, year out and
  year in,
While from earth's farthest corner there
  comes not a breeze
But wafts her the buzz of her gold-glean-
  ing bees:
What though those horn hands have as yet
  found small time
For painting and sculpture and music and
  rhyme ?
These will come in due order; the need
  that pressed sorest
Was to vanquish the seasons, the ocean
  the forest,
To bridle and harness the rivers, the steam,
Making those whirl her mill-wheels, this
  tug in her team,
To vassalize old tyrant Winter, and make
Him delve surlily for her on river and
  lake; —
When this New World was parted, she
  strove not to shirk
Her lot in the heirdom, the tough, silent
  Work,
The hero-share ever from Herakles down
To Odin, the Earth's iron sceptre and
  crown:
Yes, thou dear, noble Mother ! if ever
  men's praise
Could be claimed for creating heroical lays,
Thou hast won it; if ever the laurel divine
Crowned the Maker and Builder, that glory
  is thine !
Thy songs are right epic, they tell how this
  rude
Rock-rib of our earth here was tamed and
  subdued;
Thou hast written them plain on the face
  of the planet
In brave, deathless letters of iron and
  granite;
Thou hast printed them deep for all time;
  they are set
From the same runic type-fount and al-
  phabet
With thy stout Berkshire hills and the
  arms of thy Bay, —
They are staves from the burly old May-
  flower lay.

If the drones of the Old World, in querulous ease,
Ask thy Art and thy Letters, point proudly to these,
Or, if they deny these are Letters and Art,
Toil on with the same old invincible heart;
Thou art rearing the pedestal broad-based and grand
Whereon the fair shapes of the Artist shall stand,
And creating, through labors undaunted and long,
The theme for all Sculpture and Painting and Song!

"But my good mother Baystate wants no praise of mine,
She learned from *her* mother a precept divine
About something that butters no parsnips, her *forte*
In another direction lies, work is her sport
(Though she 'll curtsey and set her cap straight, that she will,
If you talk about Plymouth and red Bunker's hill).
Dear, notable goodwife! by this time of night,
Her hearth is swept neatly, her fire burning bright,
And she sits in a chair (of home plan and make) rocking,
Musing much, all the while, as she darns on a stocking,
Whether turkeys will come pretty high next Thanksgiving,
Whether flour 'll be so dear, for, as sure as she 's living,
She will use rye-and-injun then, whether the pig
By this time ain't got pretty tolerable big,
And whether to sell it outright will be best,
Or to smoke hams and shoulders and salt down the rest, —
At this minute, she 'd swop all my verses, ah, cruel!
For the last patent stove that is saving of fuel;
So I 'll just let Apollo go on, for his phiz
Shows I 've kept him awaiting too long as it is."

"If our friend, there, who seems a reporter, is done

With his burst of emotion, why, *I* will go on,"
Said Apollo; some smiled, and, indeed, I must own
There was something sarcastic, perhaps, in his tone; —

"There 's Holmes, who is matchless among you for wit;
A Leyden-jar always full-charged, from which flit
The electrical tingles of hit after hit;
In long poems 't is painful sometimes, and invites
A thought of the way the new Telegraph writes,
Which pricks down its little sharp sentences spitefully
As if you got more than you 'd title to rightfully,
And you find yourself hoping its wild father Lightning
Would flame in for a second and give you a fright'ning.
He has perfect sway of what I call a sham metre,
But many admire it, the English pentameter,
And Campbell, I think, wrote most commonly worse,
With less nerve, swing, and fire in the same kind of verse,
Nor e'er achieved aught in 't so worthy of praise
As the tribute of Holmes to the grand *Marseillaise*.
You went crazy last year over Bulwer's New Timon; —
Why, if B., to the day of his dying, should rhyme on,
Heaping verses on verses and tomes upon tomes,
He could ne'er reach the best point and vigor of Holmes.
His are just the fine hands, too, to weave you a lyric
Full of fancy, fun, feeling, or spiced with satiric
In a measure so kindly, you doubt if the toes
That are trodden upon are your own or your foes'.

"There is Lowell, who 's striving Parnassus to climb

With a whole bale of *isms* tied together
    with rhyme,
He might get on alone, spite of brambles
    and boulders,
But he can't with that bundle he has on his
    shoulders,
The top of the hill he will ne'er come nigh
    reaching
Till he learns the distinction 'twixt singing
    and preaching;
His lyre has some chords that would ring
    pretty well,
But he 'd rather by half make a drum of
    the shell,
And rattle away till he 's old as Methusalem,
At the head of a march to the last new
    Jerusalem.

" There goes Halleck, whose Fanny 's a
    pseudo Don Juan,
With the wickedness out that gave salt to
    the true one,
He 's a wit, though, I hear, of the very first
    order,
And once made a pun on the words soft
    Recorder;
More than this, he 's a very great poet, I 'm
    told,
And has had his works published in crimson
    and gold,
With something they call ' Illustrations,'
    to wit,
Like those with which Chapman obscured
    Holy Writ,[1]
Which are said to illustrate, because, as I
    view it,
Like *lucus a non*, they precisely don't do it;
Let a man who can write what himself
    understands
Keep clear, if he can, of designing men's
    hands,
Who bury the sense, if there 's any worth
    having,
And then very honestly call it engraving.
But, to quit *badinage*, which there is n't
    much wit in,
Halleck 's better, I doubt not, than all he
    has written;
In his verse a clear glimpse you will fre-
    quently find,
If not of a great, of a fortunate mind,
Which contrives to be true to its natural
    loves

[1] (Cuts rightly called wooden, as all must admit.)

In a world of back-offices, ledgers, and
    stoves.
When his heart breaks away from the
    brokers and banks,
And kneels in his own private shrine to give
    thanks,
There 's a genial manliness in him that
    earns
Our sincerest respect (read, for instance,
    his ' Burns '),
And we can't but regret (seek excuse where
    we may)
That so much of a man has been peddled
    away.

" But what 's that? a mass-meeting?
    No, there come in lots
The American Bulwers, Disraelis, and
    Scotts,
And in short the American everything elses,
Each charging the others with envies and
    jealousies; —
By the way, 't is a fact that displays what
    profusions
Of all kinds of greatness bless free institu-
    tions,
That while the Old World has produced
    barely eight
Of such poets as all men agree to call great,
And of other great characters hardly a
    score
(One might safely say less than that rather
    than more),
With you every year a whole crop is be-
    gotten,
They 're as much of a staple as corn is, or
    cotton;
Why, there 's scarcely a huddle of log-huts
    and shanties
That has not brought forth its own Miltons
    and Dantes;
I myself know ten Byrons, one Coleridge,
    three Shelleys,
Two Raphaels, six Titians (I think), one
    Apelles,
Leonardos and Rubenses plenty as lichens,
One (but that one is plenty) American
    Dickens,
A whole flock of Lambs, any number of
    Tennysons, —
In short, if a man has the luck to have any
    sons,
He may feel pretty certain that one out of
    twain
Will be some very great person over again.

There is one inconvenience in all this, which lies
In the fact that by contrast we estimate size,[1]
And, where there are none except Titans, great stature
Is only the normal proceeding of nature.
What puff the strained sails of your praise will you furl at, if
The calmest degree that you know is superlative?
At Rome, all whom Charon took into his wherry must,
As a matter of course, be well *issimust* and *errimust*,
A Greek, too, could feel, while in that famous boat he tost,
That his friends would take care he was ιστοst and ωτατοst,
And formerly we, as through graveyards we past,
Thought the world went from bad to worst fearfully fast;
Let us glance for a moment, 't is well worth the pains,
And note what an average graveyard contains;
There lie levellers levelled, duns done up themselves,
There are booksellers finally laid on their shelves,
Horizontally there lie upright politicians,
Dose-a-dose with their patients sleep faultless physicians,
There are slave-drivers quietly whipped under ground,
There bookbinders, done up in boards, are fast bound,
There card-players wait till the last trump be played,
There all the choice spirits get finally laid,
There the babe that 's unborn is supplied with a berth,
There men without legs get their six feet of earth,
There lawyers repose, each wrapped up in his case,
There seekers of office are sure of a place,
There defendant and plaintiff get equally cast,
There shoemakers quietly stick to the last,

There brokers at length become silent as stocks,
There stage-drivers sleep without quitting their box,
And so forth and so forth and so forth and so on,
With this kind of stuff one might endlessly go on;
To come to the point, I may safely assert you
Will find in each yard every cardinal virtue;[1]
Each has six truest patriots: four discoverers of ether,
Who never had thought on 't nor mentioned it either;
Ten poets, the greatest who ever wrote rhyme:
Two hundred and forty first men of their time:
One person whose portrait just gave the least hint
Its original had a most horrible squint:
One critic, most (what do they call it?) reflective,
Who never had used the phrase ob- or subjective:
Forty fathers of Freedom, of whom twenty bred
Their sons for the rice-swamps, at so much a head,
And their daughters for — faugh! thirty mothers of Gracchi:
Non-resistants who gave many a spiritual blackeye:
Eight true friends of their kind, one of whom was a jailer:
Four captains almost as astounding as Taylor:
Two dozen of Italy's exiles who shoot us his Kaisership daily, stern pen-and-ink Brutuses,
Who, in Yankee back-parlors, with crucified smile,[2]
Mount serenely their country's funereal pile:
Ninety-nine Irish heroes, ferocious rebellers
'Gainst the Saxon in cis-marine garrets and cellars,
Who shake their dread fists o'er the sea and all that, —

---

[1] That is in most cases we do, but not all,
Past a doubt, there are men who are innately small,
Such as Blank, who, without being 'minished a tittle,
Might stand for a type of the Absolute Little.

[1] (And at this just conclusion will surely arrive,
That the goodness of earth is more dead than alive.)
[2] Not forgetting their tea and their toast, though, the while.

As long as a copper drops into the hat:
Nine hundred Teutonic republicans stark
From Vaterland's battle just won — in the
Park,
Who the happy profession of martyrdom
take
Whenever it gives them a chance at a
steak:
Sixty-two second Washingtons : two or
three Jacksons :
And so many everythings-else that it racks
one's
Poor memory too much to continue the
list,
Especially now they no longer exist; —
I would merely observe that you 've taken
to giving
The puffs that belong to the dead to the
living,
And that somehow your trump-of-contem-
porary-doom's tones
Is tuned after old dedications and tomb-
stones."

Here the critic came in and a thistle pre-
sented — [1]
From a frown to a smile the god's features
relented,
As he stared at his envoy, who, swelling
with pride,
To the god's asking look, nothing daunted,
replied, —
"You 're surprised, I suppose, I was absent
so long,
But your godship respecting the lilies was
wrong;
I hunted the garden from one end to
t' other,
And got no reward but vexation and bother,
Till, tossed out with weeds in a corner to
wither,
This one lily I found and made haste to
bring hither."

"Did he think I had given him a book to
review ?
I ought to have known what the fellow
would do,"
Muttered Phœbus aside, "for a thistle will
pass
Beyond doubt for the queen of all flowers
with an ass;

[1] Turn back now to page — goodness only knows
what,
And take a fresh hold on the thread of my plot.

He has chosen in just the same way as he 'd
choose
His specimens out of the books he reviews;
And now, as this offers an excellent text,
I 'll give 'em some brief hints on criticism
next."
So, musing a moment, he turned to the
crowd,
And, clearing his voice, spoke as follows
aloud: —

"My friends, in the happier days of the
muse,
We were luckily free from such things as
reviews;
Then naught came between with its fog to
make clearer
The heart of the poet to that of his hearer;
Then the poet brought heaven to the peo-
ple, and they
Felt that they, too, were poets in hearing
his lay;
Then the poet was prophet, the past in his
soul
Precreated the future, both parts of one
whole;
Then for him there was nothing too great
or too small,
For one natural deity sanctified all;
Then the bard owned no clipper and meter
of moods
Save the spirit of silence that hovers and
broods
O'er the seas and the mountains, the rivers
and woods;
He asked not earth's verdict, forgetting the
clods,
His soul soared and sang to an audience of
gods;
'T was for them that he measured the
thought and the line,
And shaped for their vision the perfect
design,
With as glorious a foresight, a balance as
true,
As swung out the worlds in the infinite blue;
Then a glory and greatness invested man's
heart,
The universal, which now stands estranged
and apart,
In the free individual moulded, was Art;
Then the forms of the Artist seemed
thrilled with desire
For something as yet unattained, fuller,
higher,

As once with her lips, lifted hands, and
eyes listening,
And her whole upward soul in her counte-
nance glistening,
Eurydice stood — like a beacon unfired,
Which, once touched with flame, will leap
heav'nward inspired —
And waited with answering kindle to mark
The first gleam of Orpheus that pained the
red Dark.
Then painting, song, sculpture did more
than relieve
The need that men feel to create and be-
lieve,
And as, in all beauty, who listens with love
Hears these words oft repeated — 'beyond
and above,'
So these seemed to be but the visible sign
Of the grasp of the soul after things more
divine;
They were ladders the Artist erected to
climb
O'er the narrow horizon of space and of
time,
And we see there the footsteps by which
men had gained
To the one rapturous glimpse of the never-
attained,
As shepherds could erst sometimes trace in
the sod
The last spurning print of a sky-cleaving
god.

" But now, on the poet's dis-privacied
moods
With *do this* and *do that* the pert critic
intrudes;
While he thinks he's been barely fulfilling
his duty
To interpret 'twixt men and their own sense
of beauty,
And has striven, while others sought honor
or pelf,
To make his kind happy as he was him-
self,
He finds he's been guilty of horrid offences
In all kinds of moods, numbers, genders,
and tenses;
He's been *ob* and *sub*jective, what Kettle
calls Pot,
Precisely, at all events, what he ought not,
You have done this, says one judge; *done
that*, says another;
You should have done this, grumbles one; *that*,
says t' other;

Never mind what he touches, one shrieks
out *Taboo!*
And while he is wondering what he shall do,
Since each suggests opposite topics for
song,
They all shout together *you're right!* and
you're wrong!

" Nature fits all her children with some-
thing to do,
He who would write and can't write can
surely review,
Can set up a small booth as critic and sell
us his
Petty conceit and his pettier jealousies;
Thus a lawyer's apprentice, just out of his
teens,
Will do for the Jeffrey of six magazines;
Having read Johnson's lives of the poets
half through,
There's nothing on earth he's not compe-
tent to;
He reviews with as much nonchalance as he
whistles, —
He goes through a book and just picks out
the thistles;
It matters not whether he blame or com-
mend,
If he's bad as a foe, he's far worse as a
friend:
Let an author but write what's above his
poor scope,
He goes to work gravely and twists up a
rope,
And, inviting the world to see punishment
done,
Hangs himself up to bleach in the wind and
the sun;
'T is delightful to see, when a man comes
along
Who has anything in him peculiar and
strong,
Every cockboat that swims clear its fierce
(pop) gundeck at him,
And make as he passes its ludicrous Peck
at him — "

Here Miranda came up and began, " As
to that — "
Apollo at once seized his gloves, cane, and
hat,
And, seeing the place getting rapidly
cleared,
I too snatched my notes and forthwith
disappeared.

THE UNHAPPY LOT OF MR. KNOTT

PART I

SHOWING HOW HE BUILT HIS HOUSE AND
HIS WIFE MOVED INTO IT

MY worthy friend, A. Gordon Knott,
From business snug withdrawn,
Was much contented with a lot
That would contain a Tudor cot
'Twixt twelve feet square of garden-plot,
And twelve feet more of lawn.

He had laid business on the shelf
To give his taste expansion,
And, since no man, retired with pelf,
The building mania can shun,
Knott, being middle-aged himself,
Resolved to build (unhappy elf!)
A mediæval mansion.

He called an architect in counsel;
"I want," said he, "a — you know
what,
(You are a builder, I am Knott,)
A thing complete from chimney-pot
Down to the very grounsel;
Here's a half-acre of good land;
Just have it nicely mapped and planned
And make your workmen drive on;
Meadow there is, and upland too,
And I should like a water-view,
D' you think you could contrive one?
(Perhaps the pump and trough would
do,
If painted a judicious blue?)
The woodland I've attended to;"
[He meant three pines stuck up askew,
Two dead ones and a live one.]
"A pocket-full of rocks 't would take
To build a house of freestone,
But then it is not hard to make
What nowadays is *the* stone;
The cunning painter in a trice
Your house's outside petrifies,
And people think it very gneiss
Without inquiring deeper;
My money never shall be thrown
Away on such a deal of stone,
When stone of deal is cheaper."

And so the greenest of antiques
Was reared for Knott to dwell in:
The architect worked hard for weeks
In venting all his private peaks
Upon the roof, whose crop of leaks
Had satisfied Fluellen;
Whatever anybody had
Out of the common, good or bad,
Knott had it all worked well in;
A donjon-keep, where clothes might dry,
A porter's lodge that was a sty,
A campanile slim and high,
Too small to hang a bell in;
All up and down and here and there,
With Lord-knows-whats of round and
square
Stuck on at random everywhere, —
It was a house to make one stare,
All corners and all gables;
Like dogs let loose upon a bear,
Ten emulous styles *staboyed* with care,
The whole among them seemed to tear,
And all the oddities to spare
Were set upon the stables.

Knott was delighted with a pile
Approved by fashion's leaders:
(Only he made the builder smile,
By asking every little while,
Why that was called the Twodoor style,
Which certainly had *three* doors?)
Yet better for this luckless man
If he had put a downright ban
Upon the thing *in limine;*
For, though to quit affairs his plan,
Ere many days, poor Knott began
Perforce accepting draughts, that ran
All ways — except up chimney;
The house, though painted stone to mock,
With nice white lines round every block,
Some trepidation stood in,
When tempests (with petrific shock,
So to speak,) made it really rock,
Though not a whit less wooden;
And painted stone, howe'er well done,
Will not take in the prodigal sun
Whose beams are never quite at one
With our terrestrial lumber;
So the wood shrank around the knots,

And gaped in disconcerting spots,
And there were lots of dots and rots
　And crannies without number,
Wherethrough, as you may well presume,
The wind, like water through a flume,
　Came rushing in ecstatic,
Leaving, in all three floors, no room
　That was not a rheumatic;
And, what with points and squares and
　　rounds
　Grown shaky on their poises,
The house at nights was full of pounds,
Thumps, bumps, creaks, scratchings, raps —
　　till — "Zounds!"
Cried Knott, "this goes beyond all bounds;
I do not deal in tongues and sounds,
Nor have I let my house and grounds
　To a family of Noyeses!"

But, though Knott's house was full of
　　airs,
　He had but one, — a daughter;
And, as he owned much stocks and shares,
Many who wished to render theirs
Such vain, unsatisfying cares,
　And needed wives to sew their tears,
　　In matrimony sought her;
They vowed her gold they wanted not,
　Their faith would never falter,
They longed to tie this single Knott
　In the Hymeneal halter;
So daily at the door they rang,
　Cards for the belle delivering,
Or in the choir at her they sang,
Achieving such a rapturous twang
　As set her nerves ashivering.

Now Knott had quite made up his mind
　That Colonel Jones should have her;
No beauty he, but oft we find
Sweet kernels 'neath a roughish rind,
So hoped his Jenny 'd be resigned
　And make no more palaver;
Glanced at the fact that love was blind,
That girls were ratherish inclined
　To pet their little crosses,
Then nosologically defined
The rate at which the system pined
In those unfortunates who dined
Upon that metaphoric kind
　Of dish — their own proboscis.

But she, with many tears and moans,
　Besought him not to mock her,
Said 't was too much for flesh and bones

To marry mortgages and loans,
That fathers' hearts were stocks and stones,
And that she 'd go, when Mrs. Jones,
　To Davy Jones's locker;
Then gave her head a little toss
That said as plain as ever was,
If men are always at a loss
　Mere womankind to bridle —
To try the thing on woman cross
　Were fifty times as idle;
For she a strict resolve had made
　And registered in private,
That either she would die a maid,
　Or else be Mrs. Doctor Slade,
　　If woman could contrive it;
And, though the wedding-day was set,
　Jenny was more so, rather,
Declaring, in a pretty pet,
That, howsoe'er they spread their net,
She would out-Jennyral them yet,
　The colonel and her father.

Just at this time the Public's eyes
　Were keenly on the watch, a stir
Beginning slowly to arise
About those questions and replies,
Those raps that unwrapped mysteries
　So rapidly at Rochester,
And Knott, already nervous grown
By lying much awake alone,
And listening, sometimes to a moan,
　And sometimes to a clatter,
Whene'er the wind at night would rouse
The gingerbread-work on his house,
Or when some hasty-tempered mouse,
Behind the plastering, made a towse
　About a family matter,
Began to wonder if his wife,
A paralytic half her life,
　Which made it more surprising,
Might not to rule him from her urn,
Have taken a peripatetic turn
　For want of exorcising.

This thought, once nestled in his head,
Erelong contagious grew, and spread
Infecting all his mind with dread,
Until at last he lay in bed
And heard his wife, with well-known tread,
Entering the kitchen through the shed,
　(Or was 't his fancy, mocking?)
Opening the pantry, cutting bread,
And then (she 'd been some ten years
　　dead)
　Closets and drawers unlocking;

Or, in his room (his breath grew thick)
He heard the long-familiar click
Of slender needles flying quick,
    As if she knit a stocking;
For whom? — he prayed that years might
      flit
With pains rheumatic shooting,
Before those ghostly things she knit
Upon his unfleshed sole might fit,
He did not fancy it a bit,
    To stand upon that footing;
At other times, his frightened hairs
Above the bedclothes trusting,
He heard her, full of household cares,
(No dream entrapped in supper's snares,
The foal of horrible nightmares,
But broad awake, as he declares,)
Go bustling up and down the stairs,
Or setting back last evening's chairs,
    Or with the poker thrusting
The raked-up sea-coal's hardened crust —
And — what! impossible! it must!
He knew she had returned to dust,
And yet could scarce his senses trust,
Hearing her as she poked and fussed
    About the parlor, dusting!

Night after night he strove to sleep
    And take his ease in spite of it;
But still his flesh would chill and creep,
And, though two night-lamps he might
      keep,
    He could not so make light of it.
At last, quite desperate, he goes
And tells his neighbors all his woes,
    Which did but their amount enhance;
They made such mockery of his fears
That soon his days were of all jeers,
    His nights of the rueful countenance;
"I thought most folks," one neighbor
      said,
"Gave up the ghost when they were
      dead?"
Another gravely shook his head,
    Adding, "From all we hear, it's
Quite plain poor Knott is going mad —
For how can he at once be sad
    And think he's full of spirits?"
A third declared he knew a knife
    Would cut this Knott much quicker,
"The surest way to end all strife,
And lay the spirit of a wife,
    Is just to take and lick her!"
A temperance man caught up the word,
"Ah yes," he groaned, "I've always heard

Our poor friend somewhat slanted
Tow'rd taking liquor overmuch;
I fear these spirits may be Dutch,
(A sort of gins, or something such,)
    With which his house is haunted;
I see the thing as clear as light, —
If Knott would give up getting tight,
    Naught farther would be wanted:"
So all his neighbors stood aloof
And, that the spirits 'neath his roof
Were not entirely up to proof,
    Unanimously granted.

Knott knew that cocks and sprites were
    foes,
And so bought up, Heaven only knows
How many, for he wanted crows
To give ghosts caws, as I suppose,
    To think that day was breaking;
Moreover what he called his park,
He turned into a kind of ark
For dogs, because a little bark
Is a good tonic in the dark,
    If one is given to waking;
But things went on from bad to worse,
His curs were nothing but a curse,
    And, what was still more shocking,
Foul ghosts of living fowl made scoff
And would not think of going off
    In spite of all his cocking.

Shanghais, Bucks-counties, Dominiques,
Malays (that did n't lay for weeks,)
    Polanders, Bantams, Dorkings,
(Waiving the cost, no trifling ill,
Since each brought in his little bill,)
By day or night were never still,
But every thought of rest would kill
    With cacklings and with quorkings;
Henry the Eighth of wives got free
    By a way he had of axing;
But poor Knott's Tudor henery
Was not so fortunate, and he
    Still found his trouble waxing;
As for the dogs, the rows they made,
And how they howled, snarled, barked and
      bayed,
    Beyond all human knowledge is;
All night, as wide awake as gnats,
The terriers rumpused after rats,
Or, just for practice, taught their brats
To worry cast-off shoes and hats,
The bull-dogs settled private spats,
All chased imaginary cats,
Or raved behind the fence's slats

At real ones, or, from their mats,
With friends, miles off, held pleasant chats,
Or, like some folks in white cravats,
Contemptuous of sharps and flats,
Sat up and sang dogsologies.
Meanwhile the cats set up a squall,
And, safe upon the garden-wall,
    All night kept cat-a-walling,
As if the feline race were all,
In one wild cataleptic sprawl,
    Into love's tortures falling.

PART II

SHOWING WHAT IS MEANT BY A FLOW OF SPIRITS

At first the ghosts were somewhat shy,
Coming when none but Knott was nigh,
And people said 't was all their eye,
(Or rather his) a flam, the sly
    Digestion's machination:
Some recommended a wet sheet,
Some a nice broth of pounded peat,
Some a cold flat-iron to the feet,
Some a decoction of lamb's-bleat,
Some a southwesterly grain of wheat;
Meat was by some pronounced unmeet,
Others thought fish most indiscreet,
And that 't was worse than all to eat
Of vegetables, sour or sweet,
(Except, perhaps, the skin of beet,)
    In such a concatenation:
One quack his button gently plucks
And murmurs, " Biliary ducks ! "
    Says Knott, " I never ate one; "
But all, though brimming full of wrath,
Homœo, Allo, Hydropath,
Concurred in this — that t' other's path
    To death's door was the straight one.
Still, spite of medical advice,
The ghosts came thicker, and a spice
    Of mischief grew apparent;
Nor did they only come at night,
But seemed to fancy broad daylight,
Till Knott, in horror and affright,
    His unoffending hair rent;
Whene'er with handkerchief on lap,
He made his elbow-chair a trap,
To catch an after-dinner nap,
The spirits, always on the tap,
Would make a sudden *rap, rap, rap*,
The half-spun cord of sleep to snap,

(And what is life without its nap
But threadbareness and mere mishap ?)
As 't were with a percussion cap
    The trouble's climax capping;
It seemed a party dried and grim
Of mummies had come to visit him,
Each getting off from every limb
    Its multitudinous wrapping;
Scratchings sometimes the walls ran round,
The merest penny-weights of sound;
Sometimes 't was only by the pound
    They carried on their dealing,
A thumping 'neath the parlor floor,
Thump-bump-thump-bumping o'er and o'er,
As if the vegetables in store
(Quiet and orderly before)
    Were all together peeling;
You would have thought the thing was done
By the spirit of some son of a gun,
    And that a forty-two-pounder,
Or that the ghost which made such sounds
Could be none other than John Pounds,
    Of Ragged Schools the founder.
Through three gradations of affright,
The awful noises reached their height;
    At first they knocked nocturnally,
Then, for some reason, changing quite,
(As mourners, after six months' flight,
Turn suddenly from dark to light,)
    Began to knock diurna'ly,
And last, combining all their stocks,
(Scotland was ne'er so full of Knox,)
Into one Chaos (father of Nox,)
Nocte pluit — they showered knocks,
    And knocked, knocked, knocked, eter-
        nally;
Ever upon the go, like buoys,
(Wooden sea-urchins,) all Knott's joys,
They turned to troubles and a noise
    That preyed on him internally.

Soon they grew wider in their scope;
Whenever Knott a door would ope,
It would ope not, or else elope
And fly back (curbless as a trope
Once started down a stanza's slope
By a bard that gave it too much rope —)
    Like a clap of thunder slamming;
And, when kind Jenny brought his hat,
(She always, when he walked, did that,)
Just as upon his head it sat,
Submitting to his settling pat,
Some unseen hand would jam it flat,
Or give it such a furious bat

That eyes and nose went cramming
Up out of sight, and consequently,
As when in life it paddled free,
  His beaver caused much damning;
If these things seem o'erstrained to be,
Read the account of Doctor Dee,
'T is in our college library;
Read Wesley's circumstantial plea,
And Mrs. Crowe, more like a bee,
Sucking the nightshade's honeyed fee,
And Stilling's Pneumatology;
Consult Scot, Glanvil, grave Wie-
rus, and both Mathers; further see,
Webster, Casaubon, James First's trea-
tise, a right royal Q. E. D.
Writ with the moon in perigee,
Bodin de la Demonomanie —
(Accent that last line gingerly)
All full of learning as the sea
Of fishes, and all disagree,
  Save in *Sathanas apage!*
Or, what will surely put a flea
In unbelieving ears — with glee,
Out of a paper (sent to me
By some friend who forgot to P...
A... Y... — I use cryptography
Lest I his vengeful pen should dree —
His P...O...S...T...A...G...E...)
  Things to the same effect I cut,
About the tantrums of a ghost,
Not more than three weeks since, at most,
  Near Stratford, in Connecticut.
Knott's Upas daily spread its roots,
Sent up on all sides livelier shoots,
And bore more pestilential fruits;
The ghosts behaved like downright brutes,
They snipped holes in his Sunday suits,
Practised all night on octave flutes,
Put peas (not peace) into his boots,
  Whereof grew corns in season,
They scotched his sheets, and, what was
    worse,
Stuck his silk nightcap full of burrs,
Till he, in language plain and terse,
(But much unlike a Bible verse,)
  Swore he should lose his reason.

The tables took to spinning, too,
Perpetual yarns, and arm-chairs grew
  To prophets and apostles;
One footstool vowed that only he
Of law and gospel held the key,
That teachers of whate'er degree
To whom opinion bows the knee

Were n't fit to teach Truth's *a b c,*
And were (the whole lot) to a T
  Mere fogies all and fossils;
A teapoy, late the property
  Of Knox's Aunt Keziah,
(Whom Jenny most irreverently
Had nicknamed her aunt-tipathy)
With tips emphatic claimed to be
  The prophet Jeremiah;
The tins upon the kitchen-wall,
Turned tintinnabulators all,
And things that used to come at call
  For simple household services
Began to hop and whirl and prance,
Fit to put out of countenance
The *Commis* and *Grisettes* of France
  Or Turkey's dancing Dervises.

Of course such doings, far and wide,
With rumors filled the country-side,
And (as it is our nation's pride
To think a Truth not verified
Till with majorities allied)
Parties sprung up, affirmed, denied,
And candidates with questions plied,
Who, like the circus-riders, tried
At once both hobbies to bestride,
And each with his opponent vied
  In being inexplicit.
Earnest inquirers multiplied;
Folks, whose tenth cousins lately died,
Wrote letters long, and Knott replied;
All who could either walk or ride
Gathered to wonder or deride,
  And paid the house a visit;
Horses were to his pine-trees tied,
Mourners in every corner sighed,
Widows brought children there that cried,
Swarms of lean Seekers, eager-eyed,
(People Knott never could abide,)
Into each hole and cranny pried
With strings of questions cut and dried
From the Devout Inquirer's Guide,
For the wise spirits to decide —
  As, for example, is it
True that the damned are fried or boiled?
Was the Earth's axis greased or oiled?
Who cleaned the moon when it was soiled?
How baldness might be cured or foiled?
  How heal diseased potatoes?
Did spirits have the sense of smell?
Where would departed spinsters dwell?
If the late Zenas Smith were well?
If Earth were solid or a shell?

Were spirits fond of Doctor Fell?
Did the bull toll Cock-Robin's knell?
What remedy would bugs expel?
If Paine's invention were a sell?
Did spirits by Webster's system spell?
Was it a sin to be a belle?
Did dancing sentence folks to hell?
If so, then where most torture fell?
    On little toes or great toes?
If life's true seat were in the brain?
Did Ensign mean to marry Jane?
By whom, in fact, was Morgan slain?
Could matter ever suffer pain?
What would take out a cherry-stain?
Who picked the pocket of Seth Crane,
Of Waldo precinct, State of Maine?
Was Sir John Franklin sought in vain?
Did primitive Christians ever train?
What was the family-name of Cain?
Them spoons, were they by Betty ta'en?
Would earth-worm poultice cure a sprain?
Was Socrates so dreadful plain?
What teamster guided Charles's wain?
Was Uncle Ethan mad or sane,
And could his will in force remain?
If not, what counsel to retain?
Did Le Sage steal Gil Blas from Spain?
Was Junius writ by Thomas Paine?
Were ducks discomforted by rain?
How did Britannia rule the main?
Was Jonas coming back again?
Was vital truth upon the wane?
Did ghosts, to scare folks, drag a chain?
Who was our Huldah's chosen swain?
Did none have teeth pulled without payin',
    Ere ether was invented?
Whether mankind would not agree,
If the universe were tuned in C?
What was it ailed Lucindy's knee?
Whether folks eat folks in Feejee?
Whether *his* name would end with T?
If Saturn's rings were two or three,
And what bump in Phrenology
    They truly represented?
These problems dark, wherein they groped,
Wherewith man's reason vainly coped,
Now that the spirit-world was oped,
In all humility they hoped
    Would be resolved *instanter;*
Each of the miscellaneous rout
Brought his, or her, own little doubt,
And wished to pump the spirits out,
Through his or her own private spout,
    Into his or her decanter.

PART III

WHEREIN IT IS SHOWN THAT THE MOST
ARDENT SPIRITS ARE MORE ORNA-
MENTAL THAN USEFUL

Many a speculating wight
Came by express-trains, day and night,
To see if Knott would "sell his right,"
Meaning to make the ghosts a sight —
    What they call a "meenaygerie;"
One threatened, if he would not "trade,"
His run of custom to invade,
(He could not these sharp folks persuade
That he was not, in some way, paid,)
    And stamp him as a plagiary,
By coming down, at one fell swoop,
With THE ORIGINAL KNOCKING TROUPE,
Come recently from Hades,
Who (for a quarter-dollar heard)
Would ne'er rap out a hasty word
Whence any blame might be incurred
    From the most fastidious ladies;
The late lamented Jesse Soule,
To stir the ghosts up with a pole
And be director of the whole,
    Who was engaged the rather
For the rare merits he 'd combine,
Having been in the spirit line,
Which trade he only did resign,
With general applause, to shine,
Awful in mail of cotton fine,
    As ghost of Hamlet's father!
Another a fair plan reveals
Never yet hit on, which, he feels,
To Knott's religious sense appeals —
" We 'll have your house set up on wheels,
    A speculation pious;
For music, we can shortly find
A barrel-organ that will grind
Psalm-tunes — an instrument designed
For the New England tour — refined
From secular drosses, and inclined
To an unworldly turn, (combined
    With no sectarian bias;)
Then, travelling by stages slow,
Under the style of Knott & Co.,
I would accompany the show
As moral lecturer, the foe
Of Rationalism; while you could throw
The rappings in, and make them go
Strict Puritan principles, you know,
(How *do* you make 'em? with your toe?)

And the receipts which thence might flow,
    We could divide between us;
Still more attractions to combine,
Beside these services of mine,
I will throw in a very fine
(It would do nicely for a sign)
    Original Titian's Venus."
Another offered handsome fees
If Knott would get Demosthenes
(Nay, his mere knuckles, for more ease)
To rap a few short sentences;
Or if, for want of proper keys,
    His Greek might make confusion,
Then just to get a rap from Burke,
To recommend a little work
    On Public Elocution.
Meanwhile, the spirits made replies
To all the reverent *whats* and *whys*,
Resolving doubts of every size,
And giving seekers grave and wise,
Who came to know their destinies,
    A rap-turous reception;
When unbelievers void of grace
Came to investigate the place,
(Creatures of Sadducistic race,
With grovelling intellects and base,)
They could not find the slightest trace
    To indicate deception;
Indeed, it is declared by some
That spirits (of this sort) are glum,
Almost, or wholly, deaf and dumb,
And (out of self-respect) quite mum
To skeptic natures cold and numb,
Who of *this* kind of Kingdom Come
    Have not a just conception:
True, there were people who demurred
That, though the raps no doubt were heard
    Both under them and o'er them,
Yet, somehow, when a search they made,
They found Miss Jenny sore afraid,
Or Jenny's lover, Doctor Slade,
Equally awestruck and dismayed,
Or Deborah, the chambermaid,
Whose terrors not to be gainsaid
In laughs hysteric were displayed,
    Was always there before them;
This had its due effect with some
Who straight departed, muttering, Hum!
    Transparent hoax! and Gammon!
But these were few: believing souls,
Came, day by day, in larger shoals,
As the ancients to the windy holes
'Neath Delphi's tripod brought their doles,
    Or to the shrine of Ammon.

The spirits seemed exceeding tame,
Call whom you fancied, and he came;
The shades august of eldest fame
    You summoned with an awful ease;
As grosser spirits gurgled out
From chair and table with a spout,
In Auerbach's cellar once, to flout
The senses of the rabble rout,
Where'er the gimlet twirled about
    Of cunning Mephistopheles,
So did these spirits seem in store,
Behind the wainscot or the door,
Ready to thrill the being's core
Of every enterprising bore
    With their astounding glamour;
Whatever ghost one wished to hear,
By strange coincidence, was near
To make the past or future clear
    (Sometimes in shocking grammar)
By raps and taps, now there, now here —
It seemed as if the spirit queer
Of some departed auctioneer
Were doomed to practise by the year
    With the spirit of his hammer:
Whate'er you asked was answered, yet
One could not very deeply get
Into the obliging spirits' debt,
Because they used the alphabet
    In all communications,
And new revelings (though sublime)
Rapped out, one letter at a time,
    With boggles, hesitations,
Stoppings, beginnings o'er again,
And getting matters into train,
Could hardly overload the brain
    With too excessive rations,
Since just to ask *if two and two
Really make four?* or, *How d' ye do?*
And get the fit replies thereto
In the tramundane rat-tat-too,
    Might ask a whole day's patience.

'T was strange ('mongst other things) to find
In what odd sets the ghosts combined,
    Happy forthwith to thump any
Piece of intelligence inspired,
The truth whereof had been inquired
    By some one of the company;
For instance, Fielding, Mirabeau,
Orator Henley, Cicero,
Paley, John Ziska, Marivaux,
Melancthon, Robertson, Junot,
Scaliger, Chesterfield, Rousseau,
Hakluyt, Boccaccio, South, De Foe,

Diaz, Josephus, Richard Roe,
Odin, Arminius, Charles *le gros*,
Tiresias, the late James Crow,
Casabianca, Grose, Prideaux,
Old Grimes, Young Norval, Swift, Brissot,
Maimonides, the Chevalier D'O,
Socrates, Fénelon, Job, Stow,
The inventor of *Elixir pro*,
Euripides, Spinoza, Poe,
Confucius, Hiram Smith, and Fo,
Came (as it seemed, somewhat *de trop*)
With a disembodied Esquimaux,
To say that it was so and so,
    With Franklin's expedition;
One testified to ice and snow,
One that the mercury was low,
One that his progress was quite slow,
One that he much desired to go,
One that the cook had frozen his toe,
(Dissented from by Dandolo,
Wordsworth, Cynaegirus, Boileau,
La Hontan, and Sir Thomas Roe,)
One saw twelve white bears in a row,
One saw eleven and a crow,
With other things we could not know
(Of great statistic value, though,)
    By our mere mortal vision.

Sometimes the spirits made mistakes,
And seemed to play at ducks and drakes
With bold inquiry's heaviest stakes
    In science or in mystery;
They knew so little (and that wrong)
Yet rapped it out so bold and strong,
One would have said the unnumbered
    throng
Had been Professors of History;
What made it odder was, that those
Who, you would naturally suppose,
Could solve a question, if they chose,
As easily as count their toes,
    Were just the ones that blundered;
One day, Ulysses happening down,
A reader of Sir Thomas Browne
And who (with him) had wondered
What song it was the Sirens sang,
Asked the shrewd Ithacan — *bang! bang!*
With this response the chamber rang,
    "I guess it was Old Hundred."
And Franklin, being asked to name
The reason why the lightning came,
    Replied, "Because it thundered."

On one sole point the ghosts agreed,
One fearful point, than which, indeed,

    Nothing could seem absurder;
Poor Colonel Jones they all abused
And finally downright accused
    The poor old man of murder;
'T was thus; by dreadful raps was shown
Some spirit's longing to make known
A bloody fact, which he alone
Was privy to, (such ghosts more prone
    In Earth's affairs to meddle are;)
Who are you? with awe-stricken looks,
All ask: his airy knuckles he crooks,
And raps, "I *was* Eliab Snooks,
    That used to be a pedler;
Some on ye still are on my books!"
Whereat, to inconspicuous nooks;
(More fearing this than common spooks,)
    Shrank each indebted meddler;
Further the vengeful ghost declared
That while his earthly life was spared,
About the country he had fared,
    A duly licensed follower
Of that much-wandering trade that
    wins
Slow profit from the sale of tins
    And various kinds of hollow-ware;
That Colonel Jones enticed him in,
Pretending that he wanted tin,
There slew him with a rolling-pin,
Hid him in a potato-bin,
    And (the same night) him ferried
Across Great Pond to t' other shore,
And there, on land of Widow Moore,
Just where you turn to Larkin's store,
    Under a rock him buried;
Some friends (who happened to be by)
He called upon to testify
That what he said was not a lie,
    And that he did not stir this
Foul matter, out of any spite
But from a simple love of right; —
    Which statements the Nine Worthies,
Rabbi Akiba, Charlemagne,
Seth, Colley Cibber, General Wayne,
Cambyses, Tasso, Tubal-Cain,
The owner of a castle in Spain,
Jehanghire, and the Widow of Nain,
(The friends aforesaid,) made more plain
    And by loud raps attested;
To the same purport testified
Plato, John Wilkes, and Colonel Pride
Who knew said Snooks before he died,
    Had in his wares invested,
Thought him entitled to belief
And freely could concur, in brief,
    In everything the rest did.

Eliab this occasion seized,
(Distinctly here the spirit sneezed,)
To say that he should ne'er be eased
Till Jenny married whom she pleased,
    Free from all checks and urgin's,
(This spirit dropt his final g's)
And that, unless Knott quickly sees
This done, the spirits to appease,
They would come back his life to tease,
As thick as mites in ancient cheese,
And let his house on an endless lease
To the ghosts (terrific rappers these
And veritable Eumenides)
    Of the Eleven Thousand Virgins!

Knott was perplexed and shook his head,
He did not wish his child to wed
    With a suspected murderer,
(For, true or false, the rumor spread,)
But as for this roiled life he led,
" It would not answer," so he said,
    " To have it go no furderer."
At last, scarce knowing what it meant,
Reluctantly he gave consent
That Jenny, since 't was evident
That she *would* follow her own bent,
    Should make her own election;
For that appeared the only way
These frightful noises to allay
Which had already turned him gray
    And plunged him in dejection.

Accordingly, this artless maid
Her father's ordinance obeyed,
And, all in whitest crape arrayed,
(Miss Pulsifer the dresses made
And wishes here the fact displayed
That she still carries on the trade,
The third door south from Bagg's Arcade,)
A very faint " I do " essayed
And gave her hand to Hiram Slade,
From which time forth, the ghosts were
        laid,
And ne'er gave trouble after;
But the Selectmen, be it known,
Dug underneath the aforesaid stone,
Where the poor pedler's corpse was
        thrown,
And found thereunder a jaw-bone,
Though, when the crowner sat thereon,
He nothing hatched, except alone
    Successive broods of laughter;
It was a frail and dingy thing,
In which a grinder or two did cling,

In color like molasses,
Which surgeons, called from far and wide,
Upon the horror to decide,
    Having put on their glasses,
Reported thus: " To judge by looks,
These bones, by some queer hooks or
        crooks,
May have belonged to Mr. Snooks,
But, as men deepest-read in books
    Are perfectly aware, bones,
If buried fifty years or so,
Lose their identity and grow
    From human bones to bare bones."

Still, if to Jaalam you go down,
You 'll find two parties in the town,
One headed by Benaiah Brown,
    And one by Perez Tinkham;
The first believe the ghosts all through
And vow that they shall never rue
The happy chance by which they knew
That people in Jupiter are blue,
And very fond of Irish stew,
Two curious facts which Prince Lee Boo
Rapped clearly to a chosen few —
    Whereas the others think 'em
A trick got up by Doctor Slade
With Deborah the chambermaid
    And that sly cretur Jinny.
That all the revelations wise,
At which the Brownites made big eyes,
Might have been given by Jared Keyes,
    A natural fool and ninny,
And, last week, did n't Eliab Snooks
Come back with never better looks,
As sharp as new-bought mackerel hooks,
    And bright as a new pin, eh?
Good Parson Wilbur, too, avers
(Though to be mixed in parish stirs
Is worse than handling chestnut-burrs)
That no case to his mind occurs
Where spirits ever did converse,
Save in a kind of guttural Erse,
    (So say the best authorities;)
And that a charge by raps conveyed
Should be most scrupulously weighed
    And searched into, before it is
Made public, since it may give pain
That cannot soon be cured again,
And one word may infix a stain
    Which ten cannot gloss over,
Though speaking for his private part,
He is rejoiced with all his heart
    Miss Knott missed not her lover.

FRAGMENTS OF AN UNFINISHED POEM

In the note introducing *Fitz Adam's Story, infra* p. 411, will be found a brief account of the unfinished poem of which this is a fragment.

I AM a man of forty, sirs, a native of East
    Haddam,
And have some reason to surmise that I
    descend from Adam;
But what 's my pedigree to you ?   That I
    will soon unravel;
I 've sucked my Haddam-Eden dry, there-
    fore desire to travel,
And, as a natural consequence, presume I
    need n't say,
I wish to write some letters home and have
    those letters p—
[I spare the word suggestive of those grim
    Next Morns that mount
Clump, Clump, the stairways of the brain
    with — " *Sir, my small account,*"
And, after every good we gain — Love,
    Fame, Wealth, Wisdom — still,
As punctual as a cuckoo clock, hold up their
    little bill,
The *garçons* in our Café of Life, by dream-
    ing us forgot —
Sitting, like Homer's heroes, full and mus-
    ing God knows what, —
Till they say, bowing, *S'il vous plait, voila,*
    Messieurs, la note!]
I would not hint at this so soon, but in our
    callous day,
The tollman Debt, who drops his bar across
    the world's highway,
Great Cæsar in mid-march would stop, if
    Cæsar could not pay;
Pilgriming 's dearer than it was : men
    cannot travel now
Scot-free from Dan to Beersheba upon a
    simple vow;
Nay, as long back as Bess's time, when
    Walsingham went over
Ambassador to Cousin France, at Canter-
    bury and Dover
He was so fleeced by innkeepers that, ere
    he quitted land,
He wrote to the Prime Minister to take the
    knaves in hand.
If I with staff and scallop-shell should try
    my way to win,
Would Bonifaces quarrel as to who should
    take me in ?

Or would my pilgrim's progress end where
    Bunyan started his on,
And my grand tour be round and round the
    backyard of a prison ?
I give you here a saying deep and therefore,
    haply true;
'T is out of Merlin's prophecies, but quite
    as good as new:
The question boath for men and meates longe
    vohages yt beginne
Lyes in a notshell, rather saye lyes in a case
    of tinne.
But, though men may not travel now, as in
    the Middle Ages,
With self-sustaining retinues of little gilt-
    edged pages,
Yet one may manage pleasantly, where'er
    he likes to roam,
By sending his small pages (at so much per
    small page) home;
And if a staff and scallop-shell won't serve
    so well as then,
Our outlay is about as small — just paper,
    ink, and pen.
Be thankful ! Humbugs never die, more
    than the wandering Jew;
Bankrupt, they publish their own deaths,
    slink for a while from view,
Then take an *alias,* change the sign, and the
    old trade renew;
Indeed, 't is wondrous how each Age,
    though laughing at the Past,
Insists on having its tight shoe made on the
    same old last;
How it is sure its system would break up
    at once without
The bunion which it *will* believe hereditary
    gout;
How it takes all its swans for geese, nay,
    stranger yet and sadder,
Sees in its treadmill's fruitless jog a heaven-
    ward Jacob's-ladder,
Shouts, *Lo, the Shining Heights are reached !*
    One moment more aspire !
Trots into cramps its poor, dear legs, gets
    never an inch the higher,
And like the others, ends with pipe **and**
    mug beside the fire.

There, 'tween each doze, it whiffs and sips
and watches with a sneer
The green recruits that trudge and sweat
where it had swinked whilere,
And sighs to think this soon spent zeal
should be in simple truth
The only interval between old Fogyhood
and Youth:
"Well," thus it muses, "well, what odds?
'T is not for us to warn;
'T will be the same when we are dead, and
was ere we were born;
Without the Treadmill, too, how grind our
store of winter's corn?
Had we no stock, nor twelve per cent. re-
ceived from Treadmill shares,
We might . . . but these poor devils at
last will get our easy-chairs.
High aims and hopes have great rewards,
they, too, serene and snug,
Shall one day have their soothing pipe and
their enlivening mug;
From Adam, empty-handed Youth hath
always heard the hum
Of Good Times Coming, and will hear un-
til the last day come;
Young ears hear forward, old ones back,
and, while the earth rolls on,
Full-handed Eld shall hear recede the steps
of Good Times Gone;
Ah what a cackle we set up whene'er an
egg was laid!
Cack-cack-cack-cackle! rang around, the
scratch for worms was stayed,
Cut-cut-ca-dah-cut! from this egg the com-
ing cock shall stalk!
The great New Era dawns, the age of
Deeds and not of Talk!
And every stupid hen of us hugged close
his egg of chalk,
Thought, — sure, I feel life stir within,
each day with greater strength,
When lo, the chick! from former chicks
he differed not a jot,
But grew and crew and scratched and
went, like those before, to pot!"
So muse the dim Emeriti, and, mournful
though it be,
I must confess a kindred thought hath
sometimes come to me,
Who, though but just of forty turned, have
heard the rumorous fame
Of nine and ninety Coming Men, all —
coming till they came.

Pure Mephistopheles all this? the vulgar
nature jeers?
Good friend, while I was writing it, my
eyes were dim with tears;
Thrice happy he who cannot see, or who
his eyes can shut,
Life's deepest sorrow is contained in that
small word there — But!
. . . .
We 're pretty nearly crazy here with
change and go ahead,
With flinging our caught bird away for
two i' th' bush instead,
With butting 'gainst the wall which we
declare shall be a portal,
And questioning Deeps that never yet have
oped their lips to mortal;
We 're growing pale and hollow-eyed, and
out of all condition,
With mediums and prophetic chairs, and
crickets with a mission,
(The most astounding oracles since Ba-
laam's donkey spoke, —
'T would seem our furniture was all of
Dodonean oak.)
Make but the public laugh, be sure 't will
take you to be somebody;
'T will wrench its button from your clutch,
my densely earnest glum body;
'T is good, this noble earnestness, good in
its place, but why
Make great Achilles' shield the pan to
bake a penny pie?
Why, when we have a kitchen-range, insist
that we shall stop,
And bore clear down to central fires to
broil our daily chop?
Excalibur and Durandart are swords of
price, but then
Why draw them sternly when you wish to
trim your nails or pen?
Small gulf between the ape and man; you
bridge it with your staff;
But it will be impassable until the ape can
laugh; —
No, no, be common now and then, be sen-
sible, be funny,
And, as Siberians bait their traps for bears
with pots of honey,
From which ere they 'll withdraw their
snouts, they 'll suffer many a club-
lick,
So bait your moral figure-of-fours to catch
the Orson public.

Look how the dead leaves melt their way
   down through deep-drifted snow;
They take the sun-warmth down with them
   — pearls could not conquer so;
There *is* a moral here, you see; if you
   would preach, you must
Steep all your truths in sunshine would
   you have them pierce the crust;
Brave Jeremiah, you are grand and ter-
   rible, a sign
And wonder, but were never quite a popu-
   lar divine;
Fancy the figure you would cut among the
   nuts and wine !
I, on occasion, too, could preach, but hold
   it wiser far
To give the public sermons it will take with
   its cigar,
And morals fugitive, and vague as are
   these smoke-wreaths light
In which . . . I trace . . . a . . . let me
   see — bless me ! 't is out of sight.
. . . .
There are some goodish things at sea; for
   instance, one can feel
A grandeur in the silent man forever at the
   wheel,
That bit of two-legged intellect, that par-
   ticle of drill,
Who the huge floundering hulk inspires with
   reason, brain, and will,
And makes the ship, though skies are black
   and headwinds whistle loud,
Obey her conscience there which feels the
   loadstar through the cloud;
And when by lusty western gales the full-
   sailed barque is hurled,
Towards the great moon which, setting on
   the silent underworld,
Rounds luridly up to look on ours, and
   shoots a broadening line,
Of palpitant light from crest to crest across
   the ridgy brine,
Then from the bows look back and feel a
   thrill that never stales,
In that full-bosomed, swan-white pomp of
   onward-yearning sails;
Ah, when dear cousin Bull laments that
   you can't make a poem,
Take him aboard a clipper-ship, young
   Jonathan, and show him
A work of art that in its grace and grandeur
   may compare
With any thing that any race has fashioned
   any where;

'T is not a statue, grumbles John; nay, if
   you come to that,
We think of Hyde Park Corner, and con-
   cede you beat us flat
With your equestrian statue to a Nose and
   a Cocked hat;
But 't is not a cathedral; well, e'en that we
   will allow,
Both statues and cathedrals are anachro-
   nistic now;
Your minsters, coz, the monuments of men
   who conquered you,
You 'd sell a bargain, if we 'd take the deans
   and chapters too;
No; mortal men build nowadays, as always
   heretofore,
Good temples to the gods which they in
   very truth adore;
The shepherds of this Broker Age, with all
   their willing flocks,
Although they bow to stones no more, do
   bend the knee to stocks,
And churches can't be beautiful though
   crowded, floor and gallery,
If people worship preacher, and if preacher
   worship salary;
'T is well to look things in the face, the god
   o' the modern universe,
Hermes, cares naught for halls of art and
   libraries of puny verse,
If they don't sell, he notes them thus upon
   his ledger — say, *per*
Contra to a loss of so much stone, best
   Russia duck and paper;
And, after all, about this Art men talk a
   deal of fudge,
Each nation has its path marked out, from
   which it must not budge;
The Romans had as little art as Noah in his
   ark,
Yet somehow on this globe contrived to
   make an epic mark;
Religion, painting, sculpture, song — for
   these they ran up jolly ticks
With Greece and Egypt, but they were great
   artists in their politics,
And if we make no minsters, John, nor
   epics, yet the Fates
Are not entirely deaf to men who *can* build
   ships and states;
The arts are never pioneers, but men have
   strength and health
Who, called on suddenly, can improvise a
   commonwealth,

Nay, can more easily go on and frame them
    by the dozen,
Than you can make a dinner-speech, dear
    sympathizing cousin:
And, though our restless Jonathan have not
    your graver bent, sure he
Does represent this hand-to-mouth, pert,
    rapid, nineteenth century;
This is the Age of Scramble; men move
    faster than they did
When they pried up the imperial Past's
    deep-dusted coffin-lid,
Searching for scrolls of precedent; the wire-
    leashed lightning now
Replaces Delphos — men don't leave the
    steamer for the scow;
What public, were they new to-day, would
    ever stop to read
The Iliad, the Shanàmeh, or the Nibelun-
    genlied ?

Their public's gone, the artist Greek, the
    lettered Shah, the hairy Graf —
Folio and plesiosaur sleep well; *we* weary
    o'er a paragraph;
The mind moves planet-like no more, it
    fizzes, cracks, and bustles;
From end to end with journals dry the land
    o'ershadowed rustles,
As with dead leaves a winter-beech, and,
    with their breath-roused jars
Amused, we care not if they hide the eternal
    skies and stars;
Down to the general level of the Board of
    Brokers sinking,
The Age takes in the newspapers, or, to say
    sooth unshrinking,
The newspapers take in the Age, and
    stocks do all the thinking.

AN ORIENTAL APOLOGUE

SOMEWHERE in India, upon a time,
(Read it not Injah, or you spoil the verse,)
    There dwelt two saints whose privilege
        sublime
It was to sit and watch the world grow
        worse,
    Their only care (in that delicious clime)
At proper intervals to pray and curse;
    Pracrit the dialect each prudent brother
    Used for himself, Damnonian for the
        other.

One half the time of each was spent in
    praying
For blessings on his own unworthy head,
The other half in fearfully portraying
Where certain folks would go when they
    were dead;
    This system of exchanges — there's no
        saying
To what more solid barter 't would have led,
    But that a river, vext with boils and
        swellings
    At rainy times, kept peace between their
        dwellings.

So they two played at wordy battledore
And kept a curse forever in the air,
    Flying this way or that from shore to
        shore;

Nor other labor did this holy pair,
    Clothed and supported from the lavish
        store
Which crowds lanigerous brought with
    daily care;
    They toiled not, neither did they spin;
        their bias
Was tow'rd the harder task of being
    pious.

Each from his hut rushed six score times
    a day,
Like a great canon of the Church full-
    rammed
    With cartridge theologic, (so to say,)
Touched himself off, and then, recoiling,
    slammed
His hovel's door behind him in a way
That to his foe said plainly, — *you'll* be
    damned;
    And so like Potts and Wainwright, shrill
        and strong
The two D——D'd each other all day
    long.

One was a dancing Dervise, a Moham-
    medan,
The other was a Hindoo, a gymnosophist;
    One kept his whatd'yecallit and his Ram-
        adan,

Laughing to scorn the sacred rites and laws
    of his
Transfluvial rival, who, in turn, called
    Ahmed an
Old top, and, as a clincher, shook across a
    fist
With nails six inches long, yet lifted
    not
His eyes from off his navel's mystic knot.

"Who whirls not round six thousand
    times an hour
Will go," screamed Ahmed, "to the evil
    place;
May he eat dirt, and may the dog and
    Giaour
Defile the graves of him and all his race;
    Allah loves faithful souls and gives them
    power
To spin till they are purple in the face;
    Some folks get you know what, but he
    that pure is
    Earns Paradise and ninety thousand hou-
    ries."

"Upon the silver mountain, South by
    East,
Sits Brahma fed upon the sacred bean;
    He loves those men whose nails are still
    increased,
Who all their lives keep ugly, foul, and
    lean;
'T is of his grace that not a bird or beast
Adorned with claws like mine was ever
    seen;
    The suns and stars are Brahma's
    thoughts divine,
    Even as these trees I seem to see are
    mine."

"Thou seem'st to see, indeed !" roared
    Ahmed back;
"Were I but once across this plaguy
    stream,
With a stout sapling in my hand, one
    whack
On those lank ribs would rid thee of that
    dream !
    Thy Brahma-blasphemy is ipecac
To my soul's stomach; couldst thou grasp
    the scheme
    Of true redemption, thou wouldst know
    that Deity
Whirls by a kind of blessed spontaneity.

"And this it is which keeps our earth
    here going
With all the stars." — "Oh, vile ! but
    there's a place
Prepared for such; to think of Brahma
    throwing
Worlds like a juggler's balls up into Space !
    Why, not so much as a smooth lotos
    blowing
Is e'er allowed that silence to efface
    Which broods round Brahma, and our
    earth, 't is known,
    Rests on a tortoise, moveless as this
    stone."

So they kept up their banning amœbæan,
When suddenly came floating down the
    stream
A youth whose face like an incarnate
    pæan
Glowed, 't was so full of grandeur and of
    gleam;
"If there be gods, then, doubtless, this
    must be one,"
Thought both at once, and then began to
    scream,
"Surely, whate'er immortals know, thou
    knowest,
    Decide between us twain before thou
    goest !"

The youth was drifting in a slim canoe
Most like a huge white water-lily's petal,
    But neither of our theologians knew
Whereof 't was made ; whether of heav-
    enly metal
Seldseen, or of a vast pearl split in two
And hollowed, was a point they could not
    settle;
    'T was good debate-seed, though, and
    bore large fruit
In after years of many a tart dispute.

There were no wings upon the stranger's
    shoulders,
And yet he seemed so capable of rising
    That, had he soared like thistledown,
    beholders
Had thought the circumstance noways sur-
    prising;
    Enough that he remained, and, when the
    scolders
Hailed him as umpire in their vocal prize-
    ring,

The painter of his boat he lightly threw
Around a lotos-stem, and brought her to.

The strange youth had a look as if he
        might
Have trod far planets where the atmosphere
(Of nobler temper) steeps the face with
        light,
Just as our skins are tanned and freckled
        here;
His air was that of a cosmopolite
In the wide universe from sphere to sphere;
Perhaps he was (his face had such grave
        beauty)
An officer of Saturn's guards off duty.

Both saints began to unfold their tales at
        once,
Both wished their tales, like simial ones,
        prehensile,
That they might seize his ear; *fool!
        knave!* and *dunce!*
Flew zigzag back and forth, like strokes of
        pencil
In a child's fingers; voluble as duns,
They jabbered like the stones on that
        immense hill
In the Arabian Nights; until the stranger
Began to think his ear-drums in some
        danger.

In general those who nothing have to say
Contrive to spend the longest time in doing
        it;
They turn and vary it in every way,
Hashing it, stewing it, mincing it, *ragouting*
        it;
Sometimes they keep it purposely at bay,
Then let it slip to be again pursuing it;
They drone it, groan it, whisper it and
        shout it,
Refute it, flout it, swear to 't, prove it,
        doubt it.

Our saints had practised for some thirty
        years;
Their talk, beginning with a single stem,
Spread like a banyan, sending down live
        piers,
Colonies of digression, and, in them,
Germs of yet new dispersion; once by the
        ears,
They could convey damnation in a hem,
And blow the pinch of premise-priming off
Long syllogistic batteries, with a cough.

Each had a theory that the human ear
A providential tunnel was, which led
To a huge vacuum (and surely here
They showed some knowledge of the gen-
        eral head,)
For cant to be decanted through, a mere
Auricular canal or mill-race fed
All day and night, in sunshine and in
        shower,
From their vast heads of milk-and-water-
        power.

The present being a peculiar case,
Each with unwonted zeal the other scouted,
Put his spurred hobby through its every
        pace,
Pished, pshawed, poohed, horribled, bahed,
        jeered, sneered, flouted,
Sniffed, nonsensed, infideled, fudged, with
        his face
Looked scorn too nicely shaded to be
        shouted,
And, with each inch of person and of
        vesture,
Contrived to hint some most disdainful
        gesture.

At length, when their breath's end was
        come about,
And both could now and then just gasp
        "impostor!"
Holding their heads thrust menacingly
        out,
As staggering cocks keep up their fighting
        posture,
The stranger smiled and said, "Beyond a
        doubt
'T is fortunate, my friends, that you have
        lost your
United parts of speech, or it had been
Impossible for me to get between.

"Produce! says Nature, — what have you
        produced?
A new strait-waistcoat for the human mind;
Are you not limbed, nerved, jointed,
        arteried, juiced,
As other men? yet, faithless to your
        kind,
Rather like noxious insects you are used
To puncture life's fair fruit, beneath the
        rind
Laying your creed-eggs, whence in time
        there spring
Consumers new to eat and buzz and sting.

" Work! you have no conception how
    't will sweeten
Your views of Life and Nature, God and
    Man;
  Had you been forced to earn what you
    have eaten,
Your heaven had shown a less dyspeptic
    plan;
  At present your whole function is to eat
    ten
And talk ten times as rapidly as you can;
  Were your shape true to cosmogonic laws,
  You would be nothing but a pair of jaws.

" Of all the useless beings in creation
The earth could spare most easily you
    bakers
  Of little clay gods, formed in shape and
    fashion
Precisely in the image of their makers ;
  Why, it would almost move a saint to
    passion,
To see these blind and deaf, the hourly
    breakers
  Of God's own image in their brother
    men,
  Set themselves up to tell the how, where,
    when,

" Of God's existence; one's digestion 's
    worse —
So makes a god of vengeance and of blood ;
  Another, — but no matter, they reverse
Creation's plan, out of their own vile mud
  Pat up a god, and burn, drown, hang, or
    curse
Whoever worships not; each keeps his stud
  Of texts which wait with saddle on and
    bridle
  To hunt down atheists to their ugly idol.

" This, I perceive, has been your occupa-
    tion;
You should have been more usefully em-
    ployed;
  All men are bound to earn their daily
    ration,
Where States make not that primal contract
    void
  By cramps and limits; simple devastation
Is the worm's task, and what he has de-
    stroyed
  His monument; creating is man's work
  And that, too, something more than mist
    and murk."

So having said, the youth was seen no
    more,
And straightway our sage Brahmin, the
    philosopher,
  Cried, " That was aimed at thee, thou
    endless bore,
Idle and useless as the growth of moss over
A rotting tree-trunk!" " I would square
    that score
Full soon," replied the Dervise, " could I
    cross over
  And catch thee by the beard. Thy nails
    I 'd trim
  And make thee work, as was advised by
    him."

" Work ? Am I not at work from morn
    till night
Sounding the deeps of oracles umbilical
  Which for man's guidance never come to
    light,
With all their various aptitudes, until I
    call ? "
  " And I, do I not twirl from left to right
For conscience' sake ? Is that no work?
    Thou silly gull,
  He had thee in his eye; 't was Gabriel
  Sent to reward my faith, I know him
    well."

" 'T was Vishnu, thou vile whirligig! "
  . and so
The good old quarrel was begun anew;
  One would have sworn the sky was black
    as sloe,
Had but the other dared to call it blue;
  Nor were the followers who fed them
    slow
To treat each other with their curses, too,
  Each hating t' other (moves it tears or
    laughter ?)
  Because he thought him sure of hell here-
    after.

At last some genius built a bridge of boats
Over the stream, and Ahmed's zealots filed
  Across, upon a mission to (cut throats
And) spread religion pure and undefiled;
  They sowed the propagandist's wildest
    oats,
Cutting off all, down to the smallest child,
  And came back, giving thanks for such
    fat mercies,
  To find their harvest gone past prayers
    or curses.

All gone except their saint's religious hops,
Which he kept up with more than common flourish;
But these, however satisfying crops
For the inner man, were not enough to nourish
The body politic, which quickly drops
Reserve in such sad junctures, and turns currish;
So Ahmed soon got cursed for all the famine
Where'er the popular voice could edge a damn in.

At first he pledged a miracle quite boldly,
And, for a day or two, they growled and waited;
But, finding that this kind of manna coldly
Sat on their stomachs, they erelong berated
The saint for still persisting in that old lie,
Till soon the whole machine of saintship grated,
Ran slow, creaked, stopped, and, wishing him in Tophet,

They gathered strength enough to stone the prophet.

Some stronger ones contrived (by eating leather,
Their weaker friends, and one thing or another)
The winter months of scarcity to weather;
Among these was the late saint's younger brother,
Who, in the spring, collecting them together,
Persuaded them that Ahmed's holy pother
Had wrought in their behalf, and that the place
Of Saint should be continued to his race.

Accordingly, 't was settled on the spot
That Allah favored that peculiar breed;
Beside, as all were satisfied, 't would not
Be quite respectable to have the need
Of public spiritual food forgot;
And so the tribe, with proper forms, decreed
That he, and, failing him, his next of kin,
Forever for the people's good should spin.

THE BIGLOW PAPERS

FIRST SERIES

In a letter, June 16, 1846, to Mr. Sydney Howard Gay, then editor of the *Anti-Slavery Standard*, Lowell wrote: " I mean to send all the poems I write (on whatever subject) first to the *Standard*, except such arrows as I may deem it better to shoot from the ambushment of the *Courier*, because the old enemy offers me a fairer mark from that quarter. . . . You will find a squib of mine in this week's *Courier*. I wish it to continue anonymous, for I wish slavery to think it has as many enemies as possible. If I may judge from the number of persons who have asked me if I wrote it, I have struck the old hulk of the Public between wind and water." This was the first of the *Biglow Papers*. The scheme of anonymity was preserved through the first series, and as Lowell wrote forty years later to Thomas Hughes (*Letters*, II. 334) : " I had great fun out of it. I have often wished that I could have had a literary *nom de guerre*, and kept my own to myself. I should n't have cared a doit what

happened to *him*." But as appears from the letter given above, the satire was readily fathered on Lowell, and many of the subsequent papers were published in the *Standard*. " As for Hosea," he wrote to his friend Mr. Charles F. Briggs, November 13, 1847, " I am sorry that I began by making him such a detestable speller. There is no fun in bad spelling of itself, but only where the misspelling suggests something else which is droll *per se*. You see I am getting him out of it gradually. I mean to altogether. Parson Wilbur is about to propose a subscription for fitting him for college, and has already commenced his education. Perhaps you like the last best, because it is more personal and has therefore more directness of purpose. But I confess I think that Birdofredom's attempt to explain the Anglo-Saxon theory is the best thing yet, except Parson Wilbur's letter in the *Courier* of last Saturday." The series ran at intervals for about eighteen months, when the papers were collected into a volume. Lowell's letters, written when he was busy over the equipment of the book, show him in high spirits over his *jeu d'esprit*. "I am going," he writes to Mr. Briggs, " to indulge all my fun in a volume of H. Biglow's verses which I am preparing, and which I shall edit under the character of the Rev. Mr. Wilbur. I hope you saw Mr. B.'s last production, which I consider his best hitherto. I am going to include in the volume an essay of the reverend gentleman on the Yankee dialect, and on dialects in general, and on everything else, and also an attempt at a complete natural history of the Humbug — which I think I shall write in Latin. The book will purport to be published at Jaalam (Mr. B.'s native place), and will be printed on brownish paper, with those little head and tail-pieces which used to adorn our earlier publications — such as hives, scrolls, urns, and the like."

This was written on the last day of the year 1847, but it was not until September of the next year that the actual volume got under way; for meanwhile Lowell's original design had been modified, and he turned the fun he had been devising for the volume of mock poetry into the collection of his Biglow Papers. The essay on the Yankee dialect by Mr. Wilbur was included, but it was not till the second series was published, nearly twenty years later, that there appeared the scholarly introduction, not now as a piece of affected pedantry, but as the serious and delightful study of the author delivered in his own voice.

At the beginning of September, 1848, Lowell wrote to Mr. Gay: "I am as busy as I can be with Mr. Biglow's poems, of which I have got between twenty and thirty pages already printed. It is the hardest book to print that ever I had anything to do with, and what with corrections and Mr. Wilbur's annotations, keeps me more employed than I care to be." Later in the same month he wrote to the same correspondent that he was "wearied out with Mr. Biglow and his tiresome (though wholly respectable) friend Mr. Wilbur." His notes continue to show the pressure under which he worked until the book was published, the middle of November. The first edition (1500) was gone in a week, and the book and its author became famous.

A little more than ten years afterward an English edition was to appear, and Thomas Hughes, who had it in charge, wrote to Lowell asking for a new preface. The answer, a portion of which is here given, is interesting as showing how the book appeared as a whole to its author when he was in the midst of his University service and had made a name for himself as scholar and critic as well as poet.

CAMBRIDGE, MASS., Sept. 13, 1859.

MY DEAR SIR: — I have put off from time to time writing to you, because I hardly knew what to write. To say simply that I liked your writings would have been pleasant enough (though that would have given me no claim upon you that was not shared by all the world), but I find it particularly hard to write anything about a book of my own. It has been a particular satisfaction to me to hear, now and then, some friendly voice from the old mother-island say " Well done " of the *Biglow Papers*; for, to say the truth, I like them myself, and when I was reading them over for a new edition, a year or two ago, could not help laughing. But then as I laughed I found myself asking, "Are these yours? How did you make them?" Friendly people say to me sometimes, "Write us more *Biglow Papers*," and I have even been simple enough to try, only to find that I could not. This has helped to persuade me that the book was a genuine growth, and not a manufacture, and that, therefore, I had an honest right to be pleased without blushing if people liked it. But then, this very fact makes it rather hard to write an introduction to it. All I can say is that the book was *that*; how it came is more than I can tell. I cannot, like the great Goethe, deliberately imagine what would have been a proper *Entstehungsweise* for my book, and then assume it as a fact. And as for an historical preface, I find that quite as hard after now twelve years of more cloistered interests and studies that have alienated me very much from contemporary politics. I only know that I believed our war with Mexico (though we had as just ground for it as a strong nation ever has against a weak one) to be essentially a war of false pretences, and that it would result in widening the boundaries and so prolonging the life of slavery. Believing that it is the manifest destiny of the English race to occupy this whole continent, and to display there that practical understanding in matters of government and colonization which no other race has given such proof of possessing since the Romans, I hated to see a noble hope evaporated into a lying phrase to sweeten the foul breath of demagogues. Leaving the sin of it to God, I believed, and still believe, that slavery is the Achilles-heel of our polity; that it is a temporary and false supremacy of the white races, sure to destroy that supremacy at last, because an enslaved people always prove themselves of more enduring fibre than their enslavers, as not suffering from the social vices sure to be engendered by oppression in the governing class. Against these and many other things I thought all honest men should protest. I was born and bred in the country, and the dialect was homely to me. I tried my first *Biglow* paper in a newspaper, and found that it had a great run. So I wrote the others from time to time during the year which followed, always very rapidly, and sometimes (as with " What Mr. Robinson thinks ") at one sitting.

When I came to collect them and publish them in a volume, I conceived my parson-editor, with his pedantry and verbosity, his amiable vanity and superiority to the verses he was editing, as a fitting artistic background and foil. It gave me the chance, too, of glancing obliquely at many things which were beyond the horizon of my other characters. I was told afterwards that my Parson Wilbur was only Jedediah Cleishbotham over again, and I dare say it may be so; but I drew him from the life as well as I could, and for the authentic reasons I have mentioned. I confess that I am proud of the recognition the book has received in England, because it seems to prove that, despite its intense provincialism, there is a general truth to human nature in it which justifies its having been written.

But life is too short to write about one's self in, and you see that I cannot make a suitable preface. I would rather have something of this kind: " It could not but be gratifying to the writer of the *Biglow Papers* that Mr. Trübner should deem it worth his while to publish an edition of them in England. It gives him a particular pleasure that the author of *Tom Brown's School Days* should have consented to see the work through the press, for the remarkable favor with which that work was received on both sides of the Atlantic proved that all speakers of the English tongue, however differing in other respects, agree wholly in their admiration for soundness of head and heart and manliness of character."

Now do not think this is " Buncombe."

The first series as here given retains the elaborate apparatus attached to the poem, in the order given in the book when first published by George Nichols, Cambridge.

NOTICES OF AN INDEPENDENT PRESS

[I HAVE observed, reader (bene- or malevolent, as it may happen), that it is customary to append to the second editions of books, and to the second works of authors, short sentences commendatory of the first, under the title of *Notices of the Press*. These, I have been given to understand, are procurable at certain established rates, payment being made either in money or advertising patronage by the publisher, or by an adequate outlay of servility on the part of the author. Considering these things with myself, and also that such notices are neither intended, nor generally believed, to convey any real opinions, being a purely ceremonial accompaniment of literature, and resembling certificates to the virtues of various morbiferal panaceas, I conceived that it would be not only more economical to prepare a sufficient number of such myself, but also more immediately subservient to the end in view to prefix them to this our primary edition rather than to await the contingency of a second, when they would seem to be of small utility. To delay attaching the *bobs* until the second attempt at flying the kite would indicate but a slender experience in that useful art. Neither has it escaped my notice, nor failed to afford me matter of reflection, that, when a circus or a caravan is about to visit Jaalam, the initial step is to send forward large and highly ornamented bills of performance, to be hung in the bar-room and the

post-office. These having been sufficiently gazed at, and beginning to lose their attractiveness except for the flies, and, truly, the boys also (in whom I find it impossible to repress, even during school-hours, certain oral and telegraphic communications concerning the expected show), upon some fine morning the band enters in a gayly painted wagon, or triumphal chariot, and with noisy advertisement, by means of brass, wood, and sheepskin, makes the circuit of our startled village streets. Then, as the exciting sounds draw nearer and nearer, do I desiderate those eyes of Aristarchus, " whose looks were as a breeching to a boy." Then do I perceive, with vain regret of wasted opportunities, the advantage of a pancratic or pantechnic education, since he is most reverenced by my little subjects who can throw the cleanest summerset or walk most securely upon the revolving cask. The story of the Pied Piper becomes for the first time credible to me (albeit confirmed by the Hameliners dating their legal instruments from the period of his exit), as I behold how those strains, without pretence of magical potency, bewitch the pupillary legs, nor leave to the pedagogic an entire self-control. For these reasons, lest my kingly prerogative should suffer diminution, I prorogue my restless commons, whom I follow into the street, chiefly lest some mischief may chance befall them. After the manner of such a band, I send forward the following notices of domestic manufacture, to make brazen proclamation, not unconscious of the advantage which will accrue, if our little craft, *cymbula sutilis*, shall seem to leave port with a clipping breeze, and to carry, in nautical phrase, a bone in her mouth. Nevertheless, I have chosen, as being more equitable, to prepare some also sufficiently objurgatory, that readers of every taste may find a dish to their palate. I have modelled them upon actually existing specimens, preserved in my own cabinet of natural curiosities. One, in particular, I had copied with tolerable exactness from a notice of one of my own discourses, which, from its superior tone and appearance of vast experience, I concluded to have been written by a man at least three hundred years of age, though I recollected no existing instance of such antediluvian longevity. Nevertheless, I afterwards discovered the author to be a young gentleman preparing for the ministry under the direction of one of my brethren in a neighboring town, and whom I had once instinctively corrected in a Latin quantity. But this I have been forced to omit, from its too great length. — H. W.]

From the Universal Littery Universe.

Full of passages which rivet the attention of the reader. . . . Under a rustic garb, sentiments are conveyed which should be committed to the memory and engraven on the heart of every moral and social being. . . . We consider this a *unique* performance. . . . We hope to see it soon introduced into our common schools. . . . Mr. Wilbur has performed his duties as editor with excellent taste and judgment. . . . This is a vein which we hope to see successfully prosecuted. . . . We hail the appearance of this work as a long stride toward the formation of a purely aboriginal, indigenous, native, and American literature. We rejoice to meet with an author national enough to break away from the slavish deference, too common among us, to English grammar and orthography. . . . Where all is so good, we are at a loss how to make extracts. . . . On the whole, we may call it a volume which no library, pretending to entire completeness, should fail to place upon its shelves.

From the Higginbottomopolis Snapping-turtle.

A collection of the merest balderdash and doggerel that it was ever our bad fortune to lay eyes on. The author is a vulgar buffoon, and the editor a talkative, tedious old fool. We use strong language, but should any of our readers peruse the book, (from which calamity Heaven preserve them!) they will find reasons for it thick as the leaves of Vallumbrozer, or, to use a still more expressive comparison, as the combined heads of author and editor. The work is wretchedly got up. . . . We should like to know how much *British* gold was pocketed by this libeller of our country and her purest patriots.

From the Oldfogrumville Mentor.

We have not had time to do more than glance through this handsomely printed volume, but the name of its respectable editor, the Rev. Mr. Wilbur, of Jaalam, will afford a sufficient guaranty for the worth of its contents. . . . The paper is white, the type clear, and the volume of a convenient and attractive size. . . . In reading this elegantly executed work, it has seemed to us that a passage or two might have been retrenched with advantage, and that the general style of diction was susceptible of a higher polish. . . . On the whole, we may safely leave the ungrateful task of criticism to the reader. We will barely suggest, that in volumes intended, as this is, for the illustration of a provincial dialect and turns of expression, a dash of humor or satire might be thrown in with advantage. . . . The work is admirably got up. . . . This work will form an appropriate ornament to the centre-table. It is beautifully printed, on paper of an excellent quality.

From the Dekay Bulwark.

We should be wanting in our duty as the conductor of that tremendous engine, a public press, as an American, and as a man, did we allow such an opportunity as is presented to us by "The Biglow Papers" to pass by without entering our earnest protest against such attempts (now, alas! too common) at demoralizing the public sentiment. Under a wretched mask of stupid drollery, slavery, war, the social glass, and, in short, all the valuable and time-honored institutions justly dear to our common humanity and especially to republicans, are made the butt of coarse and senseless ribaldry by this low-minded scribbler. It is time that the respectable and religious portion of our community should be aroused to the alarming inroads of foreign Jacobinism, sansculottism, and infidelity. It is a fearful proof of the wide-spread nature of this contagion, that these secret stabs at religion and virtue are given from under the cloak (*credite, posteri!*) of a clergyman. It is a mournful spectacle indeed to the patriot and Christian to see liberality and new ideas (falsely so called, — they are as old as Eden) invading the sacred precincts of the pulpit. . . . On the whole, we consider this volume as one of the first shocking results which we predicted would spring out of the late French "Revolution" (!).

From the Bungtown Copper and Comprehensive Tocsin (a tryweakly family journal).

Altogether an admirable work. . . . Full of humor, boisterous, but delicate, — of wit withering and scorching, yet combined with a pathos cool as morning dew, — of satire ponderous as the mace of Richard, yet keen as the scymitar of Saladin. . . . A work full of "mountain-mirth," mischievous as Puck, and lightsome as Ariel. . . . We know not whether to admire most the genial, fresh, and discursive concinnity of the author, or his playful fancy, weird imagination, and compass of style, at once both objective and subjective. . . . We might indulge in some criticisms, but, were the author other than he is, he would be a different being. As it is, he has a wonderful *pose*, which flits from flower to flower, and bears the reader irresistibly along on its eagle pinions (like Ganymede) to the "highest heaven of invention." . . . We love a book so purely objective. . . . Many of his pictures of natural scenery have an extraordinary subjective clearness and fidelity. . . . In fine, we consider this as one of the most extraordinary volumes of this or any age. We know of no English author who could have written it. It is a work to which the proud genius of our country, standing with one foot on the Aroostook and the other on the Rio Grande, and holding up the star-spangled banner amid the wreck of matter and the crush of worlds, may point with bewildering scorn of the punier efforts of enslaved Europe. . . . We hope soon to encounter our author among those higher walks of literature in which he is evidently capable of achieving enduring fame. Already we should be inclined to assign him a high position in the bright galaxy of our American bards.

From the Saltriver Pilot and Flag of Freedom.

A volume in bad grammar and worse taste. . . . While the pieces here collected were confined to their appropriate sphere in the corners of obscure newspapers, we considered them wholly beneath contempt, but, as the author has chosen to come forward in this public manner, he must expect the lash he so richly merits. . . . Contemptible slanders. . . . Vilest Billingsgate. . . . Has raked all the gutters of our language. . . . The most pure, upright, and consistent politicians not safe from his malignant venom. . . . General Cushing comes in for a share of his vile calumnies. . . . The *Reverend* Homer Wilbur is a disgrace to his cloth. . . .

From the World-Harmonic-Æolian-Attachment.

Speech is silver: silence is golden. No utterance more Orphic than this. While, therefore, as highest author, we reverence him whose works continue heroically unwritten, we have also our hopeful word for those who with pen (from wing of goose loud-cackling, or seraph God-commissioned) record the thing that is revealed. . . . Under mask of quaintest irony, we detect here the deep, storm-tost (nigh shipwracked) soul, thunder-scarred, semi-articulate, but ever climbing hopefully toward the peaceful summits of an Infinite Sorrow. . . . Yes, thou poor, forlorn Hosea, with Hebrew fire-flaming soul in thee, for thee also this life of ours has not been without its aspects of heavenliest pity and laughingest mirth. Conceivable enough! Through coarse Thersites-cloak, we have revelation of the heart, wild-glowing, world-clasping,

that is in him. Bravely he grapples with the life-problem as it presents itself to him, uncombed, shaggy, careless of the "nicer proprieties," inexpert of "elegant diction," yet with voice audible enough to whoso hath ears, up there on the gravelly side-hills, or down on the splashy, indiarubber-like salt-marshes of native Jaalam. To this soul also the *Necessity of Creating* somewhat has unveiled its awful front. If not Œdipuses and Electras and Alcestises, then in God's name Birdofredum Sawins ! These also shall get born into the world, and filch (if so need) a Zingali subsistence therein, these lank, omnivorous Yankees of his. He shall paint the Seen, since the Unseen will not sit to him. Yet in him also are Nibelungen-lays, and Iliads, and Ulysses-wanderings, and Divine Comedies, — if only once he could come at them ! Therein lies much, nay all ; for what truly is this which we name *All*, but that which we do *not* possess ? . . . Glimpses also are given us of an old father Ezekiel, not without paternal pride, as is the wont of such. A brown, parchment-hided old man of the geoponic or bucolic species, gray-eyed, we fancy, *queued* perhaps, with much weather-cunning and plentiful September-gale memories, bidding fair in good time to become the Oldest Inhabitant. After such hasty apparition, he vanishes and is seen no more. . . . Of "Rev. Homer Wilbur, A. M., Pastor of the First Church in Jaalam," we have small care to speak here. Spare touch in him of his Melesigenes namesake, save, haply, the — blindness ! A tolerably caliginose, nephelegeretous elderly gentleman, with infinite faculty of sermonizing, muscularized by long practice and excellent digestive apparatus, and, for the rest, well-meaning enough, and with small private illuminations (somewhat tallowy, it is to be feared) of his own. To him, there, "Pastor of the First Church in Jaalam," our Hosea presents himself as a quite inexplicable Sphinx-riddle. A rich poverty of Latin and Greek, — so far is clear enough, even to eyes peering myopic through horn-lensed editorial spectacles, — but naught farther ? O purblind, well-meaning, altogether fuscous Melesigenes-Wilbur, there are things in him incommunicable by stroke of birch ! Did it ever enter that old bewildered head of thine that there was the *Possibility of the Infinite* in him ? To thee, quite wingless (and even featherless) biped, has not so much even as a dream of wings ever come ? "Talented young parishioner " ? Among the Arts whereof thou art *Magister*, does that of *seeing* happen to be one ? Unhappy *Artium Magister !* Somehow a Nemean lion, fulvous, torrid-eyed, dry-nursed in broad-howling sand-wildernesses of a sufficiently rare spirit-Libya (it may be supposed) has got whelped among the sheep. Already he stands wild-glaring, with feet clutching the ground as with oak-roots, gathering for a Remus-spring over the walls of thy little fold. In Heaven's name, go not near him with that flybite crook of thine ! In good time, thou painful preacher, thou wilt go to the appointed place of departed Artillery - Election Sermons, Right - Hands of

Fellowship, and Results of Councils, gathered
to thy spiritual fathers with much Latin of the
Epitaphial sort; thou, too, shalt have thy re-
ward; but on him the Eumenides have looked,
not Xantippes of the pit, snake-tressed, finger-
threatening, but radiantly calm as on antique
gems; for him paws impatient the winged
courser of the gods, champing unwelcome bit;
him the starry deeps, the empyrean glooms, and
far-flashing splendors await.

From the Onion Grove Phœnix.

A talented young townsman of ours, recently
returned from a Continental tour, and who is
already favorably known to our readers by his
sprightly letters from abroad which have graced
our columns, called at our office yesterday. We
learn from him, that, having enjoyed the distin-
guished privilege, while in Germany, of an in-
troduction to the celebrated Von Humbug, he
took the opportunity to present that eminent
man with a copy of the "Biglow Papers." The
next morning he received the following note,
which he has kindly furnished us for publica-
tion. We prefer to print it *verbatim*, knowing
that our readers will readily forgive the few
errors into which the illustrious writer has
fallen, through ignorance of our language.

"HIGH-WORTHY MISTER !

"I shall also now especially happy starve, be-
cause I have more or less a work one those abo-
riginal Red-Men seen in which have I so deaf
an interest ever taken full-worthy on the self
shelf with our Gottsched to be upset.
"Pardon my in the English-speech un-prac-
tice!   VON HUMBUG."

He also sent with the above note a copy of his
famous work on "Cosmetics," to be presented
to Mr. Biglow; but this was taken from our
friend by the English custom-house officers,
probably through a petty national spite. No
doubt, it has by this time found its way into the
British Museum. We trust this outrage will be
exposed in all our American papers. We shall
do our best to bring it to the notice of the State
Department. Our numerous readers will share
in the pleasure we experience at seeing our
young and vigorous national literature thus
encouragingly patted on the head by this vener-
able and world-renowned German. We love to
see these reciprocations of good-feeling between
the different branches of the great Anglo-Saxon
race.

[The following genuine "notice" having
met my eye, I gladly insert a portion of it here,
the more especially as it contains one of Mr.
Biglow's poems not elsewhere printed.—H. W.]

From the Jaalam Independent Blunderbuss.

. . . But, while we lament to see our young
townsman thus mingling in the heated contests
of party politics, we think we detect in him the
presence of talents which, if properly directed,
might give an innocent pleasure to many. As
a proof that he is competent to the production
of other kinds of poetry, we copy for our read-
ers a short fragment of a pastoral by him, the
manuscript of which was loaned us by a friend.
The title of it is "The Courtin'."

ZEKLE crep' up, quite unbeknown,
  An' peeked in thru the winder,
An' there sot Huldy all alone,
  'ith no one nigh to hender.

Agin' the chimbly crooknecks hung,
  An' in amongst 'em rusted
The ole queen's-arm thet gran'ther Young
  Fetched back frum Concord busted.

The wannut logs shot sparkles out
  Towards the pootiest, bless her!
An' leetle fires danced all about
  The chiny on the dresser.

The very room, coz she wuz in,
  Looked warm frum floor to ceilin',
An' she looked full ez rosy agin
  Ez th' apples she wuz peelin'.

She heerd a foot an' knowed it, tu,
  Araspin' on the scraper, —
All ways to once her feelins flew
  Like sparks in burnt-up paper.

He kin' o' l'itered on the mat,
  Some doubtfle o' the seekle;
His heart kep' goin' pitypat,
  But hern went pity Zekle.

An' yet she gin her cheer a jerk
  Ez though she wished him furder,
An' on her apples kep' to work
  Ez ef a wager spurred her.

"You want to see my Pa, I spose?"
  "Wall, no; I come designin' —"
"To see my Ma? She's sprinklin' clo'es
  Agin to-morrow's i'nin'."

He stood a spell on one foot fust,
  Then stood a spell on tother,
An' on which one he felt the wust
  He could n't ha' told ye, nuther.

Sez he, "I'd better call agin;"
  Sez she, "Think likely, *Mister;*"
The last word pricked him like a pin,
  An' — wal, he up and kist her.

When Ma bimeby upon 'em slips,
  Huldy sot pale ez ashes,
All kind o' smily round the lips
  An' teary round the lashes.

Her blood riz quick, though, like the tide
  Down to the Bay o' Fundy,
An' all I know is they wuz cried
  In meetin', come nex Sunday.

Satis multis sese emptores futuros libri professis, Georgius Nichols, Cantabrigiensis, opus emittet de parte gravi sed adhuc neglecta historiæ naturalis, cum titulo sequente, videlicet:

Conatus ad Delineationem naturalem nonnihil perfectiorem Scarabœi Bombilatoris, vulgo dicti Humbug, ab Homero Wilbur, Artium Magistro, Societatis historico-naturalis Jaalamensis Præside (Secretario, Socioque (eheu!) singulo), multarumque aliarum Societatum eruditarum (sive ineruditarum) tam domesticarum quam transmarinarum Socio — forsitan futuro.

PROEMIUM

Lectori Benevolo S.

Toga scholastica nondum deposita, quum systemata varia entomologica, a viris ejus scientiæ-cultoribus studiosissimis summa diligentia ædificata, penitus indagâssem, non fuit quin luctuose omnibus in iis, quamvis aliter laude dignissimis, hiatum magni momenti perciperem. Tunc, nescio quo motu superiore impulsus, aut qua captus dulcedine operis, ad eum implendum (Curtius alter) me solemniter devovi. Nec ab isto labore, δαιμονίως imposito, abstinui antequam tractatulum sufficienter inconcinnum lingua vernacula perfeceram. Inde, juveniliter tumefactus, et barathro ineptiæ τῶν βιβλιοπωλῶν (necnon " Publici Legentis ") nusquam explorato, me composuisse quod quasi placentas præfervidas (ut sic dicam) homines ingurgitarent credidi. Sed, quum huic et alio bibliopolæ MSS. mea submisissem et nihil solidius responsione valde negativa in Musæum meum retulissem, horror ingens atque misericordia, ob crassitudinem Lambertianam in cerebris homunculorum istius muneris cœlesti quadam ira infixam, me invasere. Extemplo mei solius impensis librum edere decrevi, nihil omnino dubitans quin " Mundus Scientificus " (ut aiunt) crumenam meam campliter repleret. Nullam, attamen, ex agro illo meo parvulo segetem demessui præter gaudium vacuum bene de Republica merendi. Iste panis meus pretiosus super aquas literarias fæculentas præfidenter jactus, quasi Harpyiarum quarundam (scilicet bibliopolarum istorum facinorosorum supradictorum) tactu rancidus, intra perpaucos dies mihi domum rediit. Et, quum ipse tali victu ali non tolerarem, primum in mentem venit pistori (typographo nempe) nihilominus solvendum esse. Animum non idcirco demisi, imo æque ac pueri naviculas suas penes se lino retinent (eo ut e recto cursu delapsas ad ripam retrahant), sic ego Argô meam chartaceam fluctibus laborantem a quæsitu velleris aurei, ipse potius tonsus pelleque exutus, mente solida revocavi. Metaphoram ut mutem, *boomaran-*

gam meam a scopo aberrantem retraxi, dum majore vi, occasione ministrante, adversus Fortunam intorquerem. Ast mihi, talia volventi, et, sicut Saturnus ille παιδοβόρος, liberos intellectûs mei depascere fidenti, casus miserandus, nec antea inauditus, supervenit. Nam, ut ferunt Scythas pietatis causa et parsimoniæ, parentes suos mortuos devorâsse, sic filius hic meus primogenitus, Scythis ipsis minus mansuetus, patrem vivum totum et calcitrantem exsorbere enixus est. Nec tamen hac de causa sobolem meam esurientem exheredavi. Sed famem istam pro valido testimonio virilitatis roborisque potius habui, cibumque ad eam satiandam, salva paterna mea carne, petii. Et quia bilem illam scaturientem ad æs etiam concoquendum idoneam esse estimabam, unde æs alienum, ut minoris pretii, haberem, circumspexi. Rebus ita se habentibus, ab avunculo meo Johanne Doolittle, Armigero, impetravi ut pecunias necessarias suppeditaret, ne opus esset mihi universitatem relinquendi antequam ad gradum primum in artibus pervenissem. Tunc ego, salvum facere patronum meum munificum maxime cupiens, omnes libros primæ editionis operis mei non venditos una cum privilegio in omne ævum ejusdem imprimendi et edendi avunculo meo dicto pigneravi. Ex illo die, atro lapide notando, curæ vociferantes familiæ singulis annis crescentis eo usque insultabant ut nunquam tam carum pignus e vinculis istis aheneis solvere possem.

Avunculo vero nuper mortuo, quum inter alios consanguineos testamenti ejus lectionem audiendi causa advenissem, erectis auribus verba talia sequentia accepi: " Quoniam persuasum habeo meum dilectum nepotem Homerum, longa et intima rerum angustarum domi experientia, aptissimum esse qui divitias tueatur, beneficenterque ac prudenter iis divinis creditis utatur, — ergo, motus hisce cogitationibus, exque amore meo in illum magno, do, lego-que nepoti caro meo supranominato omnes singularesque istas possessiones nec ponderabiles nec computabiles meas quæ sequuntur, scilicet: quingentos libros quos mihi pigneravit dictus Homerus, anno lucis 1792, cum privilegio edendi e. repetendi opus istud ' scientificum' (quod dicunt) suum, si sic elegerit. Tamen D. O. M. precor oculos Homeri nepotis mei ita aperiat eumque moveat, ut libros istos in bibliotheca unius e plurimis castellis suis Hispaniensibus tuto abscondat."

His verbis (vix credibilibus, auditis, cor meum in pectore exsultavit. Deinde, quoniam tractatus Anglice scriptus spem auctoris fefellerat, quippe quum studium Historiæ Naturalis in Republica nostra inter factionis strepitum languescat, Latine versum edere statui, et eo potius quia nescio quomodo disciplina academica et duo diplomata proficiant, nisi quod peritos linguarum omnino mortuarum (et damnandarum, ut dicebat iste πανοῦργος Guilielmus Cobbett) nos faciant.

Et mihi adhuc superstes est tota illa editio prima, quam quasi crepitaculum per quod dentes caninos dentibam retineo.

OPERIS SPECIMEN

(*Ad exemplum Johannis Physiophili speciminis Monachologiæ.*)

12. S. B. *Militaris*, WILBUR. *Carnifex*, JABLONSK. *Profanus*, DESFONT.

[Male hancce speciem *Cyclopem* Fabricius vocat, ut qui singulo oculo ad quod sui interest distinguitur. Melius vero Isaacus Outis nullum inter S. milit. S. que Belzebul (Fabric. 152) discrimen esse defendit.]

Habitat civitat. Americ. austral.

Aureis lineis splendidus; plerumque tamen sordidus, utpote lanienas valde frequentans, fœtore sanguinis allectus. Amat quoque insuper septa apricari, neque inde, nisi maxima conatione detruditur. *Candidatus* ergo populariter vocatus. Caput cristam quasi pennarum ostendit. Pro cibo vaccam publicam callide mulget; abdomen enorme; facultas suctus haud facile estimanda. Otiosus, fatuus; ferox nihilominus, semperque dimicare paratus. Tortuose repit.

Capite speæ maxima cum cura dissecto, ne illud rudimentum etiam cerebri commune omnibus prope insectis detegere poteram.

Unam de hoc S. milit. rem singularem notavi; nam S. Guineens. (Fabric. 143) servos facit, et idcirco a multis summa in reverentia habitus, quasi scintillas rationis pæne humanæ demonstrans.

24. S. B. *Criticus*, WILBUR. *Zoilus*, FABRIC. *Pygmæus*, CARLSEN.

[Stultissime Johannes Stryx cum S. punctato (Fabric. 64–109) confundit. Specimina quamplurima scrutationi microscopicæ subjeci, nunquam tamen unum ulla indicia puncti cujusvis prorsus ostendentem inveni.]

Præcipue formidolosus, insectatusque, in proxima rima anonyma sese abscondit, *we, we,* creberrime stridens. Ineptus, segnipes.

Habitat ubique gentium; in sicco; nidum suum terebratione indefessa ædificans. Cibus. Libros depascit; siccos præcipue.

MELIBŒUS-HIPPONAX.

THE

Biglow Papers,

EDITED,

WITH AN INTRODUCTION, NOTES, GLOSSARY, AND COPIOUS INDEX,

BY

HOMER WILBUR, A. M.,

PASTOR OF THE FIRST CHURCH IN JAALAM, AND (PROSPECTIVE) MEMBER OF MANY LITERARY, LEARNED, AND SCIENTIFIC SOCIETIES,

(*for which see page* 173).

The ploughman's whistle, or the trivial flute,
Finds more respect than great Apollo's lute.
        Quarles's Emblems, B. ii. E. 8.

Margaritas, munde porcine, calcasti : en, siliquas accipe.
        Jac. Car. Fil. ad Pub. Leg. § 1.

NOTE TO TITLE-PAGE

IT will not have escaped the attentive eye, that I have, on the title-page, omitted those honorary appendages to the editorial name which not only add greatly to the value of every book, but whet and exacerbate the appetite of the reader. For not only does he surmise that an honorary membership of literary and scientific societies implies a certain amount of necessary distinction on the part of the recipient of such decorations, but he is willing to trust himself more entirely to an author who writes under the fearful responsibility of involving the reputation of such bodies as the *S. Archæol. Dahom.* or the *Acad. Lit. et Scient. Kamtschat.* I cannot but think that the early editions of Shakespeare and Milton would have met with more rapid and general acceptance, but for the barrenness of their respective title-pages; and I believe that, even now, a publisher of the works of either of those justly distinguished men would find his account in procuring their admission to the membership of learned bodies on the Continent, — a proceeding no whit more incongruous than the reversal of the judgment against Socrates, when he was already more than twenty centuries beyond the reach of antidotes, and when his memory had acquired a deserved respectability. I conceive that it was a feeling of the importance of this precaution which induced Mr. Locke to style himself "Gent." on the title-page of his Essay, as who should say to his readers that they could receive his metaphysics on the honor of a gentleman.

Nevertheless, finding that, without descending to a smaller size of type than would have been compatible with the dignity of the several societies to be named I could not compress my intended list within the limits of a single page, and thinking, moreover, that the act would carry with it an air of decorous modesty, I have chosen to take the reader aside, as it were, into my private closet, and there not only exhibit to him the diplomas which I already possess, but also to furnish him with a prophetic vision of those which I may, without undue presumption, hope for, as not beyond the reach of human ambition and attainment. And I am the rather induced to this from the fact that my name has been unaccountably dropped from the last triennial catalogue of our beloved *Alma Mater*. Whether this is to be attributed to the difficulty of Latinizing any of those honorary adjuncts (with a complete list of which I took care to furnish the proper persons nearly a year beforehand), or whether it had its origin in any more culpable motives, I forbear to consider in this place, the matter being in course of painful investigation. But, however this may be, I felt the omission the more keenly, as I had, in expectation of the new catalogue, enriched the library of the Jaalam Athenæum with the old one then in my possession, by which means it has come about that my children will be deprived of a never-wearying winter evening's amusement in looking out the name of their parent in that distinguished roll. Those harmless innocents had at least committed no —— but I forbear, having intrusted my reflections and animadversions on this painful topic to the safe-keeping of my private diary, intended for posthumous publication. I state this fact here, in order that certain nameless individuals, who are, perhaps, overmuch congratulating themselves upon my silence, may know that a rod is in pickle which the vigorous hand of a justly incensed posterity will apply to their memories.

The careful reader will note that, in the list which I have prepared, I have included the names of several Cisatlantic societies to which a place is not commonly assigned in processions of this nature. I have ventured to do this, not only to encourage native ambition and genius, but also because I have never been able to perceive in what way distance (unless we suppose them at the end of a lever) could increase the weight of learned bodies. As far as I have been able to extend my researches among such stuffed specimens as occasionally reach America, I have discovered no generic difference between the antipodal *Fogrum Japonicum* and the *F. Americanum* sufficiently

common in our own immediate neighborhood. Yet, with a becoming deference to the popular belief that distinctions of this sort are enhanced in value by every additional mile they travel, I have intermixed the names of some tolerably distant literary and other associations with the rest.

I add here, also, an advertisement, which, that it may be the more readily understood by those persons especially interested therein, I have written in that curtailed and otherwise maltreated canine Latin, to the writing and reading of which they are accustomed.

OMNIB. PER TOT. ORB. TERRAR. CATALOG. ACADEM. EDD.

Minim. gent. diplom. ab inclytiss. acad. vest. orans, vir. honorand. operosiss., at sol. ut sciat. quant. glor. nom. meum (dipl. fort. concess.) catal. vest. temp. futur. affer., ill. subjec., addit. omnib. titul. honorar. qu. adh. non tant. opt. quam probab. put.

** *Litt. Uncial. distinx. ut Præs. S. Hist. Nat. Jaal.*

HOMERUS WILBUR, Mr., Episc. Jaalam, S. T. D. 1850, et Yal. 1849, et Neo-Cæs. et Brun. et Gulielm. 1852, et Gul. et Mar. et Bowd. et Georgiop. et Viridimont. et Columb. Nov. Ebor. 1853, et Amherst. et Watervill. et S. Jarlath. Hib. et S. Mar. et S. Joseph. et S. And. Scot. 1854, et Nashvill. et Dart. et Dickins. et Concord. et Wash. et Columbian. et Charlest. et Jeff. et Dubl. et Oxon. et Cantab. et Cæt. 1855, P. U. N. C. H. et J. U. D. Gott. et Osnab. et Heidelb. 1860, et Acad. BORE US. Berolin. Soc., et SS. RR. Lugd. Bat. et Patav. et Lond. et Edinb. et Ins. Feejee. et Null. Terr. et Pekin. Soc. Hon. et S. H. S. et S. P. A. et A. A. S. et S. Humb. Univ. et S. Omn. Rer. Quarund. q. Aliar. Promov. Passamaquod. et H. P. C. et I. O. H, et A. Δ. Φ. et Π. K. P. et Φ. B. K. et Peucin. et Erosoph. et Philadelph. et Frat. in Unit. et Σ. T. et S. Archæolog. Athen. et Acad. Scient. et Lit. Panorm. et SS. R. H. Matrit. et Beeloochist. et Caffrar. et Caribb. et M. S. Reg. Paris. et S. Am. Antiserv. Soc. Hon. et P. D. Gott. et LL. D. 1852, et D. C. L. et Mus. Doc. Oxon. 1860, et M. M. S. S. et M. D. 1854, et Med. Fac. Univ. Harv. Soc. et S. pro Convers. Pollywog. Soc. Hon. et Higgl. Piggl. et LL. B. 1853, et S. pro Christianiz. Moschet. Soc. et SS. Ante-Diluv. ubiq. Gent. Soc. Hon. et Civit. Cleric. Jaalam. et S. pro Diffus. General. Tenebr. Secret. Corr.

INTRODUCTION

WHEN, more than three years ago, my talented young parishioner, Mr. Biglow, came to me and submitted to my animadversions the first of his poems which he intended to commit to the more hazardous trial of a city newspaper, it never so much as entered my imagination to conceive that his productions would ever be gathered into a fair volume, and ushered into the august presence of the reading public by myself. So little are we short-sighted mortals able to predict the event! I confess that there is to me a quite new satisfaction in being associated (though only as sleeping partner) in a book which can stand by itself in an independent unity on the shelves of libraries. For there is always this drawback from the pleasure of printing a sermon, that, whereas the queasy stomach of this generation will not bear a discourse long enough to make a separate volume, those religious and godly-minded children (those Samuels, if I may call them so) of the brain must at first lie buried in an undistinguished heap, and then get such resurrection as is vouchsafed to them, mummy-wrapped with a score of others in a cheap binding, with no other mark of distinction than the word "*Miscellaneous*" printed upon the back. Far be it from me to claim any credit for the quite unexpected popularity which I am pleased to find these bucolic strains have attained unto. If I know myself, I am measurably free from the itch of vanity; yet I may be allowed to say that I was not backward to recognize in them a certain wild, puckery, acidulous (sometimes even verging toward that point which, in our rustic phrase, is termed *shut-eyed*) flavor, not wholly unpleasing, nor unwholesome, to palates cloyed with the sugariness of tamed and cultivated fruit. It may be, also, that some touches of my own, here and there, may have led to their wider acceptance, albeit solely from my larger experience of literature and authorship.[1]

I was at first inclined to discourage Mr. Biglow's attempts, as knowing that the desire to poetize is one of the diseases naturally incident to adolescence, which, if the fitting remedies be not at once and with a bold hand applied, may become chronic, and render one, who might else have become in due time an ornament of the social circle, a painful object even to nearest friends and relatives. But thinking, on a further experience, that there was a germ of promise in him which required

only culture and the pulling up of weeds from about it, I thought it best to set before him the acknowledged examples of English composition in verse, and leave the rest to natural emulation. With this view, I accordingly lent him some volumes of Pope and Goldsmith, to the assiduous study of which he promised to devote his evenings. Not long afterward, he brought me some verses written upon that model, a specimen of which I subjoin, having changed some phrases of less elegancy, and a few rhymes objectionable to the cultivated ear. The poem consisted of childish reminiscences, and the sketches which follow will not seem destitute of truth to those whose fortunate education began in a country village. And, first, let us hang up his charcoal portrait of the school-dame.

" Propped on the marsh, a dwelling now, I see
The humble school-house of my A, B, C,
Where well-drilled urchins, each behind his
    tire,
Waited in ranks the wished command to fire,
Then all together, when the signal came,
Discharged their *a-b abs* against the dame.
Daughter of Danaus, who could daily pour
In treacherous pipkins her Pierian store,
She, mid the volleyed learning firm and calm,
Patted the furloughed ferule on her palm,
And, to our wonder, could divine at once
Who flashed the pan, and who was downright
    dunce.

" There young Devotion learned to climb with
    ease
The gnarly limbs of Scripture family-trees,
And he was most commended and admired
Who soonest to the topmost twig perspired ;
Each name was called as many various ways
As pleased the reader's ear on different days,
So that the weather, or the ferule's stings,
Colds in the head, or fifty other things,
Transformed the helpless Hebrew thrice a
    week
To guttural Pequot or resounding Greek,
The vibrant accent skipping here and there,
Just as it pleased invention or despair ;
No controversial Hebraist was the Dame ;
With or without the points pleased her the
    same ;
If any tyro found a name too tough,
And looked at her, pride furnished skill
    enough ;
She nerved her larynx for the desperate thing,
And cleared the five-barred syllables at a
    spring.

" Ah, dear old times ! there once it was my hap,
Perched on a stool, to wear the long-eared cap ;
From books degraded, there I sat at ease,
A drone, the envy of compulsory bees ;
Rewards of merit, too, full many a time,

---

[1] The reader curious in such matters may refer (if he can find them) to *A sermon preached on the Anniversary of the Dark Day, An Artillery Election Sermon,* *A Discourse on the Late Eclipse, Dorcas, a Funeral Sermon on the Death of Madam Submit Tidd, Relict of the late Experience Tidd, Esq., &c., &c.*

Each with its woodcut and its moral rhyme,
And pierced half-dollars hung on ribbons gay
About my neck (to be restored next day)
I carried home, rewards as shining then
As those that deck the lifelong pains of men,
More solid than the redemanded praise
With which the world beribbons later days.

" Ah, dear old times! how brightly ye re-
  turn!
How, rubbed afresh, your phosphor traces
  burn!
The ramble schoolward through dewsparkling
  meads,
The willow-wands turned Cinderella steeds,
The impromptu pin-bent hook, the deep re-
  morse
O'er the chance-captured minnow's inchlong
  corse;
The pockets, plethoric with marbles round,
That still a space for ball and pegtop found,
Nor satiate yet, could manage to confine
Horsechestnuts, flagroot, and the kite's wound
  twine,
Nay, like the prophet's carpet could take in,
Enlarging still, the popgun's magazine;
The dinner carried in the small tin pail,
Shared with some dog, whose most beseeching
  tail
And dripping tongue and eager ears belied
The assumed indifference of canine pride;
The caper homeward, shortened if the cart
Of Neighbor Pomeroy, trundling from the
  mart,
O'ertook me, — then, translated to the seat
I praised the steed, how stanch he was and
  fleet,
While the bluff farmer, with superior grin,
Explained where horses should be thick, where
  thin,
And warned me (joke he always had in store)
To shun a beast that four white stockings wore.
What a fine natural courtesy was his!
His nod was pleasure, and his full bow bliss;
How did his well-thumbed hat, with ardor
  rapt,
Its curve decorous to each rank adapt!
How did it graduate with a courtly ease
The whole long scale of social differences,
Yet so gave each his measure running o'er,
None thought his own was less, his neighbor's
  more;
The squire was flattered, and the pauper knew
Old times acknowledged 'neath the threadbare
  blue!
Dropped at the corner of the embowered lane,
Whistling I wade the knee-deep leaves again,
While eager Argus, who has missed all day
The sharer of his condescending play,
Comes leaping onward with a bark elate
And boisterous tail to greet me at the gate;
That I was true in absence to our love
Let the thick dog's-ears in my primer prove."

I add only one further extract, which will
possess a melancholy interest to all such as
have endeavored to glean the materials of rev-
olutionary history from the lips of aged per-
sons, who took a part in the actual making of
it, and, finding the manufacture profitable,
continued the supply in an adequate propor-
tion to the demand.

" Old Joe is gone, who saw hot Percy goad
His slow artillery up the Concord road,
A tale which grew in wonder, year by year,
As, every time he told it, Joe drew near
To the main fight, till, faded and grown gray,
The original scene to bolder tints gave way;
Then Joe had heard the foe's scared double-
  quick
Beat on stove drum with one uncaptured stick,
And, ere death came the lengthening tale to
  lop,
Himself had fired, and seen a red-coat drop;
Had Joe lived long enough, that scrambling
  fight
Had squared more nearly with his sense of
  right,
And vanquished Percy, to complete the tale,
Had hammered stone for life in Concord jail."

I do not know that the foregoing extracts
ought not to be called my own rather than Mr.
Biglow's, as, indeed, he maintained stoutly
that my file had left nothing of his in them. I
should not, perhaps, have felt entitled to take
so great liberties with them, had I not more
than suspected an hereditary vein of poetry in
myself, a very near ancestor having written a
Latin poem in the Harvard *Gratulatio* on the
accession of George the Third. Suffice it to
say, that, whether not satisfied with such lim-
ited approbation as I could conscientiously be-
stow, or from a sense of natural inaptitude,
certain it is that my young friend could never
be induced to any further essays in this kind.
He affirmed that it was to him like writing
in a foreign tongue, — that Mr. Pope's versifi-
cation was like the regular ticking of one of
Willard's clocks, in which one could fancy,
after long listening, a certain kind of rhythm
or tune, but which yet was only a poverty-
stricken *tick, tick*, after all, — and that he had
never seen a sweet-water on a trellis growing
so fairly, or in forms so pleasing to his eye, as
a fox-grape over a scrub-oak in a swamp. He
added I know not what, to the effect that the
sweet-water would only be the more disfigured
by having its leaves starched and ironed out,
and that Pegāsus (so he called him) hardly
looked right with his mane and tail in curl-
papers. These and other such opinions I did
not long strive to eradicate, attributing them
rather to a defective education and senses un-
tuned by too long familiarity with purely nat-
ural objects, than to a perverted moral sense.
I was the more inclined to this leniency since

sufficient evidence was not to seek, that his
verses, wanting as they certainly were in classic
polish and point, had somehow taken hold of
the public ear in a surprising manner. So,
only setting him right as to the quantity of the
proper name Pegasus, I left him to follow the
bent of his natural genius.

Yet could I not surrender him wholly to the
tutelage of the pagan (which, literally inter-
preted, signifies village) muse without yet a
further effort for his conversion, and to this
end I resolved that whatever of poetic fire yet
burned in myself, aided by the assiduous bel-
lows of correct models, should be put in requi-
sition. Accordingly, when my ingenious young
parishioner brought to my study a copy of
verses which he had written touching the ac-
quisition of territory resulting from the Mexi-
can war, and the folly of leaving the question
of slavery or freedom to the adjudication of
chance, I did myself indite a short fable or
apologue after the manner of Gay and Prior,
to the end that he might see how easily even
such subjects as he treated of were capable of
a more refined style and more elegant expres-
sion. Mr. Biglow's production was as fol-
lows : —

THE TWO GUNNERS

A FABLE

Two fellers, Isrel named and Joe,
One Sundy mornin' 'greed to go
Agunnin' soon 'z the bells wuz done
And meetin' finally begun,
So'st no one would n't be about
Ther Sabbath-breakin' to spy out.

Joe did n't want to go a mite ;
He felt ez though 't warn't skeercely right,
But, when his doubts he went to speak on,
Isrel he up and called him Deacon,
An' kep' apokin' fun like sin
An' then arubbin' on it in,
Till Joe, less skeered o' doin' wrong
Than bein' laughed at, went along.

Past noontime they went trampin' round
An' nary thing to pop at found,
Till, fairly tired o' their spree,
They leaned their guns agin a tree,
An' jest ez they wuz settin' down
To take their noonin', Joe looked roun'
And see (acrost lots in a pond
That warn't mor'n twenty rod beyond)
A goose that on the water sot
Ez ef awaitin' to be shot.

Isrel he ups and grabs his gun ;
Sez he, " By ginger, here 's some fun ! "
Don't fire," sez Joe, " it ain't no use,
Thet 's Deacon Peleg's tame wil'-goose : "
Sez Isrel, " I don't care a cent.

I 've sighted an' I 'll let her went ; "
Bang! went queen's-arm, ole gander flopped
His wings a spell, an' quorked, an' dropped.

Sez Joe, " I would n't ha' been hired
At that poor critter to ha' fired,
But sence it 's clean gin up the ghost,
We 'll hev the tallest kind o' roast ;
I guess our waistbands 'll be tight
'Fore it comes ten o'clock ternight."

" I won't agree to no such bender,"
Sez Isrel ; " keep it tell it 's tender ;
'T aint wuth a snap afore it 's ripe."
Sez Joe, " I 'd jest ez lives eat tripe ;
You *air* a buster ter suppose
I 'd eat what makes me hol' my nose ! "

So they disputed to an' fro
Till cunnin' Isrel sez to Joe,
" Don't le's stay here an' play the fool,
Le's wait till both on us git cool,
Jest for a day or two le's hide it,
An' then toss up an' so decide it."
" Agreed ! " sez Joe, an' so they did,
An' the ole goose wuz safely hid.

Now 't wuz the hottest kind o' weather,
An' when at last they come together,
It did n't signify which won,
Fer all the mischief hed been done :
The goose wuz there, but, fer his soul,
Joe would n't ha' tetched it with a pole ;
But Isrel kind o' liked the smell on 't
An' made *his* dinner very well on 't.

My own humble attempt was in manner and
form following, and I print it here, I sincerely
trust, out of no vainglory, but solely with the
hope of doing good.

LEAVING THE MATTER OPEN

A TALE

BY HOMER WILBUR, A. M.

Two brothers once, an ill-matched pair,
Together dwelt (no matter where),
To whom an Uncle Sam, or some one,
Had left a house and farm in common.
The two in principles and habits
Were different as rats from rabbits ;
Stout Farmer North, with frugal care,
Laid up provision for his heir,
Not scorning with hard sun-browned hands
To scrape acquaintance with his lands ;
Whatever thing he had to do
He did, and made it pay him, too ;
He sold his waste stone by the pound,
His drains made water-wheels spin round,
His ice in summer-time he sold,
His wood brought profit when 't was cold,
He dug and delved from morn till night,
Strove to make profit square with right,

Lived on his means, cut no great dash,
And paid his debts in honest cash.

On tother hand, his brother South
Lived very much from hand to mouth,
Played gentleman, nursed dainty hands,
Borrowed North's money on his lands,
And culled his morals and his graces
From cock-pits, bar-rooms, fights, and races;
His sole work in the farming line
Was keeping droves of long-legged swine,
Which brought great bothers and expenses
To North in looking after fences,
And, when they happened to break through,
Cost him both time and temper too,
For South insisted it was plain
He ought to drive them home again,
And North consented to the work
Because he loved to buy cheap pork.

Meanwhile, South's swine increasing fast,
His farm became too small at last;
So, having thought the matter over,
And feeling bound to live in clover
And never pay the clover's worth,
He said one day to Brother North: —

" Our families are both increasing,
And, though we labor without ceasing,
Our produce soon will be too scant
To keep our children out of want;
They who wish fortune to be lasting
Must be both prudent and forecasting;
We soon shall need more land; a lot
I know, that cheaply can be bo't;
You lend the cash, I 'll buy the acres,
And we 'll be equally partakers."

Poor North, whose Anglo-Saxon blood
Gave him a hankering after mud,
Wavered a moment, then consented,
And, when the cash was paid, repented;
To make the new land worth a pin,
Thought he, it must be all fenced in,
For, if South's swine once get the run on 't
No kind of farming can be done on 't;
If that don't suit the other side,
'T is best we instantly divide.

But somehow South could ne'er incline
This way or that to run the line,
And always found some new pretence
'Gainst setting the division fence;
At last he said: —
          " For peace's sake,
Liberal concessions I will make;
Though I believe, upon my soul,
I 've a just title to the whole,
I 'll make an offer which I call
Gen'rous, — we 'll have no fence at all;
Then both of us, whene'er we choose,
Can take what part we want to use;
If you should chance to need it first,
Pick you the best, I 'll take the worst."

" Agreed !" cried North; thought he, This fall
With wheat and rye I 'll sow it all;

In that way I shall get the start,
And South may whistle for his part.
So thought, so done, the field was sown,
And, winter having come and gone,
Sly North walked blithely forth to spy,
The progress of his wheat and rye;
Heavens, what a sight! his brother's swine
Had asked themselves all out to dine;
Such grunting, munching, rooting, shoving,
The soil seemed all alive and moving,
As for his grain, such work they 'd made on 't,
He could n't spy a single blade on 't.

Off in a rage he rushed to South,
" My wheat and rye " — grief choked his
          mouth :
" Pray don't mind me," said South, " but plant
All of the new land that you want ; "
" Yes, but your hogs," cried North;

                              " The grain
Won't hurt them," answered South again;
" But they destroy my crop ; "

                              " No doubt;
'T is fortunate you 've found it out;
Misfortunes teach, and only they,
You must not sow it in their way ; "
" Nay, you," says North, " must keep them
          out ; "
" Did I create them with a snout ? "
Asked South demurely; " as agreed,
The land is open to your seed,
And would you fain prevent my pigs
From running there their harmless rigs ?
God knows I view this compromise
With not the most approving eyes;
I gave up my unquestioned rights
For sake of quiet days and nights;
I offered then, you know 't is true,
To cut the piece of land in two,"
" Then cut it now," growls North;

                              " Abate
Your heat," says South, " 't is now too late;
I offered you the rocky corner,
But you, of your own good the scorner,
Refused to take it ; I am sorry;
No doubt you might have found a quarry,
Perhaps a gold-mine, for aught I know,
Containing heaps of native rhino;
You can't expect me to resign
My rights " —

" But where," quoth North, " are mine ? "
" Your rights," says tother, " well, that's
          funny,
I bought the land " —
                    " I paid the money ; "
" That," answered South, " is from the point,
The ownership, you 'll grant, is joint;
I 'm sure my only hope and trust is
Not law so much as abstract justice,
Though, you remember, 't was agreed
That so and so — consult the deed;
Objections now are out of date.

They might have answered once, but Fate
Quashes them at the point we 've got to ;
Obsta principiis, that 's my motto.''
So saying, South began to whistle
And looked as obstinate as gristle,
While North went homeward, each brown paw
Clenched like a knot of natural law,
And all the while, in either ear,
Heard something clicking wondrous clear.

To turn now to other matters, there are two things upon which it should seem fitting to dilate somewhat more largely in this place, — the Yankee character and the Yankee dialect. And, first, of the Yankee character, which has wanted neither open maligners, nor even more dangerous enemies in the persons of those unskilful painters who have given to it that hardness, angularity, and want of proper perspective, which, in truth, belonged, not to their subject, but to their own niggard and unskilful pencil.

New England was not so much the colony of a mother country, as a Hagar driven forth into the wilderness. The little self - exiled band which came hither in 1620 came, not to seek gold, but to found a democracy. They came that they might have the privilege to work and pray, to sit upon hard benches and listen to painful preachers as long as they would, yea, even unto thirty-seventhly, if the spirit so willed it. And surely, if the Greek might boast his Thermopylæ, where three hundred men fell in resisting the Persian, we may well be proud of our Plymouth Rock, where a handful of men, women, and children not merely faced, but vanquished, winter, famine, the wilderness, and the yet more invincible *storge* that drew them back to the green island far away. These found no lotus growing upon the surly shore, the taste of which could make them forget their little native Ithaca ; nor were they so wanting to themselves in faith as to burn their ship, but could see the fair west-wind belly the homeward sail, and then turn unrepining to grapple with the terrible Unknown.

As Want was the prime foe these hardy exodists had to fortress themselves against, so it is little wonder if that traditional feud be long in wearing out of the stock. The wounds of the old warfare were long a-healing, and an east-wind of hard times puts a new ache into every one of them. Thrift was the first lesson in their horn-book, pointed out, letter after letter, by the lean finger of the hard schoolmistress, Necessity. Neither were those plump, rosy-gilled Englishmen that came hither, but a hard-faced, atrabilious, earnest-eyed race, stiff from long wrestling with the Lord in prayer, and who had taught Satan to dread the new Puritan hug. Add two hundred years' influence of soil, climate, and exposure, with its necessary result

of idiosyncrasies, and we have the present Yankee, full of expedients, half-master of all trades, inventive in all but the beautiful, full of shifts, not yet capable of comfort, armed at all points against the old enemy Hunger, longanimous, good at patching, not so careful for what is best as for what will *do*, with a clasp to his purse and a button to his pocket, not skilled to build against Time, as in old countries, but against sore-pressing Need, accustomed to move the world with no ποῦ στῶ but his own two feet, and no lever but his own long forecast. A strange hybrid, indeed, did circumstance beget, here in the New World, upon the old Puritan stock, and the earth never before saw such mystic-practicalism, such niggard-geniality, such calculating-fanaticism, such cast-iron-enthusiasm, such sour-faced-humor, such close - fisted - generosity. This new *Græculus esuriens* will make a living out of anything. He will invent new trades as well as tools. His brain is his capital, and he will get education at all risks. Put him on Juan Fernandez, and he would make a spelling-book first, and a salt-pan afterward. *In cœlum, jusseris, ibit,* — or the other way either, — it is all one, so anything is to be got by it. Yet, after all, thin, speculative Jonathan is more like the Englishman of two centuries ago than John Bull himself is. He has lost somewhat in solidity, has become fluent and adaptable, but more of the original groundwork of character remains. He feels more at home with Fulke Greville, Herbert of Cherbury, Quarles, George Herbert, and Browne, than with his modern English cousins. He is nearer than John, by at least a hundred years, to Naseby, Marston Moor, Worcester, and the time when, if ever, there were true Englishmen. John Bull has suffered the idea of the Invisible to be very much fattened out of him. Jonathan is conscious still that he lives in the world of the Unseen as well as of the Seen. To move John you must make your fulcrum of solid beef and pudding ; an abstract idea will do for Jonathan.

*** TO THE INDULGENT READER

MY friend, the Rev. Mr. Wilbur, having been seized with a dangerous fit of illness, before this Introduction had passed through the press, and being incapacitated for all literary exertion, sent to me his notes, memoranda, &c., and requested me to fashion them into some shape more fitting for the general eye. This, owing to the fragmentary and disjointed state of his manuscripts, I have felt wholly unable to do ; yet being unwilling that the reader should be deprived of such parts of his lucubrations as seemed more finished, and not well discerning how to segregate these from the rest, I have concluded to send them all to the press precisely as they are.

COLUMBUS NYE,
Pastor of a Church in Bungtown Corner.

It remains to speak of the Yankee dialect. And, first, it may be premised, in a general way, that any one much read in the writings of the early colonists need not be told that the far greater share of the words and phrases now esteemed peculiar to New England, and local there, were brought from the mother country. A person familiar with the dialect of certain portions of Massachusetts will not fail to recognize, in ordinary discourse, many words now noted in English vocabularies as archaic, the greater part of which were in common use about the time of the King James translation of the Bible. Shakespeare stands less in need of a glossary to most New-Englanders than to many a native of the Old Country. The peculiarities of our speech, however, are rapidly wearing out. As there is no country where reading is so universal and newspapers are so multitudinous, so no phrase remains long local, but is transplanted in the mail-bags to every remotest corner of the land. Consequently our dialect approaches nearer to uniformity than that of any other nation.

The English have complained of us for coining new words. Many of those so stigmatized were old ones by them forgotten, and all make now an unquestioned part of the currency, wherever English is spoken. Undoubtedly, we have a right to make new words, as they are needed by the fresh aspects under which life presents itself here in the New World; and, indeed, wherever a language is alive, it grows. It might be questioned whether we could not establish a stronger title to the ownership of the English tongue than the mother-islanders themselves. Here, past all question, is to be its great home and centre. And not only is it already spoken here by greater numbers, but with a far higher popular average of correctness than in Britain. The great writers of it, too, we might claim as ours, were ownership to be settled by the number of readers and lovers.

As regards the provincialisms to be met with in this volume, I may say that the reader will not find one which is not (as I believe) either native or imported with the early settlers, nor one which I have not, with my own ears, heard in familiar use. In the metrical portion of the book, I have endeavored to adapt the spelling as nearly as possible to the ordinary mode of pronunciation. Let the reader who deems me over-particular remember this caution of Martial : —

*" Quem recitas, meus est, O Fidentine, libellus ;
Sed male cum recitas, incipit esse tuus."*

A few further explanatory remarks will not be impertinent.

I shall barely lay down a few general rules for the reader's guidance.

1. The genuine Yankee never gives the rough sound to the *r* when he can help it, and often displays considerable ingenuity in avoiding it even before a vowel.

2. He seldom sounds the final *g*, a piece of self-denial, if we consider his partiality for nasals. The same of the final *d*, as *han'* and *stan'* for *hand* and *stand*.

3. The *h* in such words as *while, when, where,* he omits altogether.

4. In regard to *a*, he shows some inconsistency, sometimes giving a close and obscure sound, as *hev* for *have, hendy* for *handy, ez* for *as, thet* for *that,* and again giving it the broad sound it has in *father,* as *hânsome* for *handsome.*

5. To the sound *ou* he prefixes an *e* (hard to exemplify otherwise than orally).

The following passage in Shakespeare he would recite thus : —

" Neow is the winta uv eour discontent
Med glorious summa by this sun o' Yock,
An' all the cleouds thet leowered upun eour
    heouse
In the deep buzzum o' the oshin buried ;
Neow air eour breows beound 'ith victorious
    wreaths ;
Eour breused arms hung up fer monimunce ;
Eour starn alarums changed to merry meetins,
Eour dreffle marches to delighfle masures.
Grim-visaged war heth smeuthed his wrinkled
    front,
An' neow, instid o' mountin' barebid steeds
To fright the souls o' ferfle edverseries,
He capers nimly in a lady's chāmber,
To the lascivious pleasin' uv a loot."

6. *Au*, in such words as *daughter* and *slaughter,* he pronounces *ah.*

7. To the dish thus seasoned add a drawl *ad libitum.*

[Mr. Wilbur's notes here become entirely fragmentary. — C. N.]

a. Unable to procure a likeness of Mr. Biglow, I thought the curious reader might be gratified with a sight of the editorial effigies. And here a choice between two was offered,— the one a profile (entirely black) cut by Doyle, the other a portrait painted by a native artist of much promise. The first of these seemed wanting in expression, and in the second a slight obliquity of the visual organs has been heightened (perhaps from an over-desire of force on the part of the artist) into too close

an approach to actual *strabismus*. This slight
divergence in my optical apparatus from the
ordinary model — however I may have been
taught to regard it in the light of a mercy
rather than a cross, since it enabled me to give
as much of directness and personal application
to my discourses as met the wants of my con-
gregation, without risk of offending any by
being supposed to have him or her in my eye
(as the saying is) — seemed yet to Mrs. Wil-
bur a sufficient objection to the engraving of
the aforesaid painting. We read of many who
either absolutely refused to allow the copying
of their features, as especially did Plotinus and
Agesilaus among the ancients, not to mention
the more modern instances of Scioppius, Palæ-
ottus, Pinellus, Velserus, Gataker, and others,
or were indifferent thereto, as Cromwell.

β. Yet was Cæsar desirous of concealing his
baldness. *Per contra*, my Lord Protector's
carefulness in the matter of his wart might be
cited. Men generally more desirous of being
improved in their portraits than characters.
Shall probably find very unflattered likenesses
of ourselves in Recording Angel's gallery.

γ. Whether any of our national peculiarities
may be traced to our use of stoves, as a certain
closeness of the lips in pronunciation, and a
smothered smoulderingness of disposition sel-
dom roused to open flame ? An unrestrained
intercourse with fire probably conducive to
generosity and hospitality of soul. Ancient
Mexicans used stoves, as the friar Augustin
Ruiz reports, Hakluyt, III. 468, — but Popish
priests not always reliable authority.
To-day picked my Isabella grapes. Crop
injured by attacks of rose-bug in the spring.
Whether Noah was justifiable in preserving
this class of insects ?

δ. Concerning Mr. Biglow's pedigree. Tol-
erably certain that there was never a poet
among his ancestors. An ordination hymn
attributed to a maternal uncle, but perhaps a
sort of production not demanding the creative
faculty.
His grandfather a painter of the grandiose
or Michael Angelo school. Seldom painted ob-
jects smaller than houses or barns, and these
with uncommon expression.

ε. Of the Wilburs no complete pedigree.
The crest said to be a *wild boar*, whence, per-
haps, the name. (?) A connection with the
Earls of Wilbraham (*quasi* wild boar ham)
might be made out. This suggestion worth
following up. In 1677, John W. m. Expect
——, had issue, 1. John, 2. Haggai, 3. Expect,
4. Ruhamah, 5. Desire.

" Hear lyes yᵉ bodye of Mrs Expect Wilber,
Yᵉ crewell salvages they kil'd her
Together wᵗʰ other Christian soles eleaven,
October yᵉ ix daye, 1707.
Yᵉ stream of Jordan sh' as crost ore
And now expeacts me on yᵉ other shore :
I live in hope her soon to join ;
Her earthlye yeeres were forty and nine."
From Gravestone in Pekussett, North Parish.

This is unquestionably the same John who
afterward (1711) married Tabitha Hagg or
Ragg.
But if this were the case, she seems to have
died early ; for only three years after, namely,
1714, we have evidence that he married Wini-
fred, daughter of Lieutenant Tipping.
He seems to have been a man of substance,
for we find him in 1696 conveying " one un-
divided eightieth part of a salt-meadow " in
Yabbok, and he commanded a sloop in 1702.
Those who doubt the importance of genea-
logical studies *fuste potius quam argumento eru-
diendi.*
I trace him as far as 1723, and there lose
him. In that year he was chosen selectman.
No gravestone. Perhaps overthrown when
new hearse-house was built, 1802.
He was probably the son of John, who came
from Bilham Comit. Salop. circa 1642.
This first John was a man of considerable
importance, being twice mentioned with the
honorable prefix of *Mr.* in the town records.
Name spelt with two *l*-s.

" Hear lyeth yᵉ bod [*stone unhappily broken.*]
Mr. Ihon Willber [Esq.] [*I inclose this in
   brackets as doubtful. To me it seems
   clear.*]
Ob't die [*illegible ; looks like xviii.*] iii
   [*prob.* 1693.]

.   .   .   .   .   paynt
.   .   .   .   deseased seinte :
A friend and [fath]er untoe all yᵉ opreast,
Hee gave yᵉ wicked familists noe reast,
When Sat[an bl]ewe his Antinomian blaste,
Wee clong to [Willber as a steadf]ast maste.
[A] gaynst yᵉ horrid Qua[kers] . . . . . "

It is greatly to be lamented that this curious
epitaph is mutilated. It is said that the sacri-
legious British soldiers made a target of the
stone during the war of Independence. How
odious an animosity which pauses not at the
grave ! How brutal that which spares not
the monuments of authentic history.! This is
not improbably from the pen of Rev. Moody
Pyram, who is mentioned by Hubbard as hav-
ing been noted for a silver vein of poetry. If
his papers be still extant, a copy might possi-
bly be recovered.

THE BIGLOW PAPERS

No. I

A LETTER

FROM MR. EZEKIEL BIGLOW OF JAALAM
TO THE HON. JOSEPH T. BUCKINGHAM,
EDITOR OF THE BOSTON COURIER, IN-
CLOSING A POEM OF HIS SON, MR.
HOSEA BIGLOW

JAYLEM, june 1846.

MISTER EDDYTER : — Our Hosea wuz
down to Boston last week, and he see a
cruetin Sarjunt a struttin round as popler
as a hen with 1 chicking, with 2 fellers a
drummin and fifin arter him like all nater.
the sarjunt he thout Hosea hed n't gut his
i teeth cut cos he looked a kindo 's though
he 'd jest com down, so he cal'lated to hook
him in, but Hosy wood n't take none o' his
sarse for all he hed much as 20 Rooster's
tales stuck onto his hat and eenamost enuf
brass a bobbin up and down on his shoul-
ders and figureed onto his coat and trousis,
let alone wut nater hed sot in his featers,
to make a 6 pounder out on.

wal, Hosea he com home considerabal
riled, and arter I 'd gone to bed I heern
Him a thrashin round like a short-tailed
Bull in fli-time. The old Woman ses she
to me ses she, Zekle, ses she, our Hosee 's
gut the chollery or suthin anuther ses she,
don't you Bee skeered, ses I, he 's oney
amakin pottery[1] ses i, he 's ollers on hand
at that ere busynes like Da & martin, and
shure enuf, cum mornin, Hosy he cum down
stares full chizzle, hare on eend and cote
tales flyin, and sot rite of to go reed his
varses to Parson Wilbur bein he haint aney
grate shows o' book larnin himself, bimeby
he cum back and sed the parson wuz dreffle
tickled with 'em as i hoop you will Be, and
said they wuz True grit.

Hosea ses taint hardly fair to call 'em
hisn now, cos the parson kind o' slicked off
sum o' the last varses, but he told Hosee
he did n't want to put his ore in to tetch to
the Rest on 'em, bein they wuz verry well
As thay wuz, and then Hosy ses he sed
suthin a nuther about Simplex Mundishes
or sum sech feller, but I guess Hosea kind
o' did n't hear him, for I never hearn o'
nobody o' that name in this villadge, and

[1] *Aut insanit, aut versos facit.* — H. W.

I 've lived here man and boy 76 year cum
next tater diggin, and thair aint no wheres
a kitting spryer 'n I be.

If you print 'em I wish you 'd jest let
folks know who hosy's father is, cos my ant
Keziah used to say it 's nater to be curus
ses she, she aint livin though and he 's
a likely kind o' lad.

EZEKIEL BIGLOW.

THRASH away, you 'll *hev* to rattle
  On them kittle-drums o' yourn, —
'Taint a knowin' kind o' cattle
  Thet is ketched with mouldy corn ;
Put in stiff, you fifer feller,
  Let folks see how spry you be, —
Guess you 'll toot till you are yeller
  'Fore you git ahold o' me !

Thet air flag 's a leetle rotten,
  Hope it aint your Sunday's best ; —
Fact ! it takes a sight o' cotton
  To stuff out a soger's chest :
Sence we farmers hev to pay fer 't,
  Ef you must wear humps like these,
S'posin' you should try salt hay fer 't,
  It would du ez slick ez grease.

'T would n't suit them Southun fellers,
  They 're a dreffle graspin' set,
We must ollers blow the bellers
  Wen they want their irons het ;
May be it 's all right ez preachin',
  But *my* narves it kind o' grates,
Wen I see the overreachin'
  O' them nigger-drivin' States.

Them thet rule us, them slave-traders
  Haint they cut a thunderin' swarth
(Helped by Yankee renegaders),
  Thru the vartu o' the North !
We begin to think it 's nater
  To take sarse an' not be riled ; —
Who 'd expect to see a tater
  All on eend at bein' biled ?

Ez fer war, I call it murder, —
  There you hev it plain an' flat ;
I don't want to go no furder
  Than my Testyment fer that ;
God hez sed so plump an' fairly,
  It 's ez long ez it is broad,
An' you 've gut to git up airly
  Ef you want to take in God.

'Taint your eppyletts an' feathers
  Make the thing a grain more right;
'Taint afollerin' your bell-wethers
  Will excuse ye in His sight;
Ef you take a sword an' dror it,
  An' go stick a feller thru,
Guv'ment aint to answer for it,
  God 'll send the bill to you.

Wut 's the use o' meetin'-goin'
  Every Sabbath, wet or dry,
Ef it 's right to go amowin'
  Feller-men like oats an' rye ?
I dunno but wut it 's pooty
  Trainin' round in bobtail coats, —
But it 's curus Christian dooty
  This 'ere cuttin' folks's throats.

They may talk o' Freedom's airy
  Tell they 're pupple in the face, —
It 's a grand gret cemetary
  Fer the barthrights of our race;
They jest want this Californy
  So 's to lug new slave-states in
To abuse ye, an' to scorn ye,
  An' to plunder ye like sin.

Aint it cute to see a Yankee
  Take sech everlastin' pains,
All to get the Devil's thankee
  Helpin' on 'em weld their chains ?
Wy, it 's jest ez clear ez figgers,
  Clear ez one an' one make two,
Chaps thet make black slaves o' niggers
  Want to make wite slaves o' you.

Tell ye jest the eend I 've come to
  Arter cipherin' plaguy smart,
An' it makes a handy sum, tu,
  Any gump could larn by heart;
Laborin' man an' laborin' woman
  Hev one glory an' one shame.
Ev'y thin' thet 's done inhuman
  Injers all on 'em the same.

'Taint by turnin' out to hack folks
  You 're agoin' to git your right,
Nor by lookin' down on black folks
  Coz you 're put upon by wite;
Slavery aint o' nary color,
  'Taint the hide thet makes it wus,
All it keers fer in a feller
  'S jest to make him fill its pus.

Want to tackle *me* in, du ye ?
  I expect you 'll hev to wait ;
Wen cold lead puts daylight thru ye
  You 'll begin to kal'late;
S'pose the crows wun't fall to pickin'
  All the carkiss from your bones,
Coz you helped to give a lickin'
  To them poor half-Spanish drones ?

Jest go home an' ask our Nancy
  Wether I 'd be sech a goose
Ez to jine ye, — guess you 'd fancy
  The etarnal bung wuz loose !
She wants me fer home consumption,
  Let alone the hay 's to mow, —
Ef you 're arter folks o' gumption,
  You 've a darned long row to hoe.

Take them editors thet 's crowin'
  Like a cockerel three months old, —
Don't ketch any on 'em goin',
  Though they *be* so blasted bold;
Aint they a prime lot o' fellers ?
  'Fore they think on 't guess they 'll
    sprout
(Like a peach thet 's got the yellers),
  With the meanness bustin' out.

Wal, go 'long to help 'em stealin'
  Bigger pens to cram with slaves,
Help the men thet 's ollers dealin'
  Insults on your fathers' graves;
Help the strong to grind the feeble,
  Help the many agin the few,
Help the men thet call your people
  Witewashed slaves an' peddlin' crew !

Massachusetts, God forgive her,
  She 's akneelin' with the rest,
She, thet ough' to ha' clung ferever
  In her grand old eagle-nest;
She thet ough' to stand so fearless
  W'ile the wracks are round her hurled,
Holdin' up a beacon peerless
  To the oppressed of all the world !

Ha'n't they sold your colored seamen ?
  Ha'n't they made your env'ys w'iz ?
Wut 'll make ye act like freemen ?
  Wut 'll git your dander riz ?
Come, I 'll tell ye wut I 'm thinkin'
  Is our dooty in this fix,
They 'd ha' done 't ez quick ez winkin'
  In the days o' seventy-six.

Clang the bells in every steeple,
Call all true men to disown
The tradoocers of our people,
The enslavers o' their own;
Let our dear old Bay State proudly
Put the trumpet to her mouth,
Let her ring this messidge loudly
In the ears of all the South: —

" I 'll return ye good fer evil
Much ez we frail mortils can,
But I wun't go help the Devil
Makin' man the cus o' man;
Call me coward, call me traiter,
Jest ez suits your mean idees, —
Here I stand a tyrant-hater,
An' the friend o' God an' Peace! "

Ef I 'd *my* way I hed ruther
We should go to work an' part,
They take one way, we take t' other,
Guess it would n't break my heart;
Man hed ough' to put asunder
Them thet God has noways jined;
An' I should n't gretly wonder
Ef there 's thousands o' my mind.

[The first recruiting sergeant on record I
conceive to have been that individual who is
mentioned in the Book of Job as *going to and
fro in the earth, and walking up and down in it.*
Bishop Latimer will have him to have been a
bishop, but to me that other calling would ap-
pear more congenial. The sect of Cainites is
not yet extinct, who esteemed the first-born of
Adam to be the most worthy, not only because
of that privilege of primogeniture, but inasmuch
as he was able to overcome and slay his younger
brother. That was a wise saying of the famous
Marquis Pescara to the Papal Legate, that *it
was impossible for men to serve Mars and Christ
at the same time.* Yet in time past the profession
of arms was judged to be κατ' ἐξοχήν that of a
gentleman, nor does this opinion want for stren-
uous upholders even in our day. Must we sup-
pose, then, that the profession of Christianity
was only intended for losels, or, at best, to
afford an opening for plebeian ambition? Or
shall we hold with that nicely metaphysical
Pomeranian, Captain Vratz, who was Count
Königsmark's chief instrument in the murder
of Mr. Thynne, that the Scheme of Salvation
has been arranged with an especial eye to the
necessities of the upper classes, and that " God
would consider *a gentleman* and deal with him
suitably to the condition and profession he had
placed him in"? It may be said of us all,
Exemplo plus quam ratione vivimus. — H. W.]

No. II

A LETTER

FROM MR. HOSEA BIGLOW TO THE HON. J.
T. BUCKINGHAM, EDITOR OF THE BOS-
TON COURIER, COVERING A LETTER
FROM MR. B. SAWIN, PRIVATE IN THE
MASSACHUSETTS REGIMENT

[THIS letter of Mr. Sawin's was not origi-
nally written in verse. Mr. Biglow, thinking it
peculiarly susceptible of metrical adornment,
translated it, so to speak, into his own vernacu-
lar tongue. This is not the time to consider
the question, whether rhyme be a mode of ex-
pression natural to the human race. If leisure
from other and more important avocations be
granted, I will handle the matter more at large
in an appendix to the present volume. In this
place I will barely remark, that I have some-
times noticed in the unlanguaged prattlings of
infants a fondness for alliteration, assonance,
and even rhyme, in which natural predisposition
we may trace the three degrees through which
our Anglo-Saxon verse rose to its culmination
in the poetry of Pope. I would not be under-
stood as questioning in these remarks that pious
theory which supposes that children, if left
entirely to themselves, would naturally dis-
course in Hebrew. For this the authority of
one experiment is claimed, and I could, with
Sir Thomas Browne, desire its establishment,
inasmuch as the acquirement of that sacred
tongue would thereby be facilitated. I am aware
that Herodotus states the conclusion of Psam-
meticus to have been in favor of a dialect of
the Phrygian. But, beside the chance that a
trial of this importance would hardly be blessed
to a Pagan monarch whose only motive was
curiosity, we have on the Hebrew side the
comparatively recent investigation of James
the Fourth of Scotland. I will add to this pre-
fatory remark, that Mr. Sawin, though a native
of Jaalam, has never been a stated attendant
on the religious exercises of my congregation.
I consider my humble efforts prospered in that
not one of my sheep hath ever indued the wolf's
clothing of war, save for the comparatively
innocent diversion of a militia training. Not
that my flock are backward to undergo the
hardships of *defensive* warfare. They serve
cheerfully in the great army which fights, even
unto death *pro aris et focis*, accoutred with the
spade, the axe, the plane, the sledge, the spell-
ing-book, and other such effectual weapons
against want and ignorance and unthrift. I
have taught them (under God) to esteem our
human institutions as but tents of a night, to
be stricken whenever Truth puts the bugle to

her lips and sounds a march to the heights of wider-viewed intelligence and more perfect organization. — H. W.]

MISTER BUCKINUM, the follerin Billet was writ hum by a Yung feller of our town that wuz cussed fool enuff to goe atrottin inter Miss Chiff arter a Drum and fife. it ain't Nater for a feller to let on that he 's sick o' any bizness that He went intu off his own free will and a Cord, but I rather cal'late he 's middlin tired o' voluntearin By this Time. I bleeve u may put dependunts on his statemence. For I never heered nothin bad on him let Alone his havin what Parson Wilbur cals a *pong shong* for cocktales, and he ses it wuz a soshiashun of idees sot him agoin arter the Crootin Sargient cos he wore a cocktale onto his hat.

his Folks gin the letter to me and i shew it to parson Wilbur and he ses it oughter Bee printed. send It to mister Buckinum, ses he, i don't ollers agree with him, ses he, but by Time,[1] ses he, I *du* like a feller that aint a Feared.

I have intusspussed a Few refleckshuns hear and thair. We 're kind o' prest with Hayin.

Ewers respecfly
HOSEA BIGLOW.

THIS kind o' sogerin' aint a mite like our
  October trainin',
A chap could clear right out from there ef
  't only looked like rainin',
An' th' Cunnles, tu, could kiver up their
  shappoes with bandanners,
An' send the insines skootin' to the bar-
  room with their banners
(Fear o' gittin' on 'em spotted), an' a feller
  could cry quarter
Ef he fired away his ramrod arter tu much
  rum an' water.
Recollect wut fun we hed, you 'n' I an'
  Ezry Hollis,
Up there to Waltham plain last fall, along
  o' the Cornwallis ?[2]
This sort o' thing aint *jest* like thet, — I
  wish thet I wuz furder,[3] —

Nimepunce a day fer killin' folks comes
  kind o' low fer murder,
(Wy I 've worked out to slarterin' some
  fer Deacon Cephas Billins,
An' in the hardest times there wuz I ollers
  tetched ten shillins,)
There 's sutthin' gits into my throat thet
  makes it hard to swaller,
It comes so nateral to think about a hempen
  collar;
It 's glory, — but, in spite o' all my tryin'
  to git callous,
I feel a kind o' in a cart, aridin' to the
  gallus.
But wen it comes to *bein'* killed, — I tell ye
  I felt streaked
The fust time 't ever I found out wy bag-
  gonets wuz peaked;
Here 's how it wuz: I started out to go to
  a fandango,
The sentinul he ups an' sez, " Thet 's fur-
  der 'an you can go."
" None o' your sarse," sez I; sez he,
  " Stan' back !" " Aint you a bus-
  ter ? "
Sez I, " I 'm up to all thet air, I guess
  I 've ben to muster;
I know wy sentinuls air sot; you aint agoin'
  to eat us;
Caleb haint no monopoly to court the
  seenoreetas;
My folks to hum air full ez good ez his'n
  be, by golly !"
An' so ez I wuz goin' by, not thinkin' wut
  would folly,
The everlastin' cus he stuck his one-
  pronged pitchfork in me
An' made a hole right thru my close ez ef
  I wuz an in'my.

Wal, it beats all how big I felt hoorawin'
  in ole Funnel
Wen Mister Bolles he gin the sword to our
  Leftenant Cunnle,
(It 's Mister Secondary Bolles,[4] thet writ
  the prize peace essay;
Thet 's wy he did n't list himself along o'
  us, I dessay,)

---

[1] In relation to this expression, I cannot but think that Mr. Biglow has been too hasty in attributing it to me. Though Time be a comparatively innocent personage to swear by, and though Longinus in his discourse Περὶ Ὕψους have commended timely oaths as not only a useful but sublime figure of speech, yet I have always kept my lips free from that abomination. *Odi*

profanum vulgus, I hate your swearing and hectoring fellows. — H. W.

[2] i hait the Site of a feller with a muskit as I du pizn But their *is* fun to a cornwallis I aint agoin' to deny it. — H. B.

[3] he means Not quite so fur I guess. — H. B.

[4] the ignerant creeter means Sekketary ; but he ollers stuck to his books like cobbler's wax to an ilestone. — H. B.

An' Rantoul, tu, talked pooty loud, but
    don't put *his* foot in it,
Coz human life 's so sacred thet he 's
    principled agin it, —
Though I myself can't rightly see it 's any
    wus achokin' on 'em,
Than puttin' bullets thru their lights, or
    with a bagnet pokin' on 'em;
How dreffle slick he reeled it off (like
    Blitz at our lyceum
Ahaulin' ribbins from his chops so quick
    you skeercely see 'em),
About the Anglo-Saxon race (an' saxons
    would be handy
To du the buryin' down here upon the Rio
    Grandy),
About our patriotic pas an' our star-
    spangled banner,
Our country's bird alookin' on an' singin'
    out hosanner,
An' how he (Mister B. himself) wuz happy
    fer Ameriky, —
I felt, ez sister Patience sez, a leetle mite
    histericky.
I felt, I swon, ez though it wuz a dreffle
    kind o' privilege
Atrampin' round thru Boston streets
    among the gutter's drivelage;
I act'lly thought it wuz a treat to hear a
    little drummin',
An' it did bonyfidy seem millanyum wuz
    acomin'
Wen all on us got suits (darned like them
    wore in the state prison)
An' every feller felt ez though all Mexico
    wuz hisn.[1]

This 'ere 's about the meanest place a
    skunk could wal diskiver
(Saltillo 's Mexican, I b'lieve, fer wut we
    call Salt-river);
The sort o' trash a feller gits to eat doos
    beat all nater,
I 'd give a year's pay fer a smell o' one
    good blue-nose tater;
The country here thet Mister Bolles de-
    clared to be so charmin'

Throughout is swarmin' with the most
    alarmin' kind o' varmin.
He talked about delishis froots, but then
    it wuz a wopper all,
The holl on 't 's mud an' prickly pears,
    with here an' there a chapparal;
You see a feller peekin' out, an', fust you
    know, a lariat
Is round your throat an' you a copse, 'fore
    you can say, " Wut air ye at ? "[2]
You never see sech darned gret bugs (it
    may not be irrelevant
To say I 've seen a *scarabæus pilularius*[3]
    big ez a year old elephant),
The rigiment come up one day in time to
    stop a red bug
From runnin' off with Cunnle Wright, — 't
    wuz jest a common *cimex lectularius*.

One night I started up on eend an' thought
    I wuz to hum agin,
I heern a horn, thinks I it 's Sol the fisher-
    man hez come agin,
His bellowses is sound enough, — ez I 'm a
    livin' creeter,
I felt a thing go thru my leg, — 't wuz
    nothin' more 'n a skeeter !
Then there 's the yaller fever, tu, they call
    it here el vomito, —
(Come, thet wun't du, you landcrab there,
    I tell ye to le' *go* my toe !
My gracious ! it 's a scorpion thet 's took
    a shine to play with 't,
I darsn't skeer the tarnal thing fer fear
    he 'd run away with 't.)
Afore I come away from hum I hed a
    strong persuasion
Thet Mexicans worn't human beans,[4] — an
    ourang outang nation,
A sort o' folks a chap could kill an' never
    dream on 't arter,
No more 'n a feller 'd dream o' pigs thet
    he hed hed to slarter;
I 'd an idee thet they were built arter the
    darkie fashion all,
An' kickin' colored folks about, you know,
    's a kind o' national;

---

[1] it must be aloud that thare 's a streak of nater in lovin' sho, but it sartinly is 1 of the curusest things in nater to see a rispecktable dri goods dealer (deekon off a chutch maybe) a riggin' himself out in the Weigh they du and struttin' round in the Reign aspilin' his trowsis and makin' wet goods of himself. Ef any thin's foolisher and moor dicklus than militerry gloary it is milishy gloary. — H. B.

[2] these fellers are verry proppilly called Rank Heroes, and the more tha kill the ranker and more Herowick tha bekum. — H. B.

[3] it wuz " tumblebug " as he Writ it, but the parson put the Latten instid. i sed tother maid better meeter, but he said tha was eddykated peepl to Boston and tha would n't stan' it no how. idnow as tha *wood* and idnow *as* tha wood. — H. B.

[4] he means human beins, that 's wut he means. i spose he kinder thought tha wuz human beans ware the Xisle Poles comes from. — H. B.

But wen I jined I worn't so wise ez thet
air queen o' Sheby,
Fer, come to look at 'em, they aint much
diff'rent from wut we be,
An' here we air ascrougin' 'em out o' thir
own dominions,
Ashelterin' 'em, ez Caleb sez, under our
eagle's pinions,
Wich means to take a feller up jest by the
slack o' 's trowsis
An' walk him Spanish clean right out o'
all his homes an' houses;
Wal, it doos seem a curus way, but then
hooraw fer Jackson !
It must be right, fer Caleb sez it 's reg'lar
Anglo-saxon.
The Mex'cans don't fight fair, they say,
they piz'n all the water,
An' du amazin' lots o' things thet is n't
wut they ough' to;
Bein' they haint no lead, they make their
bullets out o' copper
An' shoot the darned things at us, tu, wich
Caleb sez aint proper;
He sez they 'd ough' to stan' right up an'
let us pop 'em fairly
(Guess wen he ketches 'em at thet he 'll
hev to git up airly),
Thet our nation 's bigger 'n theirn an' so
its rights air bigger,
An' thet it 's all to make 'em free thet we
air pullin' trigger,
Thet Anglo Saxondom's idee 's abreakin'
'em to pieces,
An' thet idee 's thet every man doos jest
wut he damn pleases;
Ef I don't make his meanin' clear, perhaps
in some respex I can,
I know thet " every man " don't mean a
nigger or a Mexican;
An' there 's another thing I know, an' thet
is, ef these creeturs,
Thet stick an Anglosaxon mask onto State-
prison feeturs,
Should come to Jaalam Centre fer to
argify an' spout on 't,
The gals 'ould count the silver spoons the
minnit they cleared out on 't.

This goin' ware glory waits ye haint one
agreeable feetur,
An' ef it worn't fer wakin' snakes, I 'd
home agin short meter;
O, would n't I be off, quick time, ef
't worn't thet I wuz sartin

They 'd let the daylight into me to pay me
fer desartin !
I don't approve o' tellin' tales, but jest to
you I may state
Our ossifers aint wut they wuz afore they
left the Bay-state;
Then it wuz " Mistei Sawin, sir, you 're
middlin' well now, be ye ?
Step up an' take a nipper, sir; I 'm dreffle
glad to see ye ; "
But now it 's " Ware 's my eppylet ? here,
Sawin, step an' fetch it !
An' mind your eye, be thund'rin' spry, or,
damn ye, you shall ketch it ! "
Wal, ez the Doctor sez, some pork will bile
so, but by mighty,
Ef I hed some on 'em to hum, I 'd give
'em linkum vity,
I 'd play the rogue's march on their hides
an' other music follerin' —
But I must close my letter here, fer one on
'em 's ahollerin',
These Anglosaxon ossifers, — wal, taint no
use ajawin',
I 'm safe enlisted fer the war,
 Yourn,
  BIRDOFREDUM SAWIN.

[Those have not been wanting (as, indeed,
when hath Satan been to seek for attorneys?)
who have maintained that our late inroad upon
Mexico was undertaken not so much for the
avenging of any national quarrel, as for the
spreading of free institutions and of Protestant-
ism. *Capita vix duabus Anticyris medenda!*
Verily I admire that no pious sergeant among
these new Crusaders beheld Martin Luther rid-
ing at the front of the host upon a tamed ponti-
fical bull, as, in that former invasion of Mexico,
the zealous Gomara (spawn though he were of
the Scarlet Woman) was favored with a vision
of St. James of Compostella, skewering the
infidels upon his apostolical lance. We read,
also, that Richard of the lion heart, having gone
to Palestine on a similar errand of mercy, was
divinely encouraged to cut the throats of such
Paynims as refused to swallow the bread of life
(doubtless that they might be thereafter inca-
pacitated for swallowing the filthy gobbets of
Mahound) by angels of heaven, who cried to the
king and his knights, — *Seigneurs, tuez! tuez!*
providentially using the French tongue, as
being the only one understood by their auditors.
This would argue for the pantoglottism of these
celestial intelligences, while, on the other hand,
the Devil, *teste* Cotton Mather, is unversed in
certain of the Indian dialects. Yet must he be
a semeiologist the most expert, making himself
intelligible to every people and kindred by
signs ; no other discourse, indeed, being needful,
than such as the mackerel-fisher holds with his
finned quarry, who, if other bait be wanting,

THE BIGLOW PAPERS

can by a bare bit of white rag at the end of a string captivate those foolish fishes. Such piscatorial persuasion is Satan cunning in. Before one he trails a hat and feather, or a bare feather without a hat; before another, a Presidential chair or a tide-waiter's stool, or a pulpit in the city, no matter what. To us, dangling there over our heads, they seem junkets dropped out of the seventh heaven, sops dipped in nectar, but, once in our mouths, they are all one, bits of fuzzy cotton.

This, however, by the way. It is time now *revocare gradum*. While so many miracles of this sort, vouched by eye-witnesses, have encouraged the arms of Papists, not to speak of Echetlæus at Marathon and those *Dioscuri* (whom we must conclude imps of the pit) who sundry times captained the pagan Roman soldiery, it is strange that our first American crusade was not in some such wise also signalized. Yet it is said that the Lord hath manifestly prospered our armies. This opens the question, whether, when our hands are strengthened to make great slaughter of our enemies, it be absolutely and demonstratively certain that this might is added to us from above, or whether some Potentate from an opposite quarter may not have a finger in it, as there are few pies into which his meddling digits are not thrust. Would the Sanctifier and Setter-apart of the seventh day have assisted in a victory gained on the Sabbath, as was one in the late war? Do we not know from Josephus, that, careful of His decree, a certain river in Judæa abstained from flowing on the day of Rest? Or has that day become less an object of His especial care since the year 1697, when so manifest a providence occurred to Mr. William Trowbridge, in answer to whose prayers, when he and all on shipboard with him were starving, a dolphin was sent daily, "which was enough to serve 'em; only on *Saturdays* they still catched a couple, and on the *Lord's Days* they could catch none at all"? Haply they might have been permitted, by way of mortification, to take some few sculpins (those banes of the salt-water angler), which unseemly fish would, moreover, have conveyed to them a symbolical reproof for their breach of the day, being known in the rude dialect of our mariners as *Cape Cod Clergymen.*

It has been a refreshment to many nice consciences to know that our Chief Magistrate would not regard with eyes of approval the (by many esteemed) sinful pastime of dancing, and I own myself to be so far of that mind, that I could not but set my face against this Mexican Polka, though danced to the Presidential piping with a Gubernatorial second. If ever the country should be seized with another such mania *pro propaganda fide*, I think it would be wise to fill our bombshells with alternate copies of the Cambridge Platform and the Thirty-nine Articles, which would produce a mixture of the highest explosive power, and to wrap every one of our cannon-balls in a leaf of the New Testament, the reading of which is denied to those who sit in the darkness of Popery. Those iron evangelists would thus be able to disseminate vital religion and Gospel truth in quarters inaccessible to the ordinary missionary. I have seen lads, unimpregnate with the more sublimated punctiliousness of Walton, secure pickerel, taking their unwary *siesta* beneath the lily-pads too nigh the surface, with a gun and small shot. Why not, then, since gunpowder was unknown in the time of the Apostles (not to enter here upon the question whether it were discovered before that period by the Chinese), suit our metaphor to the age in which we live, and say *shooters* as well as *fishers* of men?

I do much fear that we shall be seized now and then with a Protestant fervor, as long as we have neighbor Naboths whose wallowings in Papistical mire excite our horror in exact proportion to the size and desirableness of their vineyards. Yet I rejoice that some earnest Protestants have been made by this war, — I mean those who protested against it. Fewer they were than I could wish, for one might imagine America to have been colonized by a tribe of those nondescript African animals the Aye-Ayes, so difficult a word is *No* to us all. There is some malformation or defect of the vocal organs, which either prevents our uttering it at all, or gives it so thick a pronunciation as to be unintelligible. A mouth filled with the national pudding, or watering in expectation thereof, is wholly incompetent to this refractory monosyllable. An abject and herpetic Public Opinion is the Pope, the Anti-Christ, for us to protest against *e corde cordium.* And by what College of Cardinals is this our God's-vicar, our binder and looser, elected? Very like, by the sacred conclave of Tag, Rag, and Bobtail, in the gracious atmosphere of the grog-shop. Yet it is of this that we must all be puppets. This thumps the pulpit-cushion, this guides the editor's pen, this wags the senator's tongue. This decides what Scriptures are canonical, and shuffles Christ away into the Apocrypha. According to that sentence fathered upon Solon, Οὕτω δημόσιον κακὸν ἔρχεται οἴκαδ' ἑκάστῳ. This unclean spirit is skilful to assume various shapes. I have known it to enter my own study and nudge my elbow of a Saturday, under the semblance of a wealthy member of my congregation. It were a great blessing, if every particular of what in the sum we call popular sentiment could carry about the name of its manufacturer stamped legibly upon it. I gave a stab under the fifth rib to that pestilent fallacy, — "Our country, right or wrong," — by tracing its original to a speech of Ensign Cilley at a dinner of the Bungtown Fencibles. — H. W.]

No. III

WHAT MR. ROBINSON THINKS

[A FEW remarks on the following verses will not be out of place. The satire in them was not meant to have any personal, but only a general, application. Of the gentleman upon whose letter they were intended as a commentary Mr. Biglow had never heard, till he saw the letter itself. The position of the satirist is oftentimes one which he would not have chosen, had the election been left to himself. In attacking bad principles, he is obliged to select some individual who has made himself their exponent, and in whom they are impersonate, to the end that what he says may not, through ambiguity, be dissipated *tenues in auras*. For what says Seneca? *Longum iter per præcepta, breve et efficace per exempla.* A bad principle is comparatively harmless while it continues to be an abstraction, nor can the general mind comprehend it fully till it is printed in that large type which all men can read at sight, namely, the life and character, the sayings and doings, of particular persons. It is one of the cunningest fetches of Satan, that he never exposes himself directly to our arrows, but, still dodging behind this neighbor or that acquaintance, compels us to wound him through them, if at all. He holds our affections as hostages, the while he patches up a truce with our conscience.

Meanwhile, let us not forget that the aim of the true satirist is not to be severe upon persons, but only upon falsehood, and, as Truth and Falsehood start from the same point, and sometimes even go along together for a little way, his business is to follow the path of the latter after it diverges, and to show her floundering in the bog at the end of it. Truth is quite beyond the reach of satire. There is so brave a simplicity in her, that she can no more be made ridiculous than an oak or a pine. The danger of the satirist is, that continual use may deaden his sensibility to the force of language. He becomes more and more liable to strike harder than he knows or intends. He may be careful to put on his boxing-gloves, and yet forget that, the older they grow, the more plainly may the knuckles inside be felt. Moreover, in the heat of contest, the eye is insensibly drawn to the crown of victory, whose tawdry tinsel glitters through that dust of the ring which obscures Truth's wreath of simple leaves. I have sometimes thought that my young friend, Mr. Biglow, needed a monitory hand laid on his arm, — *aliquid sufflaminandus erat.* I have never thought it good husbandry to water the tender plants of reform with *aqua fortis*, yet, where so much is to do in the beds, he were a sorry gardener who should wage a whole day's war with an iron scuffle on those ill weeds that make the garden-walks of life unsightly, when a sprinkle of Attic salt will wither them up. *Est ars etiam maledicendi*, says Scaliger, and truly it is a hard thing to say where the graceful gentleness of the lamb merges in downright sheepishness. We may conclude with worthy and wise Dr. Fuller, that "one may be a lamb in private wrongs, but in hearing general affronts to goodness they are asses which are not lions." — H. W.]

GUVENER B. is a sensible man;
 He stays to his home an' looks arter his
  folks;
He draws his furrer ez straight ez he can,
 An' into nobody's tater-patch pokes;
  But John P.
  Robinson he
 Sez he wunt vote fer Guvener B.

My! aint it terrible? Wut shall we du?
 We can't never choose him o' course, —
  thet's flat;
Guess we shall hev to come round, (don't
  you?)
 An' go in fer thunder an' guns, an' all
  that;
  Fer John P.
  Robinson he
 Sez he wunt vote fer Guvener B.

Gineral C. is a dreffle smart man:
 He's ben on all sides thet give places or
  pelf;
But consistency still wuz a part of his
  plan, —
 He's ben true to *one* party, — an' thet is
  himself; —
  So John P.
  Robinson he
 Sez he shall vote fer Gineral C.

Gineral C. he goes in fer the war;
 He don't vally princerple more 'n an old
  cud;
Wut did God make us raytional creeturs fer,
 But glory an' gunpowder, plunder an'
  blood?
  So John P.
  Robinson he
 Sez he shall vote fer Gineral C.

We were gittin' on nicely up here to our
  village,
 With good old idees o' wut's right an'
  wut aint,
We kind o' thought Christ went agin war
  an' pillage,
 An' thet eppyletts worn't the best mark
  of a saint;
  But John P.
  Robinson he
 Sez this kind o' thing's an exploded
  idee.

The side of our country must ollers be took,
An' Presidunt Polk, you know, *he* is our
    country.
An' the angel thet writes all our sins in a
    book
Puts the *debit* to him, an' to us the *per
    contry;*
        An' John P.
        Robinson he
Sez this is his view o' the thing to a T.

Parson Wilbur he calls all these argimunts
    lies;
Sez they 're nothin' on airth but jest *fee,
    faw, fum;*
An' thet all this big talk of our destinies
Is half on it ign'ance, an' t' other half
    rum;
        But John P.
        Robinson he
Sez it aint no sech thing; an', of course,
    so must we.

Parson Wilbur sez *he* never heerd in his life
Thet th' Apostles rigged out in their
    swaller-tail coats,
An' marched round in front of a drum an'
    a fife,
To git some on 'em office, an' some on 'em
    votes;
        But John P.
        Robinson he
Sez they did n't know everythin' down
    in Judee.

Wal, it 's a marcy we 've gut folks to tell us
The rights an' the wrongs o' these mat-
    ters, I vow, —
God sends country lawyers, an' other wise
    fellers,
To start the world's team wen it gits in a
    slough;
        Fer John P.
        Robinson he
Sez the world 'll go right, ef he hollers
    out Gee!

[The attentive reader will doubtless have per-
ceived in the foregoing poem an allusion to that
pernicious sentiment, — "Our country, right or
wrong." It is an abuse of language to call a
certain portion of land, much more, certain per-
sonages, elevated for the time being to high sta-
tion, our country. I would not sever nor loosen
a single one of those ties by which we are united
to the spot of our birth, nor minish by a tittle
the respect due to the Magistrate. I love our

own Bay State too well to do the one, and as for
the other, I have myself for nigh forty years
exercised, however unworthily, the function of
Justice of the Peace, having been called thereto
by the unsolicited kindness of that most ex-
cellent man and upright patriot, Caleb Strong.
Patriæ fumus igne alieno luculentior is best
qualified with this, — *Ubi libertas, ibi patria.*
We are inhabitants of two worlds, and owe a
double, but not a divided, allegiance. In virtue
of our clay, this little ball of earth exacts a
certain loyalty of us, while, in our capacity as
spirits, we are admitted citizens of an invisible
and holier fatherland. There is a patriotism of
the soul whose claim absolves us from our other
and terrene fealty. Our true country is that ideal
realm which we represent to ourselves under the
names of religion, duty, and the like. Our terres-
trial organizations are but far-off approaches to
so fair a model, and all they are verily traitors
who resist not any attempt to divert them from
this their original intendment. When, therefore,
one would have us to fling up our caps and shout
with the multitude, — "*Our country, however
bounded!*" he demands of us that we sacrifice
the larger to the less, the higher to the lower,
and that we yield to the imaginary claims of a
few acres of soil our duty and privilege as liege-
men of Truth. Our true country is bounded on
the north and the south, on the east and the
west, by Justice, and when she oversteps that
invisible boundary-line by so much as a hair's-
breadth, she ceases to be our mother, and chooses
rather to be looked upon *quasi noverca.* That
is a hard choice when our earthly love of country
calls upon us to tread one path and our duty
points us to another. We must make as noble
and becoming an election as did Penelope be-
tween Icarius and Ulysses. Veiling our faces,
we must take silently the hand of Duty to
follow her.

Shortly after the publication of the foregoing
poem, there appeared some comments upon it
in one of the public prints which seemed to call
for animadversion. I accordingly addressed to
Mr. Buckingham, of the Boston Courier, the
following letter.

           "JAALAM, November 4, 1847.

" *To the Editor of the Courier :*
    "RESPECTED SIR, — Calling at the post-
office this morning, our worthy and efficient
postmaster offered for my perusal a paragraph
in the Boston Morning Post of the 3d instant,
wherein certain effusions of the pastoral muse
are attributed to the pen of Mr. James Russell
Lowell. For aught I know or can affirm to
the contrary, this Mr. Lowell may be a very
deserving person and a youth of parts (though
I have seen verses of his which I could never
rightly understand) ; and if he be such, he, I
am certain, as well as I, would be free from
any proclivity to appropriate to himself what-
ever of credit (or discredit) may honestly be-
long to another. I am confident, that, in pen-
ning these few lines, I am only forestalling a
disclaimer from that young gentleman, whose

silence hitherto, when rumor pointed to him-
ward, has excited in my bosom mingled emo-
tions of sorrow and surprise. Well may my
young parishioner, Mr. Biglow, exclaim with
the poet,

" ' Sic vos non vobis,' &c. ;

though, in saying this, I would not convey the
impression that he is a proficient in the Latin
tongue, — the tongue, I might add, of a Horace
and a Tully.
" Mr. B. does not employ his pen, I can safely
say, for any lucre of worldly gain, or to be ex-
alted by the carnal plaudits of men, *digito
monstrari*, &c. He does not wait upon Provi-
dence for mercies, and in his heart mean *merces*.
But I should esteem myself as verily deficient
in my duty (who am his friend and in some un-
worthy sort his spiritual *fidus Achates*, &c.), if I
did not step forward to claim for him whatever
measure of applause might be assigned to him
by the judicious.
" If this were a fitting occasion, I might ven-
ture here a brief dissertation touching the man-
ner and kind of my young friend's poetry. But
I dubitate whether this abstruser sort of specu-
lation (though enlivened by some apposite in-
stances from Aristophanes) would sufficiently
interest your oppidan readers. As regards their
satirical tone, and their plainness of speech, I
will only say, that, in my pastoral experience, I
have found that the Arch-Enemy loves nothing
better than to be treated as a religious, moral,
and intellectual being, and that there is no
apage Sathanas! so potent as ridicule. But it
is a kind of weapon that must have a button of
good-nature on the point of it.
" The productions of Mr. B. have been stig-
matized in some quarters as unpatriotic ; but I
can vouch that he loves his native soil with
that hearty, though discriminating, attachment
which springs from an intimate social inter-
course of many years' standing. In the plough-
ing season, no one has a deeper share in the
well-being of the country than he. If Dean
Swift were right in saying that he who makes
two blades of grass grow where one grew be-
fore confers a greater benefit on the state than
he who taketh a city, Mr. B. might exhibit a
fairer claim to the Presidency than General
Scott himself. I think that some of those
disinterested lovers of the hard-handed demo-
cracy, whose fingers have never touched any-
thing rougher than the dollars of our common
country, would hesitate to compare palms with
him. It would do your heart good, respected
Sir, to see that young man mow. He cuts a
cleaner and wider swath than any in this town.
" But it is time for me to be at my Post. It
is very clear that my young friend's shot has
struck the lintel, for the Post is shaken (Amos
ix. 1). The editor of that paper is a strenuous
advocate of the Mexican war, and a colonel, as
I am given to understand. I presume, that,
being necessarily absent in Mexico, he has left
his journal in some less judicious hands. At
any rate, the Post has been too swift on this

occasion. It could hardly have cited a more
incontrovertible line from any poem than that
which it has selected for animadversion,
namely, —

" ' We kind o' thought Christ went agin war an' pillage.'

" If the Post maintains the converse of this
proposition, it can hardly be considered as a
safe guide-post for the moral and religious por-
tions of its party, however many other excellent
qualities of a post it may be blessed with.
There is a sign in London on which is painted,
— ' The Green Man.' It would do very well as
a portrait of any individual who should support
so unscriptural a thesis. As regards the lan-
guage of the line in question, I am bold to say
that He who readeth the hearts of men will
not account any dialect unseemly which con-
veys a sound and pious sentiment. I could
wish that such sentiments were more common,
however uncouthly expressed. Saint Ambrose
affirms, that *veritas a quocunque* (why not, then,
quomodocunque?) *dicatur, a spiritu sancto est*.
Digest also this of Baxter : ' The plainest words
are the most profitable oratory in the weighti-
est matters.'
" When the paragraph in question was shown
to Mr. Biglow, the only part of it which seemed
to give him any dissatisfaction was that which
classed him with the Whig party. He says,
that, if resolutions are a nourishing kind of
diet, that party must be in a very hearty and
flourishing condition ; for that they have qui-
etly eaten more good ones of their own bak-
ing than he could have conceived to be possi-
ble without repletion. He has been for some
years past (I regret to say) an ardent opponent
of those sound doctrines of protective policy
which form so prominent a portion of the creed
of that party. I confess, that, in some discus-
sions which I have had with him on this point in
my study, he has displayed a vein of obstinacy
which I had not hitherto detected in his compo-
sition. He is also (*horresco referens*) infected in
no small measure with the peculiar notions of
a print called the Liberator, whose heresies I
take every proper opportunity of combating,
and of which, I thank God, I have never read
a single line.
" I did not see Mr. B.'s verses until they ap-
peared in print, and there *is* certainly one thing
in them which I consider highly improper. I
allude to the personal references to myself by
name. To confer notoriety on an humble indi-
vidual who is laboring quietly in his vocation,
and who keeps his cloth as free as he can from
the dust of the political arena (though *væ mihi
si non evangelizavero*), is no doubt an indeco-
rum. The sentiments which he attributes to
me I will not deny to be mine. They were em-
bodied, though in a different form, in a dis-
course preached upon the last day of public
fasting, and were acceptable to my entire
people (of whatever political views), except the
postmaster, who dissented *ex officio*. I observe
that you sometimes devote a portion of your
paper to a religious summary. I should be

well pleased to furnish a copy of my discourse
for insertion in this department of your instruc-
tive journal. By omitting the advertisements,
it might easily be got within the limits of a
single number, and I venture to insure you the
sale of some scores of copies in this town. I
will cheerfully render myself responsible for
ten. It might possibly be advantageous to is-
sue it as an *extra*. But perhaps you will not
esteem it an object, and I will not press it. My
offer does not spring from any weak desire of
seeing my name in print; for I can enjoy this
satisfaction at any time by turning to the Tri-
ennial Catalogue of the University, where it
also possesses that added emphasis of Italics
with which those of my calling are distin-
guished.

"I would simply add, that I continue to fit
ingenuous youth for college, and that I have
two spacious and airy sleeping apartments at
this moment unoccupied. *Ingenuas didicisse*,
&c. Terms,which vary according to the circum-
stances of the parents, may be known on appli-
cation to me by letter, post-paid. In all cases
the lad will be expected to fetch his own towels.
This rule, Mrs. W. desires me to add, has no
exceptions.

"Respectfully, your obedient servant,
"HOMER WILBUR, A. M.

"P. S. Perhaps the last paragraph may look
like an attempt to obtain the insertion of my
circular gratuitously. If it should appear to
you in that light, I desire that you would erase
it, or charge for it at the usual rates, and deduct
the amount from the proceeds in your hands
from the sale of my discourse, when it shall be
printed. My circular is much longer and more
explicit, and will be forwarded without charge
to any who may desire it. It has been very
neatly executed on a letter sheet, by a very de-
serving printer, who attends upon my ministry,
and is a creditable specimen of the typographic
art. I have one hung over my mantelpiece in
a neat frame, where it makes a beautiful and
appropriate ornament, and balances the profile
of Mrs. W., cut with her toes by the young lady
born without arms.
"H. W."

I have in the foregoing letter mentioned Gen-
eral Scott in connection with the Presidency,
because I have been given to understand that
he has blown to pieces and otherwise caused to
be destroyed more Mexicans than any other
commander. His claim would therefore be de-
servedly considered the strongest. Until accu-
rate returns of the Mexicans killed, wounded,
and maimed be obtained, it will be difficult to
settle these nice points of precedence. Should
it prove that any other officer has been more
meritorious and destructive than General S.,
and has thereby rendered himself more worthy
of the confidence and support of the conservative
portion of our community, I shall cheerfully
insert his name, instead of that of General S.,
in a future edition. It may be thought, like-

wise, that General S. has invalidated his claims
by too much attention to the decencies of ap-
parel, and the habits belonging to a gentleman.
These abstruser points of statesmanship are be-
yond my scope. I wonder not that successful
military achievement should attract the admira-
tion of the multitude. Rather do I rejoice with
wonder to behold how rapidly this sentiment is
losing its hold upon the popular mind. It is
related of Thomas Warton, the second of that
honored name who held the office of Poetry
Professor at Oxford, that, when one wished to
find him, being absconded, as was his wont,
in some obscure alehouse, he was counselled to
traverse the city with a drum and fife, the sound
of which inspiring music would be sure to draw
the Doctor from his retirement into the street.
We are all more or less bitten with this martial
insanity. *Nescio qua dulcedine . . . cunctos ducit.*
I confess to some infection of that itch myself.
When I see a Brigadier-General maintaining his
insecure elevation in the saddle under the severe
fire of the training-field, and when I remember
that some military enthusiasts, through haste,
inexperience, or an over-desire to lend reality
to those fictitious combats, will sometimes dis-
charge their ramrods, I cannot but admire,
while I deplore, the mistaken devotion of those
heroic officers. *Semel insanivimus omnes.* I
was myself, during the late war with Great
Britain, chaplain of a regiment, which was for-
tunately never called to active military duty.
I mention this circumstance with regret rather
than pride. Had I been summoned to actual
warfare, I trust that I might have been strength-
ened to bear myself after the manner of that
reverend father in our New England Israel, Dr.
Benjamin Colman, who, as we are told in Tu-
rell's life of him, when the vessel in which he
had taken passage for England was attacked
by a French privateer, "fought like a philoso-
pher and a Christian, . . . and prayed all the
while he charged and fired." As this note is
already long, I shall not here enter upon a dis-
cussion of the question, whether Christians may
lawfully be soldiers. I think it sufficiently evi-
dent, that, during the first two centuries of the
Christian era, at least, the two professions were
esteemed incompatible. Consult Jortin on this
head. — H. W.]

No. IV

REMARKS OF INCREASE D. O'PHACE, ESQUIRE,

AT AN EXTRUMPERY CAUCUS IN STATE
STREET, REPORTED BY MR. H. BIG-
LOW

[THE ingenious reader will at once understand
that no such speech as the following was ever
totidem verbis pronounced. But there are simpler
and less guarded wits, for the satisfying of which

such an explanation may be needful. For there
are certain invisible lines, which as Truth
successively overpasses, she becomes Untruth
to one and another of us, as a large river,
flowing from one kingdom into another, some-
times takes a new name, albeit the waters
undergo no change, how small soever. There is,
moreover, a truth of fiction more veracious
than the truth of fact, as that of the Poet, which
represents to us things and events as they ought
to be, rather than servilely copies them as they
are imperfectly imaged in the crooked and
smoky glass of our mundane affairs. It is this
which makes the speech of Antonius, though
originally spoken in no wider a forum than the
brain of Shakespeare, more historically valuable
than that other which Appian has reported, by
as much as the understanding of the English-
man was more comprehensive than that of the
Alexandrian. Mr. Biglow, in the present in-
stance, has only made use of a license assumed
by all the historians of antiquity, who put into
the mouths of various characters such words as
seem to them most fitting to the occasion and
to the speaker. If it be objected that no such
oration could ever have been delivered, I answer,
that there are few assemblages for speech-
making which do not better deserve the title of
Parliamentum Indoctorum than did the sixth
Parliament of Henry the Fourth, and that men
still continue to have as much faith in the Or-
acle of Fools as ever Pantagruel had. Howell,
in his letters, recounts a merry tale of a certain
ambassador of Queen Elizabeth, who, having
written two letters, — one to her Majesty, and
the other to his wife, — directed them at cross-
purposes, so that the Queen was beducked and
bedeared and requested to send a change of
hose, and the wife was beprincessed and other-
wise unwontedly besuperlatived, till the one
feared for the wits of her ambassador, and the
other for those of her husband. In like manner
it may be presumed that our speaker has misdi-
rected some of his thoughts, and given to the
whole theatre what he would have wished to
confide only to a select auditory at the back of
the curtain. For it is seldom that we can get
any frank utterance from men, who address,
for the most part, a Buncombe either in this
world or the next. As for their audiences, it
may be truly said of our people, that they enjoy
one political institution in common with the an-
cient Athenians: I mean a certain profitless
kind of *ostracism*, wherewith, nevertheless, they
seem hitherto well enough content. For in
Presidential elections, and other affairs of the
sort, whereas I observe that the *oysters* fall to
the lot of comparatively few, the *shells* (such as
the privileges of voting as they are told to do by
the *ostrivori* aforesaid, and of huzzaing at public
meetings) are very liberally distributed among

the people, as being their prescriptive and quite
sufficient portion.

The occasion of the speech is supposed to be
Mr. Palfrey's refusal to vote for the Whig can-
didate for the Speakership. — H. W.]

No? Hez he? He haint, though? Wut?
    Voted agin him?
Ef the bird of our country could ketch him,
    she 'd skin him;
I seem 's though I see her, with wrath in
    each quill,
Like a chancery lawyer, afilin' her bill,
An' grindin' her talents ez sharp ez all
    nater,
To pounce like a writ on the back o' the
    traitor.
Forgive me, my friends, ef I seem to be het,
But a crisis like this must with vigor be
    met;
Wen an Arnold the star-spangled banner
    bestains,
Holl Fourth o' Julys seem to bile in π
    veins.

Who ever 'd ha' thought sech a pisonous rig
Would be run by a chap thet wuz chose fer
    a Wig?
"We knowed wut his princerples wuz 'fore
    we sent him"?
Wut wuz there in them from this vote to
    pervent him?
A marciful Providunce fashioned us holler
O' purpose thet we might our princerples
    swaller;
It can hold any quantity on 'em, the belly
    can,
An' bring 'em up ready fer use like the
    pelican,
Or more like the kangaroo, who (wich is
    stranger)
Puts her family into her pouch wen there 's
    danger.
Aint princerple precious? then, who 's
    goin' to use it
Wen there 's resk o' some chap 's gittin' up
    to abuse it?
I can't tell the wy on't, but nothin' is *so*
    sure
Ez thet princerple kind o' gits spiled by
    exposure;[1]

[1] The speaker is of a different mind from Tully, who,
in his recently discovered tractate *De Republica*, tells
us, *Nec vero habere virtutem satis est, quasi artem
aliquam, nisi utare*, and from our Milton, who says:
"I cannot praise a fugitive and cloistered virtue, un-
exercised and unbreathed, that never sallies out and
sees her adversary, but slinks out of the race where that
immortal garland is to be run for, *not without dust and
heat*." — *Areop.* He had taken the words out of the
Roman's mouth, without knowing it, and might well

A man thet lets all sorts o' folks git a sight
 on 't
Ough' to hev it all took right away, every
 mite on 't;
Ef he can't keep it all to himself wen it 's
 wise to,
He aint one it's fit to trust nothin' so nice to.

Besides, ther 's a wonderful power in lati-
 tude
To shift a man's morril relations an' atti-
 tude;
Some flossifers think thet a fakkilty 's
 granted
The minnit it 's proved to be thoroughly
 wanted,
Thet a change o' demand makes a change
 o' condition,
An' thet everythin' 's nothin' except by
 position;
Ez, fer instance, thet rubber-trees fust be-
 gun bearin'
 en p'litikle conshunces come into wear-
 in',
Thet the fears of a monkey, whose holt
 chanced to fail,
Drawed the vertibry out to a prehensile
 tail;
So, wen one 's chose to Congriss, ez soon ez
 he 's in it,
A collar grows right round his neck in a
 minnit,
An' sartin it is thet a man cannot be strict
In bein' himself, wen he gits to the Dees-
 trict,
Fer a coat thet sets wal here in ole Massa-
 chusetts,
Wen it gits on to Washinton, somehow
 askew sets.

Resolves, do you say, o' the Springfield
 Convention ?
Thet 's percisely the pint I was goin' to
 mention;
Resolves air a thing we most gen'ally keep
 ill,
They 're a cheap kind 'o dust fer the eyes
 o' the people;
A parcel o' delligits jest git together
An' chat fer a spell o' the crops an' the
 weather,

exclaim with Donatus (if Saint Jerome's tutor may
stand sponsor for a curse), *Pereant qui ante nos nostra
dixerint !* — H. W.

Then, comin' to order, they squabble awile
An' let off the speeches they 're ferful 'll
 spile;
Then — Resolve, — Thet we wunt hev an
 inch o' slave territory;
Thet Presidunt Polk's holl perceedins air
 very tory;
Thet the war is a damned war, an' them
 thet enlist in it
Should hev a cravat with a dreffle tight
 twist in it;
Thet the war is a war fer the spreadin' o'
 slavery;
Thet our army desarves our best thanks
 fer their bravery;
Thet we 're the original friends o' the
 nation,
All the rest air a paltry an' base fabrica-
 tion;
Thet we highly respect Messrs. A, B,
 an' C,
An' ez deeply despise Messrs. E, F, an' G.
In this way they go to the eend o' the
 chapter,
An' then they bust out in a kind of a rap-
 tur
About their own vartoo, an' folks's stone-
 blindness
To the men thet 'ould actilly do 'em a
 kindness, —
The American eagle, — the Pilgrims thet
 landed, —
Till on ole Plymouth Rock they git finally
 stranded.
Wal, the people they listen an' say, " Thet 's
 the ticket;
Ez fer Mexico, 't aint no great glory to
 lick it,
But 't would be a darned shame to go pull-
 in' o' triggers
To extend the aree of abusin' the nig-
 gers."

So they march in percession, an' git up
 hooraws,
An' tramp thru the mud fer the good o' the
 cause,
An' think they 're a kind o' fulfillin' the
 prophecies,
Wen they 're on'y jest changin' the holders
 of offices;
Ware A sot afore, B is comf'tably seated,
One humbug 's victor'ous an' t' other de-
 feated,

Each honnable doughface gits jest wut he
    axes,
An' the people, — their annooal soft-sodder
    an' taxes.

Now, to keep unimpaired all these glorious
    feeturs
Thet characterize morril an' reasonin' cree-
    turs,
Thet give every paytriot all he can cram,
Thet oust the untrustworthy Presidunt
    Flam,
An' stick honest Presidunt Sham in his
    place,
To the manifest gain o' the holl human
    race,
An' to some indervidgewals on 't in par-
    tickler,
Who love Public Opinion an' know how to
    tickle her, —
I say thet a party with gret aims like these
Must stick jest ez close ez a hive full o'
    bees.

I 'm willin' a man should go tollable strong
Agin wrong in the abstract, fer thet kind
    o' wrong
Is ollers unpop'lar an' never gits pitied,
Because it 's a crime no one never com-
    mitted;
But he mus' n't be hard on partickler sins,
Coz then he 'll be kickin' the people's own
    shins;
On'y look at the Demmercrats, see wut
    they 've done
Jest simply by stickin' together like fun;
They 've sucked us right into a mis'able
    war
Thet no one on airth aint responsible for;
They 've run us a hundred cool millions in
    debt
(An' fer Demmercrat Horners ther 's good
    plums left yet);
They talk agin tayriffs, but act fer a high
    one,
An' so coax all parties to build up their
    Zion;
To the people they 're ollers ez slick ez mo-
    lasses,
An' butter their bread on both sides with
    The Masses,
Half o' whom they 've persuaded, by way
    of a joke,
Thet Washinton's mantelpiece fell upon
    Polk.

Now all o' these blessin's the Wigs might
    enjoy,
Ef they 'd gumption enough the right means
    to imploy;[1]
Fer the silver spoon born in Dermoc'acy's
    mouth
Is a kind of a scringe thet they hev to the
    South;
Their masters can cuss 'em an' kick 'em an'
    wale 'em,
An' they notice it less 'an the ass did to Ba-
    laam;
In this way they screw into second-rate
    offices
Wich the slaveholder thinks 'ould substract
    too much off his ease;
The file-leaders, I mean, du, fer they, by
    their wiles,
Unlike the old viper, grow fat on their files.
Wal, the Wigs hev been tryin' to grab all
    this prey frum 'em
An' to hook this nice spoon o' good fortin'
    away frum 'em,
An' they might ha' succeeded, ez likely ez
    not,
In lickin' the Demmercrats all round the
    lot,
Ef it warn't the't, wile all faithful Wigs
    were their knees on,
Some stuffy old codger would holler out, —
    " Treason!
You must keep a sharp eye on a dog thet
    hez bit you once,
An' *I* aint agoin' to cheat my constitoo-
    unts," —
Wen every fool knows thet a man repre-
    sents
Not the fellers thet sent him, but them on
    the fence, —
Impartially ready to jump either side
An' make the fust use of a turn o' the
    tide, —
The waiters on Providunce here in the city,
Who compose wut they call a State Centerl
    Committy.
Constitoounts air hendy to help a man in,
But arterwards don't weigh the heft of a
    pin.
Wy, the people can't all live on Uncle Sam's
    pus,
So they 've nothin' to du with 't fer better
    or wus;

---

[1] That was a pithy saying of Persius, and fits our
politicians without a wrinkle, — *Magister artis, inge-
niique largitor venter.* — H. W.

It 's the folks thet air kind o' brought up
to depend on 't
Thet hev any consarn in 't, an' thet is the
end on 't.
Now here wuz New England ahevin' the
honor
Of a chance at the Speakership showered
upon her; —
Do you say, "She don't want no more
Speakers, but fewer;
She 's hed plenty o' them, wut she wants is
a *doer* " ?
Fer the matter o' thet, it 's notorous in town
Thet her own representatives du her quite
brown.
But thet 's nothin' to du with it; wut right
hed Palfrey
To mix himself up with fanatical small
fry?
Warn't we gittin' on prime with our hot
an' cold blowin',
Acondemnin' the war wilst we kep' it
agoin' ?
We 'd assumed with gret skill a command-
in' position,
On this side or thet, no one could n't tell
wich one,
So, wutever side wipped, we 'd a chance at
the plunder
An' could sue fer infringin' our paytented
thunder;
We were ready to vote fer whoever wuz
eligible,
Ef on all pints at issoo he 'd stay unintelli-
gible.
Wal, sposin' we hed to gulp down our per-
fessions,
We were ready to come out next mornin'
with fresh ones;
Besides, ef we did, 't was our business alone,
Fer could n't we du wut we would with our
own ?
An' ef a man can, wen pervisions hev riz so,
Eat up his own words, it 's a marcy it is so.
Wy, these chaps frum the North, with back-
bones to 'em, darn 'em,
'Ould be wuth more 'an Gennle Tom Thumb
is to Barnum:
Ther 's enough thet to office on this very
plan grow,
By exhibitin' how very small a man can
grow;
But an M. C. frum here ollers hastens to
state he
Belongs to the order called invertebraty,

Wence some gret filologists judge primy
fashy
Thet M. C. is M. T. by paronomashy;
An' these few exceptions air *loosus naytury*
Folks 'ould put down their quarters to stare
at, like fury.

It 's no use to open the door o' success,
Ef a member can bolt so fer nothin' or less;
Wy, all o' them grand constitootional pillers
Our fore-fathers fetched with 'em over the
billers,
Them pillers the people so soundly hev
slep' on,
Wile to slav'ry, invasion, an' debt they were
swep' on,
Wile our Destiny higher an' higher kep'
mountin'
(Though I guess folks 'll stare wen she
hends her account in),
Ef members in this way go kickin' agin 'em,
They wunt hev so much ez a feather left in
'em.

An', ez fer this Palfrey,[1] we thought wen
we 'd gut him in,
He 'd go kindly in wutever harness we put
him in;
Supposin' we *did* know thet he wuz a peace
man ?
Doos he think he can be Uncle Sammle's
policeman,
An' wen Sam gits tipsy an kicks up a riot,
Lead him off to the lockup to snooze till
he 's quiet ?
Wy, the war is a war thet true paytriots
can bear, ef
It leads to the fat promised land of a
tayriff;
We don't go an' fight it, nor aint to be driv
on,
Nor Demmercrats nuther, thet hev wut to
live on;
Ef it aint jest the thing thet 's well pleasin'
to God,
It makes us thought highly on elsewhere
abroad;
The Rooshian black eagle looks blue in his
eerie
An' shakes both his heads wen he hears o'
Monteery;
In the Tower Victory sets, all of a fluster,

---

[1] There is truth yet in this of Juvenal, —

"Dat veniam corvis, vexat censura columbas."—H. W.

An' reads, with locked doors, how we won
　　Cherry Buster;
An' old Philip Lewis — thet come an' kep'
　　school here
Fer the mere sake o' scorin' his ryalist
　　ruler
On the tenderest part of our kings *in
　　futuro* —
Hides his crown underneath an old shut in
　　his bureau,
Breaks off in his brags to a suckle o' merry
　　kings,
How he often hed hided young native
　　Amerrikins,
An' turnin' quite faint in the midst of his
　　fooleries,
Sneaks down stairs to bolt the front door
　　o' the Tooleries.[1]
You say, " We 'd ha' scared 'em by grow-
　　in' in peace,
A plaguy sight more then by bobberies like
　　these " ?
Who is it dares say thet our naytional
　　eagle
Wun't much longer be classed with the
　　birds thet air regal,
Coz theirn be hooked beaks, an' she, arter
　　this slaughter,
'll bring back a bill ten times longer 'n
　　she 'd ough' to ?
Wut 's your name ? Come, I see ye, you
　　up-country feller,
You 've put me out severil times with your
　　beller;
Out with it ! Wut ? Biglow ? I say no-
　　thin' furder,
Thet feller would like nothin' better 'n a
　　murder;
He 's a traiter, blasphemer, an' wut ruther
　　worse is,
He puts all his ath'ism in dreffle bad verses;
Socity aint safe till sech monsters air out
　　on it,
Refer to the Post, ef you hev the least
　　doubt on it;
Wy, he goes agin war, agin indirect taxes,
Agin sellin' wild lands 'cept to settlers
　　with axes,

Agin holdin' o' slaves, though he knows
　　it 's the corner
Our libbaty rests on, the mis'able scorner !
In short, he would wholly upset with his
　　ravages
All thet keeps us above the brute critters
　　an' savages,
An' pitch into all kinds o' briles an' con-
　　fusions
The holl of our civerlized, free institu-
　　tions;
He writes fer thet ruther unsafe print, the
　　Courier,
An' likely ez not hez a squintin' to Foorier;
I 'll be ——, thet is, I mean I 'll be blest,
Ef I hark to a word frum so noted a pest;
I sha'n't talk with *him*, my religion 's too
　　fervent.
Good mornin', my friends, I 'm your most
　　humble servant.

[Into the question whether the ability to ex-
press ourselves in articulate language has been
productive of more good or evil, I shall not
here enter at large. The two faculties of speech
and of speech-making are wholly diverse in
their natures. By the first we make ourselves
intelligible, by the last unintelligible, to our
fellows. It has not seldom occurred to me (not-
ing how in our national legislature everything
runs to talk, as lettuces, if the season or the
soil be unpropitious, shoot up lankly to seed,
instead of forming handsome heads) that Babel
was the first Congress, the earliest mill erected
for the manufacture of gabble. In these days,
what with Town Meetings, School Committees,
Boards (lumber) of one kind and another, Con-
gresses, Parliaments, Diets, Indian Councils,
Palavers, and the like, there is scarce a village
which has not its factories of this description
driven by milk-and-water power. I cannot
conceive the confusion of tongues to have been
the curse of Babel, since I esteem my ignorance
of other languages as a kind of Martello-tower,
in which I am safe from the furious bombard-
ments of foreign garrulity. For this reason I
have ever preferred the study of the dead lan-
guages, those primitive formations being Ara-
rats upon whose silent peaks I sit secure and
watch this new deluge without fear, though it
rain figures (*simulacra*, semblances) of speech

no thanks to Beelzebub neither ! That of Seneca in
Medea will suit here : —

" Rapida fortuna ac levis
Præcepsque regno eripuit, exsilio dedit."

Let us allow, even to richly deserved misfortune, our
commiseration, and be not over-hasty meanwhile in our
censure of the French people, left for the first time to
govern themselves, remembering that wise sentence of
Æschylus, —

Ἅπας δὲ τραχὺς ὅστις ἂν νέον κρατῇ. — H. W.

---

[1] Jortin is willing to allow of other miracles besides
those recorded in Holy Writ, and why not of other
prophecies ? It is granting too much to Satan to sup-
pose him, as divers of the learned have done, the in-
spirer of the ancient oracles. Wiser, I esteem it, to
give chance the credit of the successful ones. What is
said here of Louis Philippe was verified in some of its
minute particulars within a few months' time. Enough
to have made the fortune of Delphi or Hammon, and

forty days and nights together, as it not uncommonly happens. Thus is my coat, as it were, without buttons by which any but a vernacular wild bore can seize me. Is it not possible that the Shakers may intend to convey a quiet reproof and hint, in fastening their outer garments with hooks and eyes ?

This reflection concerning Babel, which I find in no Commentary, was first thrown upon my mind when an excellent deacon of my congregation (being infected with the Second Advent delusion) assured me that he had received a first instalment of the gift of tongues as a small earnest of larger possessions in the like kind to follow. For, of a truth, I could not reconcile it with my ideas of the Divine justice and mercy that the single wall which protected people of other languages from the incursions of this otherwise well-meaning propagandist should be broken down.

In reading Congressional debates, I have fancied, that, after the subsidence of those painful buzzings in the brain which result from such exercises, I detected a slender residuum of valuable information. I made the discovery that *nothing* takes longer in the saying than anything else, for as *ex nihilo nihil fit*, so from one polypus *nothing* any number of similar ones may be produced. I would recommend to the attention of *viva voce* debaters and controversialists the admirable example of the monk Copres, who, in the fourth century, stood for half an hour in the midst of a great fire, and thereby silenced a Manichæan antagonist who had less of the salamander in him. As for those who quarrel in print, I have no concern with them here, since the eyelids are a divinely granted shield against all such. Moreover, I have observed in many modern books that the printed portion is becoming gradually smaller, and the number of blank or fly-leaves (as they are called) greater. Should this fortunate tendency of literature continue, books will grow more valuable from year to year, and the whole Serbonian bog yield to the advances of firm arable land.

The sagacious Lacedæmonians, hearing that Tesephone had bragged that he could talk all day long on any given subject, made no more ado, but forthwith banished him, whereby they supplied him a topic and at the same time took care that his experiment upon it should be tried out of earshot.

I have wondered, in the Representatives' Chamber of our own Commonwealth, to mark how little impression seemed to be produced by that emblematic fish suspended over the heads of the members. Our wiser ancestors, no doubt, hung it there as being the animal which the Pythagoreans reverenced for its silence, and which certainly in that particular does not so well merit the epithet *cold-blooded*, by which naturalists distinguish it, as certain bipeds, afflicted with ditch-water on the brain, who take occasion to tap themselves in Faneuil Halls, meeting-houses, and other places of public resort. — H. W.]

[THE incident which gave rise to the debate satirized in the following verses was the unsuccessful attempt of Drayton and Sayres to give freedom to seventy men and women, fellow-beings and fellow-Christians. Had Tripoli, instead of Washington, been the scene of this undertaking, the unhappy leaders in it would have been as secure of the theoretic as they now are of the practical part of martyrdom. I question whether the Dey of Tripoli is blessed with a District Attorney so benighted as ours at the seat of government. Very fitly is he named Key, who would allow himself to be made the instrument of locking the door of hope against sufferers in such a cause. Not all the waters of the ocean can cleanse the vile smutch of the jailer's fingers from off that little Key. *Ahenea clavis*, a brazen Key indeed !

Mr. Calhoun, who is made the chief speaker in this burlesque, seems to think that the light of the nineteenth century is to be put out as soon as he tinkles his little cow-bell curfew. Whenever slavery is touched, he sets up his scarecrow of dissolving the Union. This may do for the North, but I should conjecture that something more than a pumpkin-lantern is required to scare manifest and irretrievable Destiny out of her path. Mr. Calhoun cannot let go the apron-string of the Past. The Past is a good nurse, but we must be weaned from her sooner or later, even though, like Plotinus, we should run home from school to ask the breast, after we are tolerably well-grown youths. It will not do for us to hide our faces in her lap, whenever the strange Future holds out her arms and asks us to come to her.

But we are all alike. We have all heard it said, often enough, that little boys must not play with fire ; and yet, if the matches be taken away from us, and put out of reach upon the shelf, we must needs gets into our little corner, and scowl and stamp and threaten the dire revenge of going to bed without our supper. The world shall stop till we get our dangerous plaything again. Dame Earth, meanwhile, who has more than enough household matters to mind, goes bustling hither and thither as a hiss or a sputter tells her that this or that kettle of hers is boiling over, and before bedtime we are glad to eat our porridge cold, and gulp down our dignity along with it.

Mr. Calhoun has somehow acquired the name of a great statesman, and, if it be great statesmanship to put lance in rest and run a tilt at the Spirit of the Age with the certainty of being next moment hurled neck and heels into the dust amid universal laughter, he deserves the title. He is the Sir Kay of our modern chivalry. He should remember the old Scandinavian mythus. Thor was the strongest of gods, but he could not wrestle with Time, nor so much as lift up a fold of the great snake which bound the universe together; and when he smote the Earth, though with his terrible mallet, it was but as if a leaf had fallen. Yet all the while it seemed to Thor that he had only been wrestling with an old woman, striving to lift a cat, and striking a stupid giant on the head.

And in old times, doubtless, the giants *were* stupid, and there was no better sport for the Sir Launcelots and Sir Gawains than to go about cutting off their great blundering heads with enchanted swords. But things have wonderfully changed. It is the giants, nowadays, that have the science and the intelligence, while the chivalrous Don Quixotes of Conservatism still cumber themselves with the clumsy armor of a bygone age. On whirls the restless globe through unsounded time, with its cities and its silences, its births and funerals, half light, half shade, but never wholly dark, and sure to swing round into the happy morning at last. With an involuntary smile, one sees Mr. Calhoun letting slip his pack-thread cable with a crooked pin at the end of it to anchor South Carolina upon the bank and shoal of the Past. — H. W.]

TO MR. BUCKENAM

MR. EDITER, As i wuz kinder prunin round in a little nussry sot out a year or 2 a go, the Dbait in the sennit cum inter my mine An so i took & Sot it to wut I call a nussry rime. I hev made sum onnable Gentlemun speak thut dident speak in a Kind uv Poetikul lie sense the seeson is dreffle backerd up This way
ewers as ushul
HOSEA BIGLOW.

"HERE we stan' on the Constitution, by thunder!
It's a fact o' wich ther 's bushils o' proofs;
Fer how could we trample on 't so, I wonder,
Ef 't worn't thet it 's ollers under our hoofs?"
Sez John C. Calhoun, sez he;
"Human rights haint no more
Right to come on this floor,
No more 'n the man in the moon," sez he.

"The North haint no kind o' bisness with nothin',
An' you 've no idee how much bother it saves;

We aint none riled by their frettin' an' frothin',
We 're *used* to layin' the string on our slaves,"
Sez John C. Calhoun, sez he; —
Sez Mister Foote,
" I should like to shoot
The holl gang, by the gret horn spoon! " sez he.

" Freedom's Keystone is Slavery, thet ther 's no doubt on,
It 's sutthin' thet 's — wha' d' ye call it? — divine, —
An' the slaves thet we ollers *make* the most out on
Air them north o' Mason an' Dixon's line,"
Sez John C. Calhoun, sez he; —
" Fer all that," sez Mangum,
" 'T would be better to hang 'em
An' so git red on 'em soon," sez he.

" The mass ough' to labor an' we lay on soffies,
Thet 's the reason I want to spread Freedom's aree;
It puts all the cunninest on us in office,
An' reelises our Maker's orig'nal idee,"
Sez John C. Calhoun, sez he; —
" Thet 's ez plain," sez Cass,
" Ez thet some one 's an ass,
It 's ez clear ez the sun is at noon," sez he.

" Now don't go to say I 'm the friend of oppression,
But keep all your spare breath fer coolin' your broth,
Fer I ollers hev strove (at least thet 's my impression)
To make cussed free with the rights o' the North,"
Sez John C. Calhoun, sez he; —
" Yes," sez Davis o' Miss.,
" The perfection o' bliss
Is in skinnin' thet same old coon," sez he.

" Slavery 's a thing thet depends on complexion,
It 's God's law thet fetters on black skins don't chafe;
Ef brains wuz to settle it (horrid reflection!
Wich of our onnable body 'd be safe? "

Sez John C. Calhoun, sez he; —
Sez Mister Hannegan,
Afore he began agin,
" Thet exception is quite oppertoon,"
sez he.

" Gen'nle Cass, Sir, you need n't be twitchin'
your collar,
Your merit 's quite clear by the dut on
your knees,
At the North we don't make no distinctions
o' color;
You can all take a lick at our shoes wen
you please,"
Sez John C. Calhoun, sez he; —
Sez Mister Jarnagin,
" They wun't hev to larn agin,
They all on 'em know the old toon,"
sez he.

" The slavery question aint no ways bewil-
derin',
North an' South hev one int'rest, it's plain
to a glance;
No'thern men, like us patriarchs, don't sell
their childrin,
But they *du* sell themselves, ef they git a
good chance,"
Sez John C. Calhoun, sez he;—
Sez Atherton here,
" This is gittin' severe,
I wish I could dive like a loon," sez he.

" It 'll break up the Union, this talk about
freedom,
An' your fact' ry gals (soon ez we split)
'll make head,
An' gittin' some Miss chief or other to lead
'em,
'll go to work raisin' permiscoous Ned,"
Sez John C. Calhoun, sez he; —
" Yes, the North," sez Colquitt,
" Ef we Southeners all quit,
Would go down like a busted balloon,"
sez he.

" Jest look wut is doin', wut annyky 's
brewin'
In the beautiful clime o' the olive an'
vine,
All the wise aristoxy 's atumblin' to ruin,
An' the sankylots drorin' an' drinkin'
their wine,"
Sez John C. Calhoun, sez he; —
" Yes," sez Johnson, " in France

They 're beginnin' to dance
Beëlzebub's own rigadoon," sez he.

" The South 's safe enough, it don't feel a
mite skeery,
Our slaves in their darkness an' dut air
tu blest
Not to welcome with proud hallylugers the
ery
Wen our eagle kicks yourn from the nay-
tional nest,"
Sez John C. Calhoun, sez he; —
" Oh," sez Westcott o' Florida,
" Wut treason is horrider
Than our priv'leges tryin' to proon ? "
sez he.

" It 's 'coz they 're so happy, thet, wen crazy
sarpints
Stick their nose in our bizness, we git so
darned riled;
We think it 's our dooty to give pooty sharp
hints,
Thet the last crumb of Edin on airth
sha'n't be spiled,"
Sez John C. Calhoun, sez he;—
" Ah," sez Dixon H. Lewis,
" It perfectly true is
Thet slavery 's airth's grettest boon,"
sez he.

[It was said of old time, that riches have
wings; and, though this be not applicable in a
literal strictness to the wealth of our patriarchal
brethren of the South, yet it is clear that their
possessions have legs, and an unaccountable
propensity for using them in a northerly direc-
tion. I marvel that the grand jury of Washing-
ton did not find a true bill against the North
Star for aiding and abetting Drayton and Sayres.
It would have been quite of a piece with the
intelligence displayed by the South on other
questions connected with slavery. I think that
no ship of state was ever freighted with a more
veritable Jonah than this same domestic institu-
tion of ours. Mephistopheles himself could not
feign so bitterly, so satirically sad a sight as
this of three millions of human beings crushed
beyond help or hope by this one mighty argu-
ment, — *Our fathers knew no better !* Neverthe-
less, it is the unavoidable destiny of Jonahs to
be cast overboard sooner or later. Or shall we
try the experiment of hiding our Jonah in a safe
place, that none may lay hands on him to make
jetsam of him ? Let us, then, with equal fore-
thought and wisdom, lash ourselves to the an-
chor, and await, in pious confidence, the cer-
tain result. Perhaps our suspicious passenger
is no Jonah after all, being black. For it is well
known that a superintending Providence made

a kind of sandwich of Ham and his descendants, to be devoured by the Caucasian race.

In God's name, let all, who hear nearer and nearer the hungry moan of the storm and the growl of the breakers, speak out! But, alas! we have no right to interfere. If a man pluck an apple of mine, he shall be in danger of the justice; but if he steal my brother, I must be silent. Who says this? Our Constitution, consecrated by the callous consuetude of sixty years, and grasped in triumphant argument by the left hand of him whose right hand clutches the clotted slave-whip. Justice, venerable with the undethronable majesty of countless æons, says,—SPEAK! The Past, wise with the sorrows and desolations of ages, from amid her shattered fanes and wolf-housing palaces, echoes,— SPEAK! Nature, through her thousand trumpets of freedom, her stars, her sunrises, her seas, her winds, her cataracts, her mountains blue with cloudy pines, blows jubilant encouragement, and cries,—SPEAK! From the soul's trembling abysses the still, small voice not vaguely murmurs,—SPEAK! But, alas! the Constitution and the Honorable Mr. Bagowind, M. C., say—BE DUMB!

It occurs to me to suggest, as a topic of inquiry in this connection, whether, on that momentous occasion when the goats and the sheep shall be parted, the Constitution and the Honorable Mr. Bagowind, M. C., will be expected to take their places on the left as our hircine vicars,

> Quid sum miser tunc dicturus?
> Quem patronum rogaturus?

There is a point where toleration sinks into sheer baseness and poltroonery. The toleration of the worst leads us to look on what is barely better as good enough, and to worship what is only moderately good. Woe to that man, or that nation, to whom mediocrity has become an ideal!

Has our experiment of self-government succeeded, if it barely manage to rub and go? Here, now, is a piece of barbarism which Christ and the nineteenth century say shall cease, and which Messrs. Smith, Brown, and others say shall not cease. I would by no means deny the eminent respectability of these gentlemen, but I confess, that, in such a wrestling-match, I cannot help having my fears for them.

> Discite justitiam, moniti, et non temnere divos.

H. W.]

No. VI

THE PIOUS EDITOR'S CREED

[AT the special instance of Mr. Biglow, I preface the following satire with an extract from a sermon preached during the past summer, from Ezekiel xxxiv. 2: "Son of man, prophesy against the shepherds of Israel." Since the Sabbath on which this discourse was delivered,

the editor of the "Jaalam Independent Blunderbuss" has unaccountably absented himself from our house of worship.

"I know of no so responsible position as that of the public journalist. The editor of our day bears the same relation to his time that the clerk bore to the age before the invention of printing. Indeed, the position which he holds is that which the clergyman should hold even now. But the clergyman chooses to walk off to the extreme edge of the world, and to throw such seed as he has clear over into that darkness which he calls the Next Life. As if next did not mean nearest, and as if any life were nearer than that immediately present one which boils and eddies all around him at the caucus, the ratification meeting, and the polls! Who taught him to exhort men to prepare for eternity, as for some future era of which the present forms no integral part? The furrow which Time is even now turning runs through the Everlasting, and in that must he plant, or nowhere. Yet he would fain believe and teach that we are going to have more of eternity than we have now. This going of his is like that of the auctioneer, on which gone follows before we have made up our minds to bid,—in which manner, not three months back, I lost an excellent copy of Chappelow on Job. So it has come to pass that the preacher, instead of being a living force, has faded into an emblematic figure at christenings, weddings, and funerals. Or, if he exercise any other function, it is as keeper and feeder of certain theologic dogmas, which, when occasion offers, he unkennels with a staboy! 'to bark and bite as 't is their nature to,' whence that reproach of odium theologicum has arisen.

"Meanwhile, see what a pulpit the editor mounts daily, sometimes with a congregation of fifty thousand within reach of his voice, and never so much as a nodder, even, among them! And from what a Bible can he choose his text,—a Bible which needs no translation, and which no priestcraft can shut and clasp from the laity,—the open volume of the world, upon which, with a pen of sunshine or destroying fire, the inspired Present is even now writing the annals of God! Methinks the editor who should understand his calling, and be equal thereto, would truly deserve that title of ποιμὴν λαῶν, which Homer bestows upon princes. He would be the Moses of our nineteenth century; and whereas the old Sinai, silent now, is but a common mountain stared at by the elegant tourist and crawled over by the hammering geologist, he must find his tables of the new law here among factories and cities in this Wilderness of Sin (Numbers xxxiii. 12) called Progress of Civilization, and be the captain of our Exodus into the Canaan of a truer social order.

"Nevertheless, our editor will not come so far within even the shadow of Sinai as Mahomet did, but chooses rather to construe Moses by Joe Smith. He takes up the crook, not that the sheep may be fed, but that he may never want a warm woollen suit and a joint of mutton.

Immemor, O, fidei, pecorumque oblite tuorum!

For which reason I would derive the name *editor* not so much from *edo*, to publish, as from *edo*, to eat, that being the peculiar profession to which he esteems himself called. He blows up the flames of political discord for no other occasion than that he may thereby handily boil his own pot. I believe there are two thousand of these mutton-loving shepherds in the United States, and of these, how many have even the dimmest perception of their immense power, and the duties consequent thereon? Here and there, haply, one. Nine hundred and ninety-nine labor to impress upon the people the great principles of *Tweedledum*, and other nine hundred and ninety-nine preach with equal earnestness the gospel according to *Tweedledee*." — H. W.]

I DU believe in Freedom's cause,
    Ez fur away ez Payris is ;
I love to see her stick her claws
    In them infarnal Phayrisees ;
It 's wal enough agin a king
    To dror resolves an' triggers, —
But libbaty 's a kind o' thing
    Thet don't agree with niggers.

I du believe the people want
    A tax on teas an' coffees,
Thet nothin' aint extravygunt, —
    Purvidin' I 'm in office ;
Fer I hev loved my country sence
    My eye-teeth filled their sockets,
An' Uncle Sam I reverence,
    Partic'larly his pockets.

I du believe in *any* plan
    O' levyin' the texes,
Ez long ez, like a lumberman,
    I git jest wut I axes ;
I go free-trade thru thick an' thin,
    Because it kind o' rouses
The folks to vote, — an' keeps us in
    Our quiet custom-houses.

I du believe it 's wise an' good
    To sen' out furrin missions,
Thet is, on sartin understood
    An' orthydox conditions ; —
I mean nine thousan' dolls. per ann.,
    Nine thousan' more fer outfit,
An' me to recommend a man
    The place 'ould jest about fit.

I du believe in special ways
    O' prayin' an' convartin' ;
The bread comes back in many days,

    An' buttered, tu, fer sartin ;
I mean in preyin' till one busts
    On wut the party chooses,
An' in convartin' public trusts
    To very privit uses.

I du believe hard coin the stuff
    Fer 'lectioneers to spout on;
The people's ollers soft enough
    To make hard money out on;
Dear Uncle Sam pervides fer his,
    An' gives a good-sized junk to all, —
I don't care *how* hard money is,
    Ez long ez mine 's paid punctooal.

I du believe with all my soul
    In the gret Press's freedom,
To pint the people to the goal
    An' in the traces lead 'em;
Palsied the arm thet forges yokes
    At my fat contracts squintin',
An' withered be the nose thet pokes
    Inter the gov'ment printin' !

I du believe thet I should give
    Wut 's his'n unto Cæsar,
Fer it 's by him I move an' live,
    Frum him my bread an' cheese air;
I du believe thet all o' me
    Doth bear his superscription, —
Will, conscience, honor, honesty,
    An' things o' thet description.

I du believe in prayer an' praise
    To him thet hez the grantin'
O' jobs, — in every thin' thet pays,
    But most of all in CANTIN' ;
This doth my cup with marcies fill,
    This lays all thought o' sin to rest,
I *don't* believe in princerple,
    But oh, I *du* in interest.

I du believe in bein' this
    Or thet, ez it may happen
One way or 't other hendiest is
    To ketch the people nappin' ;
It aint by princerples nor men
    My preudunt course is steadied, —
I scent wich pays the best, an' then
    Go into it baldheaded.

I du believe thet holdin' slaves
    Comes nat'ral to a Presidunt,
Let 'lone the rowdedow it saves
    To hev a wal-broke precedunt;

Fer any office, small or gret,
   I could n't ax with no face,
'uthout I 'd ben, thru dry an' wet,
   Th' unrizzest kind o' doughface.

I du believe wutever trash
   'll keep the people in blindness, —
Thet we the Mexicuns can thrash
   Right inter brotherly kindness,
Thet bombshells, grape, an' powder 'n' ball
   Air good-will's strongest magnets,
Thet peace, to make it stick at all,
   Must be druv in with bagnets.

In short, I firmly du believe
   In Humbug generally,
Fer it 's a thing thet I perceive
   To hev a solid vally;
This heth my faithful shepherd ben,
   In pasturs sweet heth led me,
An' this 'll keep the people green
   To feed ez they hev fed me.

[I subjoin here another passage from my be-
fore-mentioned discourse.

"Wonderful, to him that has eyes to see it
rightly, is the newspaper. To me, for example,
sitting on the critical front bench of the pit, in
my study here in Jaalam, the advent of my
weekly journal is as that of a strolling theatre,
or rather of a puppet-show, on whose stage, nar-
row as it is, the tragedy, comedy, and farce
of life are played in little. Behold the whole
huge earth sent to me hebdomadally in a brown-
paper wrapper!
" Hither, to my obscure corner, by wind or
steam, on horseback or dromedary-back, in the
pouch of the Indian runner, or clicking over
the magnetic wires, troop all the famous per-
formers from the four quarters of the globe.
Looked at from a point of criticism, tiny pup-
pets they seem all, as the editor sets up his
booth upon my desk and officiates as showman.
Now I can truly see how little and transitory is
life. The earth appears almost as a drop of
vinegar, on which the solar microscope of the
imagination must be brought to bear in order
to make out anything distinctly. That animal-
cule there, in the pea-jacket, is Louis Philippe,
just landed on the coast of England. That
other, in the gray surtout and cocked hat, is
Napoleon Bonaparte Smith, assuring France
that she need apprehend no interference from
him in the present alarming juncture. At that
spot, where you seem to see a speck of some-
thing in motion, is an immense mass-meeting.
Look sharper, and you will see a mite brandish-
ing his mandibles in an excited manner. That
is the great Mr. Soandso, defining his position
amid tumultuous and irrepressible cheers.
That infinitesimal creature, upon whom some
score of others, as minute as he, are gazing in
open-mouthed admiration, is a famous philoso-
pher, expounding to a select audience their
capacity for the Infinite. That scarce discerni-
ble pufflet of smoke and dust is a revolution.
That speck there is a reformer, just arranging
the lever with which he is to move the world.
And lo, there creeps forward the shadow of a
skeleton that blows one breath between its
grinning teeth, and all our distinguished actors
are whisked off the slippery stage into the dark
Beyond.
"Yes, the little show-box has its solemner
suggestions. Now and then we catch a glimpse
of a grim old man, who lays down a scythe and
hour-glass in the corner while he shifts the
scenes. There, too, in the dim background, a
weird shape is ever delving. Sometimes he
leans upon his mattock, and gazes, as a coach
whirls by, bearing the newly married on their
wedding jaunt, or glances carelessly at a babe
brought home from christening. Suddenly (for
the scene grows larger and larger as we look) a
bony hand snatches back a performer in the
midst of his part, and him, whom yesterday
two infinities (past and future) would not suf-
fice, a handful of dust is enough to cover and
silence forever. Nay, we see the same fleshless
fingers opening to clutch the showman himself,
and guess, not without a shudder, that they are
lying in wait for spectator also.
"Think of it: for three dollars a year I buy
a season-ticket to this great Globe Theatre, for
which God would write the dramas (only that
we like farces, spectacles, and the tragedies of
Apollyon better), whose scene-shifter is Time,
and whose curtain is rung down by Death.
"Such thoughts will occur to me sometimes
as I am tearing off the wrapper of my news-
paper. Then suddenly that otherwise too often
vacant sheet becomes invested for me with a
strange kind of awe. Look! deaths and mar-
riages, notices of inventions, discoveries, and
books, lists of promotions, of killed, wounded,
and missing, news of fires, accidents, of sudden
wealth and as sudden poverty; — I hold in my
hand the ends of myriad invisible electric con-
ductors, along which tremble the joys, sorrows,
wrongs, triumphs, hopes, and despairs of as
many men and women everywhere. So that
upon that mood of mind which seems to isolate
me from mankind as a spectator of their puppet-
pranks, another supervenes, in which I feel that
I, too, unknown and unheard of, am yet of some
import to my fellows. For, through my news-
paper here, do not families take pains to send
me, an entire stranger, news of a death among
them? Are not here two who would have me
know of their marriage? And, strangest of all,
is not this singular person anxious to have me
informed that he has received a fresh supply of
Dimitry Bruisgins? But to none of us does the
Present continue miraculous (even if for a mo-
ment discerned as such). We glance carelessly
at the sunrise, and get used to Orion and the
Pleiades. The wonder wears off, and to-morrow
this sheet, (Acts x. 11, 12,) in which a vision was

let down to me from Heaven, shall be the wrappage to a bar of soap or the platter for a beggar's broken victuals." — H. W.]

No. VII

A LETTER

FROM A CANDIDATE FOR THE PRESI-DENCY IN ANSWER TO SUTTIN QUES-TIONS PROPOSED BY MR. HOSEA BIG-LOW, INCLOSED IN A NOTE FROM MR. BIGLOW TO S. H. GAY, ESQ., EDITOR OF THE NATIONAL ANTI - SLAVERY STANDARD

[CURIOSITY may be said to be the quality which preëminently distinguishes and segregates man from the lower animals. As we trace the scale of animated nature downward, we find this faculty (as it may truly be called) of the mind diminished in the savage, and wellnigh extinct in the brute. The first object which civilized man proposes to himself I take to be the finding out whatsoever he can concerning his neighbors. *Nihil humanum a me alienum puto;* I am curious about even John Smith. The desire next in strength to this (an opposite pole, indeed, of the same magnet) is that of communicating the unintelligence we have carefully picked up.

Men in general may be divided into the inquisitive and the communicative. To the first class belong Peeping Toms, eaves-droppers, navel-contemplating Brahmins, metaphysicians, travellers, Empedocleses, spies, the various societies for promoting Rhinothism, Columbuses, Yankees, discoverers, and men of science, who present themselves to the mind as so many marks of interrogation wandering up and down the world, or sitting in studies and laboratories. The second class I should again subdivide into four. In the first subdivision I would rank those who have an itch to tell us about themselves, — as keepers of diaries, insignificant persons generally, Montaignes, Horace Walpoles, autobiographers, poets. The second includes those who are anxious to impart information concerning other people, — as historians, barbers, and such. To the third belong those who labor to give us intelligence about nothing at all, — as novelists, political orators, the large majority of authors, preachers, lecturers, and the like. In the fourth come those who are communicative from motives of public benevolence, — as finders of mares'-nests and bringers of ill news. Each of us two-legged fowls without feathers embraces all these subdivisions in himself to a greater or less degree, for none of us so much as lays an egg, or incubates a chalk one, but straightway the whole barnyard shall know it by our cackle or our cluck. *Omnibus hoc vitium est.* There are different grades in all

these classes. One will turn his telescope toward a back-yard, another toward Uranus; one will tell you that he dined with Smith, another that he supped with Plato. In one particular, all men may be considered as belonging to the first grand division, inasmuch as they all seem equally desirous of discovering the mote in their neighbor's eye.

To one or another of these species every human being may safely be referred. I think it beyond a peradventure that Jonah prosecuted some inquiries into the digestive apparatus of whales, and that Noah sealed up a letter in an empty bottle, that news in regard to him might not be wanting in case of the worst. They had else been super or subter human. I conceive, also, that, as there are certain persons who continually peep and pry at the keyhole of that mysterious door through which, sooner or later, we all make our exits, so there are doubtless ghosts fidgeting and fretting on the other side of it, because they have no means of conveying back to this world the scraps of news they have picked up in that. For there is an answer ready somewhere to every question, the great law of *give and take* runs though all nature, and if we see a hook, we may be sure that an eye is waiting for it. I read in every face I meet a standing advertisement of information wanted in regard to A. B., or that the friends of C. D. can hear something to his disadvantage by application to such a one.

It was to gratify the two great passions of asking and answering that epistolary correspondence was first invented. Letters (for by this usurped title epistles are now commonly known) are of several kinds. First, there are those which are not letters at all — as letters-patent, letters dimissory, letters enclosing bills, letters of administration, Pliny's letters, letters of diplomacy, of Cato, of Mentor, of Lords Lyttelton, Chesterfield, and Orrery, of Jacob Behmen, Seneca (whom St. Jerome includes in his list of sacred writers), letters from abroad, from sons in college to their fathers, letters of marque, and letters generally, which are in no wise letters of mark. Second, are real letters, such as those of Gray, Cowper, Walpole, Howell, Lamb, D. Y., the first letters from children (printed in staggering capitals), Letters from New York, letters of credit, and others, interesting for the sake of the writer or the thing written. I have read also letters from Europe by a gentleman named Pinto, containing some curious gossip, and which I hope to see collected for the benefit of the curious. There are, besides, letters addressed to posterity, — as epitaphs, for example, written for their own monuments by monarchs, whereby we have lately become possessed of the names of several great conquerors and kings of kings, hitherto unheard of and still unpronounceable, but valuable to the student of the entirely dark ages. The letter of our Saviour to King Abgarus, that which St. Peter sent to King Pepin in the year of grace 755, that of the Virgin to the magistrates of Messina, that of the Sanhedrim of Toledo to Annas and Caiaphas, A. D. 35,

that of Galeazzo Sforza's spirit to his brother
Lodovico, that of St. Gregory Thaumaturgus
to the D——l, and that of this last-mentioned
active police-magistrate to a nun of Cirgenti, I
would place in a class by themselves, as also the
letters of candidates, concerning which I shall
dilate more fully in a note at the end of the
following poem. At present *sat prata biberunt*.
Only, concerning the shape of letters, they are
all either square or oblong, to which general
figures circular letters and round-robins also
conform themselves. — H. W.]

DEER SIR its gut to be the fashun now
to rite letters to the candid 8s and i wus
chose at a publick Meetin in Jaalam to du
wut wus nessary fur that town. i writ to
271 ginerals and gut ansers to 209. tha air
called candid 8s but I don't see nothin can-
did about 'em. this here 1 wich I send wus
thought satty's factory. I dunno as it 's
ushle to print Poscrips, but as all the ansers
I got hed the saim, I sposed it wus best.
times has gretly changed. Formaly to
knock a man into a cocked hat wus to use
him up, but now it ony gives him a chance
fur the cheef madgustracy. — H. B.

DEAR SIR, — You wish to know my notions
    On sartin pints thet rile the land ;
There 's nothin' thet my natur so shuns
    Ez bein' mum or underhand ;
I 'm a straight-spoken kind o' creetur
    Thet blurts right out wut 's in his head,
An' ef I 've one pecooler feetur,
    It is a nose thet wunt be led.

So, to begin at the beginnin'
    An' come direcly to the pint,
I think the country's underpinnin'
    Is some consid'ble out o' jint ;
I aint agoin' to try your patience
    By tellin' who done this or thet,
I don't make no insinooations,
    I jest let on I smell a rat.

Thet is, I mean, it seems to me so,
    But, ef the public think I 'm wrong,
I wunt deny but wut I be so, —
    An', fact, it don't smell very strong ;
My mind 's tu fair to lose its balance
    An' say wich party hez most sense ;
There may be folks o' greater talence
    Thet can't set stiddier on the fence.

I 'm an eclectic ; ez to choosin'
    'Twixt this an' thet, I 'm plaguy lawth ;

I leave a side thet looks like losin',
    But (wile there 's doubt) I stick to both ;
I stan' upon the Constitution,
    Ez preudunt statesmun say, who 've
        planned
A way to git the most profusion
    O' chances ez to *ware* they 'll stand.

Ez fer the war, I go agin it, —
    I mean to say I kind o' du, —
Thet is, I mean thet, bein' in it,
    The best way wuz to fight it thru ;
Not but wut abstract war is horrid,
    I sign to thet with all my heart, —
But civlyzation *doos* git forrid
    Sometimes upon a powder-cart.

About thet darned Proviso matter
    I never hed a grain o' doubt,
Nor I aint one my sense to scatter
    So 'st no one could n't pick it out ;
My love fer North an' South is equil,
    So I 'll jest answer plump an' frank,
No matter wut may be the sequil, —
    Yes, Sir, I *am* agin a Bank.

Ez to the answerin' o' questions,
    I 'm an off ox at bein' druv,
Though I aint one thet ary test shuns
    'Ill give our folks a helpin' shove;
Kind o' permiscoous I go it
    Fer the holl country, an' the ground
I take, ez nigh ez I can show it,
    Is pooty gen'ally all round.

I don't appruve o' givin' pledges;
    You 'd ough' to leave a feller free,
An' not go knockin' out the wedges
    To ketch his fingers in the tree;
Pledges air awfle breachy cattle
    Thet preudunt farmers don't turn out, —
Ez long 'z the people git their rattle,
    Wut is there fer 'm to grout about ?

Ez to the slaves, there 's no confusion
    In *my* idees consarnin' them, —
I think they air an Institution,
    A sort of — yes, jest so, — ahem:
Do *I* own any ? Of my merit
    On thet pint you yourself may jedge;
All is, I never drink no sperit,
    Nor I haint never signed no pledge.

Ez to my princerples, I glory
    In hevin' nothin' o' the sort;

I aint a Wig, I aint a Tory,
  I'm jest a canderdate, in short;
Thet's fair an' square an' parpendicler
But, ef the Public cares a fig
To hev me an' thin' in particler,
  Wy, I'm a kind o' peri-Wig.

P. S.

Ez we're a sort o' privateerin',
  O' course, you know, it's sheer an' sheer,
An' there is sutthin' wuth your hearin'
  I'll mention in *your* privit ear;
Ef you git *me* inside the White House,
  Your head with ile I'll kin' o' 'nint
By gittin' *you* inside the Light-house
  Down to the eend o' Jaalam Pint.

An' ez the North hez took to brustlin'
  At bein' scrouged frum off the roost,
I'll tell ye wut'll save all tusslin'
  An' give our side a harnsome boost, —
Tell 'em thet on the Slavery question
  I'm RIGHT, although to speak I'm
    lawth;
This gives you a safe pint to rest on,
  An' leaves me frontin' South by North.

[And now of epistles candidatial, which are
of two kinds, — namely, letters of acceptance,
and letters definitive of position. Our republic,
on the eve of an election, may safely enough be
called a republic of letters. Epistolary compo-
sition becomes then an epidemic, which seizes
one candidate after another, not seldom cutting
short the thread of political life. It has come
to such a pass, that a party dreads less the at-
tacks of its opponents than a letter from its can-
didate. *Litera scripta manet*, and it will go
hard if something bad cannot be made of it.
General Harrison, it is well understood, was
surrounded, during his candidacy, with the *cor-
don sanitaire* of a vigilance committee. No
prisoner in Spielberg was ever more cautiously
deprived of writing materials. The soot was
scraped carefully from the chimney-places;
outposts of expert rifle-shooters rendered it sure
death for any goose (who came clad in feathers)
to approach within a certain limited distance of
North Bend; and all domestic fowls about the
premises were reduced to the condition of Pla-
to's original man. By these precautions the
General was saved. *Parva componere magnis*,
I remember, that, when party-spirit once ran
high among my people, upon occasion of the
choice of a new deacon, I, having my prefer-
ences, yet not caring too openly to express them,
made use of an innocent fraud to bring about
that result which I deemed most desirable.
My stratagem was no other than the throwing a
copy of the Complete Letter-Writer in the way

of the candidate whom I wished to defeat. He
caught the infection, and addressed a short note
to his constituents, in which the opposite party
detected so many and so grave improprieties (he
had modelled it upon the letter of a young lady
accepting a proposal of marriage), that he not
only lost his election, but, falling under a suspi-
cion of Sabellianism and I know not what (the
widow Endive assured me that he was a Parali-
pomenon, to her certain knowledge), was forced
to leave the town. Thus it is that the letter
killeth.

The object which candidates propose to them-
selves in writing is to convey no meaning at all.
And here is a quite unsuspected pitfall into
which they successively plunge headlong. For
it is precisely in such cryptographies that man-
kind are prone to seek for and find a wonder-
ful amount and variety of significance. *Omne
ignotum pro mirifico.* How do we admire at
the antique world striving to crack those orac-
ular nuts from Delphi, Hammon, and else-
where, in only one of which can I so much as
surmise that any kernel had ever lodged; that,
namely, wherein Apollo confessed that he was
mortal. One Didymus is, moreover, related to
have written six thousand books on the single
subject of grammar, a topic rendered only more
tenebrific by the labors of his successors, and
which seems still to possess an attraction for
authors in proportion as they can make nothing
of it. A singular loadstone for theologians,
also, is the Beast in the Apocalypse, whereof,
in the course of my studies, I have noted two
hundred and three several interpretations, each
lethiferal to all the rest. *Non nostrum est
tantas componere lites,* yet I have myself ven-
tured upon a two hundred and fourth, which I
embodied in a discourse preached on occasion
of the demise of the late usurper, Napoleon
Bonaparte, and which quieted, in a large meas-
ure, the minds of my people. It is true that
my views on this important point were ardently
controverted by Mr. Shearjashub Holden, the
then preceptor of our academy, and in other
particulars a very deserving and sensible young
man, though possessing a somewhat limited
knowledge of the Greek tongue. But his heresy
struck down no deep root, and, he having been
lately removed by the hand of Providence, I
had the satisfaction of reaffirming my cherished
sentiments in a sermon preached upon the
Lord's day immediately succeeding his funeral.
This might seem like taking an unfair advan-
tage, did I not add that he had made provision
in his last will (being celibate) for the publica-
tion of a posthumous tractate in support of his
own dangerous opinions.

I know of nothing in our modern times which
approaches so nearly to the ancient oracle as
the letter of a Presidential candidate. Now,
among the Greeks, the eating of beans was
strictly forbidden to all such as had it in mind
to consult those expert amphibologists, and this
same prohibition on the part of Pythagoras to
his disciples is understood to imply an absti-
nence from politics, beans having been used as

ballots. That other explication, *quod videlicet sensus eo cibo obtundi existimaret*, though supported *pugnis et calcibus* by many of the learned, and not wanting the countenance of Cicero, is confuted by the larger experience of New England. On the whole, I think it safer to apply here the rule of interpretation which now generally obtains in regard to antique cosmogonies, myths, fables, proverbial expressions, and knotty points generally, which is, to find a common-sense meaning, and then select whatever can be imagined ,the most opposite thereto. In this way we arrive at the conclusion, that the Greeks objected to the questioning of candidates. And very properly, if, as I conceive, the chief point be not to discover what a person in that position is, or what he will do, but whether he can be elected. *Vos exemplaria Græca nocturna versate manu, versate diurna.*

But, since an imitation of the Greeks in this particular (the asking of questions being one chief privilege of freemen) is hardly to be hoped for, and our candidates will answer, whether they are questioned or not, I would recommend that these ante-electionary dialogues should be carried on by symbols, as were the diplomatic correspondences of the Scythians and Macrobii, or confined to the language of signs, like the famous interview of Panurge and Goatsnose. A candidate might then convey a suitable reply to all committees of inquiry by closing one eye, or by presenting them with a phial of Egyptian darkness to be speculated upon by their respective constituencies. These answers would be susceptible of whatever retrospective construction the exigencies of the political campaign might seem to demand, and the candidate could take his position on either side of the fence with entire consistency. Or, if letters must be written, profitable use might be made of the Dighton rock hieroglyphic or the cuneiform script, every fresh decipherer of which is enabled to educe a different meaning, whereby a sculptured stone or two supplies us, and will probably continue to supply posterity, with a very vast and various body of authentic history. For even the briefest epistle in the ordinary chirography is dangerous. There is scarce any style so compressed that superfluous words may not be detected in it. A severe critic might curtail that famous brevity of Cæsar's by two thirds, drawing his pen through the supererogatory *veni* and *vidi*. Perhaps, after all, the surest footing of hope is to be found in the rapidly increasing tendency to demand less and less of qualification in candidates. Already have statesmanship, experience, and the possession (nay, the profession, even) of principles been rejected as superfluous, and may not the patriot reasonably hope that the ability to write will follow? At present, there may be death in pot-hooks as well as pots, the loop of a letter may suffice for a bow-string, and all the dreadful heresies of Antislavery may lurk in a flourish. — H. W.]

No. VIII

A SECOND LETTER FROM B. SAWIN, ESQ.

[IN the following epistle, we behold Mr. Sawin returning, a *miles emeritus*, to the bosom of his family. *Quantum mutatus!* The good Father of us all had doubtless intrusted to the keeping of this child of his certain faculties of a constructive kind. He had put in him a share of that vital force, the nicest economy of every minute atom of which is necessary to the perfect development of Humanity. He had given him a brain and heart, and so had equipped his soul with the two strong wings of knowledge and love, whereby it can mount to hang its nest under the eaves of heaven. And this child, so dowered, he had intrusted to the keeping of his vicar, the State. How stands the account of that stewardship? The State, or Society (call her by what name you will), had taken no manner of thought of him till she saw him swept out into the street, the pitiful leavings of last night's debauch, with cigar-ends, lemon-parings, tobacco-quids, slops, vile stenches, and the whole loathsome next-morning of the bar-room, — an own child of the Almighty God! I remember him as he was brought to be christened, a ruddy, rugged babe ; and now there he wallows, reeking, seething, — the dead corpse, not of a man, but of a soul, — a putrefying lump, horrible for the life that is in it. Comes the wind of heaven, that good Samaritan, and parts the hair upon his forehead, nor is too nice to kiss those parched, cracked lips ; the morning opens upon him her eyes full of pitying sunshine, the sky yearns down to him, — and there he lies fermenting. O sleep! let me not profane thy holy name by calling that stertorous unconsciousness a slumber! By and by comes along the State, God's vicar. Does she say, "My poor, forlorn foster-child! Behold here a force which I will make dig and plant and build for me"? Not so, but, "Here is a recruit ready-made to my hand, a piece of destroying energy lying unprofitably idle." So she claps an ugly gray suit on him, puts a musket in his grasp, and sends him off, with Gubernatorial and other godspeeds, to do duty as a destroyer.

I made one of the crowd at the last Mechanics' Fair, and, with the rest, stood gazing in wonder at a perfect machine, with its soul of fire, its boiler-heart that sent the hot blood pulsing along the iron arteries, and its thews of steel. And while I was admiring the adaptation of means to end, the harmonious involutions of contrivance, and the never-bewildered complexity, I saw a grimed and greasy fellow, the imperious engine's lackey and drudge, whose sole office was to let fall, at intervals, a drop or two of oil upon a certain joint. Then my soul said within me, See there a piece of mechanism to which that other you marvel at is but as the rude first effort of a child, — a force

which not merely suffices to set a few wheels in
motion, but which can send an impulse all
through the infinite future, — a contrivance,
not for turning out pins, or stitching button-
holes, but for making Hamlets and Lears. And
yet this thing of iron shall be housed, waited
on, guarded from rust and dust, and it shall be
a crime but so much as to scratch it with a pin;
while the other, with its fire of God in it, shall
be buffeted hither and thither, and finally sent
carefully a thousand miles to be the target for a
Mexican cannon-ball. Unthrifty Mother State!
My heart burned within me for pity and indig-
nation, and I renewed this covenant with my
own soul, — *In aliis mansuetus ero, at, in blas-
phemiis contra Christum, non ita.* — H. W.

I spose you wonder ware I be; I can't tell,
    fer the soul o' me,
Exacly ware I be myself, — meanin' by
    thet the holl o' me.
Wen I left hum, I hed two legs, an' they
    worn't bad ones neither,
(The scaliest trick they ever played wuz
    bringin' on me hither,)
Now one on 'em's I dunno ware; — they
    thought I wuz adyin',
An' sawed it off because they said 't wuz
    kin' o' mortifyin';
I 'm willin' to believe it wuz, an' yit I don't
    see, nuther,
Wy one shoud take to feelin' cheap a min-
    nit sooner 'n t' other,
Sence both wuz equilly to blame; but
    things is ez they be;
It took on so they took it off, an' thet's
    enough fer me:
There 's one good thing, though, to be said
    about my wooden new one, —
The liquor can't git into it ez 't used to in
    the true one;
So it saves drink; an' then, besides, a feller
    could n't beg
A gretter blessin' then to hev one ollers
    sober peg;
It's true a chap's in want o' two fer fol-
    lerin' a drum,
But all the march I 'm up to now is jest to
    Kingdom Come.

I 've lost one eye, but thet's a loss it's easy
    to supply
Out o' the glory thet I 've gut, fer thet is
    all my eye;
An' one is big enough, I guess, by dili-
    gently usin' it,
To see all I shall ever git by way o' pay fer
    losin' it;

Off'cers I notice, who git paid fer all our
    thumps an' kickins,
Du wal by keepin' single eyes arter the
    fattest pickins;
So, ez the eye's put fairly out, I 'll larn to
    go without it,
An' not allow *myself* to be no gret put out
    about it.
Now, le' me see, thet is n't all; I used, 'fore
    leavin' Jaalam,
To count things on my finger-eends, but
    sutthin' seems to ail 'em:
Ware 's my left hand? Oh, darn it, yes,
    I recollect wut 's come on 't;
I haint no left arm but my right, an' thet's
    gut jest a thumb on 't;
It aint so hendy ez it wuz to cal'late a sum
    on 't.
I 've hed some ribs broke, — six (I b'lieve),
    — I haint kep' no account on 'em;
Wen pensions git to be the talk, I 'll settle
    the amount on 'em.
An' now I 'm speakin' about ribs, it kin' o'
    brings to mind
One thet I could n't never break, — the one
    I lef' behind;
Ef you should see her, jest clear out the
    spout o' your invention
An' pour the longest sweetnin' in about an
    annooal pension,
An' kin' o' hint (in case, you know, the
    critter should refuse to be
Consoled) I aint so 'xpensive now to keep
    ez wut I used to be;
There 's one arm less, ditto one eye, an'
    then the leg thet 's wooden
Can be took off an' sot away wenever
    ther 's a puddin'.

I spose you think I 'm comin' back ez op-
    perlunt ez thunder,
With shiploads o' gold images an' varus
    sorts o' plunder;
Wal, 'fore I vullinteered, I thought this
    country wuz a sort o'
Canaan, a reg'lar Promised Land flowin'
    with rum an' water,
Ware propaty growed up like time, without
    no cultivation,
An' gold wuz dug ez taters be among our
    Yankee nation,
Ware nateral advantages were pufficly
    amazin',
Ware every rock there wuz about with pre-
    cious stuns wuz blazin',

Ware mill-sites filled the country up ez
    thick ez you could cram 'em,
An' desput rivers run about a beggin' folks
    to dam 'em;
Then there were meetinhouses, tu, chockful
    o' gold an' silver
Thet you could take, an' no one could n't
    hand ye in no bill fer; —
Thet's wut I thought afore I went, thet's
    wut them fellers told us
Thet stayed to hum an' speechified an' to
    the buzzards sold us;
I thought thet gold-mines could be gut
    cheaper than Chiny asters,
An' see myself acomin' back like sixty Ja-
    cob Astors;
But sech idees soon melted down an' did n't
    leave a grease-spot;
I vow my holl sheer o' the spiles would n't
    come nigh a V spot;
Although, most anywares we 've ben, you
    need n't break no locks,
Nor run no kin' o' risks, to fill your pocket
    full o' rocks.
I 'xpect I mentioned in my last some o' the
    nateral feeturs
O' this all-fiered buggy hole in th' way o'
    awfle creeturs,
But I fergut to name (new things to speak
    on so abounded)
How one day you 'll most die o' thust, an'
    'fore the next git drownded.
The clymit seems to me jest like a teapot
    made o' pewter
Our Prudence hed, thet would n't pour
    (all she could du) to suit her;
Fust place the leaves 'ould choke the
    spout, so 's not a drop 'ould dreen
    out,
Then Prude 'ould tip an' tip an' tip, till the
    holl kit bust clean out,
The kiver-hinge-pin bein' lost, tea-leaves
    an' tea an' kiver
'ould all come down *kerswosh!* ez though
    the dam bust in a river.
Jest so 't is here; holl months there aint a
    day o' rainy weather,
An' jest ez th' officers 'ould be a layin'
    heads together
Ez t' how they 'd mix their drink at sech a
    milingtary deepot, —
'T would pour ez though the lid wuz off the
    everlastin' teapot.
The cons'quence is, thet I shall take, wen
    I 'm allowed to leave here,

One piece o' propaty along, an' thet 's the
    shakin' fever;
It 's reggilar employment, though, an' thet
    aint thought to harm one,
Nor 't aint so tiresome ez it wuz with
    t'other leg an' arm on;
An' it 's a consolation, tu, although it doos
    n't pay,
To hev it said you 're some gret shakes in
    any kin' o' way.
'T worn't very long, I tell ye wut, I thought
    o' fortin-makin', —
One day a reg'lar shiver-de-freeze, an' next
    ez good ez bakin', —
One day abrilin' in the sand, then smoth'rin'
    in the mashes, —
Git up all sound, be put to bed a mess o'
    hacks an' smashes.
But then, thinks I, at any rate there 's glory
    to be hed, —
Thet 's an investment, arter all, thet may n't
    turn out so bad;
But somehow, wen we 'd fit an' licked, I
    ollers found the thanks
Gut kin' o' lodged afore they come ez low
    down ez the ranks;
The Gin'rals gut the biggest sheer, the
    Cunnles next, an' so on, —
We never gut a blasted mite o' glory ez I
    know on;
An' spose we hed, I wonder how you 're
    goin' to contrive its
Division so 's to give a piece to twenty
    thousand privits;
Ef you should multiply by ten the portion
    o' the brav'st one,
You would n't git more 'n half enough to
    speak of on a grave-stun;
We git the licks, — we 're jest the grist
    thet 's put into War's hoppers;
Leftenants is the lowest grade thet helps
    pick up the coppers.
It may suit folks thet go agin a body with
    a soul in 't,
An' aint contented with a hide without a
    bagnet hole in 't;
But glory is a kin' o' thing *I* sha' n't pursue
    no furder,
Coz thet 's the offc'ers' parquisite, —yourn 's
    on'y jest the murder.

Wal, arter I gin glory up, thinks I at least
    there 's one
Thing in the bills we aint hed yit, an' thet 's
    the GLORIOUS FUN;

Ef once we git to Mexico, we fairly may
    presume we
All day an' night shall revel in the halls o'
    Montezumy.
I 'll tell ye wut *my* revels wuz, an' see how
    you would like 'em;
We never gut inside the hall: the nighest
    ever *I* come
Wuz stan'in' sentry in the sun (an', fact, it
    seemed a cent'ry)
A ketchin' smells o' biled an' roast thet
    come out thru the entry,
An' hearin' ez I sweltered thru my passes
    an' repasses,
A rat-tat-too o' knives an' forks, a clinkty-
    clink o' glasses:
I can't tell off the bill o' fare the Gin'rals
    hed inside;
All I know is, thet out o' doors a pair o'
    soles wuz fried,
An' not a hunderd miles away frum ware
    this child wuz posted,
A Massachusetts citizen wuz baked an' biled
    an' roasted;
The on'y thing like revellin' thet ever come
    to me
Wuz bein' routed out o' sleep by thet darned
    revelee.

They say the quarrel 's settled now; fer my
    part I 've some doubt on 't,
't 'll take more fish-skin than folks think to
    take the rile clean out on 't;
At any rate I 'm so used up I can't do no
    more fightin',
The on'y chance thet 's left to me is politics
    or writin';
Now, ez the people 's gut to hev a miling-
    tary man,
An' I aint nothin' else jest now, I 've hit
    upon a plan;
The can'idatin' line, you know, 'ould suit
    me to a T,
An' ef I lose, 't wunt hurt my ears to lodge
    another flea;
So I 'll set up ez can'idate fer any kin' o'
    office,
(I mean fer any thet includes good easy-
    cheers an' soffies;
Fer ez tu runnin' fer a place ware work 's
    the time o' day,
You know thet 's wut I never did, — ex-
    cept the other way;)
Ef it 's the Presidential cheer fer wich I 'd
    better run,

Wut two legs anywares about could keep
    up with my one?
There aint no kin' o' quality in can'idates,
    it 's said,
So useful ez a wooden leg, — except a
    wooden head;
There 's nothin' aint so poppylar — (wy,
    it 's a parfect sin
To think wut Mexico hez paid fer Santy
    Anny's pin;) —
Then I haint gut no princerples, an', sence
    I wuz knee-high,
I never *did* hev any gret, ez you can tes-
    tify;
I 'm a decided peace-man, tu, an' go agin
    the war, —
Fer now the holl on 't 's gone an' past, wut
    is there to go *for*?
Ef, wile you 're 'lectioneerin' round, some
    curus chaps should beg
To know my views o' state affairs, jest
    answer WOODEN LEG!
Ef they aint settisfied with thet, an' kin' o
    pry an' doubt
An' ax fer sutthin' deffynit, jest say ONE
    EYE PUT OUT!
Thet kin' o' talk I guess you 'll find 'll
    answer to a charm,
An' wen you 're druv tu nigh the wall, hol'
    up my missin' arm;
Ef they should nose round fer a pledge, put
    on a vartoous look
An' tell 'em thet 's percisely wut I never
    gin nor — took!

Then you can call me "Timbertoes," —
    thet 's wut the people likes;
Sutthin' combinin' morril truth with
    phrases sech ez strikes;
Some say the people 's fond o' this, or thet,
    or wut you please, —
I tell ye wut the people want is jest correct
    idees;
"Old Timbertoes," you see, 's a creed it 's
    safe to be quite bold on,
There 's nothin' in 't the other side can any
    ways git hold on;
It 's a good tangible idee, a sutthin' to em-
    body
Thet valooable class o' men who look thru
    brandy-toddy;
It gives a Party Platform, tu, jest level
    with the mind
Of all right-thinkin', honest folks thet
    mean to go it blind;

Then there air other good hooraws to dror
  on ez you need 'em,
Sech ez the ONE-EYED SLARTERER, the
  BLOODY BIRDOFREDUM:
Them 's wut takes hold o' folks thet think,
  ez well ez o' the masses,
An' makes you sartin o' the aid o' good
  men of all classes.

There 's one thing I 'm in doubt about; in
  order to be Presidunt,
It 's absolutely ne'ssary to be a Southern
  residunt;
The Constitution settles thet, an' also thet
  a feller
Must own a nigger o' some sort, jet black,
  or brown, or yeller.
Now I haint no objections agin particklar
  climes,
Nor agin ownin' anythin' (except the truth
  sometimes),
But, ez I haint no capital, up there among
  ye, maybe,
You might raise funds enough fer me to
  buy a low-priced baby,
An' then to suit the No'thern folks, who
  feel obleeged to say
They hate an' cus the very thing they vote
  fer every day,
Say you 're assured I go full but fer Lib-
  baty's diffusion
An' made the purchis on'y jest to spite the
  Institootion; —
But, golly ! there 's the currier's hoss upon
  the pavement pawin' !
I 'll be more 'xplicit in my next.
    Yourn,
    BIRDOFREDUM SAWIN.

[We have now a tolerably fair chance of esti-
mating how the balance-sheet stands between
our returned volunteer and glory. Supposing
the entries to be set down on both sides of the
account in fractional parts of one hundred, we
shall arrive at something like the following re-
sult: —

B. SAWIN, Esq., *in account with* (BLANK)
           GLORY.

Cr.		*Dr.*	
By loss of one leg . . .	20	To one 675th three	
" do. one arm . .	15	cheers in Fan-	
" do. four fingers	5	euil Hall	30
" do. one eye . .	10	" do. do. on oc-	
" the breaking of six		casion of presen-	
ribs	6	tation of sword	
" having served un-		to Colonel	
der Colonel Cush-		Wright	25
ing one month . .	44		
	100		55

Brought forward . . .	100	*Brought forward* . . .	55
		To one suit of gray	
		clothes (ingeni-	
		ously unbecom-	
		ing)	15
		" musical enter-	
		tainments(drum	
		and fife six	
		months)	5
		" one dinner after	
		return	1
		" chance of pen-	
		sion	1
		" privilege of draw-	
		ing longbow dur-	
		ing rest of nat-	
		ural life	23
E. E.	100		100

It should appear that Mr. Sawin found the
actual feast curiously the reverse of the bill
of fare advertised in Faneuil Hall and other
places. His primary object seems to have been
the making of his fortune. *Quœrenda pecunia
primum, virtus post nummos.* He hoisted sail
for Eldorado, and shipwrecked on Point Tribu-
lation. *Quid non mortalia pectora cogis, auri
sacra fames ?* The speculation has sometimes
crossed my mind, in that dreary interval of
drought which intervenes between quarterly
stipendiary showers, that Providence, by the
creation of a money-tree, might have simplified
wonderfully the sometimes perplexing problem
of human life. We read of bread-trees, the
butter for which lies ready-churned in Irish
bogs. Milk-trees we are assured of in South
America, and stout Sir John Hawkins testifies
to water-trees in the Canaries. Boot-trees bear
abundantly in Lynn and elsewhere ; and I have
seen, in the entries of the wealthy, hat-trees
with a fair show of fruit. A family-tree I once
cultivated myself, and found therefrom but a
scanty yield, and that quite tasteless and in-
nutritious. Of trees bearing men we are not
without examples ; as those in the park of
Louis the Eleventh of France. Who has for-
gotten, moreover, that olive-tree, growing in
the Athenian's back-garden, with its strange
úxorious crop, for the general propagation of
which, as of a new and precious variety, the
philosopher Diogenes, hitherto uninterested in
arboriculture, was so zealous ? In the *sylva* of
our own Southern States, the females of my
family have called my attention to the china-
tree. Not to multiply examples, I will barely
add to my list the birch-tree, in the smaller
branches of which has been implanted so
miraculous a virtue for communicating the
Latin and Greek languages, and which may
well, therefore, be classed among the trees pro-
ducing necessaries of life, — *venerabile donum
fatalis virgæ.* That money-trees existed in the
golden age there want not prevalent reasons for
our believing. For does not the old proverb,
when it asserts that money does not grow on
every bush, imply *a fortiori* that there were
certain bushes which did produce it ? Again,
there is another ancient saw to the effect that

money is the *root* of all evil. From which two adages it may be safe to infer that the aforesaid species of tree first degenerated into a shrub, then absconded underground, and finally, in our iron age, vanished altogether. In favorable exposures it may be conjectured that a specimen or two survived to a great age, as in the garden of the Hesperides; and, indeed, what else could that tree in the Sixth Æneid have been, with a branch whereof the Trojan hero procured admission to a territory, for the entering of which money is a surer passport than to a certain other more profitable and too foreign kingdom? Whether these speculations of mine have any force in them, or whether they will not rather, by most readers, be deemed impertinent to the matter in hand, is a question which I leave to the determination of an indulgent posterity. That there were, in more primitive and happier times, shops where money was sold, — and that, too, on credit and at a bargain, — I take to be matter of demonstration. For what but a dealer in this article was that Æolus who supplied Ulysses with motive-power for his fleet in bags? what that Ericus, King of Sweden, who is said to have kept the winds in his cap? what, in more recent times, those Lapland Nornas who traded in favorable breezes? All which will appear the more clearly when we consider, that, even to this day, *raising the wind* is proverbial for raising money, and that brokers and banks were invented by the Venetians at a later period.

And now for the improvement of this digression. I find a parallel to Mr. Sawin's fortune in an adventure of my own. For, shortly after I had first broached to myself the before-stated natural-historical and archæological theories, as I was passing, *hæc negotia penitus mecum revolvens*, through one of the obscure suburbs of our New England metropolis, my eye was attracted by these words upon a signboard, — CHEAP CASH-STORE. Here was at once the confirmation of my speculations, and the substance of my hopes. Here lingered the fragment of a happier past, or stretched out the first tremulous organic filament of a more fortunate future. Thus glowed the distant Mexico to the eyes of Sawin, as he looked through the dirty pane of the recruiting-office window, or speculated from the summit of that mirage-Pisgah which the imps of the bottle are so cunning to raise up. Already had my Alnaschar-fancy (even during that first half-believing glance) expended in various useful directions the funds to be obtained by pledging the manuscript of a proposed volume of discourses. Already did a clock ornament the tower of the Jaalam meeting-house, a gift appropriately, but modestly, commemorated in the parish and town records, both, for now many years, kept by myself. Already had my son Seneca completed his course at the University. Whether, for the moment, we may not be considered as actually lording it over those Baratarias with the viceroyalty of which Hope invests us, and whether we are ever so warmly housed as in our Spanish castles, would afford

matter of argument. Enough that I found that signboard to be no other than a bait to the trap of a decayed grocer. Nevertheless, I bought a pound of dates (getting short weight by reason of immense flights of harpy flies who pursued and lighted upon their prey even in the very scales), which purchase I made not only with an eye to the little ones at home, but also as a figurative reproof of that too frequent habit of my mind, which, forgetting the due order of chronology, will often persuade me that the happy sceptre of Saturn is stretched over this Astræa-forsaken nineteenth century.

Having glanced at the ledger of Glory under the title *Sawin, B.*, let us extend our investigations, and discover if that instructive volume does not contain some charges more personally interesting to ourselves. I think we should be more economical of our resources, did we thoroughly appreciate the fact, that, whenever Brother Jonathan seems to be thrusting his hand into his own pocket, he is, in fact, picking ours. I confess that the late *muck* which the country has been running has materially changed my views as to the best method of raising revenue. If, by means of direct taxation, the bills for every extraordinary outlay were brought under our immediate eye, so that, like thrifty housekeepers, we could see where and how fast the money was going, we should be less likely to commit extravagances. At present, these things are managed in such a hugger-mugger way, that we know not what we pay for; the poor man is charged as much as the rich; and, while we are saving and scrimping at the spigot, the government is drawing off at the bung. If we could know that a part of the money we expend for tea and coffee goes to buy powder and balls, and that it is Mexican blood which makes the clothes on our backs more costly, it would set some of us athinking. During the present fall, I have often pictured to myself a government official entering my study and handing me the following bill: —

WASHINGTON, Sept. 30, 1848.

REV. HOMER WILBUR to 𝔘ncle 𝔖amuel,

Dr.

To his share of work done in Mexico on partnership account, sundry jobs, as below.	
" killing, maiming and wounding about 5,000 Mexicans	$2.00
" slaughtering one woman carrying water to wounded	.10
" extra work on two different Sabbaths (one bombardment and one assault), whereby the Mexicans were prevented from defiling themselves with the idolatries of high mass	3.50
" throwing an especially fortunate and Protestant bombshell into the Cathedral at Vera Cruz, whereby several female Papists were slain at the altar	.50
" his proportion of cash paid for conquered territory	1.75
" do. do. for conquering do.	1.50
" manuring do. with new superior compost called " American Citizen "	.50
	$9.85

Brought forward	$9.85
To extending the area of freedom and Protestantism	.01
" glory	.01
	$9.87

Immediate payment is requested.

N. B. Thankful for former favors, U. S. requests a continuance of patronage. Orders executed with neatness and despatch. Terms as low as those of any other contractor for the same kind and style of work.

I can fancy the official answering my look of horror with — " Yes, Sir, it looks like a high charge, Sir ; but in these days slaughtering is slaughtering." Verily, I would that every one understood that it was ; for it goes about obtaining money under the false pretence of being glory. For me, I have an imagination which plays me uncomfortable tricks. It happens to me sometimes to see a slaughterer on his way home from his day's work, and forthwith my imagination puts a cocked-hat upon his head and epaulettes upon his shoulders, and sets him up as a candidate for the Presidency. So, also, on a recent public occasion, as the place assigned to the " Reverend Clergy" is just behind that of " Officers of the Army and Navy " in processions, it was my fortune to be seated at the dinner-table over against one of these respectable persons. He was arrayed as (out of his own profession) only kings, court-officers, and footmen are in Europe, and Indians in America. Now what does my over-officious imagination but set to work upon him, strip him of his gay livery, and present him to me coatless, his trousers thrust into the tops of a pair of boots thick with clotted blood, and a basket on his arm out of which lolled a gore-smeared axe, thereby destroying my relish for the temporal mercies upon the board before me ! — H. W.]

No. IX

A THIRD LETTER FROM B. SAWIN, ESQ.

[UPON the following letter slender comment will be needful. In what river Selemnus has Mr. Sawin bathed, that he has become so swiftly oblivious of his former loves ? From an ardent and (as befits a soldier) confident wooer of that coy bride, the popular favor, we see him subside of a sudden into the (I trust not jilted) Cincinnatus, returning to his plough with a goodly sized branch of willow in his hand ; figuratively returning, however, to a figurative plough, and from no profound affection for that honored implement of husbandry (for which, indeed, Mr. Sawin never displayed any decided predilection), but in order to be gracefully summoned therefrom to more congenial labors. It should seem that the character of the ancient

Dictator had become part of the recognized stock of our modern political comedy, though, as our term of office extends to a quadrennial length, the parallel is not so minutely exact as could be desired. It is sufficiently so, however, for purposes of scenic representation. An humble cottage (if built of logs, the better) forms the Arcadian background of the stage. This rustic paradise is labelled Ashland, Jaalam, North Bend, Marshfield, Kinderhook, or Bâton Rouge, as occasion demands. Before the door stands a something with one handle (the other painted in proper perspective), which represents, in happy ideal vagueness, the plough. To this the defeated candidate rushes with delirious joy, welcomed as a father by appropriate groups of happy laborers, or from it the successful one is torn with difficulty, sustained alone by a noble sense of public duty. Only I have observed, that, if the scene be laid at Bâton Rouge or Ashland, the laborers are kept carefully in the background, and are heard to shout from behind the scenes in a singular tone resembling ululation, and accompanied by a sound not unlike vigorous clapping. This, however, may be artistically in keeping with the habits of the rustic population of those localities. The precise connection between agricultural pursuits and statesmanship I have not been able, after diligent inquiry, to discover. But, that my investigations may not be barren of all fruit, I will mention one curious statistical fact, which I consider thoroughly established, namely, that no real farmer ever attains practically beyond a seat in the General Court, however theoretically qualified for more exalted station.

It is probable that some other prospect has been opened to Mr. Sawin, and that he has not made this great sacrifice without some definite understanding in regard to a seat in the cabinet or a foreign mission. It may be supposed that we of Jaalam were not untouched by a feeling of villatic pride in beholding our townsman occupying so large a space in the public eye. And to me, deeply revolving the qualifications necessary to a candidate in these frugal times, those of Mr. S. seemed peculiarly adapted to a successful campaign. The loss of a leg, an arm, an eye, and four fingers reduced him so nearly to the condition of a *vox et prœterea nihil* that I could think of nothing but the loss of his head by which his chance could have been bettered. But since he has chosen to balk our suffrages, we must content ourselves with what we can get, remembering *lactucas non esse dandas, dum cardui sufficiant.* — H. W.]

I SPOSE you recollect thet I explained my gennle views
In the last billet thet I writ, 'way down frum Veery Cruze,
Jest arter I 'd a kin' o' ben spontanously sot up
To run unannermously fer the Preserdential cup ;

O' course it worn't no wish o' mine, 't wuz
  ferflely distressin',
But poppiler enthusiasm gut so almighty
  pressin'
Thet, though like sixty all along I fumed
  an' fussed an' sorrered,
There did n't seem no ways to stop their
  bringin' on me forrerd:
Fact is, they udged the matter so, I
  could n't help admittin'
The Father o' his Country's shoes no feet
  but mine 'ould fit in,
Besides the savin' o' the soles fer ages to
  succeed,
Seein' thet with one wannut foot, a pair 'd
  be more 'n I need;
An', tell ye wut, them shoes 'll want a
  thund'rin sight o' patchin',
Ef this ere fashion is to last we 've gut into
  o' hatchin'
A pair o' second Washintons fer every new
  election, —
Though, fer ez number one 's consarned, I
  don't make no objection.

I wuz agoin' on to say thet wen at fust I saw
The masses would stick to 't I wuz the
  Country's father-'n-law,
(They would ha' hed it *Father*, but I told
  'em 't would n't du,
Coz thet wuz sutthin' of a sort they
  could n't split in tu,
An' Washinton hed hed the thing laid
  fairly to his door,
Nor dars n't say 't worn't his'n, much ez
  sixty year afore,)
But 't aint no matter ez to thet; wen I wuz
  nomernated,
'T worn't natur but wut I should feel con-
  sid'able elated,
An' wile the hooraw o' the thing wuz kind
  o' noo an' fresh,
I thought our ticket would ha' caird the
  country with a resh.

Sence I 've come hum, though, an' looked
  round, I think I seem to find
Strong argimunts ez thick ez fleas to make
  me change my mind;
It 's clear to any one whose brain aint fur
  gone in a phthisis,
Thet hail Columby's happy land is goin'
  thru a crisis,
An' 't would n't noways du to hev the
  people's mind distracted

By bein' all to once by sev'ral pop'lar
  names attackted;
'T would save holl haycartloads o' fuss an'
  three four months o' jaw,
Ef some illustrous paytriot should back out
  an' withdraw;
So, ez I aint a crooked stick, jest like —
  like ole (I swow,
I dunno ez I know his name) — I 'll go
  back to my plough.
Wenever an Amerikin distinguished poli-
  tishin
Begins to try et wut they call definin' his
  posishin,
Wal, I, fer one, feel sure he aint gut nothin'
  to define;
It 's so nine cases out o' ten, but jest that
  tenth is mine;
An' 't aint no more 'n is proper 'n' right in
  sech ɔ sitooation
To hint the course you think 'll be the
  savin' o' the nation;
To funk right out o' p'lit'cal strife aint
  thought to be the thing,
Without you deacon off the toon you want
  your folks should sing;
So I edvise the noomrous friends thet 's in
  one boat with me
To jest up killick, jam right down their
  hellum hard alee,
Haul the sheets taut, an', layin' out upon
  the Suthun tack,
Make fer the safest port they can, wich, *I*
  think, is Ole Zack.

Next thing you 'll want to know, I spose,
  wut argimunts I seem
To see thet makes me think this ere 'll be
  the strongest team;
Fust place, I 've ben consid'ble round in
  bar-rooms an' saloons
Agetherin' public sentiment, 'mongst Dem-
  mercrats and Coons,
An' 't aint ve'y offen thet I meet a chap
  but wut goes in
Fer Rough an' Ready, fair an' square, hufs,
  taller, horns, an' skin;
I don't deny but wut, fer one, ez fur ez I
  could see,
I did n't like at fust the Pheladelphy nom-
  ernee:
I could ha' pinted to a man thet wuz, I
  guess, a peg
Higher than him, — a soger, tu, an' with a
  wooden leg;

But every day with more an' more o' Tay-
lor zeal I'm burnin',
Seein' wich way the tide thet sets to office
is aturnin';
Wy, into Bellers's we notched the votes
down on three sticks, —
'T wuz Birdofredum *one*, Cass *aught*, an'
Taylor *twenty-six*,
An' bein' the on'y canderdate thet wuz
upon the ground,
They said 't wuz no more 'n right thet I
should pay the drinks all round;
Ef I 'd expected sech a trick, I would n't
ha' cut my foot
By goin' an' votin' fer myself like a con-
sumed coot;
It did n't make no deff'rence, though; I
wish I may be cust,
Ef Bellers wuz n't slim enough to say he
would n't trust !

Another pint thet influences the minds o'
sober jedges
Is thet the Gin'ral hez n't gut tied hand an'
foot with pledges;
He hez n't told ye wut he is, an' so there
aint no knowin'
But wut he may turn out to be the best
there is agoin' ;
This, at the on'y spot thet pinched, the shoe
directly eases,
Coz every one is free to 'xpect percisely
wut he pleases:
I want free-trade; you don't; the Gin'ral
is n't bound to neither; —
I vote my way; you, yourn; an' both air
sooted to a T there.
Ole Rough an' Ready, tu, 's a Wig, but
without bein' ultry;
He 's like a holsome hayin' day, thet 's
warm, but is n't sultry;
He 's jest wut I should call myself, a kin'
o' *scratch* ez 't ware,
Thet aint exacly all a wig nor wholly your
own hair;
I 've ben a Wig three weeks myself, jest o'
this mod'rate sort,
An' don't find them an' Demmercrats so
defferent ez I thought;
They both act pooty much alike, an' push
an' scrouge an' cus;
They 're like two pickpockets in league fer
Uncle Samwell's pus;
Each takes a side, an' then they squeeze
the ole man in between 'em,

Turn all his pockets wrong side out an'
quick ez lightnin' clean 'em;
To nary one on 'em I'd trust a secon'-
handed rail
No furder off 'an I could sling a bullock
by the tail.

Webster sot matters right in thet air Mash-
fiel' speech o' his'n; —
"Taylor," sez he, "aint nary ways the one
thet I 'd a chizzen,
Nor he aint fittin' fer the place, an' like
ez not he aint
No more 'n a tough ole bullethead, an' no
gret of a saint;
But then," sez he, "obsarve my pint, he 's
jest ez good to vote fer
Ez though the greasin' on him worn't a
thing to hire Choate fer;
Aint it ez easy done to drop a ballot in a
box
Fer one ez 't is fer t' other, fer the bull-dog
ez the fox ? "
It takes a mind like Dannel's, fact, ez big
ez all ou' doors,
To find out thet it looks like rain arter it
fairly pours;
I 'gree with him, it aint so dreffle trouble-
some to vote
Fer Taylor arter all, — it 's jest to go an'
change your coat;
Wen he 's once greased, you 'll swaller him
an' never know on 't, scurce,
Unless he scratches, goin' down, with them
'ere Gin'ral's spurs.
I 've ben a votin' Demmercrat, ez reg'lar
as a clock,
But don't find goin' Taylor gives my narves
no gret 'f a shock;
Truth is, the cutest leadin' Wigs, ever sence
fust they found
Wich side the bread gut buttered on, hev
kep' a edgin' round;
They kin' o' slipt the planks frum out th'
ole platform one by one
An' made it gradooally noo, 'fore folks
know'd wut wuz done,
Till, fur 'z I know, there aint an inch thet
I could lay my han' on,
But I, or any Demmercrat, feels comf'table
to stan' on,
An' ole Wig doctrines act'lly look, their
occ'pants bein' gone,
Lonesome ez steddles on a mash without no
hayricks on.

I spose it 's time now I should give my
    thoughts upon the plan,
Thet chipped the shell at Buffalo, o' settin'
    up ole Van.
I used to vote fer Martin, but, I swan, I 'm
    clean disgusted, —
He aint the man thet I can say is fittin' to
    be trusted;
He aint half antislav'ry 'nough, nor I aint
    sure, ez some be,
He 'd go in fer abolishin' the Deestrick o'
    Columby;
An', now I come to racollec', it kin' o' makes
    me sick 'z
A horse, to think o' wut he wuz in eighteen
    thirty-six.
An' then, another thing; — I guess, though
    mebby I am wrong,
This Buff'lo plaster aint agoin' to dror al-
    mighty strong;
Some folks, I know, hev gut th' idee thet
    No'thun dough 'll rise,
Though, 'fore I see it riz an' baked, I
    would n't trust my eyes;
'T will take more emptins, a long chalk,
    than this noo party 's gut,
To give sech heavy cakes ez them a start, I
    tell ye wut.
But even ef they caird the day, there would
    n't be no endurin'
To stan' upon a platform with sech critters
    ez Van Buren; —
An' his son John, tu, I can't think how thet
    'ere chap should dare
To speak ez he doos; wy, they say he used
    to cuss an' swear !
I spose he never read the hymn thet tells
    how down the stairs
A feller with long legs wuz throwed thet
    would n't say his prayers.
This brings me to another pint: the leaders
    o' the party
Aint jest sech men ez I can act along with
    free an' hearty;
They aint not quite respectable, an' wen a
    feller's morrils
Don't toe the straightest kin' o' mark, wy,
    him an' me jest quarrils.
I went to a free soil meetin' once, an' wut
    d' ye think I see ?
A feller was aspoutin' there thet act'lly
    come to me,
About two year ago last spring, ez nigh ez
    I can jedge,

An' axed me ef I did n't want to sign the
    Temprunce pledge!
He 's one o' them that goes about an' sez
    you hed n't oughter
Drink nothin', mornin', noon, or night,
    stronger 'an Taunton water.
There 's one rule I 've ben guided by, in
    settlin' how to vote, ollers, —
I take the side thet *is n't* took by them
    consarned teetotallers.

Ez fer the niggers, I 've ben South, an' thet
    hez changed my min';
A lazier, more ongrateful set you could n't
    nowers fin'.
You know I mentioned in my last thet I
    should buy a nigger,
Ef I could make a purchase at a pooty
    mod'rate figger;
So, ez there 's nothin' in the world I 'm
    fonder of 'an gunnin',
I closed a bargain finally to take a feller
    runnin'.
I shou'dered queen's-arm an' stumped out,
    an' wen I come t' th' swamp,
'T worn't very long afore I gut upon the
    nest o' Pomp;
I come acrost a kin' o' hut, an', playin round
    the door,
Some little woolly-headed cubs, ez many 'z
    six or more.
At fust I thought o' firin', but *think twice* is
    safest ollers;
There aint, thinks I, not one on 'em but 's
    wuth his twenty dollars,
Or would be, ef I hed 'em back into a
    Christian land, —
How temptin' all on 'em would look upon
    an auction-stand!
(Not but wut *I* hate Slavery, in th' abstract,
    stem to starn, —
I leave it ware our fathers did, a privit
    State consarn.)
Soon 'z they see me, they yelled an' run,
    but Pomp wuz out ahoein'
A leetle patch o' corn he hed, or else there
    aint no knowin'
He would n't ha' took a pop at me; but I
    hed gut the start,
An' wen he looked, I vow I groaned ez
    though he 'd broke his heart;
He done it like a wite man, tu, ez nat'ral ez
    a pictur,
The imp'dunt, pis'nous hypocrite! wus 'an
    a boy constrictur.

"You can't gum *me*, I tell ye now, an' so
    you need n't try,
I 'xpect my eye-teeth every mail, so jest
    shet up," sez I.
"Don't go to actin' ugly now, or else I 'll
    let her strip,
You 'd best draw kindly, seein' 'z how I 've
    gut ye on the hip;
Besides, you darned ole fool, it aint no gret
    of a disaster
To be benev'lently druv back to a contented
    master,
Ware you hed Christian priv'ledges you
    don't seem quite aware on,
Or you 'd ha' never run away from bein'
    well took care on;
Ez fer kin' treatment, wy, he wuz so fond
    on ye, he said
He 'd give a fifty spot right out, to git ye,
    'live or dead;
Wite folks aint sot by half ez much; 'mem-
    ber I run away,
Wen I wuz bound to Cap'n Jakes, to Mat-
    tysqumscot Bay;
Don' know him, likely? Spose not; wal,
    the mean old codger went
An' offered — wut reward, think? Wal,
    it worn't no *less* 'n a cent."

Wal, I jest gut 'em into line, an' druv 'em
    on afore me;
The pis'nous brutes, I 'd no idee o' the ill-
    will they bore me;
We walked till som'ers about noon, an'
    then it grew so hot
I thought it best to camp awile, so I chose
    out a spot
Jest under a magnoly tree, an' there right
    down I sot;
Then I unstrapped my wooden leg, coz it
    begun to chafe,
An' laid it down 'longside o' me, supposin'
    all wuz safe;
I made my darkies all set down around me
    in a ring,
An' sot an' kin' o' ciphered up how much
    the lot would bring;
But, wile I drinked the peaceful cup of a
    pure heart an' min'
(Mixed with some whiskey, now an' then),
    Pomp he snaked up behin',
An' creepin' grad'lly close tu, ez quiet ez a
    mink,
Jest grabbed my leg, an' then pulled foot,
    quicker 'an you could wink,

An', come to look, they each on 'em hed
    gut behin' a tree,
An' Pomp poked out the leg a piece, jest
    so ez I could see,
An' yelled to me to throw away my pistils
    an' my gun,
Or else thet they 'd cair off the leg, an'
    fairly cut an' run.
I vow I did n't b'lieve there wuz a decent
    alligatur
Thet hed a heart so destitoot o' common
    human natur;
However, ez there worn't no help, I finally
    give in
An' heft my arms away to git my leg safe
    back agin.

Pomp gethered all the weapins up, an' then
    he come an' grinned,
He showed his ivory some, I guess, an' sez,
    "You 're fairly pinned;
Jest buckle on your leg agin, an' git right
    up ' come,
'T wun't du fer fammerly men like me to
    be so long frum hum."
At fust I put my foot right down an' swore
    I would n't budge.
"Jest ez you choose," sez he, quite cool,
    "either be shot or trudge."
So this black-hearted monster took an'
    act'lly druv me back
Along the very feetmarks o' my happy
    mornin' track,
An' kep' me pris'ner 'bout six months, an'
    worked me, tu, like sin,
Till I hed gut his corn an' his Carliny
    taters in;
He made me larn him readin', tu (although
    the crittur saw
How much it hut my morril sense to act
    agin the law),
So'st he could read a Bible he 'd gut; an'
    axed ef I could pint
The North Star out; but there I put his
    nose some out o' jint,
Fer I weeled roun' about sou'west, an',
    lookin' up a bit,
Picked out a middlin' shiny one an' tole
    him thet wuz it.
Fin'lly he took me to the door, an' givin'
    me a kick,
Sez, "Ef you know wut 's best fer ye, be
    off, now, double-quick;
The winter-time 's a comin' on, an' though
    I gut ye cheap,

You 're so darned lazy, I don't think you 're
    hardly wuth your keep;
Besides, the childrin 's growin' up, an' you
    aint jest the model
I 'd like to hev 'em immertate, an' so you 'd
    better toddle ! "

Now is there anythin' on airth 'll ever prove
    to me
Thet renegader slaves like him air fit fer
    bein' free ?
D' you think they 'll suck me in to jine the
    Buff'lo chaps, an' them
Rank infidels thet go agin the Scriptur'l
    cus o' Shem ?
Not by a jugfull ! sooner 'n thet, I 'd go
    thru fire an' water;
Wen I hev once made up my mind, a
    meet'nhus aint sotter;
No, not though all the crows thet flies to
    pick my bones wuz cawin', —
I guess we 're in a Christian land, —
    Yourn,
        BIRDOFREDUM SAWIN.

[Here, patient reader, we take leave of each
other, I trust with some mutual satisfaction. I
say *patient*, for I love not that kind which
skims dippingly over the surface of the page, as
swallows over a pool before rain. By such no
pearls shall be gathered. But if no pearls there
be (as, indeed, the world is not without example
of books wherefrom the longest-winded diver
shall bring up no more than his proper handful
of mud), yet let us hope than an oyster or two
may reward adequate perseverance. If neither
pearls nor oysters, yet is patience itself a gem
worth diving deeply for.

It may seem to some that too much space has
been usurped by my own private lucubrations,
and some may be fain to bring against me that
old jest of him who preached all his hearers out
of the meeting-house save only the sexton, who,
remaining for yet a little space, from a sense
of official duty, at last gave out also, and, pre-
senting the keys, humbly requested our preacher
to lock the doors, when he should have wholly
relieved himself of his testimony. I confess to
a satisfaction in the self act of preaching, nor
do I esteem a discourse to be wholly thrown
away even upon a sleeping or unintelligent
auditory. I cannot easily believe that the Gos-
pel of Saint John, which Jacques Cartier or-
dered to be read in the Latin tongue to the
Canadian savages, upon his first meeting with
them, fell altogether upon stony ground. For
the earnestness of the preacher is a sermon ap-
preciable by dullest intellects and most alien
ears. In this wise did Episcopius convert many
to his opinions, who yet understood not the
language in which he discoursed. The chief

thing is that the messenger believe that he has
an authentic message to deliver. For counter-
feit messengers that mode of treatment which
Father John de Plano Carpini relates to have
prevailed among the Tartars would seem ef-
fectual, and, perhaps, deserved enough. For
my own part, I may lay claim to so much of the
spirit of martyrdom as would have led me to
go into banishment with those clergymen whom
Alphonso the Sixth of Portugal drave out of
his kingdom for refusing to shorten their pulpit
eloquence. It is possible, that, having been in-
vited into my brother Biglow's desk, I may
have been too little scrupulous in using it for
the venting of my own peculiar doctrines to a
congregation drawn together in the expectation
and with the desire of hearing him.

I am not wholly unconscious of a peculiarity
of mental organization which impels me, like
the railroad-engine with its train of cars, to run
backward for a short distance in order to obtain
a fairer start. I may compare myself to one
fishing from the rocks when the sea runs high,
who, misinterpreting the suction of the under-
tow for the biting of some larger fish, jerks
suddenly, and finds that he has *caught bottom*,
hauling in upon the end of his line a trail of
various *algæ*, among which, nevertheless, the
naturalist may haply find somewhat to repay
the disappointment of the angler. Yet have I
conscientiously endeavored to adapt myself to
the impatient temper of the age, daily degener-
ating more and more from the high standard of
our pristine New England. To the catalogue
of lost arts I would mournfully add also that of
listening to two-hour sermons. Surely we have
been abridged into a race of pygmies. For,
truly, in those of the old discourses yet subsist-
ing to us in print, the endless spinal column of
divisions and subdivisions can be likened to
nothing so exactly as to the vertebræ of the
saurians, whence the theorist may conjecture a
race of Anakim proportionate to the withstand-
ing of these other monsters. I say Anakim
rather than Nephelim, because there seem
reasons for supposing that the race of those
whose heads (though no giants) are constantly
enveloped in clouds (which that name imports)
will never become extinct. The attempt to
vanquish the innumerable *heads* of one of those
afore-mentioned discourses may supply us with
a plausible interpretation of the second labor of
Hercules, and his successful experiment with
fire affords us a useful precedent.

But while I lament the degeneracy of the age
in this regard, I cannot refuse to succumb to its
influence. Looking out through my study-
window, I see Mr. Biglow at a distance busy in
gathering his Baldwins, of which, to judge by
the number of barrels lying about under the
trees, his crop is more abundant than my own,
— by which sight I am admonished to turn to
those orchards of the mind wherein my labors
may be more prospered, and apply myself dili-
gently to the preparation of my next Sabbath's
discourse. — H. W.]

MELIBŒUS-HIPPONAX

THE
Biglow Papers,
SECOND SERIES.

Ἔστιν ἄρ' ὁ ἰδιωτισμὸς ἐνίοτε τοῦ κόσμου παραπολὺ
ἐμφανιστικώτερον.
LONGINUS.

" J'aimerois mieulx que mon fils apprinst aux tavernes
à parler, qu'aux escholes de la parlerie."
MONTAIGNE.

„ Unſer Sprach iſt auch ein Sprach und kan ſo wohl ein
Sack nennen als die Lateiner saccus."
FISCHART.

" Vim rebus aliquando ipsa verborum humilitas affert."
QUINTILIANUS.

" O ma lengo,
Plantarèy une estèlo à toun froun encrumit ! "
JASMIN.

" Multos enim, quibus loquendi ratio non desit, in-
venias, quos curiose potius loqui dixeris quam Latine ;
quomodo et illa Attica anus Theophrastum, hominem
alioqui disertissimum, annotata unius affectatione verbi,
hospitem dixit, nec alio se id deprehendisse interrogata
respondit, quam quod nimium Attice loqueretur." —
QUINTILIANUS.

" Et Anglice sermonicari solebat populo, sed secun-
dum linguam Norfolchie ubi natus et nutritus erat."
— CRONICA JOCELINI.

" La politique est une pierre attachée au cou de la
littérature, et qui en moins de six mois la submerge.
. . . Cette politique va offenser mortellement une
moitié des lecteurs, et ennuyer l'autre qui l'a trouvée
bien autrement spéciale et énergique dans le journal du
matin." — HENRI BEYLE.

THE best introduction to the Second Series
of the Biglow Papers is to be found in Low-
ell's prose papers on political topics contributed
to the *Atlantic Monthly* and the *North Ameri-
can Review* from 1858 to 1860, some of which
have been reprinted in the fifth volume of the
Riverside edition of his Writings. Just before
Mr. Lincoln's election in 1860 he wrote : " We
are approaching a crisis in our domestic pol-
icy more momentous than any that has arisen
since we became a nation." The crisis arrived,
and during 1861 his political sagacity, his ar-
dent patriotism, his moral genius were dis-
played in a series of essays which did much to
enlighten and confirm the roused spirit of the
Northern people. But more was wanting of
him. His verse could reach more ears than
his or any other writer's prose. He was urged
to write fresh Biglow Papers, and in a letter
dated the last day of the year 1860, Lowell
wrote : " As for new Biglow Papers, God knows
how I should like to write them, if they would
only *make* me as they did before. But I am so
occupied and bothered that I have no time to

brood, which with me is as needful a prelimi-
nary to hatching anything as with a clucking
hen. However, I am going to try my hand, and
see what comes of it." It was a year, however,
before the first of the new series appeared in
the *Atlantic Monthly*, and he wrote of it to Miss
Norton : " I have been writing a *Biglow Paper*,
and I feel as nervous about it as a young au-
thor not yet weaned of public favor. It was
clean against my critical judgment, for I don't
believe in resuscitations, — we hear no good of
the *posthumous* Lazarus, — but I may get into
the vein and do some good." The first of the
series was published in January, 1862, and the
stimulus Lowell needed came quickly in the
Trent affair, which drew out of him at once
Mason and Slidell : a Yankee Idyll, which ap-
peared in February. " If I am not mistaken,"
he wrote to Mr. Fields on sending it, "it will
take." The third followed in March, and Low-
ell wrote again to Mr. Fields : " As for the
Biglow — glad you like it. If not so good as
the others, the public will be sure to. I think
well of the *Fable* and believe there is nothing
exotic therein. I am going to kill Wilbur
before long, and give a ' would-have-been '
obituary on him in the American style. That
is, for example, ' he wrote no epic, but if he
had, he would have been,' etc. I don't know
how many of these future-conditional geniuses
we have produced — many score, certainly. . . .
Good-by-yours — with a series of Biglows rising,
like the visionary kings before Macbeth, to de-
stroy all present satisfaction."

Lowell did not kill Parson Wilbur imme-
diately. Three more numbers followed, the
fourth, fifth, and sixth, in April, May, and June.
Then there was an interval when the rustic
muse refused to come at a call. " It 's no use,"
the poet wrote June 5, 1862, to Fields, who had
evidently been asking for the July portion ; " I
reverse the gospel difficulty, and while the flesh
is willing enough the spirit is weak. My
brain must lie fallow a spell — there is no su-
perphosphate for those worn-out fields. Bet-
ter no crop than small potatoes. I want to
have the *passion* of the thing on me again and
beget lusty Biglows. I am all the more de-
jected because you have treated me so well.
But I must rest awhile. My brain is out of
kilter." Mr. Fields returned to the attack the
next month, and Lowell wrote him a humorous
letter in which he expressed his amazement at
having kept his word about the six already
written, and had some hopes that two ideas he
cherished might come to something. At last
he seems to have fallen back on his scheme for
putting Parson Wilbur to death, and made it an
excuse for the seventh paper, *Latest Views of
Mr. Biglow*, which appeared in *The Atlantic* for
February, 1863. Other occupations at this time

engrossed him, and he again wrote to Mr. Fields, October 18, 1864 : "Firstly, whar's Biglow ? Let echo repeat her customary observation, adding only that I began one, but it would not go. I had ideas in plenty, but all I could do, they would not marry themselves to immortal worse. Not only did I wish to write, for there was a chance of a thousand, but I wanted money — so there can be no doubt I was in earnest." It was not till peace was imminent that he wrote again, the moving tenth satire, which was published in April, 1865. The final paper, called out by the Johnson retrograde movement, was published in *The Atlantic* for May, 1866. The papers numbered VIII. and IX. did not appear in print until the book was published in the fall of the same year.

Lowell more than once spoke of this second series of *Biglow Papers* as in his judgment better than the first. In a letter to Thomas Hughes twenty years after the book appeared, he wrote as follows : " Pray, who is ' F. T.,' who has been writing about me in so friendly a way in the *Cornhill* ? He is a little out now and then, but strikes me as in the main judicious. He is wrong about the second part of the *Biglow Papers*. I think had he read these first, he would have seen they had more permanent qualities than their predecessors, less fun and more humor perhaps. And pray what natural scenery would he have me describe but my own ? If you know him, tell him I think two European birds beat any of ours, the nightingale and the blackbird. The lark beats any of them also by sentiment and association, though not vocally. I suppose I should have been a more poetical poet if I had not been a professor. A poet should feed on nothing but poetry as they used to say a drone could be turned into a queen-bee by a diet of bee-bread."

When the book appeared it bore a dedication to E. R. Hoar, and was introduced by the essay on the Yankee form of English speech, which, as we have seen, he had long ago proposed writing. This Introduction is so distinctly an essay that it has been thought best to print it as an appendix to this volume, rather than allow it to break in upon the pages of verse. There is, however, one passage in it which may be repeated here, since it bears directly upon the poem which serves as a sort of prelude to the series.

" The only attempt I had ever made at anything like a pastoral (if that may be called an attempt which was the result almost of pure accident) was in *The Courtin'*. While the introduction to the First Series was going through the press, I received word from the printer that there was a blank page left which must be filled. I sat down at once and improvised another fictitious ' notice of the press,' in which,

because verse would fill up space more cheaply than prose, I inserted an extract from a supposed ballad of Mr. Biglow. I kept no copy of it, and the printer, as directed, cut it off when the gap was filled. Presently I began to receive letters asking for the rest of it, sometimes for the *balance* of it. I had none, but to answer such demands, I patched a conclusion upon it in a later edition. Those who had only the first continued to importune me. Afterward, being asked to write it out as an autograph for the Baltimore Sanitary Commission Fair, I added other verses, into some of which I infused a little more sentiment in a homely way, and after a fashion completed it by sketching in the characters and making a connected story. Most likely I have spoiled it, but I shall put it at the end of this Introduction, to answer once for all those kindly importunings."

THE COURTIN'

GOD makes sech nights, all white an' still
  Fur 'z you can look or listen,
Moonshine an' snow on field an' hill,
  All silence an' all glisten.

Zekle crep' up quite unbeknown
  An' peeked in thru' the winder,
An' there sot Huldy all alone,
  'ith no one nigh to hender.

A fireplace filled the room's one side
  With half a cord o' wood in —
There war n't no stoves (tell comfort died)
  To bake ye to a puddin'.

The wa'nut logs shot sparkles out
  Towards the pootiest, bless her,
An' leetle flames danced all about
  The chiny on the dresser.

Agin the chimbley crook-necks hung,
  An' in amongst 'em rusted
The ole queen's-arm thet gran'ther Young
  Fetched back f'om Concord busted.

The very room, coz she was in,
  Seemed warm f'om floor to ceilin',
An' she looked full ez rosy agin
  Ez the apples she was peelin'.

'T was kin' o' kingdom-come to look
  On sech a blessed cretur,
A dogrose blushin' to a brook
  Ain't modester nor sweeter.

He was six foot o' man, A 1,
  Clear grit an' human natur',
None could n't quicker pitch a ton
  Nor dror a furrer straighter.

He 'd sparked it with full twenty gals,
  Hed squired 'em, danced 'em, druv 'em,
Fust this one, an' then thet, by spells —
  All is, he could n't love 'em.

But long o' her his veins 'ould run
  All crinkly like curled maple,
The side she breshed felt full o' sun
  Ez a south slope in Ap'il.

She thought no v'ice hed sech a swing
  Ez hisn in the choir;
My! when he made Ole Hunderd ring,
  She *knowed* the Lord was nigher.

An' she 'd blush scarlit, right in prayer,
  When her new meetin'-bunnet
Felt somehow thru' its crown a pair
  O' blue eyes sot upun it.

Thet night, I tell ye, she looked *some!*
  She seemed to 've gut a new soul,
For she felt sartin-sure he 'd come,
  Down to her very shoe-sole.

She heered a foot, an' knowed it tu,
  A-raspin' on the scraper, —
All ways to once her feelins flew
  Like sparks in burnt-up paper.

He kin' o' l'itered on the mat,
  Some doubtfle o' the sekle,
His heart kep' goin' pity-pat,
  But hern went pity Zekle.

An' yit she gin her cheer a jerk
  Ez though she wished him furder,
An' on her apples kep' to work,
  Parin' away like murder.

"You want to see my Pa, I s'pose?"
  "Wal . . . no . . . I come dasignin'"—
"To see my Ma? She 's sprinklin' clo'es
  Agin to-morrer's i'nin'."

To say why gals acts so or so,
  Or don't, 'ould be persumin';
Mebby to mean *yes* an' say *no*
  Comes nateral to women.

He stood a spell on one foot fust,
  Then stood a spell on t' other,
An' on which one he felt the wust
  He could n't ha' told ye nuther.

Says he, "I 'd better call agin;"
  Says she, "Think likely, Mister:"
Thet last word pricked him like a pin,
  An' . . . Wal, he up an' kist her.

When Ma bimeby upon 'em slips,
  Huldy sot pale ez ashes,
All kin' o' smily roun' the lips
  An' teary roun' the lashes.

For she was jes' the quiet kind
  Whose naturs never vary,
Like streams that keep a summer mind
  Snowhid in Jenooary.

The blood clost roun' her heart felt glued
  Too tight for all expressin',
Tell mother see how metters stood,
  An' gin 'em both her blessin'.

Then her red come back like the tide
  Down to the Bay o' Fundy,
An' all I know is they was cried
  In meetin' come nex' Sunday.

THE BIGLOW PAPERS

SECOND SERIES

No. I

BIRDOFREDUM SAWIN, ESQ., TO MR. HOSEA BIGLOW

LETTER FROM THE REVEREND HOMER WILBUR, M. A., ENCLOSING THE EPISTLE AFORESAID

JAALAM, 15th Nov., 1861.

.   .   .   .

IT is not from any idle wish to obtrude my humble person with undue prominence upon the publick view that I resume my pen upon the present occasion. *Juniores ad labores.* But having been a main instrument in rescuing the talent of my young parishioner from being buried in the ground, by giving it such warrant with the world as could be derived from a name already widely known by several printed discourses (all of which I may be permitted without immodesty to state have been deemed worthy of preservation in the Library of Harvard College by my esteemed friend Mr. Sibley), it seemed becoming that I should not only testify to the genuineness of the following production, but call attention to it, the more as Mr. Biglow had so long been silent as to be in danger of absolute oblivion. I insinuate no claim to any share in the authorship (*vix ea nostra voco*) of the works already published by Mr. Biglow, but merely take to myself the credit of having fulfilled toward them the office of taster (*experto crede*), who, having first tried, could afterward bear witness (*credenzen* it was aptly named by the Germans), an office always arduous, and sometimes even dangerous, as in the case of those devoted persons who venture their lives in the deglutition of patent medicines (*dolus latet in generalibus*, there is deceit in the most of them) and thereafter are wonderfully preserved long enough to append their signatures to testimonials in the diurnal and hebdomadal prints. I say not this as covertly glancing at the authors of certain manuscripts which have been submitted to my literary judgment (though an epick in twenty-four books on the "Taking of Jericho" might, save for the prudent forethought of Mrs. Wilbur in secreting the same just as I had arrived beneath the walls and was beginning a catalogue of the various horns and their blowers, too ambitiously emulous in longanimity of Homer's list of ships, might, I say, have rendered frustrate any hope I could entertain *vacare Musis* for the small remainder of my days), but only the further to secure myself against any imputation of unseemly forthputting. I will barely subjoin, in this connexion, that, whereas Job was left to desire, in the soreness of his heart, that his adversary had written a book, as perchance misanthropically wishing to indite a review thereof, yet was not Satan allowed so far to tempt him as to send Bildad, Eliphaz, and Zophar each with an unprinted work in his wallet to be submitted to his censure. But of this enough. Were I in need of other excuse, I might add that I write by the express desire of Mr. Biglow himself, whose entire winter leisure is occupied, as he assures me, in answering demands for autographs, a labor exacting enough in itself, and egregiously so to him, who, being no ready penman, cannot sign so much as his name without strange contortions of the face (his nose, even, being essential to complete success) and painfully suppressed Saint-Vitus-dance of every muscle in his body. This, with his having been put in the Commission of the Peace by our excellent Governor (*O, si sic omnes!*) immediately on his accession to office, keeps him continually employed. *Haud inexpertus loquor*, having for many years written myself J. P., and being not seldom applied to for specimens of my chirography, a request to which I have sometimes over weakly assented, believing as I do that nothing written of set purpose can properly be called an autograph, but only those unpremeditated sallies and lively runnings which betray the fireside Man instead of the hunted Notoriety doubling on his pursuers. But it is time that I should bethink me of St. Austin's prayer, *libera me a meipso*, if I would arrive at the matter in hand.

Moreover, I had yet another reason for taking up the pen myself. I am informed that "The Atlantic Monthly" is mainly indebted for its success to the contributions and editorial supervision of Dr. Holmes, whose excellent "Annals of America" occupy an honored place upon my shelves. The journal itself I have never seen; but if this be so, it might seem that the recommendation of a brother-clergyman (though *par magis quam similis*) should carry a greater weight. I suppose that you have a department for historical lucubrations, and should be glad, if deemed desirable, to forward for publication my "Collections for the Antiquities of Jaalam," and my (now happily complete) pedigree of the Wilbur family from its *fons et origo*, the Wild Boar of Ardennes. Withdrawn from the active duties of my profession by the settlement of a colleague-pastor, the Reverend Jeduthun Hitchcock, formerly of Brutus Four-Corners, I might find time for further contributions to general literature on similar topics. I have made large advances towards a completer genealogy of Mrs. Wilbur's family, the Pilcoxes, not, if I know myself, from any idle vanity, but with the sole desire of rendering myself useful in my day and generation. *Nulla dies sine lineâ.* I inclose a meteorological register, a list of the births, deaths, and marriages, and a few *memorabilia* of longevity in Jaalam East Parish for the last half-century. Though spared to the unusual period of more than eighty years, I find no diminution of my faculties or abatement of my natural vigor, except a scarcely sensible decay of memory and a necessity of recurring to younger eyesight or spectacles for the finer print in Cruden. It would gratify me to make some further provision for declining years from the emoluments of my literary labors. I had intended to effect an insurance on my life, but was deterred therefrom by a circular from one of the offices, in which the sudden death of so large a proportion of the insured was set forth as an inducement, that it seemed to me little less than a tempting of Providence. *Neque in summâ inopiâ levis esse senectus potest, ne sapienti quidem.*

Thus far concerning Mr. Biglow; and so much seemed needful (*brevis esse laboro*) by way of preliminary, after a silence of fourteen years. He greatly fears lest he may in this essay have fallen below himself, well knowing that, if exercise be dangerous on a full stomach, no less so is writing on a full reputation. Beset as he has been on all sides, he could not refrain, and would only imprecate patience till he shall again have "got the hang" (as he calls it) of an accomplishment long disused. The letter of Mr. Sawin was received some time in last June, and others have followed which will in due season be submitted to the publick. How largely his statements are to be depended on, I more than merely dubitate. He was always distinguished for a tendency to exaggeration, — it might almost be qualified by a stronger term. *Fortiter mentire, aliquid hœret,* seemed to be his favorite rule of rhetoric. That he is actually where he says he is the postmark would seem to confirm; that he was received with the publick demonstrations he describes would appear consonant with what we know of the habits of those regions; but further than this I venture not to decide. I have sometimes suspected a vein of humor in him which leads him to speak by contraries; but since, in the unrestrained intercourse of private life, I have never observed in him any striking powers of invention, I am the more

willing to put a certain qualified faith in the incidents and the details of life and manners which give to his narratives some portion of the interest and entertainment which characterizes a Century Sermon.

It may be expected of me that I should say something to justify myself with the world for a seeming inconsistency with my well-known principles in allowing my youngest son to raise a company for the war, a fact known to all through the medium of the publick prints. I did reason with the young man, but *expellas naturam furcâ, tamen usque recurrit.* Having myself been a chaplain in 1812, I could the less wonder that a man of war had sprung from my loins. It was, indeed, grievous to send my Benjamin, the child of my old age; but after the discomfiture of Manassas, I with my own hands did buckle on his armor, trusting in the great Comforter and Commander for strength according to my need. For truly the memory of a brave son dead in his shroud were a greater staff of my declining years than a living coward (if those may be said to have lived who carry all of themselves into the grave with them), though his days might be long in the land, and he should get much goods. It is not till our earthen vessels are broken that we find and truly possess the treasure that was laid up in them. *Migravi in animam meam,* I have sought refuge in my own soul; nor would I be shamed by the heathen comedian with his *Nequam illud verbum, bene vult, nisi bene facit.* During our dark days, I read constantly in the inspired book of Job, which I believe to contain more food to maintain the fibre of the soul for right living and high thinking than all pagan literature together, though I would by no means vilipend the study of the classicks. There I read that Job said in his despair, even as the fool saith in his heart there is no God, — "The tabernacles of robbers prosper, and they that provoke God are secure." (Job xii. 6.) But I sought farther till I found this Scripture also, which I would have those perpend who have striven to turn our Israel aside to the worship of strange gods: "If I did despise the cause of my man-servant or of my maid-servant when they contended with me, what then shall I do when God riseth up? and when he visiteth, what shall I answer

him?" (Job xxxi. 13, 14.) On this text
I preached a discourse on the last day of
Fasting and Humiliation with general ac-
ceptance, though there were not wanting
one or two Laodiceans who said that I
should have waited till the President an-
nounced his policy. But let us hope and
pray, remembering this of Saint Gregory,
*Vult Deus rogari, vult cogi, vult quâdam im-
portunitate vinci.*

We had our first fall of snow on Friday
last. Frosts have been unusually backward
this fall. A singular circumstance occurred
in this town on the 20th October, in the
family of Deacon Pelatiah Tinkham. On
the previous evening, a few moments be-
fore family prayers,

. . . .

[The editors of the "Atlantic" find it neces-
sary here to cut short the letter of their valued
correspondent, which seemed calculated rather
on the rates of longevity in Jaalam than for less
favored localities. They have every encourage-
ment to hope that he will write again.]

With esteem and respect,
Your obedient servant,
HOMER WILBUR, A. M.

It's some consid'ble of a spell sence I
hain't writ no letters,
An' ther' 's gret changes hez took place in
all polit'cle metters;
Some canderdates air dead an' gone, an'
some hez ben defeated,
Which 'mounts to pooty much the same;
fer it 's ben proved repeated
A betch o' bread thet hain't riz once ain't
goin' to rise agin,
An' it 's jest money throwed away to put
the emptins in:
But thet 's wut folks wun't never larn;
they dunno how to go,
Arter you want their room, no more 'n a
bullet-headed beau;
Ther' 's ollers chaps a-hangin' roun' thet
can't see peatime 's past,
Mis'ble as roosters in a rain, heads down
an' tails half-mast:
It ain't disgraceful bein' beat, when a holl
nation doos it,
But Chance is like an amberill, — it don't
take twice to lose it.

I spose you 're kin' o' cur'ous, now, to know
why I hain't writ.

Wal, I 've ben where a litt'ry taste don't
somehow seem to git
Th' encouragement a feller 'd think, thet 's
used to public schools,
An' where sech things ez paper 'n' ink air
clean agin the rules:
A kind o' vicyvarsy house, built dreffle
strong an' stout,
So 's 't honest people can't get in, ner
t' other sort git out,
An' with the winders so contrived, you 'd
prob'ly like the view
Better alookin' in than out, though it seems
sing'lar, tu;
But then the landlord sets by ye, can't bear
ye out o' sight,
And locks ye up ez reg'lar ez an outside
door at night.

This world is awfle contrary: the rope may
stretch your neck
Thet mebby kep' another chap frum washin'
off a wreck;
An' you may see the taters grow in one poor
feller's patch,
So small no self-respectin' hen thet vallied
time 'ould scratch,
So small the rot can't find 'em out, an' then
agin, nex' door,
Ez big ez wut hogs dream on when they 're
'most too fat to snore.
But groutin' ain't no kin' o' use; an' ef the
fust throw fails,
Why, up an' try agin, thet 's all, — the cop-
pers ain't all tails,
Though I *hev* seen 'em when I thought they
hed n't no more head
Than 'd sarve a nussin' Brigadier thet gits
some ink to shed.

When I writ last, I 'd ben turned loose by
thet blamed nigger, Pomp,
Ferlorner than a musquash, ef you 'd took
an' dreened his swamp:
But I ain't o' the meechin' kind, thet sets
an' thinks fer weeks
The bottom 's out o' th' univarse coz their
own gillpot leaks.
I hed to cross bayous an' criks, (wal; it did
beat all natur',)
Upon a kin' o' corderoy, fust log, then
alligator;
Luck'ly, the critters warn't sharp-sot; I
guess 't wuz overruled

They 'd done their mornin's marketin' an'
    gut their hunger cooled;
Fer missionaries to the Creeks an' runaways
    are viewed
By them an' folks ez sent express to be
    their reg'lar food;
Wutever 't wuz, they laid an' snoozed ez
    peacefully ez sinners,
Meek ez disgestin' deacons be at ordination
    dinners;
Ef any on 'em turned an' snapped, I let 'em
    kin' o' taste
My live-oak leg, an' so, ye see, ther' warn't
    no gret o' waste;
Fer they found out in quicker time than ef
    they 'd ben to college
'T warn't heartier food then though 't wuz
    made out o' the tree o' knowledge.
But *I* tell *you* my other leg hed larned wut
    pizon-nettle meant,
An' var'ous other usefle things, afore I
    reached a settlement,
An' all o' me thet wuz n't sore an' sendin'
    prickles thru me
Wuz jest the leg I parted with in lickin'
    Montezumy:
A useful limb it 's ben to me, an' more of a
    support
Than wut the other hez ben, — coz I dror
    my pension for 't.

Wal, I gut in at last where folks wuz civer-
    lized an' white,
Ez I diskivered to my cost afore 't warn't
    hardly night;
Fer 'z I wuz settin' in the bar a-takin' sun-
    thin' hot,
An' feelin' like a man agin, all over in one
    spot,
A feller thet sot oppersite, arter a squint at
    me,
Lep' up an' drawed his peacemaker, an',
    "Dash it, Sir," suz he,
"I 'm doubledashed ef you ain't him thet
    stole my yaller chettle,
(You 're all the stränger thet 's around,) so
    now you 've gut to settle;
It ain't no use to argerfy ner try to cut up
    frisky,
I know ye ez I know the smell of ole chain-
    lightnin' whiskey;
We 're lor-abidin' folks down here, we 'll fix
    ye so 's 't a bar
Would n' tech ye with a ten-foot pole;
    (Jedge, you jest warm the tar;)

You 'll think you 'd bettei ha' gut among
    a tribe o' Mongrel Tartars,
'fore we 've done showin' how we raise our
    Southun prize tar-martyrs;
A moultin' fallen cherubim, ef he should
    see ye, 'd snicker,
Thinkin' he warn't a suckemstance. Come,
    genlemun, le' 's liquor;
An', Gin'ral, when you 've mixed the drinks
    an' chalked 'em up, tote roun'
An' see ef ther' 's a feather-bed (thet 's
    borryable) in town.
We 'll try ye fair, ole Grafted-Leg, an' ef
    the tar wun't stick,
Th' ain't not a juror here but wut 'll 'quit
    ye double-quick."
To cut it short, I wun't say sweet, they gi'
    me a good dip,
(They ain't *perfessin'* Bahptists here,) then
    give the bed a rip, —
The jury 'd sot, an' quicker thin a flash
    they hetched me out, a livin'
Extemp'ry mammoth turkey-chick fer a
    Fejee Thanksgivin'.
Thet I felt some stuck up is wut it 's
    nat'ral to suppose,
When poppylar enthusiasm hed funnished
    me sech clo'es;
(Ner 't ain't without edvantiges, this kin'
    o' suit, ye see,
It 's water-proof, an' water 's wut I like
    kep' out o' me;)
But nut content with thet, they took a ker-
    ridge from the fence
An' rid me roun' to see the place, entirely
    free 'f expense,
With forty-'leven new kines o' sarse with-
    out no charge acquainted me,
Gi' me three cheers, an' vowed thet I wuz
    all their fahncy painted me;
They treated me to all their eggs; (they
    keep 'em I should think,
Fer sech ovations, pooty long, for they
    wuz mos' distinc' ;)
They starred me thick 'z the Milky-Way
    with indiscrim'nit cherity,
Fer wut we call reception eggs air sunthin'
    of a rerity;
Green ones is plentifle anough, skurce wuth
    a nigger's getherin',
But your dead-ripe ones ranges high fer
    treatin' Nothun bretherin;
A spotteder, ring streakeder child the'
    warn't in Uncle Sam's

THE BIGLOW PAPERS

Holl farm, — a cross of stripëd pig an' one
o' Jacob's lambs;
'T wuz Dannil in the lions' den, new an'
enlarged edition,
An' everythin' fust-rate o' 'ts kind; the'
warn't no impersition.
People 's impulsiver down here than wut
our folks to home be,
An' kin' o' go it 'ith a resh in raisin' Hail
Columby:
Thet 's *so:* an' they swarmed out like bees,
for your real Southun men's
Time is n't o' much more account than an
ole settin' hen's;
(They jest work semioccashnally, or else
don't work at all,
An' so their time an' 'tention both air at
saci'ty's call.)
Talk about hospatality! wut Nothun
town d' ye know
Would take a totle stranger up an' treat
him gratis so?
You 'd better b'lieve ther' 's nothin' like
this spendin' days an' nights
Along 'ith a dependent race fer civerlizin'
whites.

But this wuz all prelim'nary; it 's so Gran'
Jurors here
Fin' a true bill, a hendier way than ourn,
an' nut so dear;
So arter this they sentenced me, to make
all tight 'n' snug,
Afore a reg'lar court o' law, to ten years
in the Jug.
I did n't make no gret defence : you don't
feel much like speakin',
When, ef you let your clamshells gape, a
quart o' tar will leak in:
I *hev* hearn tell o' wingëd words, but pint
o' fact it tethers
The spoutin' gift to hev your words *tu* thick
sot on with feathers,
An' Choate ner Webster would n't ha'
made an A 1 kin' o' speech
Astride a Southun chestnut horse sharper
'n a baby's screech.
Two year ago they ketched the thief, 'n'
seein' I wuz innercent,
They jest uncorked an' le' me run, an' in
my stid the sinner sent
To see how *he* liked pork 'n' pone flavored
with wa'nut saplin',
An' nary social priv'ledge but a one-hoss,
starn-wheel chaplin.

When I come out, the folks behaved mos'
gen'manly an' harnsome;
They 'lowed it would n't be more 'n right,
ef I should cuss 'n' darn some:
The Cunnle he apolergized; suz he, "I 'll
du wut 's right,
I 'll give ye settisfection now by shootin'
ye at sight,
An' give the nigger (when he 's caught), to
pay him fer his trickin'
In gittin' the wrong man took up, a most
H fired lickin', —
It 's jest the way with all on 'em, the in-
consistent critters,
They 're 'most enough to make a man blas-
pheme his mornin' bitters;
I 'll be your frien' thru thick an' thin an'
in all kines o' weathers,
An' all you 'll hev to pay fer 's jest the
waste o' tar an' feathers:
A lady owned the bed, ye see, a widder, tu,
Miss Shennon;
It wuz her mite; we would ha' took another,
ef ther 'd ben one:
We don't make *no* charge for the ride an'
all the other fixins.
Le' 's liquor; Gin'ral, you can chalk our
friend for all the mixins."
A meetin' then wuz called, where they
"RESOLVED, Thet we respec'
B. S. Esquire for quallerties o' heart an'
intellec'
Peculiar to Columby's sile, an' not to no
one else's,
Thet makes Európean tyrans scringe in all
their gilded pel'ces,
An' doos gret honor to our race an'
Southun institootions : "
(I give ye jest the substance o' the leadin'
resolootions:)
"RESOLVED, Thet we revere in him a
soger 'thout a flor,
A martyr to the princerples o' libbaty an'
lor :
RESOLVED, Thet other nations all, ef sot
'longside o' us,
For vartoo, larnin', chivverlry, ain't noways
wuth a cuss."
They gut up a subscription, tu, but no gret
come o' *thet;*
I 'xpect in cairin' of it roun' they took a
leaky hat;
Though Southun genelmun ain't slow at
puttin' down their name,

(When they can write,) fer in the eend it
comes to jes' the same,
Because, ye see, 't 's the fashion here to
sign an' not to think
A critter 'd be so sordid ez to ax 'em for
the chink:
I did n't call but jest on one, an' *he* drawed
tooth-pick on me,
An' reckoned he warn't goin' to stan' no
sech dog-gauned econ'my;
So nothin' more wuz realized, 'ceptin' the
good-will shown,
Than ef 't had ben from fust to last a regu-
lar Cotton Loan.
It 's a good way, though, come to think,
coz ye enjy the sense
O' lendin' lib'rally to the Lord, an' nary
red o' 'xpense:
Sence then I 've gut my name up for a
gin'rous-hearted man
By jes' subscribin' right an' left on this
high-minded plan;
I 've gin away my thousans so to every
Southun sort
O' missions, colleges, an' sech, ner ain't no
poorer for 't.

I warn't so bad off, arter all; I need n't
hardly mention
That Guv'ment owed me quite a pile for
my arrears o' pension, —
I mean the poor, weak thing we *hed:* we
run a new one now,
Thet strings a feller with a claim up ta the
nighes' bough,
An' *prectises* the right o' man, purtects
down-trodden debtors,
Ner wun't hev creditors about ascrougin'
o' their betters:
Jeff 's gut the last idees ther' is, poscrip',
fourteenth edition,
He knows it takes some enterprise to run
an oppersition;
Ourn 's the fust thru-by-daylight train,
with all ou'doors for deepot;
Yourn goes so slow you 'd think 't wuz
drawed by a las' cent'ry teapot; —
Wal, I gut all on 't paid in gold afore our
State seceded,
An' done wal, for Confed'rit bonds warn't
jest the cheese I needed:
Nut but wut they 're ez *good* ez gold, but
then it 's hard a-breakin' on 'em,
An' ignorant folks is ollers sot an' wun't
git used to takin' on 'em;

They 're wuth ez much ez wut they wuz
afore ole Mem'nger signed 'em,
An' go off middlin' wal for drinks, when
ther' 's a knife behind 'em;
We *du* miss silver, jes' fer thet an' ridin' in
a bus,
Now we 've shook off the desputs thet
wuz suckin' at our pus;
An' it 's *because* the South 's so rich; 't
wuz nat'ral to expec'
Supplies o' change wuz jes' the things we
should n't recollec';
We 'd ough' to ha' thought aforehan',
though, o' thet good rule o' Crock-
ett's,
For 't 's tiresome cairin' cotton-bales an'
niggers in your pockets,
Ner 't ain't quite hendy to pass off one o'
your six-foot Guineas
An' git your halves an' quarters back in
gals an' pickaninnies:
Wal, 't ain't quite all a feller 'd ax, but
then ther 's this to say,
It 's on'y jest among ourselves thet we
expec' to pay;
Our system would ha' caird us thru in any
Bible cent'ry,
'fore this onscripterl plan come up o' books
by double entry;
We go the patriarkle here out o' all sight
an' hearin',
For Jacob warn't a suckemstance to Jeff
at financierin';
He never 'd thought o' borryin' from Esau
like all nater
An' then cornfiscatin' all debts to sech a
small pertater;
There 's p'litickle econ'my, now, combined
'ith morril beauty
Thet saycrifices privit eends (your in'my's,
tu) to dooty !
Wy, Jeff 'd ha' gin him five an' won his
eye-teeth 'fore he knowed it,
An', stid o' wastin' pottage, he 'd ha' eat it
up an' owed it.
But I wuz goin' on to say how I come here
to dwall ; —
'Nough said, thet, arter lookin' roun', I
liked the place so wal,
Where niggers doos a double good, with us
atop to stiddy 'em,
By bein' proofs o' prophecy an' suckleatin'
medium,
Where a man 's sunthin' coz he 's white,
an' whiskey 's cheap ez fleas,

An' the financial pollercy jes' sooted my
  idees,
Thet I friz down right where I wuz, mer-
  ried the Widder Shennon,
(Her thirds wuz part in cotton-land, part
  in the curse o' Canaan,)
An' here I be ez lively ez a chipmunk on a
  wall,
With nothin' to feel riled about much later
  'n Eddam's fall.

Ez fur ez human foresight goes, we made
  an even trade:
She gut an overseer, an' I a fem'ly ready-
  made,
The youngest on 'em 's 'mos' growed up,
  rugged an' spry ez weazles,
So 's 't ther' 's no resk o' doctors' bills fer
  hoopin'-cough an' measles.
Our farm 's at Turkey-Buzzard Roost,
  Little Big Boosy River,
Wal located in all respex, — fer 't ain't the
  chills 'n' fever
Thet makes my writin' seem to squirm; a
  Southuner 'd allow I 'd
Some call to shake, for I 've jest hed to
  meller a new cowhide.
Miss S. is all 'f a lady; th' ain't no better on
  Big Boosy
Ner one with more accomplishmunts 'twixt
  here an' Tuscaloosy;
She 's an F. F., the tallest kind, an' prouder
  'n the Gran' Turk,
An' never hed a relative thet done a stroke
  o' work;
Hern ain't a scrimpin' fem'ly sech ez *you*
  git up Down East,
Th' ain't a growed member on 't but owes
  his thousuns et the least:
She *is* some old; but then agin ther' 's draw-
  backs in my sheer:
Wut 's left o' me ain't more 'n enough to
  make a Brigadier:
Wust is, thet she hez tantrums ; she 's like
  Seth Moody's gun
(Him thet wuz nicknamed frum his limp
  Ole Dot an' Kerry One);
He 'd left her loaded up a spell, an' hed to
  git her clear,
So he onhitched, — Jeerusalem ! the middle
  o' last year
Wuz right nex' door compared to where she
  kicked the critter tu
(Though *jest* where he brought up wuz wut
  no human never knew);

His brother Asaph picked her up an' tied
  her to a tree,
An' then she kicked an hour 'n' a half afore
  she 'd let it be:
Wal, Miss S. *doos* hev cuttins-up an' pourins-
  out o' vials,
But then she hez her widder's thirds, an'
  all on us hez trials.
My objec', though, in writin' now warn't to
  allude to sech,
But to another suckemstance more dellykit
  to tech, —
I want thet you should grad'lly break my
  merriage to Jerushy,
An' there 's a heap of argymunts thet 's
  emple to indooce ye:
Fust place, State's Prison, — wal, it 's true
  it warn't fer crime, o' course,
But then it 's jest the same fer her in gittin'
  a divorce;
Nex' place, my State 's secedin' out hez
  leg'lly lef' me free
To merry any one I please, pervidin' it 's a
  she;
Fin'lly, I never wun't come back, she need
  n't hev no fear on 't,
But then it 's wal to fix things right fer
  fear Miss S. should hear on 't;
Lastly, I 've gut religion South, an' Rushy
  she 's a pagan
Thet sets by th' graven imiges o' the gret
  Nothun Dagon;
(Now I hain't seen one in six munts, for,
  sence our Treashry Loan,
Though yaller boys is thick anough, eagles
  hez kind o' flown;)
An' ef J wants a stronger pint than them
  thet I hev stated,
Wy, she 's an aliun in 'my now, an' I 've
  been cornfiscated, —
For sence we 've entered on th' estate o'
  the late nayshnul eagle,
She hain't no kin' o' right but jes' wut I
  allow ez legle:
Wut *doos* Secedin' mean, ef 't ain't thet
  nat'rul rights hez riz, 'n'
Thet wut is mine 's my own, but wut 's
  another man's ain't his'n ?

Besides, I could n't do no else; Miss S. suz
  she to me,
" You 've sheered my bed," [thet 's when I
  paid my interduction fee
To Southun rites,] " an' kep' your sheer,"
  [wal, I allow it sticked

So 's 't I wuz most six weeks in jail afore I
    gut me picked,]
"Ner never paid no demmiges; but thet
    wun't do no harm,
Pervidin' thet you 'll ondertake to oversee
    the farm:
(My eldes' boy he 's so took up, wut with
    the Ringtail Rangers
An' settin' in the Jestice-Court for welcomin'
    o' strangers ;")
[He sot on *me;*] "an' so, ef you 'll jest on-
    dertake the care
Upon a mod'rit sellery, we 'll up an' call it
    square;
But ef you *can't* conclude," suz she, an' give
    a kin' o' grin,
"Wy, the Gran' Jurymen, I 'xpect, 'll hev
    to set agin."
That 's the way metters stood at fust; now
    wut wuz I to du,
But jes' to make the best on 't an' off coat
    an' buckle tu ?
Ther' ain't a livin' man thet finds an income
    necessarier
Than me, — bimeby I 'll tell ye how I
    fin'lly come to merry her.

She hed another motive, tu: I mention of it
    here
T' encourage lads thet 's growin' up to
    study 'n' persevere,
An' show 'em how much better 't pays to
    mind their winter-schoolin'
Than to go off on benders 'n' sech, an' waste
    their time in foolin';
Ef 't warn't for studyin' evenins, why, I
    never 'd ha' ben here
A orn'ment o' saciety, in my approprut
    spear:
She wanted somebody, ye see, o' taste an'
    cultivation,
To talk along o' preachers when they stopt
    to the plantation ;
For folks in Dixie th't read an' rite, onless
    it is by jarks,
Is skurce ez wut they wuz among th' ori-
    genle patriarchs ;
To fit a feller f' wut they call the soshle
    higherarchy,
All thet you 've gut to know is jes' beyund
    an evrage darky;
Schoolin' 's wut they can't seem to stan',
    they 're tu consarned high-pressure,
An' knowin' t' much might spile a boy for
    bein' a Secesher.

We hain't no settled preachin' here, ner
    ministeril taxes ;
The min'ster's only settlement 's the carpet-
    bag he packs his
Razor an' soap-brush intu, with his hym-
    book an' his Bible, —
But they *du* preach, I swan to man, it 's
    puf'kly indescrib'le !
They go it like an Ericsson's ten-hoss-
    power coleric ingine,
An' make Ole Split-Foot winch an' squirm,
    for all he 's used to singein' ;
Hawkins's whetstone ain't a pinch o' primin'
    to the innards
To hearin' on 'em put free grace t' a lot o'
    tough old sinhards !
But I must eend this letter now : 'fore long
    I 'll send a fresh un ;
I 've lots o' things to write about, pertick-
    lerly Seceshun :
I 'm called off now to mission-work, to let
    a leetle law in
To Cynthy's hide : an' so, till death,
    Yourn,
        BIRDOFREDUM SAWIN.

No. II

MASON AND SLIDELL:
A YANKEE IDYLL

TO THE EDITORS OF THE ATLANTIC
MONTHLY

JAALAM, 6th Jan., 1862.

GENTLEMEN, — I was highly gratified by
the insertion of a portion of my letter in the
last number of your valuable and entertain-
ing Miscellany, though in a type which
rendered its substance inaccessible even to
the beautiful new spectacles presented to
me by a Committee of the Parish on New
Year's Day. I trust that I was able to bear
your very considerable abridgment of my
lucubrations with a spirit becoming a Chris-
tian. My third granddaughter, Rebekah,
aged fourteen years, and whom I have
trained to read slowly and with proper em-
phasis (a practice too much neglected in
our modern systems of education), read
aloud to me the excellent essay upon " Old
Age," the author of which I cannot help
suspecting to be a young man who has

never yet known what it was to have snow (*canities morosa*) upon his own roof. *Dissolve frigus, large super foco ligna reponens*, is a rule for the young, whose wood-pile is yet abundant for such cheerful lenitives. A good life behind him is the best thing to keep an old man's shoulders from shivering at every breath of sorrow or ill-fortune. But methinks it were easier for an old man to feel the disadvantages of youth than the advantages of age. Of these latter I reckon one of the chiefest to be this : that we attach a less inordinate value to our own productions, and, distrusting daily more and more our own wisdom (with the conceit whereof at twenty we wrap ourselves away from knowledge as with a garment), do reconcile ourselves with the wisdom of God. I could have wished, indeed, that room might have been made for the residue of the anecdote relating to Deacon Tinkham, which would not only have gratified a natural curiosity on the part of the publick (as I have reason to know from several letters of inquiry already received), but would also, as I think, have largely increased the circulation of your Magazine in this town. *Nihil humani alienum*, there is a curiosity about the affairs of our neighbors which is not only pardonable, but even commendable. But I shall abide a more fitting season.

As touching the following literary effort of Esquire Biglow, much might be profitably said on the topick of Idyllick and Pastoral Poetry, and concerning the proper distinctions to be made between them, from Theocritus, the inventor of the former, to Collins, the latest authour I know of who has emulated the classicks in the latter style. But in the time of a Civil War worthy a Milton to defend and a Lucan to sing, it may be reasonably doubted whether the publick, never too studious of serious instruction, might not consider other objects more deserving of present attention. Concerning the title of Idyll, which Mr. Biglow has adopted at my suggestion, it may not be improper to animadvert, that the name properly signifies a poem somewhat rustick in phrase (for, though the learned are not agreed as to the particular dialect employed by Theocritus, they are universanimous both as to its rusticity and its capacity of rising now and then to the level of more elevated

sentiments and expressions), while it is also descriptive of real scenery and manners. Yet it must be admitted that the production now in question (which here and there bears perhaps too plainly the marks of my correcting hand) does partake of the nature of a Pastoral, inasmuch as the interlocutors therein are purely imaginary beings, and the whole is little better than καπνοῦ σκιᾶς ὄναρ. The plot was, as I believe, suggested by the "Twa Briggs" of Robert Burns, a Scottish poet of the last century, as that found its prototype in the "Mutual Complaint of Plainstanes and Causey" by Fergusson, though the metre of this latter be different by a foot in each verse. Perhaps the Two Dogs of Cervantes gave the first hint. I reminded my talented young parishioner and friend that Concord Bridge had long since yielded to the edacious tooth of Time. But he answered me to this effect : that there was no greater mistake of an authour than to suppose the reader had no fancy of his own ; that, if once that faculty was to be called into activity, it were *better* to be in for the whole sheep than the shoulder ; and that he knew Concord like a book, — an expression questionable in propriety, since there are few things with which he is not more familiar than with the printed page. In proof of what he affirmed, he showed me some verses which with others he had stricken out as too much delaying the action, but which I communicate in this place because they rightly define "punkinseed" (which Mr. Bartlett would have a kind of perch, — a creature to which I have found a rod or pole not to be so easily equivalent in our inland waters as in the books of arithmetic), and because it conveys an eulogium on the worthy son of an excellent father, with whose acquaintance (*eheu, fugaces anni!*) I was formerly honoured.

"But nowadays the Bridge ain't wut they show,
So much ez Em'son, Hawthorne, an' Thoreau.
I know the village, though; was sent there once
A-schoolin', 'cause to home I played the dunce;
An' I 've ben sence a visitin' the Jedge,
Whose garding whispers with the river's edge,
Where I 've sot mornin's lazy as the bream,
Whose on'y business is to head up-stream,
(We call 'em punkin-seed,) or else in chat
Along 'th the Jedge, who covers with his hat
More wit an' gumption an' shrewd Yankee sense
Than there is mosses on an ole stone fence."

Concerning the subject-matter of the verses, I have not the leisure at present to write so fully as I could wish, my time being occupied with the preparation of a discourse for the forthcoming bicentenary celebration of the first settlement of Jaalam East Parish. It may gratify the publick interest to mention the circumstance, that my investigations to this end have enabled me to verify the fact (of much historick importance, and hitherto hotly debated) that Shearjashub Tarbox was the first child of white parentage born in this town, being named in his father's will under date August 7th, or 9th, 1662. It is well known that those who advocate the claims of Mehetable Goings are unable to find any trace of her existence prior to October of that year. As respects the settlement of the Mason and Slidell question, Mr. Biglow has not incorrectly stated the popular sentiment, so far as I can judge by its expression in this locality. For myself, I feel more sorrow than resentment: for I am old enough to have heard those talk of England who still, even after the unhappy estrangement, could not unschool their lips from calling her the Mother-Country. But England has insisted on ripping up old wounds, and has undone the healing work of fifty years; for nations do not reason, they only feel, and the *spretæ injuria formæ* rankles in their minds as bitterly as in that of a woman. And because this is so, I feel the more satisfaction that our Government has acted (as all Governments should, standing as they do between the people and their passions) as if it had arrived at years of discretion. There are three short and simple words, the hardest of all to pronounce in any language (and I suspect they were no easier before the confusion of tongues), but which no man or nation that cannot utter can claim to have arrived at manhood. Those words are, *I was wrong;* and I am proud that, while England played the boy, our rulers had strength enough from the People below and wisdom enough from God above to quit themselves like men.

The sore points on both sides have been skilfully exasperated by interested and unscrupulous persons, who saw in a war between the two countries the only hope of profitable return for their investment in Confederate stock, whether political or financial. The always supercilious, often insulting, and sometimes even brutal tone of British journals and publick men has certainly not tended to soothe whatever resentment might exist in America.

"Perhaps it was right to dissemble your love,
But why did you kick me down stairs?"

We have no reason to complain that England, as a necessary consequence of her clubs, has become a great society for the minding of other people's business, and we can smile good-naturedly when she lectures other nations on the sins of arrogance and conceit; but we may justly consider it a breach of the political *convenances* which are expected to regulate the intercourse of one well-bred government with another, when men holding places in the ministry allow themselves to dictate our domestic policy, to instruct us in our duty, and to stigmatize as unholy a war for the rescue of whatever a high-minded people should hold most vital and most sacred. Was it in good taste, that I may use the mildest term, for Earl Russell to expound our own Constitution to President Lincoln, or to make a new and fallacious application of an old phrase for our benefit, and tell us that the Rebels were fighting for independence and we for empire? As if all wars for independence were by nature just and deserving of sympathy, and all wars for empire ignoble and worthy only of reprobation, or as if these easy phrases in any way characterized this terrible struggle, — terrible not so truly in any superficial sense, as from the essential and deadly enmity of the principles that underlie it. His Lordship's bit of borrowed rhetoric would justify Smith O'Brien, Nana Sahib, and the Maori chieftains, while it would condemn nearly every war in which England has ever been engaged. Was it so very presumptuous in us to think that it would be decorous in English statesmen if they spared time enough to acquire some kind of knowledge, though of the most elementary kind, in regard to this country and the questions at issue here, before they pronounced so off-hand a judgment? Or is political information expected to come Dogberry-fashion in England, like reading and writing, by nature?

And now all respectable England is wondering at our irritability, and sees a quite satisfactory explanation of it in our national vanity. *Suave mari magno*, it is pleasant, sitting in the easy-chairs of Downing Street, to sprinkle pepper on the raw wounds of a kindred people struggling for life, and philosophical to find in self-conceit the cause of our instinctive resentment. Surely we were of all nations the least liable to any temptation of vanity at a time when the gravest anxiety and the keenest sorrow were never absent from our hearts. Nor is conceit the exclusive attribute of any one nation. The earliest of English travellers, Sir John Mandeville, took a less provincial view of the matter when he said, "For fro what partie of the erthe that men duellen, other aboven or beneathen, it semethe alweys to hem that duellen that thei gon more righte than any other folke." The English have always had their fair share of this amiable quality. We may say of them still, as the authour of the "Lettres Cabalistiques" said of them more than a century ago, "*Ces derniers disent naturellement qu'il n'y a qu'eux qui soient estimables.*" And, as he also says, "*J'aimerois presque autant tomber entre les mains d'un Inquisiteur que d'un Anglois qui me fait sentir sans cesse combien il s'estime plus que moi, et qui ne daigne me parler que pour injurier ma Nation et pour m'ennuyer du récit des grandes qualités de la sienne.*" Of *this* Bull we may safely say with Horace, *habet fœnum in cornu*. What we felt to be especially insulting was the quiet assumption that the descendants of men who left the Old World for the sake of principle, and who had made the wilderness into a New World patterned after an Idea, could not possibly be susceptible of a generous or lofty sentiment, could have no feeling of nationality deeper than that of a tradesman for his shop. One would have thought, in listening to England, that we were presumptuous in fancying that we were a nation at all, or had any other principle of union than that of booths at a fair, where there is no higher notion of government than the constable, or better image of God than that stamped upon the current coin.

It is time for Englishmen to consider whether there was nothing in the spirit of their press and of their leading public men

calculated to rouse a just indignation, and to cause a permanent estrangement on the part of any nation capable of self-respect, and sensitively jealous, as ours then was, of foreign interference. Was there nothing in the indecent haste with which belligerent rights were conceded to the Rebels, nothing in the abrupt tone assumed in the Trent case, nothing in the fitting out of Confederate privateers, that might stir the blood of a people already overcharged with doubt, suspicion, and terrible responsibility? The laity in any country do not stop to consider points of law, but they have an instinctive perception of the *animus* that actuates the policy of a foreign nation; and in our own case they remembered that the British authorities in Canada did not wait till diplomacy could send home to England for her slow official tinder-box to fire the "Caroline." Add to this, what every sensible American knew, that the moral support of England was equal to an army of two hundred thousand men to the Rebels, while it insured us another year or two of exhausting war. It was not so much the spite of her words (though the time might have been more tastefully chosen) as the actual power for evil in them that we felt as a deadly wrong. Perhaps the most immediate and efficient cause of mere irritation was the sudden and unaccountable change of manner on the other side of the water. Only six months before, the Prince of Wales had come over to call us cousins; and everywhere it was nothing but "our American brethren," that great offshoot of British institutions in the New World, so almost identical with them in laws, language, and literature, — this last of the alliterative compliments being so bitterly true, that perhaps it will not be retracted even now. To this outburst of long-repressed affection we responded with genuine warmth, if with something of the awkwardness of a poor relation bewildered with the sudden tightening of the ties of consanguinity when it is rumored that he has come into a large estate. Then came the Rebellion, and, *presto!* a flaw in our titles was discovered, the plate we were promised at the family table is flung at our head, and we were again the scum of creation, intolerably vulgar, at once cowardly and overbearing, — no relations of theirs, after all, but a dreggy hybrid of the basest bloods of Europe. Panurge was not quicker to call Friar John his *former* friend. I cannot help thinking of Walter Mapes's jingling paraphrase of Petronius, —

" Dummodo sim splendidis vestibus ornatus,
Et multa familia sim circumvallatus,
Prudens sum et sapiens et morigeratus,
Et tuus nepos sum et tu meus cognatus," —

which I may freely render thus: —

So long as I was prosperous, I 'd dinners by the dozen,
Was well-bred, witty, virtuous, and everybody's cousin;
If luck should turn, as well she may, her fancy is so flexile,
Will virtue, cousinship, and all return with her from exile ?

There was nothing in all this to exasperate a philosopher, much to make him smile rather; but the earth's surface is not chiefly inhabited by philosophers, and I revive the recollection of it now in perfect good-humour, merely by way of suggesting to our *ci-devant* British cousins, that it would have been easier for them to hold their tongues than for us to keep our tempers under the circumstances.

The English Cabinet made a blunder, unquestionably, in taking it so hastily for granted that the United States had fallen forever from their position as a first-rate power, and it was natural that they should vent a little of their vexation on the people whose inexplicable obstinacy in maintaining freedom and order, and in resisting degradation, was likely to convict them of their mistake. But if bearing a grudge be the sure mark of a small mind in the individual, can it be a proof of high spirit in a nation ? If the result of the present estrangement between the two countries shall be to make us more independent of British twaddle (*Indomito nec dira ferens stipendia Tauro*), so much the better; but if it is to make us insensible to the value of British opinion in matters where it gives us the judgment of an impartial and cultivated outsider, if we are to shut ourselves out from the advantages of English culture, the loss will be ours, and not theirs. Because the door of the old homestead has been once slammed in our faces, shall we in a huff reject all future advances of conciliation, and cut ourselves foolishly off from any share in the human-

izing influences of the place, with its ineffable riches of association, its heirlooms of immemorial culture, its historic monuments, ours no less than theirs, its noble gallery of ancestral portraits ? We have only to succeed, and England will not only respect, but, for the first time, begin to understand us. And let us not, in our justifiable indignation at wanton insult, forget that England is not the England only of snobs who dread the democracy they do not comprehend, but the England of history, of heroes, statesmen, and poets, whose names are dear, and their influence as salutary to us as to her.

Let us strengthen the hands of those in authority over us, and curb our own tongues, remembering that General Wait commonly proves in the end more than a match for General Headlong, and that the Good Book ascribes safety to a multitude, indeed, but not to a mob, of counsellours. Let us remember and perpend the words of Paulus Emilius to the people of Rome ; that, "if they judged they could manage the war to more advantage by any other, he would willingly yield up his charge ; but if they confided in him, *they were not to make themselves his colleagues in his office, or raise reports, or criticise his actions, but, without talking, supply him with means and assistance necessary to the carrying on of the war ; for, if they proposed to command their own commander, they would render this expedition more ridiculous than the former."* (*Vide Plutarchum in Vitâ P. E.*) Let us also not forget what the same excellent authour says concerning Perseus's fear of spending money, and not permit the covetousness of Brother Jonathan to be the good fortune of Jefferson Davis. For my own part, till I am ready to admit the Commander-in-Chief to my pulpit, I shall abstain from planning his battles. If courage be the sword, yet is patience the armour of a nation ; and in our desire for peace, let us never be willing to surrender the Constitution bequeathed us by fathers at least as wise as ourselves (even with Jefferson Davis to help us), and, with those degenerate Romans, *tuta et præsentia quam vetera et periculosa malle.*

And not only should we bridle our own tongues, but the pens of others, which are swift to convey useful intelligence to the enemy. This is no new inconvenience ; for, under date, 3d June, 1745, General Pepperell wrote thus to Governor Shirley from Louisbourg : "What your Excellency observes of the *army's being made acquainted with any plans proposed, until ready to be put in execution,* has always been disagreeable to me, and I have given many cautions relating to it. But when your Excellency considers that *our Council of War consists of more than twenty members,* I am persuaded you will think it *impossible for me to hinder it,* if any of them will persist in communicating to inferior officers and soldiers what ought to be kept secret. I am informed that the Boston newspapers are filled with paragraphs from private letters relating to the expedition. Will your Excellency permit me to say I think it may be of ill consequence ? Would it not be convenient, if your Excellency should forbid the Printers' inserting such news ? " Verily, if *tempora mutantur,* we may question the *et nos mutamur in illis ;* and if tongues be leaky, it will need all hands at the pumps to save the Ship of State. Our history dotes and repeats itself. If Sassycus (rather than Alcibiades) find a parallel in Beauregard, so Weakwash, as he is called by the brave Lieutenant Lion Gardiner, need not seek far among our own Sachems for his antitype.

With respect,
Your ob* humble serv*,
HOMER WILBUR, A. M.

I LOVE to start out arter night 's begun,
An' all the chores about the farm are done,
The critters milked an' foddered, gates shet fast,
Tools cleaned aginst to-morrer, supper past,
An' Nancy darnin' by her ker'sene lamp, —
I love, I say, to start upon a tramp,
To shake the kinkles out o' back an' legs,
An' kind o' rack my life off from the dregs
Thet 's apt to settle in the buttery-hutch
Of folks thet foller in one rut too much :
Hard work is good an' wholesome, past all doubt ;
But 't ain't so, ef the mind gits tuckered out.
Now, bein' born in Middlesex, you know,
There 's certin spots where I like best to go :

The Concord road, for instance (I, for one,
Most gin'lly ollers call it *John Bull's Run*),
The field o' Lexin'ton where England tried
The fastest colours thet she ever dyed,
An' Concord Bridge, thet Davis, when he came,
Found was the bee-line track to heaven an' fame,
Ez all roads be by natur', ef your soul
Don't sneak thru shun-pikes so 's to save the toll.

They 're 'most too fur away, take too much time
To visit of'en, ef it ain't in rhyme ;
But the' 's a walk thet 's hendier, a sight,
An' suits me fust-rate of a winter's night, —
I mean the round whale's-back o' Prospect Hill.
I love to l'iter there while night grows still,
An' in the twinklin' villages about,
Fust here, then there, the well-saved lights goes out,
An' nary sound but watch - dogs' false alarms,
Or muffled cock-crows from the drowsy farms,
Where some wise rooster (men act jest thet way)
Stands to 't thet moon-rise is the break o' day :
(So Mister Seward sticks a three-months' pin
Where the war 'd oughto eend, then tries agin ;
My gran'ther's rule was safer 'n 't is to crow :
Don't never prophesy — onless ye know.)
I love to muse there till it kind o' seems
Ez ef the world went eddyin' off in dreams;
The northwest wind thet twitches at my baird
Blows out o' sturdier days not easy scared,
An' the same moon thet this December shines
Starts out the tents an' booths o' Putnam's lines ;
The rail-fence posts, acrost the hill thet runs,
Turn ghosts o' sogers should'rin' ghosts o' guns ;
Ez wheels the sentry, glints a flash o' light,
Along the firelock won at Concord Fight,

An', 'twixt the silences, now fur, now nigh,
Rings the sharp chellenge, hums the low
    reply.

Ez I was settin' so, it warn't long sence,
Mixin' the puffict with the present tense,
I heerd two voices som'ers in the air,
Though, ef I was to die, I can't tell where:
Voices I call 'em: 't was a kind o' sough
Like pine-trees thet the wind 's ageth'rin'
    through ;
An', fact, I thought it *was* the wind a spell,
Then some misdoubted, could n't fairly tell,
Fust sure, then not, jest as you hold an eel,
I knowed, an' did n't, — fin'lly seemed to
    feel
'T was Concord Bridge a talkin' off to kill
With the Stone Spike thet 's druv thru
    Bunker's Hill ;
Whether 't was so, or ef I on'y dreamed,
I could n't say; I tell it ez it seemed.

THE BRIDGE

Wal, neighbor, tell us wut 's turned up
    thet 's new ?
You 're younger 'n I be, — nigher Bos-
    ton, tu :
An' down to Boston, ef you take their
    showin',
Wut they don't know ain't hardly wuth
    the knowin'.
There 's *sunthin'* goin' on, I know : las'
    night
The British sogers killed in our gret fight
(Nigh fifty year they hed n't stirred nor
    spoke)
Made sech a coil you 'd thought a dam hed
    broke :
Why, one he up an' beat a revellee
With his own crossbones on a holler tree,
Till all the graveyards swarmed out like a
    hive
With faces I hain't seen sence Seventy-
    five.
Wut *is* the news ? 'T ain't good, or they 'd
    be cheerin'.
Speak slow an' clear, for I 'm some hard o'
    hearin'.

THE MONIMENT

I don't know hardly ef it 's good or bad, —

THE BRIDGE

At wust, it can't be wus than wut we 've
    had.

THE MONIMENT

You know them envys thet the Rebbles
    sent,
An' Cap'n Wilkes he borried o' the Trent ?

THE BRIDGE

Wut ! they ha'n't hanged 'em ? Then their
    wits is gone !
Thet 's the sure way to make a goose a
    swan !

THE MONIMENT

No : England she *would* hev 'em, *Fee, Faw,
    Fum !*
(Ez though she hed n't fools enough to
    home,)
So they 've returned 'em —

THE BRIDGE

         Hev they ? Wal, by heaven,
Thet 's the wust news I 've heerd sence
    Seventy-seven !
By George, I meant to say, though I de-
    clare
It 's 'most enough to make a deacon swear.

THE MONIMENT

Now don't go off half-cock : folks never
    gains
By usin' pepper-sarse instid o' brains.
Come, neighbor, you don't understan' —

THE BRIDGE

                How ? Hey ?
Not understan' ? Why, wut 's to hender,
    pray ?
Must I go huntin' round to find a chap
To tell me when my face hez hed a slap ?

THE MONIMENT

See here : the British they found out a
    flaw
In Cap'n Wilkes's readin' o' the law :
(They *make* all laws, you know, an' so, o'
    course,
It 's nateral they should understan' their
    force :)
He 'd oughto ha' took the vessel into port,
An' hed her sot on by a reg'lar court ;
She was a mail-ship, an' a steamer, tu,
An' thet, they say, hez changed the pint o'
    view,
Coz the old practice, bein' meant for sails,
Ef tried upon a steamer, kind o' fails ;

You *may* take out despatches, but you mus' n't
Take nary man —

THE BRIDGE

You mean to say, you dus' n't !
Changed pint o' view ! No, no, — it 's overboard
With law an' gospel, when their ox is gored !
I tell ye, England's law, on sea an' land,
Hez ollers ben, " *I 've gut the heaviest hand.*"
Take nary man ? Fine preachin' from *her* lips !
Why, she hez taken hunderds from our ships,
An' would agin, an' swear she had a right to,
Ef we warn't strong enough to be perlite to.
Of all the sarse thet I can call to mind,
England *doos* make the most onpleasant kind :
It 's you 're the sinner ollers, she 's the saint ;
Wut 's good 's all English, all thet is n't ain't ;
Wut profits her is ollers right an' just,
An' ef you don't read Scriptur so, you must ;
She 's praised herself ontil she fairly thinks
There ain't no light in Natur when she winks ;
Hain't she the Ten Comman'ments in her pus ?
Could the world stir 'thout she went, tu, ez nus ?
She ain't like other mortals, thet 's a fact :
She never stopped the habus-corpus act,
Nor specie payments, nor she never yet
Cut down the int'rest on her public debt ;
She don't put down rebellions, lets 'em breed,
An' 's ollers willin' Ireland should secede ;
She 's all thet 's honest, honnable, an' fair,
An' when the vartoos died they made her heir.

THE MONIMENT

Wal, wal, two wrongs don't never make a right ;
Ef we 're mistaken, own up, an' don't fight :
For gracious' sake, ha'n't we enough to du
'thout gettin' up a fight with England, tu ?
She thinks we 're rabble-rid —

THE BRIDGE

An' so we can't
Distinguish 'twixt *You ought n't* an' *You sha'n't !*
She jedges by herself ; she 's no idear
How 't stiddies folks to give 'em their fair sheer :
The odds 'twixt her an' us is plain 's a steeple, —
Her People 's turned to Mob, our Mob 's turned People.

THE MONIMENT

She 's riled jes' now —

THE BRIDGE

Plain proof her cause ain't strong, —
The one thet fust gits mad 's 'most ollers wrong.
Why, sence she helped in lickin' Nap the Fust,
An' pricked a bubble jest agoin' to bust,
With Rooshy, Prooshy, Austry, all assistin',
Th' ain't nut a face but wut she 's shook her fist in,
Ez though she done it all, an' ten times more,
An' nothin' never hed gut done afore,
Nor never could agin, 'thout she wuz spliced
On to one eend an' gin th' old airth a hoist.
She *is* some punkins, thet I wun't deny,
(For ain't she some related to you 'n' I ?)
But there 's a few small intrists here below
Outside the counter o' John Bull an' Co,
An' though they can't conceit how 't should be so,
I guess the Lord druv down Creation's spiles
'thout no *gret* helpin' from the British Isles,
An' could contrive to keep things pooty stiff
Ef they withdrawed from business in a miff ;
I ha'n't no patience with sech swellin' fellers ez
Think God can't forge 'thout them to blow the bellerses.

THE MONIMENT

You 're ollers quick to set your back aridge,
Though 't suits a tom-cat more 'n a sober bridge :

Don't you git het : they thought the thing
was planned ;
They 'll cool off when they come to under-
stand.

THE BRIDGE

Ef *thet*'s wut you expect, you 'll *hev* to wait ;
Folks never understand the folks they hate:
She 'll fin' some other grievance jest ez good,
'fore the month 's out, to git misunderstood.
England cool off ! She 'll do it, ef she sees
She 's run her head into a swarm o' bees.
I ain't so prejudiced ez wut you spose :
I hev thought England was the best thet
goes ;
Remember (no, you can't), when *I* was
reared,
God save the King was all the tune you
heerd :
But it 's enough to turn Wachuset roun'
This stumpin' fellers when you think
they 're down.

THE MONIMENT

But, neighbor, ef they prove their claim at
law,
The best way is to settle, an' not jaw.
An' don't le' 's mutter 'bout the awfle bricks
We 'll give 'em, ef we ketch 'em in a fix :
That 'ere 's most frequently the kin' o' talk
Of critters can't be kicked to toe the chalk;
Your "You 'll see *nex*' time !" an' "Look
out bumby ! "
'Most ollers ends in eatin' umble-pie.
'T wun't pay to scringe to England : will it
pay
To fear thet meaner bully, old "They 'll
say " ?
Suppose they *du* say : words are dreffle
bores,
But they ain't quite so bad ez seventy-fours.
Wut England wants is jest a wedge to fit
Where it 'll help to widen out our split :
She 's found her wedge, an' 't ain't for us to
come
An' lend thé beetle thet 's to drive it home.
For growed-up folks like us 't would be a
scandle,
When we git sarsed, to fly right off the
handle.
England ain't *all* bad, coz she thinks us
blind :
Ef she can't change her skin, she can her
mind ;
An' we shall see her change it double-quick,

Soon ez we 've proved thet we 're a-goin' to
lick.
She an' Columby 's gut to be fas' friends:
For the world prospers by their privit ends:
'T would put the clock back all o' fifty years
Ef they should fall together by the ears.

THE BRIDGE

I 'gree to thet ; she 's nigh us to wut
France is ;
But then she 'll hev to make the fust ad-
vances ;
We 've gut pride, tu, an' gut it by good
rights,
An' ketch *me* stoopin' to pick up the mites
O' condescension she 'll be lettin' fall
When she finds out we ain't dead arter all !
I tell ye wut, it takes more 'n one good week
Afore *my* nose forgits it 's hed a tweak.

THE MONIMENT

She 'll come out right bumby, thet I 'll
engage,
Soon ez she gits to seein' we 're of age ;
This talkin' down o' hers ain't wuth a fuss ;
It 's nat'ral ez nut likin' 't is to us ;
Ef we 're agoin' to prove we *be* growed-up,
'T wun't be by barkin' like a tarrier pup,
But turnin' to an' makin' things ez good
Ez wut we 're ollers braggin' that we could;
We 're boun' to be good friends, an' so
we 'd oughto,
In spite of all the fools both sides the water.

THE BRIDGE

I b'lieve thet 's so ; but hearken in your
ear, —
I 'm older 'n you, — Peace wun't keep house
with Fear :
Ef you want peace, the thing you 've gut tu
du
Is jes' to show you 're up to fightin', tu.
I recollect how sailors' rights was won,
Yard locked in yard, hot gun-lip kissin'
gun :
Why, afore thet, John Bull sot up thet he
Hed gut a kind o' mortgage on the sea;
You 'd thought he held by Gran'ther
Adam's will,
An' ef you knuckle down, *he* 'll think so still.
Better thet all our ships an' all their crews
Should sink to rot in ocean's dreamless ooze,
Each torn flag wavin' chellenge ez it went,
An' each dumb gun a brave man's moni-
ment,

Than seek sech peace ez only cowards
  crave :
Give *me* the peace of dead men or of brave!

THE MONIMENT

I say, ole boy, it ain't the Glorious Fourth:
You'd oughto larned 'fore this wut talk wuz
  worth.
It ain't *our* nose thet gits put out o' jint;
It's England thet gives up her dearest pint.
We've gut, I tell ye now, enough to du
In our own fem'ly fight, afore we're thru.
I hoped, las' spring, jest arter Sumter's
  shame,
When every flag-staff flapped its tethered
  flame,
An' all the people, startled from their
  doubt,
Come must'rin' to the flag with sech a
  shout, —
I hoped to see things settled 'fore this fall,
The Rebbles licked, Jeff Davis hanged, an'
  all;
Then come Bull Run, an' *sence* then I've
  ben waitin'
Like boys in Jennooary thaw for skatin',
Nothin' to du but watch my shadder's trace
Swing, like a ship at anchor, roun' my base,
With daylight's flood an' ebb: it's gittin'
  slow,
An' I 'most think we'd better let 'em go.
I tell ye wut, this war's a-goin' to cost —

THE BRIDGE

An' I tell *you* it wun't be money lost;
Taxes milks dry, but, neighbor, you'll allow
Thet havin' things onsettled kills the cow:
We've gut to fix this thing for good an' all;
It's no use buildin' wut's a-goin' to fall.
I'm older 'n you, an' I've seen things an'
  men,
An' *my* experunce, — tell ye wut it's ben:
Folks thet worked thorough was the ones
  thet thriv,
But bad work follers ye ez long 's ye live;
You can't git red on 't; jest ez sure ez sin,
It's ollers askin' to be done agin:
Ef we should part, it would n't be a week
'Fore your soft-soddered peace would spring
  aleak.
We've turned our cuffs up, but, to put her
  thru,
We must git mad an' off with jackets, tu;
'T wun't du to think thet killin' ain't per-
  lite, —

You've gut to be in airnest, ef you fight;
Why, two thirds o' the Rebbles 'ould cut
  dirt,
Ef they once thought thet Guv'ment meant
  to hurt;
An' I *du* wish our Gin'rals hed in mind
The folks in front more than the folks be-
  hind;
You wun't do much ontil you think it 's God,
An' not constitoounts, thet holds the rod;
We want some more o' Gideon's sword, I
  jedge,
For proclamations ha'n't no gret of edge;
There's nothin' for a cancer but the knife,
Onless you set by 't more than by your life.
I've seen hard times; I see a war begun
Thet folks thet love their bellies never'd
  won;
Pharo's lean kine hung on for seven long
  year;
But when't was done, we did n't count it
  dear;
Why, law an' order, honor, civil right,
Ef they *ain't* wuth it, wut *is* wuth a fight?
I'm older 'n you: the plough, the axe, the
  mill,
All kin's o' labor an' all kin's o' skill,
Would be a rabbit in a wile-cat's claw,
Ef 't warn't for thet slow critter, 'stablished
  law;
Onsettle *thet*, an' all the world goes whiz,
A screw's gut loose in everythin' there is:
Good buttresses once settled, don't you fret
An' stir 'em; take a bridge's word for thet!
Young folks are smart, but all ain't good
  thet 's new;
I guess the gran'thers they knowed sunthin',
  tu.

THE MONIMENT

Amen to thet! build sure in the beginnin':
An' then don't never tech the underpinnin':
Th' older a guv'ment is, the better 't suits;
New ones hunt folks's corns out like new
  boots:
Change jes' for change, is like them big
  hotels
Where they shift plates, an' let ye live on
  smells.

THE BRIDGE

Wal, don't give up afore the ship goes
  down:
It's a stiff gale, but Providence wun't
  drown;

An' God wun't leave us yit to sink or swim,
Ef we don't fail to du wut 's right by Him.
This land o' ourn, I tell ye, 's gut to be
A better country than man ever see.
I feel my sperit swellin' with a cry
Thet seems to say, "Break forth an' pro-
    phesy!"
O strange New World, thet yit wast never
    young,
Whose youth from thee by gripin' need was
    wrung,
Brown foundlin' o' the woods, whose baby-
    bed
Was prowled roun' by the Injun's cracklin'
    tread,
An' who grew'st strong thru shifts an' wants
    an' pains,
Nussed by stern men with empires in their
    brains,
Who saw in vision their young Ishmel strain
With each hard hand a vassal ocean's mane,
Thou, skilled by Freedom an' by gret events
To pitch new States ez Old-World men
    pitch tents,
Thou, taught by Fate to know Jehovah's
    plan
Thet man's devices can't unmake a man,
An' whose free latch-string never was
    drawed in
Against the poorest child of Adam's kin, —
The grave 's not dug where traitor hands
    shall lay
In fearful haste thy murdered corse away!
I see —

Jest here some dogs begun to bark,
So thet I lost old Concord's last remark:
I listened long, but all I seemed to hear
Was dead leaves gossipin' on some birch-
    trees near;
But ez they hed n't no gret things to say,
An' sed 'em often, I come right away,
An', walkin' home'ards, jest to pass the
    time,
I put some thoughts thet bothered me in
    rhyme;
I hain't hed time to fairly try 'em on,
But here they be — it 's

JONATHAN TO JOHN

IT don't seem hardly right, John,
    When both my hands was full,
To stump me to a fight, John, —
    Your cousin, tu, John Bull!

Ole Uncle S. sez he, "I guess
    We know it now," sez he,
"The lion's paw is all the law,
    Accordin' to J. B.,
    Thet 's fit for you an' me!"

You wonder why we 're hot, John?
    Your mark wuz on the guns,
The neutral guns, thet shot, John,
    Our brothers an' our sons:
    Ole Uncle S. sez he, "I guess
    There 's human blood," sez he,
"By fits an' starts, in Yankee hearts,
    Though 't may surprise J. B.
    More 'n it would you an' me."

Ef *I* turned mad dogs loose, John,
    On *your* front-parlor stairs,
Would it jest meet your views, John,
    To wait an' sue their heirs?
    Ole Uncle S. sez he, "I guess,
    I on'y guess," sez he,
"Thet ef Vattel on *his* toes fell,
    'T would kind o' rile J. B.,
    Ez wal ez you an' me!"

Who made the law thet hurts, John,
    Heads I win, — ditto tails?
"*J. B.*" was on his shirts, John,
    Onless my memory fails.
    Ole Uncle S. sez he, "I guess
    (I 'm good at thet)," sez he,
"Thet sauce for goose ain't *jest* the juice
    For ganders with J. B.,
    No more 'n with you or me!"

When your rights was our wrongs, John,
    You did n't stop for fuss, —
Britanny's trident prongs, John,
    Was good 'nough law for us.
    Ole Uncle S. sez he, "I guess,
    Though physic 's good," sez he,
"It does n't foller thet he can swaller
    Prescriptions signed 'J. B.,'
    Put up by you an' me!"

We own the ocean, tu, John:
    You mus' n' take it hard,
Ef we can't think with you, John,
    It 's jest your own back-yard.
    Ole Uncle S. sez he, "I guess,
    Ef *thet* 's his claim," sez he,
"The fencin'-stuff 'll cost enough
    To bust up friend J. B.,
    Ez wal ez you an' me!"

Why talk so dreffle big, John,
Of honor when it meant
You did n't care a fig, John,
But jest for *ten per cent?*
Ole Uncle S. sez he, " I guess
He 's like the rest," sez he :
" When all is done, it 's number one
Thet 's nearest to J. B.,
Ez wal ez t' you an' me !"

We give the critters back, John,
Cos Abram thought 't was right ;
It warn't your bullyin' clack, John,
Provokin' us to fight.
Ole Uncle S. sez he, " I guess
We 've a hard row," sez he,
" To hoe jest now ; but thet, somehow,
May happen to J. B.,
Ez wal ez you an' me !"

We ain't so weak an' poor, John,
With twenty million people,
An' close to every door, John,
A school-house an' a steeple.
Ole Uncle S. sez he, " I guess,
It is a fact," sez he,
" The surest plan to make a Man
Is, think him so, J. B.,
Ez much ez you or me !"

Our folks believe in Law, John ;
An' it 's for her sake, now,
They 've left the axe an' saw, John,
The anvil an' the plough.
Ole Uncle S. sez he, " I guess,
Ef 't warn't for law," sez he,
" There 'd be one shindy from here to
Indy ;
An' thet don't suit J. B.
(When 't ain't 'twixt you an' me !) "

We know we 've got a cause, John,
Thet 's honest, just, an' true ;
We thought 't would win applause, John,
Ef nowheres else, from you.
Ole Uncle S. sez he, " I guess
His love of right," sez he,
" Hangs by a rotten fibre o' cotton :
There 's natur' in J. B.,
Ez wal 'z in you an' me !"

The South says, *"Poor folks down !"* John,
An' *" All men up !"* say we, —
White, yaller, black, an' brown, John :
Now which is your idee ?

Ole Uncle S. sez he, " I guess,
John preaches wal," sez he ;
" But, sermon thru, an' come to *du,*
Why, there 's the old J. B.
A-crowdin' you an' me !"

Shall it be love, or hate, John?
It 's you thet 's to decide ;
Ain't *your* bonds held by Fate, John,
Like all the world's beside ?
Ole Uncle S. sez he, " I guess
Wise men forgive," sez he,
" But not forgit ; an' some time yit
Thet truth may strike J. B.,
Ez wal ez you an' me !"

God means to make this land, John,
Clear thru, from sea to sea,
Believe an' understand, John,
The *wuth* o' bein' free.
Ole Uncle S. sez he, " I guess,
God's price is high," sez he ;
" But nothin' else than wut He sells
Wears long, an' thet J. B.
May larn, like you an' me !"

No. III

BIRDOFREDUM SAWIN, ESQ., TO
MR. HOSEA BIGLOW

With the following Letter from the REV-
EREND HOMER WILBUR, A. M.

TO THE EDITORS OF THE ATLANTIC
MONTHLY

JAALAM, 7th Feb., 1862.

RESPECTED FRIENDS, — If I know my-
self, — and surely a man can hardly be
supposed to have overpassed the limit of
fourscore years without attaining to some
proficiency in that most useful branch of
learning (*e cœlo descendit,* says the pagan
poet), — I have no great smack of that
weakness which would press upon the pub-
lick attention any matter pertaining to my
private affairs. But since the following
letter of Mr. Sawin contains not only a
direct allusion to myself, but that in con-
nection with a topick of interest to all
those engaged in the publick ministrations
of the sanctuary, I may be pardoned for
touching briefly thereupon. Mr. Sawin
was never a stated attendant upon my

preaching, — never, as I believe, even an occasional one, since the erection of the new house (where we now worship) in 1845. He did, indeed, for a time, supply a not unacceptable bass in the choir ; but, whether on some umbrage (*omnibus hoc vitium est cantoribus*) taken against the bass-viol, then, and till his decease in 1850 (*æt.* 77,) under the charge of Mr. Asaph Perley, or, as was reported by others, on account of an imminent subscription for a new bell, he thenceforth absented himself from all outward and visible communion. Yet he seems to have preserved (*altâ mente repostum*), as it were, in the pickle of a mind soured by prejudice, a lasting *scunner*, as he would call it, against our staid and decent form of worship ; for I would rather in that wise interpret his fling, than suppose that any chance tares sown by my pulpit discourses should survive so long, while good seed too often fails to root itself. I humbly trust that I have no personal feeling in the matter ; though I know that, if we sound any man deep enough, our lead shall bring up the mud of human nature at last. The Bretons believe in an evil spirit which they call *ar c'houskezik*, whose office it is to make the congregation drowsy ; and though I have never had reason to think that he was specially busy among my flock, yet have I seen enough to make me sometimes regret the hinged seats of the ancient meeting-house, whose lively clatter, not unwillingly intensified by boys beyond eye-shot of the tithing-man, served at intervals as a wholesome *réveil*. It is true, I have numbered among my parishioners some who are proof against the prophylactick fennel, nay, whose gift of somnolence rivalled that of the Cretan Rip Van Winkle, Epimenides, and who, nevertheless, complained not so much of the substance as of the length of my (by them unheard) discourses. Some ingenious persons of a philosophick turn have assured us that our pulpits were set too high, and that the soporifick tendency increased with the ratio of the angle in which the hearer's eye was constrained to seek the preacher. This were a curious topick for investigation. There can be no doubt that some sermons are pitched too high, and I remember many struggles with the drowsy fiend in

my youth. Happy Saint Anthony of Padua, whose finny acolytes, however they might profit, could never murmur ! *Quare fremuerunt gentes?* Who is he that can twice a week be inspired, or has eloquence (*ut ita dicam*) always on tap ? A good man, and, next to David, a sacred poet (himself, haply, not inexpert of evil in this particular), has said, —

" The worst speak something good : if all want sense,
God takes a text and preacheth patience."

There are one or two other points in Mr. Sawin's letter which I would also briefly animadvert upon. And first, concerning the claim he sets up to a certain superiority of blood and lineage in the people of our Southern States, now unhappily in rebellion against lawful authority and their own better interests. There is a sort of opinions, anachronisms at once and anachorisms, foreign both to the age and the country, that maintain a feeble and buzzing existence, scarce to be called life, like winter flies, which in mild weather crawl out from obscure nooks and crannies to expatiate in the sun, and sometimes acquire vigor enough to disturb with their enforced familiarity the studious hours of the scholar. One of the most stupid and pertinacious of these is the theory that the Southern States were settled by a class of emigrants from the Old World socially superior to those who founded the institutions of New England. The Virginians especially lay claim to this generosity of lineage, which were of no possible account, were it not for the fact that such superstitions are sometimes not without their effect on the course of human affairs. The early adventurers to Massachusetts at least paid their passages ; no felons were ever shipped thither ; and though it be true that many deboshed younger brothers of what are called good families may have sought refuge in Virginia, it is equally certain that a great part of the early deportations thither were the sweepings of the London streets and the leavings of the London stews. It was this my Lord Bacon had in mind when he wrote : " It is a shameful and unblessed thing to take the scum of people and wicked condemned men to be the people with whom you plant." That certain names are found there is nothing to the purpose, for, even had an *alias* been beyond the invention of the knaves of that generation, it is known that servants were often called by their masters' names, as slaves are now. On what the heralds call the spindle side, some, at least, of the oldest Virginian families are descended from matrons who were exported and sold for so many hogsheads of tobacco the head. So notorious was this, that it became one of the jokes of contemporary playwrights, not only that men bankrupt in purse and character were "food for the Plantations" (and this before the settlement of New England), but also that any drab would suffice to wive such pitiful adventurers. "Never choose a wife as if you were going to Virginia," says Middleton in one of his comedies. The mule is apt to forget all but the equine side of his pedigree. How early the counterfeit nobility of the Old Dominion became a topick of ridicule in the Mother Country may be learned from a play of Mrs. Behn's, founded on the Rebellion of Bacon : for even these kennels of literature may yield a fact or two to pay the raking. Mrs. Flirt, the keeper of a Virginia ordinary, calls herself the daughter of a baronet, "undone in the late rebellion," — her father having in truth been a tailor, — and three of the Council, assuming to themselves an equal splendor of origin, are shown to have been, one "a broken exciseman who came over a poor servant," another a tinker transported for theft, and the third "a common pickpocket often flogged at the cart's tail." The ancestry of South Carolina will as little pass muster at the Herald's Visitation, though I hold them to have been more reputable, inasmuch as many of them were honest tradesmen and artisans, in some measure exiles for conscience' sake, who would have smiled at the high-flying nonsense of their descendants. Some of the more respectable were Jews. The absurdity of supposing a population of eight millions all sprung from gentle loins in the course of a century and a half is too manifest for confutation. But of what use to discuss the matter ? An expert genealogist will provide any solvent man with a *genus et proavos* to order. My Lord Burleigh used to say, with Aristotle and the Emperor Frederick II. to back him, that

"nobility was ancient riches," whence also the Spanish were wont to call their nobles *ricos hombres*, and the aristocracy of America are the descendants of those who first became wealthy, by whatever means. Petroleum will in this wise be the source of much good blood among our posterity. The aristocracy of the South, such as it is, has the shallowest of all foundations, for it is only skin-deep, — the most odious of all, for, while affecting to despise trade, it traces its origin to a successful traffick in men, women, and children, and still draws its chief revenues thence. And though, as Doctor Chamberlayne consolingly says in his "Present State of England," "to become a Merchant of Foreign Commerce, without serving any Apprentisage, hath been allowed no disparagement to a Gentleman born, especially to a younger Brother," yet I conceive that he would hardly have made a like exception in favour of the particular trade in question. Oddly enough this trade reverses the ordinary standards of social respectability no less than of morals, for the retail and domestick is as creditable as the wholesale and foreign is degrading to him who follows it. Are our morals, then, no better than *mores* after all ? I do not believe that such aristocracy as exists at the South (for I hold with Marius, *fortissimum quemque generosissimum*) will be found an element of anything like persistent strength in war, — thinking the saying of Lord Bacon (whom one quaintly called *inductionis dominus et Verulamii*) as true as it is pithy, that "the more gentlemen, ever the lower books of subsidies." It is odd enough as an historical precedent, that, while the fathers of New England were laying deep in religion, education, and freedom the basis of a polity which has substantially outlasted any then existing, the first work of the founders of Virginia, as may be seen in Wingfield's "Memorial," was conspiracy and rebellion, — odder yet, as showing the changes which are wrought by circumstance, that the first insurrection in South Carolina was against the aristocratical scheme of the Proprietary Government. I do not find that the cuticular aristocracy of the South has added anything to the refinements of civilization except the carrying of bowie-knives and the chewing of tobacco, — a high-toned

Southern gentleman being commonly not only *quadrumanous* but *quidruminant.*

I confess that the present letter of Mr. Sawin increases my doubts as to the sincerity of the convictions which he professes, and I am inclined to think that the triumph of the legitimate Government, sure sooner or later to take place, will find him and a large majority of his newly adopted fellow-citizens (who hold with Dædalus, the primal sitter-on-the-fence, that *medium tenere tutissimum*) original Union men. The criticisms towards the close of his letter on certain of our failings are worthy to be seriously perpended; for he is not, as I think, without a spice of vulgar shrewdness. *Fas est et ab hoste doceri:* there is no reckoning without your host. As to the good-nature in us which he seems to gird at, while I would not consecrate a chapel, as they have not scrupled to do in France, to *Nôtre Dame de la Haine* (Our Lady of Hate), yet I cannot forget that the corruption of good-nature is the generation of laxity of principle. Good-nature is our national characteristick; and though it be, perhaps, nothing more than a culpable weakness or cowardice, when it leads us to put up tamely with manifold impositions and breaches of implied contracts (as too frequently in our publick conveyances) it becomes a positive crime when it leads us to look unresentfully on peculation, and to regard treason to the best Government that ever existed as something with which a gentleman may shake hands without soiling his fingers. I do not think the gallows-tree the most profitable member of our *Sylva ;* but, since it continues to be planted, I would fain see a Northern limb ingrafted on it, that it may bear some other fruit than loyal Tennesseeans.

A relick has recently been discovered on the east bank of Bushy Brook in North Jaalam, which I conceive to be an inscription in Runick characters relating to the early expedition of the Northmen to this continent. I shall make fuller investigations, and communicate the result in due season. Respectfully,

Your obedient servant,
HOMER WILBUR, A. M.

P. S. — I inclose a year's subscription from Deacon Tinkham.

I HED it on my min' las' time, when I to
    write ye started,
To tech the leadin' featurs o' my gittin' me
    convarted ;
But, ez my letters hez to go clearn roun'
    by way o' Cuby,
'T wun't seem no staler now than then, by
    th' time it gits where you be.
You know up North, though secs an' things
    air plenty ez you please,
Ther' warn't nut one on 'em thet come jes'
    square with my idees :
They all on 'em wuz too much mixed with
    Covenants o' Works,
An' would hev answered jest ez wal for
    Afrikins an' Turks,
Fer where 's a Christian's privilege an' his
    rewards ensuin',
Ef 't ain't perfessin' right and eend 'thout
    nary need o' doin' ?
I dessay they suit workin'-folks thet ain't
    noways pertic'lar,
But nut your Southun gen'leman thet
    keeps his parpendic'lar ;
I don't blame nary man thet casts his lot
    along o' *his* folks,
But ef you cal'late to save *me*, 't must be
    with folks thet *is* folks ;
Cov'nants o' works go 'ginst my grain, but
    down here I 've found out
The true fus'-fem'ly A 1 plan, — here 's
    how it come about.
When I fus' sot up with Miss S., sez she to
    me, sez she,
" Without you git religion, Sir, the thing
    can't never be ;
Nut but wut I respeck," sez she, " your
    intellectle part,
But you wun't noways du for me athout a
    change o' heart :
Nothun religion works wal North, but it 's
    ez soft ez spruce,
Compared to ourn, for keepin' sound," sez
    she, " upon the goose ;
A day's experunce 'd prove to ye, ez easy 'z
    pull a trigger,
It takes the Southun pint o' view to raise
    ten bales a nigger ;
You 'll fin' thet human natur', South, ain't
    wholesome more 'n skin-deep,
An' once 't a darkie 's took with it, he wun't
    be wuth his keep."
" How *shell* I git it, Ma'am ? " — sez
    I. " Attend the nex' camp-meet-
    in',"

Sez she, "an' it 'll come to ye ez cheap ez
    onbleached sheetin'.'"
Wal, so I went along an' hearn most an
    impressive sarmon
About besprinklin' Afriky with fourth-
    proof dew o' Harmon :
He did n't put no weaknin' in, but gin it tu
    us hot,
'Z ef he an' Satan 'd ben two bulls in one
    five-acre lot :
I don't purtend to foller him, but give ye
    jes' the heads;
For pulpit ellerkence, you know, 'most
    ollers kin' o' spreads.
Ham's seed wuz gin to us in chairge, an'
    should n't we be li'ble
In Kingdom Come, ef we kep' back their
    priv'lege in the Bible ?
The cusses an' the promerses make one gret
    chain, an' ef
You snake one link out here, one there, how
    much on 't ud be lef' ?
All things wuz gin to man for 's use, his
    sarvice, an' delight;
An' don't the Greek an' Hebrew words thet
    mean a Man mean White ?
Ain't it belittlin' the Good Book in all its
    proudes' featurs
To think 't wuz wrote for black an' brown
    an' 'lasses-colored creaturs,
Thet could n' read it, ef they would, nor
    ain't by lor allowed to,
But ough' to take wut we think suits their
    naturs, an' be proud to ?
Warn't it more prof'table to bring your raw
    materil thru
Where you can work it inta grace an' inta
    cotton, tu,
Than sendin' missionaries out where fevers
    might defeat 'em,
An' ef the butcher did n' call, their p'rish-
    ioners might eat 'em ?
An' then, agin, wut airthly use ? Nor
    'twarn't our fault, in so fur
Ez Yankee skippers would keep on atotin'
    on 'em over.
'T improved the whites by savin' 'em from
    ary need o' workin',
An' kep' the blacks from bein' lost thru
    idleness an' shirkin' ;
We took to 'em ez nat'ral ez a barn-owl
    doos to mice,
An' hed our hull time on our hands to keep
    us out o' vice;

It made us feel ez pop'lar ez a hen doos
    with one chicken,
An' fill our place in Natur's scale by givin'
    'em a lickin':
For why should Cæsar git his dues more 'n
    Juno, Pomp, an' Cuffy ?
It 's justifyin' Ham to spare a nigger when
    he 's stuffy.
Where 'd their soles go tu, like to know, ef
    we should let 'em ketch
Freeknowledgism an' Fourierism an' Speri-
    toolism an' sech ?
When Satan sets himself to work to raise
    his very bes' muss,
He scatters roun' onscriptur'l views relatin'
    to Ones'mus.
You 'd ough' to seen, though, how his facs
    an' argymunce an' figgers
Drawed tears o' real conviction from a lot
    o' pen'tent niggers!
It warn't like Wilbur's meetin', where
    you 're shet up in a pew,
Your dickeys sorrin' off your ears, an' bilin'
    to be thru;
Ther' wuz a tent clost by thet hed a kag o'
    sunthin' in it,
Where you could go, ef you wuz dry, an'
    damp ye in a minute;
An' ef you did dror off a spell, ther' wuz
    n't no occasion
To lose the thread, because, ye see, he
    bellered like all Bashan.
It 's dry work follerin' argymunce an' so,
    'twix' this an' thet,
I felt conviction weighin' down somehow
    inside my hat;
It growed an' growed like Jonah's gourd,
    a kin' o' whirlin' ketched me,
Ontil I fin'lly clean gin out an' owned up
    thet he 'd fetched me;
An' when nine tenths o' th' perrish took to
    tumblin' roun' an' hollerin',
I did n' fin' no gret in th' way o' turnin' tu
    an' follerin'.
Soon ez Miss S. see thet, sez she, "Thet 's
    wut I call wuth seein' !
Thet 's actin' like a reas'nable an' intellectle
    bein' ! "
An' so we fin'lly made it up, concluded to
    hitch hosses,
An' here I be 'n my ellermunt among crea-
    tion's bosses;
Arter I 'd drawed sech heaps o' blanks,
    Fortin at last hez sent a prize,

An' chose me for a shinin' light o' mission-
ary entaprise.

This leads me to another pint on which I 've
changed my plan
O' thinkin' so 's 't I might become a
straight-out Southun man.
Miss S. (her maiden name wuz Higgs, o'
the fus' fem'ly here)
On her Ma's side 's all Juggernot, on Pa's
all Cavileer,
An' sence I 've merried into her an' stept
into her shoes,
It ain't more 'n nateral thet I should mod-
derfy my views:
I 've ben a-readin' in Debow ontil I 've
fairly gut
So 'nlightened thet I 'd full ez lives ha' ben
a Dook ez nut;
An' when we 've laid ye all out stiff, an'
Jeff hez gut his crown,
An' comes to pick his nobles out, *wun't* this
child be in town!
We 'll hev an Age o' Chivverlry surpassin'
Mister Burke's,
Where every fem'ly is fus'-best an' nary
white man works:
Our system 's sech, the thing 'll root ez easy
ez a tater;
For while your lords in furrin parts ain't
noways marked by natur',
Nor sot apart from ornery folks in featurs
nor in figgers,
Ef ourn 'll keep their faces washed, you 'll
know 'em from their niggers.
Ain't *sech* things wuth secedin' for, an'
gittin' red o' you
Thet waller in your low idees, an' will tell
all is blue?
Fact is, we *air* a diff'rent race, an' I, for
one, don't see,
Sech havin' ollers ben the case, how w' ever
did agree.
It 's sunthin' thet you lab'rin'-folks up
North hed ough' to think on,
Thet Higgses can't bemean themselves to
rulin' by a Lincoln, —
Thet men, (an' guv'nors, tu,) thet hez sech
Normal names ez Pickens,
Accustomed to no kin' o' work, 'thout 't is
to givin' lickins,
Can't measure votes with folks thet get
their livins from their farms,
An' prob'ly think thet Law 's ez good ez
hevin' coats o' arms.

Sence I 've ben here, I 've hired a chap to
look about for me
To git me a transplantable an' thrifty
fem'ly-tree,
An' he tells *me* the Sawins is ez much o'
Normal blood
Ez Pickens an' the rest on 'em, an' older 'n
Noah's flood.
Your Normal schools wun 't turn ye into
Normals, for it 's clear,
Ef eddykatin' done the thing, they 'd be
some skurcer here.
Pickenses, Boggses, Pettuses, Magoffins,
Letchers, Polks, —
Where can you scare up names like them
among your mudsill folks?
Ther 's nothin' to compare with 'em, you 'd
fin', ef you should glance,
Among the tip-top femerlies in Englan',
nor in France:
I 've hearn frum 'sponsible men whose
word wuz full ez good 's their
note,
Men thet can run their face for drinks, an'
keep a Sunday coat,
That they wuz all on 'em come down, an'
come down pooty fur,
From folks thet, 'thout their crowns
wuz on, ou' doors would n' never
stir,
Nor thet ther' warn't a Southun man but
wut wuz *primy fashy*
O' the bes' blood in Europe, yis, an' Afriky
an' Ashy:
Sech bein' the case, is 't likely we should
bend like cotton wickin',
Or set down under anythin' so low-lived ez
a lickin'?
More 'n this, — hain't we the literatoor an
science, tu, by gorry?
Hain't we them intellectle twins, them
giants, Simms an' Maury,
Each with full twice the ushle brains, like
nothin' thet I know,
'thout 't wuz a double-headed calf I see
once to a show?

For all thet, I warn't jest at fust in favor
o' secedin';
I wuz for layin' low a spell to find out
where 't wuz leadin',
For hevin' South-Carliny try her hand at
sepritnationin',
She takin' resks an' findin' funds, an' we co-
operationin', —

I mean a kin' o' hangin' roun' an' settin' on
the fence,
Till Prov'dunce pinted how to jump an'
save the most expense;
I recollected thet 'ere mine o' lead to
Shiraz Centre
Thet bust up Jabez Pettibone, an' did n't
want to ventur'
'Fore I wuz sartin wut come out ud pay for
wut went in,
For swappin' silver off for lead ain't the
sure way to win;
(An', fact, it *doos* look now ez though —
but folks must live an' larn —
We should git lead, an' more 'n we want,
out o' the Old Consarn;)
But when I see a man so wise an' honest
ez Buchanan
A-lettin' us hev all the forts an' all the
arms an' cannon,
Admittin' we wuz nat'lly right an' you wuz
nat'lly wrong,
Coz you wuz lab'rin'-folks an' we wuz wut
they call *bong-tong*,
An' coz there warn't no fight in ye more 'n
in a mashed potater,
While two o' *us* can't skurcely meet but
wut we fight by natur',
An' th' ain't a bar-room here would pay for
openin' on 't a night,
Without it giv the priverlege o' bein' shot
at sight,
Which proves we 're Natur's noblemen,
with whom it don't surprise
The British aristoxy should feel boun' to
sympathize, —
Seein' all this, an' seein', tu, the thing wuz
strikin' roots
While Uncle Sam sot still in hopes thet
some one 'd bring his boots,
I thought th' ole Union's hoops wuz off,
an' let myself be sucked in
To rise a peg an' jine the crowd thet went
for reconstructin', —
Thet is to hev the pardnership under th'
ole name continner
Jest ez it wuz, we drorrin' pay, you findin'
bone an' sinner, —
On'y to put it in the bond, an' enter 't in
the journals,
Thet you 're the nat'ral rank an' file, an'
we the nat'ral kurnels.

Now this I thought a fees'ble plan, thet
'ud work smooth ez grease,

Suitin' the Nineteenth Century an' Upper
Ten idees,
An' there I meant to stick, an' so did most
o' th' leaders, tu;
Coz we all thought the chance wuz good o'
puttin' on it thru ;
But Jeff he hit upon a way o' helpin' on us
forrard
By bein' unannermous, — a trick you ain't
quite up to, Norrard.
A Baldin hain't no more 'f a chance with
them new apple-corers
Than folks's oppersition views aginst the
Ringtail Roarers ;
They 'll take 'em out on him 'bout east, —
one canter on a rail
Makes a man feel unannermous ez Jonah
in the whale ;
Or ef he 's a slow-moulded cuss thet can't
seem quite t' 'gree,
He gits the noose by tellergraph upon the
nighes' tree :
Their mission-work with Afrikins hez put
'em up, thet 's sartin,
To all the mos' across-lot ways o' preachin'
an' convartin' ;
I 'll bet my hat th' ain't nary priest, nor all
on 'em together,
Thet cairs conviction to the min' like Rev-
eren' Taranfeather ;
Why, he sot up with me one night, an' la-
bored to sech purpose,
Thet (ez an owl by daylight 'mongst a
flock o' teazin' chirpers
Sees clearer 'n mud the wickedness o' eatin'
little birds)
I see my error an' agreed to shen it arter-
wurds ;
An' I should say, (to jedge our folks by
facs in my possession,)
Thet three 's Unannermous where one 's a
'Riginal Secession ;
So it 's a thing you fellers North may safely
bet your chink on,
Thet we 're all water-proofed agin th'
usurpin' reign o' Lincoln.

Jeff 's *some*. He 's gut another plan thet hez
pertic'lar merits,
In givin' things a cheerfle look an' stiffnin'
loose-hung sperits ;
For while your million papers, wut with
lyin' an' discussin',
Keep folks's tempers all on eend a-fumin'
an' a-fussin',

A-wondrin' this an' guessin' thet, an'
dreadin' every night
The breechin' o' the Univarse 'll break
afore it 's light,
Our papers don't purtend to print on'y wut
Guv'ment choose,
An' thet insures us all to git the very best
o' noose :
Jeff hez it of all sorts an' kines, an' sarves
it out ez wanted,
So 's 't every man gits wut he likes an' no-
body ain't scanted ;
Sometimes it 's vict'ries (they 're 'bout
all ther' is that 's cheap down
here,)
Sometimes it 's France an' England on the
jump to interfere.
Fact is, the less the people know o' wut
ther' is a-doin',
The hendier 't is for Guv'ment, sence it
henders trouble brewin' ;
An' noose is like a shinplaster, — it 's good,
ef you believe it,
Or, wut 's all same, the other man thet 's
goin' to receive it :
Ef you 've a son in th' army, wy, it 's com-
fortin' to hear
He 'll hev no gretter resk to run than seein'
th' in'my's rear,
Coz, ef an F. F. looks at 'em, they ollers
break an' run,
Or wilt right down ez debtors will thet
stumble on a dun,
(An' this, ef an'thin', proves the wuth o'
proper fem'ly pride,
Fer sech mean shucks ez creditors are all
on Lincoln's side) ;
Ef I hev scrip thet wun't go off no more 'n
a Belgin rifle,
An' read thet it 's at par on 'Change, it
makes me feel deli'fle;
It 's cheerin', tu, where every man mus'
fortify his bed,
To hear thet Freedom 's the one thing our
darkies mos'ly dread,
An' thet experunce, time 'n' agin, to Dixie's
Land hez shown
Ther' 's nothin' like a powder-cask fer a
stiddy corner-stone ;
Ain't it ez good ez nuts, when salt is sellin'
by the ounce
For its own weight in Treash'ry-bons, (ef
bought in small amounts,)
When even whiskey 's gittin' skurce an
sugar can't be found,

To know thet all the ellerments o' luxury
abound ?
An' don't it glorify sal'-pork, to come to
understand
It 's wut the Richmon' editors call fatness
o' the land !
Nex' thing to knowin' you 're well off is
nut to know when y' ain't ;
An' ef Jeff says all 's goin' wal, who 'll
ventur' t' say it ain't ?

This cairn the Constitooshun roun' ez Jeff
doos in his hat
Is hendier a dreffle sight, an' comes more
kin' o' pat.
I tell ye wut, my jedgment is you 're pooty
sure to fail,
Ez long 'z the head keeps turnin' back for
counsel to the tail :
Th' advantiges of our consarn for bein'
prompt air gret,
While, 'long o' Congress, you can't strike,
'f you git an iron het ;
They bother roun' with argooin', an' va-
r'ous sorts o' foolin',
To make sure ef it 's leg'lly het, an' all the
while it 's coolin',
So 's 't when you come to strike, it ain't no
gret to wish ye j'y on,
An' hurts the hammer 'z much or more ez
wut it doos the iron,
Jeff don't allow no jawin'-sprees for three
months at a stretch,
Knowin' the ears long speeches suits air
mostly made to metch ;
He jes' ropes in your tonguey chaps an'
reg'lar ten-inch bores
An' lets 'em play at Congress, ef they 'll
du it with closed doors ;
So they ain't no more bothersome than ef
we 'd took an' sunk 'em,
An' yit enj'y th' exclusive right to one
another's Buncombe
'thout doin' nobody no hurt, an' 'thout its
costin' nothin',
Their pay bein' jes' Confedrit funds, they
findin' keep an' clothin' ;
They taste the sweets o' public life, an'
plan their little jobs,
An' suck the Treash'ry (no gret harm, for
it 's ez dry ez cobs,)
An' go thru all the motions jest ez safe ez
in a prison,
An' hev their business to themselves, while
Buregard hez hisn :

Ez long 'z he gives the Hessians fits, com-
  mittees can't make bother
'bout whether 't 's done the legle way or
  whether 't 's done tother.
An' *I* tell *you* you 've gut to larn thet War
  ain't one long teeter
Betwixt *I wan' to* an' *'T wun't du*, debatin'
  like a skeetur
Afore he lights, — all is, to give the other
  side a millin',
An' arter thet 's done, th' ain't no resk but
  wut the lor 'll be willin' ;
No metter wut the guv'ment is, ez nigh ez
  I can hit it,
A lickin' 's constitooshunal, pervidin' *We*
  don't git it.
Jeff don't stan' dilly-dallyin', afore he takes
  a fort,
(With no one in,) to git the leave o' the
  nex' Soopreme Court,
Nor don't want forty-'leven weeks o' jawin'
  an' expoundin',
To prove a nigger hez a right to save him,
  ef he 's drowndin' ;
Whereas ole Abe 'ud sink afore he 'd let a
  darkie boost him,
Ef Taney should n't come along an' hed n't
  interdooced him.
It ain't your twenty millions thet 'll ever
  block Jeff's game,
But one Man thet wun't let 'em jog jest ez
  he 's takin' aim :
Your numbers they may strengthen ye or
  weaken ye, ez 't heppens
They 're willin' to be helpin' hands or
  wuss-'n-nothin' cap'ns.

I 've chose my side, an' 't ain't no odds ef I
  wuz drawed with magnets,
Or ef I thought it prudenter to jine the
  nighes' bagnets ;
I 've made my ch'ice, an' ciphered out,
  from all I see an' heard,
Th' ole Constitooshun never 'd git her decks
  for action cleared,
Long 'z you elect for Congressmen poor
  shotes thet want to go
Coz they can't seem to git their grub no
  otherways than so,
An' let your bes' men stay to home coz they
  wun't show ez talkers,
Nor can't be hired to fool ye an' sof'-soap
  ye at a caucus, —
Long 'z ye set by Rotashun more 'n ye do
  by folks's merits,

Ez though experunce thriv by change o'
  sile, like corn an' kerrits, —
Long 'z you allow a critter's "claims" coz,
  spite o' shoves an' tippins,
He 's kep' his private pan jest where
  't would ketch mos' public drip-
  pin's,
Long 'z A. 'll turn tu an' grin' B. 's exe, ef
  B. 'll help him grin' hisn,
(An' thet 's the main idee by which your
  leadin' men hev risen,) —
Long 'z you let *ary* exe be groun', 'less 't is
  to cut the weasan'
O' sneaks thet dunno till they 're told wut
  is an' wut ain't Treason, —
Long 'z ye give out commissions to a lot o'
  peddlin' drones
Thet trade in whiskey with their men an'
  skin 'em to their bones, —
Long 'z ye sift out "safe" canderdates thet
  no one ain't afeard on
Coz they 're so thund'rin' eminent for bein'
  never heard on,
An' hain't no record, ez it 's called, for
  folks to pick a hole in,
Ez ef it hurt a man to hev a body with a
  soul in,
An' it wuz ostentashun to be showin' on 't
  about,
When half his feller-citizens contrive to du
  without, —
Long 'z you suppose your votes can turn
  biled kebbage into brain,
An' ary man thet 's pop'lar 's fit to drive a
  lightnin'-train, —
Long 'z you believe democracy means *I 'm
  ez good ez you be*,
An' that a feller from the ranks can't be a
  knave or booby, —
Long 'z Congress seems purvided, like yer
  street-cars an' yer 'busses,
With ollers room for jes' one more o' your
  spiled-in-bakin' cusses,
Dough 'thout the emptins of a soul, an' yit
  with means about 'em
(Like essence-peddlers [1]) thet 'll make
  folks long to be without 'em,
Jes heavy 'nough to turn a scale thet 's
  doubtfle the wrong way,
An' make their nat'ral arsenal o' bein' nasty
  pay, —
Long 'z them things last, (an' *I* don't see
  no gret signs of improvin',)

[1] A rustic euphemism for the American variety of
the *Mephitis*.   H. W.

I sha'n't up stakes, not hardly yit, nor 't
 would n't pay for movin';
For, 'fore you lick us, it 'll be the long'st
 day ever *you* see.
Yourn, (ez I 'xpec' to be nex' spring,)
 B., MARKISS O' BIG BOOSY.

No. IV

A MESSAGE OF JEFF DAVIS IN SECRET SESSION

Conjecturally reported by H. BIGLOW

TO THE EDITORS OF THE ATLANTIC
MONTHLY

JAALAM, 10 March, 1862.

GENTLEMEN, — My leisure has been so
entirely occupied with the hitherto fruitless
endeavour to decypher the Runick inscrip-
tion whose fortunate discovery I mentioned
in my last communication, that I have not
found time to discuss, as I had intended,
the great problem of what we are to do with
slavery, — a topick on which the publick
mind in this place is at present more than
ever agitated. What my wishes and hopes
are I need not say, but for safe conclusions
I do not conceive that we are yet in posses-
sion of facts enough on which to bottom
them with certainty. Acknowledging the
hand of Providence, as I do, in all events,
I am sometimes inclined to think that they
are wiser than we, and am willing to wait
till we have made this continent once more
a place where freemen can live in security
and honour, before assuming any further
responsibility. This is the view taken by
my neighbour Habakkuk Sloansure, Esq.,
the president of our bank, whose opinion in
the practical affairs of life has great weight
with me, as I have generally found it to be
justified by the event, and whose counsel,
had I followed it, would have saved me
from an unfortunate investment of a con-
siderable part of the painful economies of
half a century in the Northwest-Passage
Tunnel. After a somewhat animated discus-
sion with this gentleman a few days since, I
expanded, on the *audi alteram partem* prin-
ciple, something which he happened to say
by way of illustration, into the following
fable.

FESTINA LENTE

ONCE on a time there was a pool
Fringed all about with flag-leaves cool
And spotted with cow-lilies garish,
Of frogs and pouts the ancient parish.
Alders the creaking redwings sink on,
Tussocks that house blithe Bob o' Lincoln
Hedged round the unassailed seclusion,
Where muskrats piled their cells Carthusian;
And many a moss-embroidered log,
The watering-place of summer frog,
Slept and decayed with patient skill,
As watering-places sometimes will.

Now in this Abbey of Theleme,
Which realized the fairest dream
That ever dozing bull-frog had,
Sunned on a half-sunk lily-pad,
There rose a party with a mission
To mend the polliwogs' condition,
Who notified the sélectmen
To call a meeting there and then.
"Some kind of steps," they said, "are needed:
They don't come on so fast as we did:
Let 's dock their tails; if that don't make 'em
Frogs by brevet, the Old One take 'em!
That boy, that came the other day
To dig some flag-root down this way,
His jack-knife left, and 't is a sign
That Heaven approves of our design:
'T were wicked not to urge the step on,
When Providence has sent the weapon."

Old croakers, deacons of the mire,
That led the deep batrachian choir,
Uk! Uk! Caronk! with bass that might
Have left Lablache's out of sight,
Shook nobby heads, and said, "No go!
You 'd better let 'em try to grow:
Old Doctor Time is slow, but still
He does know how to make a pill."

But vain was all their hoarsest bass,
Their old experience out of place,
And spite of croaking and entreating,
The vote was carried in marsh-meeting.

"Lord knows," protest the polliwogs,
"We 're anxious to be grown-up frogs;
But don't push in to do the work
Of Nature till she prove a shirk;
'T is not by jumps that she advances,
But wins her way by circumstances:
Pray, wait awhile, until you know
We 're so contrived as not to grow;
Let Nature take her own direction,
And she 'll absorb our imperfection;
You might n't like 'em to appear with,
But we must have the things to steer with."

"No," piped the party of reform,
"All great results are ta'en by storm;
Fate holds her best gifts till we show
We 've strength to make her let them go;
The Providence that works in history,

And seems to some folks such a mystery,
Does not creep slowly on *incog.*,
But moves by jumps, a mighty frog;
No more reject the Age's chrism,
Your queues are an anachronism;
No more the Future's promise mock,
But lay your tails upon the block,
Thankful that we the means have voted
To have you thus to frogs promoted."

The thing was done, the tails were cropped,
And home each philotadpole hopped,
In faith rewarded to exult,
And wait the beautiful result.
Too soon it came; our pool, so long
The theme of patriot bull-frog's song,
Next day was reeking, fit to smother,
With heads and tails that missed each other, —
Here snoutless tails, there tailless snouts;
The only gainers were the pouts.

MORAL

From lower to the higher next,
Not to the top, is Nature's text;
And embryo Good, to reach full stature,
Absorbs the Evil in its nature.

I think that nothing will ever give permanent peace and security to this continent but the extirpation of Slavery therefrom, and that the occasion is nigh; but I would do nothing hastily or vindictively, nor presume to jog the elbow of Providence. No desperate measures for me till we are sure that all others are hopeless, — *flectere si nequeo* SUPEROS, *Acheronta movebo.* To make Emancipation a reform instead of a revolution is worth a little patience, that we may have the Border States first, and then the non-slaveholders of the Cotton States, with us in principle, — a consummation that seems to be nearer than many imagine. *Fiat justitia, ruat cœlum,* is not to be taken in a literal sense by statesmen, whose problem is to get justice done with as little jar as possible to existing order, which has at least so much of heaven in it that it is not chaos. Our first duty toward our enslaved brother is to educate him, whether he be white or black. The first need of the free black is to elevate himself according to the standard of this material generation. So soon as the Ethiopian goes in his chariot, he will find not only Apostles, but Chief Priests and Scribes and Pharisees willing to ride with him.

"Nil habet infelix paupertas durius in se
Quam quod ridiculos homines facit."

I rejoice in the President's late Message, which at last proclaims the Government on the side of freedom, justice, and sound policy.

As I write, comes the news of our disaster at Hampton Roads. I do not understand the supineness which, after fair warning, leaves wood to an unequal conflict with iron. It is not enough merely to have the right on our side, if we stick to the old flint-lock of tradition. I have observed in my parochial experience (*haud ignarus mali*) that the Devil is prompt to adopt the latest inventions of destructive warfare, and may thus take even such a three-decker as Bishop Butler at an advantage. It is curious, that, as gunpowder made armour useless on shore, so armour is having its revenge by baffling its old enemy at sea; and that, while gunpowder robbed land warfare of nearly all its picturesqueness to give even greater stateliness and sublimity to a sea-fight, armour bids fair to degrade the latter into a squabble between two iron-shelled turtles.

Yours, with esteem and respect,
HOMER WILBUR, A. M.

P. S. — I had wellnigh forgotten to say that the object of this letter is to enclose a communication from the gifted pen of Mr. Biglow.

I SENT you a messige, my friens, t' other
    day,
To tell you I 'd nothin' pertickler to say:
't wuz the day our new nation gut kin' o'
    stillborn,
So 't wuz my pleasant dooty t' acknow-
    ledge the corn,
An' I see clearly then, ef I did n't before,
Thet the *augur* in inauguration means *bore.*
I need n't tell *you* thet my messige wuz
    written
To diffuse correc' notions in France an'
    Gret Britten,
An' agin to impress on the poppylar mind
The comfort an' wisdom o' goin' it blind, —
To say thet I did n't abate not a hooter
O' my faith in a happy an' glorious futur',
Ez rich in each soshle an' p'litickle blessin'
Ez them thet we now hed the joy o' pos-
    sessin',
With a people united, an' longin' to die
For wut *we* call their country, without ask-
    in' why,

An' all the gret things we concluded to
    slope for
Ez much within reach now ez ever — to
    hope for.
We 've gut all the ellerments, this very
    hour,
Thet make up a fus'-class, self-governin'
    power:
We 've a war, an' a debt, an' a flag; an' ef
    this
Ain't to be inderpendunt, why, wut on airth
    is ?
An' nothin' now henders our takin' our
    station
Ez the freest, enlightenedest, civerlized
    nation,
Built up on our bran'-new politickle thesis
Thet a Gov'ment's fust right is to tumble
    to pieces, —
I say nothin' henders our takin' our place
Ez the very fus'-best o' the whole human
    race,
A spittin' tobacker ez proud ez you please
On Victory's bes' carpets, or loafin' at
    ease
In the Tool'ries front-parlor, discussin' af-
    fairs
With our heels on the backs o' Napoleon's
    new chairs,
An' princes a-mixin' our cocktails an'
    slings, —
Excep', wal, excep' jest a very few things,
Sech ez navies an' armies an' wherewith to
    pay,
An' gettin' our sogers to run t' other way,
An' not be too over-pertickler in tryin'
To hunt up the very las' ditches to die in.

Ther' are critters so base thet they want it
    explained
Jes' wut is the totle amount thet we 've
    gained,
Ez ef we could maysure stupenjious events
By the low Yankee stan'ard o' dollars an'
    cents:
They seem to forgit, thet, sence last year
    revolved,
We 've succeeded in gittin' seceshed an'
    dissolved,
An' thet no one can't hope to git thru dis-
    solootion
'thout some kin' o' strain on the best Con-
    stitootion.
Who asks for a prospec' more flettrin' an'
    bright,

When from here clean to Texas it 's all
    one free fight ?
Hain't we rescued from Seward the gret
    leadin' featurs
Thet makes it wuth while to be reasonin'
    creaturs ?
Hain't we saved Habus Coppers, improved
    it in fact,
By suspendin' the Unionists 'stid o' the
    Act ?
Ain't the laws free to all ? Where on
    airth else d' ye see
Every freeman improvin' his own rope an'
    tree ?
Ain't our piety sech (in our speeches an'
    messiges)
Ez t' astonish ourselves in the bes'-com-
    posed pessiges,
An' to make folks thet knowed us in th'
    ole state o' things
Think convarsion ez easy ez drinkin' gin-
    slings ?

It 's ne'ssary to take a good confident tone
With the public; but here, jest amongst
    us, I own
Things look blacker 'n thunder. Ther' 's
    no use denyin'
We 're clean out o' money, an' 'most out o'
    lyin' ;
Two things a young nation can't mennage
    without,
Ef she wants to look wal at her fust comin'
    out;
For the fust supplies physickle strength,
    while the second
Gives a morril edvantage thet 's hard to be
    reckoned:
For this latter I 'm willin' to du wut I
    can;
For the former you 'll hev to consult on a
    plan, —
Though our *fust* want (an' this pint I want
    your best views on)
Is plausible paper to print I. O. U.s on.
Some gennlemen think it would cure all
    our cankers
In the way o' finance, ef we jes' hanged
    the bankers;
An' I own the proposle 'ud square with my
    views,
Ef their lives wuz n't all thet we 'd left
    'em to lose.
Some say thet more confidence might be
    inspired,

Ef we voted our cities an' towns to be
  fired, —
A plan thet 'ud suttenly tax our endurance,
Coz 't would be our own bills we should
  git for th' insurance;
But cinders, no metter how sacred we
  think 'em,
Might n't strike furrin minds ez good
  sources of income,
Nor the people, perhaps, would n't like the
  eclaw
O' bein' all turned into paytriots by law.
Some want we should buy all the cotton
  an' burn it,
On a pledge, when we 've gut thru the
  war, to return it, —
Then to take the proceeds an' hold *them* ez
  security
For an issue o' bonds to be met at maturity
With an issue o' notes to be paid in hard
  cash
On the fus' Monday follerin' the 'tarnal
  Allsmash:
This hez a safe air, an', once hold o' the
  gold,
'ud leave our vile plunderers out in the
  cold,
An' *might* temp' John Bull, ef it warn't for
  the dip he
Once gut from the banks o' my own Mas-
  sissippi.
Some think we could make, by arrangin'
  the figgers,
A hendy home-currency out of our niggers;
But it wun't du to lean much on ary sech
  staff,
For they 're gittin' tu current a'ready, by
  half.

One gennleman says, ef we lef' our loan
  out
Where Floyd could git hold on 't *he* 'd take
  it, no doubt;
But 't ain't jes' the takin, though 't hez a
  good look,
We mus' git sunthin' out on it arter it 's
  took,
An' we need now more 'n ever, with sorrer
  I own,
Thet some one another should let us a loan,
Sence a soger wun't fight, on'y jes' while
  he draws his
Pay down on the nail, for the best of all
  causes,

'thout askin' to know wut the quarrel 's
  about, —
An' once come to thet, why, our game is
  played out.
It 's ez true ez though I should n't never
  hev said it,
Thet a hitch hez took place in our system
  o' credit;
I swear it 's all right in my speeches an'
  messiges,
But ther' 's idees afloat, ez ther' is about
  sessiges :
Folks wun't take a bond ez a basis to trade
  on,
Without nosin' round to find out wut it 's
  made on,
An' the thought more an' more thru the
  public min' crosses
Thet our Treshry hez gut 'mos' too many
  dead hosses.
Wut 's called credit, you see, is some like
  a balloon,
Thet looks while it 's up 'most ez harn-
  some 'z a moon,
But once git a leak in 't, an' wut looked so
  grand
Caves righ' down in a jiffy ez flat ez your
  hand.
Now the world is a dreffle mean place, for
  our sins,
Where ther' ollus is critters about with
  long pins
A-prickin' the bubbles we 've blowed with
  sech care,
An' provin' ther' 's nothin' inside but bad
  air :
They 're all Stuart Millses, poor-white trash,
  an' sneaks,
Without no more chivverlry 'n Choctaws or
  Creeks,
Who think a real gennleman's promise to
  pay
Is meant to be took in trade's ornery way :
Them fellers an' I could n' never agree ;
They 're the nateral foes o' the Southun
  Idee ;
I 'd gladly take all of our other resks on
  me
To be red o' this low-lived politikle 'con-
  'my !

Now a dastardly notion is gittin' about
Thet our bladder is bust an' the gas oozin'
  out,

An' onless we can mennage in some way to stop it,
Why, the thing 's a gone coon, an' we might ez wal drop it.
Brag works wal at fust, but it ain't jes' the thing
For a stiddy inves'ment the shiners to bring,
An' votin' we 're prosp'rous a hundred times over
Wun't change bein' starved into livin' in clover.
Manassas done sunthin' tow'rds drawin' the wool
O'er the green, antislavery eyes o' John Bull:
Oh, *warn't* it a godsend, jes' when sech tight fixes
Wuz crowdin' us mourners, to throw double-sixes !
I wuz tempted to think, an' it wuz n't no wonder,
Ther' wuz reelly a Providence, — over or under, —
When, all packed for Nashville, I fust ascertained
From the papers up North wut a victory we 'd gained.
't wuz the time for diffusin' correc' views abroad
Of our union an' strength an' relyin' on God ;
An', fact, when I 'd gut thru my fust big surprise,
I much ez half b'lieved in my own tallest lies,
An' conveyed the idee thet the whole Southun popperlace
Wuz Spartans all on the keen jump for Thermopperlies,
Thet set on the Lincolnites' bombs till they bust,
An' fight for the priv'lege o' dyin' the fust ;
But Roanoke, Bufort, Millspring, an' the rest
Of our recent starn-foremost successes out West,
Hain't left us a foot for our swellin' to stand on, —
We 've showed *too* much o' wut Buregard calls *abandon*,
For all our Thermopperlies (an' it 's a marcy

We hain't hed no more) hev ben clean vicy-varsy,
An' wut Spartans wuz lef' when the battle wuz done
Wuz them thet wuz too unambitious to run.

Oh, ef we hed on'y jes' gut Reecognition,
Things now would ha' ben in a different position !
You 'd ha' hed all you wanted : the paper blockade
Smashed up into toothpicks ; unlimited trade
In the one thing thet 's needfle, till niggers, I swow,
Hed ben thicker 'n provisional shin-plasters now ;
Quinine by the ton 'ginst the shakes when they seize ye ;
Nice paper to coin into C. S. A. specie ;
The voice of the driver 'd be heerd in our land,
An' the univarse scringe, ef we lifted our hand :
Would n't thet be some like a fulfillin' the prophecies,
With all the fus' fem'lies in all the fust offices ?
't wuz a beautiful dream, an' all sorrer is idle, —
But *ef* Lincoln *would* ha' hanged Mason an' Slidell !
For would n't the Yankees hev found they 'd ketched Tartars,
Ef they 'd raised two sech critters as them into martyrs ?
Mason *wuz* F. F. V., though a cheap card to win on,
But t' other was jes' New York trash to begin on ;
They ain't o' no good in European pellices,
But think wut a help they 'd ha' ben on their gallowses !
They 'd ha' felt they wuz truly fulfillin' their mission,
An' oh, how dog-cheap we 'd ha' gut Ree-cognition !

But somehow another, wutever we 've tried,
Though the the'ry 's fust-rate, the facs *wun't* coincide :
Facs are contrary 'z mules, an' ez hard in the mouth,

An' they allus hev showed a mean spite to the South.
Sech bein' the case, we hed best look about
For some kin' o' way to slip *our* necks out :
Le' 's vote our las' dollar, ef one can be found,
(An', at any rate, votin' it hez a good sound,) —
Le' 's swear thet to arms all our people is flyin',
(The critters can't read, an' wun't know how we 're lyin',) —
Thet Toombs is advancin' to sack Cincinnater,
With a rovin' commission to pillage an' slahter, —
Thet we 've throwed to the winds all regard for wut 's lawfle,
An' gone in for sunthin' promiscu'sly awfle.
Ye see, hitherto, it 's our own knaves an' fools
Thet we 've used, (those for whetstones, an' t' others ez tools,)
An' now our las' chance is in puttin' to test
The same kin' o' cattle up North an' out West, —
Your Belmonts, Vallandighams, Woodses, an' sech,
Poor shotes thet ye couldn't persuade us to tech,
Not in ornery times, though we 're willin' to feed 'em
With a nod now an' then, when we happen to need 'em ;
Why, for my part, I 'd ruther shake hands with a nigger
Than with cusses that load an' don't darst dror a trigger;
They 're the wust wooden nutmegs the Yankees perdooce,
Shaky everywheres else, an' jes' sound on the goose;
They ain't wuth a cuss, an' I set nothin' by 'em,
But we 're in sech a fix thet I s'pose we mus' try 'em.
I — But, Gennlemen, here 's a despatch jes' come in
Which shows thet the tide 's begun turnin' agin', —
Gret Cornfedrit success ! C'lumbus eevacooated!
I mus' run down an' hev the thing properly stated,
An' show wut a triumph it is, an' how lucky
To fin'lly git red o' thet cussed Kentucky, —
An' how, sence Fort Donelson, winnin' the day
Consists in triumphantly gittin' away.

No. V

SPEECH OF HONOURABLE PRESERVED DOE IN SECRET CAUCUS

TO THE EDITORS OF THE ATLANTIC MONTHLY

JAALAM, 12th April, 1862.

GENTLEMEN, — As I cannot but hope that the ultimate, if not speedy, success of the national arms is now sufficiently ascertained, sure as I am of the righteousness of our cause and its consequent claim on the blessing of God, (for I would not show a faith inferior to that of the Pagan historian with his *Facile evenit quod Dis cordi est*,) it seems to me a suitable occasion to withdraw our minds a moment from the confusing din of battle to objects of peaceful and permanent interest. Let us not neglect the monuments of preterite history because what shall be history is so diligently making under our eyes. *Cras ingens iterabimus æquor ;* to-morrow will be time enough for that stormy sea ; to-day let me engage the attention of your readers with the Runick inscription to whose fortunate discovery I have heretofore alluded. Well may we say with the poet, *Multa renascuntur quæ jam cecidere.* And I would premise, that, although I can no longer resist the evidence of my own senses from the stone before me to the ante-Columbian discovery of this continent by the Northmen, *gens inclytissima*, as they are called in a Palermitan inscription, written fortunately in a less debatable character than that which I am about to decipher, yet I would by no means be understood as wishing to vilipend the merits of the great Genoese, whose name will never be forgotten so long as the inspiring strains of "Hail Columbia" shall continue to be heard. Though he must be stripped also of whatever praise may belong to the experiment of the egg, which I find proverbially attributed by Castilian authors to a certain Juanito or Jack, (perhaps an offshoot of our giant-killing mythus,) his name will still remain one of the most illustrious of modern times. But the impartial historian owes a duty likewise to obscure merit, and my solicitude to render a tardy justice is perhaps quickened by my having known those who, had their own field of labour been less secluded, might have found a readier acceptance with the reading publick. I could give an example, but I forbear: *forsitan nostris ex ossibus oritur ultor.*

Touching Runick inscriptions, I find that they may be classed under three general heads: 1°. Those which are understood by the Danish Royal Society of Northern Antiquaries, and Professor Rafn, their Secretary; 2°. Those which are comprehensible only by Mr. Rafn; and 3°. Those which neither the Society, Mr. Rafn, nor anybody else can be said in any definite sense to understand, and which accordingly offer peculiar temptations to enucleating sagacity. These last are naturally deemed the most valuable by intelligent antiquaries, and to this class the stone now in my possession fortunately belongs. Such give a picturesque variety to ancient events, because susceptible oftentimes of as many interpretations as there are individual archæologists; and since facts are only the pulp in which the Idea or event-seed is softly imbedded till it ripen, it is of little consequence what colour or flavour we attribute to them, provided it be agreeable. Availing myself of the obliging assistance of Mr. Arphaxad Bowers, an ingenious photographick artist, whose house-on-wheels has now stood for three years on our Meeting-House Green, with the somewhat contradictory inscription, — "*our motto is onward*," — I have sent accurate copies of my treasure to many learned men and societies, both native and European. I may hereafter communicate their different and (*me judice*) equally erroneous solutions. I solicit also, Messrs. Editors, your own acceptance of the copy herewith enclosed. I need only premise further, that the stone itself is a goodly block of metamorphick sandstone, and that the Runes resemble very nearly the ornithichnites or fossil bird-tracks of Dr. Hitchcock, but with less regularity or apparent design than is displayed by those remarkable geological monuments. These are rather the *non bene junctarum discordia semina rerum.* Resolved to leave no door

open to cavil, I first of all attempted the elucidation of this remarkable example of lithick literature by the ordinary modes, but with no adequate return for my labour. I then considered myself amply justified in resorting to that heroick treatment the felicity of which, as applied by the great Bentley to Milton, had long ago enlisted my admiration. Indeed, I had already made up my mind, that, in case good fortune should throw any such invaluable record in my way, I would proceed with it in the following simple and satisfactory method. After a cursory examination, merely sufficing for an approximative estimate of its length, I would write down a hypothetical inscription based upon antecedent probabilities, and then proceed to extract from the characters engraven on the stone a meaning as nearly as possible conformed to this *a priori* product of my own ingenuity. The result more than justified my hopes, inasmuch as the two inscriptions were made without any great violence to tally in all essential particulars. I then proceeded, not without some anxiety, to my second test, which was, to read the Runick letters diagonally, and again with the same success. With an excitement pardonable under the circumstances, yet tempered with thankful humility, I now applied my last and severest trial, my *experimentum crucis.* I turned the stone, now doubly precious in my eyes, with scrupulous exactness upside down. The physical exertion so far displaced my spectacles as to derange for a moment the focus of vision. I confess that it was with some tremulousness that I readjusted them upon my nose, and prepared my mind to bear with calmness any disappointment that might ensue. But, *Ô albo dies notanda lapillo!* what was my delight to find that the change of position had effected none in the sense of the writing, even by so much as a single letter! I was now, and justly, as I think, satisfied of the conscientious exactness of my interpretation. It is as follows:

HERE
BJARNA GRIMOLFSSON
FIRST DRANK CLOUD-BROTHER
THROUGH CHILD-OF-LAND-AND-
WATER:

that is, drew smoke through a reed stem. In other words, we have here a record of the first smoking of the herb *Nicotiana Ta-*

bacum by an European on this continent. The probable results of this discovery are so vast as to baffle conjecture. If it be objected, that the smoking of a pipe would hardly justify the setting up of a memorial stone, I answer, that even now the Moquis Indian, ere he takes his first whiff, bows reverently toward the four quarters of the sky in succession, and that the loftiest monuments have been reared to perpetuate fame, which is the dream of the shadow of smoke. The *Saga*, it will be remembered, leaves this Bjarna to a fate something like that of Sir Humphrey Gilbert, on board a sinking ship in the "wormy sea," having generously given up his place in the boat to a certain Icelander. It is doubly pleasant, therefore, to meet with this proof that the brave old man arrived safely in Vinland, and that his declining years were cheered by the respectful attentions of the dusky denizens of our then uninvaded forest. Most of all was I gratified, however, in thus linking forever the name of my native town with one of the most momentous occurrences of modern times. Hitherto Jaalam, though in soil, climate, and geographical position as highly qualified to be the theatre of remarkable historical incidents as any spot on the earth's surface, has been, if I may say it without seeming to question the wisdom of Providence, almost maliciously neglected, as it might appear, by occurrences of world-wide interest in want of a situation. And in matters of this nature it must be confessed that adequate events are as necessary as the *vates sacer* to record them. Jaalam stood always modestly ready, but circumstances made no fitting response to her generous intentions. Now, however, she assumes her place on the historick roll. I have hitherto been a zealous opponent of the Circean herb, but I shall now reëxamine the question without bias.

I am aware that the Rev. Jonas Tutchel, in a recent communication to the "Bogus Four Corners Weekly Meridian," has endeavored to show that this is the sepulchral inscription of Thorwald Eriksson, who, as is well known, was slain in Vinland by the natives. But I think he has been misled by a preconceived theory, and cannot but feel that he has thus made an ungracious return for my allowing him to inspect the stone with the aid of my own glasses (he having by accident left his at home) and in my own study. The heathen ancients might have instructed this Christian minister in the rites of hospitality; but much is to be pardoned to the spirit of self-love. He must indeed be ingenious who can make out the words *hèr hvilir* from any characters in the inscription in question, which, whatever else it may be, is certainly not mortuary. And even should the reverend gentleman succeed in persuading some fantastical wits of the soundness of his views, I do not see what useful end he will have gained. For if the English Courts of Law hold the testimony of gravestones from the burial-grounds of Protestant dissenters to be questionable, even where it is essential in proving a descent, I cannot conceive that the epitaphial assertions of heathens should be esteemed of more authority by any man of orthodox sentiments.

At this moment, happening to cast my eyes upon the stone, whose characters a transverse light from my southern window brings out with singular distinctness, another interpretation has occurred to me, promising even more interesting results. I hasten to close my letter in order to follow at once the clue thus providentially suggested.

I inclose, as usual, a contribution from Mr. Biglow, and remain,

Gentlemen, with esteem and respect,

Your Obedient Humble Servant,

HOMER WILBUR, A. M.

I THANK ye, my frien's, for the warmth o'
    your greetin':
Ther' 's few airthly blessin's but wut 's vain
    an' fleetin';
But ef ther' is one thet hain't *no* cracks an'
    flaws,
An' is wuth goin' in for, it 's pop'lar ap-
    plause;
It sends up the sperits ez lively ez rockets,
An' I feel it — wal, down to the eend o' my
    pockets.
Jes' lovin' the people is Canaan in view,
But it 's Canaan paid quarterly t' hev 'em
    love you;
It 's a blessin' thet 's breakin' out ollus in
    fresh spots;
It 's a-follerin' Moses 'thout losin' the flesh-
    pots.

But, Gennlemen, 'scuse me, I ain't sech a
    raw cus
Ez to go luggin' ellerkence into a caucus, —
Thet is, into one where the call compre-
    hen's
Nut the People in person, but on'y their
    frien's;
I 'm so kin' o' used to convincin' the masses
Of th' edvantage o' bein' self-governin'
    asses,
I forgut thet *we* 're all o' the sort thet pull
    wires
An' arrange for the public their wants an'
    desires,
An' thet wut we hed met for wuz jes' to
    agree
Wut the People's opinions in futur' should
    be.

Now, to come to the nub, we 've ben all
    disappinted,
An' our leadin' idees are a kind o' disjinted,
Though, fur ez the nateral man could
    discern,
Things ough' to ha' took most an oppersite
    turn.
But The'ry is jes' like a train on the rail,
Thet, weather or no, puts her thru without
    fail,
While Fac' 's the ole stage thet gits
    sloughed in the ruts,
An' hez to allow for your darned efs an'
    buts,
An' so, nut intendin' no pers'nal reflections,
They don't — don't nut allus, thet is, —
    make connections:
Sometimes, when it really doos seem thet
    they 'd oughter
Combine jest ez kindly ez new rum an'
    water,
Both 'll be jest ez sot in their ways ez a
    bagnet,
Ez otherwise-minded ez th' eends of a mag-
    net,
An' folks like you 'n' me, thet ain't ept to
    be sold,
Git somehow or 'nother left out in the cold.

I expected 'fore this, 'thout no gret of a row,
Jeff D. would ha' ben where A. Lincoln is
    now,
With Taney to say 't wuz all legle an' fair,
An' a jury o' Deemocrats ready to swear
Thet the ingin o' State gut throwed into
    the ditch

By the fault o' the North in misplacin' the
    switch.
Things wuz ripenin' fust-rate with Buchanan
    to nuss 'em;
But the People — they would n't be Mexi-
    cans, cuss 'em!
Ain't the safeguards o' freedom upsot, 'z
    you may say,
Ef the right o' rev'lution is took clean
    away?
An' doos n't the right primy-fashy include
The bein' entitled to nut be subdued?
The fect is, we 'd gone for the Union so
    strong,
When Union meant South ollus right an'
    North wrong,
Thet the People gut fooled into thinkin' it
    might
Worry on middlin' wal with the North in
    the right.
We might ha' ben now jest ez prosp'rous ez
    France,
Where p'litikle enterprise hez a fair chance,
An' the People is heppy an' proud et this
    hour,
Long ez they hev the votes, to let Nap hev
    the power;
But *our* folks they went an' believed wut
    we 'd told 'em
An', the flag once insulted, no mortle could
    hold 'em.
'T wuz pervokin' jest when we wuz cert'in
    to win, —
An' I, for one, wun't trust the masses agin:
For a People thet knows much ain't fit to
    be free
In the self-cockin', back-action style o'
    J. D.

I can't believe now but wut half on 't is
    lies;
For who 'd thought the North wuz agoin'
    to rise,
Or take the pervokin'est kin' of a stump,
'thout 't wuz sunthin' ez pressin' ez Ga-
    br'el's las' trump?
Or who 'd ha' supposed, arter *sech* swell
    an' bluster
'bout the lick-ary-ten-on-ye fighters they 'd
    muster,
Raised by hand on briled lightnin', ez
    op'lent 'z you please
In a primitive furrest o' femmily-trees, —
Who 'd ha' thought thet them Southun-
    ers ever 'ud show

Starns with pedigrees to 'em like theirn to
    the foe,
Or, when the vamosin' come, ever to find
Nat'ral masters in front an' mean white
    folks behind ?
By ginger, ef I 'd ha' known half I know
    now,
When I wuz to Congress, I would n't, I
    swow,
Hev let 'em cair on so high-minded an'
    sarsy,
'thout *some* show o' wut you may call vicy-
    varsy.
To be sure, we wuz under a contrac' jes' then
To be dreffle forbearin' towards Southun
    men ;
We hed to go sheers in preservin' the bel-
    lance :
An' ez they seemed to feel they wuz wastin'
    their tellents
'thout some un to kick, 't warn't more 'n
    proper, you know,
Each should funnish his part ; an' sence
    they found the toe,
An' we wuz n't cherubs — wal, we found
    the buffer,
For fear thet the Compromise System
    should suffer.

I wun't say the plan hed n't onpleasant
    featurs, —
For men are perverse an' onreasonin' crea-
    turs,
An' forgit thet in this life 't ain't likely to
    heppen
Their own privit fancy should ollus be
    cappen, —
But it worked jest ez smooth ez the key of
    a safe,
An' the gret Union bearin's played free
    from all chafe.
They warn't hard to suit, ef they hed their
    own way,
An' we (thet is, some on us) made the
    thing pay :
't wuz a fair give-an'-take out of Uncle
    Sam's heap ;
Ef they took wut warn't theirn, wut we
    give come ez cheap ;
The elect gut the offices down to tide-
    waiter,
The people took skinnin' ez mild ez a
    tater,
Seemed to choose who they wanted tu,
    footed the bills,

An' felt kind o' 'z though they wuz havin'
    their wills,
Which kep' 'em ez harmless an' cherfle ez
    crickets,
While all we invested wuz names on the
    tickets :
Wal, ther' 's nothin', for folks fond o'
    lib'ral consumption
Free o' charge, like democ'acy tempered
    with gumption !

Now warn't thet a system wuth pains in
    presarvin',
Where the people found jints an' their
    frien's done the carvin', —
Where the many done all o' their thinkin'
    by proxy,
An' were proud on 't ez long ez 't wuz
    christened Democ'cy, —
Where the few let us sap all o' Freedom's
    foundations,
Ef you call it reformin' with prudence an'
    patience,
An' were willin' Jeff's snake-egg should
    hetch with the rest,
Ef you writ " Constitootional " over the
    nest ?
But it 's all out o' kilter, ('t wuz too good to
    last,)
An' all jes' by J. D.'s perceedin' too fast ;
Ef he 'd on'y hung on for a month or two
    more,
We 'd ha' gut things fixed nicer 'n they hed
    ben before :
Afore he drawed off an' lef' all in confu-
    sion,
We wuz safely entrenched in the ole Con-
    stitootion,
With an outlyin', heavy-gun, casemated
    fort
To rake all assailants, — I mean th' S. J.
    Court.
Now I never 'll acknowledge (nut ef you
    should skin me)
't wuz wise to abandon sech works to the
    in'my,
An' let him fin' out thet wut scared him so
    long,
Our whole line of argyments, lookin' so
    strong,
All our Scriptur an' law, every the'ry an'
    fac',
Wuz Quaker -guns daubed with Pro-sla-
    very black.
Why, ef the Republicans ever should git

Andy Johnson or some one to lend 'em the
    wit
An' the spunk jes' to mount Constitootion
    an' Court
With Columbiad guns, your real ekle-rights
    sort,
Or drill out the spike from the ole Declara-
    tion
Thet can kerry a solid shot clearn roun'
    creation,
We 'd better take maysures for shettin' up
    shop,
An' put off our stock by a vendoo or swop.

But they wun't never dare tu ; you 'll see
    'em in Edom
'fore they ventur' to go where their doc-
    trines 'ud lead 'em :
They 've ben takin' our princerples up ez
    we dropt 'em,
An' thought it wuz terrible 'cute to adopt
    'em ;
But they 'll fin' out 'fore long thet their
    hope 's ben deceivin' 'em,
An' thet princerples ain't o' no good, ef
    you b'lieve in 'em ;
It makes 'em tu stiff for a party to use,
Where they 'd ough' to be easy 'z an ole
    pair o' shoes.
If *we* say 'n our pletform thet all men are
    brothers,
We don't mean thet some folks ain't more
    so 'n some others ;
An' it 's wal understood thet we make a
    selection,
An' thet brotherhood kin' o' subsides arter
    'lection.
The fust thing for sound politicians to
    larn is,
Thet Truth, to dror kindly in all sorts o'
    harness,
Mus' be kep' in the abstract, — for, come
    to apply it,
You 're ept to hurt some folks's interists
    by it.
Wal, these 'ere Republicans (some on 'em)
    ects
Ez though gineral mexims 'ud suit speshle
    facts ;
An' there 's where we 'll nick 'em, there 's
    where they 'll be lost :
For applyin' your princerple 's wut makes
    it cost,
An' folks don't want Fourth o' July t' in-
    terfere

With the business-consarns o' the rest o'
    the year,
No more 'n they want Sunday to pry an'
    to peek
Into wut they are doin' the rest o' the
    week.

A ginooine statesman should be on his
    guard,
Ef he *must* hev beliefs, nut to b'lieve 'em
    tu hard ;
For, ez sure ez he does, he 'll be blartin'
    'em out
'thout regardin' the natur' o' man more 'n
    a spout,
Nor it don't ask much gumption to pick
    out a flaw
In a party whose leaders are loose in the
    jaw :
An' so in our own case I ventur' to hint
Thet we 'd better nut air our perceedin's in
    print,
Nor pass resserlootions ez long ez your arm
Thet may, ez things heppen to turn, du us
    harm ;
For when you 've done all your real mean-
    in' to smother,
The darned things 'll up an' mean sunthin'
    or 'nother.
Jeff'son prob'ly meant wal with his "born
    free an' ekle,"
But it 's turned out a real crooked stick in
    the sekle ;
It 's taken full eighty-odd year — don't you
    see ? —
From the pop'lar belief to root out thet
    idee,
An', arter all, suckers on 't keep buddin'
    forth
In the nat'lly onprincipled mind o' the
    North.
No, never say nothin' without you 're com-
    pelled tu,
An' then don't say nothin' thet you can be
    held tu,
Nor don't leave no friction-idees layin'
    loose
For the ign'ant to put to incend'ary use.

You know I 'm a feller thet keeps a skinned
    eye
On the leetle events thet go skurryin' by,
Coz it 's of'ner by them than by gret ones
    you 'll see
Wut the p'litickle weather is likely to be.

Now I don't think the South's more 'n
    begun to be licked,
But I *du* think, ez Jeff says, the wind-bag 's
    gut pricked ;
It 'll blow for a spell an' keep puffin' an'
    wheezin',
The tighter our army an' navy keep
    squeezin', —
For they can't help spread-eaglein' long 'z
    ther' 's a mouth
To blow Enfield's Speaker thru lef' at the
    South.
But it 's high time for us to be settin' our
    faces
Towards reconstructin' the national basis,
With an eye to beginnin' agin on the jolly
    ticks
We used to chalk up 'hind the back-door o'
    politics ;
An' the fus' thing 's to save wut of Slav'ry
    ther' 's lef'
Arter this (I mus' call it) imprudence o'
    Jeff :
For a real good Abuse, with its roots fur
    an' wide,
Is the kin' o' thing *I* like to hev on my
    side ;
A Scriptur' name makes it ez sweet ez a
    rose,
An' it 's tougher the older an' uglier it
    grows —
(I ain't speakin' now o' the righteousness
    of it,
But the p'litickle purchase it gives an' the
    profit).

Things look pooty squally, it must be
    allowed,
An' I don't see much signs of a bow in the
    cloud :
Ther' 's too many Deemocrats — leaders
    wut 's wuss —
Thet go for the Union 'thout carin' a
    cuss
Ef it helps ary party thet ever wuz heard
    on,
So our eagle ain't made a split Austrian
    bird on.
But ther' 's still some consarvative signs to
    be found
Thet shows the gret heart o' the People is
    sound :
(Excuse me for usin' a stump-phrase agin,
But, once in the way on 't, they *will* stick
    like sin :)

There 's Phillips, for instance, hez jes'
    ketched a Tartar
In the Law-'n'-Order Party of ole Cincin-
    nater ;
An' the Compromise System ain't gone out
    o' reach,
Long 'z you keep the right limits on free-
    dom o' speech.
'T warn't none too late, neither, to put on
    the gag,
For he 's dangerous now he goes in for the
    flag.
Nut thet I altogether approve o' bad eggs,
They 're mos' gin'lly argymunt on its las'
    legs, —
An' their logic is ept to be tu indiscrimi-
    nate,
Nor don't ollus wait the right objecs to
    'liminate ;
But there is a variety on 'em, you 'll find,
Jest ez usefle an' more, besides bein' re-
    fined, —
I mean o' the sort thet are laid by the dic-
    tionary,
Sech ez sophisms an' cant, thet 'll kerry
    conviction ary
Way thet you want to the right class o'
    men,
An' are staler than all 't ever come from a
    hen :
" Disunion " done wal till our resh Southun
    friends
Took the savor all out on 't for national
    ends ;
But I guess " Abolition " 'll work a spell
    yit,
When the war 's done, an' so will " Forgive-
    an'-forgit."
Times mus' be pooty thoroughly out o' all
    jint,
Ef we can't make a good constitootional
    pint ;
An' the good time 'll come to be grindin'
    our exes,
When the war goes to seed in the nettle o'
    texes :
Ef Jon'than don't squirm, with sech helps
    to assist him,
I give up my faith in the free-suffrage sys-
    tem ;
Democ'cy wun't be nut a mite interestin',
Nor p'litikle capital much wuth investin' ;
An' my notion is, to keep dark an' lay low
Till we see the right minute to put in our
    blow. —

But I 've talked longer now 'n I hed any
   idee,
An' ther' 's others you want to hear more 'n
   you du me ;
So I 'll set down an' give thet 'ere bottle a
   skrimmage,
For I 've spoke till I 'm dry ez a real graven
   image.

No. VI

SUNTHIN' IN THE PASTORAL LINE

TO THE EDITORS OF THE ATLANTIC
MONTHLY

JAALAM, 17th May, 1862.

GENTLEMEN, — At the special request of
Mr. Biglow, I intended to inclose, together
with his own contribution, (into which, at
my suggestion, he has thrown a little more
of pastoral sentiment than usual,) some pas-
sages from my sermon on the day of the
National Fast, from the text, "Remember
them that are in bonds, as bound with
them," Heb. xiii. 3. But I have not leisure
sufficient at present for the copying of
them, even were I altogether satisfied with
the production as it stands. I should pre-
fer, I confess, to contribute the entire dis-
course to the pages of your respectable
miscellany, if it should be found acceptable
upon perusal, especially as I find the diffi-
culty in selection of greater magnitude
than I had anticipated. What passes with-
out challenge in the fervour of oral deliv-
ery, cannot always stand the colder crit-
icism of the closet. I am not so great
an enemy of Eloquence as my friend Mr.
Biglow would appear to be from some pas-
sages in his contribution for the current
month. I would not, indeed, hastily sus-
pect him of covertly glancing at myself in
his somewhat caustick animadversions, al-
beit some of the phrases he girds at are
not entire strangers to my lips. I am a
more hearty admirer of the Puritans than
seems now to be the fashion, and believe,
that, if they Hebraized a little too much in
their speech, they showed remarkable prac-
tical sagacity as statesmen and founders.
But such phenomena as Puritanism are the
results rather of great religious than of

merely social convulsions, and do not long
survive them. So soon as an earnest con-
viction has cooled into a phrase, its work is
over, and the best that can be done with it
is to bury it. *Ite, missa est.* I am inclined
to agree with Mr. Biglow that we cannot
settle the great political questions which
are now presenting themselves to the nation
by the opinions of Jeremiah or Ezekiel as
to the wants and duties of the Jews in their
time, nor do I believe that an entire com-
munity with their feelings and views would
be practicable or even agreeable at the
present day. At the same time I could
wish that their habit of subordinating the
actual to the moral, the flesh to the spirit,
and this world to the other, were more
common. They had found out, at least,
the great military secret that soul weighs
more than body. — But I am suddenly
called to a sick-bed in the household of a
valued parishioner.
With esteem and respect,
   Your obedient servant,
     HOMER WILBUR.

ONCE git a smell o' musk into a draw,
An' it clings hold like precerdents in law:
Your gra'ma'am put it there, — when,
   goodness knows, —
To jes' this-worldify her Sunday-clo'es;
But the old chist wun't sarve her gran'son's
   wife,
(For, 'thout new funnitoor, wut good in
   life ?)
An' so ole clawfoot, from the precinks
   dread
O' the spare chamber, slinks into the shed,
Where, dim with dust, it fust or last sub-
   sides
To holdin' seeds an' fifty things besides;
But better days stick fast in heart an' husk,
An' all you keep in 't gits a scent o' musk.

Jes' so with poets: wut they 've airly read
Gits kind o' worked into their heart an'
   head,
So 's 't they can't seem to write but jest on
   sheers
With furrin countries or played-out ideers,
Nor hev a feelin', ef it doos n't smack
O' wut some critter chose to feel 'way
   back:
This makes 'em talk o' daisies, larks, an'
   things,

Ez though we 'd nothin' here that blows an'
 sings, —
(Why, I 'd give more for one live bobolink
Than a square mile o' larks in printer's
 ink,) —
This makes 'em think our fust o' May is
 May,
Which 't ain't, for all the almanicks can
 say.

O little city-gals, don't never go it
Blind on the word o' noospaper or poet!
They 're apt to puff, an' May-day seldom
 looks
Up in the country ez it doos in books;
They 're no more like than hornets'-nests
 an' hives,
Or printed sarmons be to holy lives.
I, with my trouses perched on cowhide
 boots,
Tuggin' my foundered feet out by the roots,
Hev seen ye come to fling on April's hearse
Your muslin nosegays from the milliner's,
Puzzlin' to find dry ground your queen to
 choose,
An' dance your throats sore in morocker
 shoes:
I 've seen ye an' felt proud, thet, come wut
 would,
Our Pilgrim stock wuz pethed with hardi-
 hood.
Pleasure doos make us Yankees kind o'
 winch,
Ez though 't wuz sunthin' paid for by the
 inch;
But yit we du contrive to worry thru,
Ef Dooty tells us thet the thing 's to du,
An' kerry a hollerday, ef we set out,
Ez stiddily ez though 't wuz a redoubt.

I, country-born an' bred, know where to
 find
Some blooms thet make the season suit the
 mind,
An' seem to metch the doubtin' bluebird's
 notes, —
Half-vent'rin' liverworts in furry coats,
Bloodroots, whose rolled-up leaves ef you
 oncurl,
Each on 'em 's cradle to a baby-pearl, —
But these are jes' Spring's pickets; sure ez
 sin,
The rebble frosts 'll try to drive 'em in;
For half our May 's so awfully like May n't,
't would rile a Shaker or an evrige saint;

Though I own up I like our back'ard
 springs
Thet kind o' haggle with their greens an'
 things,
An' when you 'most give up, 'uthout more
 words
Toss the fields full o' blossoms, leaves, an'
 birds;
Thet 's Northun natur', slow an' apt to
 doubt,
But when it *doos* git stirred, ther' 's no gin-
 out!

Fust come the blackbirds clatt'rin' in tall
 trees,
An' settlin' things in windy Congresses, —
Queer politicians, though, for I 'll be
 skinned
Ef all on 'em don't head aginst the wind.
'fore long the trees begin to show belief, —
The maple crimsons to a coral-reef,
Then saffern swarms swing off from all the
 willers
So plump they look like yaller caterpil-
 lars,
Then gray hossches'nuts leetle hands unfold
Softer 'n a baby's be at three days old:
Thet 's robin - redbreast's almanick; he
 knows
Thet arter this ther' 's only blossom-snows;
So, choosin' out a handy crotch an' spouse,
He goes to plast'rin' his adobe house.

Then seems to come a hitch, — things lag
 behind,
Till some fine mornin' Spring makes up her
 mind,
An' ez, when snow-swelled rivers cresh
 their dams
Heaped-up with ice thet dovetails in an'
 jams,
A leak comes spirtin' thru some pin-hole
 cleft,
Grows stronger, fercer, tears out right an'
 left,
Then all the waters bow themselves an'
 come,
Suddin, in one gret slope o' shedderin' foam,
Jes' so our Spring gits everythin' in tune
An' gives one leap from Aperl into June :
Then all comes crowdin' in ; afore you
 think,
Young oak-leaves mist the side-hill woods
 with pink ;
The catbird in the laylock-bush is loud ;

The orchards turn to heaps o' rosy cloud ;
Red-cedars blossom tu, though few folks
    know it,
An' look all dipt in sunshine like a poet ;
The lime-trees pile their solid stacks o'
    shade
An' drows'ly simmer with the bees' sweet
    trade ;
In ellum-shrouds the flashin' hangbird
    clings
An' for the summer vy'ge his hammock
    slings ;
All down the loose-walled lanes in archin'
    bowers
The barb'ry droops its strings o' golden
    flowers,
Whose shrinkin' hearts the school-gals love
    to try
With pins, — they 'll worry yourn so, boys,
    bimeby !
But I don't love your cat'logue style, — do
    you ? —
Ez ef to sell off Natur' by vendoo ;
One word with blood in 't 's twice ez good
    ez two :
'nuff sed, June's bridesman, poet o' the
    year,
Gladness on wings, the bobolink, is here ;
Half-hid in tip-top apple-blooms he swings,
Or climbs aginst the breeze with quiverin'
    wings,
Or, givin' way to 't in a mock despair,
Runs down, a brook o' laughter, thru the
    air.

I ollus feel the sap start in my veins
In Spring, with curus heats an' prickly
    pains,
Thet drive me, when I git a chance, to
    walk
Off by myself to hev a privit talk
With a queer critter thet can't seem to
    'gree
Along o' me like most folks, — Mister
    Me.
Ther' 's times when I 'm unsoshle ez a stone,
An' sort o' suffercate to be alone, —
I 'm crowded jes' to think thet folks are
    nigh,
An' can't bear nothin' closer than the
    sky ;
Now the wind 's full ez shifty in the mind
Ez wut it is ou'-doors, ef I ain't blind,
An' sometimes, in the fairest sou'west
    weather,

My innard vane pints east for weeks to-
    gether,
My natur' gits all goose-flesh, an' my sins
Come drizzlin' on my conscience sharp ez
    pins :
Wal, et sech times I jes' slip out o' sight
An' take it out in a fair stan'-up fight
With the one cuss I can't lay on the shelf,
The crook'dest stick in all the heap, — My-
    self.

'T wuz so las' Sabbath arter meetin'-time :
Findin' my feelin's would n't noways rhyme
With nobody's, but off the hendle flew
An' took things from an east-wind pint o'
    view,
I started off to lose me in the hills
Where the pines be, up back o' 'Siah's
    Mills :
Pines, ef you 're blue, are the best friends
    I know,
They mope an' sigh an' sheer your feelin's
    so, —
They hesh the ground beneath so, tu, I
    swan,
You half-forgit you 've gut a body on.
Ther' 's a small school'us' there where four
    roads meet,
The door-steps hollered out by little feet,
An' side-posts carved with names whose
    owners grew
To gret men, some on 'em, an' deacons, tu ;
't ain't used no longer, coz the town hez gut
A high-school, where they teach the Lord
    knows wut :
Three-story larnin' 's pop'lar now ; I guess
We thriv' ez wal on jes' two stories less,
For it strikes me ther' 's sech a thing ez
    sinnin'
By overloadin' children's underpinnin' :
Wal, here it wuz I larned my A B C,
An' it 's a kind o' favorite spot with me.

We 're curus critters : Now ain't jes' the
    minute
Thet ever fits us easy while we 're in it ;
Long ez 't wuz futur', 't would be perfect
    bliss, —
Soon ez it 's past, *thet* time 's wuth ten o'
    this ;
An' yit there ain't a man thet need be told
Thet Now 's the only bird lays eggs o' gold.
A knee-high lad, I used to plot an' plan
An' think 't wuz life's cap-sheaf to be a
    man;

Now, gittin' gray, there 's nothin' I enjoy
Like dreamin' back along into a boy :
So the ole school'us' is a place I choose
Afore all others, ef I want to muse ;
I set down where I used to set, an' git
My boyhood back, an' better things with
  it, —
Faith, Hope, an' sunthin', ef it is n't Cher-
  rity,
It 's want o' guile, an' thet 's ez gret a rer-
  rity, —
While Fancy's cushin', free to Prince and
  Clown,
Makes the hard bench ez soft ez milk-
  weed-down.

Now, 'fore I knowed, thet Sabbath arter-
  noon
When I sot out to tramp myself in tune,
I found me in the school'us' on my seat,
Drummin' the march to No-wheres with my
  feet.
Thinkin' o' nothin', I 've heerd ole folks
  say
Is a hard kind o' dooty in its way:
It 's thinkin' everythin' you ever knew,
Or ever hearn, to make your feelin's blue.
I sot there tryin' thet on for a spell :
I thought o' the Rebellion, then o' Hell,
Which some folks tell ye now is jest a met-
  terfor
(A the'ry, p'raps, it wun't *feel* none the
  better for);
I thought o' Reconstruction, wut we 'd win
Patchin' our patent self-blow-up agin :
I thought ef this 'ere milkin' o' the wits,
So much a month, warn't givin' Natur'
  fits, —
Ef folks warn't druv, findin' their own milk
  fail,
To work the cow thet hez an iron tail,
An' ef idees 'thout ripenin' in the pan
Would send up cream to humor ary man :
From this to thet I let my worryin' creep,
Till finally I must ha' fell asleep.

Our lives in sleep are some like streams
  thet glide
'twixt flesh an' sperrit boundin' on each side,
Where both shores' shadders kind o' mix
  an' mingle
In sunthin' thet ain't jes' like either sin-
  gle;
An' when you cast off moorin's from To-
  day,

An' down towards To-morrer drift away,
The imiges thet tengle on the stream
Make a new upside-down'ard world o'
  dream :
Sometimes they seem like sunrise-streaks
  an' warnin's
O' wut 'll be in Heaven on Sabbath-morn-
  in's,
An', mixed right in ez ef jest out o' spite,
Sunthin' thet says your supper ain't gone
  right.
I 'm gret on dreams, an' often when I
  wake,
I 've lived so much it makes my mem'ry
  ache,
An' can't skurce take a cat-nap in my
  cheer
'thout hevin' 'em, some good, some bad, all
  queer.

Now I wuz settin' where I 'd ben, it
  seemed,
An' ain't sure yit whether I r'ally dreamed,
Nor, ef I did, how long I might ha' slep',
When I hearn some un stompin' up the
  step,
An' lookin' round, ef two an' two make four,
I see a Pilgrim Father in the door.
He wore a steeple-hat, tall boots, an' spurs
With rowels to 'em big ez ches'nut-burrs,
An' his gret sword behind him sloped away
Long 'z a man's speech thet dunno wut to
  say. —
"Ef your name 's Biglow, an' your given-
  name
Hosee," sez he, " it 's arter you I came;
I 'm your gret-gran'ther multiplied by
  three." —
"My *wut?*" sez I. — "Your gret-gret-
  gret," sez he:
"You would n't ha' never ben here but for
  me.
Two hundred an' three year ago this May
The ship I come in sailed up Boston Bay;
I 'd been a cunnle in our Civil War, —
But wut on airth hev *you* gut up one for ?
Coz we du things in England, 't ain't for
  you
To git a notion you can du 'em tu:
I 'm told you write in public prints: ef
  true,
It 's nateral you should know a thing or
  two." —
"Thet air 's an argymunt I can't en-
  dorse, —

't would prove, coz you wear spurs, you
  kep' a horse:
For brains," sez I, "wutever you may
  think,
Ain't boun' to cash the drafs o' pen-an'-
  ink, —
Though mos' folks write ez ef they hoped
  jes' quickenin'
The churn would argoo skim-milk into
  thickenin';
But skim-milk ain't a thing to change its
  view
O' wut it 's meant for more 'n a smoky
  flue.
But du pray tell me, 'fore we furder go,
How in all Natur' did you come to know
'bout our affairs," sez I, "in Kingdom-
  Come ? " —
" Wal, I worked round at sperrit-rappin'
  some,
An' danced the tables till their legs wuz
  gone,
In hopes o' larnin' wut wuz goin' on,"
Sez he, " but mejums lie so like all-split
Thet I concluded it wuz best to quit.
But, come now, ef you wun't confess to
  knowin',
You 've some conjectures how the thing 's
  a-goin'." —
" Gran'ther," sez I, " a vane warn't never
  known
Nor asked to hev a jedgment of its own;
An' yit, ef 't ain't gut rusty in the jints,
It 's safe to trust its say on certin pints:
It knows the wind's opinions to a T,
An' the wind settles wut the weather 'll be."
" I never thought a scion of our stock
Could grow the wood to make a weather-
  cock;
When I wuz younger 'n you, skurce more
  'n a shaver,
No airthly wind," sez he, "could make me
  waver ! "
(Ez he said this, he clinched his jaw an'
  forehead,
Hitchin' his belt to bring his sword-hilt
  forrard.) —
" Jes so it wuz with me," sez I, " I swow,
When I wuz younger 'n wut you see me
  now, —
Nothin' from Adam's fall to Huldy's bon-
  net,
Thet I warn't full-cocked with my jedg-
  ment on it;
But now I 'm gittin' on in life, I find

It 's a sight harder to make up my mind, —
Nor I don't often try tu, when events
Will du it for me free of all expense.
The moral question 's ollus plain enough, —
It 's jes' the human - natur' side thet 's
  tough;
Wut 's best to think may n't puzzle me nor
  you, —
The pinch comes in decidin' wut to du ;
Ef you read History, all runs smooth ez
  grease,
Coz there the men ain't nothin' more 'n
  idees, —
But come to make it, ez we must to-day,
Th' idees hev arms an' legs an' stop the
  way:
It 's easy fixin' things in facts an' figgers, —
They can't resist, nor warn't brought up
  with niggers;
But come to try your the'ry on, — why.
  then
Your facts an' figgers change to ign'ant
  men
Actin' ez ugly — " " — " Smite 'em hip an'
  thigh ! "
Sez gran'ther, " and let every man-child
  die !
Oh for three weeks o' Crommle an' the
  Lord !
Up, Isr'el, to your tents an' grind the
  sword ! " —
" Thet kind o' thing worked wal in ole
  Judee,
But you forgit how long it 's ben A. D.;
You think thet 's ellerkence, — I call it
  shoddy,
A thing," sez I, " wun't cover soul nor
  body ;
I like the plain all-wool o' common-sense,
Thet warms ye now, an' will a twelve-
  month hence.
You took to follerin' where the Prophets
  beckoned,
An', fust you knowed on, back come Charles
  the Second;
Now wut I want 's to hev all we gain
  stick,
An' not to start Millennium too quick;
We hain't to punish only, but to keep,
An' the cure 's gut to go a cent'ry deep."
" Wall, milk-an'-water ain't the best o'
  glue,"
Sez he, " an' so you 'll find afore you 're
  thru;
Ef reshness venters sunthin', shilly-shally

Loses ez often wut 's ten times the vally.
Thet exe of ourn, when Charles's neck gut
split,
Opened a gap thet ain't bridged over yit:
Slav'ry 's your Charles, the Lord hez gin
the exe " —
" Our Charles," sez I, " hez gut eight mil-
lion necks.
The hardest question ain't the black man's
right,
The trouble is to 'mancipate the white ;
One 's chained in body an' can be sot free,
But t' other 's chained in soul to an idee:
It 's a long job, but we shall worry thru it;
Ef bagnets fail, the spellin'-book must
du it."
" Hosee," sez he, " I think you 're goin' to
fail:
The rettlesnake ain't dangerous in the tail;
This 'ere rebellion 's nothing but the ret-
tle, —
You 'll stomp on thet an' think you 've won
the bettle;
It 's Slavery thet 's the fangs an' thinkin'
head,
An' ef you want selvation, cresh it dead, —
An' cresh it suddin, or you 'll larn by
waitin'
Thet Chance wun't stop to listen to de-
batin' ! " —
"God's truth ! " sez I, — " an' ef I held the
club,
An' knowed jes' where to strike, — but
there 's the rub ! " —
" Strike soon," sez he, " or you 'll be deadly
ailin', —
Folks thet 's afeared to fail are sure o'
failin' ;
God hates your sneakin' creturs thet be-
lieve
He 'll settle things they run away an'
leave ! "
He brought his foot down fercely, ez he
spoke,
An' give me sech a startle thet I woke.

No. VII

LATEST VIEWS OF MR. BIGLOW

PRELIMINARY NOTE

[It is with feelings of the liveliest pain that
we inform our readers of the death of the Rev-
erend Homer Wilbur, A. M., which took place
suddenly, by an apoplectic stroke, on the after-

noon of Christmas day, 1862. Our venerable
friend (for so we may venture to call him,
though we never enjoyed the high privilege of
his personal acquaintance) was in his eighty-
fourth year, having been born June 12, 1779, at
Pigsgusset Precinct (now West Jerusha) in the
then District of Maine. Graduated with dis-
tinction at Hubville College in 1805, he pursued
his theological studies with the late Reverend
Preserved Thacker, D. D., and was called to
the charge of the First Society in Jaalam in
1809, where he remained till his death.
" As an antiquary he has probably left no
superior, if, indeed, an equal," writes his friend
and colleague, the Reverend Jeduthun Hitch-
cock, to whom we are indebted for the above
facts ; " in proof of which I need only allude to
his ' History of Jaalam, Genealogical, Topo-
graphical, and Ecclesiastical,' 1849, which has
won him an eminent and enduring place in our
more solid and useful literature. It is only to
be regretted that his intense application to his-
torical studies should have so entirely with-
drawn him from the pursuit of poetical compo-
sition, for which he was endowed by Nature
with a remarkable aptitude. His well-known
hymn, beginning ' With clouds of care encom-
passed round,' has been attributed in some col-
lections to the late President Dwight, and it is
hardly presumptuous to affirm that the simile
of the rainbow in the eighth stanza would do no
discredit to that polished pen."
We regret that we have not room at present
for the whole of Mr. Hitchcock's exceedingly
valuable communication. We hope to lay more
liberal extracts from it before our readers at an
early day. A summary of its contents will give
some notion of its importance and interest. It
contains : 1st, A biographical sketch of Mr.
Wilbur, with notices of his predecessors in the
pastoral office, and of eminent clerical contem-
poraries ; 2d, An obituary of deceased, from
the Punkin-Falls " Weekly Parallel ; " 3d, A
list of his printed and manuscript productions
and of projected works ; 4th, Personal anec-
dotes and recollections, with specimens of table-
talk ; 5th, A tribute to his relict, Mrs. Dorcas
(Pilcox) Wilbur ; 6th, A list of graduates fitted
for different colleges by Mr. Wilbur, with bio-
graphical memoranda touching the more dis-
tinguished ; 7th, Concerning learned, charitable,
and other societies, of which Mr. Wilbur was a
member, and of those with which, had his life
been prolonged, he would doubtless have been
associated, with a complete catalogue of such
Americans as have been Fellows of the Royal
Society ; 8th, A brief summary of Mr. Wilbur's
latest conclusions concerning the Tenth Horn
of the Beast in its special application to recent
events, for which the public, as Mr. Hitchcock
assures us, have been waiting with feelings of
lively anticipation ; 9th, Mr. Hitchcock's own
views on the same topic ; and, 10th, A brief
essay on the importance of local histories. It
will be apparent that the duty of preparing Mr.
Wilbur's biography could not have fallen into
more sympathetic hands.

In a private letter with which the reverend gentleman has since favored us, he expresses the opinion that Mr. Wilbur's life was shortened by our unhappy civil war. It disturbed his studies, dislocated all his habitual associations and trains of thought, and unsettled the foundations of a faith, rather the result of habit than conviction, in the capacity of man for self-government. "Such has been the felicity of my life," he said to Mr. Hitchcock, on the very morning of the day he died, "that, through the divine mercy, I could always say, *Summum nec metuo diem, nec opto.* It has been my habit, as you know, on every recurrence of this blessed anniversary, to read Milton's 'Hymn of the Nativity' till its sublime harmonies so dilated my soul and quickened its spiritual sense that I seemed to hear that other song which gave assurance to the shepherds that there was One who would lead them also in green pastures and beside the still waters. But to-day I have been unable to think of anything but that mournful text, 'I came not to send peace, but a sword,' and, did it not smack of Pagan presumptuousness, could almost wish I had never lived to see this day."

Mr. Hitchcock also informs us that his friend "lies buried in the Jaalam graveyard, under a large red-cedar which he specially admired. A neat and substantial monument is to be erected over his remains, with a Latin epitaph written by himself; for he was accustomed to say, pleasantly, 'that there was at least one occasion in a scholar's life when he might show the advantages of a classical training.'"

The following fragment of a letter addressed to us, and apparently intended to accompany Mr. Biglow's contribution to the present number, was found upon his table after his decease. — EDITORS ATLANTIC MONTHLY.]

TO THE EDITORS OF THE ATLANTIC MONTHLY

JAALAM, 24th Dec., 1862.

RESPECTED SIRS, — The infirm state of my bodily health would be a sufficient apology for not taking up the pen at this time, wholesome as I deem it for the mind to apricate in the shelter of epistolary confidence, were it not that a considerable, I might even say a large, number of individuals in this parish expect from their pastor some publick expression of sentiment at this crisis. Moreover, *Qui tacitus ardet magis uritur.* In trying times like these, the besetting sin of undisciplined minds is to seek refuge from inexplicable realities in the dangerous stimulant of angry partisanship or the indolent narcotick of vague and hopeful vaticination : *fortunamque suo temperat arbitrio.* Both by reason of my age

and my natural temperament, I am unfitted for either. Unable to penetrate the inscrutable judgments of God, I am more than ever thankful that my life has been prolonged till I could in some small measure comprehend His mercy. As there is no man who does not at some time render himself amenable to the one, — *quum vix justus sit securus,* — so there is none that does not feel himself in daily need of the other.

I confess I cannot feel, as some do, a personal consolation for the manifest evils of this war in any remote or contingent advantages that may spring from it. I am old and weak, I can bear little, and can scarce hope to see better days ; nor is it any adequate compensation to know that Nature is young and strong and can bear much. Old men philosophize over the past, but the present is only a burthen and a weariness. The one lies before them like a placid evening landscape ; the other is full of the vexations and anxieties of housekeeping. It may be true enough that *miscet hæc illis, prohibetque Clotho fortunam stare,* but he who said it was fain at last to call in Atropos with her shears before her time ; and I cannot help selfishly mourning that the fortune of our Republick could not at least stay till my days were numbered.

Tibullus would find the origin of wars in the great exaggeration of riches, and does not stick to say that in the days of the beechen trencher there was peace. But averse as I am by nature from all wars, the more as they have been especially fatal to libraries, I would have this one go on till we are reduced to wooden platters again, rather than surrender the principle to defend which it was undertaken. Though I believe Slavery to have been the cause of it, by so thoroughly demoralizing Northern politicks for its own purposes as to give opportunity and hope to treason, yet I would not have our thought and purpose diverted from their true object, — the maintenance of the idea of Government. We are not merely suppressing an enormous riot, but contending for the possibility of permanent order coexisting with democratical fickleness; and while I would not superstitiously venerate form to the sacrifice of substance, neither would I forget that an adherence to precedent and prescription can alone give

that continuity and coherence under a demo-
cratical constitution which are inherent in
the person of a despotick monarch and the
selfishness of an aristocratical class. *Stet
pro ratione voluntas* is as dangerous in a ma-
jority as in a tyrant.

I cannot allow the present production of
my young friend to go out without a protest
from me against a certain extremeness in
his views, more pardonable in the poet than
in the philosopher. While I agree with him,
that the only cure for rebellion is suppres-
sion by force, yet I must animadvert upon
certain phrases where I seem to see a coin-
cidence with a popular fallacy on the sub-
ject of compromise. On the one hand there
are those who do not see that the vital prin-
ciple of Government and the seminal prin-
ciple of Law cannot properly be made a
subject of compromise at all, and on the
other those who are equally blind to the
truth that without a compromise of indi-
vidual opinions, interests, and even rights,
no society would be possible. *In medio
tutissimus.* For my own part, I would
gladly——

Ef I a song or two could make
Like rockets druv by their own burnin',
All leap an' light, to leave a wake
Men's hearts an' faces skyward turn-
in'!—
But, it strikes me, 't ain't jest the time
Fer stringin' words with settisfaction:
Wut 's wanted now 's the silent rhyme
'Twixt upright Will an' downright Ac-
tion.

Words, ef you keep 'em, pay their keep,
But gabble 's the short cut to ruin;
It 's gratis, (gals half-price,) but cheap
At no rate, ef it henders doin';
Ther' 's nothin' wuss, 'less 't is to set
A martyr-prem'um upon jawrin':
Teapots git dangerous, ef you shet
Their lids down on 'em with Fort War-
ren.

'Bout long enough it 's ben discussed
Who sot the magazine afire,
An' whether, ef Bob Wickliffe bust,
'T would scare us more or blow us
higher.
D' ye s'pose the Gret Foreseer's plan
Wuz settled fer him in town-meetin'?

Or thet ther' 'd ben no Fall o' Man,
Ef Adam 'd on'y bit a sweetin'?

Oh, Jon'than, ef you want to be
A rugged chap agin an' hearty,
Go fer wutever 'll hurt Jeff D.,
Nut wut 'll boost up ary party.
Here 's hell broke loose, an' we lay flat
With half the univarse a-singein',
Till Sen'tor This an' Gov'nor Thet
Stop squabblin' fer the garding-ingin.

It 's war we 're in, not politics;
It 's systems wrastlin' now, not parties;
An' victory in the eend 'll fix
Where longest will an' truest heart is.
An' wut 's the Guv'ment folks about?
Tryin' to hope ther' 's nothin' doin',
An' look ez though they did n't doubt
Sunthin' pertickler wuz a-brewin'.

Ther' 's critters yit thet talk an' act
Fer wut they call Conciliation;
They 'd hand a buff'lo-drove a tract
When they wuz madder than all Ba-
shan.
Conciliate? it jest means *be kicked*,
No metter how they phrase an' tone it;
It means thet we 're to set down licked,
Thet we 're poor shotes an' glad to own
it!

A war on tick 's ez dear 'z the deuce,
But it wun't leave no lastin' traces,
Ez 't would to make a sneakin' truce
Without no moral specie-basis:
Ef greenbacks ain't nut jest the cheese,
I guess ther' 's evils thet 's extremer,—
Fer instance,—shinplaster idees
Like them put out by Gov'nor Seymour.

Last year, the Nation, at a word,
When tremblin' Freedom cried to shield
her,
Flamed weldin' into one keen sword
Waitin' an' longin' fer a wielder:
A splendid flash!—but how 'd the grasp
With sech a chance ez thet wuz tally?
Ther' warn't no meanin' in our clasp,—
Half this, half thet, all shilly-shally.

More men? More Man! It 's there we
fail;
Weak plans grow weaker yit by length-
enin':

Wut use in addin' to the tail,
  When it 's the head 's in need o' strength-
    enin' ?
We wanted one thet felt all Chief
  From roots o' hair to sole o' stockin',
Square-sot with thousan'-ton belief
  In him an' us, ef earth went rockin'!

Ole Hick'ry would n't ha' stood see-saw
  'Bout doin' things till they wuz done
    with, —
He 'd smashed the tables o' the Law
  In time o' need to load his gun with;
He could n't see but jest one side, —
  Ef his, 't wuz God's, an' thet wuz plenty ;
An' so his " *Forrards!* " multiplied
  An army's fightin' weight by twenty.

But this 'ere histin', creak, creak, creak,
  Your cappen's heart up with a derrick,
This tryin' to coax a lightnin'-streak
  Out of a half-discouraged hay-rick,
This hangin' on mont' arter mont'
  Fer one sharp purpose 'mongst the
    twitter, —
I tell ye, it doos kind o' stunt
  The peth and sperit of a critter.

In six months where 'll the People be,
  Ef leaders look on revolution
Ez though it wuz a cup o' tea, —
  Jest social el'ments in solution ?
This weighin' things doos wal enough
  When war cools down, an' comes to
    writin';
But while it 's makin', the true stuff
  Is pison-mad, pig-headed fightin'.

Democ'acy gives every man
  The right to be his own oppressor ;
But a loose Gov'ment ain't the plan,
  Helpless ez spilled beans on a dresser :
I tell ye one thing we might larn
  From them smart critters, the Seced-
    ers, —
Ef bein' right 's the fust consarn,
  The 'fore-the-fust 's cast-iron leaders.

But 'pears to me I see some signs
  Thet we 're a-goin' to use our senses :
Jeff druv us into these hard lines,
  An' ough' to bear his half th' expenses ;
Slavery 's Secession's heart an' will,
  South, North, East, West, where'er you
    find it,

An' ef it drors into War's mill,
  D' ye say them thunder-stones sha'n't
    grind it ?

D' ye s'pose, ef Jeff giv *him* a lick,
  Ole Hick'ry 'd tried his head to sof'n
So 's 't would n't hurt thet ebony stick
  Thet 's made our side see stars so of'n ?
"No !" he 'd ha' thundered, "on your
    knees,
  An' own one flag, one road to glory !
Soft-heartedness, in times like these,
  Shows sof'ness in the upper story !"

An' why should we kick up a muss
  About the Pres'dunt's proclamation ?
It ain't a-goin' to lib'rate us,
  Ef we don't like emancipation :
The right to be a cussed fool
  Is safe from all devices human,
It 's common (ez a gin'l rule)
  To every critter born o' woman.

So *we* 're all right, an' I, fer one,
  Don't think our cause 'll lose in vally
By rammin' Scriptur' in our gun,
  An' gittin' Natur' fer an ally :
Thank God, say I, fer even a plan
  To lift one human bein's level,
Give one more chance to make a man,
  Or, anyhow, to spile a devil !

Not thet I 'm one thet much expec'
  Millennium by express to-morrer;
They *will* miscarry, — I rec'lec'
  Tu many on 'em, to my sorrer :
Men ain't made angels in a day,
  No matter how you mould an' labor
    'em,
Nor 'riginal ones, I guess, don't stay
  With Abe so of'n ez with Abraham.

The'ry thinks Fact a pooty thing,
  An' wants the banns read right en-
    suin';
But fact wun't noways wear the ring,
  'Thout years o' settin' up an' wooin':
Though, arter all, Time's dial-plate
  Marks cent'ries with the minute-finger,
An' Good can't never come tu late,
  Though it doos seem to try an' linger.

An' come wut will, I think it 's grand
  Abe 's gut his will et last bloom-fur-
    naced

In trial-flames till it 'll stand
The strain o' bein' in deadly earnest :
Thet 's wut we want, — we want to know
The folks on our side hez the bravery
To b'lieve ez hard, come weal, come woe,
In Freedom ez Jeff doos in Slavery.

Set the two forces foot to foot,
An' every man knows who 'll be winner,
Whose faith in God hez ary root
Thet goes down deeper than his dinner:
Then 't will be felt from pole to pole,
Without no need o' proclamation,
Earth's biggest Country 's gut her soul
An' risen up Earth's Greatest Nation !

No. VIII

KETTELOPOTOMACHIA

PRELIMINARY NOTE

[IN the month of February, 1866, the editors of the "Atlantic Monthly" received from the Rev. Mr. Hitchcock of Jaalam a letter enclosing the macaronic verses which follow, and promising to send more, if more should be communicated. "They were rapped out on the evening of Thursday last past," he says, "by what claimed to be the spirit of my late predecessor in the ministry here, the Rev. Dr. Wilbur, through the medium of a young man at present domiciled in my family. As to the possibility of such spiritual manifestations, or whether they be properly so entitled, I express no opinion, as there is a division of sentiment on that subject in the parish, and many persons of the highest respectability in social standing entertain opposing views. The young man who was improved as a medium submitted himself to the experiment with manifest reluctance, and is still unprepared to believe in the authenticity of the manifestations. During his residence with me his deportment has always been exemplary ; he has been constant in his attendance upon our family devotions and the public ministrations of the Word, and has more than once privately stated to me, that the latter had often brought him under deep concern of mind. The table is an ordinary quadrupedal one, weighing about thirty pounds, three feet seven inches and a half in height, four feet square on the top, and of beech or maple, I am not definitely prepared to say which. It had once belonged to my respected predecessor, and had been, so far as I can learn upon careful inquiry, of perfectly regular and correct habits up to the evening in question. On that occasion the young man previously alluded to had been sitting with his hands resting carelessly upon it, while I read over to him at his request certain portions of my last Sabbath's discourse. On a sudden the rappings, as they are called, commenced to render themselves audible, at first faintly, but in process of time more distinctly and with violent agitation of the table. The young man expressed himself both surprised and pained by the wholly unexpected, and, so far as he was concerned, unprecedented occurrence. At the earnest solicitation, however, of several who happened to be present, he consented to go on with the experiment, and with the assistance of the alphabet commonly employed in similar emergencies, the following communication was obtained and written down immediately by myself. Whether any, and if so, how much weight should be attached to it, I venture no decision. That Dr. Wilbur had sometimes employed his leisure in Latin versification I have ascertained to be the case, though all that has been discovered of that nature among his papers consists of some fragmentary passages of a version into hexameters of portions of the Song of Solomon. These I had communicated about a week or ten days previous[ly] to the young gentleman who officiated as medium in the communication afterwards received. I have thus, I believe, stated all the material facts that have any elucidative bearing upon this mysterious occurrence."

So far Mr. Hitchcock, who seems perfectly master of Webster's unabridged quarto, and whose flowing style leads him into certain further expatiations for which we have not room. We have since learned that the young man he speaks of was a sophomore, put under his care during a sentence of rustication from —— College, where he had distinguished himself rather by physical experiments on the comparative power of resistance in window-glass to various solid substances, than in the more regular studies of the place. In answer to a letter of inquiry, the professor of Latin says, "There was no harm in the boy that I know of beyond his loving mischief more than Latin, nor can I think of any spirits likely to possess him except those commonly called animal. He was certainly not remarkable for his Latinity, but I see nothing in the verses you enclose that would lead me to think them beyond his capacity, or the result of any special inspiration whether of beech or maple. Had that of *birch* been tried upon him earlier and more faithfully, the verses would perhaps have been better in quality and certainly in quantity." This exact and thorough scholar then goes on to point out many false quantities and barbarisms. It is but fair to say, however, that the author, whoever he was, seems not to have been unaware of some of them himself, as is shown by a great many notes appended to the verses as we received them, and purporting to be by Scaliger, Bentley, and others, — among them the *Esprit de Voltaire!* These we have omitted as clearly meant to be humorous and altogether failing therein.

Though entirely satisfied that the verses are altogether unworthy of Mr. Wilbur, who seems to have been a tolerable Latin scholar after the fashion of his day, yet we have determined to print them here, partly as belonging to the *res gestæ* of this collection, and partly as a warning to their putative author which may keep him from such indecorous pranks for the future.

KETTELOPOTOMACHIA

P. Ovidii Nasonis carmen heroicum macaronicum perplexametrum, inter Getas getico more compostum, denuo per medium ardentispiritualem adjuvante mensâ diabolice obsessâ, recuperatum, curâque Jo. Conradi Schwarzii umbræ, aliis necnon plurimis adjuvantibus, restitutum.

LIBER I.

PUNCTORUM garretos colens et cellara Quinque,
Gutteribus quæ et gaudes sundayam abstingere frontem,
Plerumque insidos solita fluitare liquore
Tanglepedem quem homines appellant Di quoque rotgut,
Pimpliidis, rubicundaque, Musa, O, bourbonolensque,　　　5
Fenianas rixas procul, alma, brogipotentis
Patricii cyathos iterantis et horrida bella,
Backos dum virides viridis Brigitta remittit,
Linquens, eximios celebrem, da, Virginienses
Rowdes, præcipue et TE, heros alte, Polarde!　　　10
Insignes juvenesque, illo certamine lictos,
Colemane, Tylere, nec vos oblivione relinquam.

Ampla aquilæ invictæ fausto est sub tegmine terra,
Backyfer, ooiskeo pollens, ebenoque bipede,
Socors præsidum et altrix (denique quidruminantium),　　　15

Duplefveorum uberrima; illis et integre cordi est
Deplere assidue et sine proprio incommodo fiscum;
Nunc etiam placidum hoc opus invictique secuti,
Goosam aureos ni eggos voluissent immo necare
Quæ peperit, saltem ac de illis meliora merentem.　　　20
Condidit hanc Smithius Dux, Captinus inclytus ille
Regis Ulyssæ instar, docti arcum intendere longum;
Condidit ille Johnsmith, Virginiamque vocavit,
Settledit autem Jacobus rex, nomine primus,
Rascalis implens ruptis, blagardisque deboshtis,　　　25
Militibusque ex Falstaffi legione fugatis
Wenchisque illi quas poterant seducere nuptas;
Virgineum, ah, littus matronis talibus impar!
Progeniem stirpe ex hoc non sine stigmate ducunt
Multi sese qui jactant regum esse nepotes:
Haud omnes, Mater, genitos quæ nuper habebas　　　31
Bello fortes, consilio cautos, virtute decoros,
Jamque et habes, sparso si patrio in sanguine virtus,
Mostrabisque iterum, antiquis sub astris reducta!
De illis qui upkikitant, dicebam, rumpora tanta,　　　35
Letcheris et Floydis magnisque Extra ordine Billis;
Est his prisca fides jurare et breakere wordum;
Poppere fellerum a tergo, aut stickere clam bowiknifo,
Haud sane facinus, dignum sed victrice lauro;
Larrupere et nigerum, factum præstantius ullo:　　　40
Ast chlamydem piciplumatam, Icariam, flito et ineptam,
Yanko gratis induere, illum et valido railo
Insuper acri equitare docere est hospitio uti.
Nescio an ille Polardus duplefveoribus ortus,
Sed reputo potius de radice poorwitemanorum;　　　45

Fortuiti proles, ni fallor, Tylerus erat
Præsidis, omnibus ab Whiggis nominatus a
    poor cuss ;
Et nobilem tertium evincit venerabile no-
    men.
Ast animosi omnes bellique ad tympana ha !
    ha !
Vociferant læti, procul et si prœlia, sive   50
Hostem incautum atsito possint shootere
    salvi ;
Imperiique capaces, esset si stylus agmen,
Pro dulci spoliabant et sine dangere fito.
Præ ceterisque Polardus : si Secessia licta,
Se nunquam licturum jurat, res et unheard-
    of,   55
Verbo hæsit, similisque audaci roosteri in-
    victo,
Dunghilli solitus rex pullos whoppere
    molles,
Grantum, hirelingos stripes quique et splen-
    dida tollunt
Sidera, et Yankos, territum et omnem sars-
    uit orbem.
    Usque dabant operam isti omnes, noctes-
    que diesque,   60
Samuelem demulgere avunculum, id vero
    siccum ;
Uberibus sed ejus, et horum est culpa, re-
    motis,
Parvam domi vaccam, nec mora minima,
    quærunt,
Lacticarentem autem et droppam vix in die
    dantem ;
Reddite avunculi, et exclamabant, reddite
    pappam !   65
Polko ut consule, gemens, Billy immur-
    murat Extra ;
Echo respondit, thesauro ex vacuo, pap-
    pam !
Frustra explorant pocketa, ruber nare re-
    pertum ;
Officia expulsi aspiciunt rapta, et Para-
    disum
Occlusum, viridesque haud illis nascere
    backos ;   70
Stupent tunc oculis madidis spittantque si-
    lenter.
Adhibere usu ast longo vires prorsus in-
    epti,
Si non ut qui grindeat axve trabemve re-
    uolvat,
Virginiam excruciant totis nunc mightibu'
    matrem ;
Non melius, puta, nono panis dimidiumne
    est ?   75

Readere ibi non posse est casus commoner
    ullo ;
Tanto intentius imprimere est opus ergo
    statuta;
Nemo propterea pejor, melior, sine doubto,
Obtineat qui contractum, si et postea rhino ;
Ergo Polardus, si quis, inexsuperabilis he-
    ros,   80
Colemanus impavidus nondum, atque in
    purpure natus
Tylerus Iohanides celerisque in flito Na-
    thaniel,
Quisque optans digitos in tantum stickere
    pium,
Adstant accincti imprimere aut perrumpere
    leges:
Quales os miserum rabidi tres ægre mo-
    lossi,   85
Quales aut dubium textum atra in veste
    ministri,
Tales circumstabant nunc nostri inopes hoc
    job.
    Hisque Polardus voce canoro talia fatus:
Primum autem, veluti est mos, præceps
    quisque liquorat,
Quisque et Nicotianum ingens quid inserit
    atrum,   90
Heroûm nitidum decus et solamen avi-
    tum,
Masticat ac simul altisonans, spittatque
    profuse:
Quis de Virginia meruit præstantius un-
    quam ?
Quis se pro patria curavit impigre tu-
    tum ?
Speechisque articulisque hominum quis for-
    tior ullus,   95
Ingeminans pennæ lickos et vulnera vo-
    cis ?
Quisnam putidius (hic) sarsuit Yankinimi-
    cos,
Sæpius aut dedit ultro datam et broke his
    parolam ?
Mente inquassatus solidâque, tyranno mi-
    nante,
Horrisonis (hic) bombis mœnia et alta qua-
    tente,   100
Sese promptum (hic) jactans Yankos lickere
    centum,
Atque ad lastum invictus non surrendidit
    unquam ?
Ergo haud meddlite, posco, mique relinquite
    (hic) hoc job,
Si non — knifumque enormem mostrat spit-
    tatque tremendus.

Dixerat : ast alii reliquorant et sine
pauso   105
Pluggos incumbunt maxillis, uterque vicis-
sim
Certamine innocuo valde madidam inquinat
assem:
Tylerus autem, dumque liquorat aridus
hostis,
Mirum aspicit duplumque bibentem, astante
Lyæo;
Ardens impavidusque edidit tamen impia
verba;   110
Duplum quamvis te aspicio, esses atque
viginti,
Mendacem dicerem totumque (hic) thrash-
erem acervum;
Nempe et thrasham, doggonatus (hic) sim
nisi faxem;
Lambastabo omnes catawompositer-(hic)
que chawam!
Dixit et impulsus Ryeo ruitur bene ti-
tus,   115
Illi nam gravidum caput et laterem habet
in hatto.
Hunc inhiat titubansque Polardus, optat
et illum
Stickere inermem, protegit autem rite
Lyæus,
Et pronos geminos, oculis dubitantibus, he-
ros
Cernit et irritus hostes, dumque excogitat
utrum   120
Primum inpitchere, corruit, inter utrosque
recumbit,
Magno asino similis nimio sub pondere quas-
sus:
Colemanus hos mœstus, triste ruminansque
solamen,
Inspicit hiccans, circumspittat terque cu-
bantes;
Funereisque his ritibus humidis inde solu-
tis,   125
Sternitur, invalidusque illis superincidit in-
fans;
Hos sepelit somnus et snorunt cornisonan-
tes,
Watchmanus inscios ast calybooso deinde
reponit.

No. IX

[THE Editors of the "Atlantic" have re-
ceived so many letters of inquiry concerning the
literary remains of the late Mr. Wilbur, men-
tioned by his colleague and successor, Rev.

Jeduthun Hitchcock, in a communication from
which we made some extracts in our number
for February, 1863, and have been so repeatedly
urged to print some part of them for the grati-
fication of the public, that they felt it their duty
at least to make some effort to satisfy so urgent
a demand. They have accordingly carefully
examined the papers intrusted to them, but find
most of the productions of Mr. Wilbur's pen so
fragmentary, and even chaotic, written as they
are on the backs of letters in an exceedingly
cramped chirography, — here a memorandum
for a sermon; there an observation of the
weather; now the measurement of an extraor-
dinary head of cabbage, and then of the cerebral
capacity of some reverend brother deceased; a
calm inquiry into the state of modern literature,
ending in a method of detecting if milk be im-
poverished with water, and the amount thereof;
one leaf beginning with a genealogy, to be inter-
rupted halfway down with an entry that the
brindle cow had calved, — that any attempts at
selection seemed desperate. His only complete
work, "An Enquiry concerning the Tenth Horn
of the Beast," even in the abstract of it given
by Mr. Hitchcock, would, by a rough computa-
tion of the printers, fill five entire numbers of
our journal, and as he attempts, by a new appli-
cation of decimal fractions, to identify it with
the Emperor Julian, seems hardly of immediate
concern to the general reader. Even the Table-
Talk, though doubtless originally highly inter-
esting in the domestic circle, is so largely made
up of theological discussion and matters of local
or preterite interest, that we have found it hard
to extract anything that would at all satisfy ex-
pectation. But, in order to silence further in-
quiry, we subjoin a few passages as illustrations
of its general character.]

I think I could go near to be a perfect Chris-
tian if I were always a visitor, as I have some-
times been, at the house of some hospitable
friend. I can show a great deal of self-denial
where the best of everything is urged upon me
with kindly importunity. It is not so very
hard to turn the other cheek for a kiss. And
when I meditate upon the pains taken for our
entertainment in this life, on the endless va-
riety of seasons, of human character and for-
tune, on the costliness of the hangings and
furniture of our dwelling here, I sometimes
feel a singular joy in looking upon myself as
God's guest, and cannot but believe that we
should all be wiser and happier, because more
grateful, if we were always mindful of our priv-
ilege in this regard. And should we not rate
more cheaply any honor that men could pay us,
if we remembered that every day we sat at the
table of the Great King? Yet must we not
forget that we are in strictest bonds His ser-
vants also; for there is no impiety so abject
as that which expects to be *dead-headed* (*ut ita
dicam*) through life, and which, calling itself
trust in Providence, is in reality asking Provi-

dence to trust us and taking up all our goods on false pretences. It is a wise rule to take the world as we find it, not always to leave it so.

It has often set me thinking when I find that I can always pick up plenty of empty nuts under my shagbark-tree. The squirrels know them by their lightness, and I have seldom seen one with the marks of their teeth in it. What a school-house is the world, if our wits would only not play truant! For I observe that men set most store by forms and symbols in proportion as they are mere shells. It is the outside they want and not the kernel. What stores of such do not many, who in material things are as shrewd as the squirrels, lay up for the spiritual winter-supply of themselves and their children! I have seen churches that seemed to me garners of these withered nuts, for it is wonderful how prosaic is the apprehension of symbols by the minds of most men. It is not one sect nor another, but all, who, like the dog of the fable, have let drop the spiritual substance of symbols for their material shadow. If one attribute miraculous virtues to mere holy water, that beautiful emblem of inward purification at the door of God's house, another cannot comprehend the significance of baptism without being ducked over head and ears in the liquid vehicle thereof.

[Perhaps a word of historical comment may be permitted here. My late revered predecessor was, I would humbly affirm, as free from prejudice as falls to the lot of the most highly favored individuals of our species. To be sure, I have heard him say that "what were called strong prejudices were in fact only the repulsion of sensitive organizations from that moral and even physical effluvium through which some natures by providential appointment, like certain unsavory quadrupeds, gave warning of their neighborhood. Better ten mistaken suspicions of this kind than one close encounter." This he said somewhat in heat, on being questioned as to his motives for always refusing his pulpit to those itinerant professors of vicarious benevolence who end their discourses by taking up a collection. But at another time I remember his saying, "that there was one large thing which small minds always found room for, and that was great prejudices." This, however, by the way. The statement which I purposed to make was simply this. Down to A. D. 1830, Jaalam had consisted of a single parish, with one house set apart for religious services. In that year the foundations of a Baptist Society were laid by the labors of Elder Joash Q. Balcom, 2d. As the members of the new body were drawn from the First Parish, Mr. Wilbur was for a time considerably exercised in mind. He even went so far as on one occasion to follow the reprehensible practice of the earlier Puritan divines in choosing a punning text, and preached from Hebrews xiii. 9: "Be not carried about with *divers* and strange doctrines." He afterwards, in accordance with one of his own maxims, — "to get a dead injury out of the mind as soon as is decent, bury it, and then ventilate," — in accordance with this maxim, I say, he lived on very friendly terms with Rev. Shearjashub Scrimgour, present pastor of the Baptist Society in Jaalam. Yet I think it was never unpleasing to him that the church edifice of that society (though otherwise a creditable specimen of architecture) remained without a bell, as indeed it does to this day. So much seemed necessary to do away with any appearance of acerbity toward a respectable community of professing Christians, which might be suspected in the conclusion of the above paragraph. — J. H.]

In lighter moods he was not averse from an innocent play upon words. Looking up from his newspaper one morning, as I entered his study, he said, "When I read a debate in Congress, I feel as if I were sitting at the feet of Zeno in the shadow of the Portico." On my expressing a natural surprise, he added, smiling, "Why, at such times the only view which honorable members give me of what goes on in the world is through their intercalumniations." I smiled at this after a moment's reflection, and he added gravely, "The most punctilious refinement of manners is the only salt that will keep a democracy from stinking; and what are we to expect from the people, if their representatives set them such lessons? Mr. Everett's whole life has been a sermon from this text. There was, at least, this advantage in duelling, that it set a certain limit on the tongue. When Society laid by the rapier, it buckled on the more subtle blade of etiquette wherewith to keep obtrusive vulgarity at bay." In this connection, I may be permitted to recall a playful remark of his upon another occasion. The painful divisions in the First Parish, A. D. 1844, occasioned by the wild notions in respect to the rights of (what Mr. Wilbur, so far as concerned the reasoning faculty, always called) the unfairer part of creation, put forth by Miss Parthenia Almira Fitz, are too well known to need more than a passing allusion. It was during these heats, long since happily allayed, that Mr. Wilbur remarked that "the Church had more trouble in dealing with one *she*resiarch than with twenty *he*resiarchs," and that the men's *conscia recti*, or certainty of being right, was nothing to the women's.

When I once asked his opinion of a poetical composition on which I had expended no little pains, he read it attentively, and then remarked, "Unless one's thought pack more neatly in verse than in prose, it is wiser to refrain. Commonplace gains nothing by being translated into rhyme, for it is something which no hocus-pocus can transubstantiate with the real presence of living thought. You entitle your piece, ' My Mother's Grave,' and expend four pages of useful paper in detailing your emotions there. But, my dear sir, watering does not improve the quality of ink, even though you should do it with tears. To publish a sorrow to Tom, Dick, and Harry is in some sort to advertise its unreality, for I have observed in my intercourse with the afflicted that the deepest grief instinctively hides its face with its hands and is silent. If your piece were printed, I have no doubt it would be popular, for people like to fancy that they feel much better than the trouble of feeling. I would put all poets on oath whether they have striven to say everything they possibly could think of, or to leave out all they could not help saying. In your own case, my worthy young friend, what you have written is merely a deliberate exercise, the gymnastic of sentiment. For your excellent maternal relative is still alive, and is to take tea with me this evening, D. V. Beware of simulated feeling; it is hypocrisy's first cousin; it is especially dangerous to a preacher; for he who says one day, ' Go to, let me seem to be pathetic,' may be nearer than he thinks to saying, ' Go to, let me seem to be virtuous, or earnest, or under sorrow for sin.' Depend upon it, Sappho loved her verses more sincerely than she did Phaon, and Petrarch his sonnets better than Laura, who was indeed but his poetical stalking-horse. After you shall have once heard that muffled rattle of clods on the coffin-lid of an irreparable loss, you will grow acquainted with a pathos that will make all elegies hateful. When I was of your age, I also for a time mistook my desire to write verses for an authentic call of my nature in that direction. But one day as I was going forth for a walk, with my head full of an ' Elegy on the Death of Flirtilla,' and vainly groping after a rhyme for *lily* that should not be *silly* or *chilly*, I saw my eldest boy Homer busy over the rain-water hogshead, in that childish experiment at parthenogenesis, the changing a horse-hair into a water-snake. An immersion of six weeks showed no change in the obstinate filament. Here was a stroke of unintended sarcasm. Had I not been doing in my study precisely what my boy was doing out of doors? Had my thoughts any more chance of coming to life by being submerged in rhyme than his hair by soaking in water? I burned my elegy and took a course of Edwards on the Will. People do not make poetry; it is made out of *them* by a process for which I do not find myself fitted. Nevertheless, the writing of verses is a good rhetorical exercitation, as teaching us what to shun most carefully in prose. For prose bewitched is like window-glass with bubbles in it, distorting what it should show with pellucid veracity."

It is unwise to insist on doctrinal points as vital to religion. The Bread of Life is wholesome and sufficing in itself, but gulped down with these kickshaws cooked up by theologians, it is apt to produce an indigestion, nay, even at last an incurable dyspepsia of scepticism.

One of the most inexcusable weaknesses of Americans is in signing their names to what are called credentials. But for my interposition, a person who shall be nameless would have taken from this town a recommendation for an office of trust subscribed by the selectmen and all the voters of both parties, ascribing to him as many good qualities as if it had been his tombstone. The excuse was that it would be well for the town to be rid of him, as it would erelong be obliged to maintain him. I would not refuse my name to modest merit, but I would be as cautious as in signing a bond. [I trust I shall be subjected to no imputation of unbecoming vanity, if I mention the fact that Mr. W. indorsed my own qualifications as teacher of the high-school at Pequash Junction. J. H.] When I see a certificate of character with everybody's name to it, I regard it as a letter of introduction from the Devil. Never give a man your name unless you are willing to trust him with your reputation.

There seem nowadays to be two sources of literary inspiration, — fulness of mind and emptiness of pocket.

I am often struck, especially in reading Montaigne, with the obviousness and familiarity of a great writer's thoughts, and the freshness they gain because said by him. The truth is, we mix their greatness with all they say and give it our best attention. Johannes Faber sic cogitavit would be no enticing preface to a book, but an accredited name gives credit like the signature to a note of hand. It is the advantage of fame that it is always privileged to take the world by the button, and a thing is weightier for Shakespeare's uttering it by the whole amount of his personality.

It is singular how impatient men are with overpraise of others, how patient with overpraise of themselves; and yet the one does them no injury while the other may be their ruin.

People are apt to confound mere alertness of mind with attention. The one is but the flying abroad of all the faculties to the open doors and windows at every passing rumor; the other is the concentration of every one of them in a single focus, as in the alchemist over his alembic at the moment of expected projection. Attention is the stuff that memory is made of, and memory is accumulated genius.

Do not look for the Millennium as imminent. One generation is apt to get all the wear it can out of the cast clothes of the last, and is always sure to use up every paling of the old fence that will hold a nail in building the new.

You suspect a kind of vanity in my genealogical enthusiasm. Perhaps you are right; but it is a universal foible. Where it does not show itself in a personal and private way, it becomes public and gregarious. We flatter ourselves in the Pilgrim Fathers, and the Virginian offshoot of a transported convict swells with the fancy of a cavalier ancestry. Pride of birth, I have noticed, takes two forms. One complacently traces himself up to a coronet; another, defiantly, to a lapstone. The sentiment is precisely the same in both cases, only that one is the positive and the other the negative pole of it.

Seeing a goat the other day kneeling in order to graze with less trouble, it seemed to me a type of the common notion of prayer. Most people are ready enough to go down on their knees for material blessings, but how few for those spiritual gifts which alone are an answer to our orisons, if we but knew it!

Some people, nowadays, seem to have hit upon a new moralization of the moth and the candle. They would lock up the light of Truth, lest poor Psyche should put it out in her effort to draw nigh to it.

No. X

MR. HOSEA BIGLOW TO THE EDITOR OF THE ATLANTIC MONTHLY

DEAR SIR, — Your letter come to han'
  Requestin' me to please be funny;
But I ain't made upon a plan
  Thet knows wut 's comin', gall or honey:
Ther' 's times the world doos look so queer,
  Odd fancies come afore I call 'em;

An' then agin, for half a year,
  No preacher 'thout a call 's more solemn.

You 're 'n want o' sunthin' light an' cute,
  Rattlin' an' shrewd an' kin' o' jingle-
    ish,
An' wish, pervidin' it 'ould suit,
  I 'd take an' citify my English.
I *ken* write long-tailed, ef I please, —
  But when I 'm jokin', no, I thankee;
Then, 'fore I know it, my idees
  Run helter-skelter into Yankee.

Sence I begun to scribble rhyme,
  I tell ye wut, I hain't ben foolin';
The parson's books, life, death, an' time
  Hev took some trouble with my school-
    in';
Nor th' airth don't git put out with me,
  Thet love her 'z though she wuz a wo-
    man;
Why, th' ain't a bird upon the tree
  But half forgives my bein' human.

An' yit I love th' unhighschooled way
  Ol' farmers hed when I wuz younger;
Their talk wuz meatier, an' 'ould stay,
  While book-froth seems to whet your
    hunger;
For puttin' in a downright lick
  'twixt Humbug's eyes, ther' 's few can
    metch it,
An' then it helves my thoughts ez slick
  Ez stret-grained hickory doos a hetchet.

But when I can't, I can't, thet 's all,
  For Natur' won't put up with gullin';
Idees you hev to shove an' haul
  Like a druv pig ain't wuth a mullein:
Live thoughts ain't sent for; thru all
    rifts
  O' sense they pour an' resh ye onwards,
Like rivers when south-lyin' drifts
  Feel thet th' old airth 's a-wheelin' sun-
    wards.

Time wuz, the rhymes come crowdin' thick
  Ez office-seekers arter' lection,
An' into ary place 'ould stick
  Without no bother nor objection;
But sence the war my thoughts hang back
  Ez though I wanted to enlist 'em,
An' subs'tutes, — *they* don't never lack,
  But then they 'll slope afore you 've
    mist 'em.

Nothin' don't seem like wut it wuz;
  I can't see wut there is to hender,
An' yit my brains jes' go buzz, buzz,
  Like bumblebees agin a winder;
'fore these times come, in all airth's row,
  Ther' wuz one quiet place, my head in,
Where I could hide an' think, — but now
  It's all one teeter, hopin', dreadin'.

Where 's Peace ?   I start, some clear-
      blown night,
    When gaunt stone walls grow numb an'
      number,
An', creakin' 'cross the snow-crus' white,
  Walk the col' starlight into summer;
Up grows the moon, an' swell by swell
  Thru the pale pasturs silvers dimmer
Than the last smile thet strives to tell
    O' love gone heavenward in its shim-
      mer.

I hev been gladder o' sech things
  Than cocks o' spring or bees o' clover,
They filled my heart with livin' springs,
  But now they seem to freeze 'em over;
Sights innercent ez babes on knee,
  Peaceful ez eyes o' pastur'd cattle,
Jes' coz they be so, seem to me
    To rile me more with thoughts o' bat-
      tle.

Indoors an' out by spells I try;
  Ma'am Natur' keeps her spin-wheel
      goin',
But leaves my natur' stiff and dry
  Ez fiel's o' clover arter mowin';
An' her jes' keepin' on the same,
  Calmer 'n a clock, an' never carin',
An' findin' nary thing to blame,
  Is wus than ef she took to swearin'.

Snow-flakes come whisperin' on the pane
  The charm makes blazin' logs so pleas-
      ant,
But I can't hark to wut they 're say'n',
  With Grant or Sherman ollers present;
The chimbleys shudder in the gale,
  Thet lulls, then suddin takes to flap-
      pin'
Like a shot hawk, but all 's ez stale
  To me ez so much sperit-rappin'.

Under the yaller-pines I house,
  When sunshine makes 'em all sweet-
      scented,

An' hear among their furry boughs
  The baskin' west-wind purr contented,
While 'way o'erhead, ez sweet an' low
  Ez distant bells thet ring for meetin',
The wedged wil' geese their bugles blow,
  Further an' further South retreatin'.

Or up the slippery knob I strain
  An' see a hundred hills like islan's
Lift their blue woods in broken chain
  Out o' the sea o' snowy silence;
The farm-smokes, sweetes' sight on airth,
  Slow thru the winter air a-shrinkin'
Seem kin' o' sad, an' roun' the hearth
  Of empty places set me thinkin'.

Beaver roars hoarse with meltin' snows,
  An' rattles di'mon's from his granite;
Time wuz, he snatched away my prose,
  An' into psalms or satires ran it;
But he, nor all the rest thet once
  Started my blood to country-dances,
Can't set me goin' more 'n a dunce
    Thet hain't no use for dreams an'
      fancies.

Rat-tat-tat-tattle thru the street
  I hear the drummers makin' riot,
An' I set thinkin' o' the feet
  Thet follered once an' now are quiet, —
White feet ez snowdrops innercent,
  Thet never knowed the paths o' Satan,
Whose comin' step ther' 's ears thet won't,
  No, not lifelong, leave off awaitin'.

Why, hain't I held 'em on my knee ?
  Did n't I love to see 'em growin',
Three likely lads ez wal could be,
  Hahnsome an' brave an' not tu knowin' ?
I set an' look into the blaze
    Whose natur', jes' like theirn, keeps
      climbin',
Ez long 'z it lives, in shinin' ways,
  An' half despise myself for rhymin'.

Wut 's words to them whose faith an'
      truth
  On War's red techstone rang true metal,
Who ventered life an' love an' youth
  For the gret prize o' death in battle ?
To him who, deadly hurt, agen
    Flashed on afore the charge's thunder,
Tippin' with fire the bolt of men
  Thet rived the Rebel line asunder ?

'Tain't right to hev the young go fust,
  All throbbin' full o' gifts an' graces,
Leavin' life's paupers dry ez dust
  To try an' make b'lieve fill their places:
Nothin' but tells us wut we miss,
  Ther' 's gaps our lives can't never fay in,
An' *thet* world seems so fur from this
  Lef' for us loafers to grow gray in !

My eyes cloud up for rain; my mouth
  Will take to twitchin' roun' the corners;
I pity mothers, tu, down South,
  For all they sot among the scorners:
I 'd sooner take my chance to stan'
  At Jedgment where your meanest slave
    is,
Than at God's bar hol' up a han'
  Ez drippin' red ez yourn, Jeff Davis !

Come, Peace ! not like a mourner bowed
  For honor lost an' dear ones wasted,
But proud, to meet a people proud,
  With eyes thet tell o' triumph tasted !
Come, with han' grippin' on the hilt,
  An' step thet proves ye Victory's daugh-
    ter !
Longin' for you, our sperits wilt
  Like shipwrecked men's on raf's for
    water.

Come, while our country feels the lift
  Of a gret instinct shoutin' " Forwards ! "
An' knows thet freedom ain't a gift
  Thet tarries long in han's o' cowards !
Come, sech ez mothers prayed for, when
  They kissed their cross with lips thet
    quivered,
An' bring fair wages for brave men,
  A nation saved, a race delivered !

No. XI

MR. HOSEA BIGLOW'S SPEECH
IN MARCH MEETING

TO THE EDITOR OF THE ATLANTIC
MONTHLY

JAALAM, April 5, 1866.
MY DEAR SIR, —
  (an' noticin' by your kiver thet you 're
some dearer than wut you wuz, I enclose
the deffrence) I dunno ez I know jest how
to interdooce this las' perduction of my

mews, ez Parson Willber allus called 'em,
which is goin' to *be* the last an' *stay* the last
onless sunthin' pertikler sh'd interfear
which I don't expec' ner I wun't yield tu
ef it wuz ez pressin' ez a deppity Shiriff.
Sence Mr. Wilbur's disease I hev n't hed
no one thet could dror out my talons. He
ust to kind o' wine me up an' set the
penderlum agoin' an' then somehow I
seemed to go on tick as it wear tell I run
down, but the noo minister ain't of the
same brewin' nor I can't seem to git ahold
of no kine of huming nater in him but sort
of slide rite off as you du on the eedge of a
mow. Minnysteeril natur is wal enough
an' a site better 'n most other kines I know
on, but the other sort sech as Welbor hed
wuz of the Lord's makin' an' naterally more
wonderfle an' sweet tastin' leastways to
me so fur as heerd from. He used to in-
terdooce 'em smooth ez ile athout sayin'
nothin' in pertickler an' I misdoubt he
did n't set so much by the sec'nd Ceres as
wut he done by the Fust, fact, he let on
onct thet his mine misgive him of a sort of
fallin' off in spots. He wuz as outspoken
as a norwester *he* wuz, but I tole him I
hoped the fall wuz from so high up thet a
feller could ketch a good many times fust
afore comin' bunt onto the ground as I see
Jethro C. Swett from the meetin' house
steeple up to th' old perrish, an' took up
for dead but he 's alive now an' spry as wut
you be. Turnin' of it over I recclected
how they ust to put wut they called Argy-
munce onto the frunts of poymns, like
poorches afore housen whare you could rest
ye a spell whilst you wuz concludin'
whether you 'd go in or nut espeshully ware
tha wuz darters, though I most allus found
it the best plen to go in fust an' think after-
wards an' the gals likes it best tu. I dno
as speechis ever hez any argimunts to 'em,
I never see none thet hed an' I guess they
never du but tha must allus be a B'ginnin'
to everythin' athout it is Etarnity so I 'll
begin rite away an' anybody may put it
afore any of his speeches ef it soots an'
welcome. I don't claim no paytent.

THE ARGYMUNT

Interducshin, w'ich may be skipt. Be-
gins by talkin' about himself : thet 's jest
natur an' most gin'ally allus pleasin', I

b'leeve I 've notist, to *one* of the cumpany, an' thet 's more than wut you can say of most speshes of talkin'. Nex' comes the gittin' the goodwill of the orjunce by lettin' 'em gether from wut you kind of ex'dentally let drop thet they air about East, A one, an' no mistaik, skare 'em up an' take 'em as they rise. Spring interdooced with a fiew approput flours. Speach finally begins witch nobuddy need n't feel obolygated to read as I never read 'em an' never shell this one ag'in. Subjick staited ; expanded; delayted; extended. Pump lively. Subjick staited ag'in so 's to avide all mistaiks. Ginnle remarks ; continooed ; kerried on; pushed furder ; kind o' gin out. Subjick *r*estaited ; dielooted ; stirred up permiscoous. Pump ag'in. Gits back to where he sot out. Can't seem to stay thair. Ketches into Mr. Seaward's hair. Breaks loose ag'in an' staits his subjick ; stretches it ; turns it ; folds it ; onfolds it ; folds it ag'in so 's 't no one can't find it. Argoos with an imedginary bean thet ain't aloud to say nothin' in repleye. Gives him a real good dressin' an' is settysfide he 's rite. Gits into Johnson's hair. No use tryin' to git into his head. Gives it up. Hez to stait his subjick ag'in ; doos it back'ards, sideways, eendways, criss-cross, bevellin', noways. Gits finally red on it. Concloods. Concloods more. Reads some xtrax. Sees his subjick a-nosin' round arter him ag'in. Tries to avide it. Wun't du. *Mis*states it. Can't conjectur' no other plawsable way of staytin' on it. Tries pump. No fx. Finely concloods to conclood. Yeels the flore.

You kin spall an' punctooate thet as you please. I allus do, it kind of puts a noo soot of close onto a word, thisere funattick spellin' doos an' takes 'em out of the prissen dress they wair in the Dixonary. Ef I squeeze the cents out of 'em it 's the main thing, an' wut they wuz made for ; wut 's left 's jest pummis.

Mistur Wilbur sez he to me onct, sez he, "Hosee," sez he, "in litterytoor the only good thing is Natur. It 's amazin' hard to come at," sez he, "but onct git it an' you 've gut everythin'. Wut 's the sweetest small on airth ? " sez he. " Noomone hay," sez I, pooty bresk, for he wuz allus hankerin' round in hayin'. " Nawthin' of the kine," sez he. " My leetle Huldy's

breath," sez I ag'in. " You 're a good lad," sez he, his eyes sort of ripplin' like, for he lost a babe onct nigh about her age, — " you 're a good lad ; but 't ain't thet nuther," sez he. " Ef you want to know," sez he, " open your winder of a mornin' et ary season, and you 'll larn thet the best of perfooms is jest fresh air, *fresh air*," sez he, emphysizin', " athout no mixtur. Thet 's wut *I* call natur in writin', and it bathes my lungs and washes 'em sweet whenever I git a whiff on 't," sez he. I offen think o' thet when I set down to write, but the winders air *so* ept to git stuck, an' breakin' a pane costs sunthin'.

Yourn for the last time,
Nut to be continooed,
HOSEA BIGLOW.

I DON'T much s'pose, hows'ever I should plen it,
I could git boosted into th' House or Sennit, —
Nut while the twolegged gab-machine 's so plenty,
'nablin' one man to du the talk o' twenty ;
I 'm one o' them thet finds it ruther hard
To mannyfactur' wisdom by the yard,
An' maysure off, accordin' to demand,
The piece-goods el'kence that I keep on hand,
The same ole pattern runnin' thru an' thru,
An' nothin' but the customer thet 's new.
I sometimes think, the furder on I go,
Thet it gits harder to feel sure I know,
An' when I 've settled my idees, I find
't warn't I sheered most in makin' up my mind ;
't wuz this an' thet an' t' other thing thet done it,
Sunthin' in th' air, I could n' seek nor shun it.
Mos' folks go off so quick now in discussion,
All th' ole flint-locks seems altered to percussion,
Whilst I in agin' sometimes git a hint,
Thet I 'm percussion changin' back to flint;
Wal, ef it 's so, I ain't agoin' to werrit,
For th' ole Queen's-arm hez this pertickler merit, —
It gives the mind a hahnsome wedth o' margin
To kin' o make its will afore dischargin' :

I can't make out but jest one ginnle
rule, —
No man need go an' *make* himself a fool,
Nor jedgment ain't like mutton, thet can't
bear
Cookin' tu long, nor be took up tu rare.

Ez I wuz say'n', I hain't no chance to
speak
So 's 't all the country dreads me onct a
week,
But I 've consid'ble o' thet sort o' head
Thet sets to home an' thinks wut *might* be
said,
The sense thet grows an' werrits under-
neath,
Comin' belated like your wisdom-teeth,
An' git so el'kent, sometimes, to my gardin
Thet I don' vally public life a fardin'.
Our Parson Wilbur (blessin's on his head !)
'mongst other stories of ole times he hed,
Talked of a feller thet rehearsed his
spreads
Beforehan' to his rows o' kebbige-heads,
(Ef 't warn't Demossenes, I guess 't wuz
Sisro,)
Appealin' fust to thet an' then to this
row,
Accordin' ez he thought thet his idees
Their diff'runt ev'riges o' brains 'ould
please ;
" An'," sez the Parson, " to hit right, you
must
Git used to maysurin' your hearers fust ;
For, take my word for 't, when all 's come
an' past,
The kebbige-heads 'll cair the day et last ;
Th' ain't ben a meetin' sence the worl'
begun
But they made (raw or biled ones) ten to
one."

I 've allus foun' 'em, I allow, sence then
About ez good for talkin' tu ez men ;
They 'll take edvice, like other folks, to
keep,
(To use it 'ould be holdin' on 't tu cheap,)
They listen wal, don' kick up when you
scold 'em,
An' ef they 've tongues, hev sense enough
to hold 'em;
Though th' ain't no denger we shall lose
the breed,
I gin'lly keep a score or so for seed,
An' when my sappiness gits spry in spring,

So 's 't my tongue itches to run on full
swing,
I fin' 'em ready-planted in March-meetin',
Warm ez a lýceum - audience in their
greetin',
An' pleased to hear my spoutin' frum the
fence,
Comin', ez 't doos, entirely free 'f expense.
This year I made the follerin' observations
Extrump'ry, like most other tri'ls o' pa-
tience,
An', no reporters bein' sent express
To work their abstrac's up into a mess
Ez like th' oridg'nal ez a woodcut pictur'
Thet chokes the life out like a boy-constric-
tor,
I 've writ 'em out, an' so avide all jeal'sies
'twixt nonsense o' my own an' some one's
else's.

(N. B. Reporters gin'lly git a hint
To make dull orjunces seem 'live in print,
An', ez I hev t' report myself, I vum,
I 'll put th' applauses where they 'd *ough'*
to come !)

MY FELLER KEBBIGE-HEADS, who look so
green,
I vow to gracious thet ef I could dreen
The world of all its hearers but jest you,
't would leave 'bout all tha' is wuth talkin'
to,
An' you, my ven'able ol' frien's, thet show
Upon your crowns a sprinklin' o' March
snow,
Ez ef mild Time had christened every sense
For wisdom's church o' second innocence,
Nut Age's winter, no, no sech a thing,
But jest a kin' o' slippin'-back o' spring, —
[Sev'ril noses blowed.]
We 've gathered here, ez ushle, to decide
Which is the Lord's an' which is Satan's
side,
Coz all the good or evil thet can heppen
Is 'long o' which on 'em you choose for
Cappen.
[Cries o' " Thet 's so."]

Aprul 's come back ; the swellin' buds of
oak
Dim the fur hillsides with a purplish
smoke ;
The brooks are loose an', singing to be seen,
(Like gals,) make all the hollers soft an'
green ;

The birds are here, for all the season's
   late;
They take the sun's height an' don' never
   wait;
Soon 'z he officially declares it 's spring
Their light hearts lift 'em on a north'ard
   wing,
An' th' ain't an acre, fur ez you can hear,
Can't by the music tell the time o' year;
But thet white dove Carliny scared away,
Five year ago, jes' sech an Aprul day;
Peace, that we hoped 'ould come an' build
   last year
An' coo by every housedoor, is n't here, —
No, nor wun't never be, for all our jaw,
Till we 're ez brave in pol'tics ez in war!
O Lord, ef folks wuz made so 's 't they
   could see
The begnet-pint there is to an idee!
                              [Sensation.]
Ten times the danger in 'em th' is in steel;
They run your soul thru an' you never feel,
But crawl about an' seem to think you 're
   livin',
Poor shells o' men, nut wuth the Lord's
   forgivin',
Tell you come bunt ag'in a real live fect,
An' go to pieces when you 'd ough' to ect!
Thet kin' o' begnet's wut we 're crossin'
   now,
An' no man, fit to nevvigate a scow,
'ould stan' expectin' help from Kingdom
   Come,
While t' other side druv their cold iron
   home.

My frien's, you never gethered from my
   mouth,
No, nut one word ag'in the South ez South,
Nor th' ain't a livin' man, white, brown,
   nor black,
Gladder 'n wut I should be to take 'em
   back;
But all I ask of Uncle Sam is fust
To write up on his door, " No goods on
   trust " ;
                        [Cries o' " Thet 's the ticket! "]
Give us cash down in ekle laws for all,
An' they 'll be snug inside afore nex' fall.
Give wut they ask, an' we shell hev Jama-
   ker,
Wuth minus some consid'able an acre ;
Give wut they need, an' we shell git 'fore
   long
A nation all one piece, rich, peacefle, strong;

Make 'em Amerikin, an' they 'll begin
To love their country ez they loved their
   sin ;
Let 'em stay Southun, an' you 've kep' a
   sore
Ready to fester ez it done afore.
No mortle man can boast of perfic' vision,
But the one moleblin' thing is Indecision,
An' th' ain't no futur' for the man nor state
Thet out of j-u-s-t can't spell great.
Some folks 'ould call thet reddikle ; do
   you ?
'T was commonsense afore the war wuz
   thru;
Thet loaded all our guns an' made 'em
   speak
So 's 't Europe heared 'em clearn acrost
   the creek ;
" They 're drivin' o' their spiles down now,"
   sez she,
" To the hard grennit o' God's fust idee ;
Ef they reach thet, Democ'cy need n't fear
The tallest airthquakes *we* can git up here."
Some call 't insultin' to ask *ary* pledge,
An' say 't will only set their teeth on edge,
But folks you 've jest licked, fur 'z I ever
   see,
Are 'bout ez mad 'z they wal know how to be;
It 's better than the Rebs themselves ex-
   pected
'fore they see Uncle Sam wilt down hen-
   pected;
Be kind 'z you please, but fustly make
   things fast,
For plain Truth 's all the kindness thet 'll
   last;
Ef treason is a crime, ez *some* folks say,
How could we punish it in a milder way
Than sayin' to 'em, " Brethren, lookee here,
We 'll jes' divide things with ye, sheer an'
   sheer,
An' sence both come o' pooty strong-backed
   daddies,
You take the Darkies, ez we 've took the
   Paddies;
Ign'ant an' poor we took 'em by the hand,
An' they 're the bones an' sinners o' the
   land."
I ain't o' them thet fancy there 's a loss on
Every inves'ment thet don't start from
   Bos'on;
But I know this: our money 's safest trusted
In sunthin', come wut will, thet *can't* be
   busted,
An' thet 's the old Amerikin idee,

To make a man a Man an' let him be.

[Gret applause.]

Ez for their l'yalty, don't take a goad to 't,
But I do' want to block their only road
    to 't
By lettin' 'em believe thet they can git
Mor 'n wut they lost, out of our little wit:
I tell ye wut, I 'm 'fraid we 'll drif' to lee-
    ward
'thout we can put more stiffenin' into
    Seward;
He seems to think Columby 'd better ect
Like a scared widder with a boy stiff-
    necked
Thet stomps an' swears he wun't come in
    to supper,
She mus' set up for him, ez weak ez
    Tupper,
Keepin' the Constitootion on to warm,
Tell he 'll eccept her 'pologies in form:
The neighbors tell her he 's a cross-grained
    cuss
Thet needs a hidin' 'fore he comes to wus;
" No," sez Ma Seward, " he 's ez good 'z
    the best,
All he wants now is sugar-plums an' rest; "
" He sarsed my Pa," sez one; " He stoned
    my son,"
Another edds. " Oh wal, 't wus jes' his
    fun."
" He tried to shoot our Uncle Samwell
    dead."
" 'T wuz only tryin' a noo gun he hed."
" Wal, all we ask 's to hev it understood
You 'll take his gun away from him for
    good;
We don't, wal, nut exac'ly, like his play,
Seein' he allus kin' o' shoots our way.
You kill your fatted calves to no good
    eend,
'thout his fust sayin', 'Mother, I hev
    sinned! ' "

[" Amen ! " frum Deac'n Greenleaf.]

The Pres'dunt *he* thinks thet the slickest
    plan
'ould be t' allow thet he 's our on'y man,
An' thet we fit thru all thet dreffle war
Jes' for his private glory an' eclor;
" Nobody ain't a Union man," sez he,
" 'thout he agrees, thru thick an' thin, with
    me;
Warn't Andrew Jackson's 'nitials jes' like
    mine ?
An' ain't thet sunthin like a right divine

To cut up ez kentenkerous ez I please,
An' treat your Congress like a nest o'
    fleas ? "
Wal, I expec' the People would n' care, if
The question now wuz techin' bank or
    tariff,
But I conclude they 've 'bout made up
    their min'
This ain't the fittest time to go it blin',
Nor these ain't metters thet with pol'tics
    swings,
But goes 'way down amongst the roots o'
    things;
Coz Sumner talked o' whitewashin' one
    day
They wun't let four years' war be throwed
    away.
" Let the South hev her rights ? " They
    say, " Thet's you !
But nut greb hold of other folks's tu."
Who owns this country, is it they or Andy ?
Leastways it ough' to be the People *and*
    he;
Let him be senior pardner, ef he 's so,
But let them kin' o' smuggle in ez Co;

[Laughter.]

Did he diskiver it ? Consid'ble numbers
Think thet the job wuz taken by Columbus.
Did he set tu an' make it wut it is ?
Ef so, I guess the One-Man-power *hez* riz.
Did he put thru the rebbles, clear the
    docket,
An' pay th' expenses out of his own pocket ?
Ef thet 's the case, then everythin' I exes
Is t' hev him come an' pay my ennooal
    texes.   [Profoun' sensation.]
Was 't he thet shou'dered all them million
    guns ?
Did he lose all the fathers, brothers, sons ?
Is this ere pop'lar gov'ment thet we run
A kin' o' sulky, made to kerry one ?
An' is the country goin' to knuckle down
To hev Smith sort their letters 'stid o'
    Brown ?
Who wuz the 'Nited States 'fore Richmon'
    fell ?
Wuz the South needfle their full name to
    spell ?
An' can't we spell it in thet short-han' way
Till th' underpinnin' 's settled so 's to
    stay ?
Who cares for the Resolves of '61,
Thet tried to coax an airthquake with a
    bun ?
Hez act'ly nothin' taken place sence then

To larn folks they must hendle fects like
 men ?
Ain't *this* the true p'int ? Did the Rebs
 accep' 'em ?
Ef nut, whose fault is 't thet we hev n't
 kep 'em ?
War n't there *two* sides ? an' don't it stend
 to reason
Thet this week's 'Nited States ain't las'
 week's treason ?
When all these sums is done, with nothin'
 missed,
An' nut afore, this school 'll be dismissed.

I knowed ez wal ez though I 'd seen 't with
 eyes
Thet when the war wuz over copper 'd
 rise,
An' thet we 'd hev a rile-up in our kettle
't would need Leviathan's whole skin to
 settle:
I thought 't would take about a generation
'fore we could wal begin to be a nation,
But I allow I never did imegine
't would be our Pres'dunt thet 'ould drive
 a wedge in
To keep the split from closin' ef it could,
An' healin' over with new wholesome wood;
For th' ain't no chance o' healin' while they
 think
Thet law an' gov'ment 's only printer's ink;
I mus' confess I thank him for discoverin'
The curus way in which the States are sov-
 ereign;
They ain't nut *quite* enough so to rebel,
But, when they fin' it 's costly to raise h—,
 [A groan from Deac'n G.]
Why, then, for jes' the same superl'tive
 reason,
They 're 'most too much so to be tetched
 for treason;
They *can't* go out, but ef they somehow *du*,
Their sovereignty don't noways go out tu;
The State goes out, the sovereignty don't
 stir,
But stays to keep the door ajar for her.
He thinks secession never took 'em out,
An' mebby he 's correc', but I misdoubt;
Ef they war'n't out, then why, 'n the name
 o' sin,
Make all this row 'bout lettin' of 'em in ?
In law, p'r'aps nut; but there 's a diffur-
 ence, ruther,
Betwixt your mother-'n-law an' real mother,
 [Derisive cheers.]

An' I, for one, shall wish they 'd all ben
 som'eres,
Long 'z U. S. Texes are sech reg'lar comers.
But, O my patience ! must we wriggle
 back
Into th' ole crooked, pettyfoggin' track,
When our artil'ry-wheels a road hev cut
Stret to our purpose ef we keep the rut ?
War 's jes' dead waste excep' to wipe the
 slate
Clean for the cyph'rin' of some nobler fate.
 [Applause.]
Ez for dependin' on their oaths an' thet,
't wun't bind 'em mor 'n the ribbin roun'
 my het:
I heared a fable once from Othniel Starns,
That pints it slick ez weathercocks do
 barns:
Onct on a time the wolves hed certing
 rights
Inside the fold ; they used to sleep there
 nights,
An', bein' cousins o' the dogs, they took
Their turns et watchin', reg'lar ez a book;
But somehow, when the dogs hed gut
 asleep,
Their love o' mutton beat their love o'
 sheep,
Till gradily the shepherds come to see
Things war'n't agoin' ez they 'd ough' to be;
So they sent off a deacon to remonstrate
Along 'th the wolves an' urge 'em to go on
 straight;
They did n' seem to set much by the dea-
 con,
Nor preachin' did n' cow 'em, nut to speak
 on;
Fin'ly they swore thet they 'd go out an'
 stay,
An' hev their fill o' mutton every day;
Then dogs an' shepherds, after much hard
 dammin',
 [Groan from Deac'n G.]
Turned tu an' give 'em a tormented lam-
 min',
An' sez, " Ye sha'n't go out, the murrain
 rot ye,
To keep us wastin' half our time to watch
 ye ! "
But then the question come, How live to-
 gether
'thout losin' sleep, nor nary yew nor
 wether ?
Now there wuz some dogs (noways wuth
 their keep)

Thet sheered their cousins' tastes an'
  sheered the sheep;
They sez, " Be gin'rous, let 'em swear right
  in,
An', ef they backslide, let 'em swear ag'in;
Jes' let 'em put on sheep-skins whilst
  they 're swearin' ;
To ask for more 'ould be beyond all bear-
  in'."
" Be gin'rous for yourselves, where *you* 're
  to pay,
Thet 's the best prectice," sez a shepherd
  gray;
" Ez for their oaths they wun't be wuth a
  button,
Long 'z you don't cure 'em o' their taste
  for mutton;
Th' ain't but one solid way, howe'er you
  puzzle:
Tell they 're convarted, let 'em wear a
  muzzle."   [Cries of " Bully for you ! "]

I 've noticed thet each half-baked scheme's
  abetters
Are in the hebbit o' producin' letters
Writ by all sorts o' never-heared-on fel-
  lers,
'bout ez oridge'nal ez the wind in bellers;
I 've noticed, tu, it 's the quack med'cine
  gits
(An' needs) the grettest heaps o' stiffykits;
              [Two pothekeries goes out.]
Now, sence I lef' off creepin' on all fours,
I hain't ast no man to endorse my course;
It 's full ez cheap to be your own endorser,
An' ef I 've made a cup, I 'll fin' the
  saucer;
But I 've some letters here from t' other side,
An' them 's the sort thet helps me to decide;
Tell me for wut the copper-comp'nies
  hanker,
An' I 'll tell you jest where it 's safe to
  anchor.   [Faint hiss.]
Fus'ly the Hon'ble B. O. Sawin writes
Thet for a spell he could n't sleep o'
  nights,
Puzzlin' which side wuz preudentest to pin
  to,
Which wuz th' ole homestead, which the
  temp'ry leanto;
Et fust he jedged 't would right-side-up
  his pan
To come out ez a 'ridge'nal Union man,
" But now," he sez, " I ain't nut quite so
  fresh;

The winnin' horse is goin' to be Secesh;
You might, las' spring, hev eas'ly walked
  the course,
'fore we contrived to doctor th' Union
  horse;
Now *we* 're the ones to walk aroun' the
  nex' track:
Jest you take hol' an' read the follerin' ex-
  trac',
Out of a letter I received last week
From an ole frien' thet never sprung a
  leak,
A Nothun Dem'crat o' th' ole Jarsey blue,
Born copper-sheathed an' copper-fastened
  tu."

" These four years past it hez ben tough
To say which side a feller went for;
Guideposts all gone, roads muddy 'n' rough,
An' nothin' duin' wut 't wuz meant for;
Pickets a-firin' left an' right,
Both sides a lettin' rip et sight, —
Life warn't wuth hardly payin' rent for.

" Columby gut her back up so,
It warn't no use a-tryin' to stop her, —
War's emptin's riled her very dough
An' made it rise an' act improper;
'T wuz full ez much ez I could du
To jes' lay low an' worry thru,
'Thout hevin' to sell out my copper.

" Afore the war your mod'rit men
Could set an' sun 'em on the fences,
Cyph'rin' the chances up, an' then
Jump off which way bes' paid expenses;
Sence, 't wuz so resky ary way,
I did n't hardly darst to say
I 'greed with Paley's Evidences.
              [Groan from Deac'n G.]

" Ask Mac ef tryin' to set the fence
Warn't like bein' rid upon a rail on 't,
Headin' your party with a sense
O' bein' tipjint in the tail on 't,
An' tryin' to think thet, on the whole,
You kin' o' quasi own your soul
When Belmont 's gut a bill o' sale on 't ?
              [Three cheers for Grant and Sherman.]

" Come peace, I sposed thet folks 'ould
  like
Their pol'tics done ag'in by proxy
Give their noo loves the bag an' strike
A fresh trade with their reg'lar doxy;

But the drag 's broke, now slavery 's gone,
An' there 's gret resk they 'll blunder on,
Ef they ain't stopped, to real Democ'cy.

" We 've gut an awful row to hoe
In this 'ere job o' reconstructin' ;
Folks dunno skurce which way to go,
Where th' ain't some boghole to be ducked
        in;
But one thing 's clear; there *is* a crack,
Ef we pry hard, 'twixt white an' black,
Where the ole makebate can be tucked in.

" No white man sets in airth's broad aisle
Thet I ain't willin' t' own ez brother,
An' ef he 's heppened to strike ile,
I dunno, fin'ly, but I 'd ruther;
An' Paddies, long 'z they vote all right,
Though they ain't jest a nat'ral white,
I hold one on 'em good 'z another.
                              [Applause.]

" Wut *is* there lef' I 'd like to know,
Ef 't ain't the defference o' color,
To keep up self-respec' an' show
The human natur' of a fullah ?
Wut good in bein' white, onless
It 's fixed by law, nut lef' to guess,
We 're a heap smarter an' they duller ?

" Ef we 're to hev our ekle rights,
't wun't du to 'low no competition;
Th' ole debt doo us for bein' whites
Ain't safe onless we stop th' emission
O' these noo notes, whose specie base
Is human natur', 'thout no trace
O' shape, nor color, nor condition.
                        [Continood applause.]

" So fur I 'd writ an' could n' jedge
Aboard wut boat I 'd best take pessige,
My brains all mincemeat, 'thout no edge
Upon 'em more than tu a sessige,
But now it seems ez though I see
Sunthin' resemblin' an idee,
Sence Johnson's speech an' veto message.

" I like the speech best, I confess,
The logic, preudence, an' good taste on 't,
An' it 's so mad, I ruther guess
There 's some dependence to be placed on' t;
                              [Laughter.]
It 's narrer, but 'twixt you an' me,
Out o' the allies o' J. D.
A temp'ry party can be based on 't.

" Jes' to hold on till Johnson 's thru
An' dug his Presidential grave is,
An' *then!* — who knows but we could
        slew
The country roun' to put in —— ?
Wun't some folks rare up when we pull
Out o' their eyes our Union wool
An' larn 'em wut a p'lit'cle shave is !

" Oh, did it seem 'z ef Providunce
Could ever send a second Tyler ?
To see the South all back to once,
Reapin' the spiles o' the Freesiler,
Is cute ez though an ingineer
Should claim th' old iron for his sheer
Coz 't was himself that bust the biler ! "
                              [Gret laughter.]

Thet tells the story ! Thet 's wut we shall
        git
By tryin' squirtguns on the burnin' Pit;
For the day never comes when it 'll du
To kick off Dooty like a worn-out shoe.
I seem to hear a whisperin' in the air,
A sighin' like, of unconsoled despair,
Thet comes from nowhere an' from every-
        where,
An' seems to say, " Why died we ? warn't
        it, then,
To settle, once for all, thet men wuz men ?
Oh, airth's sweet cup snetched from us
        barely tasted,
The grave's real chill is feelin' life wuz
        wasted !
Oh, you we lef', long-lingerin' et the door,
Lovin' you best, coz we loved Her the
        more,
Thet Death, not we, had conquered, we
        should feel
Ef she upon our memory turned her heel,
An' unregretful throwed us all away
To flaunt it in a Blind Man's Holiday ! "

My frien's, I 've talked nigh on to long
        enough.
I hain't no call to bore ye coz ye 're tough;
My lungs are sound, an' our own v'ice
        delights
Our ears, but even kebbige-heads hez
        rights.
It 's the las' time thet I shell e'er address ye,
But you 'll soon fin' some new tormentor:
        bless ye !

[Tumult'ous applause and cries of " Go on ! " " Don't
stop ! "]

UNDER THE WILLOWS AND OTHER POEMS

"THE WILLOWS," as was pointed out in the introductory note to *An Indian-Summer Reverie*, was a clump of trees not far from Elmwood. Lowell took a peculiar pleasure in their gnarled and umbrageous forms, and wrote to Fields while the volume which took its title from the trees was in press: "My heart was almost broken yesterday by seeing nailed to *my* willow a board with these words on it, 'These trees for sale.' The wretch is going to peddle them for firewood! If I had the money, I would buy the piece of ground they stand on to save them — the dear friends of a lifetime. They would be a loss to the town. But what can one do? They belong to a man who values them by the cord. I wish Fenn had sketched them at least. One of them I hope will stand a few years yet in my poem — but he might just as well have outlasted me and my works, making his own green ode every summer." Not all the trees have been destroyed, for some yet remain, and it is a pleasure to record the refusal of a new comer into the neighborhood to have one destroyed which was inconveniently near the site of the house she was to build. She changed, instead, the site.

The varying minds Lowell was in regarding the title of the volume may be learned from the following letter to C. E. Norton, dated

ELMWOOD, October 7, 1868.

... "The summer is past, the harvest is ended," and I have not yet written to you! Well, I was resolved I would not write till the printers had in their hands all the copy of my new volume of old poems. And that has taken longer than I expected. I have been Marthaized by many small troubles. But last night I fairly ended my work. ... I had decided to put the "June Idyl" in the forefront and call it "A June Idyl, and Other Poems." But Fields told me that Whittier's new volume was to be called "A Summer Idyl" — so I was blocked there. Then I took "Appledore," merely because it was a pretty name, though I did not wish to put that in the van. So it was all settled for the second time. Then I was suddenly moved to finish my "Voyage to Vinland,"... and, as I liked the poem, thought no title so good as "The Voyage to Vinland, and Other Poems." But Fields would not hear of it, and proposed that I should rechristen the Idyl "Elmwood," and name the book after that. But the more I thought of it the less I liked it. It was throwing my sanctuary open and making a showhouse of my hermitage. It was indecent. So I fumed and worried. I was *riled*. Then it occurred to me that I had taken the name of "June Idyl" as a *pis-aller*, because in my haste I could think of nothing else. Why not name it over? So I hit upon "Under the Willows," and that it is to be. ... But it is awfully depressing work. They call back so many moods, and they are so bad. I think, though, there is a suggestion of something good in them at least, and they are not silly. But how much the public will stand! I sometimes wonder they don't drive all us authors into a corner and make a *battue* of the whole concern at once.

In making the collection, the first miscellaneous one since the *Poems* published in 1849, Lowell gathered not only those published meanwhile in magazines and other periodicals, but went back and recovered some earlier verses.

TO CHARLES ELIOT NORTON
AGRO DOLCE

THE wind is roistering out of doors,
My windows shake and my chimney roars;
My Elmwood chimneys seem crooning to me,
As of old, in their moody, minor key,
And out of the past the hoarse wind blows,
As I sit in my arm-chair, and toast my toes.

"Ho! ho! nine-and-forty," they seem to sing,
"We saw you a little toddling thing.

We knew you child and youth and man,
A wonderful fellow to dream and plan,
With a great thing always to come, — who knows?
Well, well! 't is some comfort to toast one's toes.

"How many times have you sat at gaze
Till the mouldering fire forgot to blaze,
Shaping among the whimsical coals
Fancies and figures and shining goals!
What matters the ashes that cover those?
While hickory lasts you can toast your toes.

"O dream-ship-builder! where are they all,
Your grand three-deckers, deep-chested and tall,
That should crush the waves under canvas piles,
And anchor at last by the Fortunate Isles?
There's gray in your beard, the years turn foes,
While you muse in your arm-chair, and toast your toes."

I sit and dream that I hear, as of yore,
My Elmwood chimneys' deep-throated roar;
If much be gone, there is much remains;
By the embers of loss I count my gains,
You and yours with the best, till the old hope glows
In the fanciful flame, as I toast my toes.

Instead of a fleet of broad-browed ships,
To send a child's armada of chips!
Instead of the great guns, tier on tier,
A freight of pebbles and grass-blades sere!
"Well, maybe more love with the less gift goes,"
I growl, as, half moody, I toast my toes.

UNDER THE WILLOWS

FRANK-HEARTED hostess of the field and wood,
Gypsy, whose roof is every spreading tree,
June is the pearl of our New England year.
Still a surprisal, though expected long,
Her coming startles. Long she lies in wait,
Makes many a feint, peeps forth, draws coyly back,
Then, from some southern ambush in the sky,
With one great gush of blossom storms the world.
A week ago the sparrow was divine;
The bluebird, shifting his light load of song
From post to post along the cheerless fence,
Was as a rhymer ere the poet come;
But now, oh rapture! sunshine winged and voiced,

Pipe blown through by the warm wild breath of the West
Shepherding his soft droves of fleecy cloud,
Gladness of woods, skies, waters, all in one,
The bobolink has come, and, like the soul
Of the sweet season vocal in a bird,
Gurgles in ecstasy we know not what
Save *June! Dear June! Now God be praised for June.*

May is a pious fraud of the almanac,
A ghastly parody of real Spring
Shaped out of snow and breathed with eastern wind;
Or if, o'er-confident, she trust the date,
And, with her handful of anemones,
Herself as shivery, steal into the sun,
The season need but turn his hour-glass round,
And Winter suddenly, like crazy Lear,
Reels back, and brings the dead May in his arms,
Her budding breasts and wan dislustred front
With frosty streaks and drifts of his white beard
All overblown. Then, warmly walled with books,
While my wood-fire supplies the sun's defect,
Whispering old forest-sagas in its dreams,
I take my May down from the happy shelf
Where perch the world's rare song-birds in a row,
Waiting my choice to open with full breast,
And beg an alms of springtime, ne'er denied
Indoors by vernal Chaucer, whose fresh woods
Throb thick with merle and mavis all the year.

July breathes hot, sallows the crispy fields,
Curls up the wan leaves of the lilac-hedge,
And every eve cheats us with show of clouds
That braze the horizon's western rim, or hang
Motionless, with heaped canvas drooping idly,
Like a dim fleet by starving men besieged,
Conjectured half, and half descried afar,
Helpless of wind, and seeming to slip back
Adown the smooth curve of the oily sea.

But June is full of invitations sweet,
Forth from the chimney's yawn and thrice-
    read tomes
To leisurely delights and sauntering
    thoughts
That brook no ceiling narrower than the
    blue.
The cherry, drest for bridal, at my pane
Brushes, then listens, *Will he come?* The
    bee,
All dusty as a miller, takes his toll
Of powdery gold, and grumbles. What a
    day
To sun me and do nothing ! Nay, I think
Merely to bask and ripen is sometimes
The student's wiser business ; the brain
That forages all climes to line its cells,
Ranging both worlds on lightest wings of
    wish,
Will not distil the juices it has sucked
To the sweet substance of pellucid thought,
Except for him who hath the secret learned
To mix his blood with sunshine, and to
    take
The winds into his pulses. Hush! 't is
    he!
My oriole, my glance of summer fire,
Is come at last, and, ever on the watch,
Twitches the packthread I had lightly
    wound
About the bough to help his housekeep-
    ing, —
Twitches and scouts by turns, blessing his
    luck,
Yet fearing me who laid it in his way,
Nor, more than wiser we in our affairs,
Divines the providence that hides and helps.
Heave, ho! Heave, ho! he whistles as the
    twine
Slackens its hold; *once more, now!* and a
    flash
Lightens across the sunlight to the elm
Where his mate dangles at her cup of
    felt.
Nor all his booty is the thread; he trails
My loosened thought with it along the
    air,
And I must follow, would I ever find
The inward rhyme to all this wealth of
    life.

I care not how men trace their ancestry,
To ape or Adam: let them please their
    whim;
But I in June am midway to believe

A tree among my far progenitors,
Such sympathy is mine with all the race,
Such mutual recognition vaguely sweet
There is between us. Surely there are
    times
When they consent to own me of their
    kin,
And condescend to me, and call me cousin,
Murmuring faint lullabies of eldest time,
Forgotten, and yet dumbly felt with thrills
Moving the lips, though fruitless of all
    words.
And I have many a lifelong leafy friend,
Never estranged nor careful of my soul,
That knows I hate the axe, and welcomes
    me
Within his tent as if I were a bird,
Or other free companion of the earth,
Yet undegenerate to the shifts of men.
Among them one, an ancient willow,
    spreads
Eight balanced limbs, springing at once all
    round
His deep-ridged trunk with upward slant
    diverse,
In outline like enormous beaker, fit
For hand of Jotun, where mid snow and
    mist
He holds unwieldy revel. This tree, spared,
I know not by what grace, — for in the
    blood
Of our New World subduers lingers yet
Hereditary feud with trees, they being
(They and the red-man most) our fathers'
    foes, —
Is one of six, a willow Pleiades,
The seventh fallen, that lean along the
    brink
Where the steep upland dips into the marsh,
Their roots, like molten metal cooled in
    flowing,
Stiffened in coils and runnels down the
    bank.
The friend of all the winds, wide-armed he
    towers
And glints his steely aglets in the sun,
Or whitens fitfully with sudden bloom
Of leaves breeze-lifted, much as when a
    shoal
Of devious minnows wheel from where a
    pike
Lurks balanced 'neath the lily-pads, and
    whirl
A rood of silver bellies to the day.
Alas! no acorn from the British oak

'Neath which slim fairies tripping wrought
    those rings
Of greenest emerald, wherewith fireside life
Did with the invisible spirit of Nature
    wed,
Was ever planted here! No darnel fancy
Might choke one useful blade in Puritan
    fields;
With horn and hoof the good old Devil
    came,
The witch's broomstick was not contra-
    band,
But all that superstition had of fair,
Or piety of native sweet, was doomed.
And if there be who nurse unholy faiths,
Fearing their god as if he were a wolf
That snuffed round every home and was
    not seen,
There should be some to watch and keep
    alive
All beautiful beliefs. And such was that, —
By solitary shepherd first surmised
Under Thessalian oaks, loved by some maid
Of royal stirp, that silent came and van-
    ished,
As near her nest the hermit thrush, nor
    dared
Confess a mortal name, — that faith which
    gave
A Hamadryad to each tree; and I
Will hold it true that in this willow dwells
The open-handed spirit, frank and blithe,
Of ancient Hospitality, long since,
With ceremonious thrift, bowed out of
    doors.

In June 't is good to lie beneath a tree
While the blithe season comforts every
    sense,
Steeps all the brain in rest, and heals the
    heart,
Brimming it o'er with sweetness unawares,
Fragrant and silent as that rosy snow
Wherewith the pitying apple-tree fills up
And tenderly lines some last-year robin's
    nest.
There muse I of old times, old hopes, old
    friends, —
Old friends! The writing of those words
    has borne
My fancy backward to the gracious past,
The generous past, when all was possible,
For all was then untried; the years between
Have taught some sweet, some bitter lessons,
    none

Wiser than this, — to spend in all things
    else,
But of old friends to be most miserly.
Each year to ancient friendships adds a
    ring,
As to an oak, and precious more and more,
Without deservingness or help of ours,
They grow, and, silent, wider spread, each
    year,
Their unbought ring of shelter or of shade.
Sacred to me the lichens on the bark,
Which Nature's milliners would scrape
    away;
Most dear and sacred every withered limb!
'T is good to set them early, for our faith
Pines as we age, and, after wrinkles come,
Few plant, but water dead ones with vain
    tears.

This willow is as old to me as life;
And under it full often have I stretched,
Feeling the warm earth like a thing alive,
And gathering virtue in at every pore
Till it possessed me wholly, and thought
    ceased,
Or was transfused in something to which
    thought
Is coarse and dull of sense. Myself was
    lost,
Gone from me like an ache, and what re-
    mained
Become a part of the universal joy.
My soul went forth, and, mingling with the
    tree,
Danced in the leaves; or, floating in the
    cloud,
Saw its white double in the stream below;
Or else, sublimed to purer ecstasy,
Dilated in the broad blue over all.
I was the wind that dappled the lush
    grass,
The tide that crept with coolness to its
    roots,
The thin-winged swallow skating on the
    air;
The life that gladdened everything was
    mine.
Was I then truly all that I beheld?
Or is this stream of being but a glass
Where the mind sees its visionary self,
As, when the kingfisher flits o'er his bay,
Across the river's hollow heaven below
His picture flits, — another, yet the same?
But suddenly the sound of human voice
Or footfall, like the drop a chemist pours,

Doth in opacous cloud precipitate
The consciousness that seemed but now
    dissolved
Into an essence rarer than its own,
And I am narrowed to myself once more.

For here not long is solitude secure,
Nor Fantasy left vacant to her spell.
Here, sometimes, in this paradise of shade,
Rippled with western winds, the dusty
    Tramp,
Seeing the treeless causey burn beyond,
Halts to unroll his bundle of strange food
And munch an unearned meal. I cannot
    help
Liking this creature, lavish Summer's
    bedesman,
Who from the almshouse steals when nights
    grow warm,
Himself his large estate and only charge,
To be the guest of haystack or of hedge,
Nobly superior to the household gear
That forfeits us our privilege of nature.
I bait him with my match-box and my
    pouch,
Nor grudge the uncostly sympathy of
    smoke,
His equal now, divinely unemployed.
Some smack of Robin Hood is in the man,
Some secret league with wild wood-wander-
    ing things;
He is our ragged Duke, our barefoot Earl,
By right of birth exonerate from toil,
Who levies rent from us his tenants all,
And serves the state by merely being.
    Here
The Scissors-grinder, pausing, doffs his hat,
And lets the kind breeze, with its delicate
    fan,
Winnow the heat from out his dank gray
    hair, —
A grimy Ulysses, a much-wandered man,
Whose feet are known to all the populous
    ways,
And many men and manners he hath seen,
Not without fruit of solitary thought.
He, as the habit is of lonely men, —
Unused to try the temper of their mind
In fence with others, — positive and shy,
Yet knows to put an edge upon his speech,
Pithily Saxon in unwilling talk.
Him I entrap with my long-suffering
    knife,
And, while its poor blade hums away in
    sparks,

Sharpen my wit upon his gritty mind,
In motion set obsequious to his wheel,
And in its quality not much unlike.

Nor wants my tree more punctual visitors.
The children, they who are the only rich,
Creating for the moment, and possessing
Whate'er they choose to feign, — for still
    with them
Kind Fancy plays the fairy godmother,
Strewing their lives with cheap material
For wingëd horses and Aladdin's lamps,
Pure elfin-gold, by manhood's touch pro-
    fane
To dead leaves disenchanted, — long ago
Between the branches of the tree fixed
    seats,
Making an o'erturned box their table. Oft
The shrilling girls sit here between school
    hours,
And play at *What's my thought like?* while
    the boys,
With whom the age chivalric ever bides,
Pricked on by knightly spur of female eyes,
Climb high to swing and shout on perilous
    boughs,
Or, from the willow's armory equipped
With musket dumb, green banner, edge-
    less sword,
Make good the rampart of their tree-
    redoubt
'Gainst eager British storming from below,
And keep alive the tale of Bunker's Hill.

Here, too, the men that mend our village
    ways,
Vexing Macadam's ghost with pounded
    slate,
Their nooning take ; much noisy talk they
    spend
On horses and their ills; and, as John Bull
Tells of Lord This or That, who was his
    friend,
So these make boast of intimacies long
With famous teams, and add large esti-
    mates,
By competition swelled from mouth to
    mouth,
Of how much they could draw, till one, ill
    pleased
To have his legend overbid, retorts :
"You take and stretch truck-horses in a
    string
From here to Long Wharf end, one thing
    I know,

Not heavy neither, they could never draw, —
Ensign's long bow!" Then laughter loud
  and long.
So they in their leaf-shadowed microcosm
Image the larger world; for wheresoe'er
Ten men are gathered, the observant eye
Will find mankind in little, as the stars
Glide up and set, and all the heavens re-
  volve
In the small welkin of a drop of dew.

I love to enter pleasure by a postern,
Not the broad popular gate that gulps the
  mob;
To find my theatres in roadside nooks,
Where men are actors, and suspect it not;
Where Nature all unconscious works her
  will,
And every passion moves with easy gait,
Unhampered by the buskin or the train.
Hating the crowd, where we gregarious
  men
Lead lonely lives, I love society,
Nor seldom find the best with simple souls
Unswerved by culture from their native
  bent,
The ground we meet on being primal man
And nearer the deep bases of our lives.

But oh, half heavenly, earthly half, my
  soul,
Canst thou from those late ecstasies de-
  scend,
Thy lips still wet with the miraculous wine
That transubstantiates all thy baser stuff
To such divinity that soul and sense,
Once more commingled in their source, are
  lost, —
Canst thou descend to quench a vulgar
  thirst
With the mere dregs and rinsings of the
  world ?
Well, if my nature find her pleasure so,
I am content, nor need to blush; I take
My little gift of being clean from God,
Not haggling for a better, holding it
Good as was ever any in the world,
My days as good and full of miracle.
I pluck my nutriment from any bush,
Finding out poison as the first men did
By tasting and then suffering, if I must.
Sometimes my bush burns, and sometimes
  it is
A leafless wilding shivering by the wall;
But I have known when winter barberries

Pricked the effeminate palate with sur-
  prise
Of savor whose mere harshness seemed
  divine.

Oh, benediction of the higher mood
And human-kindness of the lower ! for
  both
I will be grateful while I live, nor question
The wisdom that hath made us what we
  are,
With such large range as from the ale-
  house bench
Can reach the stars and be with both at
  home.
They tell us we have fallen on prosy days,
Condemned to glean the leavings of earth's
  feast
Where gods and heroes took delight of
  old;
But though our lives, moving in one dull
  round
Of repetition infinite, become
Stale as a newspaper once read, and though
History herself, seen in her workshop,
  seem
To have lost the art that dyed those glori-
  ous panes,
Rich with memorial shapes of saint and
  sage,
That pave with splendor the Past's dusky
  aisles, —
Panes that enchant the light of common day
With colors costly as the blood of kings,
Till with ideal hues it edge our thought, —
Yet while the world is left, while nature
  lasts,
And man the best of nature, there shall be
Somewhere contentment for these human
  hearts,
Some freshness, some unused material
For wonder and for song. I lose myself
In other ways where solemn guide-posts
  say,
This way to Knowledge, This way to Repose,
But here, here only, I am ne'er betrayed,
For every by-path leads me to my love.

God's passionless reformers, influences,
That purify and heal and are not seen,
Shall man say whence your virtue is, or
  how
Ye make medicinal the wayside weed ?
I know that sunshine, through whatever
  rift

How shaped it matters not, upon my walls
Paints discs as perfect - rounded as its
source,
And, like its antitype, the ray divine,
However finding entrance, perfect still,
Repeats the image unimpaired of God.

We, who by shipwreck only find the shores
Of divine wisdom, can but kneel at first;
Can but exult to feel beneath our feet,
That long stretched vainly down the yield-
ing deeps,
The shock and sustenance of solid earth;
Inland afar we see what temples gleam
Through immemorial stems of sacred
groves,
And we conjecture shining shapes there-
in;
Yet for a space we love to wander here
Among the shells and seaweed of the
beach.

So mused I once within my willow-tent
One brave June morning, when the bluff
northwest,
Thrusting aside a dank and snuffling day
That made us bitter at our neighbors' sins,
Brimmed the great cup of heaven with
sparkling cheer
And roared a lusty stave ; the sliding
Charles,
Blue toward the west, and bluer and more
blue,
Living and lustrous as a woman's eyes
Look once and look no more, with south-
ward curve
Ran crinkling sunniness, like Helen's hair
Glimpsed in Elysium, insubstantial gold;
From blossom-clouded orchards, far away
The bobolink tinkled; the deep meadows
flowed
With multitudinous pulse of light and
shade
Against the bases of the southern hills,
While here and there a drowsy island rick
Slept and its shadow slept; the wooden
bridge
Thundered, and then was silent; on the
roofs
The sun-warped shingles rippled with the
heat;
Summer on field and hill, in heart and
brain,
All life washed clean in this high tide of
June.

DARA

WHEN Persia's sceptre trembled in a hand
Wilted with harem-heats, and all the land
Was hovered over by those vulture ills
That snuff decaying empire from afar,
Then, with a nature balanced as a star,
Dara arose, a shepherd of the hills.

He who had governed fleecy subjects well
Made his own village by the selfsame
spell
Secure and quiet as a guarded fold;
Then, gathering strength by slow and wise
degrees
Under his sway, to neighbor villages
Order returned, and faith and justice old.

Now when it fortuned that a king more wise
Endued the realm with brain and hands
and eyes,
He sought on every side men brave and
just ;
And having heard our mountain shepherd's
praise,
How he refilled the mould of elder days,
To Dara gave a satrapy in trust.

So Dara shepherded a province wide,
Nor in his viceroy's sceptre took more
pride
Than in his crook before ; but envy finds
More food in cities than on mountains
bare ;
And the frank sun of natures clear and
rare
Breeds poisonous fogs in low and marish
minds.

Soon it was hissed into the royal ear,
That, though wise Dara's province, year
by year,
Like a great sponge, sucked wealth and
plenty up,
Yet, when he squeezed it at the king's be-
hest,
Some yellow drops, more rich than all the
rest,
Went to the filling of his private cup.

For proof, they said, that, wheresoe'er he
went,
A chest, beneath whose weight the camel
bent,

Went with him ; and no mortal eye had
    seen
What was therein, save only Dara's own ;
But, when 't was opened, all his tent was
    known
To glow and lighten with heaped jewels'
    sheen.

The King set forth for Dara's province
    straight ;
There, as was fit, outside the city's gate,
The viceroy met him with a stately train,
And there, with archers circled, close at
    hand,
A camel with the chest was seen to stand :
The King's brow reddened, for the guilt
    was plain.

" Open me here," he cried, " this treasure-
    chest ! "
'T was done ; and only a worn shepherd's
    vest
Was found therein. Some blushed and
    hung the head ;
Not Dara ; open as the sky's blue roof
He stood, and " O my lord, behold the
    proof
That I was faithful to my trust," he said.

" To govern men, lo all the spell I had !
My soul in these rude vestments ever clad
Still to the unstained past kept true and leal,
Still on these plains could breathe her
    mountain air,
And fortune's heaviest gifts serenely bear,
Which bend men from their truth and
    make them reel.

" For ruling wisely I should have small
    skill,
Were I not lord of simple Dara still ;
That sceptre kept, I could not lose my
    way."
Strange dew in royal eyes grew round and
    bright,
And strained the throbbing lids ; before
    't was night
Two added provinces blest Dara's sway.

THE FIRST SNOW-FALL

One of the " earlier verses " sent to the *Anti-
Slavery Standard*. In a letter to Mr. Gay,
dated Elmwood, December 22, 1849, Lowell

wrote : " Print that as if you loved it. Let not
a comma be blundered. Especially I fear they
will put 'gleaming' for 'gloaming' in the first
line unless you look to it. May you never
have the key which shall unlock the whole
meaning of the poem to you ! "

THE snow had begun in the gloaming,
    And busily all the night
Had been heaping field and highway
    With a silence deep and white.

Every pine and fir and hemlock
    Wore ermine too dear for an earl,
And the poorest twig on the elm-tree
    Was ridged inch deep with pearl.

From sheds new-roofed with Carrara
    Came Chanticleer's muffled crow,
The stiff rails softened to swan's-down,
    And still fluttered down the snow.

I stood and watched by the window
    The noiseless work of the sky,
And the sudden flurries of snow-birds,
    Like brown leaves whirling by.

I thought of a mound in sweet Auburn
    Where a little headstone stood ;
How the flakes were folding it gently,
    As did robins the babes in the wood.

Up spoke our own little Mabel,
    Saying, " Father, who makes it snow ? "
And I told of the good All-father
    Who cares for us here below.

Again I looked at the snow-fall,
    And thought of the leaden sky
That arched o'er our first great sorrow,
    When that mound was heaped so high.

I remembered the gradual patience
    That fell from that cloud like snow,
Flake by flake, healing and hiding
    The scar that renewed our woe.

And again to the child I whispered,
    " The snow that husheth all,
Darling, the merciful Father
    Alone can make it fall ! "

Then, with eyes that saw not, I kissed her ;
    And she, kissing back, could not know
That *my* kiss was given to her sister,
    Folded close under deepening snow.

THE SINGING LEAVES

A BALLAD

I

" WHAT fairings will ye that I bring? "
  Said the King to his daughters three;
" For I to Vanity Fair am boun,
  Now say what shall they be? "

Then up and spake the eldest daughter,
  That lady tall and grand:
" Oh, bring me pearls and diamonds great,
  And gold rings for my hand."

Thereafter spake the second daughter,
  That was both white and red:
" For me bring silks that will stand alone,
  And a gold comb for my head."

Then came the turn of the least daughter,
  That was whiter than thistle-down,
And among the gold of her blithesome hair
  Dim shone the golden crown.

" There came a bird this morning,
  And sang 'neath my bower eaves,
Till I dreamed, as his music made me,
  ' Ask thou for the Singing Leaves.' "

Then the brow of the King swelled crimson
  With a flush of angry scorn:
" Well have ye spoken, my two eldest,
  And chosen as ye were born;

" But she, like a thing of peasant race,
  That is happy binding the sheaves; "
Then he saw her dead mother in her face,
  And said, " Thou shalt have thy leaves."

II

He mounted and rode three days and nights
  Till he came to Vanity Fair,
And 't was easy to buy the gems and the silk,
  But no Singing Leaves were there.

Then deep in the greenwood rode he,
  And asked of every tree,
" Oh, if you have ever a Singing Leaf,
  I pray you give it me! "

But the trees all kept their counsel,
  And never a word said they,

Only there sighed from the pine-tops
  A music of seas far away.

Only the pattering aspen
  Made a sound of growing rain,
That fell ever faster and faster,
  Then faltered to silence again.

" Oh, where shall I find a little foot-page
  That would win both hose and shoon,
And will bring to me the Singing Leaves
  If they grow under the moon? "

Then lightly turned him Walter the page,
  By the stirrup as he ran:
" Now pledge you me the truesome word
  Of a king and gentleman,

" That you will give me the first, first thing
  You meet at your castle-gate,
And the Princess shall get the Singing Leaves,
  Or mine be a traitor's fate."

The King's head dropt upon his breast
  A moment, as it might be;
'T will be my dog, he thought, and said,
  " My faith I plight to thee."

Then Walter took from next his heart
  A packet small and thin,
" Now give you this to the Princess Anne,
  The Singing Leaves are therein."

III

As the King rode in at his castle-gate,
  A maiden to meet him ran,
And " Welcome, father! " she laughed and cried
  Together, the Princess Anne.

" Lo, here the Singing Leaves," quoth he,
  " And woe, but they cost me dear! "
She took the packet, and the smile
  Deepened down beneath the tear.

It deepened down till it reached her heart,
  And then gushed up again,
And lighted her tears as the sudden sun
  Transfigures the summer rain.

And the first Leaf, when it was opened,
  Sang: " I am Walter the page,
And the songs I sing 'neath thy window
  Are my only heritage."

And the second Leaf sang: "But in the
   land
That is neither on earth nor sea,
My lute and I are lords of more
   Than thrice this kingdom's fee."

And the third Leaf sang, "Be mine! Be
   mine!"
And ever it sang, "Be mine!"
Then sweeter it sang and ever sweeter,
   And said, "I am thine, thine, thine!"

At the first Leaf she grew pale enough,
   At the second she turned aside,
At the third, 't was as if a lily flushed
   With a rose's red heart's tide.

"Good counsel gave the bird," said she,
   "I have my hope thrice o'er,
For they sing to my very heart," she said,
   "And it sings to them evermore."

She brought to him her beauty and truth,
   But and broad earldoms three,
And he made her queen of the broader lands
   He held of his lute in fee.

SEAWEED

NOT always unimpeded can I pray,
Nor, pitying saint, thine intercession claim;
Too closely clings the burden of the day,
And all the mint and anise that I pay
But swells my debt and deepens my self-
   blame.

Shall I less patience have than Thou, who
   know
That Thou revisit'st all who wait for thee,
Nor only fill'st the unsounded deeps be-
   low,
But dost refresh with punctual overflow
The rifts where unregarded mosses be?

The drooping seaweed hears, in night
   abyssed,
Far and more far the wave's receding
   shocks,
Nor doubts, for all the darkness and the
   mist,
That the pale shepherdess will keep her
   tryst,
And shoreward lead again her foam-fleeced
   flocks.

For the same wave that rims the Carib
   shore
With momentary brede of pearl and gold,
Goes hurrying thence to gladden with its
   roar
Lorn weeds bound fast on rocks of Labra-
   dor,
By love divine on one sweet errand rolled.

And, though Thy healing waters far with-
   draw,
I, too, can wait and feed on hope of Thee
And of the dear recurrence of Thy law,
Sure that the parting grace my morning
   saw
Abides its time to come in search of me.

THE FINDING OF THE LYRE

THERE lay upon the ocean's shore
What once a tortoise served to cover;
A year and more, with rush and roar,
The surf had rolled it over,
Had played with it, and flung it by,
As wind and weather might decide it,
Then tossed it high where sand-drifts dry
Cheap burial might provide it.

It rested there to bleach or tan,
The rains had soaked, the suns had burned
   it;
With many a ban the fisherman
Had stumbled o'er and spurned it;
And there the fisher-girl would stay,
Conjecturing with her brother
How in their play the poor estray
Might serve some use or other.

So there it lay, through wet and dry
As empty as the last new sonnet,
Till by and by came Mercury,
And, having mused upon it,
"Why, here," cried he, "the thing of
   things
In shape, material, and dimension!
Give it but strings, and, lo, it sings,
A wonderful invention!"

So said, so done; the chords he strained,
And, as his fingers o'er them hovered,
The shell disdained a soul had gained,
The lyre had been discovered.
O empty world that round us lies,
Dead shell, of soul and thought forsaken,

Brought we but eyes like Mercury's,
In thee what songs should waken !

NEW-YEAR'S EVE, 1850

THIS is the midnight of the century, —
    hark !
Through aisle and arch of Godminster have
    gone
Twelve throbs that tolled the zenith of the
    dark,
And mornward now the starry hands move
    on;
" Mornward ! " the angelic watchers say,
" Passed is the sorest trial;
No plot of man can stay
The hand upon the dial;
Night is the dark stem of the lily Day."

If we, who watched in valleys here below,
Toward streaks, misdeemed of morn, our
    faces turned
When volcan glares set all the east aglow,
We are not poorer that we wept and
    yearned,
Though earth swing wide from God's in-
    tent,
And though no man nor nation
Will move with full consent
In heavenly gravitation,
Yet by one Sun is every orbit bent.

FOR AN AUTOGRAPH

THOUGH old the thought and oft exprest,
'T is his at last who says it best, —
I 'll try my fortune with the rest.

Life is a leaf of paper white
Whereon each one of us may write
His word or two, and then comes night.

" Lo, time and space enough," we cry,
" To write an epic ! " so we try
Our nibs upon the edge, and die.

Muse not which way the pen to hold,
Luck hates the slow and loves the bold,
Soon come the darkness and the cold.

Greatly begin ! though thou have time
But for a line, be that sublime, —
Not failure, but low aim, is crime.

Ah, with what lofty hope we came !
But we forget it, dream of fame,
And scrawl, as I do here, a name.

AL FRESCO

THE dandelions and buttercups
Gild all the lawn; the drowsy bee
Stumbles among the clover-tops,
And summer sweetens all but me:
Away, unfruitful lore of books,
For whose vain idiom we reject
The soul's more native dialect,
Aliens among the birds and brooks,
Dull to interpret or conceive
What gospels lost the woods retrieve !
Away, ye critics, city-bred,
Who springes set of thus and so,
And in the first man's footsteps tread,
Like those who toil through drifted snow !
Away, my poets, whose sweet spell
Can make a garden of a cell !
I need ye not, for I to-day
Will make one long sweet verse of play.

Snap, chord of manhood's tenser strain !
To-day I will be a boy again;
The mind's pursuing element,
Like a bow slackened and unbent,
In some dark corner shall be leant.
The robin sings, as of old, from the limb !
The cat-bird croons in the lilac-bush,
Through the dim arbor, himself more dim,
Silently hops the hermit-thrush,
The withered leaves keep dumb for him;
The irreverent buccaneering bee
Hath stormed and rifled the nunnery
Of the lily, and scattered the sacred floor
With haste - dropt gold from shrine to
    door;
There, as of yore,
The rich, milk-tingeing buttercup
Its tiny polished urn holds up,
Filled with ripe summer to the edge,
The sun in his own wine to pledge;
And our tall elm, this hundredth year
Doge of our leafy Venice here,
Who, with an annual ring, doth wed
The blue Adriatic overhead,
Shadows with his palatial mass
The deep canals of flowing grass.

O unestrangëd birds and bees !
O face of Nature always true !

O never-unsympathizing trees !
O never-rejecting roof of blue,
Whose rash disherison never falls
On us unthinking prodigals,
Yet who convictest all our ill,
So grand and unappeasable !
Methinks my heart from each of these
Plucks part of childhood back again,
Long there imprisoned, as the breeze
Doth every hidden odor seize
Of wood and water, hill and plain ;
Once more am I admitted peer
In the upper house of Nature here,
And feel through all my pulses run
The royal blood of wind and sun.

Upon these elm-arched solitudes
No hum of neighbor toil intrudes;
The only hammer that I hear
Is wielded by the woodpecker,
The single noisy calling his
In all our leaf-hid Sybaris;
The good old time, close-hidden here,
Persists, a loyal cavalier,
While Roundheads prim, with point of fox,
Probe wainscot-chink and empty box;
Here no hoarse-voiced iconoclast
Insults thy statues, royal Past;
Myself too prone the axe to wield,
I touch the silver side of the shield
With lance reversed, and challenge peace,
A willing convert of the trees.

How chanced it that so long I tost
A cable's length from this rich coast,
With foolish anchors hugging close
The beckoning weeds and lazy ooze,
Nor had the wit to wreck before
On this enchanted island's shore,
Whither the current of the sea,
With wiser drift, persuaded me ?

Oh, might we but of such rare days
Build up the spirit's dwelling-place !
A temple of so Parian stone
Would brook a marble god alone,
The statue of a perfect life,
Far-shrined from earth's bestaining strife.
Alas ! though such felicity
In our vext world here may not be,
Yet, as sometimes the peasant's hut
Shows stones which old religion cut
With text inspired, or mystic sign
Of the Eternal and Divine,
Torn from the consecration deep

Of some fallen nunnery's mossy sleep,
So, from the ruins of this day
Crumbling in golden dust away,
The soul one gracious block may draw,
Carved with some fragment of the law,
Which, set in life's prosaic wall,
Old benedictions may recall,
And lure some nunlike thoughts to take
Their dwelling here for memory's sake.

MASACCIO

IN THE BRANCACCI CHAPEL

HE came to Florence long ago,
And painted here these walls, that shone
For Raphael and for Angelo,
With secrets deeper than his own,
Then shrank into the dark again,
And died, we know not how or when.

The shadows deepened, and I turned
Half sadly from the fresco grand;
"And is this," mused I, "all ye earned,
High-vaulted brain and cunning hand,
That ye to greater men could teach
The skill yourselves could never reach ? "

"And who were they," I mused, "that
      wrought
Through pathless wilds, with labor long,
The highways of our daily thought ?
Who reared those towers of earliest song
That lift us from the crowd to peace
Remote in sunny silences ? "

Out clanged the Ave Mary bells,
And to my heart this message came:
Each clamorous throat among them tells
What strong-souled martys died in flame
To make it possible that thou
Shouldst here with brother sinners bow.

Thoughts that great hearts once broke for,
      we
Breathe cheaply in the common air ;
The dust we trample heedlessly
Throbbed once in saints and heroes rare,
Who perished, opening for their race
New pathways to the commonplace.

Henceforth, when rings the health to those
Who live in story and in song,
O nameless dead, that now repose

Safe in Oblivion's chambers strong,
One cup of recognition true
Shall silently be drained to you !

WITHOUT AND WITHIN

"Madrid, January 15, 1879. I wrote some
verses thirty odd years ago called *Without and
Within*, and they originally ended with the
author's looking up at the stars through six
feet of earth and feeling dreadfully bored,
while a passer-by deciphers the headstone and
envies the supposed sleeper beneath. I was per-
suaded to leave out this ending as too grim —
but I often think of it. They have a fine name
for this kind of feeling nowadays, and would
fain make out pessimism to be a monstrous
birth of our century. I suspect it has always
been common enough, especially with naughty
children who get tired of their playthings as
soon as I do — the absurdity being that then
we are not content with smashing the toy
which turns out to be finite — but everything
else into the bargain." J. R. L. to Miss Grace
Norton. *Letters* II. 236.

My coachman, in the moonlight there,
    Looks through the side-light of the door;
I hear him with his brethren swear,
    As I could do, — but only more.

Flattening his nose against the pane,
    He envies me my brilliant lot,
Breathes on his aching fists in vain,
    And dooms me to a place more hot.

He sees me in to supper go,
    A silken wonder by my side,
Bare arms, bare shoulders, and a row
    Of flounces, for the door too wide.

He thinks how happy is my arm
    'Neath its white-gloved and jewelled
        load;
And wishes me some dreadful harm,
    Hearing the merry corks explode.

Meanwhile I inly curse the bore
    Of hunting still the same old coon,
And envy him, outside the door,
    In golden quiets of the moon.

The winter wind is not so cold
    As the bright smile he sees me win,
Nor the host's oldest wine so old
    As our poor gabble sour and thin.

I envy him the ungyved prance
    With which his freezing feet he warms,
And drag my lady's-chains and dance
    The galley-slave of dreary forms.

Oh, could he have my share of din,
    And I his quiet ! — past a doubt
'T would still be one man bored within,
    And just another bored without.

Nay, when, once paid my mortal fee,
    Some idler on my headstone grim
Traces the moss-blurred name, will he
    Think me the happier, or I him ?

GODMINSTER CHIMES

WRITTEN IN AID OF A CHIME OF BELLS
FOR CHRIST CHURCH, CAMBRIDGE

Godminster ? Is it Fancy's play ?
    I know not, but the word
Sings in my heart, nor can I say
    Whether 't was dreamed or heard;
Yet fragrant in my mind it clings
    As blossoms after rain,
And builds of half-remembered things
    This vision in my brain.

Through aisles of long-drawn centuries
    My spirit walks in thought,
And to that symbol lifts its eyes
    Which God's own pity wrought;
From Calvary shines the altar's gleam,
    The Church's East is there,
The Ages one great minster seem,
    That throbs with praise and prayer.

And all the way from Calvary down
    The carven pavement shows
Their graves who won the martyr's crown
    And safe in God repose;
The saints of many a warring creed
    Who now in heaven have learned
That all paths to the Father lead
    Where Self the feet have spurned.

And, as the mystic aisles I pace,
    By aureoled workmen built,
Lives ending at the Cross I trace
    Alike through grace and guilt;
One Mary bathes the blessed feet
    With ointment from her eyes,

With spikenard one, and both are sweet,
For both are sacrifice.

Moravian hymn and Roman chant
In one devotion blend,
To speak the soul's eternal want
Of Him, the inmost friend;
One prayer soars cleansed with martyr
    fire,
One choked with sinner's tears,
In heaven both meet in one desire,
And God one music hears.

Whilst thus I dream, the bells clash out
Upon the Sabbath air,
Each seems a hostile faith to shout,
    A selfish form of prayer;
My dream is shattered, yet who knows
But in that heaven so near
These discords find harmonious close
In God's atoning ear ?

O chime of sweet Saint Charity,
Peal soon that Easter morn
When Christ for all shall risen be,
And in all hearts new-born !
That Pentecost when utterance clear
To all men shall be given,
When all shall say *My Brother* here,
And hear *My Son* in heaven !

THE PARTING OF THE WAYS

Who hath not been a poet ? Who hath not,
With life's new quiver full of wingèd
    years,
Shot at a venture, and then, following on,
Stood doubtful at the Parting of the Ways ?

There once I stood in dream, and as I
    paused,
Looking this way and that, came forth
    to me
The figure of a woman veiled, that said,
"My name is Duty, turn and follow me;"
Something there was that chilled me in
    her voice;
I felt Youth's hand grow slack and cold in
    mine,
As if to be withdrawn, and I exclaimed:
"Oh, leave the hot wild heart within my
    breast !
Duty comes soon enough, too soon comes
    Death;

This slippery globe of life whirls of itself,
Hasting our youth away into the dark;
These senses, quivering with electric heats,
Too soon will show, like nests on wintry
    boughs
Obtrusive emptiness, too palpable wreck,
Which whistling north-winds line with
    downy snow
Sometimes, or fringe with foliaged rime,
    in vain,
Thither the singing birds no more return."

Then glowed to me a maiden from the
    left,
With bosom half disclosed, and naked
    arms
More white and undulant than necks of
    swans;
And all before her steps an influence ran
Warm as the whispering South that opens
    buds
And swells the laggard sails of Northern
    May.
"I am called Pleasure, come with me!"
    she said,
Then laughed, and shook out sunshine from
    her hair,
Nor only that, but, so it seemed, shook out
All memory too, and all the moonlit past,
Old loves, old aspirations, and old dreams,
More beautiful for being old and gone.

So we two went together; downward
    sloped
The path through yellow meads, or so I
    dreamed,
Yellow with sunshine and young green,
    but I
Saw naught nor heard, shut up in one close
    joy;
I only felt the hand within my own,
Transmuting all my blood to golden fire,
Dissolving all my brain in throbbing mist.

Suddenly shrank the hand; suddenly burst
A cry that split the torpor of my brain,
And as the first sharp thrust of lightning
    loosens
From the heaped cloud its rain, loosened
    my sense:
"Save me !" it thrilled; "oh, hide me !
    there is Death !
Death the divider, the unmerciful,
That digs his pitfalls under Love and
    Youth,

And covers Beauty up in the cold ground;
Horrible Death ! bringer of endless dark;
Let him not see me ! hide me in thy
    breast ! "
Thereat I strove to clasp her, but my arms
Met only what slipped crumbling down,
    and fell,
A handful of gray ashes, at my feet.

I would have fled, I would have followed
    back
That pleasant path we came, but all was
    changed;
Rocky the way, abrupt, and hard to find;
Yet I toiled on, and, toiling on, I thought,
" That way lies Youth, and Wisdom, and
    all Good;
For only by unlearning Wisdom comes
And climbing backward to diviner Youth;
What the world teaches profits to the
    world,
What the soul teaches profits to the soul,
Which then first stands erect with God-
    ward face,
When she lets fall her pack of withered
    facts,
The gleanings of the outward eye and
    ear,
And looks and listens with her finer sense;
Nor Truth nor Knowledge cometh from
    without."

After long, weary days I stood again
And waited at the Parting of the Ways;
Again the figure of a woman veiled
Stood forth and beckoned, and I followed
    now:
Down to no bower of roses led the path,
But through the streets of towns where
    chattering Cold
Hewed wood for fires whose glow was
    owned and fenced,
Where Nakedness wove garments of warm
    wool
Not for itself; — or through the fields it
    led
Where Hunger reaped the unattainable
    grain,
Where idleness enforced saw idle lands,
Leagues of unpeopled soil, the common
    earth,
Walled round with paper against God and
    Man.
" I cannot look," I groaned, " at only
    these;

The heart grows hardened with perpetual
    wont,
And palters with a feigned necessity,
Bargaining with itself to be content;
Let me behold thy face."
                The Form replied:
" Men follow Duty, never overtake;
Duty nor lifts her veil nor looks behind."
But, as she spake, a loosened lock of hair
Slipped from beneath her hood, and I, who
    looked
To see it gray and thin, saw amplest gold;
Not that dull metal dug from sordid earth,
But such as the retiring sunset flood
Leaves heaped on bays and capes of island
    cloud.
" O Guide divine," I prayed, " although not
    yet
I may repair the virtue which I feel
Gone out at touch of untuned things and
    foul
With draughts of Beauty, yet declare how
    soon ! "

" Faithless and faint of heart," the voice
    returned,
" Thou seest no beauty save thou make it
    first;
Man, Woman, Nature each is but a glass
Where the soul sees the image of herself,
Visible echoes, offsprings of herself.
But, since thou need'st assurance of how
    soon,
Wait till that angel comes who opens all,
The reconciler, he who lifts the veil,
The reuniter, the rest-bringer, Death."

I waited, and methought he came; but
    how,
Or in what shape, I doubted, for no sign,
By touch or mark, he gave me as he
    passed:
Only I knew a lily that I held
Snapt short below the head and shrivelled
    up;
Then turned my Guide and looked at me
    unveiled,
And I beheld no face of matron stern,
But that enchantment I had followed erst,
Only more fair, more clear to eye and brain,
Heightened and chastened by a household
    charm;
She smiled, and " Which is fairer," said
    her eyes,
" The hag's unreal Florimel or mine ? "

ALADDIN

WHEN I was a beggarly boy,
  And lived in a cellar damp,
I had not a friend nor a toy,
  But I had Aladdin's lamp;
When I could not sleep for the cold,
  I had fire enough in my brain,
And builded, with roofs of gold,
  My beautiful castles in Spain!

Since then I have toiled day and night,
  I have money and power good store,
But I'd give all my lamps of silver bright
  For the one that is mine no more;
Take, Fortune, whatever you choose,
  You gave, and may snatch again;
I have nothing 't would pain me to lose,
  For I own no more castles in Spain!

AN INVITATION

TO J[OHN] F[RANCIS] H[EATH]

NINE years have slipt like hour-glass sand
From life's still-emptying globe away,
Since last, dear friend, I clasped your
    hand,
And stood upon the impoverished land,
Watching the steamer down the bay.

I held the token which you gave,
While slowly the smoke-pennon curled
O'er the vague rim 'tween sky and wave,
And shut the distance like a grave,
Leaving me in the colder world;

The old, worn world of hurry and heat,
The young, fresh world of thought and
    scope;
While you, where beckoning billows fleet
Climb far sky-beaches still and sweet,
Sank wavering down the ocean-slope.

You sought the new world in the old,
I found the old world in the new,
All that our human hearts can hold,
The inward world of deathless mould,
The same that Father Adam knew.

He needs no ship to cross the tide,
Who, in the lives about him, sees
Fair window-prospects opening wide

O'er history's fields on every side,
To Ind and Egypt, Rome and Greece.

Whatever moulds of various brain
E'er shaped the world to weal or woe,
Whatever empires' wax and wane,
To him that hath not eyes in vain,
Our village-microcosm can show.

Come back our ancient walks to tread,
Dear haunts of lost or scattered friends,
Old Harvard's scholar-factories red,
Where song and smoke and laughter sped
The nights to proctor-haunted ends.

Constant are all our former loves,
Unchanged the icehouse-girdled pond,
Its hemlock glooms, its shadowy coves,
Where floats the coot and never moves,
Its slopes of long-tamed green beyond.

Our old familiars are not laid,
Though snapt our wands and sunk our
    books;
They beckon, not to be gainsaid,
Where, round broad meads that mowers
    wade,
The Charles his steel-blue sickle crooks.

Where, as the cloudbergs eastward blow,
From glow to gloom the hillsides shift
Their plumps of orchard-trees arow,
Their lakes of rye that wave and flow,
Their snowy whiteweed's summer drift.

There have we watched the West unfurl
A cloud Byzantium newly born,
With flickering spires and domes of pearl,
And vapory surfs that crowd and curl
Into the sunset's Golden Horn.

There, as the flaming occident
Burned slowly down to ashes gray,
Night pitched o'erhead her silent tent,
And glimmering gold from Hesper sprent
Upon the darkened river lay,

Where a twin sky but just before
Deepened, and double swallows skimmed,
And from a visionary shore
Hung visioned trees, that more and more
Grew dusk as those above were dimmed.

Then eastward saw we slowly grow
Clear-edged the lines of roof and spire,

While great elm-masses blacken slow,
And linden-ricks their round heads show
Against a flush of widening fire.

Doubtful at first and far away,
The moon-flood creeps more wide and
    wide;
Up a ridged beach of cloudy gray,
Curved round the east as round a bay,
It slips and spreads its gradual tide.

Then suddenly, in lurid mood,
The disk looms large o'er town and field
As upon Adam, red like blood,
'Tween him and Eden's happy wood,
Glared the commissioned angel's shield.

Or let us seek the seaside, there
To wander idly as we list,
Whether, on rocky headlands bare,
Sharp cedar-horns, like breakers, tear
The trailing fringes of gray mist,

Or whether, under skies full flown,
The brightening surfs, with foamy din,
Their breeze-caught forelocks backward
    blown,
Against the beach's yellow zone
Curl slow, and plunge forever in.

And, as we watch those canvas towers
That lean along the horizon's rim,
" Sail on," I'll say; " may sunniest hours
Convoy you from this land of ours,
Since from my side you bear not him ! "

For years thrice three, wise Horace said,
A poem rare let silence bind ;
And love may ripen in the shade,
Like ours, for nine long seasons laid
In deepest arches of the mind.

Come back ! Not ours the Old World's
    good,
The Old World's ill, thank God, not ours ;
But here, far better understood,
The days enforce our native mood,
And challenge all our manlier powers.

Kindlier to me the place of birth
That first my tottering footsteps trod ;
There may be fairer spots of earth,
But all their glories are not worth
The virtue in the native sod.

Thence climbs an influence more benign
Through pulse and nerve, through heart
    and brain ;
Sacred to me those fibres fine
That first clasped earth. Oh, ne'er be
    mine
The alien sun and alien rain !

These nourish not like homelier glows
Or waterings of familiar skies,
And nature fairer blooms bestows
On the heaped hush of wintry snows,
In pastures dear to childhood's eyes,

Than where Italian earth receives
The partial sunshine's ampler boons,
Where vines carve friezes 'neath the eaves,
And, in dark firmaments of leaves,
The orange lifts its golden moons.

THE NOMADES

WHAT Nature makes in any mood
To me is warranted for good,
Though long before I learned to see
She did not set us moral theses,
And scorned to have her sweet caprices
Strait-waistcoated in you or me.

I, who take root and firmly cling,
Thought fixedness the only thing ;
Why Nature made the butterflies,
(Those dreams of wings that float and
    hover
At noon the slumberous poppies over,)
Was something hidden from mine eyes,

Till once, upon a rock's brown bosom,
Bright as a thorny cactus-blossom,
I saw a butterfly at rest ;
Then first of both I felt the beauty;
The airy whim, the grim-sèt duty,
Each from the other took its best.

Clearer it grew than winter sky
That Nature still had reasons why ;
And, shifting sudden as a breeze,
My fancy found no satisfaction,
No antithetic sweet attraction,
So great as in the Nomades.

Scythians, with Nature not at strife,
Light Arabs of our complex life,
They build no houses, plant no mills

To utilize Time's sliding river,
Content that it flow waste forever,
If they, like it, may have their wills.

An hour they pitch their shifting tents
In thoughts, in feelings, and events ;
Beneath the palm-trees, on the grass,
They sing, they dance, make love, and
    chatter,
Vex the grim temples with their clatter,
And make Truth's fount their looking-
    glass.

A picnic life ; from love to love,
From faith to faith they lightly move,
And yet, hard-eyed philosopher,
The flightiest maid that ever hovered
To me your thought-webs fine discovered,
No lens to see them through like her.

So witchingly her finger-tips
To Wisdom, as away she trips,
She kisses, waves such sweet farewells
To Duty, as she laughs " To-morrow ! "
That both from that mad contrast borrow
A perfectness found nowhere else.

The beach-bird on its pearly verge
Follows and flies the whispering surge,
While, in his tent, the rock-stayed shell
Awaits the flood's star-timed vibrations,
And both, the flutter and the patience,
The sauntering poet loves them well.

Fulfil so much of God's decree
As works its problem out in thee,
Nor dream that in thy breast alone
The conscience of the changeful seasons,
The Will that in the planets reasons
With space-wide logic, has its throne.

Thy virtue makes not vice of mine,
Unlike, but none the less divine ;
Thy toil adorns, not chides, my play ;
Nature of sameness is so chary,
With such wild whim the freakish fairy
Picks presents for the christening-day.

SELF-STUDY

A presence both by night and day,
    That made my life seem just begun,
Yet scarce a presence, rather say
    The warning aureole of one.

And yet I felt it everywhere ;
    Walked I the woodland's aisles along.
It seemed to brush me with its hair ;
    Bathed I, I heard a mermaid's song.

How sweet it was ! A buttercup
    Could hold for me a day's delight,
A bird could lift my fancy up
    To ether free from cloud or blight.

Who was the nymph ? Nay, I will see,
    Methought, and I will know her near;
If such, divined, her charm can be,
    Seen and possessed, how triply dear!

So every magic art I tried,
    And spells as numberless as sand,
Until, one evening, by my side
    I saw her glowing fulness stand.

I turned to clasp her, but " Farewell,"
    Parting she sighed, " we meet no more;
Not by my hand the curtain fell
    That leaves you conscious, wise, and poor.

" Since you have found me out, I go ;
    Another lover I must find,
Content his happiness to know,
    Nor strive its secret to unwind."

PICTURES FROM APPLEDORE

In 1854 Lowell contributed to *The Crayon*,
then just started by W. J. Stillman, a poem,
My Appledore Gallery, which reappears in part
in the following poem under a slightly changed
title. In sending the first portion to Mr. Still-
man, he wrote : " You may add a note, if you
like, saying that Appledore is one of the Isles
of Shoals, off Portsmouth, N. H., discovered by
the *great* Captain Smith, and once named after
him. A cairn on the apex of Appledore is
said to be of his building."

I

A heap of bare and splintery crags
Tumbled about by lightning and frost,
With rifts and chasms and storm-bleached
    jags,
That wait and growl for a ship to be lost;
No island, but rather the skeleton
Of a wrecked and vengeance-smitten one,
Where, æons ago, with half-shut eye,
The sluggish saurian crawled to die,
Gasping under titanic ferns;

Ribs of rock that seaward jut,
Granite shoulders and boulders and snags,
Round which, though the winds in heaven
    be shut,
The nightmared ocean murmurs and yearns,
Welters, and swashes, and tosses, and turns,
And the dreary black seaweed lolls and
    wags;
Only rock from shore to shore,
Only a moan through the bleak clefts
    blown,
With sobs in the rifts where the coarse kelp
    shifts,
Falling and lifting, tossing and drifting,
And under all a deep, dull roar,
Dying and swelling, forevermore, —
Rock and moan and roar alone,
And the dread of some nameless thing un-
    known,
These make Appledore.

These make Appledore by night:
Then there are monsters left and right;
Every rock is a different monster;
All you have read of, fancied, dreamed,
When you waked at night because you
    screamed,
There they lie for half a mile,
Jumbled together in a pile,
And (though you know they never once
    stir)
If you look long, they seem to be moving
Just as plainly as plain can be,
Crushing and crowding, wading and shov-
    ing
Out into the awful sea,
Where you can hear them snort and spout
With pauses between, as if they were listen-
    ing,
Then tumult anon when the surf breaks
    glistening
In the blackness where they wallow about.

II

All this you would scarcely comprehend,
Should you see the isle on a sunny day ;
Then it is simple enough in its way, —
Two rocky bulges, one at each end,
With a smaller bulge and a hollow between;
Patches of whortleberry and bay;
Accidents of open green,
Sprinkled with loose slabs square and gray,
Like graveyards for ages deserted; a few
Unsocial thistles ; an elder or two,
Foamed over with blossoms white as spray;

And on the whole island never a tree
Save a score of sumachs, high as your knee,
That crouch in hollows where they may,
(The cellars where once stood a village,
    men say,)
Huddling for warmth, and never grew
Tall enough for a peep at the sea;
A general dazzle of open blue;
A breeze always blowing and playing rat-
    tat
With the bow of the ribbon round your hat;
A score of sheep that do nothing but stare
Up or down at you everywhere;
Three or four cattle that chew the cud
Lying about in a listless despair;
A medrick that makes you look overhead
With short, sharp scream, as he sights his
    prey,
And, dropping straight and swift as lead,
Splits the water with sudden thud; —
This is Appledore by day.

A common island, you will say;
But stay a moment: only climb
Up to the highest rock of the isle,
Stand there alone for a little while,
And with gentle approaches it grows sub-
    lime,
Dilating slowly as you win
A sense from the silence to take it in.
So wide the loneness, so lucid the air,
The granite beneath you so savagely bare,
You well might think you were looking
    down
From some sky-silenced mountain's crown,
Whose waist-belt of pines is wont to tear
Locks of wool from the topmost cloud.
Only be sure you go alone,
For Grandeur is inaccessibly proud,
And never yet has backward thrown
Her veil to feed the stare of a crowd;
To more than one was never shown
That awful front, nor is it fit
That she, Cothurnus-shod, stand bowed
Until the self-approving pit
Enjoy the gust of its own wit
In babbling plaudits cheaply loud;
She hides her mountains and her sea
From the harriers of scenery,
Who hunt down sunsets, and huddle and
    bay,
Mouthing and mumbling the dying day.

Trust me, 't is something to be cast
Face to face with one's Self at last,

To be taken out of the fuss and strife,
The endless clatter of plate and knife,
The bore of books and the bores of the
  street,
From the singular mess we agree to call
  Life,
Where that is best which the most fools
  vote is,
And planted firm on one's own two feet
So nigh to the great warm heart of God,
You almost seem to feel it beat
Down from the sunshine and up from the
  sod;
To be compelled, as it were, to notice
All the beautiful changes and chances
Through which the landscape flits and
  glances,
And to see how the face of common day
Is written all over with tender histories,
When you study it that intenser way
In which a lover looks at his mistress.

Till now you dreamed not what could be
  done
With a bit of rock and a ray of sun ;
But look, how fade the lights and shades
Of keen bare edge and crevice deep !
How doubtfully it fades and fades,
And glows again, yon craggy steep,
O'er which, through color's dreamiest
  grades,
The musing sunbeams pause and creep !
Now pink it blooms, now glimmers gray,
Now shadows to a filmy blue,
Tries one, tries all, and will not stay,
But flits from opal hue to hue,
And runs through every tenderest range
Of change that seems not to be change,
So rare the sweep, so nice the art,
That lays no stress on any part,
But shifts and lingers and persuades;
So soft that sun-brush in the west,
That asks no costlier pigments' aids,
But mingling knobs, flaws, angles, dints,
Indifferent of worst or best,
Enchants the cliffs with wraiths and hints
And gracious preludings of tints,
Where all seems fixed, yet all evades,
And indefinably pervades
Perpetual movement with perpetual rest !

III

Away northeast is Boone Island light;
You might mistake it for a ship,
Only it stands too plumb upright,

And like the others does not slip
Behind the sea's unsteady brink;
Though, if a cloud-shade chance to dip
Upon it a moment, 't will suddenly sink,
Levelled and lost in the darkened main,
Till the sun builds it suddenly up again,
As if with a rub of Aladdin's lamp.
On the mainland you see a misty camp
Of mountains pitched tumultuously:
That one looming so long and large
Is Saddleback, and that point you see
Over yon low and rounded marge,
Like the boss of a sleeping giant's targe
Laid over his breast, is Ossipee;
That shadow there may be Kearsarge;
That must be Great Haystack; I love
  these names,
Wherewith the lonely farmer tames
Nature to mute companionship
With his own mind's domestic mood,
And strives the surly world to clip
In the arms of familiar habitude.
'T is well he could not contrive to make
A Saxon of Agamenticus:
He glowers there to the north of us,
Wrapt in his blanket of blue haze,
Unconvertibly savage, and scorns to take
The white man's baptism or his ways.
Him first on shore the coaster divines
Through the early gray, and sees him
  shake
The morning mist from his scalp-lock of
  pines;
Him first the skipper makes out in the
  west,
Ere the earliest sunstreak shoots tremu-
  lous,
Plashing with orange the palpitant lines
Of mutable billow, crest after crest,
And murmurs *Agamenticus!*
As if it were the name of a saint.
But is that a mountain playing cloud,
Or a cloud playing mountain, just there,
  so faint ?
Look along over the low right shoulder
Of Agamenticus into that crowd
Of brassy thunderheads behind it;
Now you have caught it, but, ere you are
  older
By half an hour, you will lose it and find it
A score of times; while you look 't is gone,
And, just as you 've given it up, anon
It is there again, till your weary eyes
Fancy they see it waver and rise,
With its brother clouds; it is Agiochook,

There if you seek not, and gone if you
    look,
Ninety miles off as the eagle flies.

But mountains make not all the shore
The mainland shows to Appledore;
Eight miles the heaving water spreads
To a long, low coast with beaches and
    heads
That run through unimagined mazes,
As the lights and shades and magical hazes
Put them away or bring them near,
Shimmering, sketched out for thirty miles
Between two capes that waver like threads,
And sink in the ocean, and reappear,
Crumbled and melted to little isles,
With filmy trees, that seem the mere
Half-fancies of drowsy atmosphere;
And see the beach there, where it is
Flat as a threshing-floor, beaten and packed
With the flashing flails of weariless seas,
How it lifts and looms to a precipice,
O'er whose square front, a dream, no
    more,
The steepened sand-stripes seem to pour,
A murmurless vision of cataract;
You almost fancy you hear a roar,
Fitful and faint from the distance wander-
    ing;
But 't is only the blind old ocean maunder-
    ing,
Raking the shingle to and fro,
Aimlessly clutching and letting go
The kelp-haired sedges of Appledore,
Slipping down with a sleepy forgetting,
And anon his ponderous shoulder setting,
With a deep, hoarse pant against Apple-
    dore.

IV

Eastward as far as the eye can see,
Still eastward, eastward, endlessly,
The sparkle and tremor of purple sea
That rises before you, a flickering hill,
On and on to the shut of the sky,
And beyond, you fancy it sloping until
The same multitudinous throb and thrill
That vibrate under your dizzy eye
In ripples of orange and pink are sent
Where the poppied sails doze on the yard,
And the clumsy junk and proa lie
Sunk deep with precious woods and nard,
'Mid the palmy isles of the Orient.
Those leaning towers of clouded white
On the farthest brink of doubtful ocean,

That shorten and shorten out of sight,
Yet seem on the selfsame spot to stay,
Receding with a motionless motion,
Fading to dubious films of gray,
Lost, dimly found, then vanished wholly,
Will rise again, the great world under,
First films, then towers, then high-heaped
    clouds,
Whose nearing outlines sharpen slowly
Into tall ships with cobweb shrouds,
That fill long Mongol eyes with wonder,
Crushing the violet wave to spray
Past some low headland of Cathay; —
What was that sigh which seemed so near,
Chilling your fancy to the core?
'T is only the sad old sea you hear,
That seems to seek forevermore
Something it cannot find, and so,
Sighing, seeks on, and tells its woe
To the pitiless breakers of Appledore.

V

How looks Appledore in a storm?
    I have seen it when its crags seemed
        frantic,
    Butting against the mad Atlantic,
When surge on surge would heap enorme,
    Cliffs of emerald topped with snow,
    That lifted and lifted, and then let go
A great white avalanche of thunder,
    A grinding, blinding, deafening ire
Monadnock might have trembled under;
    And the island, whose rock-roots pierce
        below
    To where they are warmed with the cen-
        tral fire,
You could feel its granite fibres racked,
    As it seemed to plunge with a shudder
        and thrill
Right at the breast of the swooping hill,
And to rise again snorting a cataract
Of rage-froth from every cranny and ledge,
    While the sea drew its breath in hoarse
        and deep,
And the next vast breaker curled its edge,
    Gathering itself for a mightier leap.

North, east, and south there are reefs and
    breakers
    You would never dream of in smooth
        weather,
That toss and gore the sea for acres,
    Bellowing and gnashing and snarling to-
        gether;
Look northward, where Duck Island lies,

And over its crown you will see arise,
Against a background of slaty skies,
A row of pillars still and white,
That glimmer, and then are gone from
sight,
As if the moon should suddenly kiss,
While you crossed the gusty desert by
night,
The long colonnades of Persepolis;
Look southward for White Island light,
The lantern stands ninety feet o'er the
tide;
There is first a half-mile of tumult and
fight,
Of dash and roar and tumble and fright,
And surging bewilderment wild and wide,
Where the breakers struggle left and right,
Then a mile or more of rushing sea,
And then the lighthouse slim and lone;
And whenever the weight of ocean is
thrown
Full and fair on White Island head,
A great mist-jotun you will see
Lifting himself up silently
High and huge o'er the lighthouse top,
With hands of wavering spray outspread,
Groping after the little tower,
That seems to shrink and shorten and
cower,
Till the monster's arms of a sudden drop,
And silently and fruitlessly
He sinks back into the sea.

You, meanwhile, where drenched you stand,
Awaken once more to the rush and roar,
And on the rock-point tighten your hand,
As you turn and see a valley deep,
That was not there a moment before,
Suck rattling down between you and a heap
Of toppling billow, whose instant fall
Must sink the whole island once for all,
Or watch the silenter, stealthier seas
Feeling their way to you more and more;
If they once should clutch you high as the
knees,
They would whirl you down like a sprig of
kelp,
Beyond all reach of hope or help; —
And such in a storm is Appledore.

VI

'T is the sight of a lifetime to behold
The great shorn sun as you see it now,
Across eight miles of undulant gold
That widens landward, weltered and rolled,

With freaks of shadow and crimson stains;
To see the solid mountain brow
As it notches the disk, and gains and gains,
Until there comes, you scarce know when,
A tremble of fire o'er the parted lips
Of cloud and mountain, which vanishes;
then
From the body of day the sun-soul slips
And the face of earth darkens; but now the
strips
Of western vapor, straight and thin,
From which the horizon's swervings win
A grace of contrast, take fire and burn
Like splinters of touchwood, whose edges a
mould
Of ashes o'erfeathers; northward turn
For an instant, and let your eye grow cold
On Agamenticus, and when once more
You look, 't is as if the land-breeze, grow-
ing,
From the smouldering brands the film
were blowing,
And brightening them down to the very
core;
Yet they momently cool and dampen and
deaden,
The crimson turns golden, the gold turns
leaden,
Hardening into one black bar
O'er which, from the hollow heaven afar,
Shoots a splinter of light like diamond,
Half seen, half fancied; by and by
Beyond whatever is most beyond
In the uttermost waste of desert sky,
Grows a star;
And over it, visible spirit of dew, —
Ah, stir not, speak not, hold your breath,
Or surely the miracle vanisheth, —
The new moon, tranced in unspeakable
blue !
No frail illusion; this were true,
Rather, to call it the canoe
Hollowed out of a single pearl,
That floats us from the Present's whirl
Back to those beings which were ours,
When wishes were wingèd things like pow-
ers !
Call it not light, that mystery tender,
Which broods upon the brooding ocean
That flush of ecstasied surrender
To indefinable emotion,
That glory, mellower than a mist
Of pearl dissolved with amethyst,
Which rims Square Rock, like what they
paint

Of mitigated heavenly splendor
Round the stern forehead of a Saint !

No more a vision, reddened, largened,
The moon dips toward her mountain nest,
And, fringing it with palest argent,
Slow sheathes herself behind the margent
Of that long cloud-bar in the West,
Whose nether edge, erelong, you see
The silvery chrism in turn anoint,
And then the tiniest rosy point
Touched doubtfully and timidly
Into the dark blue's chilly strip,
As some mute, wondering thing below,
Awakened by the thrilling glow,
Might, looking up, see Dian dip
One lucent foot's delaying tip
In Latmian fountains long ago.

Knew you what silence was before ?
Here is no startle of dreaming bird
That sings in his sleep, or strives to sing;
Here is no sough of branches stirred,
Nor noise of any living thing,
Such as one hears by night on shore;
Only, now and then, a sigh,
With fickle intervals between,
Sometimes far, and sometimes nigh,
Such as Andromeda might have heard,
And fancied the huge sea-beast unseen
Turning in sleep; it is the sea
That welters and wavers uneasily
Round the lonely reefs of Appledore.

THE WIND-HARP

"Your inspiration is still to you a living
mistress — make her immortal in her prompt-
ings and her consolations by imaging her
truly in art. Mine looks at me with eyes of
paler flame and beckons across a gulf. You
came into my loneliness like an incarnate as-
piration. And it is dreary enough sometimes,
for a mountain-peak on whose snow your foot
makes the first mortal print is not so lonely as
a room full of happy faces from which *one* is
missing forever. This was originally the fifth
stanza of *The Windharp*.

O tress ! that so oft in my heart hast lain,
  Rocked to rest within rest by its thankful beating,
Say, which is harder — to bear the pain
Of laughter and light, or to wait in vain
  'Neath the unleaved tree the impossible meeting ?
If Death's lips be icy, Life gives, iwis,
Some kisses more clay-cold and darkening than his !

Forgive me, but you spoke of it first." J. R. L.
to W. J. Stillman, December 7, 1854.

I TREASURE in secret some long, fine
    hair
  Of tenderest brown, but so inwardly
    golden
I half used to fancy the sunshine there,
So shy, so shifting, so waywardly rare,
  Was only caught for the moment and
    holden
While I could say *Dearest !* and kiss it,
    and then
In pity let go to the summer again.

I twisted this magic in gossamer strings
  Over a wind-harp's Delphian hollow;
Then called to the idle breeze that swings
All day in the pine-tops, and clings, and
    sings
  'Mid the musical leaves, and said, " Oh,
    follow
The will of those tears that deepen my
    words,
And fly to my window to waken these
    chords."

So they trembled to life, and, doubtfully
  Feeling their way to my sense, sang,
    " Say whether
They sit all day by the greenwood tree,
The lover and loved, as it wont to be,
  When we — " But grief conquered, and
    all together
They swelled such weird murmur as haunts
    a shore
Of some planet dispeopled, — " Never-
    more ! "

Then from deep in the past, as seemed to
    me,
  The strings gathered sorrow and sang
    forsaken,
" One lover still waits 'neath the green-
    wood tree,
But 't is dark," and they shuddered,
  " where lieth she
Dark and cold ! Forever must one be
    taken ? "
But I groaned, " O harp of all ruth be-
    reft,
This Scripture is sadder, — 'the other
    left' ! "

There murmured, as if one strove to speak,
  And tears came instead; then the sad
    tones wandered
And faltered among the uncertain chords

In a troubled doubt between sorrow and
  words;
  At last with themselves they questioned
    and pondered,
"Hereafter? — who knoweth?" and so
    they sighed
Down the long steps that lead to silence
  and died.

AUF WIEDERSEHEN

SUMMER

THE little gate was reached at last,
  Half hid in lilacs down the lane;
She pushed it wide, and, as she past,
A wistful look she backward cast,
  And said, — "Auf wiedersehen!"

With hand on latch, a vision white
  Lingered reluctant, and again
Half doubting if she did aright,
Soft as the dews that fell that night,
  She said, — "Auf wiedersehen!"

The lamp's clear gleam flits up the stair;
  I linger in delicious pain;
Ah, in that chamber, whose rich air
To breathe in thought I scarcely dare,
  Thinks she, — "Auf wiedersehen?" . . .

'T is thirteen years; once more I press
  The turf that silences the lane;
I hear the rustle of her dress,
I smell the lilacs, and — ah, yes,
  I hear "Auf wiedersehen!"

Sweet piece of bashful maiden art!
  The English words had seemed too
    fain,
But these — they drew us heart to heart,
Yet held us tenderly apart;
  She said, "Auf wiedersehen!"

PALINODE

AUTUMN

STILL thirteen years: 't is autumn now
  On field and hill, in heart and brain;
The naked trees at evening sough;
The leaf to the forsaken bough
  Sighs not, — "Auf wiedersehen!"

Two watched yon oriole's pendent dome,
  That now is void, and dank with rain,
And one, — oh, hope more frail than foam!
The bird to his deserted home
  Sings not, — "Auf wiedersehen!"

The loath gate swings with rusty creak;
  Once, parting there, we played at pain;
There came a parting, when the weak
And fading lips essayed to speak
  Vainly, — "Auf wiedersehen!"

Somewhere is comfort, somewhere faith,
  Though thou in outer dark remain;
One sweet sad voice ennobles death,
And still, for eighteen centuries saith
  Softly, — "Auf wiedersehen!"

If earth another grave must bear,
  Yet heaven hath won a sweeter strain,
And something whispers my despair,
That, from an orient chamber there,
  Floats down, "Auf wiedersehen!"

AFTER THE BURIAL

Lowell's second child, Rose, died after a
week's illness in the spring of 1850. Her father
wrote shortly after her death to Mr. Gay:
"She was very beautiful — fair, with large
dark-gray eyes and fine features. Her smile
was especially charming, and she was full of
smiles till her sickness began. Dear little
child, she had never spoken, only smiled. To
show you that I am not unable to go along
with you in the feeling expressed in your let-
ter, I will copy a few verses out of my com-
mon-place book." The verses were the first
form of the following poem, and will be found
in the notes at the end of this volume. The
poem, with its personal feeling over a universal
human experience, found its way into many
hearts. It "has roused," Lowell wrote in 1875,
"strange echoes in men who assured me they
were generally insensible to poetry. After all,
the only stuff a solitary man has to spin is
himself."

YES, faith is a goodly anchor;
  When skies are sweet as a psalm,
At the bows it lolls so stalwart,
  In its bluff, broad-shouldered calm.

And when over breakers to leeward
  The tattered surges are hurled,
It may keep our head to the tempest,
  With its grip on the base of the world.

But, after the shipwreck, tell me
　What help in its iron thews,
Still true to the broken hawser,
　Deep down among sea-weed and ooze ?

In the breaking gulfs of sorrow,
　When the helpless feet stretch out
And find in the deeps of darkness
　No footing so solid as doubt,

Then better one spar of Memory,
　One broken plank of the Past,
That our human heart may cling to,
　Though hopeless of shore at last !

To the spirit its splendid conjectures,
　To the flesh its sweet despair,
Its tears o'er the thin-worn locket
　With its anguish of deathless hair !

Immortal ?　I feel it and know it,
　Who doubts it of such as she ?
But that is the pang's very secret, —
　Immortal away from me.

There 's a narrow ridge in the graveyard
　Would scarce stay a child in his race,
But to me and my thought it is wider
　Than the star-sown vague of Space.

Your logic, my friend, is perfect,
　Your moral most drearily true;
But, since the earth clashed on *her* coffin,
　I keep hearing that, and not you.

Console if you will, I can bear it;
　'T is a well-meant alms of breath;
But not all the preaching since Adam
　Has made Death other than Death.

It is pagan; but wait till you feel it, —
　That jar of our earth, that dull shock
When the ploughshare of deeper passion
　Tears down to our primitive rock.

Communion in spirit !　Forgive me,
　But I, who am earthly and weak,
Would give all my incomes from dream-
　　land
For a touch of her hand on my cheek.

That little shoe in the corner,
　So worn and wrinkled and brown,
With its emptiness confutes you,
　And argues your wisdom down.

THE DEAD HOUSE

"I have a notion that the inmates of a house should never be changed. When the first occupants go out it should be burned, and a stone set up with 'Sacred to the Memory of a Home' on it. Suppose the body were eternal, and that when one spirit went out another took the lease. How frightful the strange expression of the eyes would be ! I fancy sometimes that the look in the eyes of a familiar house changes when aliens have come into it. For certainly a dwelling adapts itself to its occupants. The front door of a hospitable man opens easily and looks broad, and you can read Welcome ! on every step that leads to it.

"I stopped there and tried to put that into verse. I have only half succeeded, and I shall not give it to you. I shall copy it and thrust it into Jane's letter." J. R. L. to C. E. Norton, August 31, 1858.

A similar fancy appears in an earlier letter to Mrs. Francis G. Shaw, to whom Lowell wrote January 11, 1853: "I spent Sunday with Edmund Quincy at Dedham, and, as I came back over the rail yesterday, I was roused from a reverie by seeing 'West Roxbury Station' written up over the door of a kind of Italian villa at which we stopped. I almost twisted my head off looking for the house on the hill. There it stood in mourning still, just as Frank painted it. The color suited my mood exactly. The eyes of the house were shut, the welcoming look it had was gone ; it was dead. I am a Platonist about houses. They get to my eye a shape from the souls that inhabit them. My friends' dwellings seem as peculiar to them as their bodies, looks, and motions. People have no right to sell their dead houses; they should burn them as they used to burn corpses. . . . I have buried that house now and flung my pious handful of earth over it and set up a headstone — and I shall never look up to the hill-top again, let me pass it never so often."

Here once my step was quickened,
　Here beckoned the opening door,
And welcome thrilled from the threshold
　To the foot it had known before.

A glow came forth to meet me
　From the flame that laughed in the grate,
And shadows adance on the ceiling,
　Danced blither with mine for a mate.

"I claim you, old friend," yawned the arm-
　　chair,
　"This corner, you know, is your seat;"

"Rest your slippers on me," beamed the
    fender,
  "I brighten at touch of your feet."

"We know the practised finger,"
  Said the books, "that seems like brain;"
And the shy page rustled the secret
  It had kept till I came again.

Sang the pillow, "My down once quivered
  On nightingales' throats that flew
Through moonlit gardens of Hafiz
  To gather quaint dreams for you."

Ah me, where the Past sowed heart's-ease,
  The Present plucks rue for us men!
I come back: that scar unhealing
  Was not in the churchyard then.

But, I think, the house is unaltered,
  I will go and beg to look
At the rooms that were once familiar
  To my life as its bed to a brook.

Unaltered! Alas for the sameness
  That makes the change but more!
'T is a dead man I see in the mirrors,
  'T is his tread that chills the floor!

To learn such a simple lesson,
  Need I go to Paris and Rome,
That the many make the household,
  But only one the home?

'T was just a womanly presence,
  An influence unexprest,
But a rose she had worn, on my grave-
    sod
Were more than long life with the rest!

'T was a smile, 't was a garment's rustle,
  'T was nothing that I can phrase,
But the whole dumb dwelling grew con-
    scious,
  And put on her looks and ways.

Were it mine I would close the shutters,
  Like lids when the life is fled,
And the funeral fire should wind it,
  This corpse of a home that is dead.

For it died that autumn morning
  When she, its soul, was borne
To lie all dark on the hillside
  That looks over woodland and corn.

A MOOD

I GO to the ridge in the forest
I haunted in days gone by,
But thou, O Memory, pourest
No magical drop in mine eye,
Nor the gleam of the secret restorest
That hath faded from earth and sky:
A Presence autumnal and sober
Invests every rock and tree,
And the aureole of October
Lights the maples, but darkens me.

Pine in the distance,
Patient through sun or rain,
Meeting with graceful persistence,
With yielding but rooted resistance,
The northwind's wrench and strain,
No memory of past existence
Brings thee pain;
Right for the zenith heading,
Friendly with heat or cold,
Thine arms to the influence spreading
Of the heavens, just from of old,
Thou only aspirest the more,
Unregretful the old leaves shedding
That fringed thee with music before,
And deeper thy roots embedding
In the grace and the beauty of yore;
Thou sigh'st not, "Alas, I am older,
The green of last summer is sear!"
But loftier, hopefuller, bolder,
Winnest broader horizons each year.

To me 't is not cheer thou art singing:
There's a sound of the sea,
O mournful tree,
In thy boughs forever clinging,
And the far-off roar
Of waves on the shore
A shattered vessel flinging.

As thou musest still of the ocean
On which thou must float at last,
And seem'st to foreknow
The shipwreck's woe
And the sailor wrenched from the broken
    mast,
Do I, in this vague emotion,
This sadness that will not pass,
Though the air throb with wings,
And the field laughs and sings,
Do I forebode, alas!
The ship-building longer and wearier,

The voyage's struggle and strife,
And then the darker and drearier
Wreck of a broken life ?

THE VOYAGE TO VINLAND

In the letter to Mr. Norton, quoted at the beginning of this section, reference is made to *The Voyage to Vinland*, which Lowell had some thought of making the title-poem of the volume. In the same letter he says further regarding it : " Part of [this poem], you remember, was written eighteen years ago. I meant to have made it much longer, but maybe it is better as it is. I clapt a beginning upon it, patched it in the middle, and then got to what has always been my favorite part of the plan. This was to be a prophecy by Gudrida, a woman who went with them, of the future America. I have written in an unrhymed alliterated measure, in very short verse and stanzas of five lines each. It does not aim at following the law of the Icelandic alliterated stave, but hints at it and also at the *asonante*, without being properly either. But it runs well and is melodious, and we think it pretty good here, as does also Howells. Well, after that, of course, I was all for alliteration." The poem had apparently first borne the title of *Leif's Voyage*, as he writes of that poem to Mr. Briggs in 1850.

I

BIÖRN'S BECKONERS

Now Biörn, the son of Heriulf, had ill days
Because the heart within him seethed with
    blood
That would not be allayed with any toil,
Whether of war or hunting or the oar,
But was anhungered for some joy untried:
For the brain grew not weary with the
    limbs,
But, while they slept, still hammered like a
    Troll,
Building all night a bridge of solid dream
Between him and some purpose of his soul,
Or will to find a purpose. With the dawn
The sleep-laid timbers, crumbled to soft
    mist,
Denied all foothold. But the dream remained,
And every night with yellow-bearded kings
His sleep was haunted, — mighty men of
    old,
Once young as he, now ancient like the
    gods,

And safe as stars in all men's memories.
Strange sagas read he in their sea-blue eyes
Cold as the sea, grandly compassionless;
Like life, they made him eager and then
    mocked.
Nay, broad awake, they would not let him
    be;
They shaped themselves gigantic in the
    mist,
They rose far-beckoning in the lamps of
    heaven,
They whispered invitation in the winds,
And breath came from them, mightier than
    the wind,
To strain the lagging sails of his resolve,
Till that grew passion which before was
    wish,
And youth seemed all too costly to be
    staked
On the soiled cards wherewith men played
    their game,
Letting Time pocket up the larger life,
Lost with base gain of raiment, food, and
    roof.
" What helpeth lightness of the feet ? "
    they said,
" Oblivion runs with swifter foot than
    they;
Or strength of sinew ? New men come as
    strong,
And those sleep nameless; or renown in
    war ?
Swords grave no name on the long-memoried rock
But moss shall hide it; they alone who
    wring
Some secret purpose from the unwilling
    gods
Survive in song for yet a little while
To vex, like us, the dreams of later men,
Ourselves a dream, and dreamlike all we
    did."

II

THORWALD'S LAY

So Biörn went comfortless but for his
    thought,
And by his thought the more discomforted,
Till Eric Thurlson kept his Yule-tide feast:
And thither came he, called among the rest,
Silent, lone-minded, a church-door to mirth:
But, ere deep draughts forbade such serious song
As the grave Skald might chant nor after
    blush,

Then Eric looked at Thorwald where he sat
Mute as a cloud amid the stormy hall,
And said: " O Skald, sing now an olden
    song,
Such as our fathers heard who led great
    lives;
And, as the bravest on a shield is borne
Along the waving host that shouts him king,
So rode their thrones upon the thronging
    seas ! "
Then the old man arose; white-haired he
    stood,
White-bearded, and with eyes that looked
    afar
From their still region of perpetual snow,
Beyond the little smokes and stirs of men:
His head was bowed with gathered flakes
    of years,
As winter bends the sea-foreboding pine,
But something triumphed in his brow and
    eye,
Which whoso saw it could not see and
    crouch:
Loud rang the emptied beakers as he mused,
Brooding his eyried thoughts; then, as an
    eagle
Circles smooth - winged above the wind-
    vexed woods,
So wheeled his soul into the air of song
High o'er the stormy hall; and thus he
    sang:
" The fletcher for his arrow-shaft picks out
Wood   closest - grained, long - seasoned,
    straight as light;
And from a quiver full of such as these
The wary bowman, matched against his
    peers,
Long doubting, singles yet once more the
    best.
Who is it needs such flawless shafts as
    Fate ?
What archer of his arrows is so choice,
Or hits the white so surely ? They are men,
The chosen of her quiver; nor for her
Will every reed suffice, or cross-grained
    stick
At random from life's vulgar fagot plucked:
Such answer household ends; but she will
    have
Souls straight and clear, of toughest fibre,
    sound
Down to the heart of heart; from these she
    strips
All needless stuff, all sapwood; seasons
    them;

From   circumstance   untoward   feathers
    plucks
Crumpled and cheap; and barbs with iron
    will:
The hour that passes is her quiver-boy:
When she draws bow, 't is not across the
    wind,
Nor 'gainst the sun her haste - snatched
    arrow sings,
For sun and wind have plighted faith to
    her:
Ere men have heard the sinew twang, be-
    hold
In the butt's heart her trembling messen-
    ger !

" The song is old and simple that I sing;
But old and simple are despised as cheap,
Though hardest to achieve of human things:
Good were the days of yore, when men
    were tried
By ring of shields, as now by ring of words;
But while the gods are left, and hearts of
    men,
And wide-doored ocean, still the days are
    good.
Still o'er the earth hastes Opportunity,
Seeking the hardy soul that seeks for her.
Be not abroad, nor deaf with household
    cares
That chatter loudest as they mean the
    least;
Swift-willed is thrice - willed; late means
    nevermore;
Impatient is her foot, nor turns again."
He ceased; upon his bosom sank his beard
Sadly, as one who oft had seen her pass
Nor stayed her: and forthwith the frothy
    tide
Of interrupted wassail roared along.
But Biörn, the son of Heriulf, sat apart
Musing, and, with his eyes upon the fire,
Saw shapes of arrows, lost as soon as seen.
" A ship," he muttered, "is a wingëd bridge
That leadeth every way to man's desire,
And ocean the wide gate to manful luck."
And then with that resolve his heart was
    bent,
Which, like a humming shaft, through
    many a stripe
Of day and night, across the unpathwayed
    seas
Shot the brave prow that cut on Vinland
    sands
The first rune in the Saga of the West.

III

GUDRIDA'S PROPHECY

Four weeks they sailed, a speck in sky-shut
    seas,
Life, where was never life that knew itself,
But tumbled lubber-like in blowing whales;
Thought, where the like had never been
    before
Since Thought primeval brooded the abyss;
Alone as men were never in the world.
They saw the icy foundlings of the sea,
White cliffs of silence, beautiful by day,
Or looming, sudden-perilous, at night
In monstrous hush; or sometimes in the dark
The waves broke ominous with paly gleams
Crushed by the prow in sparkles of cold fire.
Then came green stripes of sea that prom-
    ised land
But brought it not, and on the thirtieth day
Low in the west were wooded shores like
    cloud.
They shouted as men shout with sudden
    hope;
But Biörn was silent, such strange loss
    there is
Between the dream's fulfilment and the
    dream,
Such sad abatement in the goal attained.
Then Gudrida, that was a prophetess,
Rapt with strange influence from Atlantis,
    sang:
Her words: the vision was the dreaming
    shore's.

Looms there the New Land:
Locked in the shadow
Long the gods shut it,
Niggards of newness
They, the o'er-old.

Little it looks there,
Slim as a cloud-streak;
It shall fold peoples
Even as a shepherd
Foldeth his flock.

Silent it sleeps now;
Great ships shall seek it,
Swarming as salmon;
Noise of its numbers
Two seas shall hear.

Men from the Northland,
Men from the Southland,
Haste empty-handed;
No more than manhood
Bring they, and hands.

Dark hair and fair hair,
Red blood and blue blood,
There shall be mingled;
Force of the ferment
Makes the New Man.

Pick of all kindreds,
Kings' blood shall theirs be,
Shoots of the eldest
Stock upon Midgard,
Sons of the poor.

Them waits the New Land;
They shall subdue it,
Leaving their sons' sons
Space for the body,
Space for the soul.

Leaving their sons' sons
All things save song-craft,
Plant long in growing,
Thrusting its tap-root
Deep in the Gone.

Here men shall grow up
Strong from self-helping;
Eyes for the present
Bring they as eagles',
Blind to the Past.

They shall make over
Creed, law, and custom;
Driving-men, doughty
Builders of empire,
Builders of men.

Here is no singer;
What should they sing of?
They, the unresting?
Labor is ugly,
Loathsome is change.

These the old gods hate,
Dwellers in dream-land,
Drinking delusion
Out of the empty
Skull of the Past.

These hate the old gods,
Warring against them;
Fatal to Odin,
Here the wolf Fenrir
Lieth in wait.

Here the gods' Twilight
Gathers, earth-gulfing;
Blackness of battle,
Fierce till the Old World
Flare up in fire.

Doubt not, my Northmen;
Fate loves the fearless;
Fools, when their roof-tree
Falls, think it doomsday;
Firm stands the sky.

Over the ruin
See I the promise;
Crisp waves the cornfield,
Peace-walled, the homestead
Waits open-doored.

There lies the New Land;
Yours to behold it,
Not to possess it;
Slowly Fate's perfect
Fulness shall come.

Then from your strong loins
Seed shall be scattered,
Men to the marrow,
Wilderness tamers,
Walkers of waves.

Jealous, the old gods
Shut it in shadow,
Wisely they ward it,
Egg of the serpent,
Bane to them all.

Stronger and sweeter
New gods shall seek it,
Fill it with man-folk
Wise for the future,
Wise from the past.

Here all is all men's,
Save only Wisdom;
King he that wins her;
Him hail they helmsman,
Highest of heart.

Might makes no master
Here any longer;
Sword is not swayer;
Here e'en the gods are
Selfish no more.

Walking the New Earth,
Lo, a divine One
Greets all men godlike,
Calls them his kindred,
He, the Divine.

Is it Thor's hammer
Rays in his right hand?
Weaponless walks he;
It is the White Christ,
Stronger than Thor.

Here shall a realm rise
Mighty in manhood;
Justice and Mercy
Here set a stronghold
Safe without spear.

Weak was the Old World,
Wearily war-fenced;
Out of its ashes,
Strong as the morning,
Springeth the New.

Beauty of promise,
Promise of beauty,
Safe in the silence
Sleep thou, till cometh
Light to thy lids!

Thee shall awaken
Flame from the furnace,
Bath of all brave ones,
Cleanser of conscience,
Welder of will.

Lowly shall love thee,
Thee, open-handed!
Stalwart shall shield thee,
Thee, worth their best blood,
Waif of the West!

Then shall come singers,
Singing no swan-song,
Birth-carols, rather,
Meet for the man child
Mighty of bone.

MAHMOOD THE IMAGE-BREAKER

OLD events have modern meanings; only
that survives
Of past history which finds kindred in all
hearts and lives.

Mahmood once, the idol-breaker, spreader
of the Faith,
Was at Sumnat tempted sorely, as the
legend saith.

In the great pagoda's centre, monstrous
and abhorred,
Granite on a throne of granite, sat the
temple's lord.

Mahmood paused a moment, silenced by
the silent face
That, with eyes of stone unwavering, awed
the ancient place.

Then the Brahmins knelt before him, by
his doubt made bold,
Pledging for their idol's ransom countless
gems and gold.

Gold was yellow dirt to Mahmood, but of
precious use,
Since from it the roots of power suck a
potent juice.

"Were yon stone alone in question, this
would please me well,"
Mahmood said; "but, with the block there,
I my truth must sell.

"Wealth and rule slip down with Fortune,
as her wheel turns round;
He who keeps his faith, he only cannot be
discrowned.

"Little were a change of station, loss of
life or crown,
But the wreck were past retrieving if the
Man fell down."

So his iron mace he lifted, smote with
might and main,
And the idol, on the pavement tumbling,
burst in twain.

Luck obeys the downright striker; from
the hollow core,
Fifty times the Brahmins' offer deluged
all the floor.

INVITA MINERVA

THE Bardling came where by a river grew
The pennoned reeds, that, as the west-
wind blew,
Gleamed and sighed plaintively, as if they
knew
What music slept enchanted in each stem,
Till Pan should choose some happy one of
them,
And with wise lips enlife it through and
through.

The Bardling thought, "A pipe is all I
need;
Once I have sought me out a clear, smooth
reed,
And shaped it to my fancy, I proceed
To breathe such strains as, yonder mid the
rocks,
The strange youth blows, that tends Ad-
metus' flocks,
And all the maidens shall to me pay heed."

The summer day he spent in questful
round,
And many a reed he marred, but never
found
A conjuring-spell to free the imprisoned
sound;
At last his vainly wearied limbs he laid
Beneath a sacred laurel's flickering shade,
And sleep about his brain her cobweb
wound.

Then strode the mighty Mother through
his dreams,
Saying: "The reeds along a thousand
streams
Are mine, and who is he that plots and
schemes
To snare the melodies wherewith my breath
Sounds through the double pipes of Life
and Death,
Atoning what to men mad discord seems?

"He seeks not me, but I seek oft in vain
For him who shall my voiceful reeds con-
strain,

And make them utter their melodious pain;
He flies the immortal gift, for well he
    knows
His life of life must with its overflows
Flood the unthankful pipe, nor come again.

"Thou fool, who dost my harmless subjects
    wrong,
'T is not the singer's wish that makes the
    song:
The rhythmic beauty wanders dumb, how
    long,
Nor stoops to any daintiest instrument,
Till, found its mated lips, their sweet con-
    sent
Makes mortal breath than Time and Fate
    more strong."

THE FOUNTAIN OF YOUTH

This poem, written apparently in the win-
ter of 1849–50, was to have been included in
the projected work, *The Nooning.*

I

'T is a woodland enchanted!
By no sadder spirit
Than blackbirds and thrushes,
That whistle to cheer it
All day in the bushes,
This woodland is haunted:
And in a small clearing,
Beyond sight or hearing
Of human annoyance,
The little fount gushes,
First smoothly, then dashes
And gurgles and flashes,
To the maples and ashes
Confiding its joyance;
Unconscious confiding,
Then, silent and glossy,
Slips winding and hiding
Through alder-stems mossy,
Through gossamer roots
Fine as nerves,
That tremble, as shoots
Through their magnetized curves
The allurement delicious
Of the water's capricious
Thrills, gushes, and swerves.

II

'T is a woodland enchanted!
I am writing no fiction;

And this fount, its sole daughter,
To the woodland was granted
To pour holy water
And win benediction;
In summer-noon flushes,
When all the wood hushes,
Blue dragon-flies knitting
To and fro in the sun,
With sidelong jerk flitting
Sink down on the rushes,
And, motionless sitting,
Hear it bubble and run,
Hear its low inward singing,
With level wings swinging
On green tasselled rushes,
To dream in the sun.

III

'T is a woodland enchanted!
The great August noonlight!
Through myriad rifts slanted,
Leaf and bole thickly sprinkles
With flickering gold;
There, in warm August gloaming,
With quick, silent brightenings,
From meadow-lands roaming,
The firefly twinkles
His fitful heat-lightnings;
There the magical moonlight
With meek, saintly glory
Steeps summit and wold;
There whippoorwills plain in the soli-
    tudes hoary
With lone cries that wander
Now hither, now yonder,
Like souls doomed of old
To a mild purgatory;
But through noonlight and moonlight
The little fount tinkles
Its silver saints'-bells,
That no sprite ill-boding
May make his abode in
Those innocent dells.

IV

'T is a woodland enchanted!
When the phebe scarce whistles
Once an hour to his fellow,
And, where red lilies flaunted,
Balloons from the thistles
Tell summer's disasters,
The butterflies yellow,
As caught in an eddy
Of air's silent ocean,

Sink, waver, and steady
O'er goats'-beard and asters,
Like souls of dead flowers,
With aimless emotion
Still lingering unready
To leave their old bowers;
And the fount is no dumber,
But still gleams and flashes,
And gurgles and plashes,
To the measure of summer;
The butterflies hear it,
And spell-bound are holden,
Still balancing near it
O'er the goats'-beard so golden.

V

'T is a woodland enchanted!
A vast silver willow,
I know not how planted,
(This wood is enchanted,
And full of surprises,)
Stands stemming a billow,
A motionless billow
Of ankle-deep mosses;
Two great roots it crosses
To make a round basin,
And there the Fount rises;
Ah, too pure a mirror
For one sick of error
To see his sad face in!
No dew-drop is stiller
In its lupin-leaf setting
Than this water moss-bounded;
But a tiny sand-pillar
From the bottom keeps jetting,
And mermaid ne'er sounded
Through the wreaths of a shell,
Down amid crimson dulses
In some cavern of ocean,
A melody sweeter
Than the delicate pulses,
The soft, noiseless metre,
The pause and the swell
Of that musical motion:
I recall it, not see it;
Could vision be clearer?
Half I 'm fain to draw nearer
Half tempted to flee it;
The sleeping Past wake not,
Beware!
One forward step take not,
Ah! break not
That quietude rare!
By my step unaffrighted
A thrush hops before it,

And o'er it
A birch hangs delighted,
Dipping, dipping, dipping its tremulous
    hair;
Pure as the fountain, once
I came to the place,
(How dare I draw nearer?)
I bent o'er its mirror,
And saw a child's face
Mid locks of bright gold in it;
Yes, pure as this fountain once, —
Since, how much error!
Too holy a mirror
For the man to behold in it
His harsh, bearded countenance!

VI

'T is a woodland enchanted!
Ah, fly unreturning!
Yet stay; —
'T is a woodland enchanted,
Where wonderful chances
Have sway;
Luck flees from the cold one,
But leaps to the bold one
Half-way;
Why should I be daunted?
Still the smooth mirror glances,
Still the amber sand dances,
One look, — then away!
O magical glass!
Canst keep in thy bosom
Shades of leaf and of blossom
When summer days pass,
So that when thy wave hardens
It shapes as it pleases,
Unharmed by the breezes,
Its fine hanging gardens?
Hast those in thy keeping,
And canst not uncover,
Enchantedly sleeping,
The old shade of thy lover?
It is there! I have found it!
He wakes, the long sleeper!
The pool is grown deeper,
The sand dance is ending,
The white floor sinks, blending
With skies that below me
Are deepening and bending,
And a child's face alone
That seems not to know me,
With hair that fades golden
In the heaven-glow round it,
Looks up at my own;
Ah, glimpse through the portal

That leads to the throne,
That opes the child's olden
Regions Elysian!
Ah, too holy vision
For thy skirts to be holden
By soiled hand of mortal!
It wavers, it scatters,
'T is gone past recalling!
A tear's sudden falling
The magic cup shatters,
Breaks the spell of the waters,
And the sand cone once more,
With a ceaseless renewing,
Its dance is pursuing
On the silvery floor,
O'er and o'er,
With a noiseless and ceaseless renew-
    ing.

VII

'T is a woodland enchanted!
If you ask me, *Where is it?*
I can but make answer,
" 'T is past my disclosing; "
Not to choice is it granted
By sure paths to visit
The still pool enclosing
Its blithe little dancer;
But in some day, the rarest
Of many Septembers,
When the pulses of air rest,
And all things lie dreaming
In drowsy haze steaming
From the wood's glowing embers,
Then, sometimes, unheeding,
And asking not whither,
By a sweet inward leading
My feet are drawn thither,
And, looking with awe in the magical
    mirror,
I see through my tears,
Half doubtful of seeing,
The face unperverted,
The warm golden being
Of a child of five years;
And spite of the mists and the error,
And the days overcast,
Can feel that I walk undeserted,
But forever attended
By the glad heavens that bended
O'er the innocent past;
Toward fancy or truth
Doth the sweet vision win me?
Dare I think that I cast

In the fountain of youth
The fleeting reflection
Of some bygone perfection
That still lingers in me?

YUSSOUF

A STRANGER came one night to Yussouf's
    tent,
Saying, " Behold, one outcast and in dread,
Against whose life the bow of power is
    bent,
Who flies, and hath not where to lay his
    head;
I come to thee for shelter and for food,
To Yussouf, called through all our tribes
    ' The Good.' "

" This tent is mine," said Yussouf, " but no
    more
Than it is God's; come in and be at peace;
Freely shalt thou partake of all my store
As I of His who buildeth over these
Our tents his glorious roof of night and
    day,
And at whose door none ever yet heard
    Nay."

So Yussouf entertained his guest that night,
And, waking him ere day, said: " Here is
    gold;
My swiftest horse is saddled for thy flight;
Depart before the prying day grow bold."
As one lamp lights another, nor grows
    less,
So nobleness enkindleth nobleness.

That inward light the stranger's face made
    grand,
Which shines from all self-conquest; kneel-
    ing low,
He bowed his forehead upon Yussouf's
    hand,
Sobbing: " O Sheik, I cannot leave thee
    so;
I will repay thee; all this thou hast done
Unto that Ibrahim who slew thy son ! "

" Take thrice the gold," said Yussouf, " for
    with thee
Into the desert, never to return,
My one black thought shall ride away from
    me ;

First-born, for whom by day and night I
   yearn,
Balanced and just are all of God's de-
   crees;
Thou art avenged, my first-born, sleep in
   peace!"

THE DARKENED MIND

THE fire is burning clear and blithely,
Pleasantly whistles the winter wind;
We are about thee, thy friends and kin-
   dred,
On us all flickers the firelight kind;
There thou sittest in thy wonted corner
Lone and awful in thy darkened mind.

There thou sittest; now and then thou
   moanest;
Thou dost talk with what we cannot see,
Lookest at us with an eye so doubtful,
It doth put us very far from thee;
There thou sittest; we would fain be nigh
   thee,
But we know that it can never be.

We can touch thee, still we are no nearer;
Gather round thee, still thou art alone;
The wide chasm of reason is between us;
Thou confutest kindness with a moan;
We can speak to thee, and thou canst an-
   swer,
Like two prisoners through a wall of stone.

Hardest heart would call it very awful
When thou look'st at us and seest — oh,
   what?
If we move away, thou sittest gazing
With those vague eyes at the selfsame
   spot,
And thou mutterest, thy hands thou wring-
   est,
Seeing something, — us thou seest not.

Strange it is that, in this open bright-
   ness,
Thou shouldst sit in such a narrow cell;
Strange it is that thou shouldst be so lone-
   some
Where those are who love thee all so
   well;
Not so much of thee is left among us
As the hum outliving the hushed bell.

WHAT RABBI JEHOSHA SAID

Originally written for a Fair in St. Louis.

RABBI JEHOSHA used to say
That God made angels every day,
Perfect as Michael and the rest
First brooded in creation's nest,
Whose only office was to cry
Hosanna! once, and then to die;
Or rather, with Life's essence blent,
To be led home from banishment.

Rabbi Jehosha had the skill
To know that Heaven is in God's will;
And doing that, though for a space
One heart-beat long, may win a grace
As full of grandeur and of glow
As Princes of the Chariot know.

'T were glorious, no doubt, to be
One of the strong-winged Hierarchy,
To burn with Seraphs, or to shine
With Cherubs, deathlessly divine;
Yet I, perhaps, poor earthly clod,
Could I forget myself in God,
Could I but find my nature's clue
Simply as birds and blossoms do,
And but for one rapt moment know
'T is Heaven must come, not we **must**
   go,
Should win my place as near the throne
As the pearl-angel of its zone,
And God would listen mid the throng
For my one breath of perfect song,
That, in its simple human way,
Said all the Host of Heaven could say.

ALL–SAINTS

ONE feast, of holy days the crest,
   I, though no Churchman, love to keep,
All-Saints, — the unknown good that rest
   In God's still memory folded deep;
The bravely dumb that did their deed,
   And scorned to blot it with a name,
Men of the plain heroic breed,
   That loved Heaven's silence more than
      fame.

Such lived not in the past alone,
   But thread to-day the unheeding street,

And stairs to Sin and Famine known
  Sing with the welcome of their feet;
The den they enter grows a shrine,
  The grimy sash an oriel burns,
Their cup of water warms like wine,
  Their speech is filled from heavenly urns.

About their brows to me appears
  An aureole traced in tenderest light,
The rainbow-gleam of smiles through tears
  In dying eyes, by them made bright,
Of souls that shivered on the edge
  Of that chill ford repassed no more,
And in their mercy felt the pledge
  And sweetness of the farther shore.

A WINTER-EVENING HYMN TO MY FIRE

I

BEAUTY on my hearth-stone blazing !
To-night the triple Zoroaster
Shall my prophet be and master:
To-night will I pure Magian be,
Hymns to thy sole honor raising,
While thou leapest fast and faster,
Wild with self-delighted glee,
Or sink'st low and glowest faintly
As an aureole still and saintly,
Keeping cadence to my praising
Thee ! still thee ! and only thee !

II

Elfish daughter of Apollo !
Thee, from thy father stolen and bound
To serve in Vulcan's clangorous smithy,
Prometheus (primal Yankee) found,
And, when he had tampered with thee,
(Too confiding little maid !)
In a reed's precarious hollow
To our frozen earth conveyed:
For he swore I know not what;
Endless ease should be thy lot,
Pleasure that should never falter,
Lifelong play, and not a duty
Save to hover o'er the altar,
Vision of celestial beauty,
Fed with precious woods and spices ;
Then, perfidious ! having got
Thee in the net of his devices,
Sold thee into endless slavery,
Made thee a drudge to boil the pot,
Thee, Helios' daughter, who dost bear
His likeness in thy golden hair;

Thee, by nature wild and wavery,
Palpitating, evanescent
As the shade of Dian's crescent,
Life, motion, gladness, everywhere !

III

Fathom deep men bury thee
In the furnace dark and still,
There, with dreariest mockery,
Making thee eat, against thy will,
Blackest Pennsylvanian stone;
But thou dost avenge thy doom,
For, from out thy catacomb,
Day and night thy wrath is blown
In a withering simoom,
And, adown that cavern drear,
Thy black pitfall in the floor,
Staggers the lusty antique cheer,
Despairing, and is seen no more !

IV

Elfish I may rightly name thee;
We enslave, but cannot tame thee;
With fierce snatches, now and then,
Thou pluckest at thy right again,
And thy down-trod instincts savage
To stealthy insurrection creep
While thy wittol masters sleep,
And burst in undiscerning ravage:
Then how thou shak'st thy bacchant locks !
While brazen pulses, far and near,
Throb thick and thicker, wild with fear
And dread conjecture, till the drear
Disordered clangor every steeple rocks !

V

But when we make a friend of thee,
And admit thee to the hall
On our nights of festival,
Then, Cinderella, who could see
In thee the kitchen's stunted thrall ?
Once more a Princess lithe and tall,
Thou dancest with a whispering tread,
While the bright marvel of thy head
In crinkling gold floats all abroad,
And gloriously dost vindicate
The legend of thy lineage great,
Earth-exiled daughter of the Pythian god !
Now in the ample chimney-place,
To honor thy acknowledged race,
We crown thee high with laurel good,
Thy shining father's sacred wood,
Which, guessing thy ancestral right,
Sparkles and snaps its dumb delight,
And, at thy touch, poor outcast one,

Feels through its gladdened fibres go
The tingle and thrill and vassal glow
Of instincts loyal to the sun.

VI

O thou of home the guardian Lar,
And, when our earth hath wandered far
Into the cold, and deep snow covers
The walks of our New England lovers,
Their sweet secluded evening-star !
'T was with thy rays the English Muse
Ripened her mild domestic hues;
'T was by thy flicker that she conned
The fireside wisdom that enrings
With light from heaven familiar things;
By thee she found the homely faith
In whose mild eyes thy comfort stay'th,
When Death, extinguishing his torch,
Gropes for the latch-string in the porch ;
The love that wanders not beyond
His earliest nest, but sits and sings
While children smooth his patient wings;
Therefore with thee I love to read
Our brave old poets: at thy touch how
    stirs
Life in the withered words ! how swift
    recede
Time's shadows ! and how glows again
Through its dead mass the incandescent
    verse,
As when upon the anvils of the brain
It glittering lay, cyclopically wrought
By the fast-throbbing hammers of the
    poet's thought!
Thou murmurest, too, divinely stirred,
The aspirations unattained,
The rhythms so rathe and delicate,
They bent and strained
And broke, beneath the sombre weight
Of any airiest mortal word.

VII

What warm protection dost thou bend
Round curtained talk of friend with friend,
While the gray snow-storm, held aloof,
To softest outline rounds the roof,
Or the rude North with baffled strain
Shoulders the frost-starred window-pane !
Now the kind nymph to Bacchus born
By Morpheus' daughter, she that seems
Gifted upon her natal morn
By him with fire, by her with dreams,
Nicotia, dearer to the Muse
Than all the grape's bewildering juice,
We worship, unforbid of thee;

And, as her incense floats and curls
In airy spires and wayward whirls,
Or poises on its tremulous stalk
A flower of frailest revery,
So winds and loiters, idly free,
The current of unguided talk,
Now laughter-rippled, and now caught
In smooth, dark pools of deeper thought.
Meanwhile thou mellowest every word,
A sweetly unobtrusive third;
For thou hast magic beyond wine,
To unlock natures each to each;
The unspoken thought thou canst divine;
Thou fill'st the pauses of the speech
With whispers that to dream-land reach
And frozen fancy-springs unchain
In Arctic outskirts of the brain :
Sun of all inmost confidences,
To thy rays doth the heart unclose
Its formal calyx of pretences,
That close against rude day's offences,
And open its shy midnight rose !

VIII

Thou holdest not the master key
With which thy Sire sets free the mystic
    gates
Of Past and Future: not for common fates
Do they wide open fling,
And, with a far-heard ring,
Swing back their willing valves melodi-
    ously;
Only to ceremonial days,
And great processions of imperial song
That set the world at gaze,
Doth such high privilege belong:
But thou a postern-door canst ope
To humbler chambers of the selfsame
    palace
Where Memory lodges, and her sister
    Hope,
Whose being is but as a crystal chalice
Which, with her various mood, the elder
    fills
Of joy or sorrow,
So coloring as she wills
With hues of yesterday the unconscious
    morrow.

IX

Thou sinkest, and my fancy sinks with
    thee:
For thee I took the idle shell,
And struck the unused chords again,
But they are gone who listened well;

Some are in heaven, and all are far from
    me:
Even as I sing, it turns to pain,
And with vain tears my eyelids throb and
    swell:
Enough; I come not of the race
That hawk their sorrows in the market-
    place.
Earth stops the ears I best had loved to
    please;
Then break, ye untuned chords, or rust in
    peace!
As if a white-haired actor should come
    back
Some midnight to the theatre void and
    black,
And there rehearse his youth's great part
Mid thin applauses of the ghosts,
So seems it now: ye crowd upon my
    heart,
And I bow down in silence, shadowy hosts!

FANCY'S CASUISTRY

How struggles with the tempest's swells
That warning of tumultuous bells!
The fire is loose! and frantic knells
    Throb fast and faster,
As tower to tower confusedly tells
    News of disaster.

But on my far-off solitude
No harsh alarums can intrude;
The terror comes to me subdued
    And charmed by distance,
To deepen the habitual mood
    Of my existence.

Are those, I muse, the Easter chimes?
And listen, weaving careless rhymes
While the loud city's griefs and crimes
    Pay gentle allegiance
To the fine quiet that sublimes
    These dreamy regions.

And when the storm o'erwhelms the shore,
I watch entranced as, o'er and o'er,
The light revolves amid the roar
    So still and saintly,
Now large and near, now more and more
    Withdrawing faintly.

This, too, despairing sailors see
Flash out the breakers 'neath their lee

In sudden snow, then lingeringly
    Wane tow'rd eclipse,
While through the dark the shuddering
    sea
    Gropes for the ships.

And is it right, this mood of mind
That thus, in revery enshrined,
Can in the world mere topics find
    For musing stricture,
Seeing the life of humankind
    Only as picture?

The events in line of battle go;
In vain for me their trumpets blow
As unto him that lieth low
    In death's dark arches,
And through the sod hears throbbing slow
    The muffled marches.

O Duty, am I dead to thee
In this my cloistered ecstasy,
In this lone shallop on the sea
    That drifts tow'rd Silence?
And are those visioned shores I see
    But sirens' islands?

My Dante frowns with lip-locked mien,
As who would say, "'T is those, I ween,
Whom lifelong armor-chafe makes lean
    That win the laurel;"
But where *is* Truth? What does it mean,
    The world-old quarrel?

Such questionings are idle air:
Leave what to do and what to spare
To the inspiring moment's care,
    Nor ask for payment
Of fame or gold, but just to wear
    Unspotted raiment.

TO MR. JOHN BARTLETT

WHO HAD SENT ME A SEVEN-POUND
TROUT

Mr. Bartlett, the editor of *Familiar Quota-
tions*, was a near neighbor of Lowell, and with
him was long a member of a whist-party.

FIT for an Abbot of Theleme,
    For the whole Cardinals' College, or
The Pope himself to see in dream
Before his lenten vision gleam,
    He lies there, the sogdologer!

His precious flanks with stars besprent,
　Worthy to swim in Castaly !
The friend by whom such gifts are sent,
For him shall bumpers full be spent,
　His health ! be Luck his fast ally !

I see him trace the wayward brook
　Amid the forest mysteries,
Where at their shades shy aspens look,
Or where, with many a gurgling crook,
　It croons its woodland histories.

I see leaf-shade and sun-fleck lend
　Their tremulous, sweet vicissitude
To smooth, dark pool, to crinkling bend, —
(Oh, stew him, Ann, as 't were your friend,
　With amorous solicitude !)

I see him step with caution due,
　Soft as if shod with moccasins,
Grave as in church, for who plies you,
Sweet craft, is safe as in a pew
　From all our common stock o' sins.

The unerring fly I see him cast,
　That as a rose-leaf falls as soft,
A flash ! a whirl ! he has him fast !
We tyros, how that struggle last
　Confuses and appalls us oft.

Unfluttered he : calm as the sky
　Looks on our tragi-comedies,
This way and that he lets him fly,
A sunbeam-shuttle, then to die
　Lands him, with cool *aplomb*, at ease.

The friend who gave our board such gust,
　Life's care may he o'erstep it half,
And, when Death hooks him, as he must,
He 'll do it handsomely, I trust,
　And John H—— write his epitaph !

Oh, born beneath the Fishes' sign,
　Of constellations happiest,
May he somewhere with Walton dine,
May Horace send him Massic wine,
　And Burns Scotch drink, the nappi-
　　est!

And when they come his deeds to weigh,
　And how he used the talents his,
One trout-scale in the scales he 'll lay
(If trout had scales), and 't will out-
　sway
　The wrong side of the balances.

ODE TO HAPPINESS

SPIRIT, that rarely comest now
　And only to contrast my gloom,
　Like rainbow-feathered birds that bloom
A moment on some autumn bough
That, with the spurn of their farewell,
Sheds its last leaves, — thou once didst
　dwell
　With me year-long, and make intense
To boyhood's wisely vacant days
Their fleet but all-sufficing grace
　Of trustful inexperience,
　While soul could still transfigure sense,
And thrill, as with love's first caress,
At life's mere unexpectedness.
　Days when my blood would leap and run
　　As full of sunshine as a breeze,
　　Or spray tossed up by Summer seas
　That doubts if it be sea or sun!
Days that flew swiftly like the band
　That played in Grecian games at strife,
　And passed from eager hand to hand
　The onward-dancing torch of life!

Wing-footed! thou abid'st with him
　Who asks it not; but he who hath
　Watched o'er the waves thy waning path,
Shall nevermore behold returning
Thy high-heaped canvas shoreward yearn-
　ing!
Thou first reveal'st to us thy face
Turned o'er the shoulder's parting grace,
　A moment glimpsed, then seen no
　　more, —
Thou whose swift footsteps we can trace
　Away from every mortal door.

Nymph of the unreturning feet,
　How may I win thee back ?　But no,
　I do thee wrong to call thee so;
'T is I am changed, not thou art fleet:
The man thy presence feels again,
Not in the blood, but in the brain,
Spirit, that lov'st the upper air
Serene and passionless and rare,
　Such as on mountain heights we find
　And wide-viewed uplands of the mind;
Or such as scorns to coil and sing
Round any but the eagle's wing
　Of souls that with long upward beat
　Have won an undisturbed retreat
Where, poised like wingèd victories,
They mirror in relentless eyes

The life broad - basking 'neath their
  feet, —
Man ever with his Now at strife,
  Pained with first gasps of earthly air,
  Then praying Death the last to spare,
Still fearful of the ampler life.

Not unto them dost thou consent
  Who, passionless, can lead at ease
A life of unalloyed content
  A life like that of land-locked seas,
Who feel no elemental gush
Of tidal forces, no fierce rush
  Of storm deep-grasping scarcely spent
  'Twixt continent and continent.
Such quiet souls have never known
  Thy truer inspiration, thou
  Who lov'st to feel upon thy brow
Spray from the plunging vessel thrown
  Grazing the tusked lee shore, the cliff
That o'er the abrupt gorge holds its breath,
  Where the frail hair-breadth of an *if*
Is all that sunders life and death:
These, too, are cared for, and round these
Bends her mild crook thy sister Peace;
  These in unvexed dependence lie,
  Each 'neath his strip of household sky;
O'er these clouds wander, and the blue
Hangs motionless the whole day through;
  Stars rise for them, and moons grow
    large
And lessen in such tranquil wise
As joys and sorrows do that rise
  Within their nature's sheltered marge;
Their hours into each other flit
  Like the leaf-shadows of the vine
And fig-tree under which they sit,
  And their still lives to heaven incline
With an unconscious habitude,
  Unhistoried as smokes that rise
From happy hearths and sight elude
  In kindred blue of morning skies.

Wayward! when once we feel thy lack,
'T is worse than vain to woo thee back!
  Yet there is one who seems to be
Thine elder sister, in whose eyes
A faint far northern light will rise
  Sometimes, and bring a dream of thee;
She is not that for which youth hoped,
  But she hath blessings all her own,
Thoughts pure as lilies newly oped,
  And faith to sorrow given alone:
Almost I deem that it is thou
Come back with graver matron brow,

With deepened eyes and bated breath,
  Like one that somewhere hath met Death:
But "No," she answers, " I am she
Whom the gods love, Tranquillity;
  That other whom you seek forlorn
  Half earthly was; but I am born
Of the immortals, and our race
Wears still some sadness on its face:
He wins me late, but keeps me long,
Who, dowered with every gift of passion,
In that fierce flame can forge and fashion
  Of sin and self the anchor strong;
Can thence compel the driving force
Of daily life's mechanic course,
Nor less the nobler energies
Of needful toil and culture wise;
Whose soul is worth the tempter's lure
Who can renounce, and yet endure,
To him I come, not lightly wooed,
But won by silent fortitude."

VILLA FRANCA

1859

WAIT a little: do *we* not wait ?
Louis Napoleon is not Fate,
Francis Joseph is not Time;
There 's One hath swifter feet than Crime;
Cannon-parliaments settle naught;
Venice is Austria's, — whose is Thought ?
Minié is good, but, spite of change,
Gutenberg's gun has the longest range.
  Spin, spin, Clotho, spin !
  Lachesis, twist! and, Atropos, sever!
  In the shadow, year out, year in,
  The silent headsman waits forever.

Wait, we say: our years are long;
Men are weak, but Man is strong;
Since the stars first curved their rings,
We have looked on many things;
Great wars come and great wars go,
Wolf-tracks light on polar snow;
We shall see him come and gone,
This second-hand Napoleon.
  Spin, spin, Clotho, spin!
  Lachesis, twist! and, Atropos, sever!
  In the shadow, year out, year in,
  The silent headsman waits forever.

We saw the elder Corsican,
And Clotho muttered as she span,
While crowned lackeys bore the train,

Of the pinchbeck Charlemagne :
" Sister, stint not length of thread!
Sister, stay the scissors dread!
On Saint Helen's granite bleak,
Hark, the vulture whets his beak!"
    Spin, spin, Clotho, spin!
    Lachesis, twist! and, Atropos, sever!
    In the shadow, year out, year in,
    The silent headsman waits forever.

The Bonapartes, we know their bees
That wade in honey red to the knees;
Their patent reaper, its sheaves sleep sound
In dreamless garners underground:
We know false glory's spendthrift race
Pawning nations for feathers and lace;
It may be short, it may be long,
" 'T is reckoning - day!" sneers unpaid
    Wrong.
    Spin, spin, Clotho, spin!
    Lachesis, twist! and, Atropos, sever!
    In the shadow, year out, year in,
    The silent headsman waits forever.

The Cock that wears the Eagle's skin
Can promise what he ne'er could win;
Slavery reaped for fine words sown,
System for all, and rights for none,
Despots atop, a wild clan below,
Such is the Gaul from long ago;
Wash the black from the Ethiop's face,
Wash the past out of man or race !
    Spin, spin, Clotho, spin!
    Lachesis, twist ! and, Atropos, sever!
    In the shadow, year out, year in,
    The silent headsman waits forever.

'Neath Gregory's throne a spider swings,
And snares the people for the kings;
" Luther is dead; old quarrels pass;
The stake's black scars are healed with
    grass; "
So dreamers prate; did man e'er live
Saw priest or woman yet forgive ?
But Luther's broom is left, and eyes
Peep o'er their creeds to where it lies.
    Spin, spin, Clotho, spin!
    Lachesis, twist! and, Atropos, sever!
    In the shadow, year out, year in,
    The silent headsman waits forever.

Smooth sails the ship of either realm,
Kaiser and Jesuit at the helm ;
We look down the depths, and mark
Silent workers in the dark

Building slow the sharp-tusked reefs,
Old instincts hardening to new beliefs;
Patience a little; learn to wait;
Hours are long on the clock of Fate.
    Spin, spin, Clotho, spin!
    Lachesis, twist! and, Atropos, sever!
    Darkness is strong, and so is Sin,
    But surely God endures forever!

THE MINER

Down 'mid the tangled roots of things
    That coil about the central fire,
I seek for that which giveth wings
    To stoop, not soar, to my desire.

Sometimes I hear, as 't were a sigh,
    The sea's deep yearning far above,
" Thou hast the secret not," I cry,
    " In deeper deeps is hid my Love."

They think I burrow from the sun,
    In darkness, all alone, and weak;
Such loss were gain if He were won,
    For 't is the sun's own Sun I seek.

" The earth," they murmur, " is the tomb
    That vainly sought his life to prison;
Why grovel longer in the gloom ?
    He is not here; he hath arisen."

More life for me where he hath lain
    Hidden while ye believed him dead,
Than in cathedrals cold and vain,
    Built on loose sands of *It is said.*

My search is for the living gold;
    Him I desire who dwells recluse,
And not his image worn and old,
    Day-servant of our sordid use.

If him I find not, yet I find
    The ancient joy of cell and church,
The glimpse, the surety undefined,
    The unquenched ardor of the search.

Happier to chase a flying goal
    Than to sit counting laurelled gains,
To guess the Soul within the soul
    Than to be lord of what remains.

Hide still, best Good, in subtile wise,
    Beyond my nature's utmost scope;
Be ever absent from mine eyes
    To be twice present in my hope !

GOLD EGG: A DREAM-FANTASY

HOW A STUDENT IN SEARCH OF THE
BEAUTIFUL FELL ASLEEP IN DRESDEN
OVER HERR PROFESSOR DOCTOR VI-
SCHER'S WISSENSCHAFT DES SCHÖNEN,
AND WHAT CAME THEREOF

I SWAM with undulation soft,
 Adrift on Vischer's ocean,
And, from my cockboat up aloft,
Sent down my mental plummet oft
 In hope to reach a notion.

But from the metaphysic sea
 No bottom was forthcoming,
And all the while (how drearily!)
In one eternal note of B
 My German stove kept humming.

"What's Beauty?" mused I; "is it told
 By synthesis? analysis?
Have you not made us lead of gold?
To feed your crucible, not sold
 Our temple's sacred chalices?"

Then o'er my senses came a change;
 My book seemed all traditions,
Old legends of profoundest range,
Diablery, and stories strange
 Of goblins, elves, magicians.

Old gods in modern saints I found,
 Old creeds in strange disguises;
I thought them safely underground,
And here they were, all safe and sound,
 Without a sign of phthisis.

Truth was, my outward eyes were closed,
 Although I did not know it;
Deep into dream-land I had dozed,
And thus was happily transposed
 From proser into poet.

So what I read took flesh and blood,
 And turned to living creatures:
The words were but the dingy bud
That bloomed, like Adam, from the mud,
 To human forms and features.

I saw how Zeus was lodged once more
 By Baucis and Philemon;
The text said, "Not alone of yore,
But every day, at every door
 Knocks still the masking Demon."

DAIMON 't was printed in the book
 And, as I read it slowly,
The letters stirred and changed, and took
Jove's stature, the Olympian look
 Of painless melancholy.

He paused upon the threshold worn:
 "With coin I cannot pay you;
Yet would I fain make some return;
The gift for cheapness do not spurn,
 Accept this hen, I pray you.

"Plain feathers wears my Hemera,
 And has from ages olden;
She makes her nest in common hay,
And yet, of all the birds that lay,
 Her eggs alone are golden."

He turned, and could no more be seen;
 Old Baucis stared a moment,
Then tossed poor Partlet on the green,
And with a tone, half jest, half spleen,
 Thus made her housewife's comment:

"The stranger had a queerish face,
 His smile was hardly pleasant,
And, though he meant it for a grace,
Yet this old hen of barnyard race
 Was but a stingy present.

"She's quite too old for laying eggs,
 Nay, even to make a soup of;
One only needs to see her legs, —
You might as well boil down the pegs
 I made the brood-hen's coop of!

"Some eighteen score of such do I
 Raise every year, her sisters;
Go, in the woods your fortunes try,
All day for one poor earthworm pry,
 And scratch your toes to blisters!"

Philemon found the rede was good,
 And, turning on the poor hen,
He clapt his hands, and stamped, and
 shooed,
Hunting the exile tow'rd the wood,
 To house with snipe and moor-hen.

A poet saw and cried: "Hold! hold!
 What are you doing, madman?
Spurn you more wealth than can be
 told,
The fowl that lays the eggs of gold,
 Because she's plainly clad, man?"

To him Philemon: "I 'll not balk
  Thy will with any shackle;
Wilt add a burden to thy walk?
There! take her without further talk:
  You 're both but fit to cackle!"

But scarce the poet touched the bird,
  It swelled to stature regal;
And when her cloud-wide wings she stirred,
A whisper as of doom was heard,
  'T was Jove's bolt-bearing eagle.

As when from far-off cloud-bergs springs
  A crag, and, hurtling under,
From cliff to cliff the rumor flings,
So she from flight-foreboding wings
  Shook out a murmurous thunder.

She gripped the poet to her breast,
  And ever, upward soaring,
Earth seemed a new moon in the west,
And then one light among the rest
  Where squadrons lie at mooring.

How tell to what heaven hallowed seat
  The eagle bent his courses?
The waves that on its bases beat,
The gales that round it weave and fleet,
  Are life's creative forces.

Here was the bird's primeval nest,
  High on a promontory
Star-pharosed, where she takes her rest
To brood new æons 'neath her breast,
  The future's unfledged glory.

I know not how, but I was there
  All feeling, hearing, seeing;
It was not wind that stirred my hair
But living breath, the essence rare
  Of unembodied being.

And in the nest an egg of gold
  Lay soft in self-made lustre,
Gazing whereon, what depths untold
Within, what marvels manifold,
  Seemed silently to muster!

Daily such splendors to confront
  Is still to me and you sent?
It glowed as when Saint Peter's front,
Illumed, forgets its stony wont,
  And seems to throb translucent.

One saw therein the life of man,
  (Or so the poet found it,)
The yolk and white, conceive who can,
Were the glad earth, that, floating, span
  In the glad heaven around it.

I knew this as one knows in dream,
  Where no effects to causes
Are chained as in our work-day scheme,
And then was wakened by a scream
  That seemed to come from Baucis.

"Bless Zeus!" she cried, "I 'm safe be-
    low!"
First pale, then red as coral;
And I, still drowsy, pondered slow,
And seemed to find, but hardly know,
  Something like this for moral.

Each day the world is born anew
  For him who takes it rightly;
Not fresher that which Adam knew,
Not sweeter that whose moonlit dew
  Entranced Arcadia nightly.

Rightly? That 's simply: 't is to see
Some substance casts these shadows
Which we call Life and History,
That aimless seem to chase and flee
  Like wind-gleams over meadows.

Simply? That 's nobly: 't is to know
  That God may still be met with,
Nor groweth old, nor doth bestow
These senses fine, this brain aglow,
  To grovel and forget with.

Beauty, Herr Doctor, trust in me,
  No chemistry will win you;
Charis still rises from the sea:
If you can't find her, *might* it be
  Because you seek within you?

A FAMILIAR EPISTLE TO A FRIEND

The friend was Miss Jane Norton, sister of Mr. C. E. Norton.

ALIKE I hate to be your debtor,
Or write a mere perfunctory letter;
For letters, so it seems to me,
Our careless quintessence should be,
Our real nature's truant play

When Consciousness looks t' other way;
Not drop by drop, with watchful skill,
Gathered in Art's deliberate still,
But life's insensible completeness
Got as the ripe grape gets its sweetness,
As if it had a way to fuse
The golden sunlight into juice.
Hopeless my mental pump I try,
The boxes hiss, the tube is dry;
As those petroleum wells that spout
Awhile like M. C.'s, then give out,
My spring, once full as Arethusa,
Is a mere bore as dry 's Creusa;
And yet you ask me why I 'm glum,
And why my graver Muse is dumb.
Ah me ! I 've reasons manifold
Condensed in one, — I 'm getting old !

When life, once past its fortieth year,
Wheels up its evening hemisphere,
The mind's own shadow, which the boy
Saw onward point to hope and joy,
Shifts round, irrevocably set
Tow'rd morning's loss and vain regret
And, argue with it as we will,
The clock is unconverted still.

" But count the gains," I hear you say,
" Which far the seeming loss outweigh;
Friendships built firm 'gainst flood and
    wind
On rock-foundations of the mind;
Knowledge instead of scheming hope;
For wild adventure, settled scope;
Talents, from surface-ore profuse,
Tempered and edged to tools for use;
Judgment, for passion's headlong whirls;
Old sorrows crystalled into pearls;
Losses by patience turned to gains,
Possessions now, that once were pains;
Joy's blossom gone, as go it must,
To ripen seeds of faith and trust ;
Why heed a snow-flake on the roof
If fire within keep Age aloof,
Though blundering north-winds push and
    strain
With palms benumbed against the pane ? "

My dear old Friend, you 're very wise;
We always are with others' eyes,
And see so clear ! (our neighbor's deck on)
What reef the idiot 's sure to wreck on;
Folks when they learn how life has quizzed
    'em
Are fain to make a shift with Wisdom,

And, finding she nor breaks nor bends,
Give her a letter to their friends.
Draw passion's torrent whoso will
Through sluices smooth to turn a mill,
And, taking solid toll of grist,
Forget the rainbow in the mist,
The exulting leap, the aimless haste
Scattered in iridescent waste;
Prefer who likes the sure esteem
To cheated youth's midsummer dream,
When every friend was more than Damon,
Each quicksand safe to build a fame on;
Believe that prudence snug excels
Youth's gross of verdant spectacles,
Through which earth's withered stubble
    seen
Looks autumn-proof as painted green, —
I side with Moses 'gainst the masses,
Take you the drudge, give me the glasses !
And, for your talents shaped with practice,
Convince me first that such the fact is;
Let whoso likes be beat, poor fool,
On life's hard stithy to a tool,
Be whoso will a ploughshare made,
Let me remain a jolly blade !

What 's Knowledge, with her stocks and
    lands,
To gay Conjecture's yellow strands ?
What 's watching her slow flock's increase
To ventures for the golden fleece ?
What her deep ships, safe under lee,
To youth's light craft, that drinks the sea,
For Flying Islands making sail,
And failing where 't is gain to fail ?
Ah me ! Experience (so we 're told),
Time's crucible, turns lead to gold;
Yet what 's experience won but dross,
Cloud-gold transmuted to our loss ?
What but base coin the best event
To the untried experiment ?

'T was an old couple, says the poet,
That lodged the gods and did not know it;
Youth sees and knows them as they were
Before Olympus' top was bare;
From Swampscot's flats his eye divine
Sees Venus rocking on the brine,
With lucent limbs, that somehow scatter a
Charm that turns Doll to Cleopatra ;
Bacchus (that now is scarce induced
To give Eld's lagging blood a boost),
With cymbals' clang and pards to draw
    him,
Divine as Ariadne saw him,

Storms through Youth's pulse with all his
train
And wins new Indies in his brain;
Apollo (with the old a trope,
A sort of finer Mister Pope),
Apollo — but the Muse forbids:
At his approach cast down thy lids,
And think it joy enough to hear
Far off his arrows singing clear;
He knows enough who silent knows
The quiver chiming as he goes;
He tells too much who e'er betrays
The shining Archer's secret ways.

Dear Friend, you 're right and I am
wrong;
My quibbles are not worth a song,
And I sophistically tease
My fancy sad to tricks like these.
I could not cheat you if I would;
You know me and my jesting mood,
Mere surface-foam, for pride concealing
The purpose of my deeper feeling.
I have not spilt one drop of joy
Poured in the senses of the boy,
Nor Nature fails my walks to bless
With all her golden inwardness;
And as blind nestlings, unafraid,
Stretch up wide-mouthed to every shade
By which their downy dream is stirred,
Taking it for the mother-bird,
So, when God's shadow, which is light,
Unheralded, by day or night,
My wakening instincts falls across,
Silent as sunbeams over moss,
In my heart's nest half-conscious things
Stir with a helpless sense of wings,
Lift themselves up, and tremble long
With premonitions sweet of song.

Be patient, and perhaps (who knows?)
These may be winged one day like those;
If thrushes, close-embowered to sing,
Pierced through with June's delicious sting;
If swallows, their half-hour to run
Star-breasted in the setting sun.
At first they 're but the unfledged proem,
Or songless schedule of a poem;
When from the shell they 're hardly dry
If some folks thrust them forth, must I?

But let me end with a comparison
Never yet hit upon by e'er a son
Of our American Apollo,

(And there 's where I shall beat them hol-
low,
If he indeed 's no courtly St. John,
But, as West said, a Mohawk Injun.)
A poem 's like a cruise for whales:
Through untried seas the hunter sails,
His prow dividing waters known
To the blue iceberg's hulk alone;
At last, on farthest edge of day,
He marks the smoky puff of spray;
Then with bent oars the shallop flies
To where the basking quarry lies;
Then the excitement of the strife,
The crimsoned waves, — ah, this is life!

But, the dead plunder once secured
And safe beside the vessel moored,
All that had stirred the blood before
Is so much blubber, nothing more,
(I mean no pun, nor image so
Mere sentimental verse, you know,)
And all is tedium, smoke, and soil,
In trying out the noisome oil.

Yes, this *is* life! And so the bard
Through briny deserts, never scarred
Since Noah's keel, a subject seeks,
And lies upon the watch for weeks;
That once harpooned and helpless lying,
What follows is but weary trying.

Now I 've a notion, if a poet
Beat up for themes, his verse will show it;
I wait for subjects that hunt me,
By day or night won't let me be,
And hang about me like a curse,
Till they have made me into verse,
From line to line my fingers tease
Beyond my knowledge, as the bees
Build no new cell till those before
With limpid summer-sweet run o'er;
Then, if I neither sing nor shine,
Is it the subject's fault, or mine?

AN EMBER PICTURE

How strange are the freaks of memory!
The lessons of life we forget,
While a trifle, a trick of color,
In the wonderful web is set, —

Set by some mordant of fancy,
And, spite of the wear and tear

Of time or distance or trouble,
  Insists on its right to be there.

A chance had brought us together;
  Our talk was of matters-of-course;
We were nothing, one to the other,
  But a short half-hour's resource.

We spoke of French acting and actors,
  And their easy, natural way:
Of the weather, for it was raining
  As we drove home from the play.

We debated the social nothings
  We bore ourselves so to discuss;
The thunderous rumors of battle
  Were silent the while for us.

Arrived at her door, we left her
  With a drippingly hurried adieu,
And our wheels went crunching the gravel
  Of the oak-darkened avenue.

As we drove away through the shadow,
  The candle she held in the door
From rain-varnished tree-trunk to tree-
    trunk
  Flashed fainter, and flashed no more; —

Flashed fainter, then wholly faded
  Before we had passed the wood;
But the light of the face behind it
  Went with me and stayed for good.

The vision of scarce a moment,
  And hardly marked at the time,
It comes unbidden to haunt me,
  Like a scrap of ballad-rhyme.

Had she beauty? Well, not what they call
    so;
  You may find a thousand as fair;
And yet there 's her face in my memory
  With no special claim to be there.

As I sit sometimes in the twilight,
  And call back to life in the coals
Old faces and hopes and fancies
  Long buried, (good rest to their souls!)

Her face shines out in the embers;
  I see her holding the light,
And hear the crunch of the gravel
  And the sweep of the rain that night.

'T is a face that can never grow older,
  That never can part with its gleam,
'T is a gracious possession forever,
  For is it not all a dream?

TO H. W. L.

ON HIS BIRTHDAY, 27TH FEBRUARY, 1867

"ELMWOOD, February 27, 1867.

"MY DEAR LONGFELLOW, — On looking back, I find that our personal intercourse is now of nearly thirty years' date. It began on your part in a note acknowledging my *Class Poem* much more kindly than it deserved. Since then it has ripened into friendship, and there has never been a jar between us. If there had been, it would certainly have been my fault and not yours. Friendship is called the wine of life, and there certainly is a stimulus in it that warms and inspires as we grow older. Ours should have some body to have kept so long.

"I planned you a little surprise in the *Advertiser* for your birthday breakfast. I hope my nosegay did not spoil the flavor of your coffee. It is a hard thing to make one that will wholly please, for some flowers will not bear to be handled without wilting, and the kind I have tried to make a pretty bunch of is of that variety. But let me hope the best from your kindness, if not from their color or perfume.

"In case they should please you (and because there was one misprint in the *Advertiser*, and two phrases which I have now made more to my mind), I have copied them that you might have them in my own handwriting. In print, you see, I have omitted the tell-tale ciphers — not that there was anything to regret in them, for we have a proverbial phrase 'like sixty' which implies not only unabated but extraordinary vigor.

"Wishing you as many happy returns as a wise man should desire, I remain always affectionately yours, J. R. L." *Letters* I. 378, 379.

I NEED not praise the sweetness of his song,
  Where limpid verse to limpid verse
    succeeds
Smooth as our Charles, when, fearing lest
    he wrong
  The new moon's mirrored skiff, he slides
    along,
    Full without noise, and whispers in his
    reeds.

With loving breath of all the winds his
name
Is blown about the world, but to his
friends
A sweeter secret hides behind his fame,
And Love steals shyly through the loud
acclaim
To murmur a *God bless you!* and there
ends.

As I muse backward up the checkered
years
Wherein so much was given, so much
was lost,
Blessings in both kinds, such as cheapen
tears, —
But hush! this is not for profaner ears;
Let them drink molten pearls nor dream
the cost.

Some suck up poison from a sorrow's core,
As naught but nightshade grew upon
earth's ground;
Love turned all his to heart's-ease, and the
more
Fate tried his bastions, she but forced a
door
Leading to sweeter manhood and more
sound.

Even as a wind-waved fountain's swaying
shade
Seems of mixed race, a gray wraith shot
with sun,
So through his trial faith translucent rayed
Till darkness, half disnatured so, betrayed
A heart of sunshine that would fain
o'errun.

Surely if skill in song the shears may stay
And of its purpose cheat the charmed
abyss,
If our poor life be lengthened by a lay,
He shall not go, although his presence
may,
And the next age in praise shall double
this.

Long days be his, and each as lusty-sweet
As gracious natures find his song to be;
May Age steal on with softly-cadenced feet
Falling in music, as for him were meet
Whose choicest verse is harsher-toned
than he!

THE NIGHTINGALE IN THE STUDY

" While I was most unwell," Lowell wrote
to a friend, September 21, 1875, " I could not
find any reading that would seclude me from
myself till one day I bethought me of Cal-
deron. I took down a volume of his plays,
and in half an hour was completely absorbed.
He is surely one of the most marvellous of
poets. I have recorded my debt to him in a
poem, *The Nightingale in the Study*."

" Come forth! " my catbird calls to me,
" And hear me sing a cavatina
That, in this old familar tree,
Shall hang a garden of Alcina.

" These buttercups shall brim with wine
Beyond all Lesbian juice or Massic;
May not New England be divine?
My ode to ripening summer classic?

" Or, if to me you will not hark,
By Beaver Brook a thrush is ringing
Till all the alder-coverts dark
Seem sunshine-dappled with his sing-
ing.

" Come out beneath the unmastered sky,
With its emancipating spaces,
And learn to sing as well as I,
Without premeditated graces.

" What boot your many-volumed gains,
Those withered leaves forever turning,
To win, at best, for all your pains,
A nature mummy-wrapt in learning?

" The leaves wherein true wisdom lies
On living trees the sun are drinking;
Those white clouds, drowsing through the
skies,
Grew not so beautiful by thinking.

" ' Come out! ' with me the oriole cries,
Escape the demon that pursues you!
And, hark, the cuckoo weatherwise,
Still hiding farther onward, wooes you."

" Alas, dear friend, that, all my days,
Hast poured from that syringa thicket
The quaintly discontinuous lays
To which I hold a season-ticket,

" A season-ticket cheaply bought
  With a dessert of pilfered berries,
And who so oft my soul hast caught
  With morn and evening voluntaries,

" Deem me not faithless, if all day
  Among my dusty books I linger,
No pipe, like thee, for June to play
  With fancy-led, half-conscious finger.

" A bird is singing in my brain
  And bubbling o'er with mingled fancies,
Gay, tragic, rapt, right heart of Spain
  Fed with the sap of old romances.

" I ask no ampler skies than those
  His magic music rears above me,
No falser friends, no truer foes, —
  And does not Doña Clara love me ?

" Cloaked shapes, a twanging of guitars,
  A rush of feet, and rapiers clashing,
Then silence deep with breathless stars,
  And overhead a white hand flashing.

" O music of all moods and climes,
  Vengeful, forgiving, sensuous, saintly,
Where still, between the Christian chimes,
  The Moorish cymbal tinkles faintly !

" O life borne lightly in the hand,
  For friend or foe with grace Castilian !
O valley safe in Fancy's land,
  Not tramped to mud yet by the million !

" Bird of to-day, thy songs are stale
  To his, my singer of all weathers,
My Calderon, my nightingale,
  My Arab soul in Spanish feathers.

" Ah, friend, these singers dead so long,
  And still, God knows, in purgatory,
Give its best sweetness to all song,
  To Nature's self her better glory."

IN THE TWILIGHT

Men say the sullen instrument,
  That, from the Master's bow,
  With pangs of joy or woe,

Feels music's soul through every fibre sent,
  Whispers the ravished strings
More than he knew or meant ;
  Old summers in its memory glow ;
  The secrets of the wind it sings ;
  It hears the April-loosened springs ;
    And mixes with its mood
    All it dreamed when it stood
    In the murmurous pine-wood
      Long ago !

The magical moonlight then
  Steeped every bough and cone ;
The roar of the brook in the glen
  Came dim from the distance blown ;
The wind through its glooms sang low,
  And it swayed to and fro
    With delight as it stood,
    In the wonderful wood,
      Long ago !

O my life, have we not had seasons
  That only said, Live and rejoice ?
That asked not for causes and reasons,
  But made us all feeling and voice ?
When we went with the winds in their blowing,
  When Nature and we were peers,
And we seemed to share in the flowing
  Of the inexhaustible years ?
Have we not from the earth drawn juices
Too fine for earth's sordid uses ?
    Have I heard, have I seen
    All I feel, all I know ?
    Doth my heart overween ?
    Or could it have been
      Long ago ?

Sometimes a breath floats by me,
  An odor from Dreamland sent,
That makes the ghost seem nigh me
  Of a splendor that came and went,
Of a life lived somewhere, I know not
  In what diviner sphere,
Of memories that stay not and go not,
  Like music heard once by an ear
    That cannot forget or reclaim it,
A something so shy, it would shame it
  To make it a show,
A something too vague, could I name it,
  For others to know,
As if I had lived it or dreamed it,
As if I had acted or schemed it,
      Long ago !

And yet, could I live it over,
　This life that stirs in my brain,
Could I be both maiden and lover,
Moon and tide, bee and clover,
　As I seem to have been, once again,
Could I but speak it and show it,
　This pleasure more sharp than pain,
　That baffles and lures me so,
The world should once more have a poet,
　　Such as it had
　　In the ages glad,
　　　Long ago!

THE FOOT-PATH

It mounts athwart the windy hill
　Through sallow slopes of upland bare,
And Fancy climbs with foot-fall still
　Its narrowing curves that end in air.

By day, a warmer-hearted blue
　Stoops softly to that topmost swell ;
Its thread-like windings seem a clue
　To gracious climes where all is well.

By night, far yonder, I surmise
　An ampler world than clips my ken,
Where the great stars of happier skies
　Commingle nobler fates of men.

I look and long, then haste me home,
　Still master of my secret rare ;
Once tried, the path would end in Rome,
　But now it leads me everywhere.

Forever to the new it guides,
　From former good, old overmuch ;
What Nature for her poets hides,
　'T is wiser to divine than clutch.

The bird I list hath never come
　Within the scope of mortal ear ;
My prying step would make him dumb,
　And the fair tree, his shelter, sear.

Behind the hill, behind the sky,
　Behind my inmost thought, he sings ;

No feet avail ; to hear it nigh,
　The song itself must lend the wings.

Sing on, sweet bird close hid, and raise
　Those angel stairways in my brain,
That climb from these low-vaulted days
　To spacious sunshines far from pain.

Sing when thou wilt, enchantment fleet,
　I leave thy covert haunt untrod,
And envy Science not her feat
　To make a twice-told tale of God.

They said the fairies tript no more,
　And long ago that Pan was dead;
'T was but that fools preferred to bore
　Earth's rind inch-deep for truth instead.

Pan leaps and pipes all summer long,
　The fairies dance each full-mooned night,
Would we but doff our lenses strong,
　And trust our wiser eyes' delight.

City of Elf-land, just without
　Our seeing, marvel ever new,
Glimpsed in fair weather, a sweet doubt
　Sketched-in, mirage-like, on the blue,

I build thee in yon sunset cloud,
　Whose edge allures to climb the height;
I hear thy drowned bells, inly-loud,
　From still pools dusk with dreams of
　　night.

Thy gates are shut to hardiest will,
　Thy countersign of long-lost speech, —
Those fountained courts, those chambers
　　still,
　Fronting Time's far East,who shall reach?

I know not, and will never pry,
　But trust our human heart for all;
Wonders that from the seeker fly
　Into an open sense may fall.

Hidé in thine own soul, and surprise
　The password of the unwary elves;
Seek it, thou canst not bribe their spies;
　Unsought, they whisper it themselves.

POEMS OF THE WAR

THE WASHERS OF THE SHROUD

OCTOBER, 1861

Lowell wrote at some length to C. E. Norton concerning the production of this poem.

ELMWOOD, Oct. 12, 1861.

. . . You urged me to read poetry — to feed myself on bee bread — so that I might get into the mood of writing some. Well, I have n't been reading any, but I *have* written something — whether poetry or no I cannot tell yet. But I want you to like it if you can. Leigh Hunt speaks somewhere of our writing things for particular people, and wondering as we write if such or such a one will like it. Just so I thought of you, *after* I had written — for while I was writing I was wholly absorbed. I had just two days allowed me by Fields for the November *Atlantic*, and I got it done. It had been in my head some time, and when you see it you will remember my having spoken to you about it. Indeed, I owe it to you, for the hint came from one of those books of Souvestre's you lent me — the Breton legends. The writing took hold of me enough to leave me tired out and to satisfy me entirely as to what was the original of my head and back pains. But whether it is good or not, I am not yet far enough off to say. But *do* like it, if you can. Fields says it is " splendid," with tears in his eyes — but then I read it to him, which is half the battle. I began it as a lyric, but it *would* be too aphoristic for that, and finally flatly refused to sing at any price. So I submitted, took to pentameters, and only hope the thoughts are good enough to be preserved in the ice of the colder and almost glacier-slow measure. I think I have done well — in some stanzas at least — and not wasted words. It is about present matters — but abstract enough to be above the newspapers. . . .

ALONG a river-side, I know not where,
I walked one night in mystery of dream;
A chill creeps curdling yet beneath my
      hair,
To think what chanced me by the pallid
      gleam
Of a moon-wraith that waned through
      haunted air.

Pale fireflies pulsed within the meadow-
      mist
Their halos, wavering thistle downs of
      light;
The loon, that seemed to mock some goblin
      tryst,
Laughed; and the echoes, huddling in af-
      fright,
Like Odin's hounds, fled baying down the
      night.

Then all was silent, till there smote my
      ear
A movement in the stream that checked
      my breath:
Was it the slow plash of a wading deer ?
But something said, "This water is of
      Death !
The Sisters wash a shroud, — ill thing to
      hear ! "

I, looking then, beheld the ancient Three
Known to the Greek's and to the North-
      man's creed,
That sit in shadow of the mystic Tree,
Still crooning, as they weave their endless
      brede,
One song: "Time was, Time is, and Time
      shall be."

No wrinkled crones were they, as I had
      deemed,
But fair as yesterday, to-day, to-morrow,
To mourner, lover, poet, ever seemed;
Something too high for joy, too deep for
      sorrow,
Thrilled in their tones, and from their
      faces gleamed.

" Still men and nations reap as they have
      strawn,"
So sang they, working at their task the
      while;
" The fatal raiment must be cleansed ere
      dawn:
For Austria ? Italy ? the Sea - Queen's
      isle ?
O'er what quenched grandeur must our
      shroud be drawn ?

"Or is it for a younger, fairer corse,
That gathered States like children round
  his knees,
That tamed the wave to be his posting-
  horse,
Feller of forests, linker of the seas,
Bridge-builder, hammerer, youngest son of
  Thor's?

"What make we, murmur'st thou? and
  what are we?
When empires must be wound, we bring
  the shroud,
The time-old web of the implacable Three:
Is it too coarse for him, the young and
  proud?
Earth's mightiest deigned to wear it, —
  why not he?"

"Is there no hope?" I moaned, "so strong,
  so fair!
Our Fowler whose proud bird would brook
  erewhile
No rival's swoop in all our western air!
Gather the ravens, then, in funeral file
For him, life's morn yet golden in his hair?

"Leave me not hopeless, ye unpitying
  dames!
I see, half seeing. Tell me, ye who scanned
The stars, Earth's elders, still must noblest
  aims
Be traced upon oblivious ocean-sands?
Must Hesper join the wailing ghosts of
  names?"

"When grass-blades stiffen with red battle-
  dew,
Ye deem we choose the victor and the slain:
Say, choose we them that shall be leal and
  true
To the heart's longing, the high faith of
  brain?
Yet there the victory lies, if ye but knew.

"Three roots bear up Dominion: Know-
  ledge, Will, —
These twain are strong, but stronger yet
  the third, —
Obedience, — 't is the great tap-root that
  still,
Knit round the rock of Duty, is not stirred,
Though Heaven - loosed tempests spend
  their utmost skill.

"Is the doom sealed for Hesper? 'T is not
  we
Denounce it, but the Law before all time:
The brave makes danger opportunity;
The waverer, paltering with the chance sub-
  lime,
Dwarfs it to peril: which shall Hesper be?

"Hath he let vultures climb his eagle's
  seat
To make Jove's bolts purveyors of their
  maw?
Hath he the Many's plaudits found more
  sweet
Than Wisdom? held Opinion's wind for
  Law?
Then let him hearken for the doomster's
  feet!

"Rough are the steps, slow-hewn in flint-
  iest rock,
States climb to power by; slippery those
  with gold
Down which they stumble to eternal mock:
No chafferer's hand shall long the sceptre
  hold,
Who, given a Fate to shape, would sell the
  block.

"We sing old Sagas, songs of weal and woe,
Mystic because too cheaply understood;
Dark sayings are not ours; men hear and
  know,
See Evil weak, see strength alone in Good,
Yet hope to stem God's fire with walls of
  tow.

"Time Was unlocks the riddle of Time Is,
That offers choice of glory or of gloom;
The solver makes Time Shall Be surely
  his.
But hasten, Sisters! for even now the tomb
Grates its slow hinge and calls from the
  abyss."

"But not for him," I cried, "not yet for
  him,
Whose large horizon, westering, star by
  star
Wins from the void to where on Ocean's
  rim
The sunset shuts the world with golden bar,
Not yet his thews shall fail, his eye grow
  dim!

" His shall be larger manhood, saved for those
That walk unblenching through the trial-fires ;
Not suffering, but faint heart, is worst of woes,
And he no base-born son of craven sires,
Whose eye need blench confronted with his foes.

" Tears may be ours, but proud, for those who win
Death's royal purple in the foeman's lines;
Peace, too, brings tears ; and mid the battle-din,
The wiser ear some text of God divines,
For the sheathed blade may rust with darker sin.

" God, give us peace! not such as lulls to sleep,
But sword on thigh, and brow with purpose knit !
And let our Ship of State to harbor sweep,
Her ports all up, her battle-lanterns lit,
And her leashed thunders gathering for their leap! "

So cried I with clenched hands and passionate pain,
Thinking of dear ones by Potomac's side;
Again the loon laughed mocking, and again
The echoes bayed far down the night and died,
While waking I recalled my wandering brain.

TWO SCENES FROM THE LIFE OF BLONDEL

AUTUMN, 1863

SCENE I. — *Near a castle in Germany.*

'T WERE no hard task, perchance, to win
The popular laurel for my song ;
'T were only to comply with sin,
And own the crown, though snatched by wrong:
Rather Truth's chaplet let me wear,
Though sharp as death its thorns may sting;
Loyal to Loyalty, I bear
No badge but of my rightful king.

Patient by town and tower I wait,
Or o'er the blustering moorland go;
I buy no praise at cheaper rate,
Or what faint hearts may fancy so;
For me, no joy in lady's bower,
Or hall, or tourney, will I sing,
Till the slow stars wheel round the hour
That crowns my hero and my king.

While all the land runs red with strife,
And wealth is won by pedler-crimes,
Let who will find content in life
And tinkle in unmanly rhymes;
I wait and seek ; through dark and light,
Safe in my heart my hope I bring,
Till I once more my faith may plight
To him my whole soul owns her king.

When power is filched by drone and dolt,
And, with caught breath and flashing eye,
Her knuckles whitening round the bolt,
Vengeance leans eager from the sky,
While this and that the people guess,
And to the skirts of praters cling,
Who court the crowd they should compress,
I turn in scorn to seek my king.

Shut in what tower of darkling chance
Or dungeon of a narrow doom,
Dream'st thou of battle-axe and lance
That for the Cross make crashing room ?
Come! with hushed breath the battle waits
In the wild van thy mace's swing;
While doubters parley with their fates,
Make thou thine own and ours, my king!

O strong to keep upright the old,
And wise to buttress with the new,
Prudent, as only are the bold,
Clear-eyed, as only are the true,
To foes benign, to friendship stern,
Intent to imp Law's broken wing,
Who would not die, if death might earn
The right to kiss thy hand, my king ?

SCENE II. — *An Inn near the Château of Chalus.*

Well, the whole thing is over, and here I sit
With one arm in a sling and a milk-score of gashes,
And this flagon of Cyprus must e'en warm my wit,
Since what's left of youth's flame is a head flecked with ashes.

I remember I sat in this very same inn, —
  I was young then, and one young man
    thought I was handsome, —
I had found out what prison King Richard
    was in,
  And was spurring for England to push on
    the ransom.

How I scorned the dull souls that sat guz-
    zling around
  And knew not my secret nor recked my
    derision!
Let the world sink or swim, John or Richard
    be crowned,
  All one, so the beer-tax got lenient revi-
    sion.
How little I dreamed, as I tramped up and
    down,
  That granting our wish one of Fate's
    saddest jokes is!
I had mine with a vengeance, — my king
    got his crown,
  And made his whole business to break
    other folks's.

I might as well join in the safe old *tum,
    tum :*
  A hero 's an excellent loadstar, — but,
    bless ye,
What infinite odds 'twixt a hero to come
And your only too palpable hero *in esse !*
Precisely the odds (such examples are rife)
  'Twixt the poem conceived and the rhyme
    we make show of,
'Twixt the boy's morning dream and the
    wake-up of life,
'Twixt the Blondel God meant and a
    Blondel I know of!

But the world 's better off, I 'm convinced
    of it now,
  Than if heroes, like buns, could be bought
    for a penny
To regard all mankind as their haltered
    milch-cow,
  And just care for themselves. Well,
    God cares for the many;
For somehow the poor old Earth blunders
    along,
  Each son of hers adding his mite of un-
    fitness,
And, choosing the sure way of coming out
    wrong,
  Gets to port as the next generation will
    witness.

You think her old ribs have come all crash-
    ing through,
  If a whisk of Fate's broom snap your
    cobweb asunder;
But her rivets were clinched by a wiser
    than you,
  And our sins cannot push the Lord's right
    hand from under.
Better one honest man who can wait for
    God's mind
  In our poor shifting scene here though
    heroes were plenty!
Better one bite, at forty, of Truth's bitter
    rind,
  Than the hot wine that gushed from the
    vintage of twenty!

I see it all now: when I wanted a king,
  'T was the kingship that failed in myself
    I was seeking, —
'T is so much less easy to do than to sing,
  So much simpler to reign by a proxy
    than *be* king!
Yes, I think I *do* see: after all 's said and
    sung,
  Take this one rule of life and you never
    will rue it, —
'T is but do your own duty and hold your
    own tongue
  And Blondel were royal himself, if he
    knew it!

MEMORIÆ POSITUM

R. G. SHAW

In a letter to Colonel Shaw's mother, written
August 28, 1863, Lowell says: " I have been
writing something about Robert ; and if, after
keeping a little while, it should turn out to be
a poem I shall print it, but not unless I think
it some way worthy of what I feel, however,
for the best verse falls short of noble living
and dying such as his. I would rather have
my name known and blest, as his will be,
through all the hovels of an outcast race, than
blaring from all the trumpets of repute." He
kept the poem three months and then wrote
to Mr. Fields, — " You know I *owe* you a
poem — *two* in my reckoning, and here is one
of them. If this is not to your mind, I can
hammer you out another. I have a feeling
that some of it is *good* — but is it too long ? I
want to fling my leaf on dear Shaw's grave.
Perhaps I was wrong in stiffening the feet of
my verses a little, in order to give them a kind

of slow funeral tread. But I conceived it so, and so it would be. I wanted the poem a little *monumental*, perhaps I have made it *obituary*. But tell me just how it strikes you, and don't be afraid of my nerves. They can stand much in the way of friendly frankness, and besides, I find I am acquiring a vice of modesty as I grow older."

In another letter, when speaking of the distinction between odes for the closet and odes for recitation, he says: "I chose my measures with my ears open. So I did in writing the poem on Rob Shaw. That *is* regular because meant only to be read, and because also I thought it should have in the form of its stanza something of the formality of an epitaph."

When, in the last stanza, Lowell wrote

> "I write of one,
> While with dim eyes I think of three,"

the reader recalls that moving passage in No. X. of the second series of *Biglow Papers*, where Mr. Hosea Biglow in his homely speech bursts forth: —

> "Why, hain't I held 'em on my knee?
> Did n't I love to see 'em growin',
> Three likely lads ez wal could be," —

and one knows of whom Lowell was thinking.

I

Beneath the trees,
My lifelong friends in this dear spot,
Sad now for eyes that see them not,
 I hear the autumnal breeze
Wake the dry leaves to sigh for gladness
  gone,
Whispering vague omens of oblivion,
 Hear, restless as the seas,
Time's grim feet rustling through the with-
  ered grace
Of many a spreading realm and strong-
  stemmed race,
 Even as my own through these.

Why make we moan
For loss that doth enrich us yet
With upward yearnings of regret?
 Bleaker than unmossed stone
Our lives were but for this immortal gain
Of unstilled longing and inspiring pain!
 As thrills of long-hushed tone
Live in the viol, so our souls grow fine
With keen vibrations from the touch divine
 Of noble natures gone.

'T were indiscreet
To vex the shy and sacred grief
With harsh obtrusions of relief;

Yet, Verse, with noiseless feet,
Go whisper: "*This* death hath far choicer
  ends
Than slowly to impearl in hearts of friends;
 These obsequies 't is meet
Not to seclude in closets of the heart,
But, church-like, with wide doorways, to
  impart
 Even to the heedless street."

II

Brave, good, and true,
 I see him stand before me now,
 And read again on that young brow,
  Where every hope was new,
How sweet were life! Yet, by the mouth
  firm-set,
And look made up for Duty's utmost debt,
 I could divine he knew
That death within the sulphurous hostile
  lines,
In the mere wreck of nobly-pitched designs,
 Plucks heart's-ease, and not rue.

Happy their end
 Who vanish down life's evening stream
 Placid as swans that drift in dream
  Round the next river-bend!
Happy long life, with honor at the close,
Friends' painless tears, the softened thought
  of foes!
 And yet, like him, to spend
All at a gush, keeping our first faith sure
From mid-life's doubt and eld's content-
  ment poor,
 What more could Fortune send?

Right in the van,
 On the red rampart's slippery swell,
 With heart that beat a charge, he fell
  Foeward, as fits a man;
But the high soul burns on to light men's
  feet
Where death for noble ends makes dying
  sweet;
 His life her crescent's span
Orbs full with share in their undarkening
  days
Who ever climbed the battailous steeps of
  praise
 Since valor's praise began.

III

His life's expense
 Hath won him coeternal youth

With the immaculate prime of Truth ;
While we, who make pretence
At living on, and wake and eat and sleep,
And life's stale trick by repetition keep,
Our fickle permanence
(A poor leaf-shadow on a brook, whose play
Of busy idlesse ceases with our day)
Is the mere cheat of sense.

We bide our chance,
Unhappy, and make terms with Fate
A little more to let us wait ;
He leads for aye the advance,
Hope's forlorn-hopes that plant the des-
perate good
For nobler Earths and days of manlier
mood ;
Our wall of circumstance
Cleared at a bound, he flashes o'er the
fight,
A saintly shape of fame, to cheer the
right
And steel each wavering glance.

I write of one,
While with dim eyes I think of three ;
Who weeps not others fair and brave as
he ?
Ah, when the fight is won,
Dear Land, whom triflers now make bold to
scorn,
(Thee ! from whose forehead Earth awaits
her morn,)
How nobler shall the sun
Flame in thy sky, how braver breathe thy
air,
That thou bred'st children who for thee
could dare
And die as thine have done !

ON BOARD THE '76

WRITTEN FOR MR. BRYANT'S SEVEN-
TIETH BIRTHDAY

NOVEMBER 3, 1864

In a letter written to R. W. Gilder, Febru-
ary 9, 1887, Lowell characterizes this poem as
" a kind of palinode to what I said of him in
the *Fable for Critics*, which has something of
youth's infallibility in it, or at any rate of
youth's irresponsibility."

OUR ship lay tumbling in an angry sea,
Her rudder gone, her mainmast o'er the
side ;
Her scuppers, from the waves' clutch stag-
gering free,
Trailed threads of priceless crimson
through the tide ;
Sails, shrouds, and spars with pirate cannon
torn,
We lay, awaiting morn.

Awaiting morn, such morn as mocks de-
spair ;
And she that bare the promise of the
world
Within her sides, now hopeless, helmless,
bare,
At random o'er the wildering waters
hurled ;
The reek of battle drifting slow alee
Not sullener than we.

Morn came at last to peer into our woe,
When lo, a sail ! Now surely help was
nigh ;
The red cross flames aloft, Christ's pledge ;
but no,
Her black guns grinning hate, she rushes
by
And hails us : — " Gains the leak ! Ay, so
we thought !
Sink, then, with curses fraught ! "

I leaned against my gun still angry-hot,
And my lids tingled with the tears held
back :
This scorn methought was crueller than
shot:
The manly death-grip in the battle-
wrack,
Yard-arm to yard-arm, were more friendly
far
Than such fear-smothered war.

There our foe wallowed, like a wounded
brute
The fiercer for his hurt. What now
were best ?
Once more tug bravely at the peril's root,
Though death came with it ? Or evade
the test
If right or wrong in this God's world of
ours
Be leagued with mightier powers ?

Some, faintly loyal, felt their pulses lag
  With the slow beat that doubts and then
    despairs;
Some, caitiff, would have struck the starry
    flag
  That knits us with our past, and makes
    us heirs
Of deeds high-hearted as were ever done
  'Neath the all-seeing sun.

But there was one, the Singer of our crew,
  Upon whose head Age waved his peace-
    ful sign,
But whose red heart's-blood no surrender
    knew;
  And couchant under brows of massive
    line,
The eyes, like guns beneath a parapet,
  Watched, charged with lightnings yet.

The voices of the hills did his obey;
  The torrents flashed and tumbled in his
    song;
He brought our native fields from far
    away,
  Or set us 'mid the innumerable throng
Of dateless woods, or where we heard the
    calm
  Old homestead's evening psalm.

But now he sang of faith to things unseen,
  Of freedom's birthright given to us in
    trust;
And words of doughty cheer he spoke be-
    tween,
  That made all earthly fortune seem as
    dust,
Matched with that duty, old as Time and
    new,
  Of being brave and true.

We, listening, learned what makes the
    might of words, —
  Manhood to back them, constant as a
    star;
His voice rammed home our cannon, edged
    our swords,
  And sent our boarders shouting; shroud
    and spar
Heard him and stiffened; the sails heard,
    and wooed
  The winds with loftier mood.

In our dark hours he manned our guns
    again;

Remanned ourselves from his own man-
    hood's stores;
Pride, honor, country, throbbed through
    all his strain;
  And shall we praise? God's praise was
    his before;
And on our futile laurels he looks down,
  Himself our bravest crown.

ODE RECITED AT THE HAR-VARD COMMEMORATION

JULY 21, 1865

Of none of his poems did Lowell himself
write more critically, and into none, perhaps,
did he pour so much fervor in the composition.
In a playful letter to Miss Norton, written in
somewhat of a reaction four days after the de-
livery of the poem, he wrote: "Was I not so
rapt with the fervor of conception as I have
not been these ten years, losing my sleep, my
appetite and my flesh, those attributes to which
I before alluded as nobly uniting us in a com-
mon nature with our kind? Did I not for two
days exasperate everybody that came near me
by reciting passages in order to try them on?
Did I not even fall backward and downward to
the old folly of hopeful youth, and think I had
written something *really* good at last? And
am I not now enduring those retributive dumps
which ever follow such sinful exultations, the
Erynnyes of Vanity? . . . Like a boy, I mis-
took my excitement for inspiration, and here I
am in the mud. You see I am a little disap-
pointed and a little few (*un petit peu*) vexed.
I did *not* make the hit I expected, and am
ashamed at having been again tempted into
thinking I could write *poetry*, a delusion from
which I have been tolerably free these dozen
years." The next day in a postscript he added:
"I have not got cool yet (I mean as to nerves),
and lie awake at night thinking how much
better my verses might have been, only I can't
make 'em so." Twenty years later in recall-
ing the circumstances of composition he wrote
to Mr. Gilder: "The passage about Lincoln
was not in the ode as originally recited, but
added immediately after. . . . The ode itself
was an improvisation. Two days before the
Commemoration I had told my friend [F. J.]
Child that it was impossible — that I was dull
as a door-mat. But the next day something
gave me a jog and the whole thing came out
of me with a rush. I sat up all night writing
it out clear, and took it on the morning of the
day to Child. 'I have something, but don't
yet know what it is, or whether it will do.

Look at it and tell me.' He went a little way apart with it under an elm-tree in the College Yard. He read a passage here and there, brought it back to me and said : ' Do ? I should think so ! Don't you be scared.' And I was n't, but virtue enough had gone out of me to make me weak for a fortnight after. I was amazed at the praises I got. Trevelyan told me afterwards that he never could have carried through the abolition of purchase in the British Army but for the re-enforcement he got from that poem."

A few months after the delivery of the *Ode* the proposal to reprint it in *Harvard Memorial Biographies* led to a correspondence with the editor, Col. T. W. Higginson, in which some emendations and additions were proposed. " Your criticism," Lowell writes, " is perfectly just, and I am much obliged to you for it — though I might defend myself, I believe, by some constructions even looser in some of the Greek choruses. But, on the whole, where I have my choice I prefer to make sense. The fact is that the *Ode* was written at a heat — such a one, indeed, as leaves one colder than common afterwards — and I have hardly looked at it since. There is a horrible truth in the *litera scripta manet*, and the confounded things make mouths at us when we try to alter, but I think *this* may do : —

' Ere yet the sharp, decisive word
Redden the cannon's lips, and while the sword.'
                                        (Stanza v.)

On looking farther, I find to my intense disgust a verse without a mate in the last stanza but one, and I must put in a patch. If I had only kept my manuscript ! We must read

' And bid her navies, that so lately hurled
Their crashing battle, hold their thunders in,'

or else the poor ' world ' just below will have no law of gravitation to hold itself up by. I know I had something better originally, but I can't get it back. *Item*, in the eighth please make this change : —

' Virtue treads paths that end not in the grave,
But through those constellations go
That shed celestial influence on the brave.
If life were but to draw this dusty breath
That doth our wits enslave,
And with the crowd to hurry to and fro,
Seeking we know not what, and finding death,
These did unwisely ; but if living be,
As some are born to know,
The power to ennoble, and inspire
In other souls our brave desire
For fruit, not leaves, of Time's immortal tree,
These truly live, our thought's essential fire,
And to the saner,' etc.

There ! I won't open the book again, or I shall write you another ode instead of mending this. But in this latter passage the metre wanted limbering a little — it was *built* too

much with blank-verse bricks — and I think I have bettered it, at least to the ear." The second only of these emendations was incorporated in the ode at some later date.

In writing some time afterward to J. B. Thayer, who had been raising some questions regarding the structure of the *Ode*, Lowell again recurred to the manner in which he had been possessed by the poem. "I am not sure," he writes, "if I understand what you say about the tenth strophe. You will observe that it leads naturally to the eleventh, and that I there justify a certain narrowness in it as an expression of the popular feeling as well as my own. I confess I have never got over the feeling of wrath with which (just after the death of my nephew Willie) I read in an English paper that nothing was to be hoped of an army officered by tailors' apprentices and butcher-boys. The poem was written with a vehement speed, which I thought I had lost in the skirts of my professor's gown. Till within two days of the celebration I was hopelessly dumb, and then it all came with a rush, literally making me lean (*mi fece magro*) and so nervous that I was weeks in getting over it. I was longer in getting the new (eleventh) strophe to my mind than in writing the rest of the poem. In *that* I hardly changed a word, and it was so undeliberate that I did not find out till after it was printed that some of the verses lacked corresponding rhymes. . . . I doubt you are right in wishing it more historical. But then I could not have written it. I had put the ethical and political view so often in prose that I was weary of it. The motives of the war ? I had impatiently argued them again and again — but for an ode they must be in the blood and not the memory. One of my great defects (I have always been conscious of it) is an impatience of mind which makes me contemptuously indifferent about arguing matters that have once become convictions."

Once more, in 1877, in writing to the same correspondent, he quotes a passage from a paper in the *Cornhill* : " Mr. Lowell's *Commemoration Ode* is a specimen of the formless poem of unequal lines and broken stanzas supposed to be in the manner of Pindar, but truly the descendant of our royalist poet's [Cowley] ' majestick numbers.' " In animadversion on this Lowell goes on : " Whatever my other shortcomings (and they are plenty, as none knows better than I), want of reflection is not one of them. The poems [this and Lowell's other odes] were all intended for public recitation. That was the first thing to be considered. I suppose my ear (from long and painful practice on Φ B K poems) has more technical experience in this than almost any. The least tedious measure is the rhymed heroic, but this, too, palls unless relieved by passages of wit or even mere fun. A long series of uniform stanzas (I am always speaking of public recitation) with regularly recurring rhymes produces somnolence among the men and a desperate resort to their fans on the part of the women. No method has yet been invented by which the train of thought or feeling can be shunted off from the epical to the lyrical track. My ears have been jolted often enough over the sleepers on such occasions to know that. I know *something* (of course an American can't know much) about Pindar. But *his* odes had the advantage of being chanted. Now, my problem was to contrive a measure which should not be tedious by uniformity, which should vary with varying moods, in which the transitions (including those of the voice) should be managed without jar. I at first thought of mixed rhymed and blank verses of unequal measures, like those in the choruses of *Samson Agonistes*, which are in the main masterly. Of course Milton *deliberately* departed from that stricter form of the Greek Chorus to which it was bound quite as much (I suspect) by the law of its musical accompaniment as by any sense of symmetry. I wrote some stanzas of the *Commemoration Ode* on this theory at first, leaving some verses without a rhyme to match. But my ear was better pleased when the rhyme, coming at a longer interval, as a far-off echo rather than instant reverberation, produced the same effect almost, and yet was grateful by unexpectedly recalling an association and faint reminiscence of consonance."

I

WEAK-WINGED is song,
Nor aims at that clear-ethered height
Whither the brave deed climbs for light:
    We seem to do them wrong,
Bringing our robin's-leaf to deck their
    hearse
Who in warm life-blood wrote their nobler
    verse,
Our trivial song to honor those who come
With ears attuned to strenuous trump and
    drum,
And shaped in squadron-strophes their de-
    sire,
Live battle-odes whose lines were steel and
    fire:
    Yet sometimes feathered words are
        strong,
A gracious memory to buoy up and save
From Lethe's dreamless ooze, the common
    grave
    Of the unventurous throng.

II

To-day our Reverend Mother welcomes
    back
    Her wisest Scholars, those who under-
        stood
The deeper teaching of her mystic tome,
    And offered their fresh lives to make it
        good:
        No lore of Greece or Rome,
No science peddling with the names of
    things,
Or reading stars to find inglorious fates,
    Can lift our life with wings
Far from Death's idle gulf that for the
    many waits,
    And lengthen out our dates
With that clear fame whose memory sings
In manly hearts to come, and nerves them
    and dilates:
Nor such thy teaching, Mother of us all!
    Not such the trumpet-call
    Of thy diviner mood,
    That could thy sons entice
From happy homes and toils, the fruitful
    nest
Of those half-virtues which the world calls
    best,
    Into War's tumult rude;
    But rather far that stern device
The sponsors chose that round thy cradle
    stood
    In the dim, unventured wood,
    The VERITAS that lurks beneath
    The letter's unprolific sheath,
Life of whate'er makes life worth living,
Seed-grain of high emprise, immortal food,
    One heavenly thing whereof earth hath
        the giving.

III

Many loved Truth, and lavished life's best
    oil
    Amid the dust of books to find her,
Content at last, for guerdon of their toil,
    With the cast mantle she hath left be-
        hind her.
    Many in sad faith sought for her,
    Many with crossed hands sighed for
        her;
    But these, our brothers, fought for
        her,
    At life's dear peril wrought for her,
    So loved her that they died for her,
    Tasting the raptured fleetness

Of her divine completeness:
Their higher instinct knew
Those love her best who to themselves are
    true,
And what they dare to dream of, dare to
    do;
They followed her and found her
Where all may hope to find,
Not in the ashes of the burnt-out mind,
But beautiful, with danger's sweetness
    round her.
Where faith made whole with deed
Breathes its awakening breath
Into the lifeless creed,
They saw her plumed and mailed,
With sweet, stern face unveiled,
And all-repaying eyes, look proud on them
    in death.

IV

Our slender life runs rippling by, and
    glides
Into the silent hollow of the past;
    What is there that abides
To make the next age better for the last?
    Is earth too poor to give us
Something to live for here that shall
    outlive us?
Some more substantial boon
Than such as flows and ebbs with Fortune's
    fickle moon?
The little that we see
From doubt is never free;
The little that we do
Is but half-nobly true;
With our laborious hiving
What men call treasure, and the gods call
    dross,
Life seems a jest of Fate's contriving,
Only secure in every one's conniving,
A long account of nothings paid with loss,
Where we poor puppets, jerked by unseen
    wires,
After our little hour of strut and rave,
With all our pasteboard passions and de-
    sires,
Loves, hates, ambitions, and immortal fires,
Are tossed pell-mell together in the
    grave.
But stay! no age was e'er degenerate,
Unless men held it at too cheap a rate,
For in our likeness still we shape our
    fate.
Ah, there is something here
Unfathomed by the cynic's sneer,

Something that gives our feeble light
A high immunity from Night,
Something that leaps life's narrow bars
To claim its birthright with the hosts of
    heaven;
A seed of sunshine that can leaven
Our earthly dullness with the beams of
    stars,
    And glorify our clay
With light from fountains elder than the
    Day;
    A conscience more divine than we,
    A gladness fed with secret tears,
    A vexing, forward-reaching sense
Of some more noble permanence;
    A light across the sea,
Which haunts the soul and will not let it be,
Still beaconing from the heights of unde-
    generate years.

V

    Whither leads the path
    To ampler fates that leads?
    Not down through flowery meads,
    To reap an aftermath
Of youth's vainglorious weeds,
    But up the steep, amid the wrath
And shock of deadly-hostile creeds,
    Where the world's best hope and stay
By battle's flashes gropes a desperate way,
And every turf the fierce foot clings to
    bleeds.
Peace hath her not ignoble wreath,
Ere yet the sharp, decisive word
Light the black lips of cannon, and the
    sword
    Dreams in its easeful sheath;
But some day the live coal behind the
    thought,
    Whether from Baäl's stone obscene,
    Or from the shrine serene
    Of God's pure altar brought,
Bursts up in flame; the war of tongue and
    pen
Learns with what deadly purpose it was
    fraught,
And, helpless in the fiery passion caught,
Shakes all the pillared state with shock of
    men:
Some day the soft Ideal that we wooed
Confronts us fiercely, foe-beset, pursued,
And cries reproachful: "Was it, then, my
    praise,
And not myself was loved? Prove now
    thy truth;

I claim of thee the promise of thy youth;
Give me thy life, or cower in empty phrase,
The victim of thy genius, not its mate ! "
   Life may be given in many ways,
   And loyalty to Truth be sealed
As bravely in the closet as the field,
     So bountiful is Fate;
     But then to stand beside her,
     When craven churls deride her,
To front a lie in arms and not to yield,
     This shows, methinks, God's plan
     And measure of a stalwart man,
     Limbed like the old heroic breeds,
     Who stands self-poised on manhood's
        solid earth,
Not forced to frame excuses for his
     birth,
Fed from within with all the strength he
     needs.

VI

Such was he, our Martyr-Chief,
   Whom late the Nation he had led,
   With ashes on her head,
Wept with the passion of an angry grief:
Forgive me, if from present things I turn
To speak what in my heart will beat and
   burn,
And hang my wreath on his world-honored
   urn.
   Nature, they say, doth dote,
   And cannot make a man
   Save on some worn-out plan,
   Repeating us by rote:
For him her Old-World moulds aside she
   threw,
   And, choosing sweet clay from the
   breast
   Of the unexhausted West,
With stuff untainted shaped a hero new,
Wise, steadfast in the strength of God, and
   true.
   How beautiful to see
Once more a shepherd of mankind indeed,
Who loved his charge, but never loved to
   lead;
One whose meek flock the people joyed to
   be,
   Not lured by any cheat of birth,
   But by his clear-grained human worth,
And brave old wisdom of sincerity!
   They knew that outward grace is dust;
   They could not choose but trust
In that sure-footed mind's unfaltering skill,
   And supple-tempered will

That bent like perfect steel to spring again
   and thrust.
   His was no lonely mountain-peak of
   mind,
   Thrusting to thin air o'er our cloudy
   bars,
   A sea-mark now, now lost in vapors
   blind;
   Broad prairie rather, genial, level-
   lined,
   Fruitful and friendly for all human
   kind,
Yet also nigh to heaven and loved of lofti-
   est stars.
     Nothing of Europe here,
Or, then, of Europe fronting mornward
   still,
   Ere any names of Serf and Peer
   Could Nature's equal scheme deface
   And thwart her genial will;
Here was a type of the true elder race,
And one of Plutarch's men talked with us
   face to face.
   I praise him not; it were too late;
And some innative weakness there must be
In him who condescends to victory
Such as the Present gives, and cannot wait,
   Safe in himself as in a fate.
     So always firmly he:
     He knew to bide his time,
     And can his fame abide,
Still patient in his simple faith sublime,
     Till the wise years decide.
   Great captains, with their guns and
   drums,
   Disturb our judgment for the hour,
     But at last silence comes;
   These all are gone, and, standing like a
   tower,
   Our children shall behold his fame.
     The kindly-earnest, brave, foreseeing
     man,
Sagacious, patient, dreading praise, not
   blame,
New birth of our new soil, the first Amer-
   ican.

VII

Long as man's hope insatiate can discern
   Or only guess some more inspiring
   goal
   Outside of Self, enduring as the pole,
Along whose course the flying axles burn
Of spirits bravely-pitched, earth's man
   lier brood;

Long as below we cannot find
The meed that stills the inexorable mind;
So long this faith to some ideal Good,
Under whatever mortal names it masks,
Freedom, Law, Country, this ethereal
    mood
That thanks the Fates for their severer
    tasks,
Feeling its challenged pulses leap,
While others skulk in subterfuges cheap,
And, set in Danger's van, has all the boon
    it asks,
Shall win man's praise and woman's love,
Shall be a wisdom that we set above
All other skills and gifts to culture dear,
A virtue round whose forehead we in-
    wreathe
Laurels that with a living passion breathe
When other crowns grow, while we twine
    them, sear.
What brings us thronging these high
    rites to pay,
And seal these hours the noblest of our year,
Save that our brothers found this better
    way ?

VIII

We sit here in the Promised Land
That flows with Freedom's honey and
    milk;
But 't was they won it, sword in hand,
Making the nettle danger soft for us as silk.
We welcome back our bravest and our
    best; —
Ah me! not all! some come not with the
    rest,
Who went forth brave and bright as any
    here!
I strive to mix some gladness with my strain,
    But the sad strings complain,
    And will not please the ear:
I sweep them for a pæan, but they wane
    Again and yet again
Into a dirge, and die away, in pain.
In these brave ranks I only see the gaps,
Thinking of dear ones whom the dumb
    turf wraps,
Dark to the triumph which they died to
    gain:
Fitlier may others greet the living,
For me the past is unforgiving;
    I with uncovered head
    Salute the sacred dead,
Who went, and who return not. — Say not
    so!

'T is not the grapes of Canaan that repay,
But the high faith that failed not by the
    way;
Virtue treads paths that end not in the
    grave;
No ban of endless night exiles the brave;
    And to the saner mind
We rather seem the dead that stayed be-
    hind.
Blow, trumpets, all your exultations blow!
For never shall their aureoled presence lack:
I see them muster in a gleaming row,
With ever-youthful brows that nobler show;
We find in our dull road their shining
    track;
    In every nobler mood
We feel the orient of their spirit glow,
Part of our life's unalterable good,
Of all our saintlier aspiration;
    They come transfigured back,
Secure from change in their high-hearted
    ways,
Beautiful evermore, and with the rays
Of morn on their white Shields of Expecta-
    tion!

IX

    But is there hope to save
Even this ethereal essence from the
    grave ?
What ever 'scaped Oblivion's subtle
    wrong
Save a few clarion names, or golden threads
    of song ?
    Before my musing eye
    The mighty ones of old sweep by,
Disvoicëd now and insubstantial things,
As noisy once as we; poor ghosts of kings,
Shadows of empire wholly gone to dust,
And many races, nameless long ago,
To darkness driven by that imperious
    gust
Of ever-rushing Time that here doth
    blow:
O visionary world, condition strange,
Where naught abiding is but only Change,
Where the deep-bolted stars themselves
    still shift and range!
Shall we to more continuance make pre-
    tence ?
Renown builds tombs; a life-estate is Wit;
    And, bit by bit,
The cunning years steal all from us but woe;
Leaves are we, whose decays no harvest
    sow.

But, when we vanish hence,
Shall they lie forceless in the dark below,
Save to make green their little length of
sods,
Or deepen pansies for a year or two,
Who now to us are shining-sweet as gods?
Was dying all they had the skill to do?
That were not fruitless : but the Soul
resents
Such short-lived service, as if blind events
Ruled without her, or earth could so
endure;
She claims a more divine investiture
Of longer tenure than Fame's airy rents;
Whate'er she touches doth her nature
share;
Her inspiration haunts the ennobled air,
Gives eyes to mountains blind,
Ears to the deaf earth, voices to the
wind,
And her clear trump sings succor every-
where
By lonely bivouacs to the wakeful mind;
For soul inherits all that soul could dare:
Yea, Manhood hath a wider span
And larger privilege of life than man.
The single deed, the private sacrifice,
So radiant now through proudly-hidden
tears,
Is covered up erelong from mortal eyes
With thoughtless drift of the deciduous
years;
But that high privilege that makes all
men peers,
That leap of heart whereby a people rise
Up to a noble anger's height,
And, flamed on by the Fates, not shrink,
but grow more bright,
That swift validity in noble veins,
Of choosing danger and disdaining
shame,
Of being set on flame
By the pure fire that flies all contact base
But wraps its chosen with angelic might,
These are imperishable gains,
Sure as the sun, medicinal as light,
These hold great futures in their lusty
reins
And certify to earth a new imperial race.

X

Who now shall sneer?
Who dare again to say we trace
Our lines to a plebeian race?
Roundhead and Cavalier!

Dumb are those names erewhile in battle
loud;
Dream-footed as the shadow of a cloud,
They flit across the ear:
That is best blood that hath most iron
in 't.
To edge resolve with, pouring without stint
For what makes manhood dear.
Tell us not of Plantagenets,
Hapsburgs, and Guelfs, whose thin bloods
crawl
Down from some victor in a border-brawl!
How poor their outworn coronets,
Matched with one leaf of that plain civic
wreath
Our brave for honor's blazon shall bequeath,
Through whose desert a rescued Nation
sets
Her heel on treason, and the trumpet hears
Shout victory, tingling Europe's sullen ears
With vain resentments and more vain
regrets!

XI

Not in anger, not in pride,
Pure from passion's mixture rude
Ever to base earth allied,
But with far-heard gratitude,
Still with heart and voice renewed,
To heroes living and dear martyrs dead,
The strain should close that consecrates our
brave.
Lift the heart and lift the head !
Lofty be its mood and grave,
Not without a martial ring,
Not without a prouder tread
And a peal of exultation :
Little right has he to sing
Through whose heart in such an hour
Beats no march of conscious power,
Sweeps no tumult of elation !
'T is no Man we celebrate,
By his country's victories great,
A hero half, and half the whim of Fate,
But the pith and marrow of a Nation
Drawing force from all her men,
Highest, humblest, weakest, all,
For her time of need, and then
Pulsing it again through them,
Till the basest can no longer cower,
Feeling his soul spring up divinely tall,
Touched but in passing by her mantle-
hem.
Come back, then, noble pride, for 't is
her dower !

How could poet ever tower,
If his passions, hopes, and fears,
If his triumphs and his tears,
Kept not measure with his people ?
Boom, cannon, boom to all the winds and
waves !
Clash out, glad bells, from every rocking
steeple !
Banners, adance with triumph, bend your
staves !
And from every mountain-peak
Let beacon-fire to answering beacon
speak,
Katahdin tell Monadnock, Whiteface
he,
And so leap on in light from sea to sea,
Till the glad news be sent
Across a kindling continent,
Making earth feel more firm and air breathe
braver :
"Be proud ! for she is saved, and all have
helped to save her !
She that lifts up the manhood of the
poor,
She of the open soul and open door,
With room about her hearth for all
mankind !
The fire is dreadful in her eyes no
more ;
From her bold front the helm she doth
unbind,
Sends all her handmaid armies back to
spin,
And bids her navies, that so lately
hurled
Their crashing battle, hold their thun-
ders in,
Swimming like birds of calm along the
unharmful shore.

No challenge sends she to the elder
world,
That looked askance and hated ; a light
scorn
Plays o'er her mouth, as round her
mighty knees
She calls her children back, and waits
the morn
Of nobler day, enthroned between her sub-
ject seas."

XII

Bow down, dear Land, for thou hast found
release !
Thy God, in these distempered days,
Hath taught thee the sure wisdom of
His ways,
And through thine enemies hath wrought
thy peace !
Bow down in prayer and praise!
No poorest in thy borders but may now
Lift to the juster skies a man's enfran-
chised brow.
O Beautiful ! my Country ! ours once
more !
Smoothing thy gold of war-dishevelled hair
O'er such sweet brows as never other wore,
And letting thy set lips,
Freed from wrath's pale eclipse,
The rosy edges of their smile lay bare,
What words divine of lover or of poet
Could tell our love and make thee know it,
Among the Nations bright beyond com-
pare ?
What were our lives without thee ?
What all our lives to save thee ?
We reck not what we gave thee;
We will not dare to doubt thee,
But ask whatever else, and we will dare !

L'ENVOI

TO THE MUSE

WHITHER ?   Albeit I follow fast,
In all life's circuit I but find,
Not where thou art, but where thou wast,
Sweet beckoner, more fleet than wind !
I haunt the pine-dark solitudes,
With soft brown silence carpeted,
And plot to snare thee in the woods:
Peace I o'ertake, but thou art fled!

I find the rock where thou didst rest,
The moss thy skimming foot hath prest;
All Nature with thy parting thrills,
Like branches after birds new-flown;
Thy passage hill and hollow fills
With hints of virtue not their own;
In dimples still the water slips
Where thou hast dipt thy finger-tips;
Just, just beyond, forever burn
Gleams of a grace without return;

Upon thy shade I plant my foot,
And through my frame strange raptures
  shoot;
All of thee but thyself I grasp;
I seem to fold thy luring shape,
And vague air to my bosom clasp,
  Thou lithe, perpetual Escape !

One mask and then another drops,
And thou art secret as before:
  Sometimes with flooded ear I list,
  And hear thee, wondrous organist,
From mighty continental stops
A thunder of new music pour ;
Through pipes of earth and air and stone
Thy inspiration deep is blown;
Through mountains, forests, open downs,
Lakes, railroads, prairies, states, and towns,
Thy gathering fugue goes rolling on
From Maine to utmost Oregon;
The factory-wheels in cadence hum,
From brawling parties concords come;
All this I hear, or seem to hear,
But when, enchanted, I draw near
To mate with words the various theme,
Life seems a whiff of kitchen steam,
History an organ-grinder's thrum,
  For thou hast slipt from it and me
And all thine organ-pipes left dumb,
  Most mutable Perversity !

Not weary yet, I still must seek,
And hope for luck next day, next week;
I go to see the great man ride,
Shiplike, the swelling human tide
That floods to bear him into port,
Trophied from Senate-hall and Court;
Thy magnetism, I feel it there,
Thy rhythmic presence fleet and rare,
Making the Mob a moment fine
With glimpses of their own Divine,
As in their demigod they see
  Their cramped ideal soaring free;
'T was thou didst bear the fire about,
  That, like the springing of a mine,
Sent up to heaven the street-long shout;
Full well I know that thou wast here,
It was thy breath that brushed my ear;
But vainly in the stress and whirl
I dive for thee, the moment's pearl.

Through every shape thou well canst
  run,
Proteus, 'twixt rise and set of sun,
Well pleased with logger-camps in Maine

As where Milan's pale Duomo lies
A stranded glacier on the plain,
  Its peaks and pinnacles of ice
  Melted in many a quaint device,
And sees, above the city's din,
Afar its silent Alpine kin:
I track thee over carpets deep
To wealth's and beauty's inmost keep;
Across the sand of bar-room floors
Mid the stale reek of boosing boors;
Where drowse the hay-field's fragrant
  heats,
Or the flail-heart of Autumn beats;
I dog thee through the market's throngs
To where the sea with myriad tongues
Laps the green edges of the pier,
And the tall ships that eastward steer,
Curtsy their farewells to the town,
O'er the curved distance lessening down;
I follow allwhere for thy sake,
Touch thy robe's hem, but ne'er o'ertake,
Find where, scarce yet unmoving, lies,
Warm from thy limbs, thy last disguise;
But thou another shape hast donned,
And lurest still just, just beyond !

But here a voice, I know not whence,
Thrills clearly through my inward sense,
Saying : " See where she sits at home
While thou in search of her dost roam !
All summer long her ancient wheel
  Whirls humming by the open door,
Or, when the hickory's social zeal
  Sets the wide chimney in a roar,
Close-nestled by the tinkling hearth,
It modulates the household mirth
With that sweet serious undertone
Of duty, music all her own;
Still as of old she sits and spins
Our hopes, our sorrows, and our sins;
With equal care she twines the fates
Of cottages and mighty states;
She spins the earth, the air, the sea,
The maiden's unschooled fancy free,
The boy's first love, the man's first grief,
The budding and the fall o' the leaf;
The piping west-wind's snowy care
For her their cloudy fleeces spare,
Or from the thorns of evil times
She can glean wool to twist her rhymes;
Morning and noon and eve supply
To her their fairest tints for dye,
But ever through her twirling thread
There spires one line of warmest red,
Tinged from the homestead's genial heart,

The stamp and warrant of her art;
With this Time's sickle she outwears,
And blunts the Sisters' baffled shears.

" Harass her not: thy heat and stir
But greater coyness breed in her;
Yet thou mayst find, ere Age's frost,
Thy long apprenticeship not lost,
Learning at last that Stygian Fate
Unbends to him that knows to wait.
The Muse is womanish, nor deigns
Her love to him that pules and plains;
With proud, averted face she stands
To him that wooes with empty hands.
Make thyself free of Manhood's guild;
Pull down thy barns and greater build;

The wood, the mountain, and the plain
Wave breast-deep with the poet's grain;
Pluck thou the sunset's fruit of gold,
Glean from the heavens and ocean old;
From fireside lone and trampling street
Let thy life garner daily wheat;
The epic of a man rehearse,
Be something better than thy verse;
Make thyself rich, and then the Muse
Shall court thy precious interviews,
Shall take thy head upon her knee,
And such enchantment lilt to thee,
That thou shalt hear the life-blood flow
From farthest stars to grass-blades low,
And find the Listener's science still
Transcends the Singer's deepest skill ! "

THE CATHEDRAL

To

MR. JAMES T. FIELDS

MY DEAR FIELDS:

Dr. Johnson's sturdy self-respect led him to invent the Bookseller as a substitute for the Patron. My relations with you have enabled me to discover how pleasantly the Friend may replace the Bookseller. Let me record my sense of many thoughtful services by associating your name with a poem which owes its appearance in this form to your partiality.

Cordially yours,

J. R. LOWELL.

CAMBRIDGE, *November* 29, 1869.

The Cathedral was printed first in *The Atlantic Monthly* for January, 1870, but was shortly after published in a volume by itself with changes and additions. The poem was wrought at apparently with something of the loving enthusiasm which we are wont to ascribe to the builders of actual cathedrals. It was written in the summer of 1869 and returned to frequently before publication. When in the midst of the work he wrote to Mr. Howells, then editor of the *Atlantic*, " Up to time indeed! The fear is not about time, but space. You won't have room in your menagerie for such a displeaseyousaurus. The verses if stretched end to end in a continuous line would go clear round the cathedral they celebrate, and nobody (I fear) the wiser. I can't tell yet what they are. There seems a bit of clean carving here and there, a solid buttress or two, and perhaps a gleam through painted glass — but I have not copied it out yet, nor indeed read it over

consecutively." A little later he wrote to Miss Norton : " I hope it is good, for it fairly trussed me at last and bore me up as high as my poor lungs will bear into the heaven of invention. I was happy writing it, and so steeped in it that if I had written to you it would have been in blank verse. It is a kind of religious poem, and is called *A Day at Chartres*. . . . I can't tell yet how it will stand. Already I am beginning to — to — you know what I mean — to taste my champagne next morning."

The poem received some comment from two distinguished critics, Mr. Leslie Stephen and Mr. Ruskin. To the former Lowell wrote : " I am glad you liked *The Cathedral* and sorry for anything in it you did n't like. The name was none of my choosing. I called it *A Day at Chartres*, and Fields rechristened it. You see with *my* name the episode of the Britons comes in naturally enough (it is historical, by the way). The truth is, I had no notion of being satirical, but wrote what I did just as I might have said it to you in badinage. But of course the tone is lost in print. Anyhow, there is *one* Englishman I am fond enough of to balance any spite I might have against others, as you know. But I have n't a particle. If I had met two of my own countrymen at Chartres I should have been quite as free with them." In reply to some advice and strictures of Mr. Ruskin, he wrote to Mr. Norton: "I am glad to find that the poem *sticks*. Those who liked it at first like it still, some of them better than ever, some extravagantly. At any rate it wrote itself; all of a sudden it was *there*, and that is something in its favor. Now Ruskin wants me to go over it with a file. That is just what I did. I wrote in pencil, then copied it out in ink, and worked over it as I never worked over anything before. I may fairly say there is not a word in it over which I have not thought, not an objection which I did not foresee and maturely consider. Well, in my second copy I made many changes, as I thought for the better, and then put it away in my desk to cool for three weeks or so. When I came to print it, I put back, I believe, *every one* of the original readings which I had changed. Those which had come to me were far better than those I had come at. Only one change I made (for the worse), in order to escape a rhyme that had crept in without my catching it." Ruskin made some verbal criticism, which Lowell proceeded to examine, and the reader will find the discussion in the notes at the end of this volume.

FAR through the memory shines a happy day,
Cloudless of care, down-shod to every sense,
And simply perfect from its own resource,
As to a bee the new campanula's
Illuminate seclusion swung in air.
Such days are not the prey of setting suns,
Nor ever blurred with mist of after-thought;
Like words made magical by poets dead,
Wherein the music of all meaning is
The sense hath garnered or the soul divined,
They mingle with our life's ethereal part,
Sweetening and gathering sweetness ever-more,
By beauty's franchise disenthralled of time.

I can recall, nay, they are present still,
Parts of myself, the perfume of my mind,
Days that seem farther off than Homer's now
Ere yet the child had loudened to the boy,
And I, recluse from playmates, found per-force
Companionship in things that not denied
Nor granted wholly; as is Nature's wont,
Who, safe in uncontaminate reserve,
Lets us mistake our longing for her love,
And mocks with various echo of ourselves.

These first sweet frauds upon our con-sciousness,
That blend the sensual with its imaged world,
These virginal cognitions, gifts of morn,

Ere life grow noisy, and slower-footed thought
Can overtake the rapture of the sense,
To thrust between ourselves and what we feel,
Have something in them secretly divine.
Vainly the eye, once schooled to serve the brain,
With pains deliberate studies to renew
The ideal vision: second-thoughts are prose;
For beauty's acme hath a term as brief
As the wave's poise before it break in pearl.
Our own breath dims the mirror of the sense,
Looking too long and closely: at a flash
We snatch the essential grace of meaning out,
And that first passion beggars all behind,
Heirs of a tamer transport prepossessed.
Who, seeing once, has truly seen again
The gray vague of unsympathizing sea
That dragged his Fancy from her moor-ings back
To shores inhospitable of eldest time,
Till blank foreboding of earth-gendered powers,
Pitiless seigniories in the elements,
Omnipotences blind that darkling smite,
Misgave him, and repaganized the world?
Yet, by some subtler touch of sympathy,
These primal apprehensions, dimly stirred,
Perplex the eye with pictures from within.
This hath made poets dream of lives fore-gone
In worlds fantastical, more fair than ours;

So Memory cheats us, glimpsing half-
    revealed.
Even as I write she tries her wonted spell
In that continuous redbreast boding rain:
The bird I hear sings not from yonder elm;
But the flown ecstasy my childhood heard
Is vocal in my mind, renewed by him,
Haply made sweeter by the accumulate
    thrill
That threads my undivided life and steals
A pathos from the years and graves be-
    tween.

I know not how it is with other men,
Whom I but guess, deciphering myself;
For me, once felt is so felt nevermore.
The fleeting relish at sensation's brim
Had in it the best ferment of the wine.
One spring I knew as never any since:
All night the surges of the warm southwest
Boomed intermittent through the wallowing
    elms,
And brought a morning from the Gulf
    adrift,
Omnipotent with sunshine, whose quick
    charm
Startled with crocuses the sullen turf
And wiled the bluebird to his whiff of song:
One summer hour abides, what time I
    perched,
Dappled with noonday, under simmering
    leaves,
And pulled the pulpy oxhearts, while aloof
An oriole clattered and the robins shrilled,
Denouncing me an alien and a thief:
One morn of autumn lords it o'er the rest,
When in the lane I watched the ash-leaves
    fall,
Balancing softly earthward without wind,
Or twirling with directer impulse down
On those fallen yesterday, now barbed with
    frost,
While I grew pensive with the pensive year:
And once I learned how marvellous winter
    was,
When past the fence-rails, downy-gray with
    rime,
I creaked adventurous o'er the spangled
    crust
That made familiar fields seem far and
    strange
As those stark wastes that whiten endlessly
In ghastly solitude about the pole,
And gleam relentless to the unsetting sun:
Instant the candid chambers of my brain

Were painted with these sovran images ;
And later visions seem but copies pale
From those unfading frescos of the past,
Which I, young savage, in my age of flint,
Gazed at, and dimly felt a power in me
Parted from Nature by the joy in her
That doubtfully revealed me to myself.
Thenceforward I must stand outside the
    gate;
And paradise was paradise the more,
Known once and barred against satiety.

What we call Nature, all outside ourselves,
Is but our own conceit of what we see,
Our own reaction upon what we feel;
The world's a woman to our shifting mood,
Feeling with us, or making due pretence;
And therefore we the more persuade our-
    selves
To make all things our thought's confeder-
    ates,
Conniving with us in whate'er we dream.
So when our Fancy seeks analogies,
Though she have hidden what she after
    finds,
She loves to cheat herself with feigned sur-
    prise.
I find my own complexion everywhere:
No rose, I doubt, was ever, like the first,
A marvel to the bush it dawned upon,
The rapture of its life made visible,
The mystery of its yearning realized,
As the first babe to the first woman born;
No falcon ever felt delight of wings
As when, an eyas, from the stolid cliff
Loosing himself, he followed his high heart
To swim on sunshine, masterless as wind;
And I believe the brown earth takes delight
In the new snowdrop looking back at her,
To think that by some vernal alchemy
It could transmute her darkness into pearl;
What is the buxom peony after that,
With its coarse constancy of hoyden blush?
What the full summer to that wonder new?

But, if in nothing else, in us there is
A sense fastidious hardly reconciled
To the poor makeshifts of life's scenery,
Where the same slide must double all its
    parts,
Shoved in for Tarsus and hitched back for
    Tyre.
I blame not in the soul this daintiness,
Rasher of surfeit than a humming-bird,
In things indifferent by sense purveyed;

It argues her an immortality
And dateless incomes of experience,
This unthrift housekeeping that will not
    brook
A dish warmed-over at the feast of life,
And finds Twice stale, served with what-
    ever sauce.
Nor matters much how it may go with me
Who dwell in Grub Street and am proud to
    drudge
Where men, my betters, wet their crust
    with tears:
Use can make sweet the peach's shady side,
That only by reflection tastes of sun.

But she, my Princess, who will sometimes
    deign
My garret to illumine till the walls,
Narrow and dingy, scrawled with hack-
    neyed thought
(Poor Richard slowly elbowing Plato out),
Dilate and drape themselves with tapestries
Nausikaa might have stooped o'er, while,
    between,
Mirrors, effaced in their own clearness, send
Her only image on through deepening
    deeps
With endless repercussion of delight, —
Bringer of life, witching each sense to soul,
That sometimes almost gives me to believe
I might have been a poet, gives at least
A brain desaxonized, an ear that makes
Music where none is, and a keener pang
Of exquisite surmise outleaping thought, —
Her will I pamper in her luxury:
No crumpled rose-leaf of too careless choice
Shall bring a northern nightmare to her
    dreams,
Vexing with sense of exile; hers shall be
The invitiate firstlings of experience,
Vibrations felt but once and felt life long:
Oh, more than half-way turn that Grecian
    front
Upon me, while with self-rebuke I spell,
On the plain fillet that confines thy hair
In conscious bounds of seeming uncon-
    straint,
The *Naught in overplus*, thy race's badge!

One feast for her I secretly designed
In that Old World so strangely beautiful
To us the disinherited of eld, —
A day at Chartres, with no soul beside
To roil with pedant prate my joy serene
And make the minster shy of confidence.

I went, and, with the Saxon's pious care,
First ordered dinner at the pea-green inn,
The flies and I its only customers.
Eluding these, I loitered through the town,
With hope to take my minster unawares
In its grave solitude of memory.
A pretty burgh, and such as Fancy loves
For bygone grandeurs, faintly rumorous
    now
Upon the mind's horizon, as of storm
Brooding its dreamy thunders far aloof,
That mingle with our mood, but not dis-
    turb.
Its once grim bulwarks, tamed to lovers'
    walks,
Look down unwatchful on the sliding Eure,
Whose listless leisure suits the quiet place,
Lisping among his shallows homelike sounds
At Concord and by Bankside heard before.
Chance led me to a public pleasure-ground,
Where I grew kindly with the merry groups,
And blessed the Frenchman for his simple
    art
Of being domestic in the light of day.
His language has no word, we growl, for
    Home;
But he can find a fireside in the sun,
Play with his child, make love, and shriek
    his mind,
By throngs of strangers undisprivacied.
He makes his life a public gallery,
Nor feels himself till what he feels comes
    back
In manifold reflection from without;
While we, each pore alert with conscious-
    ness,
Hide our best selves as we had stolen them,
And each bystander a detective were,
Keen-eyed for every chink of undisguise.

So, musing o'er the problem which was
    best, —
A life wide-windowed, shining all abroad,
Or curtains drawn to shield from sight
    profane
The rites we pay to the mysterious I, —
With outward senses furloughed and head
    bowed
I followed some fine instinct in my feet,
Till, to unbend me from the loom of
    thought,
Looking up suddenly, I found mine eyes
Confronted with the minster's vast repose.
Silent and gray as forest-leaguered cliff
Left inland by the ocean's slow retreat,

That hears afar the breeze-borne rote and
    longs,
Remembering shocks of surf that clomb
    and fell,
Spume-sliding down the baffled decuman,
It rose before me, patiently remote
From the great tides of life it breasted once,
Hearing the noise of men as in a dream.
I stood before the triple northern port,
Where dedicated shapes of saints and kings,
Stern faces bleared with immemorial watch,
Looked down benignly grave and seemed
    to say,
Ye come and go incessant; we remain
Safe in the hallowed quiets of the past;
Be reverent, ye who flit and are forgot,
Of faith so nobly realized as this.
I seem to have heard it said by learnèd
    folk
Who drench you with æsthetics till you feel
As if all beauty were a ghastly bore,
The faucet to let loose a wash of words,
That Gothic is not Grecian, therefore worse;
But, being convinced by much experiment
How little inventiveness there is in man,
Grave copier of copies, I give thanks
For a new relish, careless to inquire
My pleasure's pedigree, if so it please,
Nobly, I mean, nor renegade to art.
The Grecian gluts me with its perfect-
    ness,
Unanswerable as Euclid, self-contained,
The one thing finished in this hasty world,
Forever finished, though the barbarous pit,
Fanatical on hearsay, stamp and shout
As if a miracle could be encored.
But ah! this other, this that never ends,
Still climbing, luring fancy still to climb,
As full of morals half-divined as life,
Graceful, grotesque, with ever new surprise
Of hazardous caprices sure to please,
Heavy as nightmare, airy-light as fern,
Imagination's very self in stone!
With one long sigh of infinite release
From pedantries past, present, or to come,
I looked, and owned myself a happy Goth.
Your blood is mine, ye architects of dream,
Builders of aspiration incomplete,
So more consummate, souls self-confident,
Who felt your own thought worthy of re-
    cord
In monumental pomp! No Grecian drop
Rebukes these veins that leap with kindred
    thrill,
After long exile, to the mother-tongue.

Ovid in Pontus, puling for his Rome
Of men invirile and disnatured dames
That poison sucked from the Attic bloom
    decayed,
Shrank with a shudder from the blue-eyed
    race
Whose force rough-handed should renew
    the world,
And from the dregs of Romulus express
Such wine as Dante poured, or he who blew
Roland's vain blast, or sang the Campeador
In verse that clanks like armor in the
    charge,
Homeric juice, though brimmed in Odin's
    horn.
And they could build, if not the columned
    fane
That from the height gleamed seaward
    many-hued,
Something more friendly with their ruder
    skies:
The gray spire, molten now in driving mist,
Now lulled with the incommunicable blue;
The carvings touched to meaning new with
    snow,
Or commented with fleeting grace of shade;
The statues, motley as man's memory,
Partial as that, so mixed of true and false,
History and legend meeting with a kiss
Across this bound-mark where their realms
    confine;
The painted windows, freaking gloom with
    glow,
Dusking the sunshine which they seem to
    cheer,
Meet symbol of the senses and the soul,
And the whole pile, grim with the North-
    man's thought
Of life and death, and doom, life's equal
    fee, —
These were before me : and I gazed
    abashed,
Child of an age that lectures, not creates,
Plastering our swallow-nests on the awful
    Past,
And twittering round the work of larger
    men,
As we had builded what we but deface.
Far up the great bells wallowed in delight,
Tossing their clangors o'er the heedless
    town,
To call the worshippers who never came,
Or women mostly, in loath twos and threes.
I entered, reverent of whatever shrine
Guards piety and solace for my kind

Or gives the soul a moment's truce of God,
And shared decorous in the ancient rite
My sterner fathers held idolatrous.
The service over, I was tranced in thought :
Solemn the deepening vaults, and most to
    me,
Fresh from the fragile realm of deal and
    paint,
Or brick mock-pious with a marble front ;
Solemn the lift of high-embowered roof,
The clustered stems that spread in boughs
    disleaved,
Through which the organ blew a dream of
    storm,
Though not more potent to sublime with
    awe
And shut the heart up in tranquillity,
Than aisles to me familiar that o'erarch
The conscious silences of brooding woods,
Centurial shadows, cloisters of the elk :
Yet here was sense of undefined regret,
Irreparable loss, uncertain what :
Was all this grandeur but anachronism,
A shell divorced of its informing life,
Where the priest housed him like a hermit-
    crab,
An alien to that faith of elder days
That gathered round it this fair shape of
    stone ?
Is old Religion but a spectre now,
Haunting the solitude of darkened minds,
Mocked out of memory by the sceptic day ?
Is there no corner safe from peeping
    Doubt,
Since Gutenberg made thought cosmopolite
And stretched electric threads from mind
    to mind ?
Nay, did Faith build this wonder ? or did
    Fear,
That makes a fetish and misnames it God
(Blockish or metaphysic, matters not),
Contrive this coop to shut its tyrant in,
Appeased with playthings, that he might
    not harm ?

I turned and saw a beldame on her knees ;
With eyes astray, she told mechanic beads
Before some shrine of saintly womanhood,
Bribed intercessor with the far-off Judge :
Such my first thought, by kindlier soon re-
    buked,
Pleading for whatsoever touches life
With upward impulse : be He nowhere
    else,
God is in all that liberates and lifts,

In all that humbles, sweetens, and con-
    soles :
Blessëd the natures shored on every side
With landmarks of hereditary thought !
Thrice happy they that wander not life
    long
Beyond near succor of the household faith,
The guarded fold that shelters, not con-
    fines !
Their steps find patience in familiar paths,
Printed with hope by loved feet gone be-
    fore
Of parent, child, or lover, glorified
By simple magic of dividing Time.
My lids were moistened as the woman
    knelt,
And — was it will, or some vibration faint
Of sacred Nature, deeper than the will ? —
My heart occultly felt itself in hers,
Through mutual intercession gently
    leagued.

Or was it not mere sympathy of brain ?
A sweetness intellectually conceived
In simpler creeds to me impossible ?
A juggle of that pity for ourselves
In others, which puts on such pretty masks
And snares self-love with bait of charity ?
Something of all it might be, or of none :
Yet for a moment I was snatched away
And had the evidence of things not seen ;
For one rapt moment ; then it all came
    back,
This age that blots out life with question-
    marks,
This nineteenth century with its knife and
    glass
That make thought physical, and thrust far
    off
The Heaven, so neighborly with man of
    old,
To voids sparse-sown with alienated stars.

'T is irrecoverable, that ancient faith,
Homely and wholesome, suited to the
    time,
With rod or candy for child-minded men :
No theologic tube, with lens on lens
Of syllogism transparent, brings it near, —
At best resolving some new nebula,
Or blurring some fixed-star of hope to
    mist.
Science was Faith once ; Faith were Science
    now,
Would she but lay her bow and arrows by

And arm her with the weapons of the
time.
Nothing that keeps thought out is safe from
thought.
For there's no virgin-fort but self-respect,
And Truth defensive hath lost hold on
God.
Shall we treat Him as if He were a child
That knew not His own purpose? nor dare
trust
The Rock of Ages to their chemic tests,
Lest some day the all-sustaining base divine
Should fail from under us, dissolved in
gas?
The armëd eye that with a glance discerns
In a dry blood-speck between ox and man
Stares helpless at this miracle called life,
This shaping potency behind the egg,
This circulation swift of deity,
Where suns and systems inconspicuous
float
As the poor blood - disks in our mortal
veins.
Each age must worship its own thought of
God,
More or less earthy, clarifying still
With subsidence continuous of the dregs ;
Nor saint nor sage could fix immutably
The fluent image of the unstable Best,
Still changing in their very hands that
wrought :
To-day's eternal truth To-morrow proved
Frail as frost-landscapes on a window-pane.
Meanwhile Thou smiledst, inaccessible,
At Thought's own substance made a cage
for Thought,
And Truth locked fast with her own mas-
ter-key ;
Nor didst Thou reck what image man
might make
Of his own shadow on the flowing world;
The climbing instinct was enough for Thee.
Or wast Thou, then, an ebbing tide that
left
Strewn with dead miracle those eldest
shores,
For men to dry, and dryly lecture on,
Thyself thenceforth incapable of flood ?
Idle who hopes with prophets to be
snatched
By virtue in their mantles left below;
Shall the soul live on other men's report,
Herself a pleasing fable of herself ?
Man cannot be God's outlaw if he would,
Nor so abscond him in the caves of sense

But Nature still shall search some crevice
out
With messages of splendor from that
Source
Which, dive he, soar he, baffles still and
lures.
This life were brutish did we not some-
times
Have intimation clear of wider scope,
Hints of occasion infinite, to keep
The soul alert with noble discontent
And onward yearnings of unstilled desire;
Fruitless, except we now and then divined
A mystery of Purpose, gleaming through
The secular confusions of the world,
Whose will we darkly accomplish, doing
ours.
No man can think nor in himself perceive,
Sometimes at waking, in the street some-
times,
Or on the hillside, always unforewarned,
A grace of being, finer than himself,
That beckons and is gone, — a larger life
Upon his own impinging, with swift
glimpse
Of spacious circles luminous with mind,
To which the ethereal substance of his
own
Seems but gross cloud to make that visible,
Touched to a sudden glory round the edge.
Who that hath known these visitations fleet
Would strive to make them trite and
ritual ?
I, that still pray at morning and at eve,
Loving those roots that feed us from the
past,
And prizing more than Plato things I
learned
At that best academe, a mother's knee,
Thrice in my life perhaps have truly
prayed,
Thrice, stirred below my conscious self,
have felt
That perfect disenthralment which is God;
Nor know I which to hold worst enemy,
Him who on speculation's windy waste
Would turn me loose, stript of the raiment
warm
By Faith contrived against our nakedness,
Or him who, cruel-kind, would fain obscure,
With painted saints and paraphrase of God,
The soul's east-window of divine surprise.
Where others worship I but look and long;
For, though not recreant to my fathers'
faith,

Its forms to me are weariness, and most
That drony vacuum of compulsory prayer,
Still pumping phrases for the Ineffable,
Though all the valves of memory gasp and
　　wheeze.
Words that have drawn transcendent mean-
　　ings up
From the best passion of all bygone time,
Steeped through with tears of triumph and
　　remorse,
Sweet with all sainthood, cleansed in mar-
　　tyr-fires,
Can they, so consecrate and so inspired,
By repetition wane to vexing wind?
Alas! we cannot draw habitual breath
In the thin air of life's supremer heights,
We cannot make each meal a sacrament,
Nor with our tailors be disbodied souls, —
We men, too conscious of earth's comedy,
Who see two sides, with our posed selves
　　debate,
And only for great stakes can be sublime!
Let us be thankful when, as I do here,
We can read Bethel on a pile of stones,
And, seeing where God *has* been, trust in
　　Him.

Brave Peter Fischer there in Nuremberg,
Moulding Saint Sebald's miracles in bronze,
Put saint and stander-by in that quaint
　　garb
Familiar to him in his daily walk,
Not doubting God could grant a miracle
Then and in Nuremberg, if so He would;
But never artist for three hundred years
Hath dared the contradiction ludicrous
Of supernatural in modern clothes.
Perhaps the deeper faith that is to come
Will see God rather in the strenuous doubt,
Than in the creed held as an infant's hand
Holds purposeless whatso is placed therein.

Say it is drift, not progress, none the less,
With the old sextant of the fathers' creed,
We shape our courses by new-risen stars,
And, still lip-loyal to what once was truth,
Smuggle new meanings under ancient
　　names,
Unconscious perverts of the Jesuit, Time.
Change is the mask that all Continuance
　　wears
To keep us youngsters harmlessly amused;
Meanwhile some ailing or more watchful
　　child,
Sitting apart, sees the old eyes gleam out,

Stern, and yet soft with humorous pity too.
Whilere, men burnt men for a doubtful
　　point,
As if the mind were quenchable with fire,
And Faith danced round them with her
　　war-paint on,
Devoutly savage as an Iroquois ;
Now Calvin and Servetus at one board
Snuff in grave sympathy a milder roast,
And o'er their claret settle Comte unread.
Fagot and stake were desperately sincere:
Our cooler martyrdoms are done in types;
And flames that shine in controversial eyes
Burn out no brains but his who kindles
　　them.
This is no age to get cathedrals built:
Did God, then, wait for one in Bethlehem?
Worst is not yet: lo, where his coming
　　looms,
Of earth's anarchic children latest born,
Democracy, a Titan who hath learned
To laugh at Jove's old-fashioned thunder-
　　bolts, —
Could he not also forge them, if he would?
He, better skilled, with solvents merciless,
Loosened in air and borne on every wind,
Saps unperceived: the calm Olympian
　　height
Of ancient order feels its bases yield,
And pale gods glance for help to gods as
　　pale.
What will be left of good or worshipful,
Of spiritual secrets, mysteries,
Of fair religion's guarded heritage,
Heirlooms of soul, passed downward un-
　　profaned
From eldest Ind? This Western giant
　　coarse,
Scorning refinements which he lacks him-
　　self,
Loves not nor heeds the ancestral hierar-
　　chies,
Each rank dependent on the next above
In orderly gradation fixed as fate.
King by mere manhood, nor allowing
　　aught
Of holier unction than the sweat of toil;
In his own strength sufficient; called to
　　solve,
On the rough edges of society,
Problems long sacred to the choicer few,
And improvise what elsewhere men re-
　　ceive
As gifts of deity; tough foundling reared
Where every man 's his own Melchisedek,

How make him reverent of a King of
    kings ?
Or Judge self-made, executor of laws
By him not first discussed and voted on ?
For him no tree of knowledge is forbid,
Or sweeter if forbid. How save the ark,
Or holy of holies, unprofaned a day
From his unscrupulous curiosity
That handles everything as if to buy,
Tossing aside what fabrics delicate
Suit not the rough - and - tumble of his
    ways ?
What hope for those fine-nerved humani-
    ties
That made earth gracious once with gentler
    arts,
Now the rude hands have caught the trick
    of thought
And claim an equal suffrage with the
    brain ?

The born disciple of an elder time,
(To me sufficient, friendlier than the new,)
Who in my blood feel motions of the
    Past,
I thank benignant nature most for this, —
A force of sympathy, or call it lack
Of character firm-planted, loosing me
From the pent chamber of habitual self
To dwell enlarged in alien modes of
    thought,
Haply distasteful, wholesomer for that,
And through imagination to possess,
As they were mine, the lives of other
    men.
This growth original of virgin soil,
By fascination felt in opposites,
Pleases and shocks, entices and perturbs.
In this brown-fisted rough, this shirt-sleeved
    Cid,
This backwoods Charlemagne of empires
    new,
Whose blundering heel instinctively finds
    out
The goutier foot of speechless dignities,
Who, meeting Cæsar's self, would slap
    his back,
Call him "Old Horse," and challenge to a
    drink,
My lungs draw braver air, my breast
    dilates
With ampler manhood, and I front both
    worlds,
Of sense and spirit, as my natural fiefs,
To shape and then reshape them as I will.

It was the first man's charter; why not
    mine ?
How forfeit ? when deposed in other hands ?

Thou shudder'st, Ovid ? Dost in him fore-
    bode
A new avatar of the large-limbed Goth,
To break, or seem to break, tradition's
    clue,
And chase to dreamland back thy gods
    dethroned ?
I think man's soul dwells nearer to the
    east,
Nearer to morning's fountains than the
    sun;
Herself the source whence all tradition
    sprang,
Herself at once both labyrinth and clue.
The miracle fades out of history,
But faith and wonder and the primal earth
Are born into the world with every child.
Shall this self-maker with the prying eyes,
This creature disenchanted of respect
By the New World's new fiend, Publicity,
Whose testing thumb leaves everywhere its
    smutch,
Not one day feel within himself the need
Of loyalty to better than himself,
That shall ennoble him with the upward
    look ?
Shall he not catch the Voice that wanders
    earth,
With spiritual summons, dreamed or heard,
As sometimes, just ere sleep seals up the
    sense,
We hear our mother call from deeps of
    Time,
And, waking, find it vision, — none the less
The benediction bides, old skies return,
And that unreal thing, preëminent,
Makes air and dream of all we see and
    feel ?
Shall he divine no strength unmade of
    votes,
Inward, impregnable, found soon as sought,
Not cognizable of sense, o'er sense su-
    preme ?
Else were he desolate as none before.
His holy places may not be of stone,
Nor made with hands, yet fairer far than
    aught
By artist feigned or pious ardor reared,
Fit altars for who guards inviolate
God's chosen seat, the sacred form of man.
Doubtless his church will be no hospital

For superannuate forms and mumping shams,
No parlor where men issue policies
Of life-assurance on the Eternal Mind,
Nor his religion but an ambulance
To fetch life's wounded and malingerers in,
Scorned by the strong; yet he, unconscious heir
To the influence sweet of Athens and of Rome,
And old Judæa's gift of secret fire,
Spite of himself shall surely learn to know
And worship some ideal of himself,
Some divine thing, large-hearted, brotherly,
Not nice in trifles, a soft creditor,
Pleased with his world, and hating only cant.
And, if his Church be doubtful, it is sure
That, in a world, made for whatever else,
Not made for mere enjoyment, in a world
Of toil but half-requited, or, at best,
Paid in some futile currency of breath,
A world of incompleteness, sorrow swift
And consolation laggard, whatsoe'er
The form of building or the creed professed,
The Cross, bold type of shame to homage turned,
Of an unfinished life that sways the world,
Shall tower as sovereign emblem over all.

The kobold Thought moves with us when we shift
Our dwelling to escape him; perched aloft
On the first load of household-stuff he went;·
For, where the mind goes, goes old furniture.
I, who to Chartres came to feed my eye
And give to Fancy one clear holiday,
Scarce saw the minster for the thoughts it stirred
Buzzing o'er past and future with vain quest.
Here once there stood a homely wooden church,
Which slow devotion nobly changed for this
That echoes vaguely to my modern steps.
By suffrage universal it was built,
As practised then, for all the country came
From far as Rouen, to give votes for God,
Each vote a block of stone securely laid
Obedient to the master's deep-mused plan.

Will what our ballots rear, responsible
To no grave forethought, stand so long as this?
Delight like this the eye of after days
Brightening with pride that here, at least, were men
Who meant and did the noblest thing they knew?
Can our religion cope with deeds like this?
We, too, build Gothic contract-shams, because
Our deacons have discovered that it pays,
And pews sell better under vaulted roofs
Of plaster painted like an Indian squaw.
Shall not that Western Goth, of whom we spoke,
So fiercely practical, so keen of eye,
Find out, some day, that nothing pays but God,
Served whether on the smoke-shut battle-field,
In work obscure done honestly, or vote
For truth unpopular, or faith maintained
To ruinous convictions, or good deeds
Wrought for good's sake, mindless of heaven or hell?
Shall he not learn that all prosperity,
Whose bases stretch not deeper than the sense,
Is but a trick of this world's atmosphere,
A desert-born mirage of spire and dome,
Or find too late, the Past's long lesson missed,
That dust the prophets shake from off their feet
Grows heavy to drag down both tower and wall?
I know not; but, sustained by sure belief
That man still rises level with the height
Of noblest opportunities, or makes
Such, if the time supply not, I can wait.
I gaze round on the windows, pride of France,
Each the bright gift of some mechanic guild
Who loved their city and thought gold well spent
To make her beautiful with piety;
I pause, transfigured by some stripe of bloom,
And my mind throngs with shining auguries,
Circle on circle, bright as seraphim,
With golden trumpets, silent, that await
The signal to blow news of good to men.

Then the revulsion came that always comes
After these dizzy elations of the mind:
And with a passionate pang of doubt I
cried,
" O mountain - born, sweet with snow-
filtered air
From uncontaminate wells of ether drawn
And never-broken secrecies of sky,
Freedom, with anguish won, misprized till
lost,
They keep thee not who from thy sacred
eyes
Catch the consuming lust of sensual good
And the brute's license of unfettered will.
Far from the popular shout and venal
breath
Of Cleon blowing the mob's baser mind
To bubbles of wind-piloted conceit,
Thou shrinkest, gathering up thy skirts, to
hide
In fortresses of solitary thought
And private virtue strong in self-restraint.
Must we too forfeit thee misunderstood,
Content with names, nor inly wise to know
That best things perish of their own ex-
cess,
And quality o'er-driven becomes defect ?
Nay, is it thou indeed that we have
glimpsed,
Or rather such illusion as of old
Through Athens glided menadlike and
Rome,
A shape of vapor, mother of vain dreams
And mutinous traditions, specious plea
Of the glaived tyrant and long-memoried
priest ? "

I walked forth saddened; for all thought
is sad,
And leaves a bitterish savor in the brain,
Tonic, it may be, not delectable,
And turned, reluctant, for a parting look
At those old weather-pitted images
Of bygone struggle, now so sternly calm.
About their shoulders sparrows had built
nests,
And fluttered, chirping, from gray perch
to perch,
Now on a mitre poising, now a crown,
Irreverently happy. While I thought
How confident they were, what careless
hearts
Flew on those lightsome wings and shared
the sun,
A larger shadow crossed; and looking up,

I saw where, nesting in the hoary towers,
The sparrow-hawk slid forth on noiseless
air,
With sidelong head that watched the joy
below,
Grim Norman baron o'er this clan of Kelts.
Enduring Nature, force conservative,
Indifferent to our noisy whims ! Men
prate
Of all heads to an equal grade cashiered
On level with the dullest, and expect
(Sick of no worse distemper than them-
selves)
A wondrous cure-all in equality;
They reason that To-morrow must be wise
Because To-day was not, nor Yesterday,
As if good days were shapen of themselves,
Not of the very lifeblood of men's souls;
Meanwhile, long-suffering, imperturbable,
Thou quietly complet'st thy syllogism,
And from the premise sparrow here below
Draw'st sure conclusion of the hawk above,
Pleased with the soft - billed songster,
pleased no less
With the fierce beak of natures aquiline.

Thou beautiful Old Time, now hid away
In the Past's valley of Avilion,
Haply, like Arthur, till thy wound be
healed,
Then to reclaim the sword and crown
again !
Thrice beautiful to us; perchance less fair
To who possessed thee, as a mountain
seems
To dwellers round its bases but a heap
Of barren obstacle that lairs the storm
And the avalanche's silent bolt holds back
Leashed with a hair, — meanwhile some
far-off clown,
Hereditary delver of the plain,
Sees it an unmoved vision of repose,
Nest of the morning, and conjectures there
The dance of streams to idle shepherds'
pipes,
And fairer habitations softly hung
On breezy slopes, or hid in valleys cool,
For happier men. No mortal ever dreams
That the scant isthmus he encamps upon
Between two oceans, one, the Stormy,
passed,
And one, the Peaceful, yet to venture on,
Has been that future whereto prophets
yearned
For the fulfilment of Earth's cheated hope,

Shall be that past which nerveless poets
　　moan
As the lost opportunity of song.

O Power, more near my life than life itself
(Or what seems life to us in sense im-
　　mured),
Even as the roots, shut in the darksome
　　earth,
Share in the tree-top's joyance, and con-
　　ceive
Of sunshine and wide air and wingëd
　　things
By sympathy of nature, so do I
Have evidence of Thee so far above,
Yet in and of me ! Rather Thou the root
Invisibly sustaining, hid in light,
Not darkness, or in darkness made by us.
If sometimes I must hear good men debate
Of other witness of Thyself than Thou,

As if there needed any help of ours
To nurse Thy flickering life, that else
　　must cease,
Blown out, as 't were a candle, by men's
　　breath,
My soul shall not be taken in their snare,
To change her inward surety for their
　　doubt
Muffled from sight in formal robes of
　　proof:
While she can only feel herself through
　　Thee,
I fear not Thy withdrawal; more I fear,
Seeing, to know Thee not, hoodwinked with
　　dreams
Of signs and wonders, while, unnoticed,
　　Thou,
Walking Thy garden still, commun'st with
　　men,
Missed in the commonplace of miracle.

THREE MEMORIAL POEMS

" Coscienza fusca
O della propria o dell' altrui vergogna
Pur sentirà la tua parola brusca."

If I let fall a word of bitter mirth
When public shames more shameful pardon won,
Some have misjudged me, and my service done,
If small, yet faithful, deemed of little worth:
Through veins that drew their life from Western earth
Two hundred years and more my blood hath run
In no polluted course from sire to son ;
And thus was I predestined ere my birth
To love the soil wherewith my fibres own
Instinctive sympathies ; yet love it so
As honor would, nor lightly to dethrone
Judgment, the stamp of manhood, nor forego
The son's right to a mother dearer grown
With growing knowledge and more chaste than snow.

To

E. L. GODKIN,

IN CORDIAL ACKNOWLEDGMENT OF HIS EMINENT SERVICE
IN HEIGHTENING AND PURIFYING THE TONE
OF OUR POLITICAL THOUGHT,

These Three Poems

ARE DEDICATED.

*** Readers, it is hoped, will remember that, by his Ode at the Harvard Commemo-
ration, the author had precluded himself from many of the natural outlets of thought
and feeling common to such occasions as are celebrated in these poems.

ODE

READ AT THE ONE HUNDREDTH ANNI-
VERSARY OF THE FIGHT AT CONCORD
BRIDGE

19TH APRIL, 1875

In the letter to Mr. Thayer quoted in the
note introducing the Commemoration Ode,
Lowell wrote at some length regarding the
structure of his odes in general. He added:
" The sentiment of the Concord Ode demanded
a larger proportion of lyrical movements, of
course, than the others. Harmony, without
sacrifice of melody, was what I had mainly in
view." He wrote to another friend that the
ode was " an improvisation written in the two
days before the celebration."

I

WHO cometh over the hills,
Her garments with morning sweet,
The dance of a thousand rills
Making music before her feet?
Her presence freshens the air;
Sunshine steals light from her face;
The leaden footstep of Care
Leaps to the tune of her pace,
Fairness of all that is fair,
Grace at the heart of all grace,
Sweetener of hut and of hall,
Bringer of life out of naught,
Freedom, oh, fairest of all
The daughters of Time and Thought!

II

She cometh, cometh to-day:
Hark! hear ye not her tread,
Sending a thrill through your clay,
Under the sod there, ye dead,
Her nurslings and champions?
Do ye not hear, as she comes,
The bay of the deep-mouthed guns,
The gathering rote of the drums?
The bells that called ye to prayer,
How wildly they clamor on her,
Crying, " She cometh! prepare
Her to praise and her to honor,
That a hundred years ago
Scattered here in blood and tears
Potent seeds wherefrom should grow
Gladness for a hundred years!"

III

Tell me, young men, have ye seen
Creature of diviner mien
For true hearts to long and cry for,
Manly hearts to live and die for?
What hath she that others want?
Brows that all endearments haunt,
Eyes that make it sweet to dare,
Smiles that cheer untimely death,
Looks that fortify despair,
Tones more brave than trumpet's breath;
Tell me, maidens, have ye known
Household charm more sweetly rare,
Grace of woman ampler blown,
Modesty more debonair,
Younger heart with wit full grown?
Oh for an hour of my prime,
The pulse of my hotter years,
That I might praise her in rhyme
Would tingle your eyelids to tears,
Our sweetness, our strength, and our star,
Our hope, our joy, and our trust,
Who lifted us out of the dust,
And made us whatever we are!

IV

Whiter than moonshine upon snow
Her raiment is, but round the hem
Crimson stained; and, as to and fro
Her sandals flash, we see on them,
And on her instep veined with blue,
Flecks of crimson, on those fair feet,
High-arched, Diana-like, and fleet,
Fit for no grosser stain than dew:
Oh, call them rather chrisms than stains,
Sacred and from heroic veins!
For, in the glory-guarded pass,
Her haughty and far-shining head
She bowed to shrive Leonidas
With his imperishable dead;
Her, too, Morgarten saw,
Where the Swiss lion fleshed his icy paw;
She followed Cromwell's quenchless star
Where the grim Puritan tread
Shook Marston, Naseby, and Dunbar:
Yea, on her feet are dearer dyes
Yet fresh, nor looked on with untearful
    eyes.

V

Our fathers found her in the woods
Where Nature meditates and broods,
The seeds of unexampled things

Which Time to consummation brings
Through life and death and man's unstable
    moods;
They met her here, not recognized,
A sylvan huntress clothed in furs,
To whose chaste wants her bow sufficed,
Nor dreamed what destinies were hers:
She taught them bee-like to create
Their simpler forms of Church and State;
She taught them to endue
The past with other functions than it knew,
And turn in channels strange the uncertain
    stream of Fate;
Better than all, she fenced them in their
    need
With iron-handed Duty's sternest creed,
'Gainst Self's lean wolf that ravens word
    and deed.

VI

Why cometh she hither to-day
To this low village of the plain
Far from the Present's loud highway,
From Trade's cool heart and seething brain?
Why cometh she? She was not far away.
Since the soul touched it, not in vain,
With pathos of immortal gain,
'T is here her fondest memories stay.
She loves yon pine-bemurmured ridge
Where now our broad-browed poet sleeps,
Dear to both Englands; near him he
Who wore the ring of Canace;
But most her heart to rapture leaps
Where stood that era-parting bridge,
O'er which, with footfall still as dew,
The Old Time passed into the New;
Where, as your stealthy river creeps,
He whispers to his listening weeds
Tales of sublimest homespun deeds.
Here English law and English thought
'Gainst the self-will of England fought;
And here were men (coequal with their
    fate),
Who did great things, unconscious they
    were great.
They dreamed not what a die was cast
With that first answering shot; what then?
There was their duty; they were men
Schooled the soul's inward gospel to obey,
Though leading to the lion's den.
They felt the habit-hallowed world give way
Beneath their lives, and on went they,
Unhappy who was last.
When Buttrick gave the word,
That awful idol of the unchallenged Past,

Strong in their love, and in their lineage
    strong,
Fell crashing: if they heard it not,
Yet the earth heard,
Nor ever hath forgot,
As on from startled throne to throne,
Where Superstition sate or conscious
    Wrong,
A shudder ran of some dread birth un-
    known.
Thrice venerable spot!
River more fateful than the Rubicon!
O'er those red planks, to snatch her diadem,
Man's Hope, star-girdled, sprang with them,
And over ways untried the feet of Doom
    strode on.

VII

Think you these felt no charms
In their gray homesteads and embowered
    farms?
In household faces waiting at the door
Their evening step should lighten up no
    more?
In fields their boyish feet had known?
In trees their fathers' hands had set,
And which with them had grown,
Widening each year their leafy coronet?
Felt they no pang of passionate regret
For those unsolid goods that seem so much
    our own?
These things are dear to every man that
    lives,
And life prized more for what it lends than
    gives.
Yea, many a tie, through iteration sweet,
Strove to detain their fatal feet;
And yet the enduring half they chose,
Whose choice decides a man life's slave or
    king,
The invisible things of God before the seen
    and known:
Therefore their memory inspiration blows
With echoes gathering on from zone to
    zone;
For manhood is the one immortal thing
Beneath Time's changeful sky,
And, where it lightened once, from age to
    age,
Men come to learn, in grateful pilgrimage,
That length of days is knowing when to die.

VIII

What marvellous change of things and men!
She, a world-wandering orphan then,

So mighty now! Those are her streams
That whirl the myriad, myriad wheels
Of all that does, and all that dreams,
Of all that thinks, and all that feels,
Through spaces stretched from sea to sea;
By idle tongues and busy brains,
By who doth right, and who refrains,
Hers are our losses and our gains;
Our maker and our victim she.

IX

Maiden half mortal, half divine,
We triumphed in thy coming; to the brinks
Our hearts were filled with pride's tumul-
tuous wine;
Better to-day who rather feels than thinks.
Yet will some graver thoughts intrude,
And cares of sterner mood;
They won thee: who shall keep thee? From
the deeps
Where discrowned empires o'er their ruins
brood,
And many a thwarted hope wrings its weak
hands and weeps,
I hear the voice as of a mighty wind
From all heaven's caverns rushing uncon-
fined,
"I, Freedom, dwell with Knowledge: I
abide
With men whom dust of faction cannot blind
To the slow tracings of the Eternal Mind;
With men by culture trained and fortified,
Who bitter duty to sweet lusts prefer,
Fearless to counsel and obey.
Conscience my sceptre is, and law my
° sword,
Not to be drawn in passion or in play,
But terrible to punish and deter;
Implacable as God's word,
Like it, a shepherd's crook to them that
blindly err.
Your firm-pulsed sires, my martyrs and my
saints,
Offshoots of that one stock whose patient
sense
Hath known to mingle flux with perma-
nence,
Rated my chaste denials and restraints
Above the moment's dear-paid paradise:
Beware lest, shifting with Time's gradual
creep,
The light that guided shine into your eyes.
The envious Powers of ill nor wink nor
sleep:
Be therefore timely wise,

Nor laugh when this one steals, and that
one lies,
As if your luck could cheat those sleepless
spies,
Till the deaf Fury comes your house to
sweep!"
I hear the voice, and unaffrighted bow;
Ye shall not be prophetic now,
Heralds of ill, that darkening fly
Between my vision and the rainbowed sky,
Or on the left your hoarse forebodings
croak
From many a blasted bough
On Yggdrasil's storm-sinewed oak,
That once was green, Hope of the West, as
thou:
Yet pardon if I tremble while I boast;
For I have loved as those who pardon most.

X

Away, ungrateful doubt, away!
At least she is our own to-day.
Break into rapture, my song,
Verses, leap forth in the sun,
Bearing the joyance along
Like a train of fire as ye run!
Pause not for choosing of words,
Let them but blossom and sing
Blithe as the orchards and birds
With the new coming of spring!
Dance in your jollity, bells;
Shout, cannon; cease not, ye drums;
Answer, ye hillside and dells;
Bow, all ye people! She comes,
Radiant, calm-fronted, as when
She hallowed that April day.
Stay with us! Yes, thou shalt stay,
Softener and strengthener of men,
Freedom, not won by the vain,
Not to be courted in play,
Not to be kept without pain.
Stay with us! Yes, thou wilt stay,
Handmaid and mistress of all,
Kindler of deed and of thought,
Thou that to hut and to hall
Equal deliverance brought!
Souls of her martyrs, draw near,
Touch our dull lips with your fire,
That we may praise without fear
Her our delight, our desire,
Our faith's inextinguishable star,
Our hope, our remembrance, our trust,
Our present, our past, our to be,
Who will mingle her life with our dust
And makes us deserve to be free!

UNDER THE OLD ELM

POEM READ AT CAMBRIDGE ON THE
HUNDREDTH ANNIVERSARY OF WASH-
INGTON'S TAKING COMMAND OF THE
AMERICAN ARMY, 3D JULY, 1775

Lowell was disposed to think this ode the
best of these three memorial odes, "mainly be-
cause," he says, "it was composed after my
college duties were over, though even in that
I was distracted by the intervention of the
Commencement dinner." Two days after de-
livering it, he wrote to a friend in another
State: "We, too, here in my birthplace, hav-
ing found out that something happened here
a hundred years ago, must have our centen-
nial; and, since my friend and townsman Dr.
Holmes could n't be had, I felt bound to do
the poetry for the day. We have still stand-
ing the elm under which Washington took
command of the *American* (till then *provin-
cial*) army, and under which also Whitefield
had preached some thirty years before. I took
advantage of the occasion to hold out a hand
of kindly reconciliation to Virginia. I could
do it with the profounder feeling, that no
family lost more than mine by the civil war.
Three nephews (the hope of our race) were
killed in one or other of the Virginia battles,
and three cousins on other of those bloody
fields." Lowell afterward, when he was in
Baltimore giving lectures at Johns Hopkins
University, read a part of this poem in public.
"I actually drew tears," he wrote, "from the
eyes of bitter secessionists — comparable with
those iron ones that rattled down Pluto's cheek.
I did n't quite like to read the invocation to
Virginia here — I was willing enough three or
four hundred miles north — but I think it did
good."

I

I.

WORDS pass as wind, but where great
    deeds were done
A power abides transfused from sire to
    son:
The boy feels deeper meanings thrill his
    ear,
That tingling through his pulse life-long
    shall run,
With sure impulsion to keep honor clear,
When, pointing down, his father whispers,
    " Here,
Here, where we stand, stood he, the purely
    great,

Whose soul no siren passion could unsphere,
Then nameless, now a power and mixed
    with fate."
Historic town, thou holdest sacred dust,
Once known to men as pious, learnèd, just,
And one memorial pile that dares to last;
But Memory greets with reverential kiss
No spot in all thy circuit sweet as this,
Touched by that modest glory as it past,
O'er which yon elm hath piously displayed
These hundred years its monumental shade.

2.

Of our swift passage through this scenery
Of life and death, more durable than we,
What landmark so congenial as a tree
Repeating its green legend every spring,
And, with a yearly ring,
Recording the fair seasons as they flee,
Type of our brief but still-renewed mortal-
    ity ?
We fall as leaves: the immortal trunk re-
    mains,
Builded with costly juice of hearts and
    brains
Gone to the mould now, whither all that
    be
Vanish returnless, yet are procreant still
In human lives to come of good or ill,
And feed unseen the roots of Destiny.

II

I.

Men's monuments, grown old, forget their
    names
They should eternize, but the place
Where shining souls have passed imbibes a
    grace
Beyond mere earth; some sweetness of
    their fames
Leaves in the soil its unextinguished trace,
Pungent, pathetic, sad with nobler aims,
That penetrates our lives and heightens
    them or shames.
This insubstantial world and fleet
Seems solid for a moment when we stand
On dust ennobled by heroic feet
Once mighty to sustain a tottering land,
And mighty still such burthen to upbear,
Nor doomed to tread the path of things
    that merely were:
Our sense, refined with virtue of the spot,
Across the mists of Lethe's sleepy stream
Recalls him, the sole chief without a blot,

No more a pallid image and a dream,
But as he dwelt with men decorously supreme.

2.

Our grosser minds need this terrestrial hint
To raise long-buried days from tombs of print:
" Here stood he," softly we repeat,
And lo, the statue shrined and still
In that gray minster-front we call the Past,
Feels in its frozen veins our pulses thrill,
Breathes living air and mocks at Death's deceit.
It warms, it stirs, comes down to us at last,
Its features human with familiar light,
A man, beyond the historian's art to kill,
Or sculptor's to efface with patient chisel-blight.

3.

Sure the dumb earth hath memory, nor for naught
Was Fancy given, on whose enchanted loom
Present and Past commingle, fruit and bloom
Of one fair bough, inseparably wrought
Into the seamless tapestry of thought.
So charmed, with undeluded eye we see
In history's fragmentary tale
Bright clues of continuity,
Learn that high natures over Time prevail,
And feel ourselves a link in that entail
That binds all ages past with all that are to be.

III

I.

Beneath our consecrated elm
A century ago he stood,
Famed vaguely for that old fight in the wood
Whose red surge sought, but could not overwhelm
The life foredoomed to wield our rough-hewn helm: —
From colleges, where now the gown
To arms had yielded, from the town,
Our rude self-summoned levies flocked to see
The new-come chiefs and wonder which was he.

No need to question long; close-lipped and tall,
Long trained in murder-brooding forests lone
To bridle others' clamors and his own,
Firmly erect, he towered above them all,
The incarnate discipline that was to free
With iron curb that armed democracy.

2.

A motley rout was that which came to stare,
In raiment tanned by years of sun and storm,
Of every shape that was not uniform,
Dotted with regimentals here and there;
An army all of captains, used to pray
And stiff in fight, but serious drill's despair,
Skilled to debate their orders, not obey;
Deacons were there, selectmen, men of note
In half-tamed hamlets ambushed round with woods,
Ready to settle Freewill by a vote,
But largely liberal to its private moods;
Prompt to assert by manners, voice, or pen,
Or ruder arms, their rights as Englishmen,
Nor much fastidious as to how and when:
Yet seasoned stuff and fittest to create
A thought-staid army or a lasting state:
Haughty they said he was, at first; severe;
But owned, as all men own, the steady hand
Upon the bridle, patient to command,
Prized, as all prize, the justice pure from fear,
And learned to honor first, then love him, then revere.
Such power there is in clear-eyed self-restraint
And purpose clean as light from every selfish taint.

3.

Musing beneath the legendary tree,
The years between furl off: I seem to see
The sun-flecks, shaken the stirred foliage through,
Dapple with gold his sober buff and blue
And weave prophetic aureoles round the head
That shines our beacon now nor darkens with the dead.
O man of silent mood,
A stranger among strangers then,

How art thou since renowned the Great,
the Good,
Familiar as the day in all the homes of
men !
The wingëd years, that winnow praise and
blame,
Blow many names out : they but fan to
flame
The self-renewing splendors of thy fame.

IV

1.

How many subtlest influences unite,
With spiritual touch of joy or pain,
Invisible as air and soft as light,
To body forth that image of the brain
We call our Country, visionary shape,
Loved more than woman, fuller of fire
than wine,
Whose charm can none define,
Nor any, though he flee it, can escape !
All party-colored threads the weaver Time
Sets in his web, now trivial, now sublime,
All memories, all forebodings, hopes and
fears,
Mountain and river, forest, prairie, sea,
A hill, a rock, a homestead, field, or tree,
The casual gleanings of unreckoned years,
Take goddess-shape at last and there is
She,
Old at our birth, new as the springing
hours,
Shrine of our weakness, fortress of our
powers,
Consoler, kindler, peerless 'mid her peers,
A force that 'neath our conscious being
stirs,
A life to give ours permanence, when we
Are borne to mingle our poor earth with
hers,
And all this glowing world goes with us on
our biers.

2.

Nations are long results, by ruder ways
Gathering the might that warrants length
of days;
They may be pieced of half-reluctant
shares
Welded by hammer-strokes of broad-
brained kings,
Or from a doughty people grow, the heirs
Of wise traditions widening cautious rings;
At best they are computable things,

A strength behind us making us feel bold
In right, or, as may chance, in wrong;
Whose force by figures may be summed
and told,
So many soldiers, ships, and dollars strong,
And we but drops that bear compulsory
part
In the dumb throb of a mechanic heart;
But Country is a shape of each man's
mind
Sacred from definition, unconfined
By the cramped walls where daily drudger-
ies grind;
An inward vision, yet an outward birth
Of sweet familiar heaven and earth;
A brooding Presence that stirs motions
blind
Of wings within our embryo being's shell
That wait but her completer spell
To make us eagle-natured, fit to dare
Life's nobler spaces and untarnished air.

3.

You, who hold dear this self-conceived
ideal,
Whose faith and works alone can make it
real,
Bring all your fairest gifts to deck her
shrine
Who lifts our lives away from Thine and
Mine
And feeds the lamp of manhood more di-
vine
With fragrant oils of quenchless constancy.
When all have done their utmost, surely he
Hath given the best who gives a character
Erect and constant, which nor any shock
Of loosened elements, nor the forceful sea
Of flowing or of ebbing fates, can stir
From its deep bases in the living rock
Of ancient manhood's sweet security :
And this he gave, serenely far from pride
As baseness, boon with prosperous stars
allied,
Part of what nobler seed shall in our loins
abide.

4.

No bond of men as common pride so
strong,
In names time-filtered for the lips of song,
Still operant, with the primal Forces bound
Whose currents, on their spiritual round,
Transfuse our mortal will nor are gain-
said :

These are their arsenals, these the exhaust-
less mines
That give a constant heart in great de-
signs;
These are the stuff whereof such dreams
are made
As make heroic men : thus surely he
Still holds in place the massy blocks he
laid
'Neath our new frame, enforcing soberly
The self-control that makes and keeps a
people free.

V

1.

Oh, for a drop of that Cornelian ink
Which gave Agricola dateless length of
days,
To celebrate him fitly, neither swerve
To phrase unkempt, nor pass discretion's
brink,
With him so statue-like in sad reserve,
So diffident to claim, so forward to de-
serve !
Nor need I shun due influence of his fame
Who, mortal among mortals, seemed as
now
The equestrian shape with unimpassioned
brow,
That paces silent on through vistas of ac-
claim.

2.

What figure more immovably august
Than that grave strength so patient and so
pure,
Calm in good fortune, when it wavered,
sure,
That mind serene, impenetrably just,
Modelled on classic lines so simple they
endure ?
That soul so softly radiant and so white
The track it left seems less of fire than
light,
Cold but to such as love distemperature ?
And if pure light, as some deem, be the
force
That drives rejoicing planets on their
course,
Why for his power benign seek an impurer
source ?
His was the true enthusiasm that burns
long,
Domestically bright,

Fed from itself and shy of human sight,
The hidden force that makes a lifetime
strong,
And not the short-lived fuel of a song.
Passionless, say you ? What is passion
for
But to sublime our natures and control
To front heroic toils with late return,
Or none, or such as shames the conqueror ?
That fire was fed with substance of the
soul
And not with holiday stubble, that could
burn,
Unpraised of men who after bonfires run,
Through seven slow years of unadvancing
war,
Equal when fields were lost or fields were
won,
With breath of popular applause or blame,
Nor fanned nor damped, unquenchably the
same,
Too inward to be reached by flaws of idle
fame.

3.

Soldier and statesman, rarest unison ;
High-poised example of great duties done
Simply as breathing, a world's honors worn
As life's indifferent gifts to all men born;
Dumb for himself, unless it were to God,
But for his barefoot soldiers eloquent,
Tramping the snow to coral where they
trod,
Held by his awe in hollow-eyed content;
Modest, yet firm as Nature's self; un-
blamed
Save by the men his nobler temper
shamed;
Never seduced through show of present
good
By other than unsetting lights to steer
New-trimmed in Heaven, nor than his
steadfast mood
More steadfast, far from rashness as from
fear;
Rigid, but with himself first, grasping still
In swerveless poise the wave-beat helm of
will;
Not honored then or now because he wooed
The popular voice, but that he still with-
stood;
Broad-minded, higher-souled, there is but
one
Who was all this and ours, and all men's,
— WASHINGTON.

4.

Minds strong by fits, irregularly great,
That flash and darken like revolving lights,
Catch more the vulgar eye unschooled to
    wait
On the long curve of patient days and
    nights
Rounding a whole life to the circle fair
Of orbed fulfilment; and this balanced
    soul,
So simple in its grandeur, coldly bare
Of draperies theatric, standing there
In perfect symmetry of self-control,
Seems not so great at first, but greater
    grows
Still as we look, and by experience learn
How grand this quiet is, how nobly stern
The discipline that wrought through life-
    long throes
That energetic passion of repose.

5.

A nature too decorous and severe,
Too self-respectful in its griefs and joys,
For ardent girls and boys
Who find no genius in a mind so clear
That its grave depths seem obvious and
    near,
Nor a soul great that made so little noise.
They feel no force in that calm-cadenced
    phrase,
The habitual full-dress of his well-bred
    mind,
That seems to pace the minuet's courtly
    maze
And tell of ampler leisures, roomier length
    of days.
His firm-based brain, to self so little kind
That no tumultuary blood could blind,
Formed to control men, not amaze,
Looms not like those that borrow height of
    haze:
It was a world of statelier movement then
Than this we fret in, he a denizen
Of that ideal Rome that made a man for
    men.

VI

I.

The longer on this earth we live
And weigh the various qualities of men,
Seeing how most are fugitive,
Or fitful gifts, at best, of now and then,

Wind-wavered corpse-lights, daughters of
    the fen,
The more we feel the high stern-featured
    beauty
Of plain devotedness to duty,
Steadfast and still, nor paid with mortal
    praise,
But finding amplest recompense
For life's ungarlanded expense
In work done squarely and unwasted days.
For this we honor him, that he could know
How sweet the service and how free
Of her, God's eldest daughter here below,
And choose in meanest raiment which was
    she.

2.

Placid completeness, life without a fall
From faith or highest aims, truth's breach-
    less wall,
Surely if any fame can bear the touch,
His will say " Here ! " at the last trumpet's
    call,
The unexpressive man whose life expressed
    so much.

VII

I.

Never to see a nation born
Hath been given to mortal man,
Unless to those who, on that summer morn,
Gazed silent when the great Virginian
Unsheathed the sword whose fatal flash
Shot union through the incoherent clash
Of our loose atoms, crystallizing them
Around a single will's unpliant stem,
And making purpose of emotion rash.
Out of that scabbard sprang, as from its
    womb,
Nebulous at first but hardening to a star,
Through mutual share of sunburst and of
    gloom,
The common faith that made us what we
    are.

2.

That lifted blade transformed our jangling
    clans,
Till then provincial, to Americans,
And made a unity of wildering plans;
Here was the doom fixed: here is marked
    the date
When this New World awoke to man's
    estate,

Burnt its last ship and ceased to look be-
    hind:
Nor thoughtless was the choice; no love or
    hate
Could from its poise move that deliberate
    mind,
Weighing between too early and too late
Those pitfalls of the man refused by Fate:
His was the impartial vision of the great
Who see not as they wish, but as they find.
He saw the dangers of defeat, nor less
The incomputable perils of success;
The sacred past thrown by, an empty rind;
The future, cloud-land, snare of prophets
    blind;
The waste of war, the ignominy of peace;
On either hand a sullen rear of woes,
Whose garnered lightnings none could
    guess,
Piling its thunder - heads and muttering
    " Cease ! "
Yet drew not back his hand, but gravely
    chose
The seeming-desperate task whence our
    new nation rose.

3.

A noble choice and of immortal seed!
Nor deem that acts heroic wait on chance
Or easy were as in a boy's romance;
The man's whole life preludes the single
    deed
That shall decide if his inheritance
Be with the sifted few of matchless breed,
Our race's sap and sustenance,
Or with the unmotived herd that only sleep
    and feed.
Choice seems a thing indifferent; thus or so,
What matters it?   The Fates with mock-
    ing face
Look on inexorable, nor seem to know
Where the lot lurks that gives life's fore-
    most place.
Yet Duty's leaden casket holds it still,
And but two ways are offered to our will,
Toil with rare triumph, ease with safe dis-
    grace,
The problem still for us and all of human
    race.
He chose, as men choose, where most dan·
    ger showed,
Nor ever faltered 'neath the load
Of petty cares, that gall great hearts the
    most,
But kept right on the strenuous up-hill road,

Strong to the end, above complaint or boast:
The popular tempest on his rock-mailed
    coast
Wasted its wind-borne spray,
The noisy marvel of a day;
His soul sate still in its unstormed abode.

VIII

Virginia gave us this imperial man
Cast in the massive mould
Of those high-statured ages old
Which into grander forms our mortal metal
    ran;
She gave us this unblemished gentleman:
What shall we give her back but love and
    praise
As in the dear old unestrangëd days
Before the inevitable wrong began?
Mother of States and undiminished men,
Thou gavest us a country, giving him,
And we owe alway what we owed thee then:
The boon thou wouldst have snatched from
    us agen
Shines as before with no abatement dim.
A great man's memory is the only thing
With influence to outlast the present whim
And bind us as when here he knit our
    golden ring.
All of him that was subject to the hours
Lies in thy soil and makes it part of ours:
Across more recent graves,
Where unresentful Nature waves
Her pennons o'er the shot-ploughed sod,
Proclaiming the sweet Truce of God,
We from this consecrated plain stretch out
Our hands as free from afterthought or
    doubt
As here the united North
Poured her embrownëd manhood forth
In welcome of our savior and thy son.
Through battle we have better learned thy
    worth,
The long-breathed valor and undaunted
    will,
Which, like his own, the day's disaster
    done,
Could, safe in manhood, suffer and be still.
Both thine and ours the victory hardly
    won;
If ever with distempered voice or pen
We have misdeemed thee, here we take it
    back,
And for the dead of both don common
    black.
Be to us evermore as thou wast then,

As we forget thou hast not always been,
Mother of States and unpolluted men,
Virginia, fitly named from England's manly
    queen!

AN ODE

FOR THE FOURTH OF JULY, 1876

I

I.

ENTRANCED I saw a vision in the cloud
That loitered dreaming in yon sunset sky,
Full of fair shapes, half creatures of the
    eye,
Half chance-evoked by the wind's fantasy
In golden mist, an ever-shifting crowd:
There, 'mid unreal forms that came and
    went
In air-spun robes, of evanescent dye,
A woman's semblance shone preëminent;
Not armed like Pallas, not like Hera proud,
But, as on household diligence intent,
Beside her visionary wheel she bent
Like Aretë or Bertha, nor than they
Less queenly in her port : about her knee
Glad children clustered confident in play:
Placid her pose, the calm of energy;
And over her broad brow in many a round
(That loosened would have gilt her gar-
    ment's hem),
Succinct, as toil prescribes, the hair was
    wound
In lustrous coils, a natural diadem.
The cloud changed shape, obsequious to the
    whim
Of some transmuting influence felt in me,
And, looking now, a wolf I seemed to see
Limned in that vapor, gaunt and hunger-
    bold,
Threatening her charge: resolve in every
    limb,
Erect she flamed in mail of sun-wove gold,
Penthesilea's self for battle dight;
One arm uplifted braced a flickering spear,
And one her adamantine shield made light;
Her face, helm-shadowed, grew a thing to
    fear,
And her fierce eyes, by danger challenged,
    took
Her trident - sceptred mother's dauntless
    look.
"I know thee now, O goddess-born!" I
    cried,

And turned with loftier brow and firmer
    stride;
For in that spectral cloud-work I had seen
Her image, bodied forth by love and pride,
The fearless, the benign, the mother-eyed,
The fairer world's toil-consecrated queen.

2.

What shape by exile dreamed elates the
    mind
Like hers whose hand, a fortress of the
    poor,
No blood in vengeance spilt, though lawful,
    stains ?
Who never turned a suppliant from her
    door ?
Whose conquests are the gains of all man-
    kind ?
To-day her thanks shall fly on every wind,
Unstinted, unrebuked, from shore to shore,
One love, one hope, and not a doubt behind !
Cannon to cannon shall repeat her praise,
Banner to banner flap it forth in flame;
Her children shall rise up to bless her
    name,
And wish her harmless length of days,
The mighty mother of a mighty brood,
Blessed in all tongues and dear to every
    blood,
The beautiful, the strong, and, best of all,
    the good.

3.

Seven years long was the bow
Of battle bent, and the heightening
Storm-heaps convulsed with the throe
Of their uncontainable lightning;
Seven years long heard the sea
Crash of navies and wave-borne thunder;
Then drifted the cloud-rack a-lee,
And new stars were seen, a world's won-
    der;
Each by her sisters made bright,
All binding all to their stations,
Cluster of manifold light
Startling the old constellations:
Men looked up and grew pale:
Was it a comet or star,
Omen of blessing or bale,
Hung o'er the ocean afar ?

4.

Stormy the day of her birth:
Was she not born of the strong,
She, the last ripeness of earth,

Beautiful, prophesied long ?
Stormy the days of her prime:
Hers are the pulses that beat
Higher for perils sublime,
Making them fawn at her feet.
Was she not born of the strong ?
Was she not born of the wise ?
Daring and counsel belong
Of right to her confident eyes:
Human and motherly they,
Careless of station or race:
Hearken ! her children to-day
Shout for the joy of her face.

II

I.

No praises of the past are hers,
No fanes by hallowing time caressed,
No broken arch that ministers
To Time's sad instinct in the breast:
She has not gathered from the years
Grandeur of tragedies and tears,
Nor from long leisure the unrest
That finds repose in forms of classic grace:
These may delight the coming race
Who haply shall not count it to our crime
That we who fain would sing are here
before our time.
She also hath her monuments;
Not such as stand decrepitly resigned
To ruin-mark the path of dead events
That left no seed of better days behind,
The tourist's pensioners that show their
scars
And maunder of forgotten wars ;
She builds not on the ground, but in the
mind,
Her open-hearted palaces
For larger-thoughted men with heaven and
earth at ease :
Her march the plump mow marks, the
sleepless wheel,
The golden sheaf, the self-swayed com-
monweal ;
The happy homesteads hid in orchard
trees
Whose sacrificial smokes through peaceful
air
Rise lost in heaven, the household's silent
prayer;
What architect hath bettered these ?
With softened eye the westward traveller
sees
A thousand miles of neighbors side by side,

Holding by toil-won titles fresh from God
The lands no serf or seigneur ever trod,
With manhood latent in the very sod,
Where the long billow of the wheatfield's
tide
Flows to the sky across the prairie wide,
A sweeter vision than the castled Rhine,
Kindly with thoughts of Ruth and Bible-
days benign.

2.

O ancient commonwealths, that we revere
Haply because we could not know you
near,
Your deeds like statues down the aisles of
Time
Shine peerless in memorial calm sublime,
And Athens is a trumpet still, and Rome;
Yet which of your achievements is not foam
Weighed with this one of hers (below you
far
In fame, and born beneath a milder star),
That to Earth's orphans, far as curves the
dome
Of death-deaf sky, the bounteous West
means home,
With dear precedency of natural ties
That stretch from roof to roof and make
men gently wise ?
And if the nobler passions wane,
Distorted to base use, if the near goal
Of insubstantial gain
Tempt from the proper race-course of the
soul
That crowns their patient breath
Whose feet, song-sandalled, are too fleet
for Death,
Yet may she claim one privilege urbane
And haply first upon the civic roll,
That none can breathe her air nor grow
humane.

3.

Oh, better far the briefest hour
Of Athens self-consumed, whose plastic
power
Hid Beauty safe from Death in words or
stone;
Of Rome, fair quarry where those eagles
crowd
Whose fulgurous vans about the world had
blown
Triumphant storm and seeds of polity;
Of Venice, fading o'er her shipless sea,
Last iridescence of a sunset cloud;

Than this inert prosperity,
This bovine comfort in the sense alone !
Yet art came slowly even to such as those,
Whom no past genius cheated of their own
With prudence of o'ermastering precedent;
Petal by petal spreads the perfect rose,
Secure of the divine event;
And only children rend the bud half-blown
To forestall Nature in her calm intent:
Time hath a quiver full of purposes
Which miss not of their aim, to us un-
  known,
And brings about the impossible with ease:
Haply for us the ideal dawn shall break
From where in legend-tinted line
The peaks of Hellas drink the morning's
  wine,
To tremble on our lids with mystic sign
Till the drowsed ichor in our veins awake
And set our pulse in tune with moods
  divine:
Long the day lingered in its sea-fringed
  nest,
Then touched the Tuscan hills with golden
  lance
And paused; then on to Spain and France
The splendor flew, and Albion's misty
  crest:
Shall Ocean bar him from his destined
  West ?
Or are we, then, arrived too late,
Doomed with the rest to grope disconsolate,
Foreclosed of Beauty by our modern date ?

III

I.

Poets, as their heads grow gray,
Look from too far behind the eyes,
Too long-experienced to be wise
In guileless youth's diviner way;
Life sings not now, but prophesies;
Time's shadows they, no more behold,
But, under them, the riddle old
That mocks, bewilders, and defies:
In childhood's face the seed of shame,
In the green tree an ambushed flame,
In Phosphor a vaunt-guard of Night,
They, though against their will, divine,
And dread the care-dispelling wine
Stored from the Muse's vintage bright,
By age imbued with second-sight.
From Faith's own eyelids there peeps out,
Even as they look, the leer of doubt;
The festal wreath their fancy loads

With care that whispers and forebodes:
Nor this our triumph-day can blunt Me-
gæra's goads.

2.

Murmur of many voices in the air
Denounces us degenerate,
Unfaithful guardians of a noble fate,
And prompts indifference or despair:
Is this the country that we dreamed in
  youth,
Where wisdom and not numbers should
  have weight,
Seed-field of simpler manners, braver truth,
Where shams should cease to dominate
In household, church, and state ?
Is this Atlantis ?   This the unpoisoned soil,
Sea-whelmed for ages and recovered late,
Where parasitic greed no more should coil
Round Freedom's stem to bend awry and
  blight
What grew so fair, sole plant of love and
  light ?
Who sit where once in crowned seclusion sate
The long-proved athletes of debate
Trained from their youth, as none thinks
  needful now ?
Is this debating club where boys dispute,
And wrangle o'er their stolen fruit,
The Senate, erewhile cloister of the few,
Where Clay once flashed and Webster's
  cloudy brow
Brooded those bolts of thought that all the
  horizon knew ?

3.

Oh, as this pensive moonlight blurs my
  pines,
Here while I sit and meditate these lines,
To gray-green dreams of what they are by
  day,
So would some light, not reason's sharp-
  edged ray,
Trance me in moonshine as before the
  flight
Of years had won me this unwelcome right
To see things as they are, or shall be soon,
In the frank prose of undissembling noon !

4.

Back to my breast, ungrateful sigh !
Whoever fails, whoever errs,
The penalty be ours, not hers !
The present still seems vulgar, seen too
  nigh;

The golden age is still the age that 's past:
I ask no drowsy opiate
To dull my vision of that only state
Founded on faith in man, and therefore
    sure to last.
For, O my country, touched by thee,
The gray hairs gather back their gold;
Thy thought sets all my pulses free;
The heart refuses to be old;
The love is all that I can see.
Not to thy natal-day belong
Time's prudent doubt or age's wrong,
But gifts of gratitude and song:
Unsummoned crowd the thankful words,
As sap in spring-time floods the tree,
Foreboding the return of birds,
For all that thou hast been to me !

IV

1.

Flawless his heart and tempered to the
    core
Who, beckoned by the forward-leaning
    wave,
First left behind him the firm-footed shore,
And, urged by every nerve of sail and
    oar,
Steered for the Unknown which gods to
    mortals gave,
Of thought and action the mysterious door,
Bugbear of fools, a summons to the brave:
Strength found he in the unsympathizing
    sun,
And strange stars from beneath the horizon
    won,
And the dumb ocean pitilessly grave:
High-hearted surely he;
But bolder they who first off-cast
Their moorings from the habitable Past
And ventured chartless on the sea
Of storm-engendering Liberty:
For all earth's width of waters is a span,
And their convulsed existence mere repose,
Matched with the unstable heart of man,
Shoreless in wants, mist-girt in all it
    knows,
Open to every wind of sect or clan,
And sudden-passionate in ebbs and flows.

2.

They steered by stars the elder shipmen
    knew,
And laid their courses where the currents
    draw

Of ancient wisdom channelled deep in law,
The undaunted few
Who changed the Old World for the New,
And more devoutly prized
Than all perfection theorized
The more imperfect that had roots and
    grew.
They founded deep and well,
Those danger-chosen chiefs of men
Who still believed in Heaven and Hell,
Nor hoped to find a spell,
In some fine flourish of a pen,
To make a better man
Than long-considering Nature will or can,
Secure against his own mistakes,
Content with what life gives or takes,
And acting still on some fore-ordered plan,
A cog of iron in an iron wheel,
Too nicely poised to think or feel,
Dumb motor in a clock-like commonweal.
They wasted not their brain in schemes
Of what man might be in some bubble-
    sphere,
As if he must be other than he seems
Because he was not what he should be
    here,
Postponing Time's slow proof to petulant
    dreams:
Yet herein they were great
Beyond the incredulous lawgivers of yore,
And wiser than the wisdom of the shelf,
That they conceived a deeper-rooted state,
Of hardier growth, alive from rind to core,
By making man sole sponsor of himself.

3.

God of our fathers, Thou who wast,
Art, and shalt be when those eye-wise who
    flout
Thy secret presence shall be lost
In the great light that dazzles them to
    doubt,
We, sprung from loins of stalwart men
Whose strength was in their trust
That Thou wouldst make thy dwelling in
    their dust
And walk with those a fellow-citizen
Who build a city of the just,
We, who believe Life's bases rest
Beyond the probe of chemic test,
Still, like our fathers, feel Thee near,
Sure that, while lasts the immutable de-
    cree,
The land to Human Nature dear
Shall not be unbeloved of Thee.

HEARTSEASE AND RUE

THIS title was given to the volume of poems collected and published in 1888 after Lowell's return to private life. He took occasion to glean after his earlier harvest and preserved in it several poems written before the publication of *Under the Willows.*

I. FRIENDSHIP

AGASSIZ

Come
Dicesti *egli ebbe?* non viv' egli ancora?
Non fiere gli occhi suoi lo dolce lome?

Lowell was in Florence when Agassiz died, and sent this poem home to Mr. Norton for publication. "His death," he says, "came home to me in a singular way, growing into my consciousness from day to day as if it were a graft new-set, that by degrees became part of my own wood and drew a greater share of my sap than belonged to it, as grafts sometimes will. I suppose that, unconsciously to myself, a great part of the ferment it produced in me was owing to the deaths of my sister Anna [Mrs. Charles R. Lowell], of Mrs. ——, whom I knew as a child in my early manhood, and of my cousin Amory, who was inextricably bound up with the primal associations of my life, associations which always have a singular sweetness for me. A very deep chord had been touched also at Florence by the sight of our old lodgings in the Casa Guidi, of the balcony Mabel used to run on, and the windows we used to look out at so long ago. I got sometimes into the mood I used to be in when I was always repeating to myself,

'King Pandion he is dead ;
All *thy* friends are lapt in lead,' —

verses which seem to me desolately pathetic. At last I began to hum over bits of my poem in my head till it took complete possession of me and worked me up to a delicious state of excitement, all the more delicious as my brain (or at any rate the musical part of it) had been lying dormant so long. My old trick of seeing things with my eyes shut after I had gone to bed (I mean whimsical things utterly alien to the train of my thoughts — for example, a hospital ward with a long row of white, untenanted beds, and on the farthest a pile of those little wooden dolls with red-painted slippers) revived in full force. Nervous, horribly nervous, but happy for the first time (I mean consciously happy) since I came over here. And so by degrees my poem worked itself out. The parts came to me as I came awake, and I wrote them down in the morning. I had all my bricks — but the mortar would n't *set,* as the masons say. However, I got it into order at last. You will see there is a logical sequence if you look sharp. It was curious to me after it was done to see how fleshly it was. This impression of Agassiz had wormed itself into my consciousness, and without my knowing it had colored my whole poem. I could not help feeling how, if I had been writing of Emerson, for example, I should have been quite otherwise ideal. But there it is, and you can judge for yourself. I think there is some go in it somehow, but it is too near me yet to be judged fairly by me. It is old-fashioned, you see, but none the worse for that." The poem was dated February, 1874.

I

1.

THE electric nerve, whose instantaneous
      thrill
Makes next-door gossips of the antipodes,
Confutes poor Hope's last fallacy of ease, —
The distance that divided her from ill:
Earth sentient seems again as when of old
      The horny foot of Pan
Stamped, and the conscious horror ran
Beneath men's feet through all her fibres
      cold:
Space's blue walls are mined; we feel the
      throe
From underground of our night-mantled
      foe:
      The flame-winged feet
Of Trade's new Mercury, that dry-shod run
Through briny abysses dreamless of the
      sun,
      Are mercilessly fleet,
      And at a bound annihilate
Ocean's prerogative of short reprieve;
      Surely ill news might wait,
And man be patient of delay to grieve:
      Letters have sympathies
      And tell-tale faces that reveal,

To senses finer than the eyes,
Their errand's purport ere we break the
    seal;
They wind a sorrow round with circum-
    stance
To stay its feet, nor all unwarned displace
The veil that darkened from our sidelong
    glance
        The inexorable face:
But now Fate stuns as with a mace;
The savage of the skies, that men have
    caught
And some scant use of language
    taught,
    Tells only what he must, —
The steel-cold fact in one laconic thrust.

2.

So thought I, as, with vague, mechanic
    eyes,
I scanned the festering news we half de-
    spise
    Yet scramble for no less,
And read of public scandal, private fraud,
Crime flaunting scot-free while the mob
    applaud,
Office made vile to bribe unworthiness,
    And all the unwholesome mess
The Land of Honest Abraham serves of
    late
    To teach the Old World how to wait,
        When suddenly,
As happens if the brain, from overweight
    Of blood, infect the eye,
Three tiny words grew lurid as I read,
And reeled commingling: *Agassiz is dead.*
As when, beneath the street's familiar jar,
An earthquake's alien omen rumbles far,
Men listen and forebode, I hung my head,
    And strove the present to recall,
As if the blow that stunned were yet to
    fall.

3.

Uprooted is our mountain oak,
That promised long security of shade
And brooding-place for many a wingëd
    thought;
    Not by Time's softly-cadenced stroke
With pauses of relenting pity stayed,
But ere a root seemed sapt, a bough de-
    cayed,
From sudden ambush by the whirlwind
    caught
And in his broad maturity betrayed !

4.

Well might I, as of old, appeal to you,
    O mountains woods and streams,
To help us mourn him, for ye loved him
    too;
    But simpler moods befit our modern
        themes,
And no less perfect birth of nature can,
Though they yearn tow'rd him, sympathize
    with man,
Save as dumb fellow-prisoners through a
    wall;
    Answer ye rather to my call,
Strong poets of a more unconscious day,
When Nature spake nor sought nice rea-
    sons why,
Too much for softer arts forgotten since
That teach our forthright tongue to lisp
    and mince,
And drown in music the heart's bitter cry !
Lead me some steps in your directer way,
Teach me those words that strike a solid
    root
        Within the ears of men;
Ye chiefly, virile both to think and feel,
Deep-chested Chapman and firm-footed
    Ben,
For he was masculine from head to heel.
Nay, let himself stand undiminished by
With those clear parts of him that will not
    die.
Himself from out the recent dark I claim
To hear, and, if I flatter him, to blame;
To show himself, as still I seem to see,
A mortal, built upon the antique plan,
Brimful of lusty blood as ever ran,
And taking life as simply as a tree !
To claim my foiled good-by let him ap-
    pear,
Large-limbed and human as I saw him
    near,
Loosed from the stiffening uniform of
    fame:
And let me treat him largely: I should
    fear,
(If with too prying lens I chanced to err,
Mistaking catalogue for character,)
His wise forefinger raised in smiling blame.
Nor would I scant him with judicial
    breath
And turn mere critic in an epitaph;
I choose the wheat, incurious of the chaff
That swells fame living, chokes it after
    death,

And would but memorize the shining half
Of his large nature that was turned to me:
Fain had I joined with those that honored
    him
With eyes that darkened because his were
    dim,
And now been silent: but it might not be.

II

I.

In some the genius is a thing apart,
    A pillared hermit of the brain,
Hoarding with incommunicable art
        Its intellectual gain;
    Man's web of circumstance and fate
    They from their perch of self observe,
Indifferent as the figures on a slate
    Are to the planet's sun-swung curve
    Whose bright returns they calculate;
    Their nice adjustment, part to part,
Were shaken from its serviceable mood
By unpremeditated stirs of heart
    Or jar of human neighborhood:
Some find their natural selves, and only
    then,
In furloughs of divine escape from men,
And when, by that brief ecstasy left bare,
    Driven by some instinct of desire,
They wander worldward, 't is to blink and
    stare,
Like wild things of the wood about a fire,
Dazed by the social glow they cannot
    share;
    His nature brooked no lonely lair,
But basked and bourgeoned in copartnery,
Companionship, and open-windowed glee:
    He knew, for he had tried,
    Those speculative heights that lure
The unpractised foot, impatient of a guide,
    Tow'rd ether too attenuately pure
For sweet unconscious breath, though dear
    to pride,
    But better loved the foothold sure
Of paths that wind by old abodes of men
Who hope at last the churchyard's peace
    secure,   ·
And follow time-worn rules, that them
    suffice,
Learned from their sires, traditionally wise,
Careful of honest custom's how and when;
His mind, too brave to look on Truth
    askance,
No more those habitudes of faith could
    share,

But, tinged with sweetness of the old Swiss
    manse,
Lingered around them still and fain would
    spare.
Patient to spy a sullen egg for weeks,
The enigma of creation to surprise,
His truer instinct sought the life that
    speaks
Without a mystery from kindly eyes;
In no self-spun cocoon of prudence wound,
He by the touch of men was best inspired,
And caught his native greatness at re-
    bound
From generosities itself had fired;
Then how the heat through every fibre ran,
Felt in the gathering presence of the man,
While the apt word and gesture came un-
    bid!
Virtues and faults it to one metal wrought,
        Fined all his blood to thought,
And ran the molten man in all he said or
    did.
All Tully's rules and all Quintilian's too
He by the light of listening faces knew,
And his rapt audience all unconscious lent
Their own roused force to make him elo-
    quent;
Persuasion fondled in his look and tone;
Our speech (with strangers prudish) he
    could bring
To find new charm in accents not her own;
Her coy constraints and icy hindrances
Melted upon his lips to natural ease,
As a brook's fetters swell the dance of
    spring.
Nor yet all sweetness: not in vain he wore,
Nor in the sheath of ceremony, controlled
By velvet courtesy or caution cold,
That sword of honest anger prized of old,
        But, with two-handed wrath,
If baseness or pretension crossed his path,
        Struck once nor needed to strike more.

2.

    His magic was not far to seek, —
He was so human! Whether strong or
    weak,
Far from his kind he neither sank nor
    soared,
But sate an equal guest at every board:
No beggar ever felt him condescend,
No prince presume; for still himself he
    bare
At manhood's simple level, and where'er
He met a stranger, there he left a friend.

How large an aspect ! nobly unsevere,
With freshness round him of Olympian
  cheer,
Like visits of those earthly gods he came;
His look, wherever its good-fortune fell,
Doubled the feast without a miracle,
And on the hearthstone danced a happier
  flame;
Philemon's crabbed vintage grew benign;
Amphitryon's gold-juice humanized to wine.

III

1.

The garrulous memories
Gather again from all their far-flown
  nooks,
Singly at first, and then by twos and threes,
Then in a throng innumerable, as the rooks
    Thicken their twilight files
Tow'rd Tintern's gray repose of roofless
  aisles:
Once more I see him at the table's head
When Saturday her monthly banquet
  spread
    To scholars, poets, wits,
All choice, some famous, loving things, not
  names,
And so without a twinge at others' fames;
Such company as wisest moods befits,
Yet with no pedant blindness to the worth
    Of undeliberate mirth,
Natures benignly mixed of air and earth,
Now with the stars and now with equal zest
Tracing the eccentric orbit of a jest.

2.

I see in vision the warm-lighted hall,
The living and the dead I see again,
And but my chair is empty; 'mid them
  all
'T is I that seem the dead: they all remain
Immortal, changeless creatures of the brain:
Wellnigh I doubt which world is real most,
Of sense or spirit, to the truly sane;
In this abstraction it were light to deem
Myself the figment of some stronger
  dream;
They are the real things, and I the ghost
That glide unhindered through the solid
  door,
Vainly for recognition seek from chair to
  chair,
And strive to speak and am but futile air,
As truly most of us are little more.

3.

Him most I see whom we most dearly miss,
    The latest parted thence,
His features poised in genial armistice
And armed neutrality of self-defence
Beneath the forehead's walled preëminence,
While Tyro, plucking facts with careless
  reach,
Settles off-hand our human how and whence;
The long-trained veteran scarcely wincing
  hears
The infallible strategy of volunteers
Making through Nature's walls its easy
  breach,
And seems to learn where he alone could
  teach.
Ample and ruddy, the board's end he fills
As he our fireside were, our light and heat,
Centre where minds diverse and various
  skills
Find their warm nook and stretch unham-
  pered feet;
I see the firm benignity of face,
Wide-smiling champaign, without tameness
  sweet,
The mass Teutonic toned to Gallic grace,
The eyes whose sunshine runs before the
  lips
While Holmes's rockets curve their long
  ellipse,
    And burst in seeds of fire that burst
      again
      To drop in scintillating rain.

4.

There too the face half-rustic, half-divine,
Self-poised, sagacious, freaked with hu-
  mor fine,
Of him who taught us not to mow and
  mope
About our fancied selves, but seek our
  scope
In Nature's world and Man's, nor fade to
  hollow trope,
Content with our New World and timely
  bold
To challenge the o'ermastery of the Old;
Listening with eyes averse I see him sit
Pricked with the cider of the Judge's wit
(Ripe-hearted homebrew, fresh and fresh
  again),
While the wise nose's firm-built aquiline
    Curves sharper to restrain
The merriment whose most unruly moods

Pass not the dumb laugh learned in listen-
    ing woods
    Of silence-shedding pine:
Hard by is he whose art's consoling spell
Hath given both worlds a whiff of
    asphodel,
His look still vernal 'mid the wintry ring
Of petals that remember, not foretell,
The paler primrose of a second spring.

5.

And more there are: but other forms
    arise
And seen as clear, albeit with dimmer
    eyes:
First he from sympathy still held apart
By shrinking over-eagerness of heart,
Cloud charged with searching fire, whose
    shadow's sweep
Heightened mean things with sense of
    brooding ill,
And steeped in doom familiar field and
    hill, —
New England's poet, soul reserved and
    deep,
November nature with a name of May,
Whom high o'er Concord plains we laid
    to sleep,
While the orchards mocked us in their
    white array
And building robins wondered at our
    tears,
Snatched in his prime, the shape august
That should have stood unbent 'neath
    fourscore years,
The noble head, the eyes of furtive trust,
    All gone to speechless dust.
    And he our passing guest,
Shy nature, too, and stung with life's
    unrest,
Whom we too briefly had but could not
    hold,
Who brought ripe Oxford's culture to our
    board,
    The Past's incalculable hoard,
Mellowed by scutcheoned panes in clois-
    ters old,
Seclusions ivy-hushed, and pavements
    sweet
With immemorial lisp of musing feet;
Young head time-tonsured smoother than
    a friar's,
Boy face, but grave with answerless
    desires,
Poet in all that poets have of best,

But foiled with riddles dark and cloudy
    aims,
    Who now hath found sure rest,
Not by still Isis or historic Thames,
Nor by the Charles he tried to love with
    me,
But, not misplaced, by Arno's hallowed
    brim,
Nor scorned by Santa Croce's neighboring
    fames,
Haply not mindless, wheresoe'er he be,
Of violets that to-day I scattered over
    him.
    He, too, is there,
After the good centurion fitly named,
Whom learning dulled not, nor convention
    tamed,
Shaking with burly mirth his hyacinthine
    hair,
Our hearty Grecian of Homeric ways,
Still found the surer friend where least he
    hoped the praise.

6.

Yea truly, as the sallowing years
Fall from us faster, like frost-loosened
    leaves
Pushed by the misty touch of shortening
    days,
    And that unwakened winter nears,
'T is the void chair our surest guest
    receives,
'T is lips long cold that give the warmest
    kiss,
'T is the lost voice comes oftenest to our
    ears;
We count our rosary by the beads we miss:
To me, at least, it seemeth so,
An exile in the land once found divine,
    While my starved fire burns low,
And homeless winds at the loose casement
    whine
Shrill ditties of the snow-roofed Apen-
    nine.

IV

1.

Now forth into the darkness all are gone,
But memory, still unsated, follows on,
Retracing step by step our homeward
    walk,
With many a laugh among our serious
    talk,
Across the bridge where, on the dimpling
    tide,

The long red streamers from the windows
glide,
    Or the dim western moon
Rocks her skiff's image on the broad lagoon,
And Boston shows a soft Venetian side
In that Arcadian light when roof and tree,
Hard prose by daylight, dream in Italy;
Or haply in the sky's cold chambers wide
Shivered the winter stars, while all below,
As if an end were come of human ill,
The world was wrapt in innocence of snow
And the cast-iron bay was blind and still;
These were our poetry; in him perhaps
Science had barred the gate that lets in
    dream,
And he would rather count the perch and
    bream
Than with the current's idle fancy lapse;
And yet he had the poet's open eye
That takes a frank delight in all it sees,
Nor was earth voiceless, nor the mystic sky,
To him the life-long friend of fields and
    trees:
Then came the prose of the suburban street,
Its silence deepened by our echoing feet,
And converse such as rambling hazard finds;
Then he who many cities knew and many
    minds,
And men once world - noised, now mere
    Ossian forms
Of misty memory, bade them live anew
As when they shared earth's manifold de-
    light,
In shape, in gait, in voice, in gesture true,
And, with an accent heightening as he
    warms,
Would stop forgetful of the shortening
    night,
Drop my confining arm, and pour profuse
Much worldly wisdom kept for others' use,
Not for his own, for he was rash and free,
His purse or knowledge all men's, like the
    sea.
Still can I hear his voice's shrilling might
(With pauses broken, while the fitful spark
He blew more hotly rounded on the dark
To hint his features with a Rembrandt
    light)
Call Oken back, or Humboldt, or Lamarck,
Or Cuvier's taller shade, and many more
Whom he had seen, or knew from others'
    sight,
And make them men to me as ne'er before:
Not seldom, as the undeadened fibre stirred
Of noble friendships knit beyond the sea,

German or French thrust by the lagging
    word,
For a good leash of mother-tongues had he.
At last, arrived at where our paths divide,
"Good night!" and, ere the distance grew
    too wide,
"Good night!" again; and now with
    cheated ear
I half hear his who mine shall never hear.

              2.

Sometimes it seemed as if New England
    air
For his large lungs too parsimonious
    were,
As if those empty rooms of dogma drear
Where the ghost shivers of a faith austere
Counting the horns o'er of the Beast,
Still scaring those whose faith in it is
    least,
As if those snaps o' th' moral atmosphere
That sharpen all the needles of the East,
Had been to him like death,
Accustomed to draw Europe's freer
    breath
    In a more stable element;
Nay, even our landscape, half the year
    morose,
Our practical horizon grimly pent,
Our air, sincere of ceremonious haze,
Forcing hard outlines mercilessly close,
Our social monotone of level days,
    Might make our best seem banish-
        ment;
    But it was nothing so;
Haply his instinct might divine,
Beneath our drift of puritanic snow,
    The marvel sensitive and fine
Of sanguinaria over-rash to blow
And trust its shyness to an air malign;
Well might he prize truth's warranty
    and pledge
In the grim outcrop of our granite edge,
Or Hebrew fervor flashing forth at need
In the gaunt sons of Calvin's iron breed,
As prompt to give as skilled to win and
    keep;
But, though such intuitions might not
    cheer,
Yet life was good to him, and, there or
    here,
With that sufficing joy, the day was never
    cheap;
Thereto his mind was its own ample
    sphere,

And, like those buildings great that
through the year
Carry one temperature, his nature large
Made its own climate, nor could any
marge
Traced by convention stay him from his
bent:
He had a habitude of mountain air;
He brought wide outlook where he went,
And could on sunny uplands dwell
Of prospect sweeter than the pastures fair
High-hung of viny Neufchâtel;
Nor, surely, did he miss
Some pale, imaginary bliss
Of earlier sights whose inner landscape still
was Swiss.

V

1.

I cannot think he wished so soon to die
With all his senses full of eager heat,
And rosy years that stood expectant by
To buckle the winged sandals on their
feet,
He that was friends with Earth, and all
her sweet
Took with both hands unsparingly:
Truly this life is precious to the root,
And good the feel of grass beneath the
foot;
To lie in buttercups and clover-bloom,
Tenants in common with the bees,
And watch the white clouds drift through
gulfs of trees,
Is better than long waiting in the tomb;
Only once more to feel the coming spring
As the birds feel it, when it bids them
sing,
Only once more to see the moon
Through leaf-fringed abbey-arches of the
elms
Curve her mild sickle in the West
Sweet with the breath of hay-cocks, were
a boon
Worth any promise of soothsayer realms
Or casual hope of being elsewhere blest;
To take December by the beard
And crush the creaking snow with springy
foot,
While overhead the North's dumb
streamers shoot,
Till Winter fawn upon the cheek en-
deared,
Then the long evening-ends

Lingered by cosy chimney-nooks,
With high companionship of books
Or slippered talk of friends
And sweet habitual looks,
Is better than to stop the ears with dust:
Too soon the spectre comes to say, "Thou
must!"

2.

When toil-crooked hands are crost upon
the breast,
They comfort us with sense of rest;
They must be glad to lie forever still;
Their work is ended with their day;
Another fills their room; 't is the World's
ancient way,
Whether for good or ill;
But the deft spinners of the brain,
Who love each added day and find it
gain,
Them overtakes the doom
To snap the half-grown flower upon the
loom
(Trophy that was to be of life-long pain),
The thread no other skill can ever knit
again.
'T was so with him, for he was glad
to live,
'T was doubly so, for he left work begun;
Could not this eagerness of Fate forgive
Till all the allotted flax were spun?
It matters not; for, go at night or noon,
A friend, whene'er he dies, has died too
soon,
And, once we hear the hopeless *He is
dead*,
So far as flesh hath knowledge, all is
said.

VI

1.

I seem to see the black procession go:
That crawling prose of death too well I
know,
The vulgar paraphrase of glorious woe;
I see it wind through that unsightly
grove,
Once beautiful, but long defaced
With granite permanence of cockney
taste
And all those grim disfigurements we
love:
There, then, we leave him: Him? such
costly waste
Nature rebels at: and it is not true

Of those most precious parts of him we
  knew:
Could we be conscious but as dreamers be,
'T were sweet to leave this shifting life
  of tents
Sunk in the changeless calm of Deity;
Nay, to be mingled with the elements,
The fellow-servant of creative powers,
Partaker in the solemn year's events,
To share the work of busy - fingered
  hours,
To be night's silent almoner of dew,
To rise, again in plants and breathe and
  grow,
To stream as tides the ocean caverns
  through,
Or with the rapture of great winds to
  blow
About earth's shaken coignes, were not a
  fate
  To leave us all-disconsolate;
Even endless slumber in the sweetening
  sod
  Of charitable earth
That takes out all our mortal stains,
And makes us cleanlier neighbors of the
  clod,
  Methinks were better worth
Than the poor fruit of most men's wake-
  ful pains,
  The heart's insatiable ache:
  But such was not his faith,
Nor mine : it may be he had trod
Outside the plain old path of *God thus
  spake,*
  But God to him was very God,
  And not a visionary wraith
Skulking in murky corners of the mind,
  And he was sure to be
Somehow, somewhere, imperishable as He,
Not with His essence mystically combined,
As some high spirits long, but whole and
  free,
A perfected and conscious Agassiz.
And such I figure him : the wise of old
Welcome and own him of their peaceful
  fold,
  Not truly with the guild enrolled
Of him who seeking inward guessed
Diviner riddles than the rest,
And groping in the darks of thought
Touched the Great Hand and knew it
  not;
  Rather he shares the daily light,
From reason's charier fountains won,

Of his great chief, the slow-paced Stagy-
  rite,
And Cuvier clasps once more his long-lost
  son.

2.

The shape erect is prone: forever stilled
The winning tongue ; the forehead's high-
  piled heap,
A cairn which every science helped to
  build,
Unvalued will its golden secrets keep:
He knows at last if Life or Death be best:
Wherever he be flown, whatever vest
The being hath put on which lately here
So many-friended was, so full of cheer
To make men feel the Seeker's noble zest,
We have not lost him all ; he is not gone
To the dumb herd of them that wholly
  die;
The beauty of his better self lives on
In minds he touched with fire, in many an
  eye
He trained to Truth's exact severity;
He was a Teacher : why be grieved for
  him
Whose living word still stimulates the air ?
In endless file shall loving scholars come
The glow of his transmitted touch to share,
And trace his features with an eye less
  dim
Than ours whose sense familiar wont
  makes numb.

TO HOLMES

ON HIS SEVENTY-FIFTH BIRTHDAY

DEAR Wendell, why need count the years
  Since first your genius made me thrill,
If what moved then to smiles or tears,
  Or both contending, move me still ?

What has the Calendar to do
  With poets ? What Time's fruitless
    tooth
With gay immortals such as you
  Whose years but emphasize your youth ?

One air gave both their lease of breath;
  The same paths lured our boyish feet;
One earth will hold us safe in death
  With dust of saints and scholars sweet.

Our legends from one source were drawn,
  I scarce distinguish yours from mine,
And *don't* we make the Gentiles yawn
  With "You   remembers?" o'er our
    wine!

If I, with too senescent air,
  Invade your elder memory's pale,
You snub me with a pitying "Where
  Were you in the September Gale?"

Both stared entranced at Lafayette,
  Saw Jackson dubbed with LL. D.
What Cambridge saw not strikes us yet
  As scarcely worth one's while to see.

Ten years my senior, when my name
  In Harvard's entrance-book was writ,
Her halls still echoed with the fame
  Of you, her poet and her wit.

'T is fifty years from then to now:
  But your Last Leaf renews its green,
Though, for the laurels on your brow
  (So thick they crowd), 't is hardly seen.

The oriole's fledglings fifty times
  Have flown from our familiar elms;
As many poets with their rhymes
  Oblivion's darkling dust o'erwhelms.

The birds are hushed, the poets gone
  Where no harsh critic's lash can reach,
And still your wingèd brood sing on
  To all who love our English speech.

Nay, let the foolish records be
  That make believe you 're seventy-five:
You 're the old Wendell still to me, —
  And that 's the youngest man alive.

The gray-blue eyes, I see them still,
  The gallant front with brown o'erhung,
The shape alert, the wit at will,
  The phrase that stuck, but never stung.

You keep your youth as yon Scotch firs,
  Whose gaunt line my horizon hems,
Though twilight all the lowland blurs,
  Hold sunset in their ruddy stems.

You with the elders? Yes, 't is true,
  But in no sadly literal sense,
With elders and coevals too,
  Whose verb admits no preterite tense.

Master alike in speech and song
  Of fame's great antiseptic — Style,
You with the classic few belong
  Who tempered wisdom with a smile.

Outlive us all! Who else like you
  Could sift the seedcorn from our chaff,
And make us with the pen we knew
  Deathless at least in epitaph?

IN A COPY OF OMAR KHAYYÁM

THESE pearls of thought in Persian gulfs
  were bred,
Each softly lucent as a rounded moon;
The diver Omar plucked them from their
  bed,
Fitzgerald strung them on an English
  thread.

Fit rosary for a queen, in shape and hue,
When Contemplation tells her pensive beads
Of mortal thoughts, forever old and new.
Fit for a queen? Why, surely then for
  you!

The moral? Where Doubt's eddies toss
  and twirl
Faith's slender shallop till her footing reel,
Plunge: if you find not peace beneath the
  whirl,
Groping, you may like Omar grasp a pearl.

ON RECEIVING A COPY OF MR. AUSTIN DOBSON'S "OLD WORLD IDYLLS"

I

AT length arrived, your book I take
To read in for the author's sake;
Too gray for new sensations grown,
Can charm to Art or Nature known
This torpor from my senses shake?

Hush! my parched ears what runnels
  slake?
Is a thrush gurgling from the brake?
Has Spring, on all the breezes blown,
At length arrived?

Long may you live such songs to make,
And I to listen while you wake.

With skill of late disused, each tone
Of the *Lesboum barbiton*,
At mastery, through long finger-ache,
At length arrived.

II

As I read on, what changes steal
O'er me and through, from head to heel ?
A rapier thrusts coat-skirt aside,
My rough Tweeds bloom to silken pride, —
Who was it laughed ? Your hand, Dick
Steele !

Down vistas long of clipt *charmille*
Watteau as Pierrot leads the reel;
Tabor and pipe the dancers guide
As I read on.

While in and out the verses wheel
The wind-caught robes trim feet reveal,
Lithe ankles that to music glide,
But chastely and by chance descried;
Art ? Nature ? Which do I most feel
As I read on ?

TO C. F. BRADFORD

ON THE GIFT OF A MEERSCHAUM PIPE

THE pipe came safe, and welcome too,
As anything must be from you;
A meerschaum pure, 't would float as light
As she the girls call Amphitrite.
Mixture divine of foam and clay,
From both it stole the best away:
Its foam is such as crowns the glow
Of beakers brimmed by Veuve Clicquot;
Its clay is but congested lymph
Jove chose to make some choicer nymph;
And here combined, — why, this must be
The birth of some enchanted sea,
Shaped to immortal form, the type
And very Venus of a pipe.

When high I heap it with the weed
From Lethe wharf, whose potent seed
Nicotia, big from Bacchus, bore
And cast upon Virginia's shore,
I 'll think, — So fill the fairer bowl
And wise alembic of thy soul,
With herbs far-sought that shall distil,
Not fumes to slacken thought and will,
But bracing essences that nerve
To wait, to dare, to strive, to serve.

When curls the smoke in eddies soft,
And hangs a shifting dream aloft,
That gives and takes, though chance-de-
signed,
The impress of the dreamer's mind,
I 'll think, — So let the vapors bred
By Passion, in the heart or head,
Pass off and upward into space,
Waving farewells of tenderest grace,
Remembered in some happier time,
To blend their beauty with my rhyme.

While slowly o'er its candid bowl
The color deepens (as the soul
That burns in mortals leaves its trace
Of bale or beauty on the face),
I 'll think, — So let the essence rare
Of years consuming make me fair;
So, 'gainst the ills of life profuse,
Steep me in some narcotic juice;
And if my soul must part with all
That whiteness which we greenness call,
Smooth back, O Fortune, half thy frown,
And make me beautifully brown !

Dream-forger, I refill thy cup
With reverie's wasteful pittance up,
And while the fire burns slow away,
Hiding itself in ashes gray,
I 'll think, — As inward Youth retreats,
Compelled to spare his wasting heats,
When Life's Ash-Wednesday comes about,
And my head 's gray with fires burnt out,
While stays one spark to light the eye,
With the last flash of memory,
'T will leap to welcome C. F. B.,
Who sent my favorite pipe to me.

BANKSIDE

(HOME OF EDMUND QUINCY)

DEDHAM, MAY 21, 1877

Edmund Quincy was eleven years the senior
of Lowell, but their common labors in the
early days of the anti-slavery movement, and
their congeniality of temper and wit, made
them very intimate friends.

I

I CHRISTENED you in happier days, before
These gray forebodings on my brow were
seen;

You are still lovely in your new-leaved
    green;
The brimming river soothes his grassy
    shore;
The bridge is there; the rock with lichens
    hoar;
And the same shadows on the water lean,
Outlasting us.   How many graves between
That day and this!   How many shadows
    more
Darken my heart, their substance from
    these eyes
Hidden forever!   So our world is made
Of life and death commingled; and the
    sighs
Outweigh the smiles, in equal balance laid:
What compensation?   None, save that the
    Allwise
So schools us to love things that cannot
    fade.

II

Thank God, he saw you last in pomp of
    May,
Ere any leaf had felt the year's regret;
Your latest image in his memory set
Was fair as when your landscape's peaceful
    sway
Charmed dearer eyes with his to make
    delay
On Hope's long prospect, — as if They for-
    get
The happy, They, the unspeakable Three,
    whose debt,
Like the hawk's shadow, blots our brightest
    day:
Better it is that ye should look so fair,
Slopes that he loved, and ever-murmuring
    pines
That make a music out of silent air,
And bloom-heaped orchard-trees in pros-
    perous lines;
In you the heart some sweeter hints divines,
And wiser, than in winter's dull despair.

III

Old Friend, farewell!   Your kindly door
    again
I enter, but the master's hand in mine
No more clasps welcome, and the temperate
    wine,
That cheered our long nights, other lips
    must stain:
All is unchanged, but I expect in vain
The face alert, the manners free and fine,

The seventy years borne lightly as the pine
Wears its first down of snow in green dis-
    dain:
Much did he, and much well; yet most of
    all
I prized his skill in leisure and the ease
Of a life flowing full without a plan;
For most are idly busy; him I call
Thrice fortunate who knew himself to
    please,
Learned in those arts that make a gentle-
    man.

IV

Nor deem he lived unto himself alone;
His was the public spirit of his sire,
And in those eyes, soft with domestic fire,
A quenchless light of fiercer temper shone
What time about the world our shame was
    blown
On every wind; his soul would not con-
    spire
With selfish men to soothe the mob's de-
    sire,
Veiling with garlands Moloch's bloody
    stone;
The high-bred instincts of a better day
Ruled in his blood, when to be citizen
Rang Roman yet, and a Free People's sway
Was not the exchequer of impoverished
    men,
Nor statesmanship with loaded votes to
    play,
Nor public office a tramps' boosing-ken.

JOSEPH WINLOCK

DIED JUNE 11, 1875

Mr. Winlock was at the head of the Harvard
Astronomical Observatory at the time of his
death.

SHY soul and stalwart, man of patient will
Through years one hair's-breadth on our
    Dark to gain,
Who, from the stars he studied not in vain,
Had learned their secret to be strong and
    still,
Careless of fames that earth's tin trum-
    pets fill;
Born under Leo, broad of build and brain,
While others slept, he watched in that
    hushed fane
Of Science, only witness of his skill:

Sudden as falls a shooting-star he fell,
But inextinguishable his luminous trace
In mind and heart of all that knew him
 well.
Happy man's doom ! To him the Fates
 were known
Of orbs dim hovering on the skirts of
 space,
Unprescient, through God's mercy, of his
 own !

SONNET

TO FANNY ALEXANDER

The daughter of an American portrait
painter who spent his life in Italy, and herself
known through her sympathetic and delicate
portraiture of Italian peasant life, especially
in her *Roadside Songs of Tuscany*. The poem
is dated at Florence in 1873.

UNCONSCIOUS as the sunshine, simply sweet
And generous as that, thou dost not close
Thyself in art, as life were but a rose
To rumple bee-like with luxurious feet;
Thy higher mind therein finds sure retreat,
But not from care of common hopes and
 woes;
Thee the dark chamber, thee the unfriended,
 knows,
Although no babbling crowds thy praise
 repeat:
Consummate artist, who life's landscape
 bleak
Hast brimmed with sun to many a clouded
 eye,
Touched to a brighter hue the beggar's
 cheek,
Hung over orphaned lives a gracious sky,
And traced for eyes, that else would vainly
 seek,
Fair pictures of an angel drawing nigh !

JEFFRIES WYMAN

DIED SEPTEMBER 4, 1874

An associate of Lowell in Cambridge, and
eminent as a man of science in the field of
comparative anatomy.

THE wisest man could ask no more of Fate
Than to be simple, modest, manly, true,

Safe from the Many, honored by the Few;
To count as naught in World, or Church,
 or State,
But inwardly in secret to be great;
To feel mysterious Nature ever new;
To touch, if not to grasp, her endless clue,
And learn by each discovery how to wait.
He widened knowledge and escaped the
 praise;
He wisely taught, because more wise to
 learn;
He toiled for Science, not to draw men's
 gaze,
But for her lore of self-denial stern.
That such a man could spring from our
 decays
Fans the soul's nobler faith until it burn.

TO A FRIEND

WHO GAVE ME A GROUP OF WEEDS AND GRASSES, AFTER A DRAWING OF DÜRER

TRUE as the sun's own work, but more
 refined,
It tells of love behind the artist's eye,
Of sweet companionships with earth and
 sky,
And summers stored, the sunshine of the
 mind.
What peace ! Sure, ere you breathe, the
 fickle wind
Will break its truce and bend that grass-
 plume high,
Scarcely yet quiet from the gilded fly
That flits a more luxurious perch to find.
Thanks for a pleasure that can never pall,
A serene moment, deftly caught and kept
To make immortal summer on my wall.
Had he who drew such gladness ever
 wept ?
Ask rather could he else have seen at all,
Or grown in Nature's mysteries an adept ?

WITH AN ARMCHAIR

I.

ABOUT the oak that framed this chair, of
 old
The seasons danced their round; delighted
 wings
Brought music to its boughs; shy wood-
 land things

Shared its broad roof, 'neath whose green
    glooms grown bold,
Lovers, more shy than they, their secret
    told;
The resurrection of a thousand springs
Swelled in its veins, and dim imaginings
Teased them, perchance, of life more mani-
    fold.
Such shall it know when its proud arms
    enclose
My Lady Goshawk, musing here at rest,
Careless of him who into exile goes,
Yet, while his gift by those fair limbs is
    prest,
Through some fine sympathy of nature
    knows
That, seas between us, she is still his guest.

2.

Yet sometimes, let me dream, the con-
    scious wood
A momentary vision may renew
Of him who counts it treasure that he
    knew,
Though but in passing, such a priceless
    good,
And, like an elder brother, felt his mood
Uplifted by the spell that kept her true,
Amid her lightsome compeers, to the few
That wear the crown of serious woman-
    hood:
Were he so happy, think of him as one
Who in the Louvre or Pitti feels his soul
Rapt by some dead face which, till then
    unseen,
Moves like a memory, and, till life outrun,
Is vexed with vague misgiving past con-
    trol,
Of nameless loss and thwarted might-have-
    been.

E. G. DE R.

WHY should I seek her spell to decompose
Or to its source each rill of influence trace
That feeds the brimming river of her
    grace ?
The petals numbered but degrade to prose
Summer's triumphant poem of the rose:
Enough for me to watch the wavering
    chase,
Like wind o'er grass, of moods across her
    face,
Fairest in motion, fairer in repose.

Steeped in her sunshine, let me, while I
    may,
Partake the bounty: ample 't is for me
That her mirth cheats my temples of their
    gray,
Her charm makes years long spent seem
    yet to be.
Wit, goodness, grace, swift flash from
    grave to gay, —
All these are good, but better far is she.

BON VOYAGE

SHIP, blest to bear such freight across the
    blue,
May stormless stars control thy horoscope;
In keel and hull, in every spar and rope,
Be night and day to thy dear office true !
Ocean, men's path and their divider too,
No fairer shrine of memory and hope
To the underworld adown thy westering
    slope
E'er vanished, or whom such regrets pur-
    sue:
Smooth all thy surges as when Jove to
    Crete
Swam with less costly burthen, and pre-
    pare
A pathway meet for her home-coming
    soon
With golden undulations such as greet
The printless summer-sandals of the moon
And tempt the Nautilus his cruise to dare !

TO WHITTIER

ON HIS SEVENTY-FIFTH BIRTHDAY

NEW ENGLAND'S poet, rich in love as
    years,
Her hills and valleys praise thee, her swift
    brooks
Dance in thy verse; to her grave sylvan
    nooks
Thy steps allure us, which the wood-thrush
    hears
As maids their lovers', and no treason
    fears;
Through thee her Merrimacs and Agio-
    chooks
And many a name uncouth win gracious
    looks,
Sweetly familiar to both Englands' ears:

Peaceful by birthright as a virgin lake,
The lily's anchorage, which no eyes behold
Save those of stars, yet for thy brother's
    sake
That lay in bonds, thou blewst a blast as
    bold
As that wherewith the heart of Roland
    brake,
Far heard across the New World and the
    Old.

ON AN AUTUMN SKETCH OF
H. G. WILD

THANKS to the artist, ever on my wall
The sunset stays: that hill in glory rolled,
Those trees and clouds in crimson and in
    gold,
Burn on, nor cool when evening's shadows
    fall.
Not round *these* splendors Midnight wraps
    her pall;
These leaves the flush of Autumn's vintage
    hold
In Winter's spite, nor can the Northwind
    bold
Deface my chapel's western window small:
On one, ah me! October struck his frost,
But not repaid him with those Tyrian
    hues;
His naked boughs but tell him what is lost,
And parting comforts of the sun refuse:
His heaven is bare, — ah, were its hollow
    crost
Even with a cloud whose light were yet to
    lose!

TO MISS D. T.

ON HER GIVING ME A DRAWING OF
LITTLE STREET ARABS

Miss Dorothy Tennant afterward married
Henry M. Stanley, the African explorer.

As, cleansed of Tiber's and Oblivion's
    slime,
Glow Farnesina's vaults with shapes again
That dreamed some exiled artist from his
    pain
Back to his Athens and the Muse's clime,
So these world-orphaned waifs of Want
    and Crime,

Purged by Art's absolution from the stain
Of the polluting city-flood, regain
Ideal grace secure from taint of time.
An Attic frieze you give, a pictured song;
For as with words the poet paints, for
    you
The happy pencil at its labor sings,
Stealing his privilege, nor does him wrong,
Beneath the false discovering the true,
And Beauty's best in unregarded things.

WITH A COPY OF AUCASSIN
AND NICOLETE

LEAVES fit to have been poor Juliet's
    cradle-rhyme,
With gladness of a heart long quenched in
    mould
They vibrate still, a nest not yet grown
    cold
From its fledged burthen. The numb
    hand of Time
Vainly his glass turns; here is endless
    prime;
Here lips their roses keep and locks their
    gold;
Here Love in pristine innocency bold
Speaks what our grosser conscience makes
    a crime.
Because it tells the dream that all have
    known
Once in their lives, and to life's end the
    few;
Because its seeds o'er Memory's desert
    blown
Spring up in heartsease such as Eden
    knew;
Because it hath a beauty all its own,
Dear Friend, I plucked this herb of grace
    for you.

ON PLANTING A TREE AT IN-
VERARAY

WHO does his duty is a question
    Too complex to be solved by me,
But he, I venture the suggestion,
    Does part of his that plants a tree.

For after he is dead and buried,
    And epitaphed, and well forgot,
Nay, even his shade by Charon ferried
    To — let us not inquire to what,

His deed, its author long outliving,
  By Nature's mother-care increased,
Shall stand, his verdant almoner, giving
  A kindly dole to man and beast.

The wayfarer, at noon reposing,
  Shall bless its shadow on the grass,
Or sheep beneath it huddle, dozing
  Until the thundergust o'erpass.

The owl, belated in his plundering,
  Shall here await the friendly night,
Blinking whene'er he wakes, and wondering
  What fool it was invented light.

Hither the busy birds shall flutter,
  With the light timber for their nests,
And, pausing from their labor, utter
  The morning sunshine in their breasts.

What though his memory shall have vanished,
  Since the good deed he did survives?
It is not wholly to be banished
  Thus to be part of many lives.

Grow, then, my foster-child, and strengthen,
  Bough over bough, a murmurous pile,
And, as your stately stem shall lengthen,
  So may the statelier of Argyll!

AN EPISTLE TO GEORGE WILLIAM CURTIS

" De prodome,
Des qu'il s'atorne a grant bonte
Ja n'iert tot dit ne tot conte,
Que leingue ne puet pas retraire
Tant d'enor com prodom set faire."
CRESTIEN DE TROIES,
Li Romans dou Chevalier au Lyon, 784-788.

1874

CURTIS, whose Wit, with Fancy arm in arm,
Masks half its muscle in its skill to charm,
And who so gently can the Wrong expose
As sometimes to make converts, never foes,
Or only such as good men must expect,
Knaves sore with conscience of their own defect,
I come with mild remonstrance. Ere I start,
A kindlier errand interrupts my heart,
And I must utter, though it vex your ears,

The love, the honor, felt so many years.
Curtis, skilled equally with voice and pen
To stir the hearts or mould the minds of men, —
That voice whose music, for I 've heard you sing
Sweet as Casella, can with passion ring,
That pen whose rapid ease ne'er trips with haste,
Nor scrapes nor sputters, pointed with good taste,
First Steele's, then Goldsmith's, next it came to you,
Whom Thackeray rated best of all our crew, —
Had letters kept you, every wreath were yours;
Had the World tempted, all its chariest doors
Had swung on flattered hinges to admit
Such high-bred manners, such good-natured wit;
At courts, in senates, who so fit to serve?
And both invited, but you would not swerve,
All meaner prizes waiving that you might
In civic duty spend your heat and light,
Unpaid, untrammelled, with a sweet disdain
Refusing posts men grovel to attain.
Good Man all own you; what is left me, then,
To heighten praise with but Good Citizen?

But why this praise to make you blush and stare,
And give a backache to your Easy-Chair?
Old Crestien rightly says no language can
Express the worth of a true Gentleman,
And I agree; but other thoughts deride
My first intent, and lure my pen aside.
Thinking of you, I see my firelight glow
On other faces, loved from long ago,
Dear to us both, and all these loves combine
With this I send and crowd in every line;
Fortune with me was in such generous mood
That all my friends were yours, and all were good;
Three generations come when one I call,
And the fair grandame, youngest of them all,
In her own Florida who found and sips
The fount that fled from Ponce's longing lips.
How bright they rise and wreathe my hearthstone round,

Divine my thoughts, reply without a sound,
And with them many a shape that memory
    sees,
As dear as they, but crowned with aureoles
    these !
What wonder if, with protest in my thought,
Arrived, I find 't was only love I brought ?
I came with protest; Memory barred the
    road
Till I repaid you half the debt I owed.

No, 't was not to bring laurels that I came,
Nor would you wish it, daily seeing fame,
(Or our cheap substitute, unknown of yore,)
Dumped like a load of coal at every door,
Mime and hetæra getting equal weight
With him whose toils heroic saved the State.
But praise can harm not who so calmly
    met
Slander's worst word, nor treasured up the
    debt,
Knowing, what all experience serves to
    show,
No mud can soil us but the mud we throw.
You have heard harsher voices and more
    loud,
As all must, not sworn liegemen of the
    crowd,
And far aloof your silent mind could keep
As when, in heavens with winter-midnight
    deep,
The perfect moon hangs thoughtful, nor
    can know
What hounds her lucent calm drives mad
    below.

But to my business, while you rub your
    eyes
And wonder how you ever thought me wise.
Dear friend and old, they say you shake
    your head
And wish some bitter words of mine un-
    said:
I wish they might be, — there we are
    agreed;
I hate to speak, still more what makes the
    need;
But I must utter what the voice within
Dictates, for acquiescence dumb were sin;
I blurt ungrateful truths, if so they be,
That none may need to say them after me.
'T were my felicity could I attain
The temperate zeal that balances your
    brain;
But nature still o'erleaps reflection's plan,

And one must do his service as he can.
Think you it were not pleasanter to speak
Smooth words that leave unflushed the
    brow and cheek ?
To sit, well-dined, with cynic smile, unseen
In private box, spectator of the scene
Where men the comedy of life rehearse,
Idly to judge which better and which
    worse
Each hireling actor spoiled his worthless
    part ?
Were it not sweeter with a careless heart,
In happy commune with the untainted
    brooks,
To dream all day, or, walled with silent
    books,
To hear nor heed the World's unmeaning
    noise,
Safe in my fortress stored with lifelong
    joys ?

I love too well the pleasures of retreat
Safe from the crowd and cloistered from
    the street;
The fire that whispers its domestic joy,
Flickering on walls that knew me still a
    boy,
And knew my saintly father; the full days,
Not careworn from the world's soul-squan-
    dering ways,
Calm days that loiter with snow-silent
    tread,
Nor break my commune with the undying
    dead;
Truants of Time, to-morrow like to-day,
That come unbid, and claimless glide away
By shelves that sun them in the indulgent
    Past,
Where Spanish castles, even, were built to
    last,
Where saint and sage their silent vigil keep,
And wrong hath ceased or sung itself to
    sleep.
Dear were my walks, too, gathering fra-
    grant store
Of Mother Nature's simple-minded lore:
I learned all weather-signs of day or night;
No bird but I could name him by his flight,
No distant tree but by his shape was
    known,
Or, near at hand, by leaf or bark alone.
This learning won by loving looks I hived
As sweeter lore than all from books derived.
I know the charm of hillside, field, and
    wood,

Of lake and stream, and the sky's downy
    brood,
Of roads sequestered rimmed with sallow
    sod,
But friends with hardhack, aster, golden-
    rod,
Or succory keeping summer long its trust
Of heaven-blue fleckless from the eddying
    dust:
These were my earliest friends, and latest
    too,
Still unestranged, whatever fate may do.
For years I had these treasures, knew their
    worth,
Estate most real man can have on earth.
I sank too deep in this soft-stuffed repose
That hears but rumors of earth's wrongs
    and woes;
Too well these Capuas could my muscles
    waste,
Not void of toils, but toils of choice and
    taste;
These still had kept me could I but have
    quelled
The Puritan drop that in my veins rebelled.
But there were times when silent were my
    books
As jailers are, and gave me sullen looks,
When verses palled, and even the woodland
    path,
By innocent contrast, fed my heart with
    wrath,
And I must twist my little gift of words
Into a scourge of rough and knotted cords
Unmusical, that whistle as they swing
To leave on shameless backs their purple
    sting.

How slow Time comes ! Gone, who so swift
    as he ?
Add but a year, 't is half a century
Since the slave's stifled moaning broke my
    sleep,
Heard 'gainst my will in that seclusion
    deep,
Haply heard louder for the silence there,
And so my fancied safeguard made my
    snare.
After that moan had sharpened to a cry,
And a cloud, hand-broad then, heaped all
    our sky
With its stored vengeance, and such thun-
    ders stirred
As heaven's and earth's remotest chambers
    heard,

I looked to see an ampler atmosphere
By that electric passion-gust blown clear.
I looked for this; consider what I see —
But I forbear, 't would please nor you nor
    me
To check the items in the bitter list
Of all I counted on and all I mist.
Only three instances I choose from all,
And each enough to stir a pigeon's gall:
Office a fund for ballot-brokers made
To pay the drudges of their gainful trade;
Our cities taught what conquered cities
    feel
By ædiles chosen that they might safely
    steal;
And gold, however got, a title fair
To such respect as only gold can bear.
I seem to see this; how shall I gainsay
What all our journals tell me every day ?
Poured our young martyrs their high-
    hearted blood
That we might trample to congenial mud
The soil with such a legacy sublimed ?
Methinks an angry scorn is here well-
    timed:
Where find retreat ? How keep reproach
    at bay ?
Where'er I turn some scandal fouls the
    way.

Dear friend, if any man I wished to please,
'T were surely you whose humor's honied
    ease
Flows flecked with gold of thought, whose
    generous mind
Sees Paradise regained by all mankind,
Whose brave example still to vanward
    shines,
Checks the retreat, and spurs our lagging
    lines.
Was I too bitter ? Who his phrase can
    choose
That sees the life-blood of his dearest
    ooze ?
I loved my Country so as only they
Who love a mother fit to die for may;
I loved her old renown, her stainless
    fame, —
What better proof than that I loathed her
    shame ?
That many blamed me could not irk me
    long,
But, if you doubted, must I not be wrong ?
'T is not for me to answer: this I know,
That man or race so prosperously low

Sunk in success that wrath they cannot
  feel,
Shall taste the spurn of parting Fortune's
  heel ;
For never land long lease of empire won
Whose sons sate silent when base deeds
  were done.

POSTSCRIPT, 1887

Curtis, so wrote I thirteen years ago,
Tost it unfinished by, and left it so ;
Found lately, I have pieced it out, or tried,
Since time for callid juncture was denied.
Some of the verses pleased me, it is true,
And still were pertinent, — those honoring
  you.
These now I offer : take them, if you
  will,
Like the old hand-grasp, when at Shady
  Hill
We met, or Staten Island, in the days
When life was its own spur, nor needed
  praise.
If once you thought me rash, no longer
  fear ;
Past my next milestone waits my seven-
  tieth year.
I mount no longer when the trumpets
  call ;
My battle-harness idles on the wall,
The spider's castle, camping - ground of
  dust,
Not without dints, and all in front, I trust.
Shivering sometimes it calls me as it hears
Afar the charge's tramp and clash of
  spears ;
But 't is such murmur only as might be
The sea-shell's lost tradition of the sea,
That makes me muse and wonder Where ?
  and When ?
While from my cliff I watch the waves of
  men
That climb to break midway their seeming
  gain,
And think it triumph if they shake their
  chain.
Little I ask of Fate ; will she refuse
Some days of reconcilement with the
  Muse ?
I take my reed again and blow it free
Of dusty silence, murmuring, " Sing to
  me ! "
And, as its stops my curious touch retries,
The stir of earlier instincts I surprise, —

Instincts, if less imperious, yet more
  strong,
And happy in the toil that ends with song.

Home am I come : not, as I hoped might
  be,
To the old haunts, too full of ghosts for me,
But to the olden dreams that time en-
  dears,
And the loved books that younger grow
  with years ;
To country rambles, timing with my tread
Some happier verse that carols in my
  head,
Yet all with sense of something vainly
  mist,
Of something lost, but when I never wist.
How empty seems to me the populous
  street,
One figure gone I daily loved to meet, —
The clear, sweet singer with the crown of
  snow
Not whiter than the thoughts that housed
  below !
And, ah, what absence feel I at my side,
Like Dante when he missed his laurelled
  guide,
What sense of diminution in the air
Once so inspiring, Emerson not there !
But life is sweet, though all that makes it
  sweet
Lessen like sound of friends' departing
  feet,
And Death is beautiful as feet of friend
Coming with welcome at our journey's
  end;
For me Fate gave, whate'er she else de-
  nied,
A nature sloping to the southern side ;
I thank her for it, though when clouds
  arise
Such natures double-darken gloomy skies.
I muse upon the margin of the sea,
Our common pathway to the new To Be,
Watching the sails, that lessen more and
  more,
Of good and beautiful embarked before;
With bits of wreck I patch the boat shall
  bear
Me to that unexhausted Otherwhere,
Whose friendly-peopled shore I sometimes
  see,
By soft mirage uplifted, beckon me,
Nor sadly hear, as lower sinks the sun,
My moorings to the past snap one by one.

II. SENTIMENT

ENDYMION

A MYSTICAL COMMENT ON TITIAN'S
"SACRED AND PROFANE LOVE"

I

My day began not till the twilight fell,
And, lo, in ether from heaven's sweetest
well,
The New Moon swam divinely isolate
In maiden silence, she that makes my fate
Haply not knowing it, or only so
As I the secrets of my sheep may know;
Nor ask I more, entirely blest if she,
In letting me adore, ennoble me
To height of what the Gods meant mak-
ing man,
As only she and her best beauty can.
Mine be the love that in itself can find
Seed of white thoughts, the lilies of the
mind,
Seed of that glad surrender of the will
That finds in service self's true purpose
still ;
Love that in outward fairness sees the tent
Pitched for an inmate far more excellent;
Love with a light irradiate to the core,
Lit at her lamp, but fed from inborn
store ;
Love thrice-requited with the single joy
Of an immaculate vision naught could
cloy,
Dearer because, so high beyond my scope,
My life grew rich with her, unbribed by
hope
Of other guerdon save to think she knew
One grateful votary paid her all her due;
Happy if she, high-radiant there, resigned
To his sure trust her image in his mind.
O fairer even than Peace is when she
comes
Hushing War's tumult, and retreating
drums
Fade to a murmur like the sough of bees
Hidden among the noon-stilled linden-trees,
Bringer of quiet, thou that canst allay
The dust and din and travail of the day,
Strewer of Silence, Giver of the dew
That doth our pastures and our souls re-
new,
Still dwell remote, still on thy shoreless sea

Float unattained in silent empery,
Still light my thoughts, nor listen to a
prayer
Would make thee less imperishably fair !

II

Can, then, my twofold nature find content
In vain conceits of airy blandishment ?
Ask I no more ?   Since yesterday I task
My storm-strewn thoughts to tell me what
I ask:
Faint premonitions of mutation strange
Steal o'er my perfect orb, and, with the
change,
Myself am changed; the shadow of my
earth
Darkens the disk of that celestial worth
Which only yesterday could still suffice
Upwards to waft my thoughts in sacrifice;
My heightened fancy with its touches
warm
Moulds to a woman's that ideal form;
Nor yet a woman's wholly, but divine
With awe her purer essence bred in mine.
Was it long brooding on their own surmise,
Which, of the eyes engendered, fools the
eyes,
Or have I seen through that translucent air
A Presence shaped in its seclusions bare,
My Goddess looking on me from above
As look our russet maidens when they love,
But high-uplifted o'er our human heat
And passion-paths too rough for her pearl
feet ?

Slowly the Shape took outline as I gazed
At her full-orbed or crescent, till, bedazed
With wonder-working light that subtly
wrought
My brain to its own substance, steeping
thought
In trances such as poppies give, I saw
Things shut from vision by sight's sober
law,
Amorphous, changeful, but defined at last
Into the peerless Shape mine eyes hold
fast.
This, too, at first I worshipt: soon, like
wine,
Her eyes, in mine poured, frenzy-philtred
mine;
Passion put Worship's priestly raiment on
And to the woman knelt, the Goddess gone.
Was I, then, more than mortal made ? or
she

Less than divine that she might mate with
me ?
If mortal merely, could my nature cope
With such o'ermastery of maddening
hope ?
If Goddess, could she feel the blissful woe
That women in their self-surrender know ?

III

Long she abode aloof there in her heaven,
Far as the grape-bunch of the Pleiad seven
Beyond my madness' utmost leap; but
here
Mine eyes have feigned of late her rapture
near,
Moulded of mind-mist that broad day dis-
pels,
Here in these shadowy woods and brook-
lulled dells.

Have no heaven-habitants e'er felt a void
In hearts sublimed with ichor unalloyed ?
E'er longed to mingle with a mortal fate
Intense with pathos of its briefer date ?
Could she partake, and live, our human
stains ?
Even with the thought there tingles through
my veins
Sense of unwarned renewal; I, the dead,
Receive and house again the ardor fled,
As once Alcestis; to the ruddy brim
Feel masculine virtue flooding every limb,
And life, like Spring returning, brings the
key
That sets my senses from their winter free,
Dancing like naked fauns too glad for
shame.
Her passion, purified to palest flame,
Can it thus kindle ? Is her purpose this ?
I will not argue, lest I lose a bliss
That makes me dream Tithonus' fortune
mine,
(Or what of it was palpably divine
Ere came the fruitlessly immortal gift;)
I cannot curb my hope's imperious drift
That wings with fire my dull mortality;
Though fancy-forged, 't is all I feel or see.

IV

My Goddess sinks; round Latmos' darken-
ing brow
Trembles the parting of her presence now,
Faint as the perfume left upon the grass
By her limbs' pressure or her feet that
pass

By me conjectured, but conjectured so
As things I touch far fainter substance
show.
Was it mine eyes' imposture I have seen
Flit with the moonbeams on from shade to
sheen
Through the wood-openings ?   Nay, I see
her now
Out of her heaven new-lighted, from her
brow
The hair breeze-scattered, like loose mists
that blow
Across her crescent, goldening as they go
High-kirtled for the chase, and what was
shown,
Of maiden rondure, like the rose half-
blown.
If dream, turn real ! If a vision, stay !
Take mortal shape, my philtre's spell obey !
If hags compel thee from thy secret sky
With gruesome incantations, why not I,
Whose only magic is that I distil
A potion, blent of passion, thought, and
will,
Deeper in reach, in force of fate more rich,
Than e'er was juice wrung by Thessalian
witch
From moon-enchanted herbs, — a potion
brewed
Of my best life in each diviner mood ?
Myself the elixir am, myself the bowl
Seething and mantling with my soul of soul.
Taste and be humanized: what though the
cup,
With thy lips frenzied, shatter ?   Drink it
up !
If but these arms may clasp, o'erquited so,
My world, thy heaven, all life means I
shall know.

V

Sure she hath heard my prayer and granted
half,
As Gods do who at mortal madness laugh.
Yet if life's solid things illusion seem,
Why may not substance wear the mask of
dream ?
In sleep she comes; she visits me in dreams,
And, as her image in a thousand streams,
So in my veins, that her obey, she sees,
Floating and flaming there, her images
Bear to my little world's remotest zone
Glad messages of her, and her alone.
With silence-sandalled Sleep she comes to
me,

(But softer-footed, sweeter-browed, than
she,)
In motion gracious as a seagull's wing,
And all her bright limbs, moving, seem to
sing.
Let me believe so, then, if so I may
With the night's bounty feed my beggared
day.
In dreams I see her lay the goddess down
With bow and quiver, and her crescent-
crown
Flicker and fade away to dull eclipse
As down to mine she deigns her longed-for
lips;
And as her neck my happy arms enfold,
Flooded and lustred with her loosened gold,
She whispers words each sweeter than a
kiss:
Then, wakened with the shock of sudden
bliss,
My arms are empty, my awakener fled,
And, silent in the silent sky o'erhead,
But coldly as on ice-plated snow, she
gleams,
Herself the mother and the child of dreams.

VI

Gone is the time when phantasms could
appease
My quest phantasmal and bring cheated
ease;
When, if she glorified my dreams, I felt
Through all my limbs a change immortal
melt
At touch of hers illuminate with soul.
Not long could I be stilled with Fancy's
dole;
Too soon the mortal mixture in me caught
Red fire from her celestial flame, and
fought
For tyrannous control in all my veins:
My fool's prayer was accepted; what re-
mains?
Or was it some eidolon merely, sent
By her who rules the shades in banishment,
To mock me with her semblance? Were
it thus,
How 'scape I shame, whose will was trai-
torous?
What shall compensate an ideal dimmed?
How blanch again my statue virgin-limbed,
Soiled with the incense-smoke her chosen
priest
Poured more profusely as within decreased
The fire unearthly, fed with coals from far

Within the soul's shrine? Could my fallen
star
Be set in heaven again by prayers and tears
And quenchless sacrifice of all my years,
How would the victim to the flamen leap,
And life for life's redemption paid hold
cheap!

But what resource when she herself de-
scends
From her blue throne, and o'er her vassal
bends
That shape thrice-deified by love, those
eyes
Wherein the Lethe of all others lies?
When my white queen of heaven's remote-
ness tires,
Herself against her other self conspires,
Takes woman's nature, walks in mortal
ways,
And finds in my remorse her beauty's
praise?
Yet all would I renounce to dream again
The dream in dreams fulfilled that made
my pain,
My noble pain that heightened all my
years
With crowns to win and prowess-breeding
tears;
Nay, would that dream renounce once more
to see
Her from her sky there looking down at
me!

VII

Goddess, reclimb thy heaven, and be once
more
An inaccessible splendor to adore,
A faith, a hope of such transcendent worth
As bred ennobling discontent with earth;
Give back the longing, back the elated
mood
That, fed with thee, spurned every meaner
good;
Give even the spur of impotent despair
That, without hope, still bade aspire and
dare;
Give back the need to worship, that still
pours
Down to the soul the virtue it adores!

Nay, brightest and most beautiful, deem
naught
These frantic words, the reckless wind of
thought:

Still stoop, still grant, — I live but in thy
    will;
Be what thou wilt, but be a woman still !
Vainly I cried, nor could myself believe
That what I prayed for I would fain re-
    ceive.
My moon is set; my vision set with her;
No more can worship vain my pulses stir.
Goddess Triform, I own thy triple spell,
My heaven's queen, — queen, too, of my
    earth and hell !

THE BLACK PREACHER

A BRETON LEGEND

At Carnac in Brittany, close on the bay,
They show you a church, or rather the
    gray
Ribs of a dead one, left there to bleach
With the wreck lying near on the crest of
    the beach,
Roofless and splintered with thunder-stone,
'Mid lichen-blurred gravestones all alone;
'T is the kind of ruin strange sights to
    see
That may have their teaching for you and
    me.

Something like this, then, my guide had to
    tell,
Perched on a saint cracked across when he
    fell;
But since I might chance give his meaning
    a wrench,
He talking his *patois* and I English-French,
I 'll put what he told me, preserving the
    tone,
In a rhymed prose that makes it half his,
    half my own.

An abbey-church stood here, once on a
    time,
Built as a death-bed atonement for crime:
'T was for somebody's sins, I know not
    whose;
But sinners are plenty, and you can choose.
Though a cloister now of the dusk-winged
    bat,
'T was rich enough once, and the brothers
    grew fat,
Looser in girdle and purpler in jowl,
Singing good rest to the founder's lost soul.

But one day came Northmen, and lithe
    tongues of fire
Lapped up the chapter-house, licked off
    the spire,
And left all a rubbish-heap, black and
    dreary,
Where only the wind sings *miserere*.

No priest has kneeled since at the altar's
    foot,
Whose crannies are searched by the night-
    shade's root,
Nor sound of service is ever heard,
Except from throat of the unclean bird,
Hooting to unassoiled shapes as they pass
In midnights unholy his witches' mass,
Or shouting "Ho ! ho !" from the belfry
    high
As the Devil's sabbath-train whirls by.

But once a year, on the eve of All-Souls,
Through these arches dishallowed the
    organ rolls,
Fingers long fleshless the bell-ropes work,
The chimes peal muffled with sea-mists
    mirk,
The skeleton windows are traced anew
On the baleful flicker of corpse-lights blue,
And the ghosts must come, so the legend
    saith,
To a preaching of Reverend Doctor Death.

Abbots, monks, barons, and ladies fair
Hear the dull summons and gather there:
No rustle of silk now, no clink of mail,
Nor ever a one greets his church-mate
    pale;
No knight whispers love in the *châtelaine's*
    ear,
His next-door neighbor this five-hundred
    year;
No monk has a sleek *benedicite*
For the great lord shadowy now as he;
Nor needeth any to hold his breath,
Lest he lose the least word of Doctor
    Death.

He chooses his text in the Book Divine,
Tenth verse of the Preacher in chapter
    nine: —
" 'Whatsoever thy hand shall find thee to
    do,
That do with thy whole might, or thou
    shalt rue;
For no man is wealthy, or wise, or brave,

In that quencher of might-be's and would-
  be's, the grave.'
Bid by the Bridegroom, 'To-morrow,' ye
  said,
And To-morrow was digging a trench for
  your bed;
Ye said, 'God can wait; let us finish our
  wine;'
Ye had wearied Him, fools, and that last
  knock was mine!'"

But I can't pretend to give you the ser-
  mon,
Or say if the tongue were French, Latin,
  or German;
Whatever he preached in, I give you my
  word
The meaning was easy to all that heard;
Famous preachers there have been and be,
But never was one so convincing as he;
So blunt was never a begging friar,
No Jesuit's tongue so barbed with fire,
Cameronian never, nor Methodist,
Wrung gall out of Scripture with such a
  twist.

And would you know who his hearers must
  be?
I tell you just what my guide told me:
Excellent teaching men have, day and
  night,
From two earnest friars, a black and a
  white,
The Dominican Death and the Carmelite
  Life;
And between these two there is never
  strife,
For each has his separate office and station,
And each his own work in the congrega-
  tion;
Whoso to the white brother deafens his
  ears,
And cannot be wrought on by blessings or
  tears,
Awake in his coffin must wait and wait,
In that blackness of darkness that means
  too late,
And come once a year, when the ghost-bell
  tolls,
As till Doomsday it shall on the eve of
  All-Souls,
To hear Doctor Death, whose words smart
  with the brine
Of the Preacher, the tenth verse of chap-
  ter nine.

ARCADIA REDIVIVA

I, WALKING the familiar street,
  While a crammed horse-car jingled
    through it,
Was lifted from my prosy feet
  And in Arcadia ere I knew it.

Fresh sward for gravel soothed my tread,
  And shepherd's pipes my ear delighted;
The riddle may be lightly read:
  I met two lovers newly plighted.

They murmured by in happy care,
  New plans for paradise devising,
Just as the moon, with pensive stare,
  O'er Mistress Craigie's pines was rising.

Astarte, known nigh threescore years,
  Me to no speechless rapture urges;
Them in Elysium she enspheres,
  Queen, from of old, of thaumaturges.

The railings put forth bud and bloom,
  The house-fronts all with myrtles twine
    them,
And light-winged Loves in every room
  Make nests, and then with kisses line
    them.

O sweetness of untasted life!
  O dream, its own supreme fulfilment!
O hours with all illusion rife,
  As ere the heart divined what ill meant!

" Et ego," sighed I to myself,
  And strove some vain regrets to bridle,
" Though now laid dusty on the shelf,
  Was hero once of such an idyl!

" An idyl ever newly sweet,
  Although since Adam's day recited,
Whose measures time them to Love's feet,
  Whose sense is every ill requited."

Maiden, if I may counsel, drain
  Each drop of this enchanted season,
For even our honeymoons must wane,
  Convicted of green cheese by Reason.

And none will seem so safe from change,
  Nor in such skies benignant hover,
As this, beneath whose witchery strange
  You tread on rose-leaves with your lover.

The glass unfilled all tastes can fit,
As round its brim Conjecture dances;
For not Mephisto's self hath wit
To draw such vintages as Fancy's.

When our pulse beats its minor key,
When play-time halves and school-time
doubles,
Age fills the cup with serious tea,
Which once Dame Clicquot starred with
bubbles.

"Fie, Mr. Graybeard! Is this wise?
Is this the moral of a poet,
Who, when the plant of Eden dies,
Is privileged once more to sow it?

"That herb of clay-disdaining root,
From stars secreting what it feeds on,
Is burnt-out passion's slag and soot
Fit soil to strew its dainty seeds on?

"Pray, why, if in Arcadia once,
Need one so soon forget the way
there?
Or why, once there, be such a dunce
As not contentedly to stay there?"

Dear child, 't was but a sorry jest,
And from my heart I hate the cynic
Who makes the Book of Life a nest
For comments staler than rabbinic.

If Love his simple spell but keep,
Life with ideal eyes to flatter,
The Grail itself were crockery cheap
To Every-day's communion-platter.

One Darby is to me well known,
Who, as the hearth between them blazes,
Sees the old moonlight shine on Joan,
And float her youthward in its hazes.

He rubs his spectacles, he stares, —
'T is the same face that witched him
early!
He gropes for his remaining hairs, —
Is this a fleece that feels so curly?

"Good heavens! but now 't was winter
gray,
And I of years had more than plenty;
The almanac 's a fool! 'T is May!
Hang family Bibles! I am twenty!

"Come, Joan, your arm; we 'll walk the
room —
The lane, I mean — do you remember?
How confident the roses bloom,
As if it ne'er could be December!

"Nor more it shall, while in your eyes
My heart its summer heat recovers,
And you, howe'er your mirror lies,
Find your old beauty in your lover's."

THE NEST

MAY

When oaken woods with buds are pink,
And new-come birds each morning sing,
When fickle May on Summer's brink
Pauses, and knows not which to fling,
Whether fresh bud and bloom again,
Or hoar-frost silvering hill and plain,

Then from the honeysuckle gray
The oriole with experienced quest
Twitches the fibrous bark away,
The cordage of his hammock-nest,
Cheering his labor with a note
Rich as the orange of his throat.

High o'er the loud and dusty road
The soft gray cup in safety swings,
To brim ere August with its load
Of downy breasts and throbbing wings,
O'er which the friendly elm-tree heaves
An emerald roof with sculptured eaves.

Below, the noisy World drags by
In the old way, because it must,
The bride with heartbreak in her eye,
The mourner following hated dust:
Thy duty, wingèd flame of Spring,
Is but to love, and fly, and sing.

Oh, happy life, to soar and sway
Above the life by mortals led,
Singing the merry months away,
Master, not slave of daily bread,
And, when the Autumn comes, to flee
Wherever sunshine beckons thee!

PALINODE — DECEMBER

Like some lorn abbey now, the wood
Stands roofless in the bitter air;

In ruins on its floor is strewed
  The carven foliage quaint and rare,
And homeless winds complain along
The columned choir once thrilled with song.

And thou, dear nest, whence joy and praise
  The thankful oriole used to pour,
Swing'st empty while the north winds chase
  Their snowy swarms from Labrador:
But, loyal to the happy past,
I love thee still for what thou wast.

Ah, when the Summer graces flee
  From other nests more dear than thou,
And, where June crowded once, I see
  Only bare trunk and disleaved bough;
When springs of life that gleamed and
      gushed
Run chilled, and slower, and are hushed;

When our own branches, naked long,
  The vacant nests of Spring betray,
Nurseries of passion, love, and song
  That vanished as our year grew gray;
When Life drones o'er a tale twice told
O'er embers pleading with the cold, —

I 'll trust, that, like the birds of Spring,
  Our good goes not without repair,
But only flies to soar and sing
Far off in some diviner air,
Where we shall find it in the calms
Of that fair garden 'neath the palms.

A YOUTHFUL EXPERIMENT IN ENGLISH HEXAMETERS

IMPRESSIONS OF HOMER

SOMETIMES come pauses of calm, when the
      rapt bard, holding his heart back,
Over his deep mind muses, as when o'er
      awe-stricken ocean
Poises a heapt cloud luridly, ripening the
      gale and the thunder;
Slow rolls onward the verse with a long
      swell heaving and swinging,
Seeming to wait till, gradually wid'ning
      from far-off horizons,
Piling the deeps up, heaping the glad-
      hearted surges before it,
Gathers the thought as a strong wind
      darkening and cresting the tumult.
Then every pause, every heave, each trough
      in the waves, has its meaning;

Full-sailed, forth like a tall ship steadies
      the theme, and around it,
Leaping beside it in glad strength, running
      in wild glee beyond it,
Harmonies billow exulting and floating the
      soul where it lists them,
Swaying the listener's fantasy hither and
      thither like driftweed.

BIRTHDAY VERSES

WRITTEN IN A CHILD'S ALBUM

'T WAS sung of old in hut and hall
How once a king in evil hour
Hung musing o'er his castle wall,
And, lost in idle dreams, let fall
Into the sea his ring of power.

Then, let him sorrow as he might,
And pledge his daughter and his throne
To who restored the jewel bright,
The broken spell would ne'er unite;
The grim old ocean held its own.

Those awful powers on man that wait,
On man, the beggar or the king,
To hovel bare or hall of state
A magic ring that masters fate
With each succeeding birthday bring.

Therein are set four jewels rare:
Pearl winter, summer's ruby blaze,
Spring's emerald, and, than all more fair,
Fall's pensive opal, doomed to bear
A heart of fire bedreamed with haze.

To him the simple spell who knows
The spirits of the ring to sway,
Fresh power with every sunrise flows,
And royal pursuivants are those
That fly his mandates to obey.

But he that with a slackened will
Dreams of things past or things to be,
From him the charm is slipping still,
And drops, ere he suspect the ill,
Into the inexorable sea.

ESTRANGEMENT

THE path from me to you that led,
  Untrodden long, with grass is grown,
Mute carpet that his lieges spread

Before the Prince Oblivion
When he goes visiting the dead.

And who are they but who forget ?
  You, who my coming could surmise
Ere any hint of me as yet
  Warned other ears and other eyes,
See the path blurred without regret.

But when I trace its windings sweet
  With saddened steps, at every spot
That feels the memory in my feet,
  Each grass-blade turns forget-me-not,
Where murmuring bees your name repeat.

PHŒBE

This poem was sent from London September
4, 1881, to Mr. Gilder for *The Century*. Its
first form was in the main the same as this,
but before the poem was published several
changes and omissions were made. The inter-
esting evolution of the final form may be seen
in detail in the *Notes and Illustrations*.

ERE pales in Heaven the morning star,
  A bird, the loneliest of its kind,
Hears Dawn's faint footfall from afar
  While all its mates are dumb and blind.

It is a wee sad-colored thing,
  As shy and secret as a maid,
That, ere in choir the robins sing,
  Pipes its own name like one afraid.

It seems pain-prompted to repeat
  The story of some ancient ill,
But *Phœbe! Phœbe!* sadly sweet
  Is all it says, and then is still.

It calls and listens. Earth and sky,
  Hushed by the pathos of its fate,
Listen : no whisper of reply
  Comes from its doom-dissevered mate.

Phœbe! it calls and calls again,
  And Ovid, could he but have heard,
Had hung a legendary pain
  About the memory of the bird ;

A pain articulate so long,
  In penance of some mouldered crime
Whose ghost still flies the Furies' thong
  Down the waste solitudes of time.

Waif of the young World's wonder-hour,
  When gods found mortal maidens fair,
And will malign was joined with power
  Love's kindly laws to overbear,

Like Progne, did it feel the stress
  And coil of the prevailing words
Close round its being, and compress
  Man's ampler nature to a bird's ?

One only memory left of all
  The motley crowd of vanished scenes,
Hers, and vain impulse to recall
  By repetition what it means.

Phœbe! is all it has to say
  In plaintive cadence o'er and o'er,
Like children that have lost their way,
  And know their names, but nothing more.

Is it a type, since Nature's Lyre
  Vibrates to every note in man,
Of that insatiable desire,
  Meant to be so since life began ?

I, in strange lands at gray of dawn,
  Wakeful, have heard that fruitless plaint
Through Memory's chambers deep with-
    drawn
  Renew its iterations faint.

So nigh ! yet from remotest years
  It summons back its magic, rife
With longings unappeased, and tears
  Drawn from the very source of life.

DAS EWIG–WEIBLICHE

How was I worthy so divine a loss,
  Deepening my midnights, kindling all
    my morns ?
Why waste such precious wood to make my
    cross,
  Such far-sought roses for my crown of
    thorns ?

And when she came, how earned I such a
    gift ?
  Why spend on me, a poor earth-delving
    mole,
The fireside sweetnesses, the heavenward
    lift,
  The hourly mercy, of a woman's soul ?

Ah, did we know to give her all her right,
  What wonders even in our poor clay
    were done !
It is not Woman leaves us to our night,
  But our brute earth that grovels from
    her sun.

Our nobler cultured fields and gracious
    domes
  We whirl too oft from her who still
    shines on
To light in vain our caves and clefts, the
    homes
  Of night-bird instincts pained till she be
    gone.

Still must this body starve our souls with
    shade ;
  But when Death makes us what we were
    before,
Then shall her sunshine all our depths
    invade,
  And not a shadow stain heaven's crystal
    floor.

THE RECALL

COME back before the birds are flown,
Before the leaves desert the tree,
And, through the lonely alleys blown,
Whisper their vain regrets to me
Who drive before a blast more rude,
The plaything of my gusty mood,
In vain pursuing and pursued !

Nay, come although the boughs be bare,
Though snowflakes fledge the summer's
    nest,
And in some far Ausonian air
The thrush, your minstrel, warm his breast.
Come, sunshine's treasurer, and bring
To doubting flowers their faith in spring,
To birds and me the need to sing !

ABSENCE

SLEEP is Death's image, — poets tell us so ;
But Absence is the bitter self of Death,
And, you away, Life's lips their red forego,
Parched in an air unfreshened by your
    breath.

Light of those eyes that made the light of
    mine,

Where shine you ?   On what happier fields
    and flowers ?
Heaven's lamps renew their lustre less
    divine,
But only serve to count my darkened hours.

If with your presence went your image too,
That brain-born ghost my path would never
    cross
Which meets me now where'er I once met
    you,
Then vanishes, to multiply my loss.

MONNA LISA

SHE gave me all that woman can,
Nor her soul's nunnery forego,
A confidence that man to man
Without remorse can never show.

Rare art, that can the sense refine
Till not a pulse rebellious stirs,
And, since she never can be mine,
Makes it seem sweeter to be hers !

THE OPTIMIST

TURBID from London's noise and smoke,
Here I find air and quiet too:
Air filtered through the beech and oak,
Quiet by nothing harsher broke
Than wood-dove's meditative coo.

The Truce of God is here; the breeze
Sighs as men sigh relieved from care,
Or tilts as lightly in the trees
As might a robin: all is ease,
With pledge of ampler ease to spare.

Time, leaning on his scythe, forgets
To turn the hour-glass in his hand,
And all life's petty cares and frets,
Its teasing hopes and weak regrets,
Are still as that oblivious sand.

Repose fills all the generous space
Of undulant plain; the rook and crow
Hush; 't is as if a silent grace,
By Nature murmured, calmed the face
Of Heaven above and Earth below.

From past and future toils I rest,
One Sabbath pacifies my year;

I am the halcyon, this my nest;
And all is safely for the best
While the World 's there and I am here.

So I turn tory for the nonce,
And think the radical a bore,
Who cannot see, thick-witted dunce,
That what was good for people once
Must be as good forevermore.

Sun, sink no deeper down the sky;
Earth, never change this summer mood;
Breeze, loiter thus forever by,
Stir the dead leaf or let it lie;
Since I am happy, all is good.

ON BURNING SOME OLD LETTERS

WITH what odorous woods and spices
Spared for royal sacrifices,
With what costly gums seld-seen,
Hoarded to embalm a queen,
With what frankincense and myrrh,
Burn these precious parts of her,
Full of life and light and sweetness
As a summer day's completeness,
Joy of sun and song of bird
Running wild in every word,
Full of all the superhuman
Grace and winsomeness of woman?

O'er these leaves her wrist has slid,
Thrilled with veins where fire is hid
'Neath the skin's pellucid veil,
Like the opal's passion pale;
This her breath has sweetened; this
Still seems trembling with the kiss
She half-ventured on my name,
Brow and cheek and throat aflame;
Over all caressing lies
Sunshine left there by her eyes;
From them all an effluence rare
With her nearness fills the air,
Till the murmur I half-hear
Of her light feet drawing near.

Rarest woods were coarse and rough,
Sweetest spice not sweet enough,
Too impure all earthly fire
For this sacred funeral-pyre;
These rich relics must suffice
For their own dear sacrifice.

Seek we first an altar fit
For such victims laid on it:
It shall be this slab brought home
In old happy days from Rome, —
Lazuli, once blest to line
Dian's inmost cell and shrine.
Gently now I lay them there,
Pure as Dian's forehead bare,
Yet suffused with warmer hue,
Such as only Latmos knew.

Fire I gather from the sun
In a virgin lens: 't is done !
Mount the flames, red, yellow, blue,
As her moods were shining through,
Of the moment's impulse born, —
Moods of sweetness, playful scorn,
Half defiance, half surrender,
More than cruel, more than tender,
Flouts, caresses, sunshine, shade,
Gracious doublings of a maid
Infinite in guileless art,
Playing hide-seek with her heart.

On the altar now, alas,
There they lie a crinkling mass,
Writhing still, as if with grief
Went the life from every leaf;
Then (heart-breaking palimpsest !)
Vanishing ere wholly guessed,
Suddenly some lines flash back,
Traced in lightning on the black,
And confess, till now denied,
All the fire they strove to hide.
What they told me, sacred trust,
Stays to glorify my dust,
There to burn through dust and damp
Like a mage's deathless lamp,
While an atom of this frame
Lasts to feed the dainty flame.

All is ashes now, but they
In my soul are laid away,
And their radiance round me hovers
Soft as moonlight over lovers,
Shutting her and me alone
In dream-Edens of our own;
First of lovers to invent
Love, and teach men what it meant.

THE PROTEST

I COULD not bear to see those eyes
On all with wasteful largess shine,

And that delight of welcome rise
Like sunshine strained through amber wine,
But that a glow from deeper skies,
From conscious fountains more divine,
Is (is it ?) mine.

Be beautiful to all mankind,
As Nature fashioned thee to be;
'T would anger me did all not find
The sweet perfection that 's in thee:
Yet keep one charm of charms behind, —
Nay, thou 'rt so rich, keep two or three
For (is it ?) me !

THE PETITION

OH, tell me less or tell me more,
Soft eyes with mystery at the core,
That always seem to meet my own
Frankly as pansies fully grown,
Yet waver still 'tween no and yes !

So swift to cavil and deny,
Then parley with concessions shy,
Dear eyes, that make their youth be mine
And through my inmost shadows shine,
Oh, tell me more or tell me less !

FACT OR FANCY?

IN town I hear, scarce wakened yet,
    My neighbor's clock behind the wall
Record the day's increasing debt,
    And *Cuckoo! Cuckoo!* faintly call.

Our senses run in deepening grooves,
    Thrown out of which they lose their tact,
And consciousness with effort moves
    From habit past to present fact.

So, in the country waked to-day,
    I hear, unwitting of the change,
A cuckoo's throb from far away
    Begin to strike, nor think it strange.

The sound creates its wonted frame:
    My bed at home, the songster hid
Behind the wainscoting, — all came
    As long association bid.

Then, half aroused, ere yet Sleep's mist
    From the mind's uplands furl away,
To the familiar sound I list,
    Disputed for by Night and Day.

I count to learn how late it is,
    Until, arrived at thirty-four,
I question, " What strange world is this
    Whose lavish hours would make me
        poor ? "

Cuckoo! Cuckoo!   Still on it went,
    With hints of mockery in its tone;
How could such hoards of time be spent
    By one poor mortal's wit alone ?

I have it !   Grant, ye kindly Powers,
    I from this spot may never stir,
If only these uncounted hours
    May pass, and seem too short, with Her !

But who She is, her form and face,
    These to the world of dream belong;
She moves through fancy's visioned space,
    Unbodied, like the cuckoo's song.

AGRO-DOLCE

ONE kiss from all others prevents me,
    And sets all my pulses astir,
And burns on my lips and torments me:
    'T is the kiss that I fain would give her.

One kiss for all others requites me,
    Although it is never to be,
And sweetens my dreams and invites me:
    'T is the kiss that she dare not give me.

Ah, could it be mine, it were sweeter
    Than honey bees garner in dream,
Though its bliss on my lips were fleeter
    Than a swallow's dip to the stream.

And yet, thus denied, it can never
    In the prose of life vanish away;
O'er my lips it must hover forever,
    The sunshine and shade of my day.

THE BROKEN TRYST

WALKING alone where we walked together
    When June was breezy and blue,
I watch in the gray autumnal weather
    The leaves fall inconstant as you.

If a dead leaf startle behind me,
    I think 't is your garment's hem,
And, oh, where no memory could find me,
    Might I whirl away with them !

CASA SIN ALMA

RECUERDO DE MADRID

SILENCIOSO por la puerta
Voy de su casa desierta
Do siempre feliz entré,
Y la encuentro en vano abierta
Cual la boca de una muerta
Despues que el alma se fué.

A CHRISTMAS CAROL

FOR THE SUNDAY-SCHOOL CHILDREN OF
THE CHURCH OF THE DISCIPLES

The Church of the Disciples in Boston was
under the ministration of the Reverend James
Freeman Clarke.

" WHAT means this glory round our feet,"
The Magi mused, "more bright than
morn ? "
And voices chanted clear and sweet,
" To-day the Prince of Peace is born ! "

" What means that star," the Shepherds
said,
" That brightens through the rocky
glen ? "
And angels, answering overhead,
Sang, " Peace on earth, good - will to
men ! "

'T is eighteen hundred years and more
Since those sweet oracles were dumb;
We wait for Him, like them of yore;
Alas, He seems so slow to come !

But it was said, in words of gold
No time or sorrow e'er shall dim,
That little children might be bold
In perfect trust to come to Him.

All round about our feet shall shine
A light like that the wise men saw,
If we our loving wills incline
To that sweet Life which is the Law.

So shall we learn to understand
The simple faith of shepherds then,
And, clasping kindly hand in hand,
Sing, " Peace on earth, good - will to
men ! "

And they who do their souls no wrong,
But keep at eve the faith of morn,
Shall daily hear the angel-song,
" To-day the Prince of Peace is born ! "

MY PORTRAIT GALLERY

OFT round my hall of portraiture I gaze,
By Memory reared, the artist wise and
holy,
From stainless quarries of deep - buried
days.
There, as I muse in soothing melancholy,
Your faces glow in more than mortal youth,
Companions of my prime, now vanished
wholly,
The loud, impetuous boy, the low-voiced
maiden,
Now for the first time seen in flawless truth.
Ah, never master that drew mortal breath
Can match thy portraits, just and generous
Death,
Whose brush with sweet regretful tints is
laden !
Thou paintest that which struggled here
below
Half understood, or understood for woe,
And with a sweet forewarning
Mak'st round the sacred front an aureole
glow
Woven of that light that rose on Easter
morning.

PAOLO TO FRANCESCA

I WAS with thee in Heaven: I cannot tell
If years or moments, so the sudden bliss,
When first we found, then lost, us in a kiss,
Abolished Time, abolished Earth and Hell,
Left only Heaven.   Then from our blue
there fell
The dagger's flash, and did not fall amiss,
For nothing now can rob my life of this, —
That once with thee in Heaven, all else is
well.
Us, undivided when man's vengeance came,
God's half - forgives that doth not here
divide;
And, were this bitter whirl-blast fanged
with flame,
To me 't were summer, we being side by
side:
This granted, I God's mercy will not blame,
For, given thy nearness, nothing is denied.

SONNET

SCOTTISH BORDER

The following letter to Mr. Howells, then editor of *The Atlantic Monthly*, in which this sonnet was printed, is a little out of proportion as a head-note to a poem of fourteen lines, but it is too characteristic and too indicative of Lowell's extreme solicitude over his verse to be omitted. " There was one verse in the *Border* sonnet which, when I came to copy it, worried me with its lack of just what I wanted. Only *one?* you will say. Yes, all; but never mind — this one *most.* Instead of

'Where the shy ballad could its leaves unfold'

read ' dared its blooms.' I had liefer ' cup,' but cup is already metaphoric when applied to flowers, and Bottom the Weaver would be sure to ask in one of the many journals he edits — ' How unfold a cup ? Does he mean one of those pocket drinking-cups — leathern inconveniences that always *stick* when you try to unfold 'em ? ' Damn Bottom ! We ought not to think of him, but then the Public is made up of him, and I wish him to know that I was thinking of a flower. Besides, the sonnet is, more than any other kind of verse, a deliberate composition, and ' susceptible of a high polish," as the dendrologists say of the woods of certain trees. Or shall we say ' grew in secret bold ' ? I write both on the opposite leaf, that you may choose one to paste over and not get the credit of tinkering my rhymes.

dared its blooms
grew in secret bold.

Perhaps, after all, it is the buzzing of that *b* in blooms and bold, answering his brother *b* in ballads that *b*-witched me, and merely changing ' could ' to ' dared ' is all that is wanted. The sentiment of this sonnet pleases me."

As sinks the sun behind yon alien hills
Whose heather-purpled slopes, in glory rolled,
Flush all my thought with momentary gold,
What pang of vague regret my fancy thrills ?
Here 't is enchanted ground the peasant tills,
Where the shy ballad dared its blooms unfold,
And memory's glamour makes new sights seem old,
As when our life some vanished dream fulfils.
Yet not to thee belong these painless tears,
Land loved ere seen: before my darkened eyes,
From far beyond the waters and the years,
Horizons mute that wait their poet rise;
The stream before me fades and disappears,
And in the Charles the western splendor dies.

SONNET

ON BEING ASKED FOR AN AUTOGRAPH IN VENICE

AMID these fragments of heroic days
When thought met deed with mutual passion's leap,
There sits a Fame whose silent trump makes cheap
What short-lived rumor of ourselves we raise.
They had far other estimate of praise
Who stamped the signet of their souls so deep
In art and action, and whose memories keep
Their height like stars above our misty ways:
In this grave presence to record my name
Something within me hangs the head and shrinks.
Dull were the soul without some joy in fame;
Yet here to claim remembrance were, methinks,
Like him who, in the desert's awful frame,
Notches his cockney initials on the Sphinx.

THE DANCING BEAR

FAR over Elf-land poets stretch their sway,
And win their dearest crowns beyond the goal
Of their own conscious purpose; they control
With gossamer threads wide-flown our fancy's play,
And so our action. On my walk to-day,
A wallowing bear begged clumsily his toll,
When straight a vision rose of Atta Troll,
And scenes ideal witched mine eyes away.
" *Merci, Mossieu !* " the astonished bearward cried,
Grateful for thrice his hope to me, the slave

Of partial memory, seeing at his side
A bear immortal. The glad dole I gave
Was none of mine; poor Heine o'er the wide
Atlantic welter stretched it from his grave.

THE MAPLE

THE Maple puts her corals on in May,
While loitering frosts about the lowlands cling,
To be in tune with what the robins sing,
Plastering new log-huts 'mid her branches gray;
But when the Autumn southward turns away,
Then in her veins burns most the blood of Spring,
And every leaf, intensely blossoming,
Makes the year's sunset pale the set of day.
O Youth unprescient, were it only so
With trees you plant, and in whose shade reclined,
Thinking their drifting blooms Fate's coldest snow,
You carve dear names upon the faithful rind,
Nor in that vernal stem the cross foreknow
That Age shall bear, silent, yet unresigned!

NIGHTWATCHES

WHILE the slow clock, as they were miser's gold,
Counts and recounts the mornward steps of Time,
The darkness thrills with conscience of each crime
By Death committed, daily grown more bold.
Once more the list of all my wrongs is told,
And ghostly hands stretch to me from my prime
Helpless farewells, as from an alien clime;
For each new loss redoubles all the old.
This morn 't was May; the blossoms were astir
With southern wind; but now the boughs are bent

With snow instead of birds, and all things freeze.
How much of all my past is dumb with her,
And of my future, too, for with her went
Half of that world I ever cared to please!

DEATH OF QUEEN MERCEDES

In a letter to his daughter from Madrid, July 26, 1878, Lowell wrote of Queen Mercedes: "Anything more tragic than the circumstances of her death it would be hard to imagine. She was actually receiving extreme unction while the guns were firing in honor of her eighteenth birthday, and four days later we saw her dragged to her dreary tomb at the Escorial, followed by the coach and its eight white horses in which she had driven in triumph from the church to the palace on the day of her wedding. The poor brutes tossed their snowy plumes as haughtily now as then. Her death is really a great public loss. She was amiable, intelligent, and simple — not beautiful but *good*-looking — and was already becoming popular."

HERS all that Earth could promise or bestow, —
Youth, Beauty, Love, a crown, the beckoning years,
Lids never wet, unless with joyous tears,
A life remote from every sordid woe,
And by a nation's swelled to lordlier flow.
What lurking-place, thought we, for doubts or fears,
When, the day's swan, she swam along the cheers
Of the Alcalá, five happy months ago?
The guns were shouting Io Hymen then
That, on her birthday, now denounce her doom;
The same white steeds that tossed their scorn of men
To-day as proudly drag her to the tomb.
Grim jest of fate! Yet who dare call it blind,
Knowing what life is, what our humankind?

PRISON OF CERVANTES

SEAT of all woes? Though Nature's firm decree
The narrowing soul with narrowing dungeon bind,

Yet was his free of motion as the wind,
And held both worlds, of spirit and sense,
    in fee.
In charmed communion with his dual mind
He wandered Spain, himself both knight
    and hind,
Redressing wrongs he knew must ever be.
His humor wise could see life's long de-
    ceit,
Man's baffled aims, nor therefore both de-
    spise;
His knightly nature could ill fortune greet
Like an old friend.   Whose ever such kind
    eyes
That pierced so deep, such scope, save his
    whose feet
By Avon ceased 'neath the same April's
    skies ?

TO A LADY PLAYING ON THE CITHERN

So dreamy-soft the notes, so far away
They seem to fall, the horns of Oberon
Blow their faint Hunt's-up from the good-
    time gone;
Or, on a morning of long-withered May,
Larks tinkle unseen o'er Claudian arches
    gray,
That Romeward crawl from Dreamland;
    and anon
My fancy flings her cloak of Darkness on,
To vanish from the dungeon of To-day.
In happier times and scenes I seem to
    be,
And, as her fingers flutter o'er the strings,
The days return when I was young as she,
And my fledged thoughts began to feel
    their wings
With all Heaven's blue before them:
    Memory
Or Music is it such enchantment sings ?

THE EYE'S TREASURY

Gold of the reddening sunset, backward
    thrown
In largess on my tall paternal trees,
Thou with false hope or fear didst never
    tease
His heart that hoards thee; nor is child-
    hood flown
From him whose life no fairer boon hath
    known

Than that what pleased him earliest still
    should please:
And who hath incomes safe from chance as
    these,
Gone in a moment, yet for life his own ?
All other gold is slave of earthward laws;
This to the deeps of ether takes its flight,
And on the topmost leaves makes glorious
    pause
Of parting pathos ere it yield to night:
So linger, as from me earth's light with-
    draws,
Dear touch of Nature, tremulously bright !

PESSIMOPTIMISM

Ye little think what toil it was to build
A world of men imperfect even as this,
Where we conceive of Good by what we
    miss,
Of Ill by that wherewith best days are
    filled;
A world whose every atom is self-willed,
Whose corner-stone is propt on artifice,
Whose joy is shorter-lived than woman's
    kiss,
Whose wisdom hoarded is but to be
    spilled.
Yet this is better than a life of caves,
Whose highest art was scratching on a
    bone,
Or chipping toilsome arrowheads of flint;
Better, though doomed to hear while Cleon
    raves,
To see wit's want eterned in paint or
    stone,
And wade the drain-drenched shoals of
    daily print.

THE BRAKES

What countless years and wealth of brain
    were spent
To bring us hither from our caves and
    huts,
And trace through pathless wilds the deep-
    worn ruts
Of faith and habit, by whose deep in-
    dent
Prudence may guide if genius be not lent,
Genius, not always happy when it shuts
Its ears against the plodder's ifs and
    buts,

Hoping in one rash leap to snatch the
   event.
The coursers of the sun, whose hoofs of
   flame
Consume morn's misty threshold, are exact
As bankers' clerks, and all this star-poised
   frame,
One swerve allowed, were with convulsion
   rackt;
This world were doomed, should Dulness
   fail, to tame
Wit's feathered heels in the stern stocks of
   fact.

A FOREBODING

WHAT were the whole void world, if thou
   wert dead,
Whose briefest absence can eclipse my
   day,
And make the hours that danced with
   Time away
Drag their funereal steps with muffled
   head ?
Through thee, meseems, the very rose is
   red,
From thee the violet steals its breath in
   May,
From thee draw life all things that grow
   not gray,
And by thy force the happy stars are sped.
Thou near, the hope of thee to overflow
Fills all my earth and heaven, as when in
   Spring,
Ere April come, the birds and blossoms
   know,
And grasses brighten round her feet to
   cling;
Nay, and this hope delights all nature so
That the dumb turf I tread on seems to
   sing.

III. FANCY

UNDER THE OCTOBER MAPLES

WHAT mean these banners spread,
These paths with royal red
So gaily carpeted ?
Comes there a prince to-day ?
Such footing were too fine
For feet less argentine
Than Dian's own or thine,
Queen whom my tides obey.

Surely for thee are meant
These hues so orient
That with a sultan's tent
Each tree invites the sun ;
Our Earth such homage pays,
So decks her dusty ways,
And keeps such holidays,
For one and only one.

My brain shapes form and face,
Throbs with the rhythmic grace
And cadence of her pace
To all fine instincts true ;
Her footsteps, as they pass,
Than moonbeams over grass
Fall lighter, — but, alas,
More insubstantial too !

LOVE'S CLOCK

A PASTORAL

DAPHNIS *waiting*

" O DRYAD feet,
Be doubly fleet,
Timed to my heart's expectant beat
While I await her !
' At four,' vowed she ;
'T is scarcely three,
Yet by *my* time it seems to be
A good hour later ! "

CHLOE

" Bid me not stay !
Hear reason, pray !
'T is striking six ! Sure never day
Was short as this is ! "

DAPHNIS

" Reason nor rhyme
Is in the chime !
It can't be five ; I 've scarce had time
To beg two kisses ! "

BOTH

" Early or late,
When lovers wait,
And Love's watch gains, if Time a gait
So snail-like chooses,
Why should his feet
Become more fleet
Than cowards' are, when lovers meet
And Love's watch loses ? "

ELEANOR MAKES MACAROONS

LIGHT of triumph in her eyes,
Eleanor her apron ties;
As she pushes back her sleeves,
High resolve her bosom heaves.
Hasten, cook ! impel the fire
To the pace of her desire;
As you hope to save your soul,
Bring a virgin casserole,
Brightest bring of silver spoons, —
Eleanor makes macaroons !

Almond-blossoms, now adance
In the smile of Southern France,
Leave your sport with sun and breeze,
Think of duty, not of ease;
Fashion, 'neath their jerkins brown,
Kernels white as thistle-down,
Tiny cheeses made with cream
From the Galaxy's mid-stream,
Blanched in light of honeymoons, —
Eleanor makes macaroons !

Now for sugar, — nay, our plan
Tolerates no work of man.
Hurry, then, ye golden bees;
Fetch your clearest honey, please,
Garnered on a Yorkshire moor,
While the last larks sing and soar,
From the heather-blossoms sweet
Where sea-breeze and sunshine meet,
And the Augusts mask as Junes, —
Eleanor makes macaroons !

Next the pestle and mortar find,
Pure rock-crystal, — these to grind
Into paste more smooth than silk,
Whiter than the milkweed's milk:
Spread it on a rose-leaf, thus,
Cate to please Theocritus;
Then the fire with spices swell,
While, for her completer spell,
Mystic canticles she croons, —
Eleanor makes macaroons !

Perfect ! and all this to waste
On a graybeard's palsied taste !
Poets so their verses write,
Heap them full of life and light,
And then fling them to the rude
Mumbling of the multitude.

Not so dire her fate as theirs,
Since her friend this gift declares
Choicest of his birthday boons, —
Eleanor's dear macaroons !

February 22, 1884.

TELEPATHY

" AND how could you dream of meet-
ing ? "
Nay, how can you ask me, sweet ?
All day my pulse had been beating
The tune of your coming feet.

And as nearer and ever nearer
I felt the throb of your tread,
To be in the world grew dearer,
And my blood ran rosier red.

Love called, and I could not linger,
But sought the forbidden tryst,
As music follows the finger
Of the dreaming lutanist.

And though you had said it and said it,
"We must not be happy to-day,"
Was I not wiser to credit
The fire in my feet than your Nay ?

SCHERZO

WHEN the down is on the chin
And the gold-gleam in the hair,
When the birds their sweethearts win
And champagne is in the air,
Love is here, and Love is there,
Love is welcome everywhere.

Summer's cheek too soon turns thin,
Days grow briefer, sunshine rare;
Autumn from his cannekin
Blows the froth to chase Despair:
Love is met with frosty stare,
Cannot house 'neath branches bare.

When new life is in the leaf
And new red is in the rose,
Though Love's Maytime be as brief
As a dragon-fly's repose,
Never moments come like those,
Be they Heaven or Hell : who knows ?

All too soon comes Winter's grief,
Spendthrift Love's false friends turn foes;
Softly comes Old Age, the thief,
Steals the rapture, leaves the throes:
Love his mantle round him throws, —
"Time to say Good-by; it snows."

"FRANCISCUS DE VERULAMIO SIC COGITAVIT"

THAT'S a rather bold speech, my Lord
  Bacon,
  For, indeed, is't so easy to know
Just how much we from others have taken,
  And how much our own natural flow?

Since your mind bubbled up at its foun-
  tain,
  How many streams made it elate,
While it calmed to the plain from the
  mountain,
  As every mind must that grows great?

While you thought 't was You thinking as
  newly
  As Adam still wet with God's dew,
You forgot in your self-pride that truly
  The whole Past was thinking through
  you.

Greece, Rome, nay, your namesake, old
  Roger,
  With Truth's nameless delvers who
  wrought
In the dark mines of Truth, helped to prod
  your
  Fine brain with the goad of their thought.

As mummy was prized for a rich hue
  The painter no elsewhere could find,
So 't was buried men's thinking with which
  you
  Gave the ripe mellow tone to your mind.

I heard the proud strawberry saying,
  "Only look what a ruby I've made!"
It forgot how the bees in their maying
  Had brought it the stuff for its trade.

And yet there's the half of a truth in it,
  And my Lord might his copyright sue;
For a thought's his who kindles new youth
  in it,
  Or so puts it as makes it more true.

The birds but repeat without ending
  The same old traditional notes,
Which some, by more happily blending,
  Seem to make over new in their throats;

And we men through our old bit of song
  run,
  Until one just improves on the rest,
And we call a thing his, in the long run,
  Who utters it clearest and best.

AUSPEX

My heart, I cannot still it,
  Nest that had song-birds in it;
And when the last shall go,
  The dreary days, to fill it,
  Instead of lark or linnet,
Shall whirl dead leaves and snow.

Had they been swallows only,
  Without the passion stronger
That skyward longs and sings, —
  Woe's me, I shall be lonely
  When I can feel no longer
The impatience of their wings!

A moment, sweet delusion,
  Like birds the brown leaves hover;
But it will not be long
  Before their wild confusion
  Fall wavering down to cover
The poet and his song.

THE PREGNANT COMMENT

OPENING one day a book of mine,
I absent, Hester found a line
Praised with a pencil-mark, and this
She left transfigured with a kiss.

When next upon the page I chance,
Like Poussin's nymphs my pulses dance,
And whirl my fancy where it sees
Pan piping 'neath Arcadian trees,
Whose leaves no winter-scenes rehearse,
Still young and glad as Homer's verse.
"What mean," I ask, "these sudden joys?
This feeling fresher than a boy's?
What makes this line, familiar long,
New as the first bird's April song?
I could, with sense illumined thus,
Clear doubtful texts in Æschylus!"

Laughing, one day she gave the key,
My riddle's open-sesame;
Then added, with a smile demure,
Whose downcast lids veiled triumph sure,
"If what I left there give you pain,
You — you — can take it off again;
'T was for *my* poet, not for him,
Your Doctor Donne there!"

      Earth grew dim
And wavered in a golden mist,
As rose, not paper, leaves I kissed.
Donne, you forgive? I let you keep
Her precious comment, poet deep.

THE LESSON

I SAT and watched the walls of night
 With cracks of sudden lightning glow,
And listened while with clumsy might
 The thunder wallowed to and fro.

The rain fell softly now; the squall,
 That to a torrent drove the trees,
Had whirled beyond us to let fall
 Its tumult on the whitening seas.

But still the lightning crinkled keen,
 Or fluttered fitful from behind
The leaden drifts, then only seen,
 That rumbled eastward on the wind.

Still as gloom followed after glare,
 While bated breath the pine-trees drew,
Tiny Salmoneus of the air,
 His mimic bolts the firefly threw.

He thought, no doubt, "Those flashes
 grand,
 That light for leagues the shuddering
 sky,
Are made, a fool could understand,
 By some superior kind of fly.

"He 's of our race's elder branch,
 His family-arms the same as ours,
Both born the twy-forked flame to launch,
 Of kindred, if unequal, powers."

And is man wiser? Man who takes
 His consciousness the law to be
Of all beyond his ken, and makes
 God but a bigger kind of Me?

SCIENCE AND POETRY

HE who first stretched his nerves of sub-
 tile wire
Over the land and through the sea-depths
 still,
Thought only of the flame-winged messen-
 ger
As a dull drudge that should encircle earth
With sordid messages of Trade, and tame
Blithe Ariel to a bagman. But the Muse
Not long will be defrauded. From her foe
Her misused wand she snatches; at a touch,
The Age of Wonder is renewed again,
And to our disenchanted day restores
The Shoes of Swiftness that give odds to
 Thought,
The Cloak that makes invisible; and with
 these
I glide, an airy fire, from shore to shore,
Or from my Cambridge whisper to Cathay.

A NEW YEAR'S GREETING

THE century numbers fourscore years;
 You, fortressed in your teens,
To Time's alarums close your ears,
And, while he devastates your peers,
 Conceive not what he means.

If e'er life's winter fleck with snow
 Your hair's deep shadowed bowers,
That winsome head an art would know
To make it charm, and wear it so
 As 't were a wreath of flowers.

If to such fairies years must come,
 May yours fall soft and slow
As, shaken by a bee's low hum,
The rose-leaves waver, sweetly dumb,
 Down to their mates below!

THE DISCOVERY

I WATCHED a moorland torrent run
 Down through the rift itself had made,
Golden as honey in the sun,
 Of darkest amber in the shade.

In this wild glen at last, methought,
 The magic's secret I surprise;
Here Celia's guardian fairy caught
 The changeful splendors of her eyes.

All else grows tame, the sky's one blue,
  The one long languish of the rose,
But these, beyond prevision new,
  Shall charm and startle to the close.

WITH A SEASHELL

SHELL, whose lips, than mine more cold,
Might with Dian's ear make bold,
Seek my Lady's; if thou win
To that portal, shut from sin,
Where commissioned angels' swords
Startle back unholy words,
Thou a miracle shalt see
Wrought by it and wrought in thee ;
Thou, the dumb one, shalt recover
Speech of poet, speech of lover.
If she deign to lift you there,
Murmur what I may not dare;
In that archway, pearly-pink
As the Dawn's untrodden brink,
Murmur, " Excellent and good,
Beauty's best in every mood,
Never common, never tame,
Changeful fair as windwaved flame " —
Nay, I maunder; this she hears
Every day with mocking ears,
With a brow not sudden-stained
With the flush of bliss restrained,
With no tremor of the pulse
More than feels the dreaming dulse
In the midmost ocean's caves,
When a tempest heaps the waves.
Thou must woo her in a phrase
Mystic as the opal's blaze,
Which pure maids alone can see
When their lovers constant be.
I with thee a secret share,
Half a hope, and half a prayer,
Though no reach of mortal skill
Ever told it all, or will;
Say, " He bids me — nothing more —
Tell you what you guessed before ! "

THE SECRET

I HAVE a fancy: how shall I bring it
Home to all mortals wherever they be ?
Say it or sing it ? Shoe it or wing it,
So it may outrun or outfly ME,
Merest cocoon-web whence it broke free ?

Only one secret can save from disaster,
Only one magic is that of the Master :

Set it to music; give it a tune, —
Tune the brook sings you, tune the breeze
    brings you,
Tune the wild columbines nod to in June !

This is the secret: so simple, you see !
Easy as loving, easy as kissing,
Easy as — well, let me ponder — as miss-
    ing,
Known, since the world was, by scarce two
    or three.

IV. HUMOR AND SATIRE

FITZ ADAM'S STORY

[The greater part of this poem was written many years ago as part of a larger one, to be called *The Nooning*, made up of tales in verse, some of them grave, some comic. It gives me a sad pleasure to remember that I was encouraged in this project by my friend the late Arthur Hugh Clough.]

Thus Lowell in the note which he prefixed to this poem when printing it in *Heartsease and Rue*. In his *Letters* are some more detailed references to the design of *The Nooning*. As far back as 1849, when issuing a new edition of his *Poems*, he wrote to Mr. Briggs: "My next volume, I think, will show an advance. It is to be called *The Nooning*. Now guess what it will be. The name suggests pleasant thoughts, does it not ? But I shall not tell you anything about it yet, and you must not mention it." A little later he wrote to the same correspondent : "Maria invented the title for me, and is it not a pleasant one ? My plan is this. I am going to bring together a party of half a dozen old friends at Elmwood. They go down to the river and bathe, and then one proposes that they shall go up into a great willow-tree (which stands at the end of the causey near our house, and has seats in it) to take their nooning. There they agree that each shall tell a story or recite a poem of some sort. In the tree they find a countryman already resting himself, who enters into the plan and tells a humorous tale, with touches of Yankee character and habits in it. *I* am to read my poem of the Voyage of Leif to Vinland, in which I mean to bring my hero straight into Boston Bay, as befits a Bay-state poet. Two of my poems are already written — one *The Fountain of Youth* (no connection with any other firm), and the other an Address to the Muse, by the Transcendentalist of the party. . . . In *The Nooning* I shall have not

even a glance towards Reform.'' Apparently
Lowell regarded the book as imminent, but
the death of his daughter Rose early in 1850
and the subsequent journey to Europe seem to
have deferred the execution of his plans, and
the book, as we know, never had a whole,
though there were several fragments of it pub-
lished. He held tenaciously, however, to his
plan. In June, 1853, he wrote again to Mr.
Briggs: " I have *The Nooning* to finish — which
shall turn out well ; " and thirteen years later
he wrote to Mr. Norton: " I have been work-
ing hard, and if my liver will let me alone, as
it does now, am likely to go on all winter.
And on *what*, do you suppose ? I have taken
up one of the unfinished tales of *The Nooning*,
and it grew to a poem of near seven hundred
lines ! [plainly this poem of *Fitz Adam's
Story*]. It is mainly descriptive. First, a
sketch of the narrator, then his ' prelude,'
then his ' tale.' I describe an old inn and its
landlord, bar-room, etc. It is very homely,
but right from nature. I have lent it to Child
and hope he will like it, for if he does n't I
shall feel discouraged. It was very interest-
ing to take up a thread dropt so long ago, and
curious as a phenomenon of memory to find
how continuous it had remained in my mind,
and how I could go on as if I had let it fall
only yesterday.''

A scheme so long persisted in and returned
to so often could scarcely be wholly unknown,
and in a letter to Professor James B. Thayer
written in December, 1868, we find Lowell
answering a query he had put: " And *The
Nooning*. Sure enough, where is it ? The
June Idyl [renamed *Under the Willows*] (writ-
ten in '51 or '52) is a part of what I had writ-
ten as the induction to it. The description of
spring in one of the *Biglow Papers* is another
fragment of the same, tagged with rhyme for
the nonce. So is a passage in *Mason and Slidell*
beginning

' Oh, strange new world.'

The *Voyage to Vinland*, the *Pictures from
Appledore*, and *Fitz Adam's Story* were written
for *The Nooning*, as originally planned. So,
you see, I had made some progress. Perhaps
it will come by and by — not in the shape I
meant at first, for something broke my life in
two, and I cannot piece it together again. Be-
sides, the Muse asks *all* of a man, and for many
years I have been unable to give myself up as I
would.'' *Fragments of an Unfinished Poem*, p.
158, is another bit of flotsam from *The Nooning*.

THE next whose fortune 't was a tale to
tell
Was one whom men, before they thought,
loved well,

And after thinking wondered why they did,
For half he seemed to let them, half for-
bid,
And wrapped him so in humors, sheath on
sheath,
'T was hard to guess the mellow soul be-
neath;
But, once divined, you took him to your
heart,
While he appeared to bear with you as
part
Of life's impertinence, and once a year
Betrayed his true self by a smile or tear,
Or rather something sweetly-shy and loath,
Withdrawn ere fully shown, and mixed of
both.
A cynic ? Not precisely: one who thrust
Against a heart too prone to love and trust,
Who so despised false sentiment he knew
Scarce in himself to part the false and
true,
And strove to hide, by roughening-o'er the
skin,
Those cobweb nerves he could not dull
within.
Gentle by birth, but of a stem decayed,
He shunned life's rivalries and hated trade;
On a small patrimony and larger pride,
He lived uneaseful on the Other Side
(So he called Europe), only coming West
To give his Old-World appetite new zest;
Yet still the New World spooked it in his
veins,
A ghost he could not lay with all his pains;
For never Pilgrims' offshoot scapes control
Of those old instincts that have shaped his
soul.
A radical in thought, he puffed away
With shrewd contempt the dust of usage
gray,
Yet loathed democracy as one who saw,
In what he longed to love, some vulgar
flaw,
And, shocked through all his delicate re-
serves,
Remained a Tory by his taste and nerves.
His fancy's thrall, he drew all ergoes
thence,
And thought himself the type of common
sense;
Misliking women, not from cross or whim,
But that his mother shared too much in
him,
And he half felt that what in them was
grace

Made the unlucky weakness of his race.
What powers he had he hardly cared to
 know,
But sauntered through the world as through
 a show;
A critic fine in his haphazard way,
A sort of mild La Bruyère on half-pay.
For comic weaknesses he had an eye
Keen as an acid for an alkali,
Yet you could feel, through his sardonic
 tone,
He loved them all, unless they were his
 own.
You might have called him, with his hu-
 morous twist,
A kind of human entomologist:
As these bring home, from every walk they
 take,
Their hat-crowns stuck with bugs of curi-
 ous make,
So he filled all the lining of his head
With characters impaled and ticketed,
And had a cabinet behind his eyes
For all they caught of mortal oddities.
He might have been a poet — many
 worse —
But that he had, or feigned, contempt of
 verse;
Called it tattooing language, and held
 rhymes
The young world's lullaby of ruder times.
Bitter in words, too indolent for gall,
He satirized himself the first of all,
In men and their affairs could find no law,
And was the ill logic that he thought he
 saw.

Scratching a match to light his pipe
 anew,
With eyes half shut some musing whiffs he
 drew
And thus began: "I give you all my word,
I think this mock-Decameron absurd;
Boccaccio's garden! how bring that to pass
In our bleak clime save under double
 glass?
The moral east-wind of New England life
Would snip its gay luxuriance like a knife;
Mile-deep the glaciers brooded here, they
 say,
Through æons numb; we feel their chill
 to-day.
These foreign plants are but half-hardy
 still,
Die on a south, and on a north wall chill.

Had we stayed Puritans! *They* had some
 heat,
(Though whence derived I have my own
 conceit,)
But you have long ago raked up their fires;
Where they had faith, you 've ten sham-
 Gothic spires.
Why more exotics? Try your native
 vines,
And in some thousand years you *may* have
 wines;
Your present grapes are harsh, all pulps
 and skins,
And want traditions of ancestral bins
That saved for evenings round the polished
 board
Old lava-fires, the sun-steeped hillside's
 hoard.
Without a Past, you lack that southern
 wall
O'er which the vines of Poesy should
 crawl;
Still they 're your only hope; no midnight
 oil
Makes up for virtue wanting in the soil;
Manure them well and prune them; 't
 won't be France,
Nor Spain, nor Italy, but there 's your
 chance.
You have one story-teller worth a score
Of dead Boccaccios, — nay, add twenty
 more, —
A hawthorn asking spring's most dainty
 breath,
And him you 're freezing pretty well to
 death.
However, since you say so, I will tease
My memory to a story by degrees,
Though you will cry, 'Enough!' I 'm well-
 nigh sure,
Ere I have dreamed through half my over-
 ture.
Stories were good for men who had no
 books,
(Fortunate race!) and built their nests
 like rooks
In lonely towers, to which the Jongleur
 brought
His pedler's-box of cheap and tawdry
 thought,
With here and there a fancy fit to see
Wrought in quaint grace in golden fili-
 gree, —
Some ring that with the Muse's finger yet
Is warm, like Aucassin and Nicolete;

The morning newspaper has spoilt his
     trade,
(For better or for worse, I leave unsaid,)
And stories now, to suit a public nice,
Must be half epigram, half pleasant vice.

   " All tourists know Shebagog County:
          there
The summer idlers take their yearly stare,
Dress to see Nature in a well-bred way,
As 't were Italian opera, or play,
Encore the sunrise (if they 're out of bed),
And pat the Mighty Mother on the head:
These have I seen, — all things are good to
     see, —
And wondered much at their complacency.
This world's great show, that took in get-
     ting-up
Millions of years, they finish ere they sup;
Sights that God gleams through with soul-
     tingling force
They glance approvingly as things of
     course,
Say, ' That 's a grand rock,' ' This a pretty
     fall,'
Not thinking, ' Are we worthy ? ' What
     if all
The scornful landscape should turn round
     and say,
' This is a fool, and that a popinjay ' ?
I often wonder what the Mountain thinks
Of French boots creaking o'er his breath-
     less brinks,
Or how the Sun would scare the chattering
     crowd,
If some fine day he chanced to think aloud.
I, who love Nature much as sinners can,
Love her where she most grandeur shows,
     — in man:
Here find I mountain, forest, cloud, and
     sun,
River and sea, and glows when day is done;
Nay, where she makes grotesques, and
     moulds in jest
The clown's cheap clay, I find unfading
     zest.
The natural instincts year by year retire,
As deer shrink northward from the settler's
     fire,
And he who loves the wild game-flavor
     more
Than city-feasts, where every man's a bore
To every other man, must seek it where
The steamer's throb and railway's iron
     blare

Have not yet startled with their punctual
     stir
The shy, wood-wandering brood of Charac-
     ter.

   " There is a village, once the county
          town,
Through which the weekly mail rolled
     dustily down,
Where the courts sat, it may be, twice a
     year,
And the one tavern reeked with rustic
     cheer;
Cheeshogquesumscot erst, now Jethro
     hight,
Red-man and pale-face bore it equal spite.
The railway ruined it, the natives say,
That passed unwisely fifteen miles away,
And made a drain to which, with steady
     ooze,
Filtered away law, stage-coach, trade, and
     news.
The railway saved it; so at least think
     those
Who love old ways, old houses, old repose.
Of course the Tavern stayed: its genial
     host
Thought not of flitting more than did the
     post
On which high-hung the fading signboard
     creaks,
Inscribed, ' The Eagle Inn, by Ezra
     Weeks.'

   " If in life's journey you should ever
          find
An inn medicinal for body and mind,
'T is sure to be some drowsy-looking house
Whose easy landlord has a bustling spouse:
He, if he like you, will not long forego
Some bottle deep in cobwebbed dust laid
     low,
That, since the War we used to call the
     ' Last,'
Has dozed and held its lang-syne memories
     fast:
From him exhales that Indian-summer air
Of hazy, lazy welcome everywhere,
While with her toil the napery is white,
The china dustless, the keen knife-blades
     bright,
Salt dry as sand, and bread that seems as
     though
'T were rather sea-foam baked than vulgar
     dough.

" In our swift country, houses trim and white
Are pitched like tents, the lodging of a night;
Each on its bank of baked turf mounted high
Perches impatient o'er the roadside dry,
While the wronged landscape coldly stands aloof,
Refusing friendship with the upstart roof.
Not so the Eagle; on a grass-green swell
That toward the south with sweet concessions fell
It dwelt retired, and half had grown to be
As aboriginal as rock or tree.
It nestled close to earth, and seemed to brood
O'er homely thoughts in a half-conscious mood,
As by the peat that rather fades than burns
The smouldering grandam nods and knits by turns,
Happy, although her newest news were old
Ere the first hostile drum at Concord rolled.
If paint it e'er had known, it knew no more
Than yellow lichens spattered thickly o'er
That soft lead-gray, less dark beneath the eaves
Which the slow brush of wind and weather leaves.
The ample roof sloped backward to the ground,
And vassal lean-tos gathered thickly round,
Patched on, as sire or son had felt the need,
Like chance growths sprouting from the old roof's seed,
Just as about a yellow-pine-tree spring
Its rough-barked darlings in a filial ring.
But the great chimney was the central thought
Whose gravitation through the cluster wrought;
For 't is not styles far-fetched from Greece or Rome,
But just the Fireside, that can make a home;
None of your spindling things of modern style,
Like pins stuck through to stay the card-built pile,
It rose broad shouldered, kindly, debonair,
Its warm breath whitening in the October air,
While on its front a heart in outline showed
The place it filled in that serene abode.

" When first I chanced the Eagle to explore,
Ezra sat listless by the open door;
One chair careened him at an angle meet,
Another nursed his hugely-slippered feet;
Upon a third reposed a shirt-sleeved arm,
And the whole man diffused tobacco's charm.
' Are you the landlord ? ' ' Wahl, I guess I be,'
Watching the smoke, he answered leisurely.
He was a stoutish man, and through the breast
Of his loose shirt there showed a brambly chest;
Streaked redly as a wind-foreboding morn,
His tanned cheeks curved to temples closely shorn;
Clean-shaved he was, save where a hedge of gray
Upon his brawny throat leaned every way
About an Adam's-apple, that beneath
Bulged like a boulder from a brambly heath.
The Western World's true child and nursling he,
Equipt with aptitudes enough for three:
No eye like his to value horse or cow,
Or gauge the contents of a stack or mow;
He could foretell the weather at a word,
He knew the haunt of every beast and bird,
Or where a two-pound trout was sure to lie,
Waiting the flutter of his home-made fly;
Nay, once in autumns five, he had the luck
To drop at fair-play range a ten-tined buck;
Of sportsmen true he favored every whim,
But never cockney found a guide in him;
A natural man, with all his instincts fresh,
Not buzzing helpless in Reflection's mesh,
Firm on its feet stood his broad-shouldered mind,
As bluffly honest as a northwest wind;
Hard-headed and soft-hearted, you 'd scarce meet
A kindlier mixture of the shrewd and sweet;
Generous by birth, and ill at saying ' No,'
Yet in a bargain he was all men's foe,
Would yield no inch of vantage in a trade,
And give away ere nightfall all he made.

" 'Can I have lodging here ? ' once more
    I said.
He blew a whiff, and, leaning back his
    head,
'You come a piece through Bailey's woods,
    I s'pose,
Acrost a bridge where a big swamp-oak
    grows ?
It don't grow, neither; it 's ben dead ten
    year,
Nor th' ain't a livin' creetur, fur nor near,
Can tell wut killed it; but I some misdoubt
'T was borers, there 's sech heaps on 'em
    about.
You did n' chance to run ag'inst my son,
A long, slab-sided youngster with a gun ?
He 'd oughto ben back more 'n an hour
    ago,
An' brought some birds to dress for supper
    — sho !
There he comes now. 'Say, Obed, wut ye
    got ?
(He 'll hev some upland plover like as not.)
Wal, them 's real nice uns, an 'll eat A 1,
Ef I can stop their bein' over-done;
Nothin' riles *me* (I pledge my fastin' word)
Like cookin' out the natur' of a bird;
(Obed, you pick 'em out o' sight an' sound,
Your ma'am don't love no feathers cluttrin'
    round;)
Jes' scare 'em with the coals, — thet 's *my*
    idee.'
Then, turning suddenly about on me,
'Wal, Square, I guess so. Callilate to
    stay ?
I 'll ask Mis' Weeks; 'bout *thet* it 's hern to
    say.'

"Well, there I lingered all October
    through,
In that sweet atmosphere of hazy blue,
So leisurely, so soothing, so forgiving,
That sometimes makes New England fit
    for living.
I watched the landscape, erst so granite
    glum,
Bloom like the south side of a ripening
    plum,
And each rock-maple on the hillside make
His ten days' sunset doubled in the lake;
The very stone walls draggling up the hills
Seemed touched, and wavered in their
    roundhead wills.
Ah ! there 's a deal of sugar in the sun !
Tap me in Indian summer, I should run

A juice to make rock-candy of, — but then
We get such weather scarce one year in
    ten.

"There was a parlor in the house, a room
To make you shudder with its prudish
    gloom.
The furniture stood round with such an air,
There seemed an old maid's ghost in
    every chair,
Which looked as it had scuttled to its
    place
And pulled extempore a Sunday face,
Too smugly proper for a world of sin,
Like boys on whom the minister comes in.
The table, fronting you with icy stare,
Strove to look witless that its legs were
    bare,
While the black sofa with its horse-hair
    pall
Gloomed like a bier for Comfort's funeral.
Each piece appeared to do its chilly best
To seem an utter stranger to the rest,
As if acquaintanceship were deadly sin,
Like Britons meeting in a foreign inn.
Two portraits graced the wall in grimmest
    truth,
Mister and Mistress W. in their youth, —
New England youth, that seems a sort of
    pill,
Half wish-I-dared, half Edwards on the
    Will,
Bitter to swallow, and which leaves a trace
Of Calvinistic colic on the face.
Between them, o'er the mantel, hung in
    state
Solomon's temple, done in copperplate;
Invention pure, but meant, we may pre-
    sume,
To give some Scripture sanction to the
    room.
Facing this last, two samplers you might
    see,
Each, with its urn and stiffly-weeping tree,
Devoted to some memory long ago
More faded than their lines of worsted woe;
Cut paper decked their frames against the
    flies,
Though none e'er dared an entrance who
    were wise,
And bushed asparagus in fading green
Added its shiver to the franklin clean.

"When first arrived, I chilled a half-
    hour there,

Nor dared deflower with use a single chair;
I caught no cold, yet flying pains could find
For weeks in me, — a rheumatism of mind.
One thing alone imprisoned there had
    power
To hold me in the place that long half-
    hour:
A scutcheon this, a helm-surmounted shield,
Three griffins argent on a sable field;
A relic of the shipwrecked past was here,
And Ezra held some Old-World lumber
    dear.
Nay, do not smile; I love this kind of thing,
These cooped traditions with a broken wing,
This freehold nook in Fancy's pipe-blown
    ball,
This less than nothing that is more than
    all !
Have I not seen sweet natures kept alive
Amid the humdrum of your business hive,
Undowered spinsters shielded from all
    harms,
By airy incomes from a coat of arms ?"

He paused a moment, and his features
    took
The flitting sweetness of that inward look
I hinted at before; but, scarcely seen,
It shrank for shelter 'neath his harder mien,
And, rapping his black pipe of ashes clear,
He went on with a self-derisive sneer:
"No doubt we make a part of God's de-
    sign,
And break the forest-path for feet divine;
To furnish foothold for this grand prevision
Is good, and yet — to be the mere transi-
    tion,
That, you will say, is also good, though I
Scarce like to feed the ogre By-and-by.
Raw edges rasp my nerves; my taste is
    wooed
By things that are, not going to be, good,
Though were I what I dreamed two lustres
    gone,
I 'd stay to help the Consummation on,
Whether a new Rome than the old more
    fair,
Or a deadflat of rascal-ruled despair;
But my skull somehow never closed the
    suture
That seems to knit yours firmly with the
    future,
So you 'll excuse me if I 'm sometimes fain
To tie the Past's warm nightcap o'er my
    brain;

I 'm quite aware 't is not in fashion here,
But then your northeast winds are so
    severe!

"But to my story: though 't is truly
    naught
But a few hints in Memory's sketchbook
    caught,
And which may claim a value on the score
Of calling back some scenery now no more.
Shall I confess ? The tavern's only Lar
Seemed (be not shocked !) its homely-fea-
    tured bar.
Here dozed a fire of beechen logs, that bred
Strange fancies in its embers golden-red,
And nursed the loggerhead whose hissing
    dip,
Timed by nice instinct, creamed the mug
    of flip
That made from mouth to mouth its genial
    round,
Nor left one nature wholly winter-bound;
Hence dropt the tinkling coal all mellow-
    ripe
For Uncle Reuben's talk-extinguished pipe;
Hence rayed the heat, as from an indoor
    sun,
That wooed forth many a shoot of rustic
    fun.
Here Ezra ruled as king by right divine;
No other face had such a wholesome shine,
No laugh like his so full of honest cheer;
Above the rest it crowed like Chanticleer.

"In this one room his dame you never
    saw,
Where reigned by custom old a Salic law;
Here coatless lolled he on his throne of oak,
And every tongue paused midway if he
    spoke.
Due mirth he loved, yet was his sway severe;
No blear-eyed driveller got his stagger
    here;
'Measure was happiness; who wanted more,
Must buy his ruin at the Deacon's store;'
None but his lodgers after ten could stay,
Nor after nine on eves of Sabbath-day.
He had his favorites and his pensioners,
The same that gypsy Nature owns for hers:
Loose-ended souls, whose skills bring scanty
    gold,
And whom the poor-house catches when
    they 're old;
Rude country-minstrels, men who doctor
    kine,

Or graft, and, out of scions ten, save nine;
Creatures of genius they, but never meant
To keep step with the civic regiment.
These Ezra welcomed, feeling in his mind
Perhaps some motions of the vagrant kind;
These paid no money, yet for them he drew
Special Jamaica from a tap they knew,
And, for their feelings, chalked behind the
    door
With solemn face a visionary score.
This thawed to life in Uncle Reuben's
    throat
A torpid shoal of jest and anecdote,
Like those queer fish that doze the droughts
    away,
And wait for moisture, wrapped in sun-
    baked clay;
This warmed the one-eyed fiddler to his
    task,
Perched in the corner on an empty cask,
By whose shrill art rapt suddenly, some
    boor
Rattled a double-shuffle on the floor;
'Hull's Victory' was, indeed, the favorite
    air,
Though 'Yankee Doodle' claimed its
    proper share.

  "'T was there I caught from Uncle
    Reuben's lips,
In dribbling monologue 'twixt whiffs and
    sips,
The story I so long have tried to tell;
The humor coarse, the persons common, —
    well,
From Nature only do I love to paint,
Whether she send a satyr or a saint,
To me Sincerity 's the one thing good,
Soiled though she be and lost to maiden-
    hood.
Quompegan is a town some ten miles south
From Jethro, at Nagumscot river-mouth,
A seaport town, and makes its title good
With lumber and dried fish and eastern
    wood.
Here Deacon Bitters dwelt and kept the
    Store,
The richest man for many a mile of shore;
In little less than everything dealt he,
From meeting-houses to a chest of tea;
So dextrous therewithal a flint to skin,
He could make profit on a single pin;
In business strict, to bring the balance true
He had been known to bite a fig in two,
And change a board-nail for a shingle-nail.

All that he had he ready held for sale,
His house, his tomb, whate'er the law allows,
And he had gladly parted with his spouse.
His one ambition still to get and get,
He would arrest your very ghost for debt.
His store looked righteous, should the Par-
    son come,
But in a dark back-room he peddled rum,
And eased Ma'am Conscience, if she e'er
    would scold,
By christening it with water ere he sold.
A small, dry man he was, who wore a queue,
And one white neckcloth all the week-days
    through, —
On Monday white, by Saturday as dun
As that worn homeward by the prodigal son.
His frosted earlocks, striped with foxy
    brown,
Were braided up to hide a desert crown;
His coat was brownish, black perhaps of
    yore;
In summer-time a banyan loose he wore;
His trousers short, through many a season
    true,
Made no pretence to hide his stockings blue;
A waistcoat buff his chief adornment was,
Its porcelain buttons rimmed with dusky
    brass.
A deacon he, you saw it in each limb,
And well he knew to deacon-off a hymn,
Or lead the choir through all its wandering
    woes
With voice that gathered unction in his
    nose,
Wherein a constant snuffle you might hear,
As if with him 't were winter all the year.
At pew-head sat he with decorous pains,
In sermon-time could foot his weekly gains,
Or, with closed eyes and heaven-abstracted
    air,
Could plan a new investment in long-
    prayer.
A pious man, and thrifty too, he made
The psalms and prophets partners in his
    trade,
And in his orthodoxy straitened more
As it enlarged the business at his store;
He honored Moses, but, when gain he
    planned,
Had his own notion of the Promised Land.

  " Soon as the winter made the sledding
    good,
From far around the farmers hauled him
    wood,

For all the trade had gathered 'neath his
    thumb.
He paid in groceries and New England
    rum,
Making two profits with a conscience
    clear, —
Cheap all he bought, and all he paid with
    dear.
With his own mete-wand measuring every
    load,
Each somehow had diminished on the
    road;
An honest cord in Jethro still would fail
By a good foot upon the Deacon's scale,
And, more to abate the price, his gimlet
    eye
Would pierce to cat-sticks that none else
    could spy;
Yet none dared grumble, for no farmer
    yet
But New Year found him in the Deacon's
    debt.

    " While the first snow was mealy under
    feet,
A team drawled creaking down Quompe-
    gan street.
Two cords of oak weighed down the grind-
    ing sled,
And cornstalk fodder rustled overhead;
The oxen's muzzles, as they shouldered
    through,
Were silver-fringed; the driver's own was
    blue
As the coarse frock that swung below his
    knee.
Behind his load for shelter waded he;
His mittened hands now on his chest he
    beat,
Now stamped the stiffened cowhides of his
    feet,
Hushed as a ghost's; his armpit scarce
    could hold
The walnut whipstock slippery-bright with
    cold.
What wonder if, the tavern as he past,
He looked and longed, and stayed his
    beasts at last,
Who patient stood and veiled themselves
    in steam
While he explored the bar-room's ruddy
    gleam ?

    " Before the fire, in want of thought
    profound,

There sat a brother-townsman weather-
    bound:
A sturdy churl, crisp-headed, bristly-eared,
Red as a pepper; 'twixt coarse brows and
    beard
His eyes lay ambushed, on the watch for
    fools,
Clear, gray, and glittering like two bay-
    edged pools;
A shifty creature, with a turn for fun,
Could swap a poor horse for a better
    one, —
He 'd a high-stepper always in his stall;
Liked far and near, and dreaded there-
    withal.
To him the in-comer, ' Perez, how d' ye
    do ? '
' Jest as I 'm mind to, Obed; how do
    you ? '
Then, his eyes twinkling such swift gleams
    as run
Along the levelled barrel of a gun
Brought to his shoulder by a man you
    know
Will bring his game down, he continued,
    ' So,
I s'pose you 're haulin' wood ? But you 're
    too late;
The Deacon 's off; Old Splitfoot could n't
    wait;
He made a bee-line las' night in the storm
To where he won't need wood to keep him
    warm.
'Fore this he 's treasurer of a fund to
    train
Young imps as missionaries; hopes to gain
That way a contract that he has in view
For fireproof pitchforks of a pattern new.
It must have tickled him, all drawbacks
    weighed,
To think he stuck the Old One in a trade;
His soul, to start with, was n't worth a
    carrot,
And all he 'd left 'ould hardly serve to
    swear at.'

    " By this time Obed had his wits thawed
    out,
And, looking at the other half in doubt,
Took off his fox-skin cap to scratch his
    head,
Donned it again, and drawled forth, ' Mean
    he 's dead ? '
' Jesso; he 's dead and t' other d that fol-
    lers

With folks that never love a thing but
    dollars.
He pulled up stakes last evening, fair and
    square,
And ever since there's been a row Down
    There.
The minute the old chap arrived, you see,
Comes the Boss-devil to him, and says
    he,
"What are you good at?   Little enough,
    I fear;
We callilate to make folks useful here."
"Well," says old Bitters, " I expect I can
Scale a fair load of wood with e'er a man."
"Wood we don't deal in; but perhaps
    you'll suit,
Because we buy our brimstone by the foot:
Here, take this measurin'-rod, as smooth as
    sin,
And keep a reckonin' of what loads comes
    in.
You'll not want business, for we need a
    lot
To keep the Yankees that you send us
    hot;
At firin' up they're barely half as spry
As Spaniards or Italians, though they're
    dry;
At first we have to let the draught on
    stronger,
But, heat 'em through, they seem to hold
    it longer."

   "'Bitters he took the rod, and pretty
    soon
A teamster comes, whistling an ex-psalm
    tune.
A likelier chap you would n't ask to see,
No different, but his limp, from you or
    me' —
'No different, Perez! Don't your mem-
    ory fail?
Why, where in thunder was his horns and
    tail?'
'They're only worn by some old-fashioned
    pokes;
They mostly aim at looking just like folks.
Sech things are scarce as queues and top-
    boots here;
'T would spoil their usefulness to look too
    queer.
Ef you could always know 'em when they
    come,
They'd get no purchase on you: now be
    mum.

On come the teamster, smart as Davy
    Crockett,
Jinglin' the red-hot coppers in his pocket,
And clost behind, ('t was gold-dust, you'd
    ha' sworn,)
A load of sulphur yallower 'n seed-corn;
To see it wasted as it is Down There
Would make a Friction-Match Co. tear its
    hair!
"Hold on!" says Bitters, "stop right
    where you be;
You can't go in athout a pass from me."
"All right," says t' other, " only step
    round smart;
I must be home by noon-time with the
    cart."
Bitters goes round it sharp-eyed as a rat,
Then with a scrap of paper on his hat
Pretends to cipher.   "By the public staff,
That load scarce rises twelve foot and a
    half."
"There's fourteen foot and over," says the
    driver,
"Worth twenty dollars, ef it's worth a
    stiver;
Good fourth-proof brimstone, that'll make
    'em squirm, —
I leave it to the Headman of the Firm;
After we masure it, we always lay
Some on to allow for settlin' by the way.
Imp and full-grown, I've carted sulphur
    here,
And gi'n fair satisfaction, thirty year."
With that they fell to quarrellin' so loud
That in five minutes they had drawed a
    crowd,
And afore long the Boss, who heard the
    row,
Comes elbowin' in with "What's to pay
    here now?"
Both parties heard, the measurin'-rod he
    takes,
And of the load a careful survey makes.
"Sence I have bossed the business here,"
    says he,
"No fairer load was ever seen by me."
Then, turnin' to the Deacon, "You mean
    cus,
None of your old Quompegan tricks with
    us!
They won't do here: we're plain old-
    fashioned folks,
And don't quite understand that kind o'
    jokes.
I know this teamster, and his pa afore him,

And the hard-working Mrs. D. that bore
him;
He would n't soil his conscience with a lie,
Though he might get the custom-house
thereby.
Here, constable, take Bitters by the queue,
And clap him into furnace ninety-two,
And try this brimstone on him; if he 's
bright,
He 'll find the masure honest afore night.
He is n't worth his fuel, and I 'll bet
The parish oven has to take him yet!"'

" This is my tale, heard twenty years
ago
From Uncle Reuben, as the logs burned
low,
Touching the walls and ceiling with that
bloom
That makes a rose's calyx of a room.
I could not give his language, where-
through ran
The gamy flavor of the bookless man
Who shapes a word before the fancy cools,
As lonely Crusoe improvised his tools.
I liked the tale, — 't was like so many told
By Rutebeuf and his brother Trouvères
bold;
Nor were the hearers much unlike to
theirs,
Men unsophisticate, rude-nerved as bears.
Ezra is gone and his large-hearted kind,
The landlords of the hospitable mind;
Good Warriner of Springfield was the last;
An inn is now a vision of the past;
One yet-surviving host my mind recalls, —
You 'll find him if you go to Trenton
Falls."

THE ORIGIN OF DIDACTIC POETRY

WHEN wise Minerva still was young
And just the least romantic,
Soon after from Jove's head she flung
That preternatural antic,
'T is said, to keep from idleness
Or flirting, those twin curses,
She spent her leisure, more or less,
In writing po——, no, verses.

How nice they were! to rhyme with *far*
A kind *star* did not tarry;
The metre, too, was regular
As schoolboy's dot and carry;

And full they were of pious plums,
So extra-super-moral, —
For sucking Virtue's tender gums
Most tooth-enticing coral.

A clean, fair copy she prepares,
Makes sure of moods and tenses,
With her own hand, — for prudence spares
A man-(or woman-)-uensis;
Complete, and tied with ribbons proud,
She hinted soon how cosy a
Treat it would be to read them loud
After next day's Ambrosia.

The Gods thought not it would amuse
So much as Homer's Odyssees,
But could not very well refuse
The properest of Goddesses;
So all sat round in attitudes
Of various dejection,
As with a *hem!* the queen of prudes
Began her grave prelection.

At the first pause Zeus said, " Well
sung! —
I mean — ask Phœbus, — *he* knows."
Says Phœbus, "Zounds! a wolf 's among
Admetus's merinos;
Fine! very fine! but I must go;
They stand in need of me there;
Excuse me!" snatched his stick, and so
Plunged down the gladdened ether.

With the next gap, Mars said, " For me
Don't wait, — naught could be finer,
But I 'm engaged at half past three, —
A fight in Asia Minor!"
Then Venus lisped, " I 'm sorely tried,
These duty-calls are vip'rous;
But I *must* go; I have a bride
To see about in Cyprus."

Then Bacchus, — " I must say good-by,
Although my peace it jeopards;
I meet a man at four, to try
A well-broke pair of leopards."
His words woke Hermes. " Ah!" he said,
" I *so* love moral theses!"
Then winked at Hebe, who turned red,
And smoothed her apron's creases.

Just then Zeus snored, — the Eagle drew
His head the wing from under;
Zeus snored, — o'er startled Greece there
flew

The many-volumed thunder.
Some augurs counted nine, some, ten;
Some said 't was war, some, famine,
And all, that other-minded men
Would get a precious ——.

Proud Pallas sighed, " It will not do;
Against the Muse I 've sinned, oh ! "
And her torn rhymes sent flying through
Olympus's back window.
Then, packing up a peplus clean,
She took the shortest path thence,
And opened, with a mind serene,
A Sunday-school in Athens.

The verses ? Some in ocean swilled,
Killed every fish that bit to 'em;
Some Galen caught, and, when distilled,
Found morphine the residuum;
But some that rotted on the earth
Sprang up again in copies,
And gave two strong narcotics birth,
Didactic verse and poppies.

Years after, when a poet asked
The Goddess's opinion,
As one whose soul its wings had tasked
In Art's clear-aired dominion,
" Discriminate," she said, " betimes;
The Muse is unforgiving;
Put all your beauty in your rhymes,
Your morals in your living."

THE FLYING DUTCHMAN

This poem appeared in *The Atlantic* for
January, 1868, and Lowell's own criticism on
it is frank. He wrote to Mr. Thayer : " You
will find some verses of mine in the next *At-
lantic*, the conception of which tickles me —
but half spoiled (and in verse half is more
than whole) in the writing ; " and in a similar
vein he wrote to Mr. Fields, the editor : " The
trouble with *The Flying Dutchman* is not in
what I left out, but in what I could n't get in.
Let us be honest with each other, my dear
Lorenzo de' Medici, if we can't be with any-
body else. The conception of the verses is
good ; the verses are bad."

DON'T believe in the Flying Dutchman ?
I 've known the fellow for years;
My button I 've wrenched from his clutch,
man:
I shudder whenever he nears !

He 's a Rip van Winkle skipper,
A Wandering Jew of the sea,
Who sails his bedevilled old clipper
In the wind's eye, straight as a bee.

Back topsails ! you can't escape him;
The man-ropes stretch with his weight,
And the queerest old toggeries drape him,
The Lord knows how long out of date !

Like a long-disembodied idea,
(A kind of ghost plentiful now,)
He stands there; you fancy you see a
Coeval of Teniers or Douw.

He greets you ; would have you take let-
ters:
You scan the addresses with dread,
While he mutters his *donners* and *wetters*, —
They 're all from the dead to the dead !

You seem taking time for reflection,
But the heart fills your throat with a
jam,
As you spell in each faded direction
An ominous ending in *dam*.

Am I tagging my rhymes to a legend ?
That were changing green turtle to
mock:
No, thank you ! I 've found out which
wedge-end
Is meant for the head of a block.

The fellow I have in my mind's eye
Plays the old Skipper's part here on
shore,
And sticks like a burr, till he finds I
Have got just the gauge of his bore.

This postman 'twixt one ghost and t' other,
With last dates that smell of the mould,
I have met him (O man and brother,
Forgive me !) in azure and gold.

In the pulpit I 've known of his preaching,
Out of hearing behind the time,
Some statement of Balaam's impeaching,
Giving Eve a due sense of her crime.

I have seen him some poor ancient thrash-
ing
Into something (God save us !) more dry,
With the Water of Life itself washing
The life out of earth, sea, and sky.

O dread fellow-mortal, get newer
  Despatches to carry, or none !
We 're as quick as the Greek and the Jew
    were
  At knowing a loaf from a stone.

Till the couriers of God fail in duty,
  We sha'n't ask a mummy for news,
Nor sate the soul's hunger for beauty
    With your drawings from casts of a
    Muse.

CREDIDIMUS JOVEM REGNARE

O DAYS endeared to every Muse,
When nobody had any Views,
Nor, while the cloudscape of his mind
By every breeze was new designed,
Insisted all the world should see
Camels or whales where none there be !
O happy days, when men received
From sire to son what all believed,
And left the other world in bliss,
Too busy with bedevilling this !

Beset by doubts of every breed
In the last bastion of my creed,
With shot and shell for Sabbath-chime,
I watch the storming-party climb,
Panting (their prey in easy reach),
To pour triumphant through the breach
In walls that shed like snowflakes tons
Of missiles from old-fashioned guns,
But crumble 'neath the storm that pours
All day and night from bigger bores.
There, as I hopeless watch and wait
The last life-crushing coil of Fate,
Despair finds solace in the praise
Of those serene dawn-rosy days
Ere microscopes had made us heirs
To large estates of doubts and snares,
By proving that the title-deeds,
Once all-sufficient for men's needs,
Are palimpsests that scarce disguise
The tracings of still earlier lies,
Themselves as surely written o'er
An older fib erased before.

So from these days I fly to those
That in the landlocked Past repose,
Where no rude wind of doctrine shakes
From bloom - flushed boughs untimely
    flakes;
Where morning's eyes see nothing strange,

No crude perplexity of change,
And morrows trip along their ways
Secure as happy yesterdays.
Then there were rulers who could trace
Through heroes up to gods their race,
Pledged to fair fame and noble use
By veins from Odin filled or Zeus,
And under bonds to keep divine
The praise of a celestial line.
Then priests could pile the altar's sods,
With whom gods spake as they with gods,
And everywhere from haunted earth
Broke springs of wonder, that had birth
In depths divine beyond the ken
And fatal scrutiny of men;
Then hills and groves and streams and
    seas
Thrilled with immortal presences,
Not too ethereal for the scope
Of human passion's dream or hope.

Now Pan at last is surely dead,
And King No-Credit reigns instead,
Whose officers, morosely strict,
Poor Fancy's tenantry evict,
Chase the last Genius from the door,
And nothing dances any more.
Nothing ? Ah, yes, our tables do,
Drumming the Old One's own tattoo,
And, if the oracles are dumb,
Have we not mediums ? Why be glum ?

Fly thither ? Why, the very air
Is full of hindrance and despair !
Fly thither ? But I cannot fly;
My doubts enmesh me if I try,
Each Liliputian, but, combined,
Potent a giant's limbs to bind.
This world and that are growing dark;
A huge interrogation mark,
The Devil's crook episcopal,
Still borne before him since the Fall,
Blackens with its ill-omened sign
The old blue heaven of faith benign.
Whence ? Whither ? Wherefore ? How ?
    Which ? Why ?
All ask at once, all wait reply.
Men feel old systems cracking under 'em;
Life saddens to a mere conundrum
Which once Religion solved, but she
Has lost — has Science found ? — the key.

What was snow-bearded Odin, trow,
The mighty hunter long ago,
Whose horn and hounds the peasant hears

Still when the Northlights shake their
    spears ?
Science hath answers twain, I 've heard;
Choose which you will, nor hope a third;
Whichever box the truth be stowed in,
There 's not a sliver left of Odin.
Either he was a pinchbrowed thing,
With scarcely wit a stone to fling,
A creature both in size and shape
Nearer than we are to the ape,
Who hung sublime with brat and spouse
By tail prehensile from the boughs,
And, happier than his maimed descendants,
The culture-curtailed independents,
Could pluck his cherries with both paws,
And stuff with both his big-boned jaws;
Or else the core his name enveloped
Was from a solar myth developed,
Which, hunted to its primal shoot,
Takes refuge in a Sanskrit root,
Thereby to instant death explaining
The little poetry remaining.

Try it with Zeus, 't is just the same;
The thing evades, we hug a name;
Nay, scarcely that, — perhaps a vapor
Born of some atmospheric caper.
All Lempriere's fables blur together
In cloudy symbols of the weather,
And Aphrodite rose from frothy seas
But to illustrate such hypotheses.
With years enough behind his back,
Lincoln will take the selfsame track,
And prove, hulled fairly to the cob,
A mere vagary of Old Prob.
Give the right man a solar myth,
And he 'll confute the sun therewith.

They make things admirably plain,
But one hard question *will* remain:
If one hypothesis you lose,
Another in its place you choose,
But, your faith gone, O man and brother,
Whose shop shall furnish you another ?
One that will wash, I mean, and wear,
And wrap us warmly from despair ?
While they are clearing up our puzzles,
And clapping prophylactic muzzles
On the Actæon's hounds that sniff
Our devious track through But and If,
Would they 'd explain away the Devil
And other facts that won't keep level,
But rise beneath our feet or fail,
A reeling ship's deck in a gale !
God vanished long ago, iwis,

A mere subjective synthesis;
A doll, stuffed out with hopes and fears,
Too homely for us pretty dears,
Who want one that conviction carries,
Last make of London or of Paris.
He gone, I felt a moment's spasm,
But calmed myself with Protoplasm,
A finer name, and, what is more,
As enigmatic as before;
Greek, too, and sure to fill with ease
Minds caught in the Symplegades
Of soul and sense, life's two conditions,
Each baffled with its own omniscience.
The men who labor to revise
Our Bibles will, I hope, be wise,
And print it without foolish qualms
Instead of God in David's psalms:
Noll had been more effective far
Could he have shouted at Dunbar,
" Rise, Protoplasm ! "   No dourest Scot
Had waited for another shot.

And yet I frankly must confess
A secret unforgivingness,
And shudder at the saving chrism
Whose best New Birth is Pessimism;
My soul — I mean the bit of phosphorus
That fills the place of what that was for
    us —
Can't bid its inward bores defiance
With the new nursery-tales of science.
What profits me, though doubt by doubt,
As nail by nail, be driven out,
When every new one, like the last,
Still holds my coffin-lid as fast ?
Would I find thought a moment's truce,
Give me the young world's Mother Goose
With life and joy in every limb,
The chimney-corner tales of Grimm !

Our dear and admirable Huxley
Cannot explain to me why ducks lay,
Or, rather, how into their eggs
Blunder potential wings and legs
With will to move them and decide
Whether in air or lymph to glide.
Who gets a hair's-breadth on by showing
That Something Else set all agoing ?
Farther and farther back we push
From Moses and his burning bush;
Cry, " Art Thou there ? "   Above, be-
    low,
All Nature mutters *yes* and *no !*
'T is the old answer: we 're agreed
Being from Being must proceed,

Life be Life's source. I might as well
Obey the meeting-house's bell,
And listen while Old Hundred pours
Forth through the summer-opened doors,
From old and young. I hear it yet,
Swelled by bass-viol and clarinet,
While the gray minister, with face
Radiant, let loose his noble bass.
If Heaven it reached not, yet its roll
Waked all the echoes of the soul,
And in it many a life found wings
To soar away from sordid things.
Church gone and singers too, the song
Sings to me voiceless all night long,
Till my soul beckons me afar,
Glowing and trembling like a star.
Will any scientific touch
With my worn strings achieve as much ?

I don't object, not I, to know
My sires were monkeys, if 't was so;
I touch my ear's collusive tip
And own the poor-relationship.
That apes of various shapes and sizes
Contained their germs that all the prizes
Of senate, pulpit, camp, and bar win
May give us hopes that sweeten Darwin.
Who knows but from our loins may spring
(Long hence) some winged sweet-throated
          thing
As much superior to us
As we to Cynocephalus ?

This is consoling, but, alas,
It wipes no dimness from the glass
Where I am flattening my poor nose,
In hope to see beyond my toes.
Though I accept my pedigree,
Yet where, pray tell me, is the key
That should unlock a private door
To the Great Mystery, such no more ?
Each offers his, but one nor all
Are much persuasive with the wall
That rises now, as long ago,
Between I wonder and I know,
Nor will vouchsafe a pin-hole peep
At the veiled Isis in its keep.
Where is no door, I but produce
My key to find it of no use.
Yet better keep it, after all,
Since Nature 's economical,
And who can tell but some fine day
(If it occur to her) she may,
In her good-will to you and me,
Make door and lock to match the key ?

TEMPORA MUTANTUR

This poem, written not long after Lowell's
return from a journey in Europe and printed
in *The Nation*, called out many angry retorts.
The reader will find a vigorous letter by Lowell
to Mr. Joel Benton, restating his position, in
The Century for November, 1891, and reprinted
in *Letters* II. 155–160.

THE world turns mild; democracy, they
          say,
Rounds the sharp knobs of character away,
And no great harm, unless at grave ex-
          pense
Of what needs edge of proof, the moral
          sense;
For man or race is on the downward path
Whose fibre grows too soft for honest
          wrath,
And there 's a subtle influence that springs
From words to modify our sense of things.
A plain distinction grows obscure of late:
Man, if he will, may pardon; but the State
Forgets its function if not fixed as Fate.
So thought our sires : a hundred years
          ago,
If men were knaves, why, people called
          them so,
And crime could see the prison-portal
          bend
Its brow severe at no long vista's end.
In those days for plain things plain words
          would serve;
Men had not learned to admire the graceful
          swerve
Wherewith the Æsthetic Nature's genial
          mood
Makes public duty slope to private good;
No muddled conscience raised the saving
          doubt;
A soldier proved unworthy was drummed
          out,
An officer cashiered, a civil servant
(No matter though his piety were fervent)
Disgracefully dismissed, and through the
          land
Each bore for life a stigma from the brand
Whose far-heard hiss made others more
          averse
To take the facile step from bad to worse.
The Ten Commandments had a meaning
          then,
Felt in their bones by least considerate
          men,

Because behind them Public Conscience
    stood,
And without wincing made their mandates
    good.
But now that "Statesmanship" is just a
    way
To dodge the primal curse and make it
    pay,
Since office means a kind of patent drill
To force an entrance to the Nation's till,
And peculation something rather less
Risky than if you spelt it with an *s;*
Now that to steal by law is grown an art,
Whom rogues the sires, their milder sons
    call smart,
And "slightly irregular" dilutes the shame
Of what had once a somewhat blunter
    name.
With generous curve we draw the moral
    line:
Our swindlers are permitted to resign;
Their guilt is wrapped in deferential names,
And twenty sympathize for one that blames.
Add national disgrace to private crime,
Confront mankind with brazen front sub-
    lime,
Steal but enough, the world is unsevere, —
Tweed is a statesman, Fisk a financier;
Invent a mine, and be — the Lord knows
    what;
Secure, at any rate, with what you 've
    got.
The public servant who has stolen or lied,
If called on, may resign with honest pride:
As unjust favor put him in, why doubt
Disfavor as unjust has turned him out ?
Even if indicted, what is that but fudge
To him who counted-in the elective judge ?
Whitewashed, he quits the politician's
    strife
At ease in mind, with pockets filled for
    life:
His "lady" glares with gems whose vul-
    gar blaze
The poor man through his heightened taxes
    pays,
Himself content if one huge Kohinoor
Bulge from a shirt-front ampler than be-
    fore,
But not too candid, lest it haply tend
To rouse suspicion of the People's Friend.
A public meeting, treated at his cost,
Resolves him back more virtue than he
    lost;
With character regilt he counts his gains;

What 's gone was air, the solid good re-
    mains;
For what is good, except what friend and
    foe
Seem quite unanimous in thinking so,
The stocks and bonds which, in our age of
    loans,
Replace the stupid pagan's stocks and
    stones ?
With choker white, wherein no cynic eye
Dares see idealized a hempen tie,
At parish-meetings he conducts in prayer,
And pays for missions to be sent else-
    where;
On 'Change respected, to his friends en-
    deared,
Add but a Sunday-school-class, he 's re-
    vered,
And his too early tomb will not be dumb
To point a moral for our youth to come.

IN THE HALF-WAY HOUSE

I

AT twenty we fancied the blest Middle
    Ages
    A spirited cross of romantic and grand,
All templars and minstrels and ladies and
    pages,
    And love and adventure in Outre-Mer
    land;
But ah, where the youth dreamed of build-
    ing a minster,
    The man takes a pew and sits reckoning
    his pelf,
And the Graces wear fronts, the Muse
    thins to a spinster,
    When Middle-Age stares from one's
    glass at oneself !

II

Do you twit me with days when I had an
    Ideal,
    And saw the sear future through spec-
    tacles green ?
Then find me some charm, while I look
    round and see all
    These fat friends of forty, shall keep me
    nineteen;
Should we go on pining for chaplets of
    laurel
    Who 've paid a perruquier for mending
    our thatch,

Or, our feet swathed in baize, with our
  Fate pick a quarrel,
If, instead of cheap bay-leaves, she sent
  a dear scratch?

III

We called it our Eden, that small patent-
  baker,
  When life was half moonshine and half
  Mary Jane;
But the butcher, the baker, the candlestick-
  maker!—
  Did Adam have duns and slip down a
  back-lane?
Nay, after the Fall did the modiste keep
  coming
  With last styles of fig-leaf to Madam
  Eve's bower?
Did Jubal, or whoever taught the girls
  thrumming,
  Make the patriarchs deaf at a dollar the
  hour?

IV

As I think what I was, I sigh *Desunt non-
  nulla!*
  Years are creditors Sheridan's self could
  not bilk;
But then, as my boy says, "What right has
  a fullah
  To ask for the cream, when himself spilt
  the milk?"
Perhaps when you 're older, my lad, you 'll
  discover
  The secret with which Auld Lang Syne
  there is gilt, —
Superstition of old man, maid, poet, and
  lover, —
  That cream rises thickest on milk that
  was spilt!

V

We sailed for the moon, but, in sad disil-
  lusion,
  Snug under Point Comfort are glad to
  make fast,
And strive (sans our glasses) to make a
  confusion
  'Twixt our rind of green cheese and the
  moon of the past.
Ah, Might-have-been, Could-have-been,
  Would-have-been! rascals,
  He 's a genius or fool whom ye cheat at
  two-score,

And the man whose boy-promise was lik-
  ened to Pascal's
  Is thankful at forty they don't call him
  bore!

VI

With what fumes of fame was each con-
  fident pate full!
  How rates of insurance should rise on
  the Charles!
And which of us now would not feel wisely
  grateful,
  If his rhymes sold as fast as the Em-
  blems of Quarles?
E'en if won, what 's the good of Life's
  medals and prizes?
  The rapture 's in what never was or is
  gone;
That we missed them makes Helens of
  plain Ann Elizys,
  For the goose of To-day still is Mem-
  ory's swan.

VII

And yet who would change the old dream
  for new treasure?
  Make not youth's sourest grapes the best
  wine of our life?
Need he reckon his date by the Almanac's
  measure
  Who is twenty life-long in the eyes of
  his wife?
Ah, Fate, should I live to be nonagenarian,
  Let me still take Hope's frail I. O. U.'s
  upon trust,
Still talk of a trip to the Islands Macarian,
  And still climb the dream-tree for —
  ashes and dust!

AT THE BURNS CENTENNIAL

JANUARY, 1859

I

A HUNDRED years! they 're quickly fled,
  With all their joy and sorrow;
Their dead leaves shed upon the dead,
  Their fresh ones sprung by morrow!
And still the patient seasons bring
  Their change of sun and shadow;
New birds still sing with every spring,
  New violets spot the meadow.

II

A hundred years ! and Nature's powers
  No greater grown nor lessened !
They saw no flowers more sweet than
    ours,
  No fairer new moon's crescent.
Would she but treat us poets so,
  So from our winter free us,
And set our slow old sap aflow
  To sprout in fresh ideas !

III

Alas, think I, what worth or parts
  Have brought me here competing,
To speak what starts in myriad hearts
  With Burns's memory beating !
Himself had loved a theme like this;
  Must I be its entomber ?
No pen save his but 's sure to miss
  Its pathos or its humor.

IV

As I sat musing what to say,
  And how my verse to number,
Some elf in play passed by that way,
  And sank my lids in slumber;
And on my sleep a vision stole,
  Which I will put in metre,
Of Burns's soul at the wicket-hole
  Where sits the good Saint Peter.

V

The saint, methought, had left his post
  That day to Holy Willie,
Who swore, " Each ghost that comes shall
    toast
  In brunstane, will he, nill he;
There 's nane need hope with phrases fine
  Their score to wipe a sin frae;
I 'll chalk a sign, to save their tryin', —
  A hand (☞) and 'Vide infra!'"

VI

Alas ! no soil 's too cold or dry
  For spiritual small potatoes,
Scrimped natures, spry the trade to ply
  Of diaboli advocatus;
Who lay bent pins in the penance-stool
  Where Mercy plumps a cushion,
Who 've just one rule for knave and fool,
  It saves so much confusion !

VII

So when Burns knocked, Will knit his
    brows,
  His window gap made scanter,
And said, " Go rouse the other house;
  We lodge no Tam O'Shanter ! "
" We lodge ! " laughed Burns. " Now well
    I see
  Death cannot kill old nature;
No human flea but thinks that he
  May speak for his Creator !

VIII

" But, Willie, friend, don't turn me forth,
  Auld Clootie needs no gauger;
And if on earth I had small worth,
  You 've let in worse I 'se wager ! "
" Na, nane has knockit at the yett
  But found me hard as whunstane;
There 's chances yet your bread to get
  Wi Auld Nick, gaugin' brunstane."

IX

Meanwhile, the Unco' Guid had ta'en
  Their place to watch the process,
Flattening in vain on many a pane
  Their disembodied noses.
Remember, please, 't is all a dream;
  One can't control the fancies
Through sleep that stream with wayward
    gleam,
  Like midnight's boreal dances.

X

Old Willie's tone grew sharp 's a knife:
  " In primis, I indite ye,
For makin' strife wi' the water o' life,
  And preferrin' aqua vitæ ! "
Then roared a voice with lusty din,
  Like a skipper's when 't is blowy,
" If that 's a sin, I 'd ne'er got in,
  As sure as my name 's Noah ! "

XI

Baulked, Willie turned another leaf, —
  " There 's many here have heard ye,
To the pain and grief o' true belief,
  Say hard things o' the clergy ! "
Then rang a clear tone over all, —
  " One plea for him allow me:
I once heard call from o'er me, 'Saul,
  Why persecutest thou me ?' "

XII

To the next charge vexed Willie turned,
  And, sighing, wiped his glasses:
" I 'm much concerned to find ye yearned
  O'er-warmly tow'rd the lasses ! "
Here David sighed ; poor Willie's face
  Lost all its self-possession:
" I leave this case to God's own grace;
  It baffles *my* discretion ! "

XIII

Then sudden glory round me broke,
  And low melodious surges
Of wings whose stroke to splendor woke
  Creation's farthest verges;
A cross stretched, ladder-like, secure
  From earth to heaven's own portal,
Whereby God's poor, with footing sure,
  Climbed up to peace immortal.

XIV

I heard a voice serene and low
  (With my heart I seemed to hear it,)
Fall soft and slow as snow on snow,
  Like grace of the heavenly spirit;
As sweet as over new-born son
  The croon of new-made mother,
The voice begun, " Sore tempted one ! "
  Then, pausing, sighed, " Our brother ! "

XV

" If not a sparrow fall, unless
  The Father sees and knows it,
Think ! recks He less his form express,
  The soul his own deposit ?
If only dear to Him the strong,
  That never trip nor wander,
Where were the throng whose morning
    song
  Thrills his blue arches yonder ?

XVI

" Do souls alone clear-eyed, strong-kneed,
  To Him true service render,
And they who need his hand to lead,
  Find they his heart untender ?
Through all your various ranks and fates
  He opens doors to duty,
And he that waits there at your gates
  Was servant of his Beauty.

XVII

" The Earth must richer sap secrete,
  (Could ye in time but know it !)

Must juice concrete with fiercer heat,
  Ere she can make her poet;
Long generations go and come,
  At last she bears a singer,
For ages dumb of senses numb
  The compensation-bringer !

XVIII

" Her cheaper broods in palaces
  She raises under glasses,
But souls like these, heav'n's hostages,
  Spring shelterless as grasses:
They share Earth's blessing and her bane,
  The common sun and shower;
What makes your pain to them is gain,
  Your weakness is their power.

XIX

" These larger hearts must feel the rolls
  Of stormier-waved temptation;
These star-wide souls between their poles
  Bear zones of tropic passion.
He loved much ! — that is gospel good,
  Howe'er the text you handle;
From common wood the cross was hewed,
  By love turned priceless sandal.

XX

" If scant his service at the kirk,
  He *paters* heard and *aves*
From choirs that lurk in hedge and birk,
  From blackbird and from mavis;
The cowering mouse, poor unroofed thing,
  In him found Mercy's angel;
The daisy's ring brought every spring
  To him Love's fresh evangel !

XXI

" Not he the threatening texts who deals
  Is highest 'mong the preachers,
But he who feels the woes and weals
  Of all God's wandering creatures.
He doth good work whose heart can find
  The spirit 'neath the letter;
Who makes his kind of happier mind,
  Leaves wiser men and better.

XXII

" They make Religion be abhorred
  Who round with darkness gulf her,
And think no word can please the Lord
  Unless it smell of sulphur.
Dear Poet-heart, that childlike guessed
  The Father's loving kindness,

Come now to rest! Thou didst his
     hest,
  If haply 't was in blindness ! "

XXIII

Then leapt heaven's portals wide apart,
  And at their golden thunder
With sudden start I woke, my heart
  Still throbbing-full of wonder.
" Father," I said, " 't is known to Thee
  How Thou thy Saints preparest;
But this I see, — Saint Charity
  Is still the first and fairest ! "

XXIV

Dear Bard and Brother ! let who may
  Against thy faults be railing,
(Though far, I pray, from us be they
  That never had a failing !)
One toast I 'll give, and that not long,
  Which thou wouldst pledge if present, —
To him whose song, in nature strong,
  Makes man of prince and peasant!

IN AN ALBUM

THE misspelt scrawl, upon the wall
By some Pompeian idler traced,
In ashes packed (ironic fact !)
Lies eighteen centuries uneffaced,
While many a page of bard and sage,
Deemed once mankind's immortal gain,
Lost from Time's ark, leaves no more mark
Than a keel's furrow through the main.

O Chance and Change ! our buzz's range
Is scarcely wider than a fly's;
Then let us play at fame to-day,
To-morrow be unknown and wise;
And while the fair beg locks of hair,
And autographs, and Lord knows what,
Quick ! let us scratch our moment's
     match,
Make our brief blaze, and be forgot !

Too pressed to wait, upon her slate
Fame writes a name or two in doubt;
Scarce written, these no longer please,
And her own finger rubs them out:
It may ensue, fair girl, that you
Years hence this yellowing leaf may see,
And put to task, your memory ask
In vain, " This Lowell, who was he ? "

AT THE COMMENCEMENT
DINNER, 1866

IN ACKNOWLEDGING A TOAST TO THE
SMITH PROFESSOR

I RISE, Mr. Chairman, as both of us know,
With the impromptu I promised you three
     weeks ago,
Dragged up to my doom by your might
     and my mane,
To do what I vowed I 'd do never again;
And I feel like your good honest dough
     when possest
By a stirring, impertinent devil of yeast.
" You must rise," says the leaven. " I
     can't," says the dough;
" Just examine my bumps, and you 'll see
     it 's no go."
" But you must," the tormentor insists,
     " 't is all right;
You must rise when I bid you, and, what 's
     more, be light."

'T is a dreadful oppression, this making
     men speak
What they 're sure to be sorry for all the
     next week;
Some poor stick requesting, like Aaron's,
     to bud
Into eloquence, pathos, or wit in cold blood,
As if the dull brain that you vented your
     spite on
Could be got, like an ox, by mere poking,
     to Brighton.

They say it is wholesome to rise with the
     sun,
And I dare say it may be if not over-
     done;
(I think it was Thomson who made the
     remark
'T was an excellent thing in its way — for
     a lark;)
But to rise after dinner and look down the
     meeting
On a distant (as Gray calls it) prospect of
     Eating,
With a stomach half full and a cerebrum
     hollow
As the tortoise-shell ere it was strung for
     Apollo,
Under contract to raise anerithmon gelasma

With rhymes so hard hunted they gasp with
the asthma,
And jokes not much younger than Jethro's
phylacteries,
Is something I leave you yourselves to
characterize.

I've a notion, I think, of a good dinner
speech,
Tripping light as a sandpiper over the
beach,
Swerving this way and that as the wave of
the moment
Washes out its slight trace with a dash of
whim's foam on 't,
And leaving on memory's rim just a sense
Something graceful had gone by, a live
present tense;
Not poetry, — no, not quite that, but as
good,
A kind of winged prose that could fly if it
would.
'T is a time for gay fancies as fleeting and
vain
As the whisper of foam-beads on fresh-
poured champagne,
Since dinners were not perhaps strictly
designed
For manœuvring the heavy dragoons of the
mind.
When I hear your set speeches that start
with a pop,
Then wander and maunder, too feeble to
stop,
With a vague apprehension from popular
rumor
There used to be something by mortals
called humor,
Beginning again when you thought they
were done,
Respectable, sensible, weighing a ton,
And as near to the present occasions of
men
As a Fast Day discourse of the year eighteen
ten,
I — well, I sit still, and my sentiments
smother,
For am I not also a bore and a brother?

And a toast, — what should that be? Light,
airy, and free,
The foam-Aphrodite of Bacchus's sea,
A fancy-tinged bubble, an orbed rainbow-
stain,

That floats for an instant 'twixt goblet and
brain;
A breath-born perfection, half something,
half naught,
And breaks if it strike the hard edge of a
thought.
Do you ask me to make such? Ah no,
not so simple;
Ask Apelles to paint you the ravishing
dimple
Whose shifting enchantment lights Venus's
cheek,
And the artist will tell you his skill is to
seek;
Once fix it, 't is naught, for the charm of
it rises
From the sudden bopeeps of its smiling
surprises.

I've tried to define it, but what mother's
son
Could ever yet do what he knows should
be done?
My rocket has burst, and I watch in the air
Its fast-fading heart's-blood drop back in
despair;
Yet one chance is left me, and, if I am
quick,
I can palm off, before you suspect me, the
stick.

Now since I've succeeded — I pray do not
frown —
To Ticknor's and Longfellow's classical
gown,
And profess four strange languages, which,
luckless elf,
I speak like a native (of Cambridge) my-
self,
Let me beg, Mr. President, leave to propose
A sentiment treading on nobody's toes,
And give, in such ale as with pump-handles
we brew,
Their memory who saved us from all talk-
ing Hebrew, —
A toast that to deluge with water is good,
For in Scripture they come in just after
the flood:
I give you the men but for whom, as I
guess, sir,
Modern languages ne'er could have had a
professor,
The builders of Babel, to whose zeal the
lungs

Of the children of men owe confusion of
    tongues;
And a name all-embracing I couple there-
    with,
Which is that of my founder — the late
    Mr. Smith.

A PARABLE

AN ass munched thistles, while a nightin-
    gale
From passion's fountain flooded all the
    vale.
"Hee-haw!" cried he, "I hearken," as
    who knew
For such ear-largess humble thanks were
    due.
"Friend," said the wingèd pain, "in vain
    you bray,
Who tunnels bring, not cisterns, for my
    lay;
None but his peers the poet rightly hear,
Nor mete we listeners by their length of
    ear."

V. EPIGRAMS

SAYINGS

I.

IN life's small things be resolute and great
To keep thy muscle trained: know'st thou
    when Fate
Thy measure takes, or when she 'll say to
    thee,
"I find thee worthy; do this deed for me"?

2.

A camel-driver, angry with his drudge,
Beating him, called him hunchback; to the
    hind
Thus spake a dervish: "Friend, the Eternal
    Judge
Dooms not his work, but ours, the crooked
    mind."

3.

Swiftly the politic goes: is it dark? — he
    borrows a lantern;
Slowly the statesman and sure, guiding his
    steps by the stars.

4.

"Where lies the capital, pilgrim, seat of
    who governs the Faithful?"
"Thither my footsteps are bent: it is where
    Saadi is lodged."

INSCRIPTIONS

FOR A BELL AT CORNELL UNIVERSITY

I CALL as fly the irrevocable hours,
    Futile as air or strong as fate to make
Your ·lives of sand or granite; awful
    powers,
Even as men choose, they either give or
    take.

FOR A MEMORIAL WINDOW TO SIR WAL-TER RALEIGH, SET UP IN ST. MARGA-RET'S, WESTMINSTER, BY AMERICAN CONTRIBUTORS

THE New World's sons, from England's
    breasts we drew
    Such milk as bids remember whence we
    came;
Proud of her Past, wherefrom our Present
    grew,
    This window we inscribe with Raleigh's
    name.

PROPOSED FOR A SOLDIERS' AND SAIL-ORS' MONUMENT IN BOSTON

To those who died for her on land and
    sea,
That she might have a country great and
    free,
Boston builds this: build ye her monument
In lives like theirs, at duty's summons
    spent.

A MISCONCEPTION

B, TAUGHT by Pope to do his good by
    stealth,
'Twixt participle and noun no difference
    feeling,
In office placed to serve the Commonwealth,
Does himself all the good he can by steal-
    ing.

THE BOSS

SKILLED to pull wires, he baffles Nature's
hope,
Who sure intended him to stretch a rope.

SUN-WORSHIP

IF I were the rose at your window,
Happiest rose of its crew,
Every blossom I bore would bend in-
ward,
They'd know where the sunshine grew.

CHANGED PERSPECTIVE

FULL oft the pathway to her door
I've measured by the selfsame track,
Yet doubt the distance more and more,
'T is so much longer coming back!

WITH A PAIR OF GLOVES LOST IN A WAGER

WE wagered, she for sunshine, I for rain,
And I should hint sharp practice if I
dared;
For was not she beforehand sure to gain
Who made the sunshine we together shared?

SIXTY-EIGHTH BIRTHDAY

As life runs on, the road grows strange
With faces new, and near the end
The milestones into headstones change,
'Neath every one a friend.

INTERNATIONAL COPYRIGHT

IN vain we call old notions fudge,
    And bend our conscience to our dealing ;
The Ten Commandments will not budge,
    And stealing will continue stealing.

LAST POEMS

THE following note was prefixed to this group when published in 1895: "This little volume contains those of the poems which Mr. Lowell wrote in his last years which, I believe, he might have wished to preserve. Three of them were published before his death. Of the rest, two appear here for the first time. C. E. N."

HOW I CONSULTED THE ORACLE OF THE GOLDFISHES

WHAT know we of the world immense
Beyond the narrow ring of sense ?
What should we know, who lounge about
The house we dwell in, nor find out,
Masked by a wall, the secret cell
Where the soul's priests in hiding dwell ?
The winding stair that steals aloof
To chapel-mysteries 'neath the roof ?

It lies about us, yet as far
From sense sequestered as a star
New launched its wake of fire to trace
In secrecies of unprobed space,
Whose beacon's lightning-pinioned spears
Might earthward haste a thousand years
Nor reach it. So remote seems this
World undiscovered, yet it is
A neighbor near and dumb as death,
So near, we seem to feel the breath
Of its hushed habitants as they
Pass us unchallenged, night and day.

Never could mortal ear nor eye
By sound or sign suspect them nigh,
Yet why may not some subtler sense
Than those poor two give evidence ?
Transfuse the ferment of their being
Into our own, past hearing, seeing,
As men, if once attempered so,
Far off each other's thought can know ?
As horses with an instant thrill
Measure their rider's strength of will ?
Comes not to all some glimpse that brings
Strange sense of sense-escaping things ?
Wraiths some transfigured nerve divines ?
Approaches, premonitions, signs,
Voices of Ariel that die out
In the dim No Man's Land of Doubt ?

Are these Night's dusky birds ? Are these
Phantasmas of the silences

Outer or inner ? — rude heirlooms
From grovellers in the cavern-glooms,
Who in unhuman Nature saw
Misshapen foes with tusk and claw,
And with those night-fears brute and blind
Peopled the chaos of their mind,
Which, in ungovernable hours,
Still make their bestial lair in ours ?

Were they, or were they not ?　Yes;
　　no;
Uncalled they come, unbid they go,
And leave us fumbling in a doubt
Whether within us or without
The spell of this illusion be
That witches us to hear and see
As in a twi-life what it will,
And hath such wonder-working skill
That what we deemed most solid-wrought
Turns a mere figment of our thought,
Which when we grasp at in despair
Our fingers find vain semblance there,
For Psyche seeks a corner-stone
Firmer than aught to matter known.

Is it illusion ?　Dream-stuff ?　Show
Made of the wish to have it so ?
'T were something, even though this were
　　all:
So the poor prisoner, on his wall
Long gazing, from the chance designs
Of crack, mould, weather-stain, refines
New and new pictures without cease,
Landscape, or saint, or altar-piece:
But these are Fancy's common brood
Hatched in the nest of solitude;
This is Dame Wish's hourly trade,
By our rude sires a goddess made.
Could longing, though its heart broke, give
Trances in which we chiefly live ?
Moments that darken all beside,
Tearfully radiant as a bride ?
Beckonings of bright escape, of wings
Purchased with loss of baser things ?
Blithe truancies from all control
Of Hylë, outings of the soul ?

The worm, by trustful instinct led,
Draws from its womb a slender thread,
And drops, confiding that the breeze
Will waft it to unpastured trees:
So the brain spins itself, and so
Swings boldly off in hope to blow
Across some tree of knowledge, fair

With fruitage new, none else shall share:
Sated with wavering in the Void,
It backward climbs, so best employed,
And, where no proof is nor can be,
Seeks refuge with Analogy;
Truth's soft half-sister, she may tell
Where lurks, seld-sought, the other's well.
With metaphysic midges sore,
My Thought seeks comfort at her door,
And, at her feet a suppliant cast,
Evokes a spectre of the past.
Not such as shook the knees of Saul,
But winsome, golden-gay withal, —
Two fishes in a globe of glass,
That pass, and waver, and re-pass,
And lighten that way, and then this,
Silent as meditation is.
With a half-humorous smile I see
In this their aimless industry,
These errands nowhere and returns
Grave as a pair of funeral urns,
This ever-seek and never-find,
A mocking image of my mind.
But not for this I bade you climb
Up from the darkening deeps of time:
Help me to tame these wild day-mares
That sudden on me unawares.
Fish, do your duty, as did they
Of the Black Island far away
In life's safe places, — far as you
From all that now I see or do.
You come, embodied flames, as when
I knew you first, nor yet knew men;
Your gold renews my golden days,
Your splendor all my loss repays.

'T is more than sixty years ago
Since first I watched your to-and-fro;
Two generations come and gone
From silence to oblivion,
With all their noisy strife and stress
Lulled in the grave's forgivingness,
While you unquenchably survive
Immortal, almost more alive.
I watched you then a curious boy,
Who in your beauty found full joy,
And, by no problem-debts distrest,
Sate at life's board a welcome guest.
You were my sister's pets, not mine;
But Property's dividing line
No hint of dispossession drew
On any map my simplesse knew;
O golden age, not yet dethroned!
What made me happy, that I owned;

You were my wonders, you my Lars,
In darkling days my sun and stars,
And over you entranced I hung,
Too young to know that I was young.
Gazing with still unsated bliss,
My fancies took some shape like this:
" I have my world, and so have you,
A tiny universe for two,
A bubble by the artist blown,
Scarcely more fragile than our own,
Where you have all a whale could wish,
Happy as Eden's primal fish.
Manna is dropt you thrice a day
From some kind heaven not far away,
And still you snatch its softening crumbs,
Nor, more than we, think whence it comes.
No toil seems yours but to explore
Your cloistered realm from shore to shore;
Sometimes you trace its limits round,
Sometimes its limpid depths you sound,
Or hover motionless midway,
Like gold-red clouds at set of day;
Erelong you whirl with sudden whim
Off to your globe's most distant rim,
Where, greatened by the watery lens,
Methinks no dragon of the fens
Flashed huger scales against the sky,
Roused by Sir Bevis or Sir Guy,
And the one eye that meets my view,
Lidless and strangely largening, too,
Like that of conscience in the dark,
Seems to make me its single mark.
What a benignant lot is yours
That have an own All-out-of-doors,
No words to spell, no sums to do,
No Nepos and no parlyvoo!
How happy you without a thought
Of such cross things as Must and Ought,—
I too the happiest of boys
To see and share your golden joys!"

So thought the child, in simpler words,
Of you his finny flocks and herds;
Now, an old man, I bid you rise
To the fine sight behind the eyes,
And, lo, you float and flash again
In the dark cistern of my brain.
But o'er your visioned flames I brood
With other mien, in other mood;
You are no longer there to please,
But to stir argument, and tease
My thought with all the ghostly shapes
From which no moody man escapes.

Diminished creature, I no more
Find Fairyland beside my door,
But for each moment's pleasure pay
With the *quart d'heure* of Rabelais!

I watch you in your crystal sphere,
And wonder if you see and hear
Those shapes and sounds that stir the wide
Conjecture of the world outside;
In your pent lives, as we in ours,
Have you surmises dim of powers,
Of presences obscurely shown,
Of lives a riddle to your own,
Just on the senses' outer verge,
Where sense-nerves into soul-nerves merge,
Where we conspire our own deceit
Confederate in deft Fancy's feat,
And the fooled brain befools the eyes
With pageants woven of its own lies?
But *are* they lies? Why more than those
Phantoms that startle your repose,
Half seen, half heard, then flit away,
And leave you your prose-bounded day?

The things ye see as shadows I
Know to be substance; tell me why
My visions, like those haunting you,
May not be as substantial too.
Alas, who ever answer heard
From fish, and dream-fish too? Absurd!
Your consciousness I half divine,
But you are wholly deaf to mine.
Go, I dismiss you; ye have done
All that ye could; our silk is spun:
Dive back into the deep of dreams,
Where what is real is what seems!
Yet I shall fancy till my grave
Your lives to mine a lesson gave;
If lesson none, an image, then,
Impeaching self-conceit in men
Who put their confidence alone
In what they call the Seen and Known.
How seen? How known? As through
        your glass
Our wavering apparitions pass
Perplexingly, then subtly wrought
To some quite other thing by thought.
Here shall my resolution be:
The shadow of the mystery
Is haply wholesomer for eyes
That cheat us to be overwise,
And I am happy in my right
To love God's darkness as His light.

TURNER'S OLD TÉMÉRAIRE

UNDER A FIGURE SYMBOLIZING THE CHURCH

THOU wast the fairest of all man-made
  things;
The breath of heaven bore up thy cloudy
  wings,
And, patient in their triple rank,
The thunders crouched about thy flank,
Their black lips silent with the doom of
  kings.

The storm-wind loved to rock him in thy
  pines,
And swell thy vans with breath of great
  designs;
Long-wildered pilgrims of the main
By thee relaid their course again,
Whose prow was guided by celestial signs.

How didst thou trample on tumultuous
  seas,
Or, like some basking sea-beast stretched
  at ease,
Let the bull-fronted surges glide
Caressingly along thy side,
Like glad hounds leaping by the hunts-
  man's knees !

Heroic feet, with fire of genius shod,
In battle's ecstasy thy deck have trod,
While from their touch a fulgor ran
Through plank and spar, from man to
  man,
Welding thee to a thunderbolt of God.

Now a black demon, belching fire and
  steam,
Drags thee away, a pale, dismantled
  dream,
And all thy desecrated bulk
Must landlocked lie, a helpless hulk,
To gather weeds in the regardless stream.

Woe 's me, from Ocean's sky-horizoned
  air
To this ! Better, the flame-cross still
  aflare,
Shot-shattered to have met thy doom
Where thy last lightnings cheered the
  gloom,
Than here be safe in dangerless despair.

Thy drooping symbol to the flagstaff
  clings,
Thy rudder soothes the tide to lazy rings,
Thy thunders now but birthdays greet,
Thy planks forget the martyrs' feet,
Thy masts what challenges the sea-wind
  brings.

Thou a mere hospital, where human
  wrecks,
Like winter-flies, crawl those renownëd
  decks,
Ne'er trodden save by captive foes,
And wonted sternly to impose
God's will and thine on bowed imperial
  necks !

Shall nevermore, engendered of thy fame,
A new sea-eagle heir thy conqueror name,
And with commissioned talons wrench
From thy supplanter's grimy clench
His sheath of steel, his wings of smoke
  and flame ?

This shall the pleased eyes of our children
  see;
For this the stars of God long even as
  we;
Earth listens for his wings; the Fates
Expectant lean; Faith cross-propt waits,
And the tired waves of Thought's insur-
  gent sea.

ST. MICHAEL THE WEIGHER

STOOD the tall Archangel weighing
All man's dreaming, doing, saying,
All the failure and the pain,
All the triumph and the gain,
In the unimagined years,
Full of hopes, more full of tears,
Since old Adam's hopeless eyes
Backward searched for Paradise,
And, instead, the flame-blade saw
Of inexorable Law.

Waking, I beheld him there,
With his fire-gold, flickering hair,
In his blinding armor stand,
And the scales were in his hand:
Mighty were they, and full well
They could poise both heaven and hell.
" Angel," asked I humbly then,
" Weighest thou the souls of men ?

That thine office is, I know."
"Nay," he answered me, "not so;
But I weigh the hope of Man
Since the power of choice began,
In the world, of good or ill."
Then I waited and was still.

In one scale I saw him place
All the glories of our race,
Cups that lit Belshazzar's feast,
Gems, the lightning of the East,
Kublai's sceptre, Cæsar's sword,
Many a poet's golden word,
Many a skill of science, vain
To make men as gods again.

In the other scale he threw
Things regardless, outcast, few,
Martyr-ash, arena sand,
Of St. Francis' cord a strand,
Beechen cups of men whose need
Fasted that the poor might feed,
Disillusions and despairs
Of young saints with grief-grayed hairs,
Broken hearts that brake for Man.

Marvel through my pulses ran
Seeing then the beam divine
Swiftly on this hand decline,
While Earth's splendor and renown
Mounted light as thistle-down.

A VALENTINE

LET others wonder what fair face
Upon their path shall shine,
And, fancying half, half hoping, trace
Some maiden shape of tenderest grace
To be their Valentine.

Let other hearts with tremor sweet
One secret wish enshrine
That Fate may lead their happy feet
Fair Julia in the lane to meet
To be their Valentine.

But I, far happier, am secure;
I know the eyes benign,
The face more beautiful and pure
Than Fancy's fairest portraiture
That mark my Valentine.

More than when first I singled thee,
This only prayer is mine,—

That, in the years I yet shall see,
As, darling, in the past, thou 'lt be
My happy Valentine.

AN APRIL BIRTHDAY — AT SEA

ON this wild waste, where never blossom
came,
Save the white wind-flower in the billow's
cap,
Or those pale disks of momentary flame,
Loose petals dropped from Dian's care-
less lap,
What far fetched influence all my fancy
fills,
With singing birds and dancing daffo-
dils ?

Why, 't is her day whom jocund April
brought,
And who brings April with her in her
eyes;
It is her vision lights my lonely thought,
Even as a rose that opes its hushed sur-
prise
In sick men's chambers, with its glow-
ing breath
Plants Summer at the glacier edge of
Death.

Gray sky, sea gray as mossy stones on
graves; —
Anon comes April in her jollity;
And dancing down the bleak vales 'tween
the waves,
Makes them green glades for all her
flowers and me.
The gulls turn thrushes, charmed are
sea and sky
By magic of my thought, and know
not why.

Ah, but I know, for never April's shine,
Nor passion gust of rain, nor all her
flowers
Scattered in haste, were seen so sudden
fine
As she in various mood, on whom the
powers
Of happiest stars in fair conjunction
smiled
To bless the birth of April's darling
child.

LOVE AND THOUGHT

WHAT hath Love with Thought to do ?
Still at variance are the two.
Love is sudden, Love is rash,
Love is like the levin flash,
Comes as swift, as swiftly goes,
And his mark as surely knows.

Thought is lumpish, Thought is slow,
Weighing long 'tween yes and no;
When dear Love is dead and gone,
Thought comes creeping in anon,
And, in his deserted nest,
Sits to hold the crowner's quest.

Since we love, what need to think ?
Happiness stands on a brink
Whence too easy 't is to fall
Whither 's no return at all;
Have a care, half-hearted lover,
Thought would only push her over !

THE NOBLER LOVER

IF he be a nobler lover, take him !
  You in you I seek, and not myself;
Love with men 's what women choose to
    make him,
  Seraph strong to soar, or fawn-eyed elf:
All I am or can, your beauty gave it,
  Lifting me a moment nigh to you,
And my bit of heaven, I fain would save
    it —
  Mine I thought it was, I never knew.

What you take of me is yours to serve
    you,
  All I give, you gave to me before;
Let him win you ! If I but deserve you,
  I keep all you grant to him and more:
You shall make me dare what others dare
    not,
  You shall keep my nature pure as snow,
And a light from you that others share
    not
  Shall transfigure me where'er I go.

Let me be your thrall ! However lowly
  Be the bondsman's service I can do,
Loyalty shall make it high and holy;
  Naught can be unworthy, done for you.

Men shall say, " A lover of this fashion
  Such an icy mistress well beseems."
Women say, " Could we deserve such pas-
    sion,
  We might be the marvel that he dreams."

ON HEARING A SONATA OF BEETHOVEN'S PLAYED IN THE NEXT ROOM

UNSEEN Musician, thou art sure to please,
  For those same notes in happier days I
    heard
Poured by dear hands that long have never
    stirred
Yet now again for me delight the keys:
Ah me, to strong illusions such as these
  What are Life's solid things ? The
    walls that gird
Our senses, lo, a casual scent or word
  Levels, and 't is the soul that hears and
    sees !
Play on, dear girl, and many be the years
  Ere some grayhaired survivor sit like
    me
And, for thy largess pay a meed of tears
  Unto another who, beyond the sea
Of Time and Change, perhaps not sadly
    hears
  A music in this verse undreamed by
    thee !

VERSES

INTENDED TO GO WITH A POSSET DISH
TO MY DEAR LITTLE GODDAUGHTER,
1882

It is of interest to know that the goddaugh-
ter was a child of Leslie Stephen.

IN good old times, which means, you know,
The time men wasted long ago,
And we must blame our brains or mood
If that we squander seems less good,
In those blest days when wish was act
And fancy dreamed itself to fact,
Godfathers used to fill with guineas
The cups they gave their pickaninnies,
Performing functions at the chrism
Not mentioned in the Catechism.
No millioner, poor I fill up
With wishes my more modest cup,
Though had I Amalthea's horn

It should be hers the newly born.
Nay, shudder not! I should bestow it
So brimming full she could n't blow it.
Wishes are n't horses: true, but still
There are worse roadsters than goodwill.
And so I wish my darling health,
And just to round my couplet, wealth,
With faith enough to bridge the chasm
'Twixt Genesis and Protoplasm,
And bear her o'er life's current vext
From this world to a better next,
Where the full glow of God puts out
Poor reason's farthing candle, Doubt.
I've wished her healthy, wealthy, wise,
What more can godfather devise?
But since there's room for countless wishes
In these old-fashioned posset dishes,
I'll wish her from my plenteous store
Of those commodities two more,
Her father's wit, veined through and
    through
With tenderness that Watts (but whew!
Celia's aflame, I mean no stricture
On his Sir Josh-surpassing picture) —
I wish her next, and 't is the soul
Of all I've dropt into the bowl,
Her mother's beauty — nay, but two
So fair at once would never do.
Then let her but the half possess,
Troy was besieged ten years for less.
Now if there's any truth in Darwin,
And we from what was, all we are win,
I simply wish the child to be
A sample of Heredity,
Enjoying to the full extent
Life's best, the Unearned Increment
Which Fate her Godfather to flout
Gave *him* in legacies of gout.
Thus, then, the cup is duly filled;
Walk steady, dear, lest all be spilled.

ON A BUST OF GENERAL GRANT

"This poem is the last, so far as is known,
written by Mr. Lowell. He laid it aside for
revision, leaving two of the verses incomplete.
In a pencilled fragment of the poem the first
verse appears as follows: —

'Strong, simple, silent, such are Nature's Laws.'

In the final copy, from which the poem is now
printed, the verse originally stood: —

'Strong, steadfast, silent are the   laws.'

but 'steadfast' is crossed out, and 'simple'
written above.

"A similar change is made in the ninth
verse of the stanza, where 'simpleness' is sub-
stituted for 'steadfastness.' The change from
'steadfast' to 'simple' was not made, prob-
ably through oversight, in the first verse of the
second stanza. There is nothing to indicate
what epithet Mr. Lowell would have chosen
to complete the first verse of the third stanza.
C. E. N."

STRONG, simple, silent are the [steadfast]
    laws
That sway this universe, of none withstood,
Unconscious of man's outcries or applause,
Or what man deems his evil or his good;
And when the Fates ally them with a cause
That wallows in the sea-trough and seems
    lost,
Drifting in danger of the reefs and sands
Of shallow counsels, this way, that way,
    tost,
Strength, silence, simpleness, of these three
    strands
They twist the cable shall the world hold
    fast
To where its anchors clutch the bed-rock of
    the Past.

Strong, simple, silent, therefore such was
    he
Who helped us in our need; the eternal law
That who can saddle Opportunity
Is God's elect, though many a mortal flaw
May minish him in eyes that closely see,
Was verified in him: what need we say
Of one who made success where others
    failed,
Who, with no light save that of common
    day,
Struck hard, and still struck on till For-
    tune quailed,
But that (so sift the Norns) a desperate
    van
Ne'er fell at last to one who was not wholly
    man.

A face all prose where Time's [benignant]
    haze
Softens no raw edge yet, nor makes all fair
With the beguiling light of vanished days;
This is relentless granite, bleak and bare,
Roughhewn, and scornful of æsthetic
    phrase;
Nothing is here for fancy, naught for
    dreams,
The Present's hard uncompromising light

Accents all vulgar outlines, flaws, and
seams,
Yet vindicates some pristine natural right
O'ertopping that hereditary grace
Which marks the gain or loss of some time-
fondled race.

So Marius looked, methinks, and Crom-
well so,
Not in the purple born, to those they led
Nearer for that and costlier to the foe,
New moulders of old forms, by nature
bred
The exhaustless life of manhood's seeds to
show,
Let but the ploughshare of portentous
times
Strike deep enough to reach them where
they lie:
Despair and danger are their fostering
climes,
And their best sun bursts from a stormy
sky:
He was our man of men, nor would abate
The utmost due manhood could claim of
fate.

Nothing ideal, a plain-people's man
At the first glance, a more deliberate ken
Finds type primeval, theirs in whose veins
ran

Such blood as quelled the dragon in his
den,
Made harmless fields, and better worlds
began:
He came grim-silent, saw and did the deed
That was to do; in his master-grip
Our sword flashed joy; no skill of words
could breed
Such sure conviction as that close-clamped
lip;
He slew our dragon, nor, so seemed it,
knew
He had done more than any simplest man
might do.

Yet did this man, war-tempered, stern as
steel
Where steel opposed, prove soft in civil
sway;
The hand hilt-hardened had lost tact to
feel
The world's base coin, and glozing knaves
made prey
Of him and of the entrusted Commonweal;
So Truth insists and will not be denied.
We turn our eyes away, and so will Fame,
As if in his last battle he had died
Victor for us and spotless of all blame,
Doer of hopeless tasks which praters shirk,
One of those still plain men that do the
world's rough work.

APPENDIX

I. INTRODUCTION TO THE SECOND SERIES OF BIGLOW PAPERS

[Lowell took occasion, when collecting in a book the several numbers of the second series of "Biglow Papers," which had appeared in the "Atlantic Monthly," to prefix an essay which not only gave a personal narrative of the origin of the whole scheme, but particularly dwelt upon the use in literature of the homely dialect in which the poems were couched. In this Cambridge Edition it has seemed expedient to print the Introduction here rather than in immediate connection with the poems themselves.]

THOUGH prefaces seem of late to have fallen under some reproach, they have at least this advantage, that they set us again on the feet of our personal consciousness and rescue us from the gregarious mock-modesty or cowardice of that *we* which shrills feebly throughout modern literature like the shrieking of mice in the walls of a house that has passed its prime. Having a few words to say to the many friends whom the "Biglow Papers" have won me, I shall accordingly take the freedom of the first person singular of the personal pronoun. Let each of the good-natured unknown who have cheered me by the written communication of their sympathy look upon this Introduction as a private letter to himself.

When, more than twenty years ago, I wrote the first of the series, I had no definite plan and no intention of ever writing another. Thinking the Mexican war, as I think it still, a national crime committed in behoof of Slavery, our common sin, and wishing to put the feeling of those who thought as I did in a way that would tell, I imagined to myself such an upcountry man as I had often seen at antislavery gatherings, capable of district-school English, but always instinctively falling back into the natural stronghold of his homely dialect when heated to the point of self-forgetfulness. When I began to carry out my conception and to write in my assumed character, I found myself in a strait between two perils. On the one hand, I was in danger of being carried beyond the limit of my own opinions, or at least of that temper with which every man should speak his mind in print, and on the other I feared the risk of seeming to vulgarize a deep and sacred conviction. I needed on occasion to rise above the level of mere *patois*, and for this purpose conceived the Rev. Mr. Wilbur, who should express the more cautious element of the New England character and its pedantry, as Mr.

Biglow should serve for its homely common-sense vivified and heated by conscience. The parson was to be the complement rather than the antithesis of his parishioner, and I felt or fancied a certain humorous element in the real identity of the two under a seeming incongruity. Mr. Wilbur's fondness for scraps of Latin, though drawn from the life, I adopted deliberately to heighten the contrast. Finding soon after that I needed some one as a mouth-piece of the mere drollery, for I conceive that true humor is never divorced from moral conviction, I invented Mr. Sawin for the clown of my little puppet-show. I meant to embody in him that half-conscious *un*morality which I had noticed as the recoil in gross natures from a puritanism that still strove to keep in its creed the intense savor which had long gone out of its faith and life. In the three I thought I should find room enough to express, as it was my plan to do, the popular feeling and opinion of the time. For the names of two of my characters, since I have received some remonstrances from very worthy persons who happen to bear them, I would say that they were purely fortuitous, probably mere unconscious memories of sign-boards or directories. Mr. Sawin's sprang from the accident of a rhyme at the end of his first epistle, and I purposely christened him by the impossible surname of Birdofredum not more to stigmatize him as the incarnation of "Manifest Destiny," in other words, of national recklessness as to right and wrong, than to avoid the chance of wounding any private sensitiveness.

The success of my experiment soon began not only to astonish me, but to make me feel the responsibility of knowing that I held in my hand a weapon instead of the mere fencing-stick I had supposed. Very far from being a popular author under my own name, so far, indeed, as to be almost unread, I found the verses of my pseudonym copied everywhere; I saw them pinned up in workshops; I heard them quoted and their authorship debated; I once even, when rumor had at length caught up my name in one of its eddies, had the satisfaction of overhearing it demonstrated, in the pauses of a concert, that *I* was utterly incompetent to have written anything of the kind. I had read too much not to know the utter worthlessness of contemporary reputation, especially as regards satire, but I knew also that by giving a certain amount of influence it also had its worth, if that influence were used on the right side. I had learned, too, that the first requisite of good writing is to have an earnest and definite purpose, whether æsthetic or moral, and that even good writing, to please long, must have more than an average amount either of imagination or common-sense. The first of these falls to the lot of scarcely one in several generations; the last is within the reach of many in every one that passes; and of this an author may fairly hope to become in part the mouthpiece. If I put on the cap and bells and made myself one of the court-fools of King Demos, it was less to make his majesty laugh than to win a passage to his royal ears for certain serious things which I had deeply at heart. I say this because there is no imputation that could be more galling to any man's self-respect than that of being a mere jester. I endeavored, by generalizing my satire, to give it what value I could beyond the passing moment and the immediate application. How far I have succeeded I cannot tell, but I have had better luck than I ever looked for in seeing my verses survive to pass beyond their nonage.

In choosing the Yankee dialect, I did not act without forethought. It had long seemed to me that the great vice of American writing and speaking was a studied want of simplicity, that we were in danger of coming to look on our mother-tongue as a dead language, to be sought in the grammar and dictionary rather than in the heart, and that our only chance of escape was by seeking it at its living sources among those who were, as Scottowe says of Major-General Gibbons, "divinely illiterate." President Lincoln, the only really great public man whom these latter days have seen, was great also in this, that he was master — witness his speech at Gettysburg — of a truly masculine English, classic, because it was of no special period, and level at once to the highest and lowest of his countrymen. I learn from the highest authority that his favorite reading was in Shakespeare and Milton, to which, of course, the Bible should be added. But whoever should read the debates in Congress might fancy himself present at a meeting of the city council of some city of Southern Gaul in the decline of the Empire, where barbarians with a Latin varnish emulated each other in being more than Ciceronian. Whether it be want of culture, for the highest outcome of that is simplicity, or for whatever reason, it is certain that very few American writers or speakers wield their native language with the directness, precision, and force that are common as the day in the mother country. We use it like Scotsmen, not as if it belonged to us, but as if we wished to prove that we belonged to it, by showing our intimacy with its written rather than with its spoken dialect. And yet all the while our popular idiom is racy with life and vigor and originality, bucksome (as Milton used the word) to our new occasions, and proves itself no mere graft by sending up new suckers from the old root in spite of us. It is only from its roots in the living generations of men that a language can be reinforced with fresh vigor for its needs; what may be called a literate dialect grows ever more and more pedantic and foreign, till it be-

comes at last as unfitting a vehicle for living thought as monkish Latin. That we should all be made to talk like books is the danger with which we are threatened by the Universal Schoolmaster, who does his best to enslave the minds and memories of his victims to what he esteems the best models of English composition, that is to say, to the writers whose style is faultily correct and has no blood-warmth in it. No language after it has faded into *diction*, none that cannot suck up the feeding juices secreted for it in the rich mother-earth of common folk, can bring forth a sound and lusty book. True vigor and heartiness of phrase do not pass from page to page, but from man to man, where the brain is kindled and the lips suppled by downright living interests and by passion in its very throe. Language is the soil of thought, and our own especially is a rich leaf-mould, the slow deposit of ages, the shed foliage of feeling, fancy, and imagination, which has suffered an earth-change, that the vocal forest, as Howell called it, may clothe itself anew with living green. There is death in the dictionary; and, where language is too strictly limited by convention, the ground for expression to grow in is limited also; and we get a *potted* literature, Chinese dwarfs instead of healthy trees.

But while the schoolmaster has been busy starching our language and smoothing it flat with the mangle of a supposed classical authority, the newspaper reporter has been doing even more harm by stretching and swelling it to suit his occasions. A dozen years ago I began a list, which I have added to from time to time, of some of the changes which may be fairly laid at his door. I give a few of them as showing their tendency, all the more dangerous that their effect, like that of some poisons, is insensibly cumulative, and that they are sure at last of effect among a people whose chief reading is the daily paper. I give in two columns the old style and its modern equivalent.

Old Style.	*New Style.*
Was hanged.	Was launched into eternity.
When the halter was put round his neck.	When the fatal noose was adjusted about the neck of the unfortunate victim of his own unbridled passions.
A great crowd came to see.	A vast concourse was assembled to witness.
Great fire.	Disastrous conflagration.
The fire spread.	The conflagration extended its devastating career.
House burned.	Edifice consumed.
The fire was got under.	The progress of the devouring element was arrested.
Man fell.	Individual was precipitated.
A horse and wagon ran against.	A valuable horse attached to a vehicle driven by J. S., in the employment of J. B., collided with.
The frightened horse.	The infuriated animal.
Sent for the doctor.	Called into requisition the services of the family physician.
The mayor of the city in a short speech welcomed.	The chief magistrate of the metropolis, in well-chosen

	and eloquent language, frequently interrupted by the plaudits of the surging multitude, officially tendered the hospitalities.
I shall say a few words.	I shall, with your permission, beg leave to offer some brief observations.
Began his answer.	Commenced his rejoinder.
Asked him to dine.	Tendered him a banquet.
A bystander advised.	One of those omnipresent characters who, as if in pursuance of some previous arrangement, are certain to be encountered in the vicinity when an accident occurs, ventured the suggestion.
He died.	He deceased, he passed out of existence, his spirit quitted its earthly habitation, winged its way to eternity, shook off its burden, etc.

In one sense this is nothing new. The school of Pope in verse ended by wire-drawing its phrase to such thinness that it could bear no weight of meaning whatever. Nor is fine writing by any means confined to America. All writers without imagination fall into it of necessity whenever they attempt the figurative. I take two examples from Mr. Merivale's "History of the Romans under the Empire," which, indeed, is full of such. "The last years of the age familiarly styled the Augustan were singularly barren of the literary glories from which its celebrity was chiefly derived. One by one the stars in its firmament had been lost to the world; Virgil and Horace, etc., had long since died; the charm which the imagination of Livy had thrown over the earlier annals of Rome had ceased to shine on the details of almost contemporary history; and if the flood of his eloquence still continued flowing, ve can hardly suppose that the stream was cs rapid, as fresh, and as clear as ever." I will not waste time in criticising the bad English or the mixture of metaphor in these sentences, but will simply cite another from the same author which is even worse. "The shadowy phantom of the Republic continued to flit before the eyes of the Cæsar. There was still, he apprehended, a germ of sentiment existing, on which a scion of his own house, or even a stranger, might boldly throw himself and raise the standard of patrician independence." Now a ghost may haunt a murderer, but hardly, I should think, to scare him with the threat of taking a new lease of its old tenement. And fancy the *scion* of a *house* in the act of *throwing itself* upon a *germ of sentiment* to *raise a standard!* I am glad, since we have so much in the same kind to answer for, that this bit of horticultural rhetoric is from beyond sea. I would not be supposed to condemn truly imaginative prose. There is a simplicity of splendor, no less than of plainness, and prose would be poor indeed if it could not find a tongue for that meaning of the mind which is behind the meaning of the words. It has sometimes seemed to me that in England there was a growing tendency to curtail language into a mere convenience, and to defecate it of all emotion as thoroughly as algebraic signs. This has arisen, no doubt, in part from that healthy national contempt of humbug which is characteristic of Englishmen, in part from that sensitiveness to the ludicrous which makes them so shy of expressing feeling, but in part also, it is to be feared, from a growing distrust, one might almost say hatred, of whatever is super-material. There is something sad in the scorn with which their journalists treat the notion of there being such a thing as a national ideal, seeming utterly to have forgotten that even in the affairs of this world the imagination is as much matter-of-fact as the understanding. If we were to trust the impression made on us by some of the cleverest and most characteristic of their periodical literature, we should think England hopelessly stranded on the good-humored cynicism of well-to-do middle-age, and should fancy it an enchanted nation, doomed to sit forever with its feet under the mahogany in that after-dinner mood which follows conscientious repletion, and which it is ill-manners to disturb with any topics more exciting than the quality of the wines. But there are already symptoms that a large class of Englishmen are getting weary of the dominion of consols and divine common-sense, and to believe that eternal three per cent is not the chief end of man, nor the highest and only kind of interest to which the powers and opportunities of England are entitled.

The quality of exaggeration has often been remarked on as typical of American character, and especially of American humor. In Dr. Petri's *Gedrängtes Handbuch der Fremdwörter*, we are told that the word *humbug* is commonly used for the exaggerations of the North-Americans. To be sure, one would be tempted to think the dream of Columbus half fulfilled, and that Europe had found in the West a nearer way to Orientalism, at least in diction. But it seems to me that a great deal of what is set down as mere extravagance is more fitly to be called intensity and picturesqueness, symptoms of the imaginative faculty in full health and strength, though producing, as yet, only the raw and formless material in which poetry is to work. By and by, perhaps, the world will see it fashioned into poem and picture, and Europe, which will be hard pushed for originality erelong, may have to thank us for a new sensation. The French continue to find Shakespeare exaggerated because he treated English just as our country-folk do when they speak of a "steep price," or say that they "freeze to" a thing. The first postulate of an original literature is that a people should use their language instinctively and unconsciously, as if it were a lively part of their growth and personality, not as the mere torpid boon of education or inheritance. Even Burns contrived to write very poor verse and prose in English. Vulgarisms are often only poetry in the egg. The late Mr. Horace Mann, in one of his public addresses, commented at some length on the beauty and moral significance of the French phrase *s'orienter*, and called on his young friends to practise upon it in life. There was not a Yankee in his audience whose problem had not always been to find out what was *about east*, and to shape his course accordingly. This charm which a familiar expression gains by being commented, as it were, and set in a new light by a foreign language, is curious and instructive. I cannot help thinking that Mr. Matthew Arnold forgets this a little too much sometimes when he writes of the beauties of French style. It would not be hard to find in the works of French Academicians phrases as coarse as those he cites from Burke, only they are veiled by the unfamiliarity of the language. But, however this may be, it is certain that poets and peasants please us in the same way by translating words back again to their primal freshness, and infusing them with a delightful strangeness which is anything but alienation. What, for example, is Milton's "*edge* of battle" but a doing into English of the Latin *acies*? *Was die Gans gedacht das der Schwan vollbracht*, what the goose but thought, that the swan full brought (or, to de-Saxonize it a little, what the goose conceived, that the swan achieved), and it may well be that the life, invention, and vigor shown by our popular speech, and the freedom with which it is shaped to the instant want of those who use it, are of the best omen for our having a swan at last. The part I have taken on myself is that of the humbler bird.

But it is affirmed that there is something innately vulgar in the Yankee dialect. M. Sainte-Beuve says, with his usual neatness: "*Je définis un patois une ancienne langue qui a eu des malheurs, ou encore une langue toute jeune et qui n'a pas fait fortune.*" The first part of his definition applies to a dialect like the Provençal, the last to the Tuscan before Dante had lifted it into a classic, and neither, it seems to me, will quite fit a *patois*, which is not properly a dialect, but rather certain archaisms, proverbial phrases, and modes of pronunciation, which maintain themselves among the uneducated side by side with the finished and universally accepted language. Norman French, for example, or Scotch down to the time of James VI., could hardly be called *patois*, while I should be half inclined to name the Yankee a *lingo* rather than a dialect. It has retained a few words now fallen into disuse in the mother country, like *to tarry, to progress, fleshy, fall*, and some others, it has changed the meaning of some, as in *freshet;* and it has clung to what I suspect to have been the broad Norman pronunciation of *e* (which Molière puts into the mouth of his rustics) in such words as *sarvant, parfect, vartoo*, and the like. It maintains something of the French sound of *a* also in words like *chāmber, dānger* (though the latter had certainly begun to take its present sound so early as 1636, when I find it sometimes

spelt *dainger*). But in general it may be said that nothing can be found in it which does not still survive in some one or other of the English provincial dialects. There is, perhaps, a single exception in the verb to *sleeve*. To *sleeve* silk means to divide or ravel out a thread of silk with the point of a needle till it becomes *floss*. (A.-S. *slćfan*, to *cleave* = divide.) This, I think, explains the "*sleeveless* errand" in "Troilus and Cressida" so inadequately, sometimes so ludicrously darkened by the commentators. Is not a "sleeveless errand" one that cannot be unravelled, incomprehensible, and therefore bootless ?

I am not speaking now of Americanisms properly so called, that is, of words or phrases which have grown into use here either through necessity, invention, or accident, such as a *carry*, a *one-horse affair*, a *prairie*, to *vamose*. Even these are fewer than is sometimes taken for granted. But I think some fair defence may be made against the charge of vulgarity. Properly speaking, vulgarity is in the thought, and not in the word or the way of pronouncing it. Modern French, the most polite of languages, is barbarously vulgar if compared with the Latin out of which it has been corrupted, or even with Italian. There is a wider gap, and one implying greater boorishness, between *ministerium* and *métier*, or *sapiens* and *sachant*, than between *druv* and *drove* or *agin* and *against*, which last is plainly an arrant superlative. Our rustic *coverlid* is nearer its French original than the diminutive *coverlet*, into which it has been ignorantly corrupted in politer speech. I obtained from three cultivated Englishmen at different times three diverse pronunciations of a single word, — *cowcumber, coocumber*, and *cucumber*. Of these the first, which is Yankee also, comes nearest to the nasality of *concombre*. Lord Ossory assures us that Voltaire saw the best society in England, and Voltaire tells his countrymen that *handkerchief* was pronounced *hankercher*. I find it so spelt in Hakluyt and elsewhere. This enormity the Yankee still persists in, and as there is always a reason for such deviations from the sound as represented by the spelling, may we not suspect two sources of derivation, and find an ancestor for *kercher* in *couverture* rather than in *couvrechef?* And what greater phonetic vagary (which Dryden, by the way, called *fegary)* in our *lingua rustica* than this *ker* for *couvre?* I copy from the fly-leaves of my books, where I have noted them from time to time, a few examples of pronunciation and phrase which will show that the Yankee often has antiquity and very respectable literary authority on his side. My list might be largely increased by referring to glossaries, but to them every one can go for himself, and I have gathered enough for my purpose.

I will take first those cases in which something like the French sound has been preserved in certain single letters and diphthongs. And this opens a curious question as to how long this Gallicism maintained itself in England.

Sometimes a divergence in pronunciation has given us two words with different meanings, as in *genteel* and *jaunty*, which I find coming in toward the close of the seventeenth century, and wavering between *genteel* and *jantee*. It is usual in America to drop the *u* in words ending in *our* — a very proper change recommended by Howell two centuries ago, and carried out by him so far as his printers would allow. This and the corresponding changes in *musique*, *musick*, and the like, which he also advocated, show that in his time the French accent indicated by the superfluous letters (for French had once nearly as strong an accent as Italian) had gone out of use. There is plenty of French accent down to the end of Elizabeth's reign. In Daniel we have *riches'* and *counsel'*, in Bishop Hall *comet'*, *chapëlain*, in Donne *pictures'*, *virtue'*, *presence'*, *mortal'*, *merit'*, *hainous'*, *giant'*, with many more, and Marston's satires are full of them. The two latter, however, are not to be relied on, as they may be suspected of Chaucerizing. Herrick writes *baptime*. The tendency to throw the accent backward began early. But the incongruities are perplexing, and perhaps mark the period of transition. In Warner's "Albion's England" we have *creator'* and *crëature'* side by side with the modern *creator* and *creature*. *E'nvy* and *e'nvying* occur in Campion (1602), and yet *envy'* survived Milton. In some cases we have gone back again nearer to the French, as in *rev'enue* for *reven'ue*. I had been so used to hearing *imbecile* pronounced with the accent on the first syllable, which is in accordance with the general tendency in such matters, that I was surprised to find *imbec'ile* in a verse of Wordsworth. The dictionaries all give it so. I asked a highly cultivated Englishman, and he declared for *imbeceel'*. In general it may be assumed that accent will finally settle on the syllable dictated by greater ease and therefore quickness of utterance. *Blas'phemous*, for example, is more rapidly pronounced than *blasphem'ous*, to which our Yankee clings, following in this the usage of many of the older poets. *Amer'ican* is easier than *Ameri'can*, and therefore the false quantity has carried the day, though the true one may be found in George Herbert, and even so late as Cowley.

To come back to the matter in hand. Our "uplandish man" retains the soft or thin sound of the *u* in some words, such as *rule*, *truth* (sometimes also pronounced *trüth*, not *trooth*), while he says *noo* for *new*, and gives to *view* and *few* so indescribable a mixture of the two sounds with a slight nasal tincture that it may be called the Yankee shibboleth. Voltaire says that the English pronounce *true* as if it rhymed with *view*, and this is the sound our rustics give to it. Spenser writes *deow* (*dew*) which can only be pronounced with the Yankee nasality. In *rule* the least sound of *a* precedes the *u*. I find *reule* in Pecock's "Repressor." He probably pronounced it *rayoolë*, as the old French word from which it is derived was very likely to be sounded at first, with a reminiscence

of its original *regula*. Tindal has *rueler*, and the Coventry Plays have *preudent*. In the "Parlyament of Byrdes" I find *reule*. As for *noo*, may it not claim some sanction in its derivation, whether from *nouveau* or *neuf*, the ancient sound of which may very well have been *noof*, as nearer *novus*? *Beef* would seem more like to have come from *buffe* than from *bœuf*, unless the two were mere varieties of spelling. The Saxon *few* may have caught enough from its French cousin *peu* to claim the benefit of the same doubt as to sound; and our slang phrase *a few* (as "I licked him a few") may well appeal to *un peu* for sense and authority. Nay, might not *lick* itself turn out to be the good old word *lam* in an English disguise, if the latter should claim descent as, perhaps, he fairly might, from the Latin *lambere*? The New England *ferce* for *fierce*, and *perce* for *pierce* (sometimes heard as *fairce* and *pairce*), are also Norman. For its antiquity I cite the rhyme of *verse* and *pierce* in Chapman and Donne, and in some commendatory verses by a Mr. Berkenhead before the poems of Francis Beaumont. Our *pairlous* for *perilous* is of the same kind, and is nearer Shakespeare's *parlous* than the modern pronunciation. One other Gallicism survives in our pronunciation. Perhaps I should rather call it a semi-Gallicism, for it is the result of a futile effort to reproduce a French sound with English lips. Thus for *joint*, *employ*, *royal*, we have *jynt*, *emply*, *ryle*, the last differing only from *rile* (*roil*) in a prolongation of the *y* sound. I find *royal* so pronounced in the "Mirror for Magistrates." In Walter de Biblesworth I find *solives* Englished by *gistes*. This, it is true, may have been pronounced *jeests*, but the pronunciation *jystes* must have preceded the present spelling, which was no doubt adopted after the radical meaning was forgotten, as analogical with other words in *oi*. In the same way after Norman-French influence had softened the *l* out of *would* (we already find *woud* for *veut* in N. F. poems), *should* followed the example, and then an *l* was foisted into *could*, where it does not belong, to satisfy the logic of the eye, which has affected the pronunciation and even the spelling of English more than is commonly supposed. I meet with *eyster* for *oyster* as early as the fourteenth century. I find *viage* in Bishop Hall and Middleton the dramatist, *bile* for *boil* in Donne and Chrononhotonthologos, *line* for *loin* in Hall, *ryall* and *chyse* (for *choice*), *dystrye* for *destroy*, in the Coventry Plays. In Chapman's "All Fools" is the misprint of *employ* for *imply*, fairly inferring an identity of sound in the last syllable. Indeed, this pronunciation was habitual till after Pope, and Rogers tells us that the elegant Gray said *naise* for *noise* just as our rustics still do. Our *cornish* (which I find also in Herrick) remembers the French better than *cornice* does. While clinging more closely to the Anglo-Saxon in dropping the *g* from the end of the present participle, the Yankee now and then pleases himself with an experiment in French nasality in words ending in *n*. It is not.

so far as my experience goes, very common, though it may formerly have been more so. *Capting*, for instance, I never heard save in jest, the habitual form being *kepp'n*. But at any rate it is no invention of ours. In that delightful old volume, "Ane Compendious Buke of Godly and Spirituall Songs," in which I know not whether the piety itself or the simplicity of its expression be more charming, I find *burding*, *garding*, and *cousing*, and in the State Trials *uncerting* used by a gentleman. I confess that I like the *n* better than the *ng*.

Of Yankee preterites I find *risse* and *rize* for *rose* in Beaumont and Fletcher, Middleton and Dryden, *clim* in Spenser, *chees* (*chose*) in Sir John Mandevil, *give* (*gave*) in the Coventry Plays, *shet* (*shut*) in Golding's Ovid, *het* in Chapman and in Weever's Epitaphs, *thriv* and *smit* in Drayton, *quit* in Ben Jonson and Henry More, and *pled* in the Paston Letters, nay, even in the fastidious Landor. *Rid* for *rode* was anciently common. So likewise was *see* for *saw*, but I find it in no writer of authority (except Golding), unless Chaucer's *seie* and Gower's *sigh* were, as I am inclined to think, so sounded. *Shew* is used by Hector Boece, Giles Fletcher, Drummond of Hawthornden, and in the Paston Letters. Similar strong preterites, like *snew*, *thew*, and even *mew*, are not without example. I find *sew* for *sewed* in "Piers Ploughman." Indeed, the anomalies in English preterites are perplexing. We have probably transferred *flew* from *flow* (as the preterite of which I have heard it) to *fly* because we had another preterite in *fled*. Of weak preterites the Yankee retains *growed*, *blowed*, for which he has good authority, and less often *knowed*. His *sot* is merely a broad sounding of *sat*, no more inelegant than the common *got* for *gat*, which he further degrades into *gut*. When he says *darst*, he uses a form as old as Chaucer.

The Yankee has retained something of the long sound of the *a* in such words as *axe*, *wax*, pronouncing them *exe*, *wex* (shortened from *aix*, *waix*). He also says *hev* and *hed* (*häve*, *häd*) for *have* and *had*. In most cases he follows an Anglo-Saxon usage. In *aix* for *axle* he certainly does. I find *wex* and *aisches* (*ashes*) in Pecock, and *exe* in the Paston Letters. Golding rhymes *wax* with *wexe* and spells *challenge chelenge*. Chaucer wrote *hendy*. Dryden rhymes *can* with *men*, as Mr. Biglow would. Alexander Gill, Milton's teacher, in his "Logonomia" cites *hez* for *hath* as peculiar to Lincolnshire. I find *hayth* in Collier's "Bibliographical Account of Early English Literature" under the date 1584, and Lord Cromwell so wrote it. Sir Christopher Wren wrote *belcony*. Our *fect* is only the O. F. *faict*. *Thaim* for *them* was common in the sixteenth century. We have an example of the same thing in the double form of the verb *thrash*, *thresh*. While the New-Englander cannot be brought to say *instead* for *instid* (commonly *'stid* where not the last word in a sentence), he changes the *i* into *e* in *red* for *rid*, *tell* for *till*, *hender* for *hinder*, *rense* for *rinse*. I find *red* in the old interlude of "Ther-

sytes," *tell* in a letter of Daborne to Henslow, and also, I shudder to mention it, in a letter of the great Duchess of Marlborough, Atossa herself! It occurs twice in a single verse of the Chester Plays,

"*Tell* the day of dome, *tell* the beames blow."

From the word *blow* (in another sense) is formed *blowth*, which I heard again this summer after a long interval. Mr. Wright [1] explains it as meaning "a blossom." With us a single blossom is a *blow*, while *blowth* means the blossoming in general. A farmer would say that there was a good blowth on his fruit-trees. The word retreats farther inland and away from the railways, year by year. Wither rhymes *hinder* with *slender*, and Shakespeare and Lovelace have *renched* for *rinsed*. In "Gammer Gurton" and "Mirror for Magistrates" is *sence* for *since;* Marlborough's Duchess so writes it, and Donne rhymes *since* with *Amiens* and *patience*, Bishop Hall and Otway with *pretence*, Chapman with *citizens*, Dryden with *providence*. Indeed, why should not *sithence* take that form? Dryden's wife (an earl's daughter) has *tell* for *till*, Margaret, mother of Henry VII., writes *seche* for *such*, and our *ef* finds authority in the old form *yeffe*.

E sometimes takes the place of *u*, as *jedge*, *tredge*, *bresh*. I find *tredge* in the interlude of "Jack Jugler," *bresh* in a citation by Collier from "London Cries" of the middle of the seventeenth century, and *resche* for *rush* (fifteenth century) in the very valuable "Volume of Vocabularies" edited by Mr. Wright. *Resce* is one of the Anglo-Saxon forms of the word in Bosworth's A.-S. Dictionary. Golding has *shet*. The Yankee always shortens the *u* in the ending *ture*, making *ventur*, *natur*, *pictur*, and so on. This was common, also, among the educated of the last generation. I am inclined to think it may have been once universal, and I certainly think it more elegant than the vile *vencher*, *naycher*, *pickcher*, that have taken its place, sounding like the invention of a lexicographer to mitigate a sneeze. Nash in his "Pierce Penniless" has *ventur*, and so spells it, and I meet it also in Spenser, Drayton, Ben Jonson, Herrick, and Prior. Spenser has *tort'rest*, which can be contracted only from *tortur* and not from *torcher*. Quarles rhymes *nature* with *creator*, and Dryden with *satire*, which he doubtless pronounced according to its older form of *satyr*. Quarles has also *torture* and *mortar*. Mary Boleyn writes *kreatur*. I find *pikter* in Izaak Walton's autograph will.

I shall now give some examples which cannot so easily be ranked under any special head. Gill charges the Eastern counties with *kiver* for *cover*, and *ta* for *to*. The Yankee pronounces both *too* and *to* like *ta* (like the *tou* in *touch*) where they are not emphatic. When they are, both become *tu*. In old spelling, *to* is the common (and indeed correct) form of *too*, which is only *to* with the sense of *in addition*. I suspect that the sound of our *too* has caught something

[1] *Dictionary of Obsolete and Provincial English.*

from the French *tout*, and it is possible that the old *too too* is not a reduplication, but a reminiscence of the feminine form of the same word (*toute*) as anciently pronounced, with the *e* not yet silenced. Gill gives a Northern origin to *geaun* for *gown* and *waund* for *wound* (*vulnus*). Lovelace has *waund*, but there is something too dreadful in suspecting Spenser (who *borealized* in his pastorals) of having ever been guilty of *geaun!* And yet some delicate mouths even now are careful to observe the Hibernicism of *ge-ard* for *guard*, and *ge-url* for *girl*. Sir Philip Sidney (*credite posteri!*) wrote *furr* for *far*. I would hardly have believed it had I not seen it in *fac-simile*. As some consolation, I find *furder* in Lord Bacon and Donne, and Wither rhymes *far* with *cur*. The Yankee, who omits the final *d* in many words, as do the Scotch, makes up for it by adding one in *geound*. The purist does not feel the loss of the *d* sensibly in *lawn* and *yon*, from the former of which it has dropped again after a wrongful adoption (retained in *laundry*), while it properly belongs to the latter. But what shall we make of *git, yit*, and *yis?* I find *yis* and *git* in Warner's "Albion's England," *yet* rhyming with *wit*, *admit*, and *fit* in Donne, with *wit* in the "Revenger's Tragedy," Beaumont, and Suckling, with *writ* in Dryden, and latest of all with *wit* in Sir Hanbury Williams. Prior rhymes *fitting* and *begetting*. Worse is to come. Among others, Donne rhymes *again* with *sin*, and Quarles repeatedly with *in*. Ben for *been*, of which our dear Whittier is so fond, has the authority of Sackville, "Gammer Gurton" (the work of a bishop), Chapman, Dryden, and many more, though *bin* seems to have been the common form. Whittier's accenting the first syllable of *rom'ance* finds an accomplice in Drayton among others, and, though manifestly wrong, is analogous with *Rom'ans*. Of other Yankeeisms, whether of form or pronunciation, which I have met with I add a few at random. Pecock writes *sowdiers* (*sogers, soudoyers*), and Chapman and Gill *sodder*. This absorption of the *l* is common in various dialects, especially in the Scottish. Pecock writes also *biyende*, and the authors of "Jack Jugler" and "Gammer Gurton" *yender*. The Yankee includes "*yon*" in the same category, and says "hither an' yen," for "to and fro." (Cf. German *jenseits*.) Pecock and plenty more have *wrastle*. Tindal has *agynste, gretter, shett, ondone, debytë*, and *scace*. "Jack Jugler" has *scacely* (which I have often heard, though *skurce* is the common form), and Donne and Dryden make *great* rhyme with *set*. In the inscription on Caxton's tomb I find *ynd* for *end*, which the Yankee more often makes *eend*, still using familiarly the old phrase "right anend" for "continuously." His "stret (straight) along" in the same sense, which I thought peculiar to him, I find in Pecock. Tindal's *debytë* for *deputy* is so perfectly Yankee that I could almost fancy the brave martyr to have been deacon of the First Parish at Jaalam Centre. "Jack Jugler" further gives us *playsent* and *sartayne*. Dry-

den rhymes *certain* with *parting*, and Chapman and Ben Jonson use *certain*, as the Yankee always does, for *certainly*. The "Coventry Mysteries" have *occupied, massage, naterallë, materal* (*material*), and *meracles*, — all excellent Yankeeisms. In the "Quatre fils, Aymon" (1504),[1] is *vertus* for *virtuous*. Thomas Fuller called *volume vollum*, I suspect, for he spells it *volumne*. However, *per contra*, Yankees habitually say *colume* for *column*. Indeed, to prove that our ancestors brought their pronunciation with them from the Old Country, and have not wantonly debased their mother tongue, I need only to cite the words *scriptur, Israll, athists*, and *cherfulness* from Governor Bradford's "History." So the good man wrote them, and so the good descendants of his fellow-exiles still pronounce them. Brampton Gurdon writes *shet* in a letter to Winthrop. *Purtend* (*pretend*) has crept like a serpent into the "Paradise of Dainty Devices;" *purvide*, which is not so bad, is in Chaucer. These, of course, are universal vulgarisms, and not peculiar to the Yankee. Butler has a Yankee phrase, and pronunciation too, in "To which these *carr'ings-on* did tend." Langham or Laneham, who wrote an account of the festivities at Kenilworth in honor of Queen Bess, and who evidently tried to spell phonetically, makes *sorrows* into *sororz*. Herrick writes *hollow* for *halloo*, and perhaps pronounced it (*horresco suggerens!*) *hollô*, as Yankees do. Why not, when it comes from *holà?* I find *ffelaschyppe* (fellowship) in the Coventry Plays. Spenser and his queen neither of them scrupled to write *afore*, and the former feels no inelegance even in *chaw* and *idee*. *'Fore* was common till after Herrick. Dryden has *do's* for *does*, and his wife spells *worse wosce*. *Afeared* was once universal. Warner has *ery* for *ever a;* nay, he also has *illy*, with which we were once ignorantly reproached by persons more familiar with Murray's Grammar than with English literature. And why not *illy?* Mr. Bartlett says it is "a word used by writers of an inferior class, who do not seem to perceive that *ill* is itself an adverb, without the termination *ly*," and quotes Dr. Messer, President of Brown University, as asking triumphantly, "Why don't you say *welly?*" I should like to have had Dr. Messer answer his own question. It would be truer to say that it was used by people who still remembered that *ill* was an adjective, the shortened form of *evil*, out of which Shakespeare and the translators of the Bible ventured to make *evilly*. This slurred *evil* is "the dram of *eale*" in "Hamlet." I find *illy* in Warner. The objection to *illy* is not an etymological one, but simply that it is contrary to good usage, — a very sufficient reason. *Ill* as an adverb was at first a vulgarism, precisely like the rustic's when he says, "I was treated *bad*." May not the reason of this exceptional form be looked for in that tendency to dodge what is hard to pronounce, to which I have already alluded? If the

[1] Cited in Collier. (I give my authority where I do not quote from the original book.)

letters were distinctly uttered, as they should be, it would take too much time to say *ill-ly*, *well-ly*, and it is to be observed that we have avoided *smally*[1] and *tally* in the same way, though we add *ish* to them without hesitation in *smallish* and *tallish*. We have, to be sure, *dully* and *fully*, but for the one we prefer *stupidly*, and the other (though this may have come from eliding the *y* before *as*) is giving way to *full*. The uneducated, whose utterance is slower, still make adverbs when they will by adding *like* to all manner of adjectives. We have had *big* charged upon us, because we use it where an Englishman would now use *great*. I fully admit that it were better to distinguish between them, allowing to *big* a certain contemptuous quality ; but as for authority, I want none better than that of Jeremy Taylor, who, in his noble sermon "On the Return of Prayer," speaks of "Jesus, whose spirit was meek and gentle up to the greatness of the *biggest* example." As for our double negative, I shall waste no time in quoting instances of it, because it was once as universal in English as it still is in the neo-Latin languages, where it does not strike us as vulgar. I am not sure that the loss of it is not to be regretted. But surely I shall admit the vulgarity of slurring or altogether eliding certain terminal consonants ? I admit that a clear and sharp-cut enunciation is one of the crowning charms and elegancies of speech. Words so uttered are like coins fresh from the mint, compared with the worn and dingy drudges of long service, — I do not mean American coins, for those look less badly the more they lose of their original ugliness. No one is more painfully conscious than I of the contrast between the rifle-crack of an Englishman's *yes* and *no*, and the wet-fuse drawl of the same monosyllables in the mouths of my countrymen. But I do not find the dropping of final consonants disagreeable in Allan Ramsay or Burns, nor do I believe that our literary ancestors were sensible of that inelegance in the fusing them together of which we are conscious. How many educated men pronounce the *t* in *chestnut?* how many say *pentise* for *penthouse*, as they should. When a Yankee skipper says that he is "boun' for Gloster" (not Gloucëster, with the leave of the Universal Schoolmaster),[2] he but speaks like Chaucer or an old ballad-singer, though they would have pronounced it *boon*. This is one of the cases where the *d* is surreptitious, and has been added in compliment to the verb *bind*, with which it has nothing to do. If we consider the root of the word (though of course I grant that every race has a right to do what it will with what is so peculiarly its own as its speech), the *d* has no more right there than at the end of *gone*, where it is often put by children, who are our best guides to the sources of linguistic corruption, and the best teachers of its processes. Cromwell, minister of Henry VIII., writes *worle*

[1] The word occurs in a letter of Mary Boleyn, in Golding, and Warner. Milton also was fond of the word.

for *world*. Chapman has *wan* for *wand*, and *lawn* has rightfully displaced *laund*, though with no thought, I suspect, of etymology. Rogers tells us that Lady Bathurst sent him some letters written to William III. by Queen Mary, in which she addresses him as "*Dear Husban.*" The old form *expoun'*, which our farmers use, is more correct than the form with a barbarous *d* tacked on which has taken its place. Of the kind opposite to this, like our *gownd* for *gown*, and the London cockney's *wind* for *wine*, I find *drownd* for *drown* in the "Misfortunes of Arthur" (1584), and in Swift. And, by the way, whence came the long sound of *wind* which our poets still retain, and which survives in "winding" a horn, a totally different word from "winding" a kite-string ? We say *behīnd* and *hīnder* (comparative) and yet to *hĭnder*. Shakespeare pronounced *kind kīnd*, or what becomes of his play on that word and *kin* in "Hamlet"? Nay, did he not even (shall I dare to hint it ?) drop the final *d* as the Yankee still does ? John Lilly plays in the same way on *kindred* and *kindness*.

But to come to some other ancient instances. Warner rhymes *bounds* with *crowns*, *grounds* with *towns*, *text* with *sex*, *worst* with *crust*, *interrupts* with *cups;* Drayton, *defects* with *sex ;* Chapman, *amends* with *cleanse;* Webster, *defects* with *checks;* Ben Jonson, *minds* with *combines;* Marston, *trust* and *obsequious*, *clothes* and *shows;* Dryden gives the same sound to *clothes*, and has also *minds* with *designs*. Of course, I do not affirm that their ears may not have told them that these were imperfect rhymes (though I am by no means sure even of that), but they surely would never have tolerated any such had they suspected the least vulgarity in them. Prior has the rhyme *first* and *trust*, but puts it into the mouth of a landlady. Swift has *stunted* and *burnt it*, an intentionally imperfect rhyme, no doubt, but which I cite as giving precisely the Yankee pronunciation of *burned*. Donne couples in unhallowed wedlock *after* and *matter*, thus seeming to give to both the true Yankee sound ; and it is not uncommon to find *after* and *daughter*. Worse than all, in one of Dodsley's Old Plays we have *onions* rhyming with *minions*, — I have tears in my eyes while I record it. And yet what is viler than the univeral *Misses* (*Mrs.*) for *Mistress?* This was once a vulgarism, and in "The Miseries of Inforced Marriage" the rhyme (printed as prose in Dodsley's Old Plays by Collier).

"To make my young *mistress*
Delighting in *kisses*,"

is put into the mouth of the clown. Our people say *Injun* for *Indian*. The tendency to make this change where *i* follows *d* is common. The Italian *giorno* and French *jour* from *diurnus* are familiar examples. And yet *Injun* is one of those depravations which the taste challenges peremptorily, though it have the authority

[2] Though I find Worcëster in the *Mirror for Magistrates*.

of Charles Cotton — who rhymes "*Indies*" with "cringes" — and four English lexicographers, beginning with Dr. Sheridan, bid us say *invidgeous*. Yet after all it is no worse than the debasement which all our terminations in *tion* and *tience* have undergone, which yet we hear with *resignashun* and *payshunce*, though it might have aroused both *impat-i-ence* and *indigna-ti-on* in Shakespeare's time. When George Herbert tells us that if the sermon be dull,

"God takes a text and preacheth pati-ence,"

the prolongation of the word seems to convey some hint at the longanimity of the virtue. Consider what a poor curtal we have made of Ocean. There was something of his heave and expanse in *o-ce-an*, and Fletcher knew how to use it when he wrote so fine a verse as the second of these, the best deep-sea verse I know, —

"In desperate storms stem with a little rudder
The tumbling ruins of the oceän."

Oceanus was not then wholly shorn of his divine proportions, and our modern *oshun* sounds like the gush of small-beer in comparison. Some other contractions of ours have a vulgar air about them. *More 'n* for *more than*, as one of the worst, may stand for a type of such. Yet our old dramatists are full of such obscurations (elisions they can hardly be called) of the *th*, making *whe'r* of *whether*, *where* of *whither*, *here* of *hither*, *bro'r* of *brother*, *smo'r* of *smother*, *mo'r* of *mother*, and so on. And dear Brer Rabbit, can I forget him? Indeed, it is this that explains the word *rare* (which has Dryden's support), and which we say of meat where an Englishman would use *underdone*. I do not believe, with the dictionaries, that it had ever anything to do with the Icelandic *hrar* (*raw*), as it plainly has not in *rareripe*, which means earlier ripe, — President Lincoln said of a precocious boy that "he was a *rareripe*." And I do not believe it, for this reason, that the earliest form of the word with us was, and the commoner now in the inland parts still is, so far as I can discover, *raredone*. Golding has "egs reere-rosted," which, whatever else it mean, cannot mean *raw*-roasted. I find *rather* as a monosyllable in Donne, and still better, as giving the sound, rhyming with *fair* in Warner. There is an epigram of Sir Thomas Browne in which the words *rather than* make a monosyllable: —

"What furie is 't to take Death's part
And rather than by Nature, die by Art!"

The contraction *more 'n* I find in the old play "Fuimus Troes," in a verse where the measure is so strongly accented as to leave it beyond doubt, —

"A golden crown whose heirs
More than half the world subdue."

It may be, however, that the contraction is in "th' orld." It is unmistakable in the "Second Maiden's Tragedy : " —

"It were but folly,
Dear soul, to boast of *more than* I can perform."

Is our *gin* for *given* more violent than *mar'l* for *marvel*, which was once common, and which I find as late as Herrick? Nay, Herrick has *gin* (spelling it *gen*), too, as do the Scotch, who agree with us likewise in preferring *chimly* to *chimney*.

I will now leave pronunciation and turn to words or phrases which have been supposed peculiar to us, only pausing to pick up a single dropped stitch, in the pronunciation of the word *súpreme*, which I had thought native till I found it in the well-languaged Daniel. I will begin with a word of which I have never met with any example in any English writer of authority. We express the first stage of withering in a green plant suddenly cut down by the verb *to wilt*. It is, of course, own cousin of the German *welken*, but I have never come upon it in literary use, and my own books of reference give me faint help. Graff gives *welhèn, marcescere*, and refers to *weih* (*weak*), and conjecturally to A.-S. *hvelan*. The A.-S. *wealwian* (*to wither*) is nearer, but not so near as two words in the Icelandic, which perhaps put us on the track of its ancestry, — *velgi, tepefacere* (and *velki*, with the derivative), meaning *contaminare*. *Wilt*, at any rate, is a good word, filling, as it does, a sensible gap between drooping and withering, and the imaginative phrase "he wilted right down," like "he caved right in," is a true Americanism. *Wilt* occurs in English provincial glossaries, but is explained by *wither*, which with us it does not mean. We have a few words such as *cache, cohog, carry* (*portage*), *shoot* (*chute*), *timber* (*forest*), *bushwhack* (to pull a boat along by the bushes on the edge of a stream), *buckeye* (a picturesque word for the horse-chestnut); but how many can we be said to have fairly brought into the language, as Alexander Gill, who first mentions Americanisms, meant it when he said, "*Sed et ab Americanis nonnulla mutuamur ut* MAIZ *et* CANOA"? Very few, I suspect, and those mostly by borrowing from the French, German, Spanish, or Indian.[1] "The Dipper" for the "Great Bear" strikes me as having a native air. *Bogus*, in the sense of *worthless*, is undoubtedly ours, but is, I more than suspect, a corruption of the French *bagasse* (from low Latin *bagasea*), which travelled up the Mississippi from New Orleans, where it was used for the refuse of the sugar-cane. It is true, we have modified the meaning of some words. We use *freshet* in the sense of *flood*, for which I have not chanced upon any authority. Our New England cross between Ancient Pistol and Dugald Dalgetty, Captain Underhill, uses the word (1638) to mean a *current*, and I do not recollect it elsewhere in that sense. I therefore leave it with a? for future explorers. *Crick* for *creek* I find in Captain John Smith and in the dedication of Fuller's "Holy Warre," and *run*, meaning a *small stream*, in Waymouth's "Voyage" (1605). *Humans* for *men*, which Mr. Bartlett includes in his "Dictionary of Americanisms," is Chapman's habitual phrase in his

---

[1] This was written twenty years ago, and now (1890) I cannot open an English journal without coming upon an Americanism.

translation of Homer. I find it also in the old play of "The Hog hath lost his Pearl." *Dogs* for *andirons* is still current in New England, and in Walter de Biblesworth I find *chiens* glossed in the margin by *andirons*. *Gunning* for *shooting* is in Drayton. We once got credit for the poetical word *fall* for *autumn*, but Mr. Bartlett and the last edition of Webster's Dictionary refer us to Dryden. It is even older, for I find it in Drayton, and Bishop Hall has *autumn fall.* Middleton plays upon the word : "May'st thou have a reasonable good *spring*, for thou art like to have many dangerous foul *falls.*" Daniel does the same, and Coleridge uses it as we do. Gray uses the archaism *picked* for *peaked*, and the word *smudge* (as our backwoodsmen do) for a smothered fire. Lord Herbert of Cherbury (more properly perhaps than even Sidney, the last *preux chevalier*) has "the Emperor's folks" just as a Yankee would say it. *Loan* for *lend*, with which we have hitherto been blackened, I must retort upon the mother island, for it appears so long ago as in "Albion's England." *Fleshy*, in the sense of *stout*, may claim Ben Jonson's warrant, and I find it also so lately as in Francklin's "Lucian." *Chore* is also Jonson's word, and I am inclined to prefer it to *chare* and *char*, because I think that I see a more natural origin for it in the French *jour* — whence it might come to mean a day's work, and thence a job — than anywhere else.[1] *At onst* for *at once* I thought a corruption of our own, till I found it in the Chester Plays. I am now inclined to suspect it no corruption at all, but only an erratic and obsolete superlative *at onest.* *To progress'* was flung in our teeth till Mr. Pickering retorted with Shakespeare's "doth pro'-gress down thy cheeks." I confess that I was never satisfied with this answer, because the accent was different, and because the word might here be reckoned a substantive quite as well as a verb. Mr. Bartlett (in his dictionary above cited) adds a surrebutter in a verse from Ford's "Broken Heart." Here the word is clearly a verb, but with the accent unhappily still on the first syllable. Mr. Bartlett says that he "cannot say whether the word was used in Bacon's time or not." It certainly was, and with the accent we give to it. Ben Jonson, in the "Alchemist," has this verse,

"Progress' so from extreme unto extreme,"

and Sir Philip Sidney,

"Progressing then from fair Turias' golden place."

Surely we may now sleep in peace, and our English cousins will forgive us, since we have cleared ourselves from any suspicion of originality in the matter! Even after I had convinced myself that the chances were desperately against our having invented any of the *Americanisms* with which we are *faulted* and which we are in the habit of *voicing*, there were one or two which had so prevailingly indigenous an accent as to stagger me a little. One of these

[1] The Rev. A. L. Mayhew of Wadham College, Oxford, has convinced me that I was astray in this.

was "the biggest *thing out.*" Alas, even this slender comfort is denied me. Old Gower has

"So harde an herte was none *oute*,"

and

"That such merveile was none *oute.*"

He also, by the way, says "a *sighte* of flowres" as naturally as our up-country folk would say it. *Poor* for *lean, thirds* for *dower,* and *dry* for *thirsty* I find in Middleton's plays. *Dry* is also in Skelton and in the "World" (1754). In a note on Middleton, Mr. Dyce thinks it needful to explain the phrase *I can't tell* (universal in America) by the gloss *I could not say.* Middleton also uses *snecked*, which I had believed an Americanism till I saw it there. It is, of course, only another form of *snatch*, analogous to *theek* and *thatch* (cf. the proper names Dekker and Thacher), *break* (*brack*) and *breach*, *make* (still common with us) and *match.* *'Long on* for *occasioned by* ("who is this 'long on?") occurs constantly in Gower and likewise in Middleton. *'Cause why* is in Chaucer. *Raising* (an English version of the French *leaven*) for *yeast* is employed by Gayton in his "Festivous Notes on Don Quixote." I have never seen an instance of our New England word *emptins* in the same sense, nor can I divine its original. Gayton has *limekill ; also shuts* for *shutters*, and the latter is used by Mrs. Hutchinson in her "Life of Colonel Hutchinson." Bishop Hall, and Purchas in his "Pilgrims," have *chist* for *chest*, and it is certainly nearer *cista*, as well as to its form in the Teutonic languages, whence probably we got it. We retain the old sound from *cist*, but *chest* is as old as Chaucer. Lovelace says *wropt* for *wrapt.* "Musicianer" I had always associated with the militia-musters of my boyhood, and too hastily concluded it an abomination of our own, but Mr. Wright calls it a Norfolk word, and I find it to be as old as 1642 by an extract in Collier. "Not worth the time of day," had passed with me for native till I saw it in Shakespeare's "Pericles." For *slick* (which is only a shorter sound of *sleek*, like *crick* and the now universal *britches* for *breeches*) I will only call Chapman and Jonson. "That's a sure card!" and "That's a stinger!" both sound like modern slang, but you will find the one in the old interlude of "Thersytes" (1537), and the other in Middleton. "Right here," a favorite phrase with our orators and with a certain class of our editors, turns up *passim* in the Chester and Coventry plays. Mr. Dickens found something very ludicrous in what he considered our neologism *right away.* But I find a phrase very like it, and which I would gladly suspect to be a misprint for it, in "Gammer Gurton : " —

"Lyght it and bring it *tite away.*"

But *tite* is the true word in this case. After all, what is it but another form of *straightway ?* *Cussedness*, meaning *wickedness, malignity*, and *cuss*, a sneaking, ill-natured fellow, in such phrases as "He done it out o' pure cussedness," and "He is a nateral cuss," have been commonly thought Yankeeisms. To vent certain contemptuously indignant moods they are admirable in their rough-and-ready way. But neither is our own. *Cursydnesse*, in the same sense of malignant wickedness, occurs in the Coventry Plays, and *cuss* may perhaps claim to have come in with the Conqueror. At least the term is also French. Saint Simon uses it and confesses its usefulness. Speaking of the Abbé Dubois, he says, "Qui étoit en plein ce qu'un mauvais françois appelle un *sacre*, mais qui ne se peut guère exprimer autrement." "Not worth a cuss," though supported by "not worth a damn," may be a mere corruption, since "not worth a *cress*" is in "Piers Ploughman." "I don't see it," was the popular slang a year or two ago, and seemed to spring from the soil; but no, it is in Cibber's "Careless Husband." *Green sauce* for *vegetables* I meet in Beaumont and Fletcher, Gayton, and elsewhere. Our rustic pronunciation *sahce* (for either the diphthong *au* was anciently pronounced *ah*, or else we have followed abundant analogy in changing it to the latter sound, as we have in *chance, dance*, and so many more) may be the older one, and at least gives some hint at its ancestor *salsa*. *Warn*, in the sense of *notify*, is, I believe, now peculiar to us, but Pecock so employs it. I find *primmer* (*primer*, as we pronounce it) in Beaumont and Fletcher, and a "square eater" too (compare our "*square* meal"), *heft* for *weight*, and "muchness" in the "Mirror for Magistrates," *bankbill* in Swift and Fielding, and *as* for *that* I might say *passim*. To *cotton to* is, I rather think, an Americanism. The nearest approach to it I have found is *cotton together*, in Congreve's "Love for Love." To *cotton* or *cotten*, in another sense, is old and common. Our word means to *cling*, and its origin, possibly, is to be sought in another direction, perhaps in A.-S. *cvead*, which means *mud, clay* (both proverbially clinging), or better yet, in the Icelandic *qvoda* (otherwise *kód*), meaning *resin* and *glue*, which are κατ' ἐξοχήν, sticky substances. To *spit cotton* is, I think, American, and also, perhaps, *to flax* for *to beat*. To *the halves* still survives among us, though apparently obsolete in England. It means either to let or to hire a piece of land, receiving half the profit in money or in kind (*partibus locare*). I mention it because in a note by some English editor, to which I have lost my reference, I have seen it wrongly explained. The editors of Nares cite Burton. To *put*, in the sense of *to go*, as *Put!* for *Begone!* would seem our own, and yet it is strictly analogous to the French *se mettre à la voie*, and the Italian *mettersi in via*. Indeed, Dante has a verse,

"*Io sarei* [for *mi sarei*] *già messo per lo sentiero*,"

which, but for the indignity, might be translated,

"I should, ere this, have *put* along the way."

I deprecate in advance any share in General Banks's notions of international law, but we may all take a just pride in his exuberant eloquence as something distinctively American. When he spoke a few years ago of "letting the Union slide," even those who, for political purposes, reproached him with the sentiment, admired the indigenous virtue of his phrase. Yet I find "let the world slide" in Heywood's "Edward IV.; " and in Beaumont and Fletcher's "Wit without Money," Valentine says,

"Will you go drink,
And let the world slide ? "

So also in Sidney's "Arcadia,"

"Let his dominion slide."

In the one case it is put into the mouth of a clown, in the other, of a gentleman, and was evidently proverbial. It has even higher sanction, for Chaucer writes,

"Well nigh all other curës *let he slide*."

Mr. Bartlett gives "above one's bend" as an Americanism; but compare Hamlet's "to the top of my bent." *In his tracks* for *immediately* has acquired an American accent, and passes where he can for a native, but is an importation nevertheless; for what is he but the Latin *e vestigio*, or at best the Norman French *enes-lespas*, both which have the same meaning ? *Hotfoot* (provincial also in England), I find in the old romance of "Tristan,"

"*Si s'en parti* CHAUT PAS."

Like for *as* is never used in New England, but is universal in the South and West. It has on its side the authority of two kings (*ego sum rex Romanorum et supra grammaticam*), Henry VIII. and Charles I. This were ample, without throwing into the scale the scholar and poet Daniel. *Them* was used as a nominative by the majesty of Edward VI., by Sir P. Hoby, and by Lord Paget (in Froude's "History"). I have never seen any passage adduced where *guess* was used as the Yankee uses it. The word was familiar in the mouths of our ancestors, but with a different shade of meaning from that we have given it, which is something like *rather think*, though the Yankee implies a confident certainty by it when he says, "I guess I *du!*" There are two examples in Otway, one of which ("So in the struggle, I guess the note was lost") perhaps might serve our purpose, and Coleridge's

"I guess 't was fearful there to see"

certainly comes very near. But I have a higher authority than either in Selden, who, in one of his notes to the "Polyolbion," writes, "The first inventor of them (I *guess* you dislike not the addition) was one Berthold Swartz." Here he must mean by it, "I take it for granted." Robert Greene, in his "Quip for an Upstart Courtier," makes Cloth-breeches say, "but I *gesse* your maistership never tried what true honor meant." In this case the word seems to be used with a meaning precisely like that which we give it. Another peculiarity almost as prominent is the beginning sentences, especially in answer to questions, with "well." Put before such a phrase as "How d'e do?" it is commonly short, and has the sound of *wul*, but in reply it is deliberative, and the various shades of meaning which can be conveyed by difference of intonation, and by prolonging or abbreviating, I should vainly attempt to describe. I have heard *ooa-ahl*, *wahl*, *ahl*, *wăl*, and something nearly approaching the sound of the *le* in *able*. Sometimes before "I" it dwindles to a mere *l*, as "'l *I* dunno." A friend of mine (why should I not please myself, though I displease him, by brightening my page with the initials of the most exquisite of humorists, J. H.?) told me that he once heard five "wells," like pioneers, precede the answer to an inquiry about the price of land. The first was the ordinary *wul*, in deference to custom; the second, the long, perpending *ooahl*, with a falling inflection of the voice; the third, the same, but with the voice rising, as if in despair of a conclusion, into a plaintively nasal whine; the fourth, *wulh*, ending in the aspirate of a sigh; and then, fifth, came a short, sharp *wal*, showing that a conclusion had been reached. I have used this latter form in the "Biglow Papers," because, if enough nasality be added, it represents most nearly the average sound of what I may call the interjection.

A locution prevails in the Southern and Middle States which is so curious that, though never heard in New England, I will give a few lines to its discussion, the more readily because it is extinct elsewhere. I mean the use of *allow* in the sense of *affirm*, as "I allow that's a good horse." I find the word so used in 1558 by Anthony Jenkinson in Hakluyt: "Corne they sowe not, neither doe eate any bread, mocking the Christians for the same, and disabling our strengthe, saying we live by eating the toppe of a weede, and drinke a drinke made of the same, *allowing* theyr great devouring of flesh and drinking of milke to be the increase of theyr strength." That is, they undervalued our strength, and affirmed their own to be the result of a certain diet. In another passage of the same narrative the word has its more common meaning of approving or praising: "The said king, much *allowing* this declaration, said." Ducange quotes Bracton *sub voce* ADLOCARE for the meaning "to admit as proved," and the transition from this to "affirm" is by no means violent. Izaak Walton has "Lebault *allows* waterfrogs to be good meat," and here the word is equivalent to *affirms*. At the same time, when we consider some of the meanings of *allow* in old English, and of *allouer* in old French, and also remember that the verbs *prize* and *praise* are from one root, I think we must admit *allaudare* to a share in the paternity of *allow*. The sentence from Hakluyt would read equally well, "contemning our strengthe, . . . and praising (or valuing) their great eating of flesh as the cause of their increase in strength." After all, if we confine ourselves to *allocare*, it

may turn out that the word was somewhere and somewhen used for *to bet*, analogously to *put up*, *put down*, *post* (cf. Spanish *apostar*), and the like. I hear boys in the street continually saying, "I bet that's a good horse," or what not, meaning by no means to risk anything beyond their opinion in the matter.

The word *improve*, in the sense of to "occupy, make use of, employ," as Dr. Pickering defines it, he long ago proved to be no neologism. He would have done better, I think, had he substituted *profit by* for *employ*. He cites Dr. Franklin as saying that the word had never, so far as he knew, been used in New England before he left it in 1723, except in Dr. Mather's "Remarkable Providences," which he oddly calls a "very old book." Franklin, as Dr. Pickering goes on to show, was mistaken. Mr. Bartlett in his "Dictionary" merely abridges Pickering. Both of them should have confined the application of the word to material things, its extension to which is all that is peculiar in the supposed American use of it. For surely "Complete Letter-Writers" have been "*improving*" this opportunity" time out of mind. I will illustrate the word a little further, because Pickering cites no English authorities. Skelton has a passage in his "Phyllyp Sparowe," which I quote the rather as it contains also the word *allowed*, and as it distinguishes *improve* from *employ*: —

> "His [Chaucer's] Englysh well alowed,
> So as it is *emprowed*,
> For as it is employd,
> There is no English voyd."

Here the meaning is *to profit by*. In Fuller's "Holy Warre" (1647), we have "The Egyptians standing on the firm ground, were thereby enabled to *improve* and enforce their darts to the utmost." Here the word might certainly mean *to make use of*. Mrs. Hutchinson (Life of Colonel H.) uses the word in the same way: "And therefore did not *emproove* his interest to engage the country in the quarrell." Swift in one of his letters says: "There is not an acre of land in Ireland turned to half its advantage; yet it is better *improved* than the people." I find it also in "Strength out of Weakness" (1652), and Plutarch's "Morals" (1714), but I know of only one example of its use in the purely American sense, and that is "a very good *improvement* for a mill" in the "State Trials" (Speech of the Attorney-General in the Lady Ivy's case, 1684). In the sense of *employ*, I could cite a dozen old English authorities.

In running over the fly-leaves of those delightful folios for this reference, I find a note which reminds me of another word, for our abuse of which we have been deservedly ridiculed. I mean *lady*. It is true I might cite the example of the Italian *donna* [1] (*domina*), which has been treated in the same way by a whole nation, and not, as *lady* among us, by the uncultivated only. It perhaps grew into use in

[1] *Dame*, in English, is a decayed gentlewoman of the same family.

the half-democratic republics of Italy in the same way and for the same reasons as with us. But I admit that our abuse of the word is villanous. I know of an orator who once said in a public meeting where bonnets preponderated, that "the ladies were last at the cross and first at the tomb"! But similar sins were committed before our day and in the mother country. In the "Harleian Miscellany" (vol. v. p. 455) I find "this *lady* is my servant; the hedger's daughter Ioan." In the "State Trials" I learn of "a *gentlewoman* that lives cook with" such a one, and I hear the Lord High Steward speaking of the wife of a waiter at a bagnio as a *gentlewoman!* From the same authority, by the way, I can state that our vile habit of chewing tobacco had the somewhat unsavory example of Titus Oates, and I know by tradition from an eye-witness that the elegant General Burgoyne partook of the same vice. Howell, in one of his letters (dated 26 August, 1623), speaks thus of another "institution" which many have thought American: "They speak much of that boisterous Bishop of Halverstadt (for so they term him here), that, having taken a place wher ther were two Monasteries of Nuns and Friers, he caus'd divers featherbeds to be rip'd, and all the feathers to be thrown in a great Hall, whither the Nuns and Friers were thrust naked with their bodies oil'd and pitch'd, and to tumble among the feathers." Howell speaks as if the thing were new to him, and I know not if the "boisterous" Bishop was the inventer of it, but I find it practised in England before our Revolution.

Before leaving the subject, I will add a few comments made from time to time on the margin of Mr. Bartlett's excellent "Dictionary," to which I am glad thus publicly to acknowledge my many obligations. "Avails" is good old English, and the *vails* of Sir Joshua Reynolds's porter are famous. A verse *from*, averse *to*, and in connection with them the English vulgarism "different *to*:" the corrupt use of *to* in these cases, as well as in the Yankee "he lives to Salem," "to home," and others, must be a very old one, for in the one case it plainly arose from confounding the two French prepositions *à* (from Latin *ad* and *ab*), and in the other from translating the first of them. I once thought "different to" a modern vulgarism, and Mr. Thackeray, on my pointing it out to him in "Henry Esmond," confessed it to be an anachronism. Mr. Bartlett refers to "the old writers quoted in Richardson's Dictionary" for "different to," though in my edition of that work all the examples are with *from*. But I find *to* used invariably by Sir R. Hawkins in Hakluyt. *Banjo* is a negro corruption of O. E. *bandore*. *Bind-weed* can hardly be modern, for *wood-bind* is old and radically right, intertwining itself through *bindan* and *windan* with classic stems. *Bobolink:* is this a contraction for Bob o' Lincoln? I find *bobolynes*, in one of the poems attributed to Skelton, where it may be rendered *giddy-pate*, a term very fit for the bird in his ecstasies. *Cruel* for *great* is in Hak-

luyt. *Bowling-alley* is in Nash's "Pierce Pennilesse." *Curious*, meaning *nice*, occurs continually in old writers, and is as old as Pecock's "Repressor." *Droger* is O. E. *drugger*. *Educational* is in Burke. *Feeze* is only a form of *fizz*. To *fix*, in the American sense, I find used by the Commissioners of the United Colonies so early as 1675, "their arms well *fixed* and fit for service." To *take the foot in the hand* is German; so is to *go under*. *Gundalow* is old; I find *gundelo* in Hakluyt, and *gundello* in Booth's reprint of the folio Shakespeare of 1623. *Gonoff* is O. E. *gnoffe*. *Heap* is in "Piers Ploughman" ("and other names *an heep*"), and in Hakluyt ("seeing such a *heap* of their enemies ready to devour them"). To *liquor* is in the "Puritan" ("call 'em in, and liquor 'em a little"). To *loaf:* this, I think, is unquestionably German. *Laufen* is pronounced *lofen* in some parts of Germany, and I once heard one German student say to another, *Ich lauf'* (lofe) *hier bis du wiederkehrest*, and he began accordingly to saunter up and down, in short, to *loaf*. To *mull*, Mr. Bartlett says, means "to soften, to dispirit," and quotes from "Margaret," — "There has been a pretty considerable *mullin* going on among the doctors," — where it surely cannot mean what he says it does. We have always heard *mulling* used for *stirring*, *bustling*, sometimes in an underhand way. It is a metaphor derived probably from *mulling* wine, and the word itself must be a corruption of *mell*, from O. F. *mesler*. *Pair* of stairs is in Hakluyt. To *pull up stakes* is in Curwen's Journal, and therefore pre-Revolutionary. I think I have met with it earlier. *Raise:* under this word Mr. Bartlett omits "to raise a house," that is, the frame of a wooden one, and also the substantive formed from it, a *raisin*. *Retire* for *go to bed* is in Fielding's "Amelia." *Setting-poles* cannot be new, for I find "some *set* [the boats] with long *poles*" in Hakluyt. *Shoulder-hitters:* I find that *shoulder-striker* is old, though I have lost the reference to my authority. *Snag* is no new word, though perhaps the Western application of it is so; but I find in Gill the proverb, "A bird in the bag is worth two on the snag." Dryden has *swop* and *to rights*. *Trail:* Hakluyt has "many wayes *traled* by the wilde beastes."

I subjoin a few phrases not in Mr. Bartlett's book which I have heard. *Bald-headed:* "to go it bald-headed;" in great haste, as where one rushes out without his hat. *Bogue:* "I don't git much done 'thout I *bogue* right in along 'th my men." *Carry:* a portage. *Catnap:* a short doze. *Cat-stick:* a small stick. *Chowder-head:* a muddle-brain. *Cling-john:* a soft cake of rye. *Cocoa-nut:* the head. *Cohees':* applied to the people of certain settlements in Western Pennsylvania, from their use of the archaic form *Quo' he*. *Dunnow'z I know:* the nearest your true Yankee ever comes to acknowledging ignorance. *Essence-pedler:* a skunk. *First-rate and a half*. *Fish-flakes*, for drying fish : O. E. *fleck* (*cratis*). *Gander-party:* a social gathering of men only. *Gawnicus:* a dolt. *Hawkins's whetstone:* rum; in derision of one Hawkins, a well-known temperance-lecturer. *Hyper:* to bustle: "I mus' *hyper* about an' git tea." *Keeler-tub:* one in which dishes are washed. ("And Greasy Joan doth *keel* the pot.") *Lap-tea:* where the guests are too many to sit at table. *Last of pea-time:* to be hard-up. *Lose-laid* (loose-laid): a weaver's term, and probably English; weak-willed. *Malahack:* to cut up hastily or awkwardly. *Moonglade:* a beautiful word: for the track of moonlight on the water. *Off-ox:* an unmanageable, cross-grained fellow. *Old Driver, Old Splitfoot:* the Devil. *Onhitch:* to pull trigger (cf. Spanish *disparar*). *Popular:* conceited. *Rote:* sound of surf before a storm. *Rot-gut:* cheap whiskey; the word occurs in Heywood's "English Traveller" and Addison's "Drummer," for a poor kind of drink. *Seem:* it is habitual with the New-Englander to put this verb to strange uses, as "I can't *seem* to be suited," "I could n't *seem* to know him." *Sidehill*, for *hillside*. *State-house:* this seems an Americanism, whether invented or derived from the Dutch *Stadhuys*, I know not. *Strike* and *string:* from the game of ninepins; to make a *strike* is to knock down all the pins with one ball, hence it has come to mean fortunate, successful. *Swampers:* men who break out roads for lumberers. *Tormented:* euphemism for damned, as, "not a tormented cent." *Virginia fence, to make a:* to walk like a drunken man.

It is always worth while to note down the erratic words or phrases which one meets with in any dialect. They may throw light on the meaning of other words, on the relationship of languages, or even on history itself. In so composite a language as ours they often supply a different form to express a different shade of meaning, as in *viol* and *fiddle*, *thrid* and *thread*, *smother* and *smoulder*, where the *l* has crept in by a false analogy with *would*. We have given back to England the excellent adjective *lengthy*, formed honestly like *earthy*, *drouthy*, and others, thus enabling their journalists to characterize our President's messages by a word civilly compromising between *long* and *tedious*, so as not to endanger the peace of the two countries by wounding our national sensitiveness to British criticism. Let me give two curious examples of the antiseptic property of dialects at which I have already glanced. Dante has *dindi* as a childish or low word for *danari* (money), and in Shropshire small Roman coins are still dug up which the peasants call *dinders*. This can hardly be a chance coincidence, but seems rather to carry the word back to the Roman soldiery. So our farmers say *chuk*, *chuk*, to their pigs, and *ciacco* is one of the Italian words for *hog*. When a countryman tells us that he "fell *all of a heap*," I cannot help thinking that he unconsciously points to an affinity between our word *tumble*, and the Latin *tumulus*, that is older than most others.

[1] Which, whether in that form, or under its aliases *witch*-grass and *cooch*-grass, points us back to its original Saxon *quick*.

I believe that words, or even the mere intonation of them, have an astonishing vitality and power of propagation by the root, like the gardener's pest, quitch-grass,[1] while the application or combination of them may be new. It is in these last that my countrymen seem to me full of humor, invention, quickness of wit, and that sense of subtle analogy which needs only refining to become fancy and imagination. Prosaic as American life seems in many of its aspects to a European, bleak and bare as it is on the side of tradition, and utterly orphaned of the solemn inspiration of antiquity, I cannot help thinking that the ordinary talk of unlettered men among us is fuller of metaphor and of phrases that suggest lively images than that of any other people I have seen. Very many such will be found in Mr. Bartlett's book, though his short list of proverbs at the end seem to me, with one or two exceptions, as un-American as possible. Most of them have no character at all but coarseness, and are quite too long-skirted for working proverbs, in which language always "takes off its coat to it," as a Yankee would say. There are plenty that have a more native and puckery flavor, seedlings from the old stock often, and yet new varieties. One hears such not seldom among us Easterners, and the West would yield many more. "Mean enough to steal acorns from a blind hog;" "Cold as the north side of a Jenooary gravestone by starlight;" "Hungry as a graven image;" "Pop'lar as a hen with one chicken;" "A hen's time ain't much;" "Quicker 'n greased lightnin';" "Ther 's sech a thing ez bein' *tu*" (our Yankee paraphrase of μηδὲν ἄγαν); hence the phrase *tooin' round*, meaning a supererogatory activity like that of flies; "Stingy enough to skim his milk at both eends"; "Hot as the Devil's kitchen;" "Handy as a pocket in a shirt;" "He 's a whole team and the dog under the wagon;" "All deacons are good, but there 's odds in deacons" (to *deacon* berries is to put the largest atop); "So thievish they hev to take in their stone walls nights;"[2] may serve as specimens. "I take my tea *barfoot*," said a backwoodsman when asked if he would have cream and sugar. (I find *barfoot*, by the way, in the Coventry Plays.) A man speaking to me once of a very rocky clearing said, "Stone 's got a pretty heavy mortgage on that land," and I overheard a guide in the woods say to his companions who were urging him to sing, "Wal, I *did* sing once, but toons gut invented, an' thet spilt my trade." Whoever has driven over a stream by a bridge made of *slabs* will feel the picturesque force of the epithet *slab-bridged* applied to a fellow of shaky character. Almost every county has some good die-sinker in phrase, whose mintage passes into the currency of the whole neighborhood. Such a one described the county jail (the one stone building where all the dwellings are of wood)

[2] And, by the way, the Yankee never says "o' nights," but uses the older adverbial form, analogous to the German *nachts*.

as " the house whose underpinnin' come up to the eaves," and called hell " the place where they did n't rake up their fires nights." I once asked a stage-driver if the other side of a hill were as steep as the one we were climbing: " Steep ? chain lightnin' could n' go down it 'thout puttin' the shoe on ! " And this brings me back to the exaggeration of which I spoke before. To me there is something very taking in the negro " so black that charcoal made a chalk-mark on him," and the wooden shingle "painted so like marble that it sank in water," as if its very consciousness or its vanity had been overpersuaded by the cunning of the painter. I heard a man, in order to give a notion of some very cold weather, say to another that a certain Joe, who had been taking mercury, found a lump of quicksilver in each boot, when he went home to dinner. This power of rapidly dramatizing a dry fact into flesh and blood and the vivid conception of Joe as a human thermometer strike me as showing a poetic sense that may be refined into faculty. At any rate there is humor here, and not mere quickness of wit, — the deeper and not the shallower quality. The *tendency* of humor is always towards overplus of expression, while the very essence of wit is its logical precision. Captain Basil Hall denied that our people had any humor, deceived, perhaps, by their gravity of manner. But this very seriousness is often the outward sign of that humorous quality of the mind which delights in finding an element of identity in things seemingly the most incongruous, and then again in forcing an incongruity upon things identical. Perhaps Captain Hall had no humor himself, and if so he would never find it. Did he always feel the point of what was said to himself ? I doubt it, because I happen to know a chance he once had given him in vain. The Captain was walking up and down the veranda of a country tavern in Massachusetts while the coach changed horses. A thunder-storm was going on, and, with that pleasant European air of indirect self-compliment in condescending to be surprised by American merit, which we find so conciliating, he said to a countryman lounging against the door, " Pretty heavy thunder you have here." The other, who had divined at a glance his feeling of generous concession to a new country, drawled gravely, " Waal, we *du*, considerin' the number of inhabitants." This, the more I analyze it, the more humorous does it seem. The same man was capable of wit also, when he would. He was a cabinet-maker, and was once employed to make some commandment-tables for the parish meeting-house. The parson, a very old man, annoyed him by looking into his workshop every morning, and cautioning him to be very sure to pick out " clear mahogany without any *knots* in it." At last, wearied out, he retorted one day : " Wal, Dr. B., I guess ef I was to leave the *nots* out o' some o' the c'man'ments, 't 'ould soot you full ez wal ! "

If I had taken the pains to write down the proverbial or pithy phrases I have heard, or if I had sooner thought of noting the Yankeeisms I met with in my reading, I might have been able to do more justice to my theme. But I have done all I wished in respect to pronunciation, if I have proved that where we are vulgar, we have the countenance of very good company. For, as to the *jus et norma loquendi*, I agree with Horace and those who have paraphrased or commented him, from Boileau to Gray. I think that a good rule for style is Galiani's definition of sublime oratory, — " l'art de tout dire sans être mis à la Bastille dans un pays où il est défendu de rien dire." I profess myself a fanatical purist, but with a hearty contempt for the speech-gilders who affect purism without any thorough, or even pedagogic, knowledge of the engendure, growth, and affinities of the noble language about whose *mésalliances* they profess (like Dean Alford) to be so solicitous. If *they* had their way — ! " Doch es sey," says Lessing, " dass jene gothische Höflichkeit eine unentbehrliche Tugend des heutigen Umganges ist. Soll sie darum unsere Schriften eben so schaal und falsch machen als unsern Umgang ? " And Drayton was not far wrong in affirming that

> " 'T is possible to climb,
> To kindle, or to slake,
> Although in Skelton's rhyme."

Cumberland in his Memoirs tells us that when, in the midst of Admiral Rodney's great sea-fight, Sir Charles Douglas said to him, " Behold, Sir George, the Greeks and Trojans contending for the body of Patroclus ! " the Admiral answered, peevishly, " Damn the Greeks and damn the Trojans ! I have other things to think of." After the battle was won, Rodney thus to Sir Charles, " Now, my dear friend, I am at the service of your Greeks and Trojans, and the whole of Homer's Iliad, or as much of it as you please ! " I had some such feeling of the impertinence of our pseudo-classicality when I chose our homely dialect to work in. Should we be nothing, because somebody had contrived to be something (and that perhaps in a provincial dialect) ages ago ? and to be nothing by our very attempt to be that something, which they had already been, and which therefore nobody could be again without being a bore ? Is there no way left, then, I thought, of being natural, of being *naïf*, which means nothing more than native, of belonging to the age and country in which you are born ? The Yankee, at least, is a new phenomenon; let us try to be *that*. It is perhaps a *pis aller*, but is not *No Thoroughfare* written up everywhere else ? In the literary world, things seemed to me very much as they were in the latter half of the last century. Pope, skimming the cream of good sense and expression wherever he could find it, had made, not exactly poetry, but an honest, salable butter of worldly wisdom which pleasantly lubricated some of the drier morsels of life's daily bread, and, seeing this, scores of harmlessly insane people went on for the next fifty years coaxing his buttermilk with the regular up and down of the pentameter churn. And in our day do we not scent everywhere, and even carry away in our clothes against our will, that faint perfume of musk which Mr. Tennyson has left behind him, or worse, of Heine's *patchouli*? And might it not be possible to escape them by turning into one of our narrow New England lanes, shut in though it were by bleak stone walls on either hand, and where no better flowers were to be gathered than goldenrod and hardhack?

Beside the advantage of getting out of the beaten track, our dialect offered others hardly inferior. As I was about to make an endeavor to state them, I remembered something that the clear-sighted Goethe had said about Hebel's "Allemannische Gedichte," which, making proper deduction for special reference to the book under review, expresses what I would have said far better than I could hope to do: "Allen diesen innern guten Eigenschaften kommt die behagliche naive Sprache sehr zu statten. Man findet mehrere sinnlich bedeutende und wohlklingende Worte . . . von einem, zwei Buchstaben, Abbreviationen, Contractionen, viele kurze, leichte Sylben, neue Reime, welches, mehr als man glaubt, ein Vortheil für den Dichter ist. Diese Elemente werden durch glückliche Constructionen und lebhafte Formen zu einem Styl zusammengedrängt der zu diesem Zwecke vor unserer Büchersprache grosse Vorzüge hat." Of course I do not mean to imply that *I* have come near achieving any such success as the great critic here indicates, but I think the success is *there*, and to be plucked by some more fortunate hand.

Nevertheless, I was encouraged by the approval of many whose opinions I valued. With a feeling too tender and grateful to be mixed with any vanity, I mention as one of these the late A. H. Clough, who more than any one of those I have known (no longer living), except Hawthorne, impressed me with the constant presence of that indefinable thing we call genius. He often suggested that I should try my hand at some Yankee Pastorals, which would admit of more sentiment and a higher tone without foregoing the advantage offered by the dialect. I have never completed anything of the kind, but, in this Second Series, both my remembrance of his counsel and the deeper feeling called up by the great interests at stake, led me to venture some passages nearer to what is called poetical than could have been admitted without incongruity into the former series. The time seemed calling to me, with the old poet, —

"Leave, then, your wonted prattle,
The oaten reed forbear ;
For I hear a sound of battle,
And trumpets rend the air !' "

The only attempt I had ever made at anything like a pastoral (if that may be called an attempt which was the result almost of pure accident) was in "The Courtin'." While the introduction to the First Series was going through the press, I received word from the printer that there was a blank page left which must be filled. I sat down at once and improvised another fictitious "notice of the press," in which, because verse would fill up space more cheaply than prose, I inserted an extract from a supposed ballad of Mr. Biglow. I kept no copy of it, and the printer, as directed, cut it off when the gap was filled. Presently I began to receive letters asking for the rest of it, sometimes for the *balance* of it. I had none, but to answer such demands, I patched a conclusion upon it in a later edition. Those who had only the first continued to importune me. Afterward, being asked to write it out as an autograph for the Baltimore Sanitary Commission Fair, I added other verses, into some of which I infused a little more sentiment in a homely way, and after a fashion completed it by sketching in the characters and making a connected story. Most likely I have spoiled it, but I shall put it at the end of this Introduction, to answer once for all those kindly importunings.

As I have seen extracts from what purported to be writings of Mr. Biglow, which were not genuine, I may properly take this opportunity to say, that the two volumes now published contain every line I ever printed under that pseudonyme, and that I have never, so far as I can remember, written an anonymous article (elsewhere than in the "North American Review" and the "Atlantic Monthly," during my editorship of it) except a review of Mrs. Stowe's "Minister's Wooing," and, some twenty years ago, a sketch of the antislavery movement in America for an English journal.

A word more on pronunciation. I have endeavored to express this so far as I could by the types, taking such pains as, I fear, may sometimes make the reading harder than need be. At the same time, by studying uniformity I have sometimes been obliged to sacrifice minute exactness. The emphasis often modifies the habitual sound. For example, *for* is commonly *fer* (a shorter sound than *fur* for *far*), but when emphatic it always becomes *for*, as "wut *for* !' " So *too* is pronounced like *to* (as it was anciently spelt), and *to* like *ta* (the sound as in the *tou* of *touch*), but *too*, when emphatic, changes into *tue*, and *to*, sometimes, in similar cases, into *toe*, as, "I did n' hardly know wut *toe* du !' " Where vowels come together, or one precedes another following an aspirate, the two melt together, as was common with the older poets who formed their versification on French or Italian models. Drayton is thoroughly Yankee when he says "I 'xpect," and Pope when he says, "t' inspire." *With* becomes sometimes *'ith*, *'üth*, or *'th*, or even disappears wholly where it comes before *the*, as, "I went along th' Square" (along with the Squire), the *are* sound being an archaism which I have noticed also in *choir*, like the old Scottish *quhair*.[1]

[1] Greene in his *Quip for an Upstart Courtier* says, "to *square* it up and downe the streetes before his mistresse."

(Herrick has, "Of flowers ne'er sucked by th' theeving bee.") *Without* becomes *athout* and *'thout*. *Afterwards* always retains its locative *s*, and is pronounced always *ahterwurds'*, with a strong accent on the last syllable. This oddity has some support in the erratic *towards'* instead of *to'wards*, which we find in the poets and sometimes hear. The sound given to the first syllable of *to'wards*, I may remark, sustains the Yankee lengthening of the *o* in *to*. At the beginning of a sentence, *ahterwurds* has the accent on the first syllable ; at the end of one, on the last ; as, "*ah'terwurds* he tol' me," "he tol' me *ahterwurds'*." The Yankee never makes a mistake in his aspirates. *U* changes in many words to *e*, always in *such*, *brush*, *tush*, *hush*, *rush*, *blush*, seldom in *much*, oftener in *trust* and *crust*, never in *mush*, *gust*, *bust*, *tumble*, or (?) *flush*, in the latter case probably to avoid confusion with *flesh*. I have heard *flush* with the *ĕ* sound, however. For the same reason, I suspect, never in *gush* (at least, I never heard it), because we have already one *gesh* for *gash*. *A* and *i* short frequently become *e* short. *U* always becomes *o* in the prefix *un* (except *unto*), and *o* in return changes to *u* short in *uv* for *of*, and in some words beginning with *om*. *T* and *d*, *b* and *p*, *v* and *w*, remain intact. So much occurs to me in addition to what I said on this head in the preface to the former volume.

Of course in what I have said I wish to be understood as keeping in mind the difference between provincialisms properly so called and *slang*. *Slang* is always vulgar, because it is not a natural but an affected way of talking, and all mere tricks of speech or writing are offensive. I do not think that Mr. Biglow can be fairly charged with vulgarity, and I should have entirely failed in my design, if I had not made it appear that high and even refined sentiment may coexist with the shrewder and more comic elements of the Yankee character. I believe that what is essentially vulgar and mean-spirited in politics seldom has its source in the body of the people, but much rather among those who are made timid by their wealth or selfish by their love of power. A democracy can *afford* much better than an aristocracy to follow out its convictions, and is perhaps better qualified to build those convictions on plain principles of right and wrong, rather than on the shifting sands of expediency. I had always thought "Sam Slick" a libel on the Yankee character, and a complete falsification of Yankee modes of speech, though, for aught I know, it may be true in both respects so far as the British provinces are concerned. To me the dialect was native, was spoken all about me when a boy, at a time when an Irish day-laborer was as rare as an American one now. Since then I have made a study of it so far as opportunity allowed. But when I write in it, it is as in a mother tongue, and I am carried back far beyond any studies of it to long-ago noonings in my father's hay-fields, and to the talk of Sam and Job over their jug of *blackstrap* under the shadow of the ash-tree which still dapples the grass whence they have been gone so long.

But life is short, and prefaces should be. And so, my good friends, to whom this introductory epistle is addressed, farewell. Though some of you have remonstrated with me, I shall never write any more "Biglow Papers," however great the temptation, — great especially at the present time, — unless it be to complete the original plan of this Series by bringing out Mr. Sawin as an "original Union man." The very favor with which they have been received is a hindrance to me, by forcing on me a self-consciousness from which I was entirely free when I wrote the First Series. Moreover, I am no longer the same careless youth, with nothing to do but live to myself, my books, and my friends, that I was then. I always hated politics, in the ordinary sense of the word, and I am not likely to grow fonder of them, now that I have learned how rare it is to find a man who can keep principle clear from party and personal prejudice, or can conceive the possibility of another's doing so. I feel as if I could in some sort claim to be an *emeritus*, and I am sure that political satire will have full justice done it by that genuine and delightful humorist, the Rev. Petroleum V. Nasby. I regret that I killed off Mr. Wilbur so soon, for he would have enabled me to bring into this preface a number of learned quotations, which must now go a-begging, and also enabled me to dispersonalize myself into a vicarious egotism. He would have helped me likewise in clearing myself from a charge which I shall briefly touch on, because my friend Mr. Hughes has found it needful to defend me in his preface to one of the English editions of the "Biglow Papers." I thank Mr. Hughes heartily for his friendly care of my good name, and were his Preface accessible to my readers here (as I am glad it is not, for its partiality makes me blush), I should leave the matter where he left it. The charge is of profanity, brought in by persons who proclaimed African slavery of Divine institution, and is based (so far as I have heard) on two passages in the First Series —

"An' you 've gut to git up airly,
  Ef you want to take in God,"

and,

"God 'll send the bill to you,"

and on some Scriptural illustrations by Mr. Sawin.

Now, in the first place, I was writing under an assumed character, and must talk as the person would whose mouthpiece I made myself. Will any one familiar with the New England countryman venture to tell me that he does *not* speak of sacred things familiarly ? that Biblical allusions (allusions, that is, to the single book with whose language, from his church-going habits, he is intimate) are *not* frequent on his lips ? If so, he cannot have pursued his studies of the character on so many long-ago musterfields and at so many cattle-shows as I. But I scorn any such line of defence, and will confess at once that one of the things I am proud of in my countrymen is (I am not speaking now of such persons as I have assumed Mr. Sawin to be) that they do not put their Maker away far from them, or interpret the fear of God into being afraid of Him. The Talmudists had conceived a deep truth when they said, that "all things were in the power of God, save the fear of God;" and when people stand in great dread of an invisible power, I suspect they mistake quite another personage for the Deity. I might justify myself for the passages criticised by many parallel ones from Scripture, but I need not. The Reverend Homer Wilbur's note-books supply me with three apposite quotations. The first is from a Father of the Roman Church, the second from a Father of the Anglican, and the third from a Father of Modern English poetry. The Puritan divines would furnish me with many more such. St. Bernard says, *Sapiens nummularius est Deus: nummum fictum non recipiet;* "A cunning money-changer is God: he will take in no base coin." Latimer says, "You shall perceive that God, by this example, shaketh us by the noses and taketh us by the ears." Familiar enough, both of them, one would say! But I should think Mr. Biglow had verily stolen the last of the two maligned passages from Dryden's "Don Sebastian," where I find

"And beg of Heaven to charge the bill on me!"

And there I leave the matter, being willing to believe that the Saint, the Martyr, and even the Poet, were as careful of God's honor as my critics are ever likely to be.

II. GLOSSARY TO THE BIGLOW PAPERS

Act'lly, *actually.*
Air, *are.*
Airth, *earth.*
Airy, *area.*
Aree, *area.*
Arter, *after.*
Ax, *ask.*

Beller, *bellow.*
Bellowses, *lungs.*
Ben, *been.*
Bile, *boil.*
Bimeby, *by and by.*
Blurt out, *to speak bluntly.*
Bust, *burst.*
Buster, *a roistering blade;* used also as a general superlative.

Caird, *carried.*
Cairn, *carrying.*
Caleb, *a turncoat.*
Cal'late, *calculate.*
Cass, *a person with two lives.*
Close, *clothes.*
Cockerel, *a young cock.*
Cocktail, *a kind of drink;* also, *an ornament peculiar to soldiers.*

Convention, *a place where people are imposed on; a juggler's show.*
Coons, *a cant term for a now defunct party;* derived, perhaps, from the fact of their being commonly *up a tree.*
Cornwallis, *a sort of muster in masquerade;* supposed to have had its origin soon after the Revolution, and to commemorate the surrender of Lord Cornwallis. It took the place of the old Guy Fawkes procession.
Crooked stick, *a perverse, froward person.*
Cunnle, *a colonel.*
Cus, *a curse;* also, *a pitiful fellow.*

Darsn't, used indiscriminately, either in singular or plural number, for *dare not, dares not,* and *dared not.*
Deacon off, *to give the cue to;* derived from a custom, once universal, but now extinct, in our New England Congregational churches. An important part of the office of deacon was to read aloud the hymns *given out* by the minister, one line at a time, the congregation singing each line as soon as read.
Demmercrat, leadin', *one in favor of extending slavery; a free-trade lecturer maintained in the custom-house.*
Desput, *desperate.*
Dō', *don't.*
Doos, *does.*
Doughface, *a contented lick-spittle;* a common variety of Northern politician.
Dror, *draw.*
Du, *do.*
Dunno, dno, *do not* or *does not know.*
Dut, *dirt.*

Eend, *end.*
Ef, *if.*
Emptins, *yeast.*
Env'y, *envoy.*
Everlasting, an intensive, without reference to duration.
Ev'y, *every.*
Ez, *as.*

Fence, on the; said of one who halts between two opinions; a trimmer.
Fer, *for.*
Ferfle, ferful, *fearful;* also an intensive.
Fin', *find.*
Fish-skin, used in New England to clarify coffee.
Fix, *a difficulty, a nonplus.*
Foller, folly, *to follow.*
Forrerd, *forward.*
Frum, *from.*
Fur, *far.*
Furder, *farther.*
Furrer, *furrow.* Metaphorically, *to draw a straight furrow* is to live uprightly or decorously.
Fust, *first.*

Gin, *gave.*
Git, *get.*
Gret, *great.*

Grit, *spirit, energy, pluck.*
Grout, *to sulk.*
Grouty, *crabbed, surly.*
Gum, *to impose on.*
Gump, *a foolish fellow, a dullard.*
Gut, *got.*

Hed, *had.*
Heern, *heard.*
Hellum, *helm.*
Hendy, *handy.*
Het, *heated.*
Hev, *have.*
Hez, *has.*
Holl, *whole.*
Holt, *hold.*
Huf, *hoof.*
Hull, *whole.*
Hum, *home.*
Humbug, *General Taylor's antislavery.*
Hut, *hurt.*

Idno, *I do not know.*
In'my, *enemy.*
Insines, *ensigns;* used to designate both the officer who carries the standard, and the standard itself.
Inter, intu, *into.*

Jedge, *judge.*
Jest, *just.*
Jine, *join.*
Jint, *joint.*
Junk, *a fragment of any solid substance.*

Keer, *care.*
Kep', *kept.*
Killock, *a small anchor.*
Kin', kin' o', kinder, *kind, kind of.*

Lawth, *loath.*
Less, *let's, let us.*
Let daylight into, *to shoot.*
Let on, *to hint, to confess, to own.*
Lick, *to beat, to overcome.*
Lights, *the bowels.*
Lily-pads, *leaves of the water-lily.*
Long-sweetening, *molasses.*

Mash, *marsh.*
Mean, *stingy, ill-natured.*
Min', *mind.*

Nimepunce, *ninepence, twelve and a half cents.*
Nowers, *nowhere.*

Offen, *often.*
Ole, *old.*
Ollers, olluz, *always.*
On, *of;* used before *it* or *them,* or at the end of a sentence, as *on 't, on 'em, nut ez ever I heerd on.*
On'y, *only.*
Ossifer, *officer* (seldom heard).

Peaked, *pointed.*
Peek, *to peep.*

Pickerel, *the pike, a fish.*
Pint, *point.*
Pocket full of rocks, *plenty of money.*
Pooty, *pretty.*
Pop'ler, *conceited, popular.*
Pus, *purse.*
Put out, *troubled, vexed.*

Quarter, *a quarter-dollar.*
Queen's-arm, *a musket.*

Resh, *rush.*
Revelee, *the réveille.*
Rile, *to trouble.*
Riled, *angry; disturbed,* as the sediment in any liquid.
Riz, *risen.*
Row, a long row to hoe, *a difficult task.*
Rugged, *robust.*

Sarse, *abuse, impertinence.*
Sartin, *certain.*
Saxon, *sacristan, sexton.*
Scaliest, *worst.*
Scringe, *cringe.*
Scrouge, *to crowd.*
Sech, *such.*
Set by, *valued.*
Shakes, great, *of considerable consequence.*
Shappoes, *chapeaux, cocked-hats.*
Sheer, *share.*
Shet, *shut.*
Shut, *shirt.*
Skeered, *scared.*
Skeeter, *mosquito.*
Skooting, *running, or moving swiftly.*
Slarterin', *slaughtering.*
Slim, *contemptible.*
Snake, *crawled like a snake;* but *to snake any one out* is to track him to his hiding-place; *to snake a thing out* is to snatch it out.
Soffies, *sofas.*
Sogerin', *soldiering;* a barbarous amusement common among men in the savage state.
Som'ers, *somewhere.*
So 'st, *so as that.*
Sot, *set, obstinate, resolute.*
Spiles, *spoils; objects of political ambition.*
Spry, *active.*
Steddles, *stout stakes driven into the salt marshes,* on which the hay-ricks are set, and thus raised out of the reach of high tides.
Streaked, *uncomfortable, discomfited.*
Suckle, *circle.*
Sutthin', *something.*
Suttin, *certain.*

Take on, *to sorrow.*
Talents, *talons.*
Taters, *potatoes.*
Tell, *till.*
Tetch, *touch.*
Tetch tu, *to be able;* used always after a negative in this sense.
Tollable, *tolerable.*
Toot, used derisively for *playing on any wind instrument.*

Thru, *through.*

Thundering, a euphemism common in New England for the profane English expression *devilish.* Perhaps derived from the belief, common formerly, that thunder was caused by the Prince of the Air, for some of whose accomplishments consult Cotton Mather.

Tu, *to, too;* commonly has this sound when used emphatically, or at the end of a sentence. At other times it has the sound of *t* in *tough,* as, *Ware ye goin' tu? Goin' ta Boston.*

Ugly, *ill-tempered, intractable.*

Uncle Sam, *United States;* the largest boaster of liberty and owner of slaves.

Unrizzest, applied to dough or bread; *heavy, most unrisen,* or *most incapable of rising.*

V-spot, *a five-dollar bill.*

Vally, *value.*

Wake snakes, *to get into trouble.*

Wal, *well;* spoken with great deliberation, and sometimes with the *a* very much flattened, sometimes (but more seldom) very much broadened.

Wannut, *walnut (hickory).*

Ware, *where.*

Ware, *were.*

Whopper, *an uncommonly large lie;* as, that General Taylor is in favor of the Wilmot Proviso.

Wig, *Whig;* a party now dissolved.

Wunt, *will not.*

Wus, *worse.*

Wut, *what.*

Wuth, *worth;* as, *Antislavery perfessions 'fore 'lection aint wuth a Bungtown copper.*

Wuz, *was,* sometimes *were.*

Yaller, *yellow.*

Yeller, *yellow.*

Yellers, *a disease of peach-trees.*

Zack, Ole, *a second Washington, an antislavery slaveholder; a humane buyer and seller of men and women, a Christian hero generally.*

III. INDEX TO THE BIGLOW PAPERS

A. wants his axe ground, 247.

A. B., information wanted concerning, 203.

Abraham (Lincoln), his constitutional scruples, 247.

Abuse, an, its usefulness, 259.

Adam, eldest son of, respected, 183 — his fall, 264 — how if he had bitten a sweet apple? 267.

Adam, Grandfather, forged will of, 236.

Æneas goes to hell, 211.

Æolus, a seller of money, as is supposed by some, 211.

Æschylus, a saying of, 196, *note.*

Alligator, a decent one conjectured to be, in some sort, humane, 216.

Allsmash, the eternal, 251.

Alphonso the Sixth of Portugal, tyrannical act of, 217.

Ambrose, Saint, excellent (but rationalistic) sentiment of, 190.

"American Citizen," new compost so called, 211.

American Eagle, a source of inspiration, 193 — hitherto wrongly classed, 196 — long bill of, *ib.*

Americans bebrothered, 231.

Amos cited, 190.

Anakim, that they formerly existed, shown, 217.

Angels providentially speak French, 186, — conjectured to be skilled in all tongues, *ib.*

Anglo-Saxondom, its idea, what, 186.

Anglo-Saxon mask, 186.

Anglo-Saxon race, 185.

Anglo-Saxon verse, by whom carried to perfection, 183.

Anthony of Padua, Saint, happy in his hearers, 240.

Antiquaries, Royal Society of Northern, 254.

Antonius, a speech of, 192 — by whom best reported, *ib.*

Apocalypse, Beast in, magnetic to theologians, 205.

Apollo, confessed mortal by his own oracle, 205.

Apollyon, his tragedies popular, 202.

Appian, an Alexandrian, not equal to Shakespeare as an orator, 192.

Applause, popular, the *summum bonum,* 255.

Ararat, ignorance of foreign tongues is an, 196.

Arcadian background, 212.

Ar c'houskezik, an evil spirit, 240.

Ardennes, Wild Boar of, an ancestor of Rev. Mr. Wilbur, 221.

Aristocracy, British, their natural sympathies, 245.

Aristophanes, 190.

Arms, profession of, once esteemed especially that of gentlemen, 183.

Arnold, 192.

Ashland, 212.

Astor, Jacob, a rich man, 208.

Astræa, nineteenth century forsaken by, 211.

Athenians, ancient, an institution of, 192.

Atherton, Senator, envies the loon, 199.

"Atlantic," editors of. See *Neptune.*

Atropos, a lady skilful with the scissors, 266.

Austin, Saint, prayer of, 221.

Austrian eagle split, 259.

Aye-aye, the, an African animal, America supposed to be settled by, 187.

B., a Congressman, *vide A.*

Babel, probably the first Congress, 196 — a gabble-mill, *ib.*

Baby, a low-priced one, 210.

Bacon, his rebellion, 241.

Bacon, Lord, quoted, 240, 241.

Bagowind, Hon. Mr., whether to be damned, 200.

Balcom, Elder Joash Q., 2d, founds a Baptist society in Jaalam, A. D. 1830, 273.

Baldwin apples, 217.

Rotation insures mediocrity and inexperience, 247.
Rough and ready, 213 — a Wig, 214 — a kind of scratch, *ib.*
Royal Society, American fellows of, 265.
Rum and water combine kindly, 256.
Runes resemble bird-tracks, 254.
Runic inscriptions, their different grades of unintelligibility and consequent value, 254.
Russell, Earl, is good enough to expound our Constitution for us, 230.
Russian eagle turns Prussian blue, 195.
Ryeus, Bacchi epitheton, 272.

Sabbath, breach of, 176.
Sabellianism, one accused of, 205.
Sailors, their rights how won, 236.
Saltillo, unfavorable view of, 185.
Salt-river, in Mexican, what, 185.
Samuel, avunculus, 271.
Samuel, Uncle, 224 — riotous, 195 — yet has qualities demanding reverence, 201 — a good provider for his family, *ib.* — an exorbitant bill of, 211 — makes some shrewd guesses, 238, 239 — expects his boots, 245.
Sansculottes, draw their wine before drinking, 199.
Santa Anna, his expensive leg, 209.
Sappho, some human nature in, 271.
Sassycus, an impudent Indian, 233.
Satan, never wants attorneys, 186 — an expert talker by signs, *ib.* — a successful fisherman with little or no bait, 187 — cunning fetch of, 188 — dislikes ridicule, 190 — ought not to have credit of ancient oracles, 196, *note* — his worst pitfall, 243.
Satirist, incident to certain dangers, 188.
Savages, Canadian, chance of redemption offered to, 217.
Sawin, B., Esquire, his letter not written in verse, 183 — a native of Jaalam, *ib.* — not regular attendant on Rev. Mr. Wilbur's preaching, *ib.* — a fool, 184 — his statements trustworthy, *ib.* — his ornithological tastes, *ib.* — letters from, 183, 206, 212 — his curious discovery in regard to bayonets, 184 — displays proper family pride, *ib.* — modestly confesses himself less wise than the Queen of Sheba, 186 — the old Adam in, peeps out, *ib.* — a *miles emeritus,* 206 — is made text for a sermon, *ib.* — loses a leg, 207 — an eye, *ib.* — left hand, *ib.* — four fingers of right hand, *ib.* — has six or more ribs broken, *ib.* — a rib of his infrangible, *ib.* — allows a certain amount of preterite greenness in himself, *ib.* — his share of spoil limited, 208 — his opinion of Mexican climate, *ib.* — acquires property of a certain sort, *ib.* — his experience of glory, *ib.* — stands sentry, and puns thereupon, 209 — undergoes martyrdom in some of its most painful forms, *ib.* — enters the candidating business, *ib.* — modestly states the (avail) abilities which qualify him for high political station, *ib.* — has no principles, *ib.* — a peace-man, *ib.* — unpledged, *ib.* — has no objections to owning *peculiar* property, but would not like to monopolize the truth, 210

— his account with glory, *ib.* — a selfish motive hinted in, *ib.* — sails for Eldorado, *ib.* — shipwrecked on a metaphorical promontory, *ib.* — parallel between, and Rev. Mr. Wilbur (not Plutarchian), 211 — conjectured to have bathed in river Selemnus, 212 — loves plough wisely, but not too well, *ib.* — a foreign mission probably expected by, *ib.* — unanimously nominated for presidency, *ib.* — his country's father-in-law, 213 — nobly emulates Cincinnatus, *ib.* — is not a crooked stick, *ib.* — advises his adherents, *ib.* — views of, on present state of politics, 213–215 — popular enthusiasm for, at Bellers's, and its disagreeable consequences, 214 — inhuman treatment of, by Bellers, *ib.* — his opinion of the two parties, *ib.* — agrees with Mr. Webster, *ib.* — his antislavery zeal, 215 — his proper self-respect, *ib.* — his unaffected piety, *ib.* — his not intemperate temperance, *ib.* — a thrilling adventure of, 215–217 — his prudence and economy, 215 — bound to Captain Jakes, but regains his freedom, 216 — is taken prisoner, *ib.* — ignominiously treated, *ib.* — his consequent resolution, 217.
Sawin, Honorable B. O'F., a vein of humor suspected in, 222 — gets into an enchanted castle, 223 — finds a wooden leg better in some respects than a living one, 224 — takes something hot, *ib.* — his experience of Southern hospitality, *ib.* — waterproof internally, *ib.* — sentenced to ten years' imprisonment, 225 — his liberal-handedness, 226 — gets his arrears of pension, *ib.* — marries the widow Shannon, 227 — confiscated, *ib.* — finds in himself a natural necessity of income, 228 — his missionary zeal, *ib.* — never a stated attendant on Mr. Wilbur's preaching, 239 — sang bass in choir, 240 — prudently avoided contribution toward bell, *ib.* — abhors a covenant of works, 242 — if saved at all, must be saved genteelly, *ib.* — reports a sermon, 243 — experiences religion, *ib.* — would consent to a dukedom, 244 — converted to unanimity, 245 — sound views of, 247 — makes himself an extempore marquis, 248 — extract of letter from, 283, 284 — his opinion of Paddies, 284 — of Johnson, *ib.*
Sayres, a martyr, 197.
Scaliger, saying of, 188.
Scarabæus pilularius, 185.
Scott, General, his claims to the presidency, 190, 191.
Scrimgour, Rev. Shearjashub, 273.
Scythians, their diplomacy commended, 206.
Sea, the wormy, 255.
Seamen, colored, sold, 182.
Secessia, licta, 271.
Secession, its legal nature defined, 227.
Secret, a great military, 260.
Selemnus, a sort of Lethean river, 212.
Senate, debate in, made readable, 197.
Seneca, saying of, 188 — another, 196, *note* — overrated by a saint (but see Lord Bolingbroke's opinion of, in a letter to Dean Swift), 203 — his letters not commended, *ib.* — a son of Rev. Mr. Wilbur, 211 — quoted, 266, 267.
Serbonian bog of literature, 197.

IV. NOTES AND ILLUSTRATIONS

Page 111. *On any pot that ever drew tea.*

When Mr. Garrison visited Edinburgh in 1846, a handsome silver tea-set was presented to him by his friends in that city. On the arrival of this gift at the Boston custom-house, it was charged with an enormous entrance duty, which would have been remitted if the articles had ever been used. It was supposed that if the owner had not been the leader of the unpopular abolitionists, this heavy impost would not have been laid on a friendly British tribute to an eminent American.

Page 111. *There jokes our Edmund.*

Edmund Quincy. [See page 383.]

Page 112. *Let Austin's total shipwreck say.*

On the occasion of the murder of Rev. Elijah P. Lovejoy, editor of an anti-slavery newspaper at Alton, Illinois, an indignation meeting was held in Boston, at which Mr. Austin, Attorney-General of Massachusetts, made a violent pro-slavery speech, which called forth a crushing reply from Wendell Phillips, who thenceforth became a main pillar of abolitionism.

Page 112. *Smiles the reviled and pelted Stephen.*

Stephen S. Foster.

Page 112. *Sits Abby in her modest dress.*

Abby Kelley.

Page 131. *There is Bryant, as quiet, as cool, and as dignified.*

[I am quite sensible now that I did not do Mr. Bryant justice in the "Fable." But there was no personal feeling in what I said — though I have regretted what I *did* say because it might seem personal. I am now asked to write a review of his poems for the *North American.* If I do, I shall try to do him justice. *Letters* I. 221.]

Page 137. *But there comes Miranda, Zeus! where shall I flee to ?*

[If it be not too late, strike out these four verses in " Miranda : "

There is one thing she owns in her own private right,
It is native and genuine — namely, her spite ;
When she acts as a censor, she privately blows
A censer of vanity, 'neath her own nose.

Lowell to C. F. Briggs, October 4, 1848.]

THE BIGLOW PAPERS

I am indebted to Mr. Frank Beverly Williams for these illustrative notes.

FIRST SERIES

This series of the Biglow Papers relates to the Mexican War. It expresses the sentiment of New England, and particularly of Massachusetts, on that conflict, which in its aim and conduct had little of honor for the American Republic. The war was begun and prosecuted in the interest of Southern slaveholders. It was essential to the vitality of slavery that fresh fields should constantly be opened to it. Agriculture was almost the sole industry in which slaves could be profitably employed. That their labor should be wasteful and careless to preserve the productive powers of the soil was inevitable. New land was ever in demand, and the history of slavery in the United States is one long series of struggles for more territory. It was with this end in view that a colony of roving, adventurous Americans, settled in the thinly populated and poorly governed region now known as Texas, revolted from the Mexican government and secured admission to the Union, thus bringing on the war with Mexico. The Northern Whigs had protested against annexation, but after the war began their resistance grew more and more feeble. In the vain effort to retain their large Southern constituent, they sacrificed justice to expediency and avoided an issue that would not be put down. The story of the Mexican War is the story of the gradual decline of the great Whig party, and of the growth of that organization, successively known as the Liberty, Free-Soil, and Republican party, whose policy was the exclusion of slavery from all new territory. One more victory was granted to the Whigs in 1848. After that their strength failed rapidly. Northern sentiment was being roused to a sense of righteous indignation by Southern aggressions and the fervid exhortations of Garrison and his co-workers in the anti-slavery cause. Few, however, followed Garrison into disloyalty to the Constitution. The greater number preferred to stay in the Union and use such lawful political means as were available for the restriction of slavery. Their wisdom was demonstrated by the election of Abraham Lincoln twelve years after the Mexican War closed.

Page 181. *A cruetin Sarjunt.*

The act of May 13, 1846, authorized President Polk to employ the militia, and call out 50,000 volunteers, if necessary. He immediately called for the full number of volunteers, asking Massachusetts for 777 men. On May 26 Governor Briggs issued a proclamation for the enrolment of the regiment. As the President's call was merely a request and not an order, many Whigs and the Abolitionists were for refusing it. *The Liberator* for June 5 severely censured the governor for complying, and accused him of not carrying out the resolutions of the last Whig Convention, which had pledged the party "to present as firm a front of opposition to the institution as was consistent with their allegiance to the Constitution."

Page 182. *Massachusetts . . . she's akneelin' with the rest.*

An allusion to the governor's call for troops (cf. note to p. 181) as well as to the vote on the War Bill. On May 11, 1846, the President sent to the House of Representatives his well-known message declaring the existence of war brought on "by the act of Mexico," and asking for a supply of $10,000,000. Of the seven members from Massachusetts, all Whigs, two, Robert C. Winthrop, of Boston, and Amos Abbott, of Andover, voted for the bill. The Whigs throughout the country, remembering the fate of the party which had opposed the last war with England, sanctioned the measure as necessary for the preservation of the army, then in peril by the unauthorized acts of the President.

Page 182.

> *Ha'n't they sold your colored seamen?*
> *Ha'n't they made your env'ys w'iz?*

South Carolina, Louisiana, and several other Southern States at an early date passed acts to prevent free persons of color from entering their jurisdictions. These acts bore with particular severity upon colored seamen, who were imprisoned, fined, or whipped, and often sold into slavery. On the petition of the Massachusetts Legislature, Governor Briggs, in 1844, appointed Mr. Samuel Hoar agent to Charleston, and Mr. George Hubbard to New Orleans, to act on behalf of oppressed colored citizens of the Bay State. Mr. Hoar was expelled from South Carolina by order of the Legislature of that State, and Mr. Hubbard was forced by threats of violence to leave Louisiana. The obnoxious acts remained in force until after the Civil War.

Page 183. *Go to work an' part.*

Propositions to secede were not uncommon in New England at this time. The rights of the States had been strongly asserted on the acquisition of Louisiana in 1803, and on the admission of the State of that name in 1812. Among the resolutions of the Massachusetts Legislature adopted in 1845, relative to the proposed annexation of Texas, was one declaring that "such an act of admission would have no binding force whatever on the people of Massachusetts." John Quincy Adams, in a discourse before the New York Historical Society, in 1839, claimed a right for the States "to part in friendship with each other . . . when the fraternal spirit shall give way," etc. The Garrisonian wing of the Abolitionists notoriously

advocated secession. There were several other instances of an expression of this sentiment, but for the most part they were not evoked by opposition to slavery.

Page 184. *Hoorawin' in ole Funnel.*

The Massachusetts regiment, though called for May 13, 1846, was not mustered into the United States' service till late in January of the next year. The officers, elected January 5, 1847, were as follows: Caleb Cushing, of Newburyport, Colonel; Isaac H. Wright, of Roxbury, Lieutenant-Colonel; Edward W. Abbott, of Andover, Major. Shortly before the troops embarked for the South, on the evening of Saturday, January 23, 1847, a public meeting was held in Faneuil Hall, where an elegant sword was presented to Mr. Wright by John A. Bolles, on behalf of the subscribers. Mr. Bolles' speech on this occasion is the one referred to.

Page 184. *Mister Bolles.*

Mr. John Augustus Bolles was the author of a prize essay on a *Congress of Nations*, published by the American Peace Society, an essay on *Usury and Usury Laws*, and of various articles in the *North American Review* and other periodicals. He was also the first editor of the *Boston Journal*. In 1843 he was Secretary of State for Massachusetts.

Page 185. *Rantoul.*

Mr. Robert Rantoul (1805-1852), a prominent lawyer and a most accomplished gentleman, was at this time United States District Attorney for Massachusetts. In 1851 he succeeded Webster in the Senate, but remained there a short time only. He was a Representative in Congress from 1851 till his death. Although a Democrat, Mr. Rantoul was strongly opposed to slavery.

Page 185. *Achokin' on 'em.*

Mr. Rantoul was an earnest advocate of the abolition of capital punishment. Public attention had recently been called to his views by some letters to Governor Briggs on the subject, written in February, 1846.

Page 186. *Caleb.*

Caleb Cushing, of Newburyport, Colonel of the Massachusetts Regiment of Volunteers.

Page 188. *Guvener B.*

George Nixon Briggs was the Whig Governor of Massachusetts from 1844 to 1851. The campaign referred to here is that of 1847. Governor Briggs was renominated by acclamation and supported by his party with great enthusiasm. His opponent was Caleb Cushing, then in Mexico, and raised by President Polk to the rank of Brigadier-General. Cushing was defeated by a majority of 14,060.

Page 188. *John P. Robinson.*

John Paul Robinson (1799-1864) was a resident of Lowell, a lawyer of considerable ability and a thorough classical scholar. He represented Lowell in the State Legislature in 1829, 1830, 1831, 1833, and 1842, and was Senator from Middlesex in 1836. Late in the gubernatorial contest of 1847 it was rumored that Robinson, heretofore a zealous Whig, and a delegate to the recent Springfield Convention, had gone over to the Democratic or, as it was then styled, the "Loco" camp. The editor of the *Boston Palladium* wrote to him to learn the truth, and Robinson replied in an open letter avowing his intention to vote for Cushing.

Page 188. *Gineral C.*
General Caleb Cushing.

Page 189. "*Our country, however bounded.*"
Mr. R. C. Winthrop, M. C., in a speech at Faneuil Hall, July 4, 1845, said in deprecation of secession: "Our country — bounded by the St. John's and the Sabine, or however otherwise bounded or described, and be the measurements more or less — still our country — to be cherished in all our hearts, to be defended by all our hands." The sentiment was at once taken up and used effectively by the "Cotton" Whigs, those who inclined to favor the Mexican War.

Page 190. *The Liberator.*
The *Liberator* was William Lloyd Garrison's anti-slavery paper, published from 1831 to 1865. The "heresies" of which Mr. Wilbur speaks were Garrison's advocacy of secession, his well-known and eccentric views on "no government," woman suffrage, etc.

Page 191. *Scott.*
General W. Scott was mentioned as a possible Whig candidate for the Presidency in the summer of 1847, but was soon overshadowed by General Taylor.

Page 192. *Palfrey.*
December 6, 1847, Mr. R. C. Winthrop, of Boston, the Whig candidate for Speaker of the House in the Thirtieth Congress, was elected after three ballots. Mr. John Gorham Palfrey, elected a Whig member from Boston, and Mr. Joshua Giddings, of Ohio, refused to vote for Winthrop, and remained firm to the last in spite of the intensity of public opinion in their party. The election of a Whig Speaker in a manner depended on their votes. Had they supported Winthrop, he could have been elected on the second ballot. At the third he could not have been elected without them had not Mr. Levin, a Native American member, changed his vote, and Mr. Holmes, a Democrat from South Carolina, left the hall. Mr. Palfrey refused to vote for Mr. Winthrop because he was assured the latter would not, through his power over the committees, exert his influence to arrest the war and obstruct the extension of slavery into new territory. So bold and decided a stand at so critical a time excited great indignation for a time among the "Cotton" Whigs of Boston.

Page 193. *Springfield Convention.*
This convention was held September 29, 1847. The substance of the resolutions is given by Mr. Biglow.

Page 195. *Monteery.*
Monterey, the capital of Nueva Leon, capitulated September 24, 1846, thus giving the United States' troops control over about two thirds of the territory and one tenth of the population of Mexico.

Page 196. *Cherry Buster.*

August 20, 1847, General Scott stormed the heights of Cherubusco, and completely routed the 30,000 Mexicans stationed there under Santa Anna. Scott could have entered the capital at once in triumph had he not preferred to delay for peace negotiations.

Page 196. *The Tooleries.*
The French Revolution of 1848, which resulted in the deposition of Louis Philippe, was at this time impending.

Page 196. *The Post.*
The *Boston Post*, a Democratic, or Loco newspaper.

Page 196. *The Courier.*
The *Boston Courier*, in which the Biglow Papers first appeared, was a "Conscience" Whig paper.

Page 197. *Drayton and Sayres.*
In April, 1848, an attempt was made to abduct seventy-seven slaves from Washington in the schooner Pearl, under the conduct of Captain Drayton and Sayres, or Sayers, his mate. The slaves were speedily recaptured and sold South, while their brave defenders barely escaped with their lives from an infuriated mob. The Abolitionists in Congress determined to evoke from that body some expression of sentiment on the subject. On the 20th of April Senator Hale introduced a resolution implying but not expressing sympathy with the oppressed. It stirred the slaveholders to unusual intemperance of language. Calhoun was "amazed that even the Senator from New Hampshire had so little regard for the Constitution," and, forgetting his usual dignity, declared he "would as soon argue with a maniac from Bedlam" as with Mr. Hale. Mr. Foote, of Mississippi, was, perhaps, the most violent of all. He denounced any attempt of Congress to legislate on the subject of slavery as "a nefarious attempt to commit grand larceny." He charged Mr. Hale with being "as guilty as if he had committed highway robbery," and went on to say, "I invite him to visit Mississippi, and will tell him beforehand, in all honesty, that he could not go ten miles into the interior before he would grace one of the tallest trees of the forest with a rope around his neck, with the approbation of all honest and patriotic citizens; and that, if necessary, I should myself assist in the operation."

Mr. Hale stood almost alone with his resolution, which was soon arrested by an adjournment. A similar resolution failed in the House.

Drayton and Sayres were convicted by the District Court and sentenced to long terms of imprisonment. In 1852 Senator Sumner secured for them an unconditional pardon from President Fillmore.

Page 198. *Mr. Foote.*
Cf. note above. Mr. Henry S. Foote was Senator from Mississippi from 1847 to 1852. He was a member of the Confederate Congress, and the author of *The War of the Rebellion*, and *Personal Recollections of Public Men.*

Page 198. *Mangum.*

W. P. Mangum (1792–1861) was Senator from North Carolina from 1831 to 1837, and from 1841 to 1847. He was President *pro tem.* of the Senate during Tyler's administration, 1842–1845.

Page 198. *Cass.*

Lewis Cass (1782–1866) was Jackson's Secretary of War from 1831 to 1836, Minister to France from 1836 to 1842, Senator from Michigan from 1845 to 1848, and candidate for the Presidency on the Democratic ticket in 1848. After his defeat by Taylor he was in 1849 returned to the Senate to fill out his unexpired term. He was Buchanan's Secretary of State until the famous message of December, 1860, when he resigned.

Page 198. *Davis.*

Jefferson Davis, the President of the so-called Confederate States, was a Senator from Mississippi from 1847 to 1850.

Page 199. *Hannegan.*

Edward A. Hannegan was Senator from Indiana from 1843 to 1849. He was afterwards Minister to Prussia and died in 1859.

Page 199. *Jarnagin.*

Spencer Jarnagin represented the State of Tennessee in the Senate from 1841 to 1847. He died in 1851.

Page 199. *Atherton.*

Charles G. Atherton (1804–1853) was Senator from New Hampshire from 1843 to 1849.

Page 199. *Colquitt.*

W. T. Colquitt (1799–1855) was Senator from Georgia, from 1843 to 1849.

Page 199. *Johnson.*

Reverdy Johnson was Senator from Maryland, 1845–1849.

Page 199. *Westcott.*

James D. Westcott, Senator from Florida, 1845–1849.

Page 199. *Lewis.*

Dixon H. Lewis represented Alabama in the House of Representatives from 1829 to 1843, and in the Senate from 1844 till his death in 1848.

Page 201. "*Payris.*"

The revolution in France was hailed with delight in the United States as a triumph of freedom and popular government. In Congress the event gave opportunity for much sounding declamation, in which the Southern members participated with as much enthusiasm as those from the North. At the same time when the Abolitionists sought to turn all this philosophy to some more practical application nearer home, the attempt was bitterly denounced at Washington and by the Democratic press generally. A striking instance of this inconsistency is afforded by a speech of Senator Foote. "The age of tyrants and slavery," said he, in allusion to France, "is drawing to a close. The happy period to be signalized by the universal emancipation of man from the fetters of civil oppression, and the recognition in all countries of the great principles of popular sovereignty, equality, and brotherhood, is at this moment visibly commencing." A few days later, when Mr. Mann, the attorney for Drayton and Sayres,

quoted these very words in palliation of his clients' offence, he was peremptorily checked by the judge for uttering "inflammatory" words that might "endanger our institutions."

Page 203. *Candidate for the Presidency.*

In the campaign of 1848 the Whigs determined to have substantially no platform or programme at all, in order to retain the Southern element in their party. Accordingly a colorless candidate was selected in the person of General Zachary Taylor, who, it was said, had never voted or made any political confession of faith. He was nominated as the "people's candidate," and men of all parties were invited to support him. He refused to pledge himself to any policy or enter into any details, unless on some such obsolete issue as that of a National Bank. After it became apparent that his followers were chiefly Whigs, he declared himself a Whig also, "although not an ultra one." He particularly avoided compromising himself on the slavery question. When, in the beginning of 1847, Mr. J. W. Taylor, of the *Cincinnati Signal*, questioned him on the Wilmot Proviso, he answered in such vague phrases that the confused editor interpreted them first as favoring and finally as opposing the measure. This declaration, together with the candidate's announcement that he was a Whig, was taken in the North to mean that he was opposed to the extension of slavery. The fact that he was a Southerner and a slaveholder was sufficient to reassure the South.

Page 203. *Pinto.*

Pseudonym of Mr. Charles F. Briggs (1810–1877), the same who was afterwards associated with Edgar A. Poe on the *Broadway Review*.

Page 204. *Thet darned Proviso.*

August 8, 1846, the President addressed a message to both Houses asking for $2,000,000 to conclude a peace with Mexico and recompense her for her proposed cession of territory. On the same day McKay, of North Carolina, introduced a bill into the lower House for this purpose. David Wilmot, of Pennsylvania, a Democrat and a zealous friend of annexation, moved as a proviso that slavery should forever be excluded from the new territory. The motion was suddenly and unexpectedly carried by a vote of 83 to 54. It did not come to a vote in the Senate, for John Davis, of Massachusetts, talked it to death by a long speech in its favor. Nevertheless it became at once a burning question in both North and South. The more pronounced antislavery men of the former section tried to make it the political test in the coming campaign. The refusal of the Whig party to take up the question caused large accessions to the old Liberty party, now known as the Free-Soil, and later to become the Republican party.

Page 212. *Ashland, etc.*

It hardly need be said that Ashland was the home of Henry Clay; North Bend, of Harrison; Marshfield, of Webster; Kinderhook, of Van Buren; and Baton Rouge, of General Taylor.

Page 213. *Pheladelphy nomernee.*

The Philadelphia nominee was General Zachary Taylor.

Page 214. *Mashfiel' speech.*

The speech here referred to is the one delivered by Webster at Marshfield, September 1, 1848. While he affirmed that the nomination of Taylor was "not fit to be made," he nevertheless declared that he would vote for him, and advised his friends to do the same. "The sagacious, wise, and far-seeing doctrine of availability," said he, "lay at the root of the whole matter."

Page 214. *Choate.*

Into none of his political addresses did Rufus Choate throw so much of his heart and soul as into those which upheld the failing policy of the Whig party from 1848 to 1852.

Page 215. *Buffalo.*

On August 9, 1848, the convention containing the consolidated elements of constitutional opposition to the extension of slavery met at Buffalo. The party, calling itself the Free-Soil party now, declared its platform to be "no more slave States and no more slave territory." Martin Van Buren and Charles Francis Adams were the candidates selected. Van Buren was chosen because it was thought he might attract Democratic votes. His opposition to the extension of slavery was not very energetic. In his letter accepting the nomination he commended the convention for having taken no decisive stand against slavery in the District of Columbia.

Page 216. *To act agin the law.*

The slaveholding States early legislated to forbid education and free religious meetings to slaves and free people of color. Stroud's *Sketch of the Slave Laws* (Philadelphia, 1827) shows that the principal acts of this character date from the period between 1740 and 1770. This was long before the oldest anti-slavery societies were organized. Thus these laws cannot be represented as having been the result of impertinent and intemperate agitation on the part of Northern Abolitionists. They were frequently defended on this ground in the heat of the anti-slavery conflict.

SECOND SERIES

Page 226. *The Cotton Loan.*

In 1861 a magnificent scheme was devised for bolstering up the Confederate government's credit. The planters signed agreements subscribing a certain portion of the next cotton and tobacco crop to the government. Using this as a basis for credit, the government issued bonds and placed about $15,000,000 in Europe, chiefly in England. A much greater loan might have been negotiated had it not suddenly appeared that the agreements made by the planters were almost worthless. By the end of the year the plan was quietly and completely abandoned. The English bondholders had the audacity to apply for aid to the United States after the war.

Page 226. *Mem'nger.*

Charles Gustavus Memminger, although he had opposed nullification, was one of the leaders in the secession movement which began in his own State, South Carolina. On the formation of the Confederate government he was made Secretary of the Treasury. Although not without experience in the management of his State's finances he showed little skill in his new position.

Page 226. *Cornfiscatin' all debts.*

After the failure of the Produce Loan and one or two other measures on a similarly grand scale, the Confederate government resorted to simpler means. Chief among these were the acts confiscating the property of and all debts due to alien enemies. No great number of reputable persons in the South could resolve to compound or wipe out debts involving their personal honor, so the results of the scheme were meagre.

Page 228. MASON AND SLIDELL.

In the latter part of 1861 President Davis undertook to send agents or commissioners to England and France to represent the Southern cause. The men chosen were James M. Mason, of Virginia, and John Slidell, of Louisiana. On the 12th of October they left Charleston, eluded the blockading squadron, and landed at Havana. Thence they embarked for St. Thomas on the British mail-steamer Trent. On the way the Trent was stopped by Captain Wilkes, of the American man-of-war San Jacinto, and the Confederate agents were transferred as prisoners to the latter vessel. The British Government at once proclaimed the act "a great outrage," and sent a peremptory demand for the release of the prisoners and reparation. At the same time, without waiting for any explanation, it made extensive preparations for hostilities. It seemed and undoubtedly was expedient for the United States to receive Lord Russell's demand as an admission that impressment of British seamen found on board neutral vessels was unwarrantable. Acting on the demand as an admission of the principle so long contended for by the United States, Mr. Seward disavowed the act of Wilkes and released the commissioners. But it was held then and has since been stoutly maintained by many jurists that the true principles of international law will not justify a neutral vessel in transporting the agents of a belligerent on a hostile mission. On the analogy of despatches they should be contraband. The difficulty of amicable settlement at that time, however, lay not so much in the point of law as in the intensity of popular feeling on both sides of the Atlantic.

Page 231. *Belligerent rights.*

One month after Sumter was attacked, on May 13, 1861, the Queen issued a proclamation of neutrality, according belligerent rights to the Confederacy. This was done even before Mr. Adams, the new minister from the Lincoln administration, could reach England. Commercial interest cannot excuse so precipitate a recognition. It cannot be regarded as anything but a deliberate expression of unfriendliness towards the United States. It coldly contemplated the dissolution of the Union, favored the establishment of an independent slave-empire, and by its moral support strengthened the hands of the Rebellion and prolonged the war.

Page 231. *Confederate privateers.*

It is notorious that Confederate cruisers were built, equipped, and even partially manned in England in open disregard of the international law respecting neutrals. Mr. Adams protested constantly and emphatically against this, but in vain for the time. No notice was taken officially of the matter until it was forced on the British government in 1864. The subsequent negotiations concerning the Alabama claims, the Treaty of Washington in 1871, and the Geneva award to the United States of some fifteen million dollars, are too well known to require any mention.

Page 231. *The Caroline.*

In 1837 an insurrection broke out in Canada, and armed bodies of men styling themselves "patriots" were in open rebellion against the government. In spite of the President's message exhorting citizens of the United States not to interfere, and in defiance of the troops sent to Buffalo to carry out his orders, numbers of sympathizers from New York crossed the Niagara River and gave assistance to the insurgents. The British authorities would have been warranted in seizing the American vessel Caroline, which was used to transport citizens to the Canadian shore, had the seizure been made *in flagrante delicto*, or out of our territorial waters. But in crossing to the American side of the river and taking the offending vessel from her moorings these authorities committed a grave breach of neutrality. After five years of negotiation the English government finally apologized and made reparation for the injury.

Page 233. *Seward sticks a three-months' pin.*

Mr. W. H. Seward, Lincoln's Secretary of State, was at the outbreak of the Rebellion an earnest advocate of conciliation. He seemed to think that if war could be averted for a time, until the people of the seceding States perceived the true intention of the administration to be the preservation of the Union, not the promoting of Abolitionism, the Southern movement would fail. In this belief he frequently declared that the trouble would all be over in sixty days.

Page 237. *Bull Run.*

On the 21st of July, 1861, the Union troops under General McDowell were completely routed by Beauregard at Bull Run in Virginia. The North was finally convinced that the South was equipped for and determined on a desperate struggle, while the victory gave immense encouragement to the insurgents.

Page 243. *Ones'mus.*

The "Scriptural" view, according to the mind of Mr. Sawin, would have been that of Jeremiah S. Black, who saw in the case of

Onesimus St. Paul's express approval of the Fugitive Slave Law of 1850.

Page 244. *Debow.*

De Bow's *Commercial Review*, published in New Orleans, Louisiana, was for some years before the war very bitter against the North, its institutions, and its society in general.

Page 244. *Simms an' Maury.*

William Gilmore Simms, the South Carolina novelist and poet, is here referred to. Matthew Fontaine Maury, of Virginia, naval officer and hydrographer, was a man of some scientific attainments. He was the author of several works on the physical geography of the sea, navigation, and astronomy. Both men were born in the same year, 1806.

Page 245. *Arms an' cannon.*

John B. Floyd, while Secretary of War in Mr. Buchanan's Cabinet, was detected in the act of stripping Northern arsenals of arms and ammunition to supply the South. He began this work as early as December, 1859, and it is not known to what extent he carried it. Pollard, a Southern historian, says the South entered the war with 150,000 small-arms of the most approved modern pattern, all of which it owed to the government at Washington. Floyd resigned because some forts and posts in the South were not given up to the rebels.

Page 245. *Admittin' we wuz nat'lly right.*

President Buchanan's message of the first Monday of December, 1860, declared "the long-continued and intemperate interference of the Northern people with the question of slavery in the Southern States" had at last produced its natural effect; disunion was impending, and if those States could not obtain redress by constitutional means, secession was justifiable and the general government had no power to prevent it. The effect these utterances had in spreading and intensifying the spirit of secession is incalculable.

Page 246. *On the jump to interfere.*

During the larger part of the war great apprehension of attempts on the part of foreign powers to interfere prevailed in the Northern States. With the exception of Russia and Denmark, all Europe inclined toward the South. Our form of government was not favored by them, and they were not unwilling to see its failure demonstrated by a complete disruption. For a long time it was very generally believed that the South would be victorious in the end. Had the Confederacy at any time had a bright prospect of success, it is likely that England or France might have offered to interfere. Indeed, the success of the French scheme to set up a military empire in Mexico in defiance of the Monroe doctrine entirely depended on the contingency of a victory for secession. Napoleon therefore was urgent for mediation. The subject was suggested several times by the French foreign minister in his correspondence with Mr. Seward, and was pressed on the British Government by France.

Page 249. *The Border States.*

The Border States, by contiguity to the North

and natural unfitness for a very profitable system of slave-labor, were slow to take a definite stand. President Lincoln's policy was to proceed cautiously at first, keep the slavery question in the background, and enlist the sympathies of these States by appeals to their attachment to the Union. Although the people of Delaware, Maryland, Kentucky, and Missouri were pretty evenly divided, the State governments were kept from seceding. Without the support of the Republican Congressmen from this section, Lincoln could not have carried out his abolition policy.

Page 249. *Hampton Roads.*

The battle of Hampton Roads, at the entrance of Chesapeake Bay in Virginia, is remarkable for the revolution in naval warfare which it began. The utter worthlessness of wooden against armored vessels was suddenly and convincingly demonstrated. On the 8th of March, 1862, the Confederate armored ram Virginia, formerly Merrimac, made terrible havoc among the old wooden men-of-war stationed about Fortress Monroe. But at nine o'clock that night the little Monitor steamed into the Roads to the assistance of the shattered Federal navy. The next day's battle is one of the romances of war. Had Mr. Wilbur waited for the next Southern mail before writing this letter, the Devil might have had less credit given him.

Page 251. *From the banks o' my own Mississippi.*

In the period from 1830 to 1840, the sudden and healthy increase of immigration and the flattering industrial prospect induced many Western and Southern States to make lavish expenditures for internal improvements. Their credit was good and they borrowed too largely. After the financial crisis of 1837, insolvency stared them in the face. A number repudiated, among whom Mississippi in particular was heavily indebted. Her securities were largely held in England. It added nothing to the credit of the Confederacy that Jefferson Davis had been an earnest advocate of repudiation.

Page 252. *Roanoke, Bufort, Millspring.*

The loss of Roanoke Island, on the coast of North Carolina, February 8, 1862, was a severe one to the South. The finest harbor on the Southern coast was that of Port Royal, South Carolina, in the centre of the sea-island cotton district. This point the North fixed on as the best for a base of operations, and on October 29, 1861, a fleet of fifty vessels, including thirty-three transports, was sent against it. A fierce attack was begun on November 7, and on the next day the two forts, Walker and Beauregard, capitulated. Without encountering further opposition the Federal troops took possession of the town of Beaufort, on an island in the harbor. January 19, 1862, the Confederates under Crittenden were defeated with considerable loss at Millspring, Kentucky, by General G. H. Thomas.

Page 252. *Reecognition.*

Recognition of independence by the European powers, particularly France and England, would of course have been of the greatest value to the South. It is said that Mr. Roebuck's motion in the House of Commons to recognize the Confederate States would have passed but for the timely news of Gettysburg. Certainly if it had, France would not have been slow to follow. It is difficult to overestimate the disastrous effect such events would have had on the Northern cause.

Page 253. *Your Belmonts, Vallandighams, Woodses.*

Mr. August Belmont, of New York, Chairman of the Democratic National Committee from 1860 to 1872, although opposed to secession, still attributed the cause and the responsibility for the continuance of the war to the Republican Administration. He led his party in clamoring for peace and conciliation, especially in 1864, and bitterly opposed reconstruction. Clement L. Vallandigham, of Dayton, Ohio, was the most conspicuous and noisy one of the Peace Democrats during the war. His treasonable and seditious utterances finally led to his banishment to the South in May, 1863. Thence he repaired to Canada, where he remained while his party made him their candidate in the next gubernatorial campaign, in which he was ignominiously defeated. The Woodses were the brothers Benjamin and Fernando Wood, prominent Democrats of New York city. The former was editor of the *Daily News* and a Representative in Congress. The latter was several times Mayor of New York, and for twelve years a Representative in Congress.

Page 253. *C'lumbus.*

After the fall of Fort Donelson, Columbus, Kentucky, was no longer tenable, and Beauregard ordered General Polk to evacuate it. March 3, 1862, a scouting party of Illinois troops, finding the post deserted, occupied it, and when Sherman approached the next day he found the Union flag flying over the town.

Page 253. *Donelson.*

The capture of Fort Donelson, in Tennessee, February 16, 1862, by General Grant, was one of several Union successes in the West, whose value was almost entirely neutralized by McClellan's dilatory conduct of the Army of the Potomac. General John B. Floyd's precipitate retreat from the fort as the Union forces approached was afterwards represented in one of his official reports as an heroic exploit.

Page 256. *Taney.*

Roger B. Taney, of Maryland, Chief Justice of the Supreme Court of the United States from 1836 to 1864. He is chiefly notable for the Dred Scott decision, in 1857, in which he held that a negro was not a "person" in the contemplation of the Constitution, and hence "had no rights a white man was bound to respect;" that the Constitution recognized property in slaves, and that this ownership was as much entitled to protection in the Territories as any other species of property. According to this, all legislation by Congress on slavery, except in its aid, was unconstitutional.

Page 257. *Compromise System.*

Henry Clay was the "great compromiser." The aim of his life was the preservation of the Union even at the cost of extending slave territory. The three compromises for which he is famous were the Missouri in 1820, the Tariff in 1833, and the California or "Omnibus" Compromise in 1850, the most conspicuous feature of which was the Fugitive Slave Law.

Page 257. *S. J. Court.*

At the beginning of Lincoln's administration, five of the Supreme Court Justices, an absolute majority, were from the South, and had always been State-rights Democrats.

Page 259. *The Law-'n'-Order Party of ole Cincinnater.*

In Cincinnati, on March 24, 1862, Wendell Phillips, while attempting to deliver one of his lectures on slavery and the war, was attacked by a mob and very roughly handled.

Page 267. *Gov'nor Seymour.*

Horatio Seymour (1810–1886), of Utica, New York, was one of the most prominent and respected men in the Democratic party, and a bitter opponent of Lincoln. He had at this time been recently elected Governor of New York on a platform that denounced almost every measure the government had found it necessary to adopt for the suppression of the Rebellion. His influence contributed not a little to the encouragement of that spirit which inspired the Draft Riot in the city of New York in July, 1863.

Page 268. *Pres'dunt's proclamation.*

In the autumn of 1862 Mr. Lincoln saw that he must either retreat or advance boldly against slavery. He had already proceeded far enough against it to rouse a dangerous hostility among Northern Democrats, and yet not far enough to injure the institution or enlist the sympathy of pronounced anti-slavery men. He determined on decisive action. On September 22, 1862, he issued a monitory proclamation giving notice that on the first day of the next year he would, in the exercise of his war-power, emancipate all slaves of those.States or parts of States in rebellion, unless certain conditions were complied with. This proclamation was at once violently assailed by the Democrats, led by such men as Seymour, and for a time the opposition threatened disaster to the administration. The elections in the five leading free States — New York, Pennsylvania, Ohio, Indiana, and Illinois — went against the Republicans. But with the aid of New England, the West, and, not least of all, the Border Slave States, the President was assured a majority of about twenty in the new House to carry out his abolition policy.

Page 269. KETTELOPOTOMACHIA.

The incident furnishing the occasion for this poem was a Virginia duel, or rather a free fight. Mr. H. R. Pollard, of the *Richmond Examiner*, had some difficulty with Messrs. Coleman and N. P. Tyler, of the *Enquirer*, concerning the public printing. On Friday,

January 5, 1866, all three gentlemen met in the rotunda of the Virginia Capitol, and proceeded to settle their dispute by an appeal to revolvers. Six shots were fired, but no damage resulted, except to a marble statue of Washington.

Page 270. *Letcheris et Floydis magnisque Extra ordine Billis.*

John Letcher (1813–1884), a Virginia lawyer and politician, was several times in Congress, and was Governor of his State from 1860 to 1864. John B. Floyd (1805–1863) was Governor of Virginia from 1849 to 1852, Secretary of War in Buchanan's Cabinet, and a brigadier in the Confederate service. William Smith, of King George County, Virginia, was the proprietor of an old line of coaches running through Virginia and the Carolinas. He was called "Extra Billy" because he charged extra for every package, large or small, which his passengers carried. Mr. Smith himself, however, attributed his nickname to his extra service to the State. He was several times a Congressman, twice Governor of Virginia, and a Confederate Brigadier-General.

Page 281. *Seward.*

Under the influence of Mr. Seward, President Andrew Johnson developed a policy of reconstruction directly opposed to the views of Congress and the mass of the Republican party. He believed in punishing individuals, if necessary, but that all the States ought to be re-installed at once in the position they had occupied in 1860. The guarantees against disloyalty he proposed to exact from the South were few and feeble. Congress, on the other hand, determined to keep the subdued States in a position somewhat resembling that of territories and under military surveillance until it could be satisfied that four years' war would not be without good results. Its chief aim was to secure the safety of the negro, who had been freed by the thirteenth Amendment in December, 1865. These differences of plan led to a protracted and bitter contest between the executive and legislative departments, culminating in the unsuccessful attempt to impeach Johnson in March, 1868. The Congressional policy was carried out over the President's vetoes. Among other conditions the Southern States were required to ratify the fourteenth and fifteenth Amendments, giving citizenship and suffrage to the blacks, before being qualified for readmission to the Union.

Page 283. *Mac.*

General George B. McClellan was one of the leaders of the Northern Democracy during the war, and the presidential nominee against Lincoln in 1864.

Page 284. *Johnson's speech an' veto message.*

The Civil Rights Act of March, 1866, had just been the occasion of an open rupture between Congress and the President. The bill, conferring extensive rights on freedmen, passed both Houses, but was vetoed by Johnson. It was quickly passed again over his veto.

Page 284. *A temp'ry party can be based on 't.*

Johnson's plan of reconstruction did, indeed,

furnish the material for the next Democratic platform in the presidential campaign of 1868.

Page 284. *Tyler.*

John Tyler, who had been chosen Vice-President in 1840, succeeded to the Presidency on the death of Harrison one month after the inauguration. He abandoned the policy of the party that elected him, and provoked just such a contest with it as Johnson did.

Page 300. AN INVITATION.

[Lowell entered this poem in his several editions as addressed to J. F. H., initials which meant nothing to the general public, but recalled to the contemporaries of his college days a Virginian gentleman, a graduate of Harvard of the class of 1840, greatly endeared by his temper and gifts to his early associates and especially to Lowell. Not long after his graduation he went to Germany to study; he disappeared from sight, turning up at odd times in odd places. He did much various study and had much varied experience. After many years he returned home. When the war broke out he joined the Confederate army as a surgeon, and died worn out with hard service in 1862.]

Page 308. AFTER THE BURIAL.

["To show you that I am not unable to go along with you in the feeling expressed in your letter, I will copy a few verses out of my commonplace book.

Yes, faith is a goodly anchor
When the skies are blue and clear;
At the bows it hangs right stalwart
With a sturdy iron cheer.

But when the ship goes to pieces,
And the tempests are all let loose,
It rushes plumb down to the sea-depths,
'Mid slimy sea-weed and ooze.

Better then one spar of memory,
One broken plank of the past,
For our human hearts to cling to,
Adrift in the whirling vast.

To the spirit the cross of the spirit,
To the flesh its blind despair,
Clutching fast the thin-worn locket
With its threads of gossamer hair.

O friend! thou reasonest bravely,
Thy preaching is wise and true;
But the earth that stops my darling's ears
Makes mine insensate, too.

That little shoe in the corner,
So worn and wrinkled and brown,
With its emptiness confutes you,
And argues your wisdom down.

"But enough, dear Sydney, of death and sorrow. They are not subjects which I think it profitable or wise to talk about, think about, or write about often. Death is a private tutor. We have no fellow-scholars, and must lay our lessons to heart alone." Lowell to Sydney Howard Gay, March 17, 1850.]

Page 350. THE CATHEDRAL.

["Now for Ruskin's criticisms. As to words,

I am something of a purist, though I like best the word that best says the thing. (You know I have studied lingo a little.) I am fifty-one years old, however, and have in one sense won my spurs. I claim the right now and then to knight a plebeian word for good service in the field. But it will almost always turn out that it has after all good blood in its veins, and can prove its claim to be put in the saddle. *Rote* is a familiar word all along our seaboard to express that dull and continuous burden of the sea heard inland before or after a great storm. The root of the word may be in *rumpere*, but it is more likely in *rotare*, from the identity of this sea-music with that of the rote — a kind of hurdy-gurdy with which the jongleurs accompanied their song. It is one of those Elizabethan words which we New-Englanders have preserved along with so many others. It occurs in the 'Mirror for Magistrates,' 'the sea's rote,' which Nares, not understanding, would change to rore! It is not to be found in any provincial glossary, but I caught it alive at Beverly and the Isles of Shoals. Like 'mobbled queen,' 't is 'good.'

"*Whiff* Ruskin calls 'an American elevation of English lower word.' Not a bit of it. I have always thought 'the whiff and wind of his fell sword' in 'Hamlet' rather fine than otherwise. Ben also has the word. *Downshod* means shod with down. I doubted about this word myself — but I wanted it. As to *misgave*, the older poets used it as an active verb, and I have done with it as all poets do with language. My meaning is clear, and that is the main point. His objection to 'spume-sliding down the baffled decuman' I do not understand. I think if he will read over his 'ridiculous Germanism' (p. 13 *seq.*) with the context he will see that he has misunderstood me. (By the way, 'in our life alone doth Nature live' is Coleridge's, not Wordsworth's.) I never hesitate to say anything I have honestly felt because some one may have said it before, for it will always get a new color from the new mind, but here I was not saying the same thing by a great deal. *Nihil in intellectu quod non prius in sensu* would be nearer — though not what I meant. Nature (inanimate), which is the image of the mind, sympathizes with all our moods. I would have numbered the lines as Ruskin suggests, only it looks as if one valued them too much. That sort of thing should be posthumous. You may do it for me, my dear Charles, if my poems survive me. Two dropt stitches I must take up which I notice on looking over what I have written. Ruskin surely remembers Carlyle's 'whiff of grape-shot.' That is one. The other is that *rote* may quite as well be from the Icelandic *at hriota* = to snore; but my studies more and more persuade me that where there is in English a Teutonic and a Romance root meaning the same thing, the two are apt to melt into each other so as to make it hard to say from which our word comes." . . . *Letters* II., pp. 65-67.]

Page 399. PHŒBE.
[The correspondence concerning this poem with the original form of the verses is here given in detail.

TO R. W. GILDER.

LEGATION OF THE UNITED STATES,
LONDON, September 4, 1881.

Dear Mr. Gilder, — Your telegram scared me, for, coming at an unusual hour, I thought it brought ill news from Washington. My relief on finding it innocent has perhaps made me too good-natured towards the verses I send you, but I have waited sixty-two years for them, and am willing to wait as many more (not here) before they are printed. Do what you like with them. They mean only my hearty good-will towards you and my hope for your success in your new undertaking. . . .

Faithfully yours,   J. R. LOWELL.

If I could see the proofs, very likely I could better it — they sober one and bring one to his bearings. Perhaps the metaphysical (or whatever they are) stanzas — what I mean is moralizing — were better away. Perhaps too many compound epithets — but I had to give up " visionary " in order to save " legendary," which was essential. Perhaps a note, saying that so long as the author can remember, a pair of these birds (give ornithological name — *muscicapa ?*) have built on jutting brick in an archway leading to the house at Elmwood — or does everybody know what a phœbe is ? I am so old that I am accustomed to people's being ignorant of whatever you please.

PHŒBE

Ere pales in heaven the morning star,
  A bird, the loneliest of its kind,
Hears Dawn's faint footfall from afar
  While all its mates are dumb and blind.

It is a wee sad-colored thing,
  As shy and secret as a maid,
That, ere in choir the robins ring,
  Pipes its own name like one afraid.

It seems pain-prompted to repeat
  The story of some ancient ill,
But *Phœbe ! Phœbe !* sadly sweet
  Is all it says, and then is still.

It calls and listens. Earth and sky,
  Hushed by the pathos of its fate,
Listen, breath held, but no reply
  Comes from its doom-divided mate.

Phœbe ! it calls and calls again,
  And Ovid, could he but have heard,
Had hung a legendary pain
  About the memory of the bird ;

A pain articulate so long
  In penance of some mouldered crime
Whose ghost still flies the Furies' thong
  Down the waste solitudes of Time ;

Or waif from young Earth's wonder-hour
  When gods found mortal maidens fair,
And will malign was joined with power
  Love's kindly laws to overbear.

Phœbe ! is all it has to say
  In plaintive cadence o'er and o'er,
Like children that have lost their way
  And know their names, but nothing more.

Is it a type, since nature's lyre
  Vibrates to every note in man,
Of that insatiable desire,
  Meant to be so, since life began ?

Or a fledged satire, sent to rasp
  Their jaded sense, who, tired so soon
With shifting life's doll-dresses, grasp,
  Gray-bearded babies, at the moon ?

I, in strange lands at gray of dawn
  Wakeful, have heard that fruitless plaint
Through Memory's chambers deep withdrawn
  Renew its iterations faint.

So nigh ! yet from remotest years
  It seems to draw its magic, rife
With longings unappeased and tears
  Drawn from the very source of life.

TO THE SAME.

LEGATION OF THE UNITED STATES,
LONDON, September 5, 1881.

Dear Mr. Gilder, — I sent off the verses yesterday, and now write in great haste to say that in my judgment the stanza beginning " Or waif from young Earth's," etc., were better away. Also for " doom-divided " print " doom-dissevered." I have not had time to mull over the poem as I should like.

Faithfully yours,   J. R. LOWELL.

P. S. I may write in a day or two suppressing more, after I have had time to think.

TO THE SAME.

LEGATION OF THE UNITED STATES,
LONDON, September 6, 1881.

Dear Mr. Gilder, — I bother you like a boy with his first essay in verse. I wrote yesterday to ask the omission of a stanza — but last night, being sleepless, as old fellows like me are too often apt to be, I contrived to make a stanza which had been tongue-tied say what I wished.

Let it go thus,

Waif of the young World's wonder-hour
  . . . .
  . . . .
  . . . . to overbear, (comma).

Then go on —

Like Progne, did it feel the stress
  And coil of the prevailing words
Close round its being and compress
  Man's ampler nature to a bird's ?

This manages the transition, which was wanting. Perhaps this might follow : —

One only memory left of all
  The motley crowd of vanished scenes,
Hers — and vain impulse to recall
  By repetition what it means.

Faithfully yours,
  J. R. LOWELL.

TO THE SAME.

LEGATION OF THE UNITED STATES,
LONDON, September 8, 1881.

Dear Mr. Gilder, — This is positively the last! I wish to omit the stanza beginning " Or a winged satire," etc. I have been convinced by a friend whom I have consulted that it was a cuckoo's egg in my nest. Item. The verse that bothered me most of all was this:

Listen, breath held, but no reply, etc.

I wished to have a distinct pause after " listen," in accordance with the sense. Somehow I could not get the right, and " breath held " was clearly the wrong one, awkward, and with the same vowel sound in both halves. Print —

Listen : no whisper of reply
Is heard of doom-dissevered mate.

No; that won't do, either, with its assonance of " heard " and " dissevered " — so, though I prefer "dissevered " for sense, I will go back to the original word " divided," which I suppose was instinctive.

This is positively my last dying speech and confession. You need fear nothing more from me. I fancy you ducking your head for fear of another rap every time the postman comes.

I hope you will like my little poem, and tell me so if you don't. Kindest regards to Mrs. Gilder.

Faithfully yours,
J. R. LOWELL.

TO THE SAME.

LEGATION OF THE UNITED STATES,
LONDON, September 12, 1881.

. . . As I am writing, I add that if you think (as I am half inclined)

No whisper of reply
Comes from its doom-dissevered mate

better than the other reading, print it so.

Faithfully yours,
J. R. LOWELL.

P. S. We are sadly anxious to-day about the President.

TO THE SAME.

HOTEL DANIELI, VENICE, October 24, 1881.
. . . Thank you for the printed copy. Of course I am disgusted with it. Print somehow is like a staring plaster-cast compared with the soft and flowing outlines, the modest nudity of the manuscript clay. But it is a real pleasure to me that you like it.

" Robins ring " is right, and whenever you spend a June night at Elmwood (as I hope you will so soon as I am safe there once more) you will recognize its truth. There are hundreds of 'em going at once, like the bells here last night (Sunday), with a perfect indecency of disregard for rhythm or each other. Mr. Burroughs, I hear, has been criticising my knowledge of out-doors. God bless his soul! I had been living in the country thirty years (I fancy

it must be) before he was born, and if anybody ever lived in the open air it was I. So be at peace. By the way, I took Progne merely because she was changed into a little bird. I should have preferred a male, and was thinking of a fellow (transformed, I think by Medea), but can't remember his name. While I am about it I question " wee." Is it English ? I had no dictionary at hand. But there is one atrocity — " moldered." Why do you give in to these absurdities ? Why abscond in to this petty creek from the great English main of orthography ? 'T is not quite so bad as " I don't know as " for " I don't know that," but grazes it and is of a piece with putting one's knife in one's mouth.]

V. A CHRONOLOGICAL LIST OF LOWELL'S POEMS

IN arranging this list the editor has relied first on the dates supplied by the author, and then on the dates of periodicals and books in which the poems otherwise undated first appeared. Whenever the first appearance of a poem has not been determined precisely, the title is printed in italics under the year when the volume first including it was published. [Scudder's list has been enlarged for this edition by the inclusion of the poems in Thelma Smith, *The Uncollected Poems of JRL* (Philadelphia, 1950), marked with an asterisk (*) ; those in Martin Duberman, "Twenty-seven Poems by JRL," (*American Literature*, Nov. 1963, pp. 322–51), marked with a dagger (†) ; and poems identified by Scudder as Lowell's but not currently in print, marked ° ; their locations in nineteenth-century periodicals are cited by Scudder in an appendix to the second volume of his biography of Lowell (Boston : Houghton, Mifflin and Co. [1901]). The initials H. P. stand for Hugh Perceval, a pseudonym frequently used by Lowell with his early poetry. M. K.]

1837. Imitation of Burns.*
Dramatic Sketch.*
What is it? *
The Serenade.*
Saratoga Lake.*

1838. Scenes from an Unpublished Drama, by the late G. A. Slimton, esq.*
Skillygoliana, II.*
Skillygoliana, III.*
Uhland's "Des Knaben Berglied." *
Translations from Uhland : I. "Das Ständchen." II. "Der Weisse Hirsch." *
A Dead Letter.*
Extracts from a "Hasty Pudding Poem." *

To Mount Washington, on a Second Visit.*
Song (A pair of black eyes).*
To the Class of '38, By their Ostracized Poet, (so called,) J. R. L.*
Class Poem.*

1839. Threnodia.
The Beggar.
Summer Storm.
Ye Yankees of the Bay State.*

1840. The Sirens.
Love.
Sonnet: To A. C. L.
Sonnet (I would not have this perfect love of ours).
Sonnet (For this true nobleness I seek in vain).
Irené.
Serenade.
With a Pressed Flower.
My Love.
The Lover's Drink-Song.*
Sonnet (Verse cannot tell thee how beautiful thou art). [Signed H. P.] °
Sonnet (My friend, I pray thee call not *this* Society). [Signed H. P.] °
Sonnet (O, child of nature! oh, most meek and free). [Signed H. P.] °
Song (What reck I of the stars when I). [Signed H. P.] °
Song (O, I must look on that sweet face once more before I die). [Signed H. P.] °
Song (Lift up the curtains of thine eyes). [Signed H. P.] °
The Serenade (Gentle, Lady, be thy sleeping). [Signed H. P.] °
Music. [Signed H. P.] °
Isabel.°
The Bobolink. [Signed H. P.] °
Ianthe. [Signed H. P.] °
Flowers. [Signed H. P.] °

1841. A Prayer.
Sonnet (What were I, Love, if I were stripped of thee).
Sonnet (Great truths are portions of the soul of man).
Sonnet (I ask not for those thoughts, that sudden leap).
Sonnet: To M. W., on her Birthday.
Sonnet (My Love, I have no fear that thou shouldst die).
Sonnet (I cannot think that thou shouldst pass away).
Sonnet (There never yet was flower so fair in vain).
Sonnet: Sub Pondere crescit.
Callirhöe.*
Merry England.*
Sonnet: "To die is gain." *
The Lesson—To Irene.*

Ballad (Gloomily the river floweth).*
The Loved One.*
"Lady, there grew a flower." †

1842. The Forlorn.
Midnight.
Song (O moonlight deep and tender).
Sonnet (Beloved, in the noisy city here).
Sonnets: On Reading Wordsworth's Sonnets in Defence of Capital Punishment (Six Sonnets).
The Shepherd of King Admetus.
An Incident in a Railroad Car.
Elegy on the Death of Dr. Channing.
Sonnet: To the Spirit of Keats.
To Perdita, Singing.
Song (Violet! sweet violet!).
Ode (In the old days of awe and keen-eyed wonder).
Rosaline.
To an Æolian Harp at Night.*
Sonnet (If some small savor creep into my rhyme).*
Sonnet (Thou art a woman, and therein thou art).*
Fancies about a Rosebud.*
Farewell.*
The True Radical.*
Hymn.*
Sonnet (Poet, if men from wisdom turn away).*
Agatha.*
The Two.*
Sonnet—to Keats.*
Sonnet: Sunset and Moonshine.*
Sonnet (I love those poets of whatever creed).*
Sonnet (Whene'er I read in mournful history).*
Sonnet (Like some black mountain glooming huge aloof).*
Sonnet (My Father, since I love, thy presence cries).*
The Ballad of the Stranger.*
Sonnet (Only as thou herein canst not see me).*
Sonnet (When in a book I find a pleasant thought).*
Sonnet (Poet! thou art most wealthy, being poor).°
Sonnet (The hope of truth grows stronger day by day).°
A Dirge.°
A Fantasy.°
Sonnet (If ye have not the one great lesson learned).°
Pierpont (The hungry flames did never yet seem hot).°
"You called my poem beautiful." †

1843. The Fountain.
The Fatherland.
Sonnet: In Absence.

Sonnet: The Street.
A Legend of Brittany.
Prometheus.
A Glance Behind the Curtain.
Stanzas on Freedom.
L'Envoi (Whether my heart hath wiser grown or not).
Allegra.
The Heritage.
A Requiem.
Sonnet: Wendell Phillips.
Sonnet (I grieve not that ripe Knowledge takes away).
Sonnet: To J. R. Giddings.
The Token.
Rhœcus.
The Moon.
The Rose: A Ballad.
A Parable (Worn and footsore was the Prophet).
Sonnet: To M. O. S.
Sonnet (Our love is not a fading earthly flower).
Voltaire.*
The Follower.*
The Poet and Apollo.*
A Love Thought.*
Wordsworth.*
In Sadness.º
Forgetfulness.º
A Reverie.º

1844. Columbus.
On the Death of a Friend's Child.
Hunger and Cold.
A Chippewa Legend.
Winter.*
A Rallying-Cry for New-England, Against the Annexation of Texas.*
Anti-Texas.*
A Mystical Ballad.*
New Year's Eve, 1844.*

1845. An Incident of the Fire at Hamburg.
To the Future.
A Contrast.
On the Capture of Fugitive Slaves near Washington.
To the Dandelion.
The Ghost-Seer.
An Interview with Miles Standish.
Remembered Music.
The Present Crisis.
The Falcon.
To a Pine Tree.
The Happy Martyrdom.*
An Epigram, on Certain Conservatives.*
Now is Always Best.*
Orpheus.*
A Song to my Wife.º
The Epitaph (What means this glosing epitaph?).º

1846. The Oak.

Letter from Boston.
To the Past.
Biglow Papers, I (17 June): A Letter from Mr. Ezekiel Biglow of Jaalam . . . inclosing a poem of his son, Mr. Hosea Biglow.
On the Death of Charles Turner Torrey.
An Indian-Summer Reverie.
The Royal Pedigree.º

1847. The Landlord.
Extreme Unction.
Above and Below.
The Growth of the Legend.
Song: To M. L.
The Search.
The Captive.
The Birch-Tree.
Studies for Two Heads.
On a Portrait of Dante by Giotto.
The Changeling.
The Pioneer.
Longing.
Hebe.
Si descendero in Infernum, ades.
Biglow Papers, II (18 August): Letter from a Volunteer in Saltillo.
Biglow Papers, III (2 November): What Mr. Robinson Thinks.
Biglow Papers, IV (28 December): Remarks of Increase D. O'Phace, esquire.

1848. The Sower.
Ambrose.
Ode to France.
A Parable (Said Christ our Lord, "I will go and see").
Freedom.
Ode written for the Celebration of the Introduction of the Cochituate Water into the City of Boston.
To Lamartine.
To the Memory of Hood.
The Vision of Sir Launfal.
A Fable for Critics.
Biglow Papers, V (3 May): The Debate in the Sennit.
Biglow Papers, VI (4 May): The Pious Editor's Creed.
Biglow Papers, VII (1 June): A Letter from a Candidate for the Presidency.
Biglow Papers, VIII (6 July): A Second Letter from B. Sawin, esq.
Biglow Papers, IX (28 September): Another Letter from B. Sawin, esq.
To W. L. Garrison (original title: The Day of Small Things).
To John Gorham Palfrey.
THE BIGLOW PAPERS, "Edited,

with an Introduction, Notes, Glossary, and Copious Index, by Homer Wilbur, A.M. . . ."
An Extract.*
The Ex-Mayor's Crumbs of Consolation: A Pathetic Ballad.*
1849. Trial.
Lines suggested by the Graves of Two English Soldiers on Concord Battle Ground.
To ——
Bibliolatres.
Beaver Brook.
Kossuth.
An Oriental Apologue.
The First Snow-Fall.
The Parting of the Ways.
The Lesson of the Pine (later, with two stanzas added, A Mood).
A Day in June (later, revised and enlarged, Al Fresco).
Sonnet (I thought our love at full, but I did err).
She came and went.
Eurydice.
King Retro.*
"Lady Bird, lady bird, fly away home !" *
The Burial of Theobald.*
1850. Dara.
New Year's Eve, 1850.
An Invitation.
Mahmood the Image-Breaker.
Out of Doors.*
The Northern Sancho Panza and His Vicarious Cork Tree.*
A Dream I Had.*
1851. Anti-Apis.
The Unhappy Lot of Mr. Knott.
On Receiving a Piece of Flax-Cotton.*
1852. A Parable (An ass munched thistles, while a nightingale).
1853. The Fountain of Youth.
Fragments from Our Own, His Wanderings and Personal Adventures.*
Rebecca's Valentine.†
1854. The Singing Leaves.
Without and Within.
Pictures from Appledore.
The Wind-Harp.
Auf Wiedersehen.
A Winter Evening Hymn to my Fire.
Sonnet on an Autumn Sketch of H. G. Wild.
Peschiera.*
Without and Within, No. II, The Restaurant.*
1855. Masaccio.
Invita Minerva.
In-doors and Out.*
Hymn: (Friends of Freedom ! ye who stand).*

Verses — Copy of verses wrote by Sir Henry Knatchbull, Bart., 1760.*
Hakon's Lay.º
1857. My Portrait Gallery.
Sonnet: The Maple.
The Origin of Didactic Poetry.
1858. The Dead House.
The Nest.
Das Ewig-Weibliche (original title, Beatrice).
Epigram on J. M.*
The Trustee's Lament.*
Happiness.º
Shipwreck.º
1859. Villa Franca.
At the Burns Centennial.
Italy, 1859.º
[Lines delivered at a dinner for Paul Morphy, May 31, 1859.] †
1860. To the Muse.º
1861. Ode to Happiness.
The Washers of the Shroud.
The Fatal Curiosity.*
1862. Biglow Papers, second series, I (January): Birdofredum Sawin, Esq., to Mr. Hosea Biglow.
Biglow Papers, second series, II (February) : Mason and Slidell : a Yankee Idyl.
Biglow Papers, second series, III (March): Birdofredum Sawin, Esq., to Mr. Hosea Biglow.
Biglow Papers, second series, IV (April) : A Message of Jeff Davis in Secret Session.
Biglow Papers, second series, V (May): Speech of Honourable Preserved Doe in Secret Caucus.
Biglow Papers, second series, VI (June) : Sunthin' in the Pastoral Line.
Before the Embers.*
Il Pesceballo. Opera Seria: in un Atto. Musica del Maestro Rossibelli-Donimozarti. Cambridge, 1862.*
1863. Two Scenes from the Life of Blondel.
In the Half-Way House.
Biglow Papers, second series, VII (February): Latest Views of Mr. Biglow.
1864. Memoriæ Positum: R. G. Shaw.
The Black Preacher
1865. Gold Egg: A Dream-Fantasy.
Ode Recited at the Harvard Commemoration.
On Board the '76.
Biglow Papers, second series, X (April) : Mr. Hosea Biglow to the Editor of the "Atlantic Monthly".
1866. What Rabbi Jehosha said.
The Miner.
To Mr. John Bartlett.

At the Commencement Dinner, 1866.
Biglow Papers, second series, XI (May): Mr. Hosea Biglow's speech in March Meeting.
THE BIGLOW PAPERS, second series (including first publication of Papers VIII and IX, a long introductory essay on "The whole scheme," as well as on "The use of homely dialects" in literature, and the complete version of "The Courtin' ").
A Worthy Ditty.*
Mr. Worsley's Nightmare.*
Dr. Longfellow's New Prescription Commended to Himself.†
"No dewdrop is stiller." †

1867. A Familiar Epistle to a Friend.
An Ember Picture.
To H.W.L.
The Nightingale in the Study.
Fitz Adam's Story.
Hob Gobbling's Song.*

1868. Under the Willows.
After the Burial.
In the Twilight.
The Foot-Path.
A Mood (earlier, The Lesson of the Pine).
To Charles Eliot Norton.
Seaweed.
The Finding of the Lyre.
For an Autograph.
Al Fresco (earlier, A Day in June).
Godminster Chimes.
Aladdin.
The Nomades.
Self-Study.
The Voyage to Vinland.
Yussouf.
The Darkened Mind.
All-Saints.
Fancy's Casuistry.

1869. The Flying Dutchman.
Sonnet (Poseidon Fields, who dost the Atlantic sway).*
[Stylistic variations on the receipt of some cheeses.] †

1870. The Cathedral.
Sonnet: Charles Dickens.*

1871. To Madame du Chatelet.*
1872. Naworth Unvisited.†
Naworth Visited.†

1873. Sonnet: To Fanny Alexander.
1874. Agassiz.
An Epistle to George William Curtis.
Sonnet: Jeffries Wyman.
An Epitaph (original title, James Fisk, Jr., An Epitaph).*

1875. Ode read at the One Hundredth Anniversary of the Fight at Concord Bridge.

Under the Old Elm.
Prison of Cervantes.
Sonnet: Scottish Border (original title, English Border).
Sonnet: On being asked for an Autograph in Venice.
Tempora Mutantur.
Sonnet: The Dancing Bear.
Sonnet: Joseph Winlock.
The World's Fair, 1876.*

1876. An Ode for the Fourth of July, 1876.
A Misconception.
The Boss (originally entitled, Defrauding Nature).
Campaign Epigrams: A Coincidence, The Widow's Mite, The Astronomer Misplaced.*

1877. Sonnets: Bankside.
Birthday Verses.
Sonnet: Nightwatches.
Sonnet: Pessimoptimism
Sonnet: The Brakes.

1878. Sonnet: Death of Queen Mercedes.
Sonnet: With a Copy of Aucassin and Nicolete.
Volverá? †
The Writing-lesson.†

1879. Sonnet: E. G. de R.
The Protest.
The Petition.
Sonnet: To a Lady Playing on the Cithern.
Auspex.
Three scenes in the Life of a Portrait.*
6th July.†
"No Se Tome El Trabajo de Contestar." †
Scene, Elmwood A.D. 1890.†
To Don J. F. de R.†
At the Photographer's.†

1880. On Planting a Tree at Inveraray.
The Turkey's Threnody.†
Yo El Rey.†

1881. Phœbe.
Sonnets: With an Armchair.
Agro-Dolce.
A New Year's Greeting.
Sun-Worship.
Cuiviscunque.*

1882. Verses intended to go with a Posset Dish to my Dear Little Goddaughter, 1882.
Sonnet: To Whittier.
The Secret.
Dedicatory Verses.*
"When through the night I sleepless lie." †

1884. To Holmes.
The Optimist.
Eleanor makes Macaroons.
Bon Voyage.
The Recall.
Changed Perspective.

Verses written in a copy of Shak-
speare [sic].*
1885. On Hearing a Sonata of Beetho-
ven's played in the Next Room.
Under the October Maples.
Street Doors.*
1886. International Copyright.
Paolo to Francesca.
With a Pair of Gloves lost in a
Wager.
1887. Postscript to An Epistle to
George William Curtis.
Credidimus Jovem regnare.
Fact or Fancy? (original title,
Fancy or Fact?).
Sixty-eighth Birthday.
1888. The Secret.
Endymion.
Turner's Old Téméraire.
St. Michael the Weigher.
Absence.
In a Copy of Omar Khayyám.
*On Receiving a Copy of Mr. Aus-
tin Dobson's "Old World
Idylls."*
To. C. F. Bradford.
Sonnet: To a Friend.
Sonnet: To Miss D. T.
Arcadia Rediviva.
*A Youthful Experiment in Eng-
lish Hexameters.*
Estrangement.
Monna Lisa.
On Burning some Old Letters.
The Broken Tryst.
Casa sin Alma.
A Christmas Carol.
Sonnet: The Eye's Treasury.
Sonnet: A Foreboding.
Love's Clock.
Telepathy.
Scherzo.
*"Franciscus de Verulamio sic
Cogitavit."*
The Pregnant Comment.

The Lesson.
Science and Poetry.
The Discovery.
With a Seashell.
In an Album.
Sayings.
Inscriptions:
  *For a Bell at Cornell Univer-
  sity.*
  *For a Memorial Window to Sir
  Walter Raleigh, set up in St.
  Margaret's Westminster, by
  American Contributors.*
  *Proposed for a Soldiers' and
  Sailors' Monument in Boston.*
1889. How I consulted the Oracle of
the Goldfishes.
Elmwood Visited.†
1890. *Fragments of an Unfinished Poem.*
The Infant Prodigy.*
My Brook.*
In a Volume of Sir Thomas
Browne.*
Inscription for a Memorial Bust
of Fielding.*
"I've tasted the fishes." †
"The newly sent fishes are." †
1891. On a Bust of General Grant.
His Ship.*
"Excellent Bartlett." †
1892. *For a Birthday.**
1894. "I am driven by my longing."
(Transl. first 82 and last 99
lines of *Kalevala*.)*
1895. A Valentine.
An April Birthday — at Sea.
Love and Thought.
The Nobler Lover.
1896. *The Power of Sound: A Rhymed
Lecture.**
1900. *More Dedicatory Verses.**
Undated. No Rewards or Punishments.†
In the Studio.†
At the Exhibition.†
The New Persephone.†

INDEX OF FIRST LINES

INDEX OF TITLES

[The titles of major works and of general divisions are set in SMALL CAPITALS.]